Consumer Reports®

EXPERT • INDEPENDENT • NONPROFIT

BUYING GUIDE

ALL NEW FOR

2005

The editors of
Consumer Reports magazine

Consumers Union • Yonkers, NY

Autos
page 149

Table of Contents

What's New for Shoppers in 2005?

LCD TVs
page 56

Read Our Latest Buying Advice

Lawn tractors
page 109

HOW TO USE THIS BOOK TO SELECT A PRODUCT

1. Read the Buying Advice (pages 27-148)
2. Check the Product Ratings (pages 224-326)
3. Study the Brand Reliability charts (pages 327-337)

Buying Advice, continued

If You're in the Market for a Car...

Product Ratings and Brand Reliability

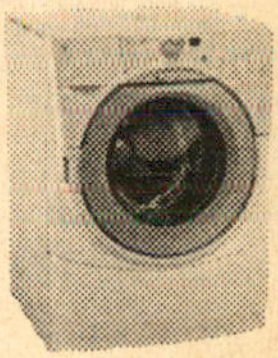

Washing machines page 324

Here's Some More Useful Buying Information...

CONSUMER REPORTS BUYING GUIDE 2005

Consumer Reports (ISSN 0010-7174) is published 13 times a year by Consumers Union of U.S., Inc., 101 Truman Avenue, Yonkers, N.Y. 10703-1057. Second-class postage paid at Yonkers, N.Y., and at additional mailing offices. Canadian postage paid at Mississauga, Ontario, Canada. Canadian publications registration no. 2665247-98. Title Consumer Reports registered in U.S. Patent Office. CU is a member of the Consumers International. Mailing lists: CU rents or exchanges its customer postal list so it can be provided to other publications, companies, and nonprofit organizations. If you wish your name deleted from lists and rentals, send your address label with a request for deletion to Consumer Reports, P.O. Box 2127, Harlan, IA 51593-0316. **U.S. Postmaster:** Send address changes to P.O. Box 2109, Harlan, IA 51593-0298. **Canada Post:** If copies are undeliverable, return to Consumer Reports, P.O. Box 1051, STN MAIN, Fort Erie ON L2A 6C7. Back issues: Single copies of 12 preceding issues, $7.95 each; Buying Guide, $10 each. Write Back Issues, Consumer Reports, Customer Relations, 101 Truman Ave., Yonkers, N.Y. 10703. Consumer Reports Buying Guide 2005 (ISBN 0-89043-991-5)

How to Use This Book

The Consumer Reports Buying Guide 2005 is your one-stop source for making intelligent, informed, money-saving purchases for all your home and personal needs. Here's how this book can help you make smart buying decisions throughout the year.

Start by learning some **Secrets of Shopping Smart,** whether you shop in stores, through catalogs, or online. This section includes two revealing surveys: **Electronics Retailers Compared** and **Computer Retailers Compared.** Each survey helps you determine the best places and methods to shop for these products.

You can then read up on **10 Great Ways to Find Bargains on the Web.** From cyber coupons to getting a great deal on a car, you'll find these tips invaluable. Then there's a section on **What's New in Home Products,** with the latest trends in the home marketplace. You'll find two handy lists here—"10 Action Points for Smart Shoppers" and a "Price Drop Alert" identifying certain products that are going down in price.

Once you're familiar with the marketplace for 2005, the **Buying Advice** sections give you guidance from the experts at Consumer Reports on more than 45 different product categories in **Home Entertainment, Kitchen and Laundry, Home and Yard,** and **Home Office.** From cooktops and microwaves to TVs and vacuum cleaners, you'll get invaluable information on what's available, important features, and how to choose the model that's best for you.

Are you in the market for a car? The **Autos** section contains the latest **Ratings** and information on new and used cars to help you make the right purchase decision. In addition to **Reviews of the 2004-05 Cars,** there's a section on the **Best and Worst Used Cars** and **Reliability Ratings** for more than 200 car models currently in the marketplace.

HOW TO SELECT A PRODUCT USING THE BUYING GUIDE

1. Read the Buying Advice for that particular product (pages 27-148).
2. Check the Product Ratings for model-specific ratings and information on test results and features (pages 224-326).
3. Study the Brand Reliability section for information on frequency of repair by brand (pages 327-337).
4. Select the brand and model that best fits your needs.

Product Ratings are given for more than 950 models in 26 categories, ranging from air conditioners to washing machines. The Ratings now include the highly useful CONSUMER REPORTS Quick Picks.

The **Brand Reliability** section presents survey results from 600,000 respondents on repairs and problems they've had with various brands in a variety of product categories.

Finally, there's a **Brand Locator** table with information for contacting manufacturers, a list of recent **Product Recalls**, and two indexes to help you find the buying advice you need.

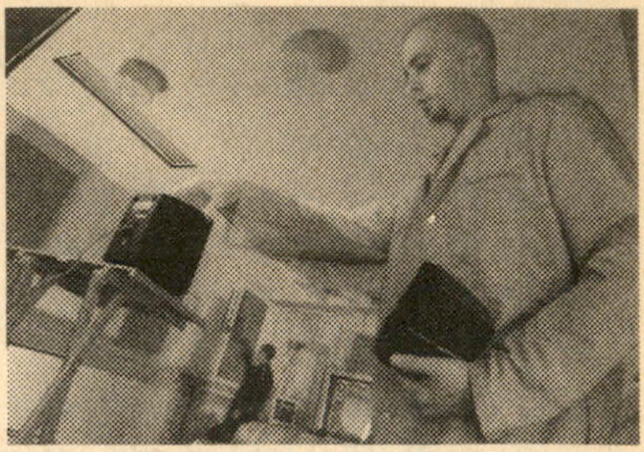

CONSUMER REPORTS tests are rigorous and objective, using constantly refined processes. Here, a technician prepares an audio speaker for testing.

WHO WE ARE

About the Consumer Reports family of products

Founded as a magazine in 1936, CONSUMER REPORTS now brings you its unbiased, trusted information in many formats. Its products and publications include CONSUMER REPORTS magazine; buying guides and magazines from Consumer Reports Publications Development; two newsletters, Consumer Reports On Health and Consumer Reports Money Adviser; and Consumer Reports TV, a nationally syndicated consumer news service.

ConsumerReports.org offers site subscribers a searchable version of our test findings and advice, now with wireless PDA accessibility. Auto prices and custom reports are available through the Consumer Reports New Car Buying Kit, Consumer Reports New Car Price Service, and Consumer Reports Used Car Price Service. You can find prices, subscription rates, and more information on all of these products and services at *www.ConsumerReports.org.* Go to "Our Publications" on the home page, then click on "More Products."

CONSUMER REPORTS specializes in head-to-head, brand-name comparisons of autos and household products. It also provides informed, impartial advice on a broad range of topics from health and nutrition to personal finance and travel.

CONSUMER REPORTS buys all the products it tests and accepts no free samples. We accept no advertising from outside entities nor do we let any company use our information or Ratings for commercial purposes.

CONSUMER REPORTS is published by Consumers Union, an independent, nonprofit testing and information organization—the largest such organization anywhere in the world.

Since 1936, Consumers Union's mission has been to test products, inform the public, and protect consumers. Our income is derived solely from the sale of our publications and services, and from nonrestrictive, noncommercial contributions, grants, and fees.

Secrets of Shopping Smart

Are you a careful researcher—someone who takes the time to shop for the best price on whatever you're buying? Or are you a time-saver, looking to get the best price as quickly as possible? Or do you window shop? Whatever your shopping style, you have lots more choices these days.

You can surf Web sites, leaf through catalogs, and visit all kinds of stores, from specialized boutiques to giant warehouse clubs. Information on just about every product is available literally at your fingertips, so chances are you'll use a combination of shopping strategies. Even if you want the immediacy of buying in a store, you may want to check models, prices, and availability online. Internet companies are now publishing catalogs as selling tools.

While shopping alternatives have grown, the basic rules for smart shopping remain the same: Do your homework and determine the best value for your needs. A good place to start is with the Consumer Reports Buying Guide. In this chapter we give you strategies for shopping smart—in the store, online, and by catalog. Next, in "10 Great Ways to Find Bargains on the Web" (page 15), we offer you tips and tools for using the Web to make smart purchases. And as you plan your purchases, consult this guide for more than 900 product Ratings (page 224) plus brand reliability information (page 327) for many product categories.

Each month, CONSUMER REPORTS magazine can also help with new product reviews and comparisons, test results, and Ratings. Our Web site, Consumer Reports.org, gives site subscribers access to the latest Ratings and archives of CONSUMER REPORTS, plus online-only content such as e-Ratings of shopping Web sites.

STORE STRATEGIES

Traditional retailers are still the principal shopping choice of most consumers. Bricks-and-mortar stores allow what online or catalog shopping can't—an in-person judgment of overall appearance and important sensory qualities. Researching your purchase before you set off for the store can pay off in valuable product knowledge, time saved, and—maybe—a lower price.

Specialty stores, special service. Need help selecting a product in a category you're not familiar with? Just want a real person to help you? Smaller stores, such as audio boutiques and Main Street shops, can provide a knowledgeable staff and personal service, including special ordering. These perks may be offset by higher prices. Determine a fair price before you go, using this guide, the Web, or a retailer's catalog. Then decide how much the extra service is worth to you. Be aware that for some products, such as computers, you can get more customization by buying online. A 2004 CONSUMER REPORTS survey found that people purchasing desktop computers over the Internet or through a catalog were generally more satisfied than people who bought them at a bricks-and-mortar retailer.

Bottom-line basics. Is finding the type of product you want at a good price more important than the latest technology and a large selection? Mass merchandisers such as Wal-Mart and Target cover many categories, with a selection of moderately priced brands from well-known manufacturers, along with their own store brands. (Wal-Mart accounts for a huge share of total sales in many categories of appliances and electronic items.)

Though return policies at most mass merchandisers are usually liberal, returns may entail time and hassle.

Big stores, big selection. Specialty chains such as Circuit City and Best Buy account for three-quarters of home-electronics sales. Home Depot and Lowe's control one-fourth of the home-improvement product market. CompUSA inhabits strip malls across the country. Sears has a network of stores and a Web site with lots of product choices for major appliances and other home products.

These chains may also feature special services, such as viewing/listening rooms for home-theater demonstrations. And although sales-staff expertise may vary, you can generally get questions answered.

Join the club. If you're willing to be flexible on brand and model, check a warehouse club: Costco, BJ's Wholesale Club, or Sam's Club (Wal-Mart's warehouse sibling). Since these stores emphasize value, not service or selection, expect long lines and little sales help. Prices are consistently low, though not necessarily the lowest.

Clubs charge an annual membership fee (generally $35 to $45). If you don't shop there frequently, that fee can undo much of your savings. But a big saving on a single purchase can pay for your membership.

YOU'RE COVERED

Consumer protection online and off

Whenever you shop at home—online, on the phone, or by mail—you have the same safety net against theft of your credit-card number as when you shop in person. If you report misuse right away, you're liable for only $50, even on international transactions. Some Web merchants will even reimburse that $50. (Check individual Web site policies.)

If a merchant misrepresents a product, Web shoppers and catalog patrons are entitled to the same protection and recourse. Unfortunately, if the merchant—Web or otherwise—is not in your state or within 100 miles of your home, some federal protections will not apply. For example, you may not be able to withhold credit-card payment if you have a dispute over the quality of a product. Many credit-card issuers will try to mediate, however, or will at least credit your account until the dispute is settled. Barring that, you'll have to file a complaint with your state attorney general's office or local consumer-protection bureau.

Note that these protections don't apply to purchases made with a debit card.

Most clubs will issue a limited-time shopping pass, letting you browse without joining, but you may have to pay a surcharge if you buy goods as a nonmember.

CATALOG STRATEGIES

Catalogs offer selection and convenience, often from established companies with proven track records and top-notch customer service. And of course they offer 24/7 access. Most catalog merchants are also online.

The catalog-Web connection can give you the best of both venues. You can browse the catalog (leafing through pages can be quicker than waiting for screens to redraw) and then order online using a catalog's "quick search" feature, or simply call the toll-free number while looking at the screen.

Online catalogs typically feature more merchandise than expensive-to-mail paper catalogs. Web sites frequently feature lines not available in the paper catalog, online-only sales and bargains, even product-selection tips and detailed enlargements of product photos. Habitués of online catalog venues can snap up specials and closeouts before items go out of stock.

Ordering from a catalog over the phone or the Web is usually quick, but popular items can still be on back-order, even if they seemed to be in stock when you placed the order. If you don't receive your purchase within the promised time, check back. And before you order, check shipping fees—they can vary widely and add significantly to the cost of the order.

WEB STRATEGIES

You can hunt down just about anything on the Web, from potato chips to vacation homes, but you'll find that some items are more e-commerce-compatible than others. Books, music, videos, DVDs, and computer software are big online successes because they're standardized products, and no bricks-and-mortar store is able to stock every title. Branded electronics items also lend themselves to online shopping because it's handy to select them by manufacturer and specific features. Shipping is another important factor: Small, lightweight purchases—books as opposed to, say, refrigerators—are top online sellers.

Perhaps even more than for buying, the Web is immensely useful for researching a purchase. Information that would previously have taken many hours and many phone calls (if it could be found at all) is now available via a simple click of your mouse. Thus armed, you can make better decisions about where to buy, what to buy, and how much to pay.

BUYING THROUGH AUCTIONS

Internet auction sites deal in anything people want to sell. Though sellers provide descriptions (and, often, digital images), details about flaws and condition may be fuzzy. Except for sites operated by retailers or businesses, most auction sites do not verify the condition of an item—or whether it really exists. Thus the largest Internet auction site, eBay, suggests you get a written statement from the seller detailing condition and value, return policy, warranty information, promised delivery date, plus an address and telephone number. Buyers should insure their items and be sure that sellers ship packages in a traceable manner to help assure a successful transaction. If a seller fails to deliver or misrepresents an item, eBay will reimburse buyers for up to $175 of their loss. Ebay also offers links to third-party companies that provide authentication and grading services.

Continued on page 14

BIGGER ISN'T ALWAYS BETTER

Electronics retailers compared

There are numerous retail outfits from which to choose when looking to buy electronic products for your home. In addition to individual and chain stores that specialize in consumer electronics, there are online sources, warehouse clubs, and mega-retailers such as Wal-Mart and Target to consider.

WHAT WE FOUND

We surveyed our readers to find out how satisfied they were with the selection, quality, price, and service that they experienced when buying home electronics. More than 10,000 responded, and they commented on over 17,000 individual visits to electronics retailers. Here's what we found:

• Our readers gave only one retailer the highest marks in each of the categories where it received a rating: Amazon.com.

The other retailers that most pleased our readers often involved trade-offs. They tended to have above-average scores either for prices or for some other attributes.

• The warehouse giants–BJ's, Costco, and Sam's Club–received relatively good scores on price, for example, but readers gave them lower marks for service and selection.

• Locally owned stores received top ratings for selection and service, but scored less well on price.

• As a group, discount chains Kmart, Target, and Wal-Mart managed only average scores on price, and received lower marks on selection, quality, and service.

The Ratings on the next page are based on our readers' overall satisfaction with the shopping experience.

Guide to the Survey

The Ratings are based on 17,153 store visits by 10,180 respondents who bought any of the following electronics products in 2002 and 2003: camcorders, cameras, DVDs, handheld PDAs, and TVs. These results from our 2003 Annual Questionnaire are based on Consumer Reports subscribers and may not reflect the experiences of the general public. There were at least 181 responses for each store. For retail chains we only had sufficient data to rate their in-store, but not online or mail order, service.

Reader Score: A score of 100 would mean all respondents had been completely satisfied with their experience; 80 means they were very satisfied, on average; 60, fairly well satisfied. Differences of less than 5 points aren't meaningful.

Prices, selection, service, and **checkout** are based on the percentage of shoppers who rated the chain as excellent or very good on each attribute. These ratings are relative and reflect how each chain compares with the average score.

Electronics retailers

Better ⊜ ⊖ ○ ◒ ● Worse

Store	Store Category	Reader Score (0–100)	Prices	Selection	Service	Checkout
Amazon.com	Online store	90	⊜	⊜	-	-
Locally owned businesses	–	88	○	⊜	⊜	⊖
AAFES	Military exchange service	87	⊜	○	○	○
Ritz Camera	Camera specialists	86	●	⊜	⊜	⊜
Costco	Price club	83	⊜	●	●	●
RadioShack	Electronics store	82	○	●	⊜	⊜
Boscov's	Department store	82	○	⊖	⊖	○
Sears	Department store	82	○	⊖	⊜	○
Circuit City	Electronics store	81	○	⊜	⊜	○
Office Depot	Office supply store	81	○	○	○	○
BJ's Wholesale	Price club	80	⊖	●	●	●
Good Guys	Electronics store	80	◒	⊖	⊜	○
Staples	Office supply store	80	○	○	○	○
Target	Discount store	80	○	●	●	○
Sam's Club	Price club	80	⊖	●	●	●
Office Max	Office supply store	78	○	○	○	○
Best Buy	Electronics store	78	○	⊜	○	◒
Wal-Mart	Discount store	78	○	◒	●	●
Kmart	Discount store	75	○	●	●	●
Fry's Electronics	Electronics store	75	○	⊜	●	●

SHOP FROM HOME

Computer retailers compared

It's now common to find fast, powerful, reasonably priced computers virtually everywhere in the marketplace. If you're looking to buy a desktop computer, be sure to check these survey results and Ratings on the best retailers for PCs to insure that you get the model and service that match your personal computing needs.

WHAT WE FOUND

According to the survey results, it's generally better to buy a desktop computer from a manufacturer or retail Web site or by mail order than in a store. The representatives tended to be more helpful and the computer selection better. Here are some of our other findings:

- Overall, respondents were less satisfied with their purchasing experiences at retail stores, which were rated relatively low for selection, knowledge, and helpfulness.
- Apple and PC/Mac Connection were the highest-rated vendors in overall satisfaction and garnered top scores on all ratings except prices.
- Wal-Mart and Best Buy were rated lower than most vendors; moreover, Wal-Mart, along with Sam's Club, scored relatively poorly on all factors except for prices, on which both stores were rated average.
- Three retailers each scored above average for prices: Costco, a warehouse store; the Web/catalog retailer PC/Mac Connection; and TigerDirect. All manufacturers were rated average for prices, except for Sony, which posted the lowest score of all vendors.
- All manufacturers and almost all retail Web sites/catalogs scored well for selection. The one exception was TigerDirect, which was average.

Guide to the Survey

Ratings are based on 43,384 responses from Consumer Reports subscribers who completed the 2004 Annual Questionnaire online, covering household computers purchased new from 2003 through June 2004. These results are based on Consumer Reports online subscribers and may not reflect the experiences of the general public. There were at least 163 responses for each vendor.

Manufacturer Direct refers to purchases from the manufacturer through Web or catalog channels only, not stores. **Retail Store** covers in-store purchases only, not those from retailers' Web sites. **Retail Web site/Catalog** includes purchases exclusively through Web or catalog channels.

Reader Score: A score of 100 would mean all respondents had been completely satisfied with their experience; 80 would mean they were very satisfied, on average; 60, fairly well satisfied. Differences of less than 4 points aren't meaningful.

Selection of PCs (models, price ranges, etc.), **prices, knowledge** of salespeople or customer-service reps, and **helpfulness** or courtesy of employees are relative and reflect how each vendor compares with the average score. (The last two ratings excluded respondents who purchased their PCs online and did not phone or e-mail the vendor.)

Computer retailers

Better ⊜ ⊖ ○ ◒ ● Worse

	Reader Score (0–100)	Selection	Prices	Knowledge	Helpfulness
MANUFACTURER DIRECT					
Apple/iMac	92	⊜	○	⊜	⊜
IBM	86	⊖	○	⊜	⊜
Dell	84	⊜	○	⊖	○
HP	83	⊖	○	⊖	○
Gateway	83	⊖	○	⊖	○
Sony	82	⊖	●	-	-
Compaq	81	⊖	○	○	○
RETAIL STORE					
Costco	82	●	⊖	●	◒
Micro Center	81	○	○	⊖	○
Office Depot	80	●	○	○	○
Sam's Club	79	●	○	●	●
Staples	77	●	◒	○	○
Circuit City	76	◒	◒	○	○
Fry's Electronics	75	○	○	◒	●
CompUSA	74	○	◒	○	○
Best Buy	73	○	○	○	◒
Wal-Mart	73	●	○	●	●
RETAIL WEB SITE/CATALOG					
PC/Mac Connection.com	91	⊜	⊖	⊜	⊜
CDW.com	87	⊜	○	-	-
PC/Mac Mall.com	84	⊜	○	⊖	○
TigerDirect.com	83	○	⊖	-	-

"-" Indicates insufficient sample.

If you purchase something at an auction site, use a credit card (not a debit card) or work out terms with an online escrow service, such as Escrow.com, which processes transactions. (Fees are based on the amount of the transaction, method of payment, and, sometimes, shipping costs.)

At pick-your-own-price sites, you name a price for, say, airline tickets, hotels, or a mortgage, and merchants come to you. Priceline originated this type of "reverse auction." The catch: You must provide a credit-card number up front. If Priceline finds the item at your price, your credit card is charged immediately, usually with no cancellation option. Nor can you request a specific brand. For airline tickets, you are only allowed to make one bid within a seven-day period for the same itinerary; for hotel rooms, within a three-day period. Simply changing your bid amount is considered a duplicate bid and will be rejected automatically. If you want to immediately bid again, you must be willing to change, say, your departure date or hotel quality level.

THANKS, BUT NO THANKS

Extended warranties are rarely a good investment. The main reason: Most big-ticket items are very dependable. The odds are heavily stacked against your collecting on an extended warranty.

SMART ORDERING

Whether catalogers or e-tailers, retailers should provide complete information about their business and policies. Here's what to look for:

Complete contact information, including a real-world location. Look for a toll-free number, e-mail and postal addresses, not a P.O. box, and 24-hour customer service. (See **Brand Locator, p. 338,** for Web addresses and phone numbers of major brands.)

Clear shipping, handling, and return policies. Review options and prices before you place an order. Shipping is extra with most catalog orders; some e-tailers offer free shipping when your total reaches a specified amount or during frequent promotions. When ordering from a catalog, remember sales tax, charged if the catalog company operates a store in your state.

A 100-percent satisfaction guarantee. Look for a merchant that allows returns for any reason, with no restocking fee. (Custom items and special orders may be excluded.) A good merchant will tell you as you order when items will arrive—or if they'll be delayed.

Security and privacy. At a Web site, look for the Trust-e symbol or a Better Business Bureau Online seal, both indicating that the merchant's business practices have passed an audit. As soon as you start the buying process, the site should show a symbol like a key or a lock, or a Web address with an "s" (for secure) after the "http." The best sites also cover the $50 maximum that credit-card companies charge if a card is used without your authorization.

When ordering from a catalog, look for a clearly stated list-sharing policy, with an easy way to opt out. If you don't see such a statement, ask for details—or assume that the company rents its customer lists to other merchants.

10 Great Ways to Find Bargains on the Web

There's no doubt that shopping on the Web is con-venient. You can shop anytime, any day, instead of fighting traffic to the local mall after work or on weekends. Some e-tailer out there in cyberspace is bound to have your desired model or size and will be happy to ship it to your door. And before you buy, you can read reviews from customers.

The Web also offers some terrific shopping bargains, if you know how and where to find them. A good place to start your search is at the CONSUMER REPORTS Web site, *www.ConsumerReports.org*. It includes expert Ratings of thousands of products and services. You can also read complete e-Ratings of online merchants' sites (supported by Consumer WebWatch, a grant-funded project of Consumers Union). ConsumerReports.org's e-Ratings take into account a site's credibility, usability, and content.

Once you're well Web-informed, try these online bargain-hunting tips:

1 Shop with a bot.

Using a bot (short for robot) to shop online is like taking the Keno twins to a flea market. Like the Kenos, from "Find!" on PBS, whose trained eyes can spot a valuable antique in a field of cast-off furniture, bots can search the Internet for the best prices on virtually any product you want. Bots then sort the results into lists so you can compare e-tailers easily.

All bots are not created equal, however. Their results depend on how many sites they check. Shoppers should also be aware that bots generally make money by charging merchants a fee when they send them customers.

The Consumer Reports Money Adviser newsletter recently put six bots to the test and recommended two sites: *www.Shopping.com* and *www.BizRate.com*. Check whichever bot you use for ratings of each merchant it lists. Before you buy from an e-tailer you're not familiar with, it pays to read what other consumers say about its reliability and service.

2 Cut car-buying costs.

Start at *www.ConsumerReports.org/carbuying*, which features a range of products designed to help you negotiate a great price with the car dealer of your choice. The interactive, online New Car Buying Kit ($39 for a three-month subscription) helps you compare models and choose the vehicle that's right for you. You also get unlimited New Car Price Reports. (If you bought each report separately, you'd pay $12 for the first vehicle and $10 for any additional models ordered at the same time.)

Consumer Reports Price Reports tell you how big a profit margin the dealer makes on a model. They also include details on current consumer rebates and unadvertised dealer sales incentives or discounts. If you're looking for a used car or want to know what your trade-in is worth, you can order a customized Consumer Reports Used Car Price Report for $10.

Once you know what you want and have an idea of what it should cost, check out these sites, which provide prices for specific new and used models and can connect you with dealers: *www.autobytel.com*, *www.autotrader.com*, *www.autovantage.com*, *www.autoweb.com*, *www.car.com*, and *www.cars.com*. For new cars, try *www.autos.msn.com*, *www.carsdirect.com*, *www.checkbook.org*, and *www.invoicedealers.com*.

For used cars, check out *www.dealernet.com*, *www.ebaymotors.com*, *www.imotors.com*, and *www.usedcars.com*.

3 Troll for the lowest travel costs.

If you have the time and patience to be your own travel agent, you can save big bucks by booking airline tickets, rental cars, cruises, and hotel rooms online. Unfortunately, no one travel Web site will consistently give you the best prices. Several studies by Consumer WebWatch have found that you have to shop around. The Web makes comparison-shopping relatively painless. You can check prices anytime you're in the mood, and you can easily change travel dates and times to see how rates vary.

To book a flight, start with the Big Three travel sites, *www.expedia.com*, *www.orbitz.com*, and *www.travelocity.com*, but also check the airlines' own sites, which frequently offer bonus frequent-flyer miles when you book directly through them. Also, check discount airlines such as JetBlue Airways *(www.jetblue.com)* and Southwest Airlines *(www.southwest.com)* that the Big Three sites don't sell tickets for.

There are even more places on the Web to find a discounted hotel room. In addition to the Big Three, you can try *www.hotels.com* and a shopping bot called SideStep.com. It searches multiple travel Web sites for the best deals. You may find an even better price on a site sponsored by a hotel chain or an individual hotel. Many chains pledge to meet or beat the best rate you can find online.

When you're researching hotels online, carefully answer all questions that pop up on your screen. You may find that you're eligible for discounts that apply to government employees, military personnel, students, seniors, children, or members of organizations like AAA or AARP.

Once you book a hotel room online, keep shopping until you hit the deadline for canceling your reservation without a penalty. If the hotel can't fill its rooms, it may drop rates or add perks like free breakfast or parking. You can stay abreast of new deals by checking an individual hotel's site or by calling the hotel directly.

4 Shop in the dark for bigger travel bargains.

If your plans are flexible, try the so-called opaque travel sites in addition to the Big Three.

Dealing with opaque sites like Hotwire.com or Priceline.com is a little like choosing the mystery vacation behind Door No. 1 on "Let's Make a Deal." Until you type in your credit-card number, you won't know which airline, car-rental company, or hotel you'll get for the price you've been quoted. On *www.hotwire.com*, you type in your itinerary. The site responds that an unnamed company can provide the flight, rental car, or hotel room you want for a specified price. With *www.priceline.com*, you name your price and wait to see if any company will meet it. If none does, you can raise your price, change your itinerary, or both.

Consumer WebWatch recently found that opaque sites provided the lowest rates about half the time. When they beat the competition, however, they did it by an impressive 16 to 25 percent, on average. But if not knowing details about a flight until after you've paid for a nonrefundable ticket gives you the willies, or you want to have a say in which hotel you'll be staying at, stick with regular travel Web sites.

5 Clip cyber coupons.

You can find coupons online for everything from mustard to pizzas made at the pizzeria around the corner. Some sites charge you for coupons or ask so many questions about you and your buying habits that they're not worth the trouble to use. Consumer Reports Money Adviser recently rated coupon sites and recommended these: *www.couponpages.com*, *www.hotcoupons.com*, *www.valpak.com*, and *www.valupage.com*.

For help in trimming your weekly grocery bill while helping to feed the hungry, click on *www.cutouthunger.org*, a site that urges you to donate your savings to the hungry. This site posts supermarket sales fliers and coupons that appear weekly in newspaper inserts around the country. First, note the sale items you plan to buy in your grocery store's weekly ad. Then check the site for coupons for those items.

6 Comparison shop 'til you drop for electronics.

Sitting and clicking is simply the best way to shop for consumer electronics and computers. Online product descriptions and customer reviews will help you pick the camera or computer that's right for you. Given all the different types of Web sites you can use to compare prices, it's easy to find great bargains.

You can try general shopping bots like BizRate.com and Shopping.com. There are also bots that specialize in electronics, like *www.shopper.com* and *www.streetprices.com*. You'll also want to check out e-tailers with a wide selection, such as *www.amazon.com*, *www.bestbuy.com*, *www.circuitcity.com*, and *www.jandr.com*. If you're in the market for a popular model, also try warehouse clubs like *www.costco.com* and *www.samsclub.com*. And when shopping for a computer, check manufacturers' sites like *www.dell.com* and *www.gateway.com*.

7 Wait for catalog companies to cut prices.

Browse the catalogs you get in the mail, but buy online. It often doesn't take long for catalog companies to offer products at cut-rate prices on the Web. Take Hanna Andersson, which specializes in pricey children's clothing with a Swedish flair. Its "late summer" catalog landed in mailboxes in midsummer 2004. By early August, a number of items in that catalog were on sale online, including a pair of zipper boots, for example, that went down 20 percent.

As an added convenience, you can ask catalog companies to send you e-mail alerts about sales.

It pays to track prices even after you've purchased an item. That's because some retailers will give you a one-time price adjustment. For example, *www.oldnavy.com* offers an adjustment if an item is marked down within seven days of the date on your invoice.

8 Search auction and online outlet sites for off-price outfits.

Granted, the big bargains are generally a season or two old. But they're often "NWT," which is eBay lingo for "new with tags." It's easier to click through hundreds of items on the Web than it is to sift through the sale racks at your local mall. You're also more likely to find the size and color you want online.

Bricks-and-mortar retailers also use the Internet to clear out inventory. At JCPenney's online outlet store, for example, you could recently buy a women's tapestry jacket for less than half the original cost. It's also worth checking your favorite stores' regular Web sites, under "sale."

9 Click for entertaining discounts.

If you're planning a trip to an amusement park or a museum, don't leave home without checking the attraction's Web site for special deals. Check even if you're traveling off the beaten path. Click on *www.outdoorhistory.org*, for instance, and you'll find discount coupons for living history museums. When we checked, a coupon for Historic Deerfield, a Colonial-era town in western Massachusetts, saved you $2 off admission prices.

Movie buffs should check the Web sites of theater chains in their neighborhoods. Regal Entertainment Group at *www.regalcinemas.com*, for example, sponsors a "Crown Club" that gives perks like free popcorn to frequent moviegoers.

If you missed your chance to buy a copy of the Entertainment Book from a student raising money for his or her school, you can buy one online at *www.entertainment.com*. These annual publications feature discount coupons for attractions, restaurants, and stores in local areas and generally cost between $25 and $45. As the months go by, the Web price goes down. Tip: Keep the book in your car, so the Burger King coupon is at your fingertips when you pull up to the take-out window.

10 Buy books used.

Sure, you can pick up a new copy of "The Da Vinci Code" on *www.amazon.com* for roughly a 40 percent discount off the publisher's list price. But why stop there? Amazon.com was recently selling used hardcover copies for several dollars less than its new copies.

If you have kids in college, send them to the Web to search for used textbook bargains. For instance, "Finance," a 500-page tome for business majors, lists for $125 but recently could be had on Amazon.com for less than half that amount. Other sites worth a look include *www.abebooks.com*, *www.alibris.com*, *www.bn.com*, and *www.powells.com*.

What's New in Home Products

I f there's one overarching trend in the marketplace today, it's that features once found only on high-priced models are trickling down to their mid- and low-priced counterparts. This more-for-less trend is also showing itself in greater energy efficiency, driven in part by competition and in part by government regulation.

While mostly good news, this trend also comes at a price. Some products are becoming more complex to learn and use as well as more difficult to choose in the first place. That's where this year's Buying Guide can help. Here's a rundown of the major developments in products for your home:

HOME ENTERTAINMENT

The digital revolution in home entertainment may still be under way, but the outcome is already clear. Digital products such as DVD players and recorders, high-definition television sets, and satellite-TV receivers have transformed the home-entertainment marketplace in recent years. Camcorders, cameras, receivers, cable boxes, and many TV sets have moved from analog to digital and, in the process, made leaps in what they promise and frequently can deliver.

Consumer Reports tests show that digital capability often results in improvements in performance. Audio CD players consistently reproduce sound better than turntables did. The typical digital camcorder offers much clearer video than the best of its older, analog cousins. Audio (or A/V) receivers supporting digital audio can provide more realism when you're watching movies at home than those using earlier, analog-audio standards. High-definition TV delivers not just the football game but the sweat glistening on the players' arms—assuming you want to see it.

Despite digital's superiority over the analog ways of cassette tape, videotape, and traditional NTSC-standard TV, those products still will be sold for some time to come. And if industry infighting and consumer confusion are any indication, it could be years before we see the last of the analog breed. Following are some of the major trends in today's home-entertainment marketplace:

Digital now dominates. DVDs, with their capacity for extra features such as director-commentary chapters and scenes cut from a movie's theatrical release, have come to dominate video—and supplant videotapes—even faster than the CD conquered audio in the 1980s and '90s. DVD players have become almost a commodity, with excellent performance the norm and prices well below $100 for an increasing number of models.

While most TV watchers are still using VCRs to record programs, the DVD is now poised to become your recording medium too. Prices for DVD recorders have fallen from more than $1,000 a few years ago to less than $500 today. Those prices and the cost of blank storage media are likely to drop further in coming years.

VCRs have not disappeared from the marketplace, however, and they may still be the best choice for many people. If you're looking to replace a VCR, you can hedge your bets with a DVD-VCR combo ($150 and up), provided you don't mind a fairly basic DVD player.

Higher definition and lower prices. The TV landscape has also changed dramatically, giving you both the luxury and the challenge of unprecedented choice. Today's market offers everything from flat-panel plasma TVs that can be mounted on a wall to thin LCD tabletop displays, wide-screen projection sets, and familiar picture tube TVs in new sizes and shapes. The gold standard for TV viewing is high-definition, or HD, the much-talked-about format that produces images with lifelike detail and clarity. If you're considering replacing your primary TV, it's probably time to upgrade to an HDTV.

Music marches to a digital drummer. The introduction of CD players in 1982 turns out to have been just phase one of the digital revolution in consumer audio—the playback part. Phase two: the current boom in digital recording options. Audio component CD player/recorders, which let you "burn" your own CDs, have been dropping in price; you can now buy one for a few hundred dollars. (The same process can also be done, often more easily, using computers with recordable CD-R drives.) MP3 players, which copy music to a hard drive rather than a CD, offer huge capacity, 5 to 80 gigabytes, in very small packages. Apple Computer, for example, boasts that its iPod digital music player lets you "easily slip up to 10,000 songs into your pocket."

Sound that surrounds. One of the biggest attractions of digital audio technology is surround sound, most commonly represented by the Dolby Digital format, which has brought multichannel audio from the movie theater to the family room. To take full advantage, you need at least five speakers (potentially more) plus a subwoofer and a Dolby Digital receiver to manage them—in addition to your TV set and DVD player.

You can buy those components completely à la carte, integrating any equipment you already own and want to keep, or as a "home theater in a box," which combines multiple speakers, a subwoofer, and a receiver (possibly with a built-in DVD player as well). See "Creating a Home Theater" on page 28 for more information.

Products are getting smaller. Manufacturers continue to shrink hard drives, batteries, and other parts of audio and video components. MP3 players can be as small as an ink pen. Portable CD and DVD players can be as thin as an inch. Many capable speakers for home theater are as small as those intended for computer use, making it possible to set up your system in a modest size room. "Executive sound systems" have shrunk minisystems into microsystems that fit readily on a desk or into flat systems that can hang on a wall.

Digital cameras, too, are continuing to get smaller and lighter. Numerous medium-size models weigh just 7 ounces, and several pocket-size compacts tip the scales at a mere 4 or 5 ounces.

Complexity abounds. One unfortunate consequence of the digital revolution is

TAKE ACTION

10 Action Points for Smart Shoppers

New models and features are arriving in today's marketplace with dizzying speed. Keep these 10 action points in mind as you make your purchases in 2005:

1. Consider switching to DVD for recording and storing movies, programs, and video. The equipment is getting better and coming down in price.

2. Falling prices and more widely available high-definition programming mean this is the time to consider HD if you're shopping for a new set.

3. A "home theater in a box" will save you the extra work of selecting separate audio and video components.

4. If you're shopping for major appliances (refrigerators, washing machines), consider buying the more energy-efficient models. They could save you money in the long run. (Be sure to consult the CONSUMER REPORTS energy-efficiency ratings.)

5. Do a lot of comparison shopping for major appliances—more and more retailers are competing in this market.

6. If personalized service is important to you for your home and yard equipment, consider paying a bit more and buying from your local hardware store or independent dealer.

7. More power tools are now battery operated. Drills and reciprocating saws now rival or exceed the performance of corded versions. You may wish to make the switch if you want to liberate yourself from these corded power tools.

8. LCD monitors are getting thinner, better, and coming down in price. Think about getting one with your next computer purchase or to replace your CRT monitor.

9. Consider getting an inkjet printer that allows you to bypass your computer and print copies of photos from your digital camera.

10. Laptop computers are now performing as well overall as desktops. You may wish to get one to handle all your computing needs.

that it now takes considerably more study to make a smart choice. Products have become more complicated, and many now involve a service provider. Not only must you choose among competing services, but once you've selected and bought the hardware, you're committed to that provider. Switching can involve paying hundreds of dollars more to buy new, provider-specific gear, as with satellite-TV equipment or digital video recorders (DVRs) such as those sold under TiVo, Replay, and other names.

More and more, electronics components need to connect with one another, requiring compatible video and audio connections for best results. And competing formats mean that early adopters cannot be sure that the format they choose will be the one that prevails, as manufacturers conjure up newer media formats, music-encoding schemes, and connection specifications.

All of this, of course, means a greater challenge for consumers shopping for these products. The section on home entertainment buying advice begins on page 27.

KITCHEN & LAUNDRY

Form is catching up with function in the kitchen and laundry room. Today's appliances, both large and small, are often more stylish than the ones most of us currently own—but their beauty isn't only skin deep. Many appliances are also smarter, more capable, and more energy-efficient than the models of just a few years ago. New technologies and an ongoing tightening of government energy standards have sparked the change. Here's a rundown on some of the current trends:

Stainless steals the show. Stainless steel is the biggest news in refrigerator design. More manufacturers are offering fridges that mimic the Sub-Zero professional-style look without the Humvee-sized price tag. You'll still pay a premium for stainless—about $150 to $300 more than for a comparable white model—but prices start at a fairly modest $650 or so. Stainless steel finishes are also increasingly popular on other kitchen appliances, including ranges, range hoods, and dishwashers.

On the color front, biscuit, bisque, or linen are replacing almond. If you prefer a splashier color for your appliance—such as cobalt blue or hunter green—look to premium brands such as Jenn-Air, KitchenAid, or Viking. Even the humble mixer is getting a livelier palette; you can find KitchenAid stand mixers, for example, in such colors as wasabi and pistachio.

Brainier appliances. Everything from dishwashers to mixers has been embellished with electronic sensors, controls, and monitors. "Smart" products are supposed to minimize the guesswork of knowing when the clothes are dry, the food is cooked, the dishes are washed, or the toast is toasty. This technology can use water and energy more efficiently, as with a washer that automatically fills to the water level the load requires, or a refrigerator that defrosts only as necessary rather than at set intervals.

Such advances, however, are just the first wave. Ready to debut: microwave ovens that scan bar codes on packaged-food labels and automatically set the precise cooking time and power level; Internet-connected refrigerators that scan labels and automatically reorder provisions when you're running low; and self-diagnosing appliances that can convey information to a repair center by computer, allowing a technician to make a preliminary diagnosis before a service call. Whether these products will truly fill a consumer need—or merely serve a manufacturer's desire to boost sales—remains to be seen.

Speed sells. Consumers seem to want food cooked ever faster, or at least manufacturers say they do. Titans such as General Electric, Maytag, and Whirlpool have introduced appliances that claim to reduce cooking times by as much as 60 percent over conventional means by combining various methods—microwave, convection, and halogen or quartz light bulbs. Such hybrid devices may offer another advantage: no preheating. The perceived need for speed has even fueled a resurgence in a category from another era—pressure cookers—in safer and more consumer-friendly designs.

Refrigerators, too, are becoming speedier. On some GE, LG, and Samsung fridges you can adjust the temperature of a drawer to "express chill" or thaw items. Higher-priced clothes dryers are adding specialty cycles such as "speed dry" (15 minutes on high heat, for example).

Lower energy costs. As of January 1, 2004, the U.S. Department of Energy mandated that new washing machines be about 35 percent more efficient than previously required. All washers manufactured after January 1, 2007, must be another 17 percent more efficient than required by the 2004 standard.

Refrigerators, which typically devour more electricity than any other kitchen appliance, are also required to be less gluttonous. If you replace a refrigerator bought in 1980 with a similar new model, your energy costs will drop about 60 percent. Over the long run, a pricier model with a low annual energy cost may prove less expensive than a cheaper model that uses more electricity. Most new fridges now cost $30 to $60 a year to run. In general, side-by-side units are less energy-efficient than either top- or bottom-freezer models.

Child-friendly features. Some manufacturers are using child lockouts to keep curious fingers out of potentially hazardous places. A number of microwave ovens let you punch in a code to prevent accidental activation. A lockout button disables the knobs on a gas range or keeps the dishwasher from shutting down midcycle if a youngster starts poking at the keypad. Such niceties are still relatively new, though, and not yet found on many products.

More places and ways to shop. Frigidaire, GE, Maytag, Sears, and Whirlpool sell almost three-fourths of all major appliances. In some categories, Sears alone sells more than several of its biggest competitors combined, and the company is trying to strengthen its position by selling online. But the competitive landscape is changing. Home Depot and Lowe's, the nation's biggest home-center chains, have publicly announced they want to dethrone Sears as the leading appliance marketer. Deep-discount warehouse membership clubs such as Costco have also expanded their selection of refrigerators, ranges, and the like.

While the Internet has become a popular way to purchase books and music and get travel deals, it's still not much of a factor in the major appliance category, at least as far as sales are concerned. Many consumers use the Internet, however, to research appliance features and availability before they buy, and so-called "multichannel retailers"—those with both a Web site and bricks-and-mortar locations—are increasingly making it possible to purchase products online and pick them up at a store. Many stores also accept returns of products that were originally purchased from their company's Web site.

Big stakes in small appliances. Coffeemakers, toasters, and blenders rule the kitchen countertop, with consumers purchasing more of them every year than any other countertop appliance. Three brands account for nearly three-quarters of small-appliance sales: Black & Decker, Hamilton Beach/Proctor-Silex, and Sunbeam/Oster.

Major mass retailers, where most of the products are sold, are trying to grab an even larger share of the business by gaining exclusive rights to established national brands. Hamilton Beach/Proctor-Silex, for example, makes products under the GE name (via a licensing agreement) for sale at Wal-Mart. Philips markets a line under its own name through Target. Black & Decker has partnered with chains such as Kmart. Sears sells small appliances under its Kenmore name.

In the case of small appliances like steam irons, manufacturers are now putting formerly high-end features on less expensive models. They hope that more features for less money will induce consumers to trade up to a new model.

The section on kitchen and laundry products begins on page 67.

HOME & YARD EQUIPMENT

The big news in this category is falling prices on products for both inside and outside your home. At the same time, innovations, often prompted by tougher state and federal environmental rules, are making home and yard gear easier and safer to use, as well as friendlier to the environment. So buying a new piece of equipment rather than putting up with an old one may be a good move. Here are trends you'll see this year:

Big boxes, lower prices. Heated competition among big-box stores such as Home Depot, Lowe's, Sears, and Wal-Mart has lowered the price of many home and yard products. Today you can buy a well-equipped automatic tractor, for example, for as little as $1,350—several hundred dollars less than comparable machines three years ago. Those same stores are also fueling competition in gas grills, resulting in more features at lower prices, and room air conditioners, where prices have dropped about 10 percent a year.

Large chains such as Sears and Wal-Mart usually have the best selection of lower-priced brands. Home centers such as Home Depot and Lowe's offer a mix of low-priced, midpriced, and upscale brands. Local hardware stores and other independent dealers tend to carry midpriced and upscale brands. Such stores often offer service that mass merchandisers and home centers don't.

Home and yard products are also sold over the Internet through sites such as Amazon.com, Home-depot.com, Lowes.com, and Sears.com. Such online sites can be useful, especially as research tools, but there's still a lot to be said for the local hardware store or home center. You can't beat hefting a vacuum cleaner or rolling a mower to see if it feels right in your hands.

Safer and simpler controls. Clutchless hydrostatic transmissions on a growing number of ride-on mowers and tractors make mowing go more smoothly. All these machines stop the blade when you leave the seat. And even the least expensive push and self-propelled power mowers stop the engine when you release the safety handle. Some higher-priced models stop the blade but not the engine, eliminating the need to restart the mower. Newer mowers also provide for easier mulching and bagging in the high grass that's typical after lots of rain or a missed week of mowing.

Inside the house, many room air conditioners now have touchpads and remote controls instead of traditional mechanical dials. Timers, energy-saver settings, and digital temperature readouts are also becoming common.

More environmentally friendly. Stricter Department of Energy rules have made today's room air conditioners more efficient. They have also become a better value, with many economical units now meeting Energy Star requirements. Energy Star is a voluntary federal program that helps identify models that are at least 10 percent more efficient than the standard.

Government rules for emissions by lawn mowers and other gasoline-powered yard tools are designed to reduce emissions by hundreds of thousands of tons per year. As of 2005, gas-powered string trimmers and other handheld tools must meet tougher emissions standards in all 50 states. Emissions aren't the only type of pollutant; dozens of towns and cities have enacted laws designed to quiet gas-powered leaf blowers.

Manufacturers are equipping a growing number of cordless drills and other tools with nickel-metal-hydride batteries that are much safer for the environment. Such batteries also delivered longer run times in our cordless-drill tests.

"Green" and "healthy" claims turn up in ads for vacuum cleaners, some of which have a high-efficiency particulate-air (HEPA) filter, designed to trap dust and allergens sucked up by vacuuming. But CONSUMER REPORTS tests have shown that many models without a HEPA filter can keep the air as free of potentially irritating particles. Some manufacturers of central vacuum systems, an increasingly popular option, also maintain that their products are cleaner than regular vacs because the base unit releases its exhaust outside the living space rather than spewing particle-laden air back into the room you're cleaning. We found that central systems did a good job of not stirring up dust within our test room, but some of the upright and canister vacs we tested did even better.

Help when you can't do it yourself. A growing number of manufacturers and retailers are providing the services of roofing, siding, and other home-product installers as well as the products themselves, typically by referral. That may reduce the risk of shoddy work, as some of these retailers and manufacturers screen and even certify the installers they recommend.

Home centers and other retailers are also pushing peace of mind for buyers when something breaks. Many stores now offer at-home repairs or servicing arrangements with local dealers.

The section on home and yard products begins on page 95.

HOME-OFFICE GEAR

The action is also fast and furious on the second front of the digital revolution, the home office. Computer gear continues to become faster and easier to use, with new features for listening to music, editing digital photos and movies, and creating your own CDs and DVDs.

Meanwhile, the added tasks performed by computers and telephones are blurring the line between products. Some cell phones take pictures and play music. Multifunction inkjet printers also scan and copy. An increasing number of telephone calls now travel over the Internet.

BARGAIN WATCH

Price Drop Alert

If you're looking to save money on purchases in 2005, keep an eye on the product categories listed below. Each one has experienced a steady decrease in price, often accompanied by increases in product quality or added features:

- Air conditioners
- CD player/recorders
- Digital cameras
- DVD recorders
- Gas grills
- HDTVs
- Lawn tractors
- LCD monitors

Among the trends that are changing computers, phones, and related gear:

More versatile products. The newest cell phones provide cameras, cutting-edge games, organizers, Web access, a walkie-talkie, and more. Some of the latest personal digital assistants (PDAs) can be easily operated with one hand, wirelessly send e-mail, or readily fit into your shirt pocket—assuming you don't have one of the tiny new digital cameras already in there.

Stand-alone telephone answering machines have pretty much disappeared, as faster, cheaper computer chips have allowed the function to be inexpensively added to cordless and corded phones.

Better and faster performance. Processors, which serve as the brains of a computer, have reached speeds of nearly 4 gigahertz, or 4 billion cycles per second. That's nearly 1,000 times the speed of the earliest personal computers. USB ports are now the primary connection for printers, scanners, and the like, replacing the confusing array of serial, parallel, and game ports. USB 2.0 connections have become the norm for scanners, providing a speed boost over USB 1.0 when used with a USB 2.0 computer.

Photo-quality color inkjet printers have become fast and affordable. In our latest tests, several printers produced excellent 8x10-inch photos in 5 to 7 minutes, as opposed to 10 to 18 minutes on models we tested the previous year. More printers also allow you to bypass your computer to print photos, some using an emerging industry standard called PictBridge for connecting digital cameras and printers via cable.

Thin is in. Svelte liquid-crystal display monitors are becoming the norm for desktop systems, as they continue to drop in price. Not only are they considerably thinner and lighter than cathode-ray tube monitors (about 15 pounds vs. 30 to 50 pounds), they also delivered better performance in our most recent tests of display quality, ease of use, and variety of features.

Computer users on the go can take advantage of laptops that are as thin as a couple of magazines. Laptops are now virtually equal to desktops in performance and features, though laptops cost slightly more and are more difficult to repair. Fortunately, according to our first-ever survey of laptops' reliability, they appear to be less repair-prone than desktops.

Buy direct and customize. In addition to the big electronics chains and other retail outlets, nearly all major computer manufacturers now sell their wares directly, through the Web, telephone orders, and factory stores. At some stores, you can custom-design your own computer at an interactive kiosk. According to the most recent CONSUMER REPORTS survey, you're likely to be better satisfied if you buy directly from the manufacturer over the Internet, where your system can be configured to order, than if you buy through a retail store.

Tech support tumbles. Home-office products may be getting better and cheaper, but when something goes wrong, consumers are frequently in for frustration. Our surveys of satisfaction with tech support showed a drop in the early 2000s, and it is now one of the lowest-rated services we evaluate. Our latest survey indicated that outsourcing—moving some tech-support call centers overseas—may contribute to that low rating. Among the 28 percent of our respondents who reported communications problems on the phone, 63 percent complained that the support staff's English was limited or very hard to understand.

The section on home-office products begins on page 125.

HOME ENTERTAINMENT

Home Entertainment: Sharper and Clearer

With new high-definition televisions and high-tech digital audio and video components easily available, staying home has become as alluring—and almost as good—as going out to the movies. There are more options every day. And prices are coming down as quality is going up.

CREATING A HOME THEATER

Even more than buying a bigger television set, adding surround sound to a TV can transform your viewing and listening experience.

Today there's plenty of surround-sound material to enjoy, and more is on the way. At last count, there were more than 4,500 films on DVD using Dolby Digital, the leading surround-sound format, along with a small but growing number of TV programs. These movies and programs are produced with at least six-channel sound that can be piped to six or more speakers around the room. And the technology is still evolving. Some new formats now offer eight channels.

Multichannel music is less prevalent, but it's starting to gain momentum. Standard music CDs have two channels, while newer discs using DVD-Audio, SACD (Super Audio CD), and DTS 5.1 music formatting can offer up to six channels of sound, simulating a concert experience.

DO YOU WANT SURROUND SOUND?

The case for surround sound is getting stronger all the time. Should you get onboard? Consider the following:

What kind of entertainment do you enjoy? If you watch mostly run-of-the-mill TV programs received via an antenna or basic cable, or if you listen to regular CDs, a stereo setup is usually enough. For DVD movies, some digital-cable or satellite programs, and multichannel music, a surround-sound setup would be better.

What equipment would you need? The typical home-theater setup includes a receiver, two to eight speakers, a TV set with cable or satellite hookup, and a DVD player. Multichannel audio discs can be played on some DVD players (or, in the case of SACD discs, on specialized players). Either the player or the receiver to which it's connected must support the appropriate format.

Assembling the requisite audio system may sound like a pricey proposition, but it doesn't have to be. You can buy components that cost thousands of dollars or opt for a prepackaged speaker system or a home theater in a box that starts at a few hundred dollars.

Do you need a big room? No. Surround sound isn't about louder sound, but more enveloping sound. You can enjoy discrete channels even in a small room at modest volume. And small speakers can be wall-mounted or set on a bookshelf, so you don't need lots of open floor space.

How 'surrounded' do you want to be? The steady evolution to more sophisticated sound processing has resulted in numerous surround options that offer anywhere from two to eight channels. Fortunately, all versions of Dolby Digital, the leading format, are backward-compatible, so you can play old material on newer equipment and vice versa.

Any new device can decode not only the latest formats but also earlier ones with fewer channels. And older equipment lacking the latest format can play new media. In either case you'll hear fewer channels and less of a surround effect.

One of the most significant upgrades you can make is to connect a TV to two speakers via a receiver. Whether you're watching regular or digital TV programs or a VHS or DVD movie, the sound will be better than that of your TV on its own. Stereo is ideal for regular CDs and tapes, which are two-channel. An investment in stereo gear won't be wasted: You can add equipment later to get surround sound. Here's how to decide what level best suits you:

Do you want to be in the midst of the action with the simplest setup possible? Basic surround sound calls for a receiver with Dolby Pro Logic or Pro Logic II decoding. Most older receivers offer this feature, so you may not need a new one. Ideally, you'd use four or five speakers to handle the front left and right channels, the center channel, and one or two rear surround channels. With any surround setup, you can use fewer speakers than that; you'll just hear less fullness. Many VHS movies and television programs are recorded in these formats, so a basic system makes the most of them. DVDs and digital programs, often recorded with more than five channels, will sound fine, minus a channel or two.

Do you relish the rumble of action movies? A typical setup requires a receiver that supports Dolby Digital 5.1 or DTS, a rival format, five full-range speakers, and a bass unit, called a subwoofer, for the lowest bass frequencies. Most new receivers support both formats, which have four full-range channels (two front and two rear), a center channel, and a low-frequency channel (the .1).

Do you want state-of-the-art sound? Dolby Digital EX and DTS-ES extended-surround formats add a center-rear channel or two, totaling 6.1 or 7.1 channels. You'll need to add one or two rear speakers to a 5.1 setup to hear the subtly smoother surround effect. Many new receivers and DVD players can handle 6.1 channels; only a few now support 7.1.

TWO PATHS TO SURROUND SOUND

Just as surround-sound technology comes in a few variations, so too do surround-sound systems. There are two basic ways to build a system: You can buy components and assemble your own system—integrating existing equipment that you'd like to keep—or you can opt for a package that includes all or most of the equipment required for surround sound.

With packages you again have two choices. A home theater in a box contains six matched speakers, a receiver, and sometimes a DVD player. Another option is a six-piece speaker set; you supply a receiver and a DVD player separately. Whether buying components or a prepackaged system, you can get amply featured equipment with the capabilities you need.

Here are some questions to help you decide what's right for you.

How much do you want to spend? You can pay anywhere from a few hundred dollars for a prepackaged system to many thousands of dollars for high-end components. A package is likely to save you money. Don't buy into the notion that expense always equals excellence. Our tests have turned up some modestly priced equipment that should be fine for most listeners.

How much time and effort are you willing to invest? Prepackaged systems offer a quick and easy route to surround sound. Buying components is more involved. You have to hand-pick them one by one, which takes time and some degree of expertise. But going with components also provides more flexibility and allows you to choose specific features.

Do you have existing equipment that you'd like to use or are you starting from scratch? If you have decent audio equipment that you'd like to keep, the component route may be the way to go. For instance, if you have a receiver and a DVD player, you could purchase just the speakers—two speakers if a stereo setup suits you, or a three-piece or six-piece speaker set, depending on how full a surround setup you want and what your receiver can support. If you have a good pair of speakers, use them for the front channel in a surround setup and add four or more speakers that have compatible sound qualities.

On the other hand, if you prefer to get a fresh start, a package can simplify the process and save you money. Just make sure any package has all the capabilities and features you want in a system.

CAMCORDERS

Fine picture quality and easy editing have improved the functionality of these moviemakers, especially for digital models.

Those grainy, jumpy home movies of yesteryear are long gone—replaced by home movies shot on digital or analog camcorders. You can edit and embellish the footage with music using your computer, then play it back on your VCR; you can even send it via e-mail.

Digital camcorders, now the dominant type, generally offer very good to excellent picture quality, along with very good sound capability, compactness, and ease of handling. Making copies of a digital recording won't result in a loss of picture or sound quality. You can even take rudimentary still photos with some digital camcorders.

Analog camcorders, now a small part of the market, generally have good picture and sound quality and are less expensive. Some analog units are about as compact and easy to handle as digital models, while others are a bit bigger and bulkier.

WHAT'S AVAILABLE

Sony dominates the camcorder market, with multiple models in a number of formats. Other top brands include Canon, JVC, Panasonic, and Samsung.

Most digital models come in the MiniDV format. New formats such as the disc-based DVD-RAM and DVD-R and tape-based MicroMV have also appeared. Some digital models weigh as little as one pound. The newest type of digital camcorder records onto the same Secure Digital (SD) memory card that many digital still cameras use.

MiniDV. Don't let their small size deceive you. Although some models can be slipped into a large pocket, MiniDV camcorders can record very high-quality images. They use a unique tape cassette, and the typical recording time is 60 minutes at standard play (SP) speed. Expect to pay $6.50 for a 60-minute tape. You'll need to use the camcorder for playback—it converts its recording to an analog signal, so it can be played directly into a TV or VCR. If the TV or VCR has an S-video input jack, use it to get a high-quality picture. Price range: $350 to more than $2,000.

Digital 8. Also known as D8, this format gives you digital quality on Hi8 or 8mm cassettes, which cost $6.50 and $3.50, respectively. The Digital 8 format records with a faster tape speed, so a "120-minute" cassette lasts only 60 minutes at SP. Most models can also play your old analog Hi8 or 8mm tapes. Price range: $350 to $800.

Disc-based. Capitalizing on the explosive growth and capabilities of DVD movie discs, these formats offer benefits tape can't provide: long-term durability, a compact medium, and random access to scenes as with a DVD. The 3¼-inch discs record standard MPEG-2 video, the same format used in commercial DVD videos. The amount of recording time varies according to the quality level you select: from 20 minutes per side at the highest-quality setting for DVD-RAM up to about 60 minutes per side at the lowest setting. DVD-RAM discs are not compatible with most DVD players, but the discs can be reused. DVD-R is supposed to be compatible with most DVD players and computer DVD drives, but the discs are write-once. We paid about $25 at a local retailer for a blank DVD-RW. Price range: $800 to $1,000.

Card-based. Camcorders in this format are very small in size and use a memory card to store video—no tape, no disk. The memory cards are expensive—approximately $85 to $100 for a 512 GB Secure Digital card, which will hold 10 to 20 minutes (depending on the model) using the highest-quality mode.

Most analog camcorders now use the Hi8 format; VHS-C and Super VHS-C are fading from the market. Blank tapes range in price from $3.50 to $6.50. Analog camcorders usually weigh around 2 pounds. Picture quality is generally good, though a notch below that of digital. Price range: $225 to $500.

IMPORTANT FEATURES

A flip-out **liquid-crystal-display** (LCD) **viewer** is becoming commonplace on all but the lowest-priced camcorders. You'll find it useful for reviewing footage you've shot and easier to use than the eyepiece viewfinder for certain shooting poses. Some LCD viewers are hard to use in sunlight, a drawback on models that have only a viewer and no eyepiece.

TECH TIP

The larger the LCD screen, the better: You can see more detail and compose scenes more easily.

Screens vary from 2½ to 4 inches measured diagonally, with a larger screen offered as a step-up feature on higher-priced models. Since an LCD viewer uses batteries faster than an eyepiece viewfinder does, you don't have as much recording time when the LCD is in use.

An **image stabilizer** automatically reduces most of the shaking that occurs from holding the camcorder as you record a scene. Most stabilizers are electronic; a few are optical. Either type can be effective, though mounting the camcorder on a tripod is the surest way to get steady images. If you're not using a tripod, you can try holding the camcorder with both hands and propping both elbows against your chest.

Full auto switch essentially lets you point and shoot. The camcorder automatically adjusts the color balance, shutter speed, focus, and aperture (also called the "iris" or "f-stop" with camcorders).

Autofocus adjusts for maximum sharpness; **manual focus override** may be needed for problem situations, such as low light. (With some camcorders, you may have to tap buttons repeatedly to get the focus just right.) With many models, you can also control exposure, shutter speed, and white balance.

The **zoom** is typically a finger control—press one way to zoom in, the other way to widen the view. The rate at which the zoom changes will depend on how hard you press the switch. Typical optical zoom ratios range from 10:1 to 26:1. The zoom relies on optical lenses, just like a film camera (hence the term "optical zoom"). Many camcorders offer a digital zoom to extend the range to 400:1 or more, but at a lower picture quality.

For tape-based formats, analog or digital, every camcorder displays **tape speeds** the same way a VCR does. Every model, for example, includes an SP (standard play) speed. Digitals have a slower, LP (long play) speed that adds 50 percent to the recording time. A few 8mm and Hi8 models have an LP speed that doubles the recording time. All VHS-C and S-VHS-C camcorders have an even slower EP (extended play) speed that triples the recording time. With analog camcorders, slower speeds worsen picture quality. Slow speed usually doesn't reduce picture quality on digital camcorders. But using slow speed means sacrificing some seldom-used editing options and may restrict playback on other camcorders.

Card-based and disc-based formats have a variety of modes that trade off recording time for image quality.

Quick review lets you view the last few seconds of a scene without having to press a lot of buttons. For special lighting situations, preset auto-exposure settings can be helpful. A "snow & sand" setting, for example, adjusts shutter speed or aperture to accommodate high reflectivity.

A **light** provides some illumination for close shots when the image would otherwise be too dark. **Backlight compensation** increases the exposure slightly when your subject is lit from behind and silhouetted. An **infrared-sensitive recording mode** (also known as night vision, zero lux, or MagicVu) allows shooting in very dim or dark situations, using infrared emitters. You can use it for nighttime shots, although colors won't register accurately in this mode.

Audio/video inputs let you record material from another camcorder or from a VCR, useful for copying part of another video onto your own. (A digital camcorder must have such an input jack if you want to record analog material digitally.) Unlike a built-in microphone, an **external microphone** that is plugged into a microphone jack won't pick up noises from the camcorder itself, and it typically improves audio performance.

A camcorder with **digital still capability** lets you take snapshots, which can be downloaded to your computer. The photo quality is generally inferior to that of a still camera.

Features that may aid editing include a **built-in title generator**, a **time-and-date stamp**, and a **time code**, which is a frame reference of exactly where you are on a tape—the hour, minute, second, and frame. A **remote control** helps when you're using the camcorder as a playback device or when you're using a tripod. **Programmed recording** (a self-timer) starts the camcorder recording at a preset time.

HOW TO CHOOSE

Pick your price range and format. The least-expensive camcorders on the market are analog. All the rest are digital.

Once you've decided which part of the price spectrum to explore, you need to pick a specific recording format. That determines not only how much you'll be spending for tapes or discs, but also how much recording time you'll get. The tape-based formats are typically superior in picture quality.

With analog, you can get 120 to 300 minutes of recording on a Hi8 cassette; with the SVHS-C or VHS-C formats, you can get only 30 to 120 minutes.

With digital formats that use MiniDV, Digital 8, or MicroMV tapes, you can get at least 60 minutes of recording on a standard cassette. MiniDV and D8 cassettes are the least expensive and easiest to find.

Digital DVD camcorders from Panasonic and Hitachi can accommodate DVD-RAM discs, which can be reused but aren't compatible with all DVD players. All brands also use DVD-R, one-use discs that work in most DVD players. The standard setting yields 60 minutes of recording; the "fine" setting, 30 minutes.

If you're replacing an older camcorder, think about what you'll do with the tapes you've accumulated. If you don't stay with the same format you've been using, you will probably want to transfer the old tapes to an easily viewed medium, such as a DVD.

If you're buying your first camcorder, concentrate on finding the best one for your budget, regardless of format.

Check the size, weight, and controls. In the store, try different camcorders to make sure they fit your hand and are comfortable to use. Some models can feel disconcertingly tiny. (You'll need to use a tripod if you want rock-steady video, no matter which camcorder you choose.) Most camcorders are designed so that the most frequently used controls—the switch to zoom in and out, and the record button—fall readily to hand. Make sure that the controls are convenient and that you can change the tape or DVD and remove the battery.

Check the flip-out LCD viewer. Most measure 2.5 inches on the diagonal, but some are larger, adding about $100 to the price. If the viewer seems small and difficult to use or suffers from too much glare, consider trading up to a similar model or a different brand to get a better screen.

Think about the lighting. A camcorder isn't always used outdoors or in a brightly lit room. You can shoot video in dim light, but don't expect miracles. In our tests, using the camcorders' default mode, most produced only fair or poor images in very low light. Many camcorders have settings that can improve performance but can be a challenge to use.

Related CR Report: November 2004
Ratings: page 231
Reliability: page 328

CAMERAS, DIGITAL

Digital photography allows you to be more involved in the creation of the print than film photography.

Digital cameras, which employ reusable memory cards instead of film, give you far more creative control than film cameras can. With a digital camera, you can transfer shots to your computer, then crop, adjust color and contrast, and add textures and other special effects. Final results can be made into cards or T-shirts, or sent via e-mail, all using the software that usually comes with the camera. You can make prints on a color inkjet printer, drop off the memory card at one of a growing number of photofinishers, or upload the file to a photo-sharing Web site for storage, viewing, or reprinting.

TECH TIP

The built-in LCD automatically displays each shot, hastening battery depletion. A model that can disable automatic display extends battery life.

Digital cameras share many features with digital camcorders, such as an electronic image sensor, LCD viewer, and a zoom lens. They also share many features with film cameras, such as focus, exposure, and flash options. Some camcorders can be used to take still pictures, but a typical camcorder's resolution is no match for a good still camera's.

WHAT'S AVAILABLE

The leading brands are Canon, Kodak, Olympus, and Sony; other brands come from consumer-electronics, computer, and traditional camera and film companies.

Digital cameras are categorized by how many pixels, or picture elements, the image sensor contains. One megapixel equals 1 million picture elements. A 2- or 3-megapixel camera can make excellent 8x10s and pleasing 11x14s. There are also 4- to 8-megapixel models for the amateur photo market; these are well suited for making larger prints or for maintaining sharpness if you want to use only a portion of the original image. Professional digital cameras use as many as 11 megapixels. Price range: $80 to $300 for 2 megapixels; $200 to $400 for 3 megapixels; $300 to $400 for 4 and 5 megapixels; $400 to $1,000 for 6 to 8 megapixels.

IMPORTANT FEATURES

Most digital cameras are highly automated, with features such as **automatic exposure control** (which manages the shutter speed, aperture, or both according to available light) and **autofocus.**

Instead of film, digital cameras typically record their shots onto **flash-memory cards.** CompactFlash and SecureDigital (SD) are the most widely used. Once quite expensive, such cards have tumbled in price—a 128-megabyte card can now cost less than $60. Some cameras store shots on a MemoryStick or on a SmartMedia or xD-picture card. Others use 3¼-inch CD-R or CD-RW discs.

To save images, you transfer them to a computer, typically by connecting the camera to the computer's USB or FireWire port or inserting the memory card into a special reader. Some printers can take memory cards and make prints without putting the images on a computer first. **Image-handling software,** such as Adobe Photoshop Elements, Jasc Paint Shop, Microsoft Picture It, and ACDSee, lets you size, touch up, and crop digital images using your computer. Most digital cameras work with both Windows and Macintosh machines.

The file format commonly used for photos is the highly compressed JPEG format. (This is also used for photos on the Internet.) Some cameras can save photos in uncompressed TIFF format, but this setting yields enormous files. Other high-end cameras have a RAW file format, which yields the image data with no processing from the camera.

Digital cameras typically have both an **optical viewfinder** and a small color **LCD viewer.** LCD viewers are very accurate in framing the actual image you get—better than most of the optical viewfinders—but they gobble up battery power and can be hard to see in bright sunlight. You can also view shots you've already taken on the LCD viewer. Many digital cameras provide a video output, so you can view your pictures on a TV set.

Certain cameras let you record an audio clip with a picture. But these clips devour storage space. Some allow you to record limited video, but the frame rate is slow and the resolution poor.

A **zoom lens** provides flexibility in framing shots and closes the distance between you and your subject—ideal if you want to quickly switch to a close shot. A 3x zoom is comparable to a 35mm to 105mm lens on a 35mm film camera; a 2x zoom approximates a 35mm to 70mm lens. **Optical zooms** are superior to **digital zooms,** which magnify the center of the frame without actually increasing picture detail, resulting in a somewhat coarser view.

Sensors in digital cameras are typically about as light-sensitive as ISO 100 film, though some let you increase that setting. (At ISO 100, you'll likely need to use a flash indoors and in low outdoor light.) A camera's **flash range** tells you how far from the camera the flash will provide proper exposure: If the subject is out of range, you'll know to close the distance. But digital cameras can tolerate some underexposure before the image suffers noticeably.

Red-eye reduction shines a light toward your subject just before the main flash. (A camera whose flash unit is farther from the lens reduces the risk of red eye. Computer editing of the image may also correct red eye.) With **automatic flash mode,** the camera fires the flash whenever the light entering the camera registers as insufficient. A few new cameras have built-in red-eye correction capability.

HOW TO CHOOSE

A digital camera for the consumer market can cost from just under $200 to more than $1,000. Consider these points, which can help you find the best combination of design and features:

Select the right size and style. For a camera that fits in your pocket, look for a compact model. Most compacts are 3 or 4 megapixels. The smallest can be almost the size of a credit card and less than an inch thick, but may feel awkward to hold. A medium-sized model is easier to handle. It's shaped like a traditional point-and-shoot, and it is available with 3 to 5 megapixels. For a camera that feels and operates more like a single-lens reflex film camera, go for a large model. Most are 5, 6, or 8 megapixels.

Decide how many megapixels you need. Narrow the field by focusing on the right combination of price and resolution—the maximum number of megapixels a camera can capture in one shot. If you're a casual photographer who prints mainly 4x6-inch snapshots, look for a 2- or 3-megapixel camera. Most cost less than $350 and are relatively compact. If you occasionally make larger prints, get a 4- or 5-megapixel model for $300 to $400. For more serious photography including cropping photos and making 8x10 prints and larger, consider a 5-megapixel camera. They range in price from $300 to $900. The highest priced are often the most feature laden and bulky.

Decide how much photographic control you want. Most digital cameras have several settings designed to give you more control over the photos than the plain point-and-shoot mode allows.

Beginners and digital veterans are likely to find very useful the controls for specific picture-taking tasks, such as action photos, close-ups, landscapes, and night shots.

Numerous 4- and 8-megapixel models have manual controls similar to those on film cameras. They allow you to control lens aperture, shutter speed, options for light-metering, and exposure compensation for tricky lighting. Many models also have a wide range of ISO (light sensitivity) settings.

Consider the optical-zoom range. Most digital cameras have at least an optical 3X zoom. A zoom lens makes it easier to compose your shots and is especially useful for portraits.

Some cameras—most of them pricey models—have a 4X, 5X, or even 10X optical zoom. New models come with image stabilizers. Choose the zoom that fits your shooting style. Longer zoom lenses present drawbacks, such as darker images and more difficulty shooting in low light. Don't confuse a camera's digital zoom with optical zoom. Digital zoom is a feature that's of very little use.

Weigh battery type and life. All digital cameras can run on rechargeable batteries of one of two types: an expensive battery pack or a set of AA batteries. In our tests of the cameras, neither battery type had a clear performance advantage. We think a camera that accepts the ubiquitous AA battery is more convenient.

Consider camera speed. Be prepared to wait after each shot as the camera processes the photo. While most cameras allow you to shoot an image every few seconds, a few models make you wait 7 seconds or more. Such slowpokes may frustrate you when you're taking photos in sequence. Camera manufacturers have claimed that some new cameras just coming to market operate more quickly.

Related CR Reports: May 2004, November 2004

Ratings: page 237

Reliability: page 328

CAMERAS, FILM

A point-and-shoot camera doesn't require elaborate setup before the shot. Single-lens reflex models offer maximum versatility and also can be easy to use.

A film camera remains a good choice if you want point-and-shoot simplicity and good quality for a relatively low price.

If you want more control over your pictures after you've taken them—for instance, you want to edit, publish, or e-mail them—buy a digital camera. But you needn't go digital to get some of a digital camera's benefits: When you drop off a roll of film for processing, you can order digital storage along with your prints. Other "digitizing" options include scanning negatives or prints using a computer and scanner.

WHAT'S AVAILABLE

Major camera companies include Canon, Fuji, KonicaMinolta, Nikon, Olympus, and Pentax. Most make point-and-shoot cameras in both 35mm and APS (advanced photo system) formats. Many of those companies also make single-lens reflex (SLR) models. Kodak makes only single-use film cameras.

No matter what the format, film cameras these days are highly automated. Practically all point-and-shoot models and some SLR models have built-in flashes. Low-priced film cameras are fixed-focus, like an old-fashioned box camera. Features that raise the price include autofocus, automatic exposure control, automatic film winding, and a zoom lens.

Compact 35mm cameras. Small, light, and inexpensive, these cameras are capable of producing exceptional photos. They're adequate for travel scenes and group shots. More expensive models include a zoom lens and many automated features. Some can shoot in panoramic mode, producing a 3½x10-inch or 4x11½-inch photo. The lens doesn't actually cover a wider angle in this mode. Instead, the panoramic shape is achieved by cropping off the top and bottom of the image. Price range: $5 to $12 for single-use cameras; $20 and up for fixed-focus models; $50 and up for automatic, nonzoom cameras; and $70 and up for a model with a zoom.

35mm SLRs. Bulkier than point-and-shoot models, SLR cameras with interchangeable lenses let you see what the camera sees. Unlike a point-and-shoot, an SLR lets you compose a shot precisely, without the uncertainty of capturing content not shown in the viewfinder. Such exactitude gives you a great deal of artistic control, and the generally high-quality optics deliver the best image quality. SLRs are typically sold without a lens or are bundled with a zoom lens. Price range: $150 and up for the camera body, $100 and up for a moderate-range zoom lens.

IMPORTANT FEATURES

A **zoom lens,** magnifying your subject two or three times or so, is available on many point-and-shoot models. The 35mm zoom lenses range from about 28 mm (fairly wide angle) to about 160 mm (a moderate telephoto). APS zoom ranges are comparable. You'll usually see the zoom lens characterized as 2x or 3x, a shorthand way of referring to the ratio of the telephoto and wide-angle focal lengths. Pricing is typically determined by the complexity of the lens design. You'll pay more for a "faster" lens, such as a 100-mm zoom that opens to f/3.5, which lets in more light than does a 100-mm lens with an f/4.5 maximum aperture.

Most cameras automate exposure partially or fully. **Aperture** governs how wide the camera should open the lens when you take a picture. Using identical-speed film and the same shutter speed, the wider the aperture a lens can manage, the better your odds of taking good pictures indoors without a flash (and the more the lens will likely cost). **Shutter speed** governs how long the shutter stays open during a shot. Fast shutter speed (1/1000 to 1/8000 of a second or so) lets you shoot fast-moving subjects.

Auto exposure regulates the shutter speed and aperture to get a properly exposed photo, whether in bright light or low light. An **exposure-compensation feature** can prevent underexposure when the background is bright, or overexposure when the background is unusually dark compared with the subject. SLRs can often set the speed or aperture automatically, after you have manually set the corresponding setting as needed for a particular shot. For example, if you set the aperture, it sets the shutter speed; if you set the speed, it sets the aperture. These and more advanced compact models may offer several preset exposure modes that suit various situations.

Autofocus frees you from having to focus the camera to ensure crisp pictures; low-end cameras typically cover preset ranges, permitting quick shots but dispensing with the more precise focusing of higher-priced models. **Multi-area autofocus** reduces the risk of unintentionally focusing on the background in a scene. **Focus lock** lets you freeze the focus onto who or what appears in the center of the viewfinder, helpful for when you'd like to focus on a subject and then shift the camera's aim. Compact film cameras typically use an infrared beam to focus. **In-the-viewfinder signals** in many models let you know when the subject is too close to be in focus or when it's out of flash range.

Motorized film handling automatically advances the film and rewinds it at the end of the roll. With a 35mm camera, you drop the film in, pull out the leader, and close the camera; with APS, you merely drop the film in. **Mid-roll change,** a feature found in some APS cameras, lets you reload partially exposed rolls of film—useful if you often switch between high- and low-speed film.

Flashes cover various distances, from 4 or 5 feet to 10 feet or more. The smartest ones work with the zoom lens to broaden or narrow the beam. **Flash on demand** lets you fill in harsh shadows in bright, sunlit portraits. "Red eye" occurs when a flash reflects off a subject's retinas; **red-eye reduction** typically uses a light before the main flash to constrict the subject's pupils. (Flashes that are farther from the lens reduce red eye to begin with.)

Some cameras are **weatherproof,** handy for the beach or boating. Certain models also offer options such as a **wireless remote shutter release** or the ability to imprint photos with the date.

HOW TO CHOOSE

Select the camera format. Most people in the market for a film camera will choose a compact point-and-shoot model rather than a single-lens reflex (SLR) camera. A point-and-shoot camera is easy to carry, capable of producing well-focused, well-exposed pictures with ease.

Select a film format. The safest choice by far is 35mm. For all its strengths, APS never caught on.

Check the features and design. The most important feature on a point-and-shoot camera is the zoom lens. Only the least expensive cameras lack one.

See how they fit your hands. Subtle differences in size, shape, and the placement of controls can make a big difference to you. At the store, spend time with each camera you're considering.

DVD PLAYERS

These devices play high-quality videos and CDs. You can get a model for less than $100.

As the fastest-growing consumer-electronics product in history—more than 21 million units were sold in 2003 alone—DVD players offer picture and sound quality that clearly surpasses what you'll get with a VCR.

DVDs are CD-sized discs that can contain a complete two-hour-plus movie with a Dolby Digital or DTS soundtrack containing six to eight audio channels, plus extra material such as multiple languages, interviews, additional camera angles for chosen scenes, behind-the-scenes documentaries, and even entire replays of the movie with commentary by the director or some of the actors.

DVD players also play standard audio CDs. Prices on multidisc models are low enough (starting at $100) for a DVD player to serve as a practical stand-in for a CD player. There is a catch if you record your own CDs: Some older DVD players may still have problems reading the CD-R and CD-RW discs that you record yourself. Some DVD players are able to play DVD-Audio or SACD, two competing high-resolution audio formats designed to offer two- to six-channel sound.

While DVD players are playback-only devices, DVD recorders record as well as play. Prices have dropped considerably in the past few years, with entry-level models now selling for less than $300. At the highest-quality record setting, DVD video recordings are better than those made to a videocassette, and DVDs offer easy access to recordings—no rewinding or fast-forwarding. However, VCRs remain the least expensive alternative for recording your favorite TV programs, and a tape made on one machine will play in any other, which isn't true of all formats used for DVD recorders.

WHAT'S AVAILABLE

Apex, Panasonic, Sony, and Toshiba are among the biggest-selling brands. DVD players are evolving as manufacturers seek to differentiate their products and come up with a winning combination of features. You can choose from a console or portable model. Many players offer built-in karaoke features, playback of MP3 files, and display of JPEG picture files. Some even have memory-card readers so you can watch slide shows of your digital photos on TV.

Most new DVD players are progressive-scan models. They provide HD-ready TVs with a slightly sharper image by redrawing 480 consecutive lines. (By comparison, a conventional TV and standard DVD player alternately redraw every other line.) You can use progressive-scan DVD players with a conventional TV, but you'll see the added benefit only with a set that supports the player's progressive-scan mode (480p), such as a high-definition or HD-ready set, or an enhanced definition (ED) set. Progressive-scan models come in single-disc and multidisc versions. Most standard players now on the market are single-disc models; these tend to be the cheapest type.

Single-disc consoles. Console models can be connected directly to your TV for viewing movies and routed through your receiver to play movies and audio CDs on your home-entertainment system. Even low-end models usually include all the video outputs you might want. Price range: less than $80 to more than $300.

Multidisc consoles. Like CD changers, these players accommodate two or more discs, often five. DVD jukeboxes that hold 400 or so discs are also available. Price range: $100 to $800.

Portables. These DVD players generally come with a small wide-screen-format LCD screen and batteries that claim to provide three hours or more of playback. Some low-priced models don't come with a screen; they're intended for users who plan to connect the device to a television. You pay extra for portability either way. Price range: $200 to $1,000.

SHOP SMART

A single-disc player is great if you mostly watch movies; a multidisc player lets you have continuous music.

IMPORTANT FEATURES

DVD-based movies often come in various formats. **Aspect-ratio control** lets you choose between the 4:3 viewing format of conventional TVs (4 inches wide for every 3 inches high) and the 16:9 ratio of newer, wide-screen sets.

A DVD player gives you all sorts of control over the picture—control you may never have known you needed. **Picture zoom** lets you zoom in on a specific frame. **Black-level adjustment** brings out the detail in dark parts of the screen image. If you've ever wanted to see certain action scenes from different angles, **multi-angle capability** gives you that opportunity. Note that this feature and some others work only with certain discs.

A DVD player enables you to navigate the disc in a number of ways. Unlike a VHS tape, DVDs are sectioned. **Chapter preview** lets you scan the opening seconds of each section or chapter until you find what you want; a related feature, **chapter gallery,** shows thumbnails of section or chapter opening scenes. **Go-to by time** lets you enter how many hours and minutes into the disc you'd like to skip to. **Marker functions** allow easy indexing of specific sections.

To get the most from a DVD player, you need to hook it up to the TV with the best available connection. A **composite-video connection** to the TV can produce a very good picture, but there will be some loss of detail and some color artifacts such as adjacent colors bleeding into each other. Using the **S-video output** can improve picture quality. It keeps the black-and-white and the color portions of the signal separated, producing more picture detail and fewer color defects than standard composite video.

Component video, sometimes not provided on the lowest-end models, improves on S-video by splitting the color signal, resulting in a wider range of color. If you connect a DVD player via an S-video or component connection, don't be surprised if you have to adjust the television-picture setup when you switch to a picture coming from a VCR or a cable box that uses a **radio-frequency** (RF, also called antenna/cable) connection or a composite connection.

Another output, **Digital Video Interface (DVI),** found on some players, is intended for a video connection to digital TVs with DVI inputs. It may be used to pass digital 480p and up-converted higher-resolution video signals. It potentially allows the content providers to control your ability to record the content.

Another benefit of DVD players is the ability to enjoy movies with **multichannel surround sound.** To reap the full sound experience of the audio encoded into DVD titles, you'll need a Dolby Digital receiver and six speakers, including a subwoofer. (For 6.1 and 7.1 soundtracks, you'll need seven or eight speakers.) **Dolby Digital decoding built-in** refers to a DVD player that decodes the multichannel audio before the audio receiver; without the built-in circuitry, you'd need to have the decoder built into the receiver or, in rare instances, use a separate decoder box to take advantage of the audio. (A Dolby Digital receiver will decode an older format, Dolby Pro Logic, as well.) Most players also support **Digital Theater System (DTS)** decoding for titles using the six-channel encoding format. When you're watching DVD-based movies, **dynamic audio-range control** helps keep explosions and other noisy sound effects from seeming too loud.

In addition to commercial DVD titles, DVD players often support playback or display of numerous other disc formats. They include CD-R; the recordable DVD formats DVD+R/RW, DVD-R/RW, and DVD-RAM; Video CD (VCD); and DVD-Audio and Super Audio CD (SACD). They can also play CD-R/RW discs containing MP3 and Windows Media Audio (WMA) files and JPEG picture files. Make sure a model you're considering plays the discs and formats you use now, or may want to use in the future.

DVD players also provide features such as **multilingual support,** which lets you choose dialog or subtitles in different languages for a given movie. **Parental control** lets parents "lock out" films by their rating code.

HOW TO CHOOSE

If you'll be using the DVD player with a regular TV, shop by price or features. All the players in our most recent tests offered comparably excellent picture and sound quality when used with regular analog TVs, so you can safely choose a DVD player by price or features.

Decide on the player type you want. We'd recommend progressive-scan models for most buyers, and they're by far the most common type of player now sold. They cost little more than standard players and can give you better video quality if you have an HDTV now or get one later. Among the models we tested, we saw the picture enhancement mostly with commercial DVD movies converted from film, as opposed to compilations of TV series or concert videos converted from videotape. Beyond that, you need to decide whether you want recording capability (in which case you need a DVD recorder, which also plays prerecorded DVDs) and whether you want to use the DVD player as your primary CD player, in which case you may want the continuous-play capability of a multidisc player.

Consider connections to your receiver. Virtually all DVD players now have the outputs for optimal connection to most TV sets, even HDTVs. Some higher-priced players have DVI connectors for use with some HDTVs. This connection may enhance picture quality and enables copy protection (to prevent the video from being copied digitally).

If a DVD player will be part of a home-theater system, consider how it and your receiver will best connect and complement one another. If you want to use digital-audio connections, make sure the DVD player's digital-audio outputs (either optical or coaxial) match the type of inputs on your receiver. If you own an older receiver that can't decode the multichannel soundtracks of most DVDs, consider a player with a built-in decoder.

Consider which, if any, special playback formats matter to you. All DVD players can play commercial DVDs and CDs. In addition, most new players play several types of DVDs you record yourself: DVD-R, DVD+R, and DVD+RW. But DVD-RAM and, in some cases, DVD-RW compatibility are harder to come by; check the player's specifications. Most play CD-audio and MP3 music recorded on CD-R and CD-RW discs you burn yourself. You'll need to shop around more if you want to play Windows Media Audio (WMA) files or video CDs. While most DVD-video players can play hybrid Super Audio CD (SACD) and DVD-Audio discs, you will hear their original high-resolution format only on an SACD or DVD-Audio player, both of which can also play DVD video discs.

Do you want to display slide shows on your TV? Many DVD players let you play CDs that you've burned on a computer to hold JPEG photos shot with a digital camera, downloaded from the Internet, or scanned from prints. These can be displayed on your TV as slide shows.

Related CR Report: December 2003

Ratings: page 253

HOME THEATER IN A BOX

All-in-one systems that you hook up to your TV and VCR or DVD player can minimize the setup hassle.

Good speakers and the components for a home-theater system cost less than ever. But selecting all those components can be time consuming, and connecting them a challenge—even for audiophiles. You can avoid some hassle by buying an all-in-one "home theater in a box" system that combines a receiver with a speaker set, wiring, and often a DVD player. Unless your needs are very demanding, you'll compromise little on quality.

WHAT'S AVAILABLE

Panasonic and Sony account for more than one-third of sales, with Sony commanding about one-fourth of the market. Home theater packages include a receiver that can decode digital-audio soundtracks and a set of six to eight compact, matched speakers—two front, one center, two to four surround, and a subwoofer. You also get all the cables and wiring you need, usually labeled and color-coded for easy setup. Most systems now include a progressive-scan DVD player (either a separate component or built into the receiver) and a powered subwoofer. Some systems also come with a VCR, but generally, the presumption is that you already own a TV and a VCR. Price range: $275 to $1,000 for typical systems with a DVD player and powered subwoofer, and $2,000 or more for systems aimed at audiophiles.

IMPORTANT FEATURES

The receivers in home-theater-in-a-box systems tend to be on the simple side. They usually include both Dolby Digital and DTS decoders. Controls should be easy to use. Look for a front panel with displays and controls grouped by function and labeled clearly. An **onscreen display** lets you control the receiver via a television screen.

Switched AC outlets let you plug in other components and turn on the whole system with one button. The receivers have about 20 or more **presets** you can use for AM and FM stations. Some receivers also offer a **sleep timer,** which turns them on or off at a preset time. **Remote controls** are most useful when they have clear labels and different-shaped and color-coded buttons grouped by function. A universal remote can control a number of devices.

A **component-video output** on the receiver that can connect to a relatively high-end TV allows for better picture quality if you choose to switch video signals through your receiver; however, not many receivers have such an output. Instead, most have **S-video output,** which is better than a **composite-video** or **RF (antenna) connection.**

Look also for an **S-video input,** which lets you pipe signals from an external DVD player, digital camcorder, or certain cable or satellite boxes through the system. Any player that you might want to connect will need the same digital-audio connections, either optical or coaxial, as those of the included receiver. And if you want to make occasional connections at the front—perhaps for a camcorder or an MP3 player—you'll need **front-panel inputs.**

DSP (digital signal processor) modes use digital circuitry to duplicate the sound measurements of, say, a concert hall. Each mode represents a different listening environment. A **bass-boost switch** amplifies the deepest sounds.

A **subwoofer** may be powered or unpowered. Either type will do the job, but a powered subwoofer requires fewer wires, provides more control over bass, and lets a powered receiver drive the other speakers.

An **integrated DVD player,** available with some models, typically has fewer features than does a stand-alone DVD player. Features to expect are **track programmability** (more useful for playing CDs than DVDs), **track repeat,** and **disc repeat.** If you want more features, a stand-alone DVD player may be the wiser choice.

HOW TO CHOOSE

Decide whether you want a DVD player. If not, you may save money by buying a system without one. If you want a DVD in the bundle, consider whether you need a multidisc model that will provide uninterrupted play of music CDs and DVD movies. Most systems have a progressive-scan player. These offer regular DVD picture quality when used with a conventional TV but can deliver a smoother, almost filmlike image when paired with a TV capable of displaying high-definition (HD) signals. Some bundled DVD players offer support for multichannel DVD-Audio and SACD music discs, although not in their original, high-resolution format.

Do you want a separate DVD player or one integrated with the receiver? Systems with separate DVD players and receivers tend to offer fuller functionality and more connections than those that integrate both units in one box. Integrated units are somewhat simpler to set up, but they may not allow you to connect video devices other than a TV to the receiver, if you want such an arrangement. Any other devices would have to be hooked up directly to the TV.

TECH TIP

For even better pictures from DVD players, digital boxes and satellite receivers, look for S-video or component-video connections.

Make sure there are enough inputs. Even home-theater systems without DVD players have fewer connections than standalone components, but they do allow you to connect the basic gear. These systems generally have enough audio and video inputs for an external DVD player, a VCR, a CD player, and a cable box or satellite receiver. Some systems have S-video inputs, which can provide better picture quality from DVD players and digital-cable or satellite boxes than composite-video inputs. Component-video inputs, better still, are less widely available.

With audio inputs, there are two points to check. Some models have either an optical or a coaxial digital-audio input, not both types. Choose a model that matches the output on your CD or DVD player, digital-cable box, or satellite receiver. If you want to connect a turntable, you'll need a phono input—hard to come by.

Get features that suit your needs. With any system, you can be assured of basics such as AM/FM tuners and Dolby Digital and DTS surround-sound support. You almost always get Dolby Pro Logic II, which offers basic surround sound from TV and VHS programs and music CDs.

Features such as front-panel inputs and onscreen displays for making adjustments on the TV screen are less common than on component receivers, so make sure a system has what you want. A few models offer Dolby Digital EX and DTS-ES, newer surround formats that process 6.1 or 7.1 channels.

Related CR Report: November 2004
Ratings: page 262

MP3 PLAYERS

These devices let you play music you've either downloaded from the Web or "ripped" from your own CD collection.

Portable MP3 players store digital music in their internal memories, on removable storage media, or a combination of both. You don't buy prerecorded discs or tapes, but instead, create your own digital files on a computer using software often supplied with a player. You can convert music from your favorite audio CDs, tapes, and even records to digital files—a process known as ripping—or download music from the Internet. In either case you can listen to the files on your computer or transfer them to a portable MP3 player so you have music to go.

The term MP3 has become shorthand for digital audio of every stripe, but it's actually just one of the formats used to encode music. The abbreviation stands for Moving Pictures Expert Group 1 Audio Layer 3, a file format that compresses music to one-tenth to one-twelfth the space it would take in uncompressed form. Other encoding schemes include Windows Media Audio (WMA), the most widely supported; Advanced Audio Codec (AAC), and Adaptive Transform Acoustic Coding (ATRAC), a proprietary format used by Sony products. Most MP3 players can handle formats in addition to MP3, typically WMA, and the software that comes with them may convert incompatible files into formats the player can handle.

Despite copyright-infringement lawsuits by the music industry, free music-sharing Web sites carry on. Online music stores, led by Apple's iTunes, allow users to download music legally for a fee. Downloaded songs from contemporary artists typically cost less than $1 per song, or $10 for an entire album. Copy-protection measures prevent these songs from being shared with other people over a network and limits the number of times users can transfer them to MP3 players or burn them onto CDs. That limitation is typically three to 10 times, depending on the service. Other legal online music sources include BuyMusic (WMA), Musicmatch (WMA), and Napster (WMA), retailers such as Wal-Mart (WMA), as well as electronics giant Sony (ATRAC). Some of these sites also offer subscription-based services, typically less than $10 per month, that allow you to listen to music on your computer in real time (streaming). Downloading music that you transfer to an MP3 player or CD costs extra, but fees are generally lower than the ones for non-subscribers.

One caveat of these services is that their copy-protected songs won't work with all players. Also keep in mind that managing MP3 files and using an MP3 player is still more demanding than using an audio CD player.

WHAT'S AVAILABLE

Major brands include Apple, Archos, Creative Labs, Dell, iRiver, Panasonic, Rio, Samsung, and Sony. Other, smaller brands are on the market as well. MP3 playback has been incorporated into other handheld portable products, including CD players, MiniDisc players, cell phones, and personal digital assistants (PDAs).

Flash-memory players. These are solid-state devices with no moving parts, which eliminates skipping, even on a bumpy road or during a grueling jog. They're also the smallest and lightest players, which makes them easier to carry around. Sizes vary, ranging from as small as a thick matchbook to the size of a deck of cards. Weight usually ranges from about 1.5 to 4 ounces. Most of the players have 128 megabytes (MB) and up of internal memory; 128 MB can hold about two hours of MP3-formatted music recorded at a CD-quality setting. You can fit more music into memory if you compress songs into smaller files, but that may result in lower audio quality.

Some flash-memory players also have expansion slots to add more memory via card slots or "backpack" modules on the player. Common expansion memory formats include Compact Flash, MultiMedia, Secure Digital, and SmartMedia. Sony players may use a MagicGate MemoryStick, a copyright-protected version of Sony's existing MemoryStick media. Memory-card capacities range from about 32 MB to 1 gigabyte (GB). Memory costs have gradually dropped. Price range: about $100 to $300 for the player; $25 to $40 for a 64-MB memory card.

Hard-disk players. These devices have

a hard drive that can hold hundreds and even thousands of songs. Storage capacity can reach 80 gigabytes (GB), enough for more than 1,000 hours of music. But often that extra capacity translates into a bulkier, heavier player. Some are bigger than a portable CD player and weigh up to a pound. The most popular hard-drive players hold about 20 GB of music files, are about the size of a deck of cards, and weigh less than a half-pound. Smaller still are microdrive players, which tend to be palm-sized and weigh about a quarter-pound. Their drives provide about 1.5 to 4 GB of storage, but that's still enough room for many hours of continuous music. Some also have memory-card slots to transfer files. Price range: $140 and up.

Disc players with "MP3" compatibility. Flash-memory and hard-disk portable players aren't the only way to enjoy digital music. Many of today's portable CD and MiniDisc players can play digital music saved on their discs, and may support the copyright-protected formats from online music stores. Controls and displays are comparable to portable MP3 players, and you can group songs on each disc according to artist, genre, and other categories. A CD, with its 650 to 800 MB storage capacity, can hold more than 10 hours of MP3-formatted music at a CD-quality setting. You can create MP3 CDs using your PC's CD burner.

Sony's MiniDisc players, the other disc option, generally have smaller dimensions than portable CD players and play music files encoded in Sony's ATRAC format. MiniDiscs are smaller, removable optical disks protected by a plastic case, similar in size and shape to a 3.5-inch floppy disk. They can be recorded over many times. According to Sony, models that accept a Hi-MD disk can store up to 45 hours of music. Price range: $100 to $200 for players; 50 cents to $4 for blank CDs; $1.50 to $7 for MiniDiscs.

IMPORTANT FEATURES

Software and hardware. Most MP3 players come with music management software to convert your CDs into files the player can handle. You can also organize your music collection according to artist, album, genre, and a variety of other categories, as well as create playlists to suit any mood or occasion. All come with software to help you shuttle music between your PC and the player via a Universal Serial Bus (USB) or FireWire connection. All players work with Windows PCs, and many support the Macintosh platform.

Player upgradability. On most models, the firmware—the built-in operating instructions—can be upgraded so the player does not become obsolete. Upgrades can add or enhance features, fix bugs, and add support for other audio formats and operating systems.

Display. Most MP3 players have a liquid crystal display (LCD) screen, sometimes color, that allows you to view the song title, track number, amount of memory remaining, battery life indicator, and other functions. Some displays present a list of tracks from which you can easily make a selection, while others show only one track at a time, requiring you to advance through individual tracks to find the desired one. On some of the models you can access the player's function controls via a wired or infrared remote control.

Sound enhancement. Expect some type of equalizer, which allows you to adjust the sound in various ways. A custom setting via separate bass and treble controls or adjustable equalizers gives you the most control over the sound.

Playback controls. Volume, track play/pause, and forward/reverse controls are standard. Most portable MP3 players let you set a play mode so you can repeat one or all music tracks, or play in a random order, also referred to as "shuffle" mode. An A-B repeat feature allows you to set bookmarks and repeat a section of the music track.

Useful extras. In addition to playing music, most MP3 players can function as external hard drives, allowing you to shuttle files from one PC to another. Some allow you to view text files, photos, and videos on their LCD screens. Other convenient features include an FM radio tuner, a built-in microphone for voice recording, and adapters for patching the player into your car's audio system.

HOW TO CHOOSE

Because MP3 music is a relatively new market, new portable MP3 players with more features and greater capabilities are continually coming out. Decide how much you're willing to spend on a unit you may want to replace in a year or two. Here are some considerations before you buy:

Be sure your computer can handle it. Make sure any player you're considering is compatible with your Windows or Macintosh computer (including the version of the operating system your computer uses). Your computer must have USB or FireWire ports. Consider high-speed Internet access if you plan to download much of your music. Also keep in mind that getting started can be tricky with some players. When used with older computers, the computer may not recognize the player, so you may have to seek help from the manufacturer.

Weigh capacity vs. size. Some MP3 players can serenade you for weeks without repeating a tune—a great feature to have on long excursions but perhaps not as necessary on short trips to the gym. Consider a flash-memory model if a lower price, smaller size, less weight and long playback time are more important to you than a vast selection of tunes. Look for models that can accept external memory cards to expand song capacity. If you have a large music collection that you want to keep with you, determine if a small sized microdrive player of 1.5 to 5 GB capacity or a deck of cards-sized player of say 20 GB of storage may make more sense. Their built-in hard drives, however, may make them more complicated to manage than a flash-memory player—and more vulnerable to damage. For some, navigating through the menus or directories (folders) of songs may also take longer.

Consider download choices. Be aware that online music sources are limited with some models. For example iPods and Sony players only work with one online music store. Owners of players that support the copy-protected WMA formats, like those from Creative, Rio, and RCA, have access to the greatest number of online stores, and, often, the best deals. Downloading "free" music from such online sources as peer-to-peer Web sites is another option. But you risk a copyright-infringement lawsuit by the music industry. You'll also increase your exposure to a host of nasty computer viruses and spyware programs that tend to hitch rides on songs swapped on these sites. Some players won't play any legally downloaded music.

Ensure upgradability. Regardless of which player you choose, look for one with upgradable firmware for adding or enhancing player features, as well as accommodating newer encoding schemes or variations of compression. The process of upgrading firmware can be a time-consuming and sometimes risky process. MP3 players use several methods for upgrading; one method, which executes the upgrade file on the computer while the player is still attached, can cause permanent damage to the player if there's even a slight interruption during execution. Upgrades may be found at the manufacturer and music-management software application Web sites.

Don't forget the batteries. With any portable device, batteries are a consideration. Our tests found a wide variation among the players. Depending upon the player settings, some will run out of power after only five hours of play, while others can play music for more than 70 hours before their batteries give out. Flash-memory players tend to have a longer playback times than hard-disk players. Many flash memory players use AA or AAA batteries and can accept either standard alkaline or rechargeable batteries—convenient when electrical outlets are hard to find. Other players use a rechargeable nonstandard "block-" or "gumstick-" shaped nickel metal-hydride (NiMH) or lithium-ion (Li-ion) removable battery, which is both more expensive and harder to find. Many hard-drive players use a non-removable rechargeable battery. When the battery can no longer hold a charge, the player has to be sent back to the manufacturer for service—a costly procedure if the product is no longer under warranty.

Look for ease of use. Whichever type of MP3 player you choose, make sure you'll be comfortable using the device. Look for a display and controls that are easy to read and that can be worked with one hand.

RECEIVERS

For a home-theater surround-sound system, look for a receiver that can decode Dolby Digital and DTS soundtracks.

The receiver is the brain of an audio/video system. It provides AM and FM tuners, amplifiers, surround sound, and switching capabilities. It's also the heart of the setup—most of the devices in a home-entertainment system connect to it, including audio components such as speakers, a CD player, cassette deck, and turntable, as well as video sources such as a TV, DVD player, VCR, and cable and satellite boxes. Even as receivers take on a bigger role in home entertainment, they're losing some audio-related features that were common years back, such as tape monitors and phono inputs. Manufacturers say they must eliminate those less-used features to make room for others.

WHAT'S AVAILABLE

Sony is by far the biggest-selling brand. Other top-selling brands include Denon, JVC, Kenwood, Onkyo, Panasonic, Pioneer, RCA, and Yamaha. Most models now are digital, designed for the six-channel surround-sound formats encoded in most DVDs and some TV fare, such as high-definition (HD) programming. Here are the types you'll see, from least to most expensive:

Stereo. Basic receivers accept the analog stereo signals from a tape deck, CD player, or turntable. They provide two channels that power a pair of stereo speakers. For a simple music setup, add a DVD or CD player to play CDs, or a cassette deck for tapes. For rudimentary home theater, add a TV and DVD player or VCR. Power typically runs 50 to 100 watts per channel. Price range: $125 to $250.

Dolby Pro Logic. Dolby Pro Logic, Pro Logic II, and Pro Logic IIx are the analog home-theater surround-sound standard. Receivers that support it can take a Dolby-encoded two-channel stereo source from your TV, DVD player, or hi-fi VCR and output them to four to six speakers—three in front, and one to three in back. Power for Dolby Pro Logic models is typically 60 to 150 watts per channel. Price range: $150 to $300 or more.

Dolby Digital. Currently the prevailing digital surround-sound standard, a Dolby Digital 5.1 receiver has a built-in decoder for six-channel audio capability—front left and right, front center, two rear with discrete wide-band signals, and a powered subwoofer for low-frequency, or bass, effects (that's where the ".1" comes in). Dolby Digital is the sound format for most DVDs, HDTV, digital cable TV, and some satellite-TV broadcast systems. Newer versions of Dolby Digital, 6.1 and 7.1, add one or two rear channels for a total of seven-channel and eight-channel sound, respectively. To take advantage of true surround-sound capability, you'll need speakers that do a good job of reproducing full-spectrum sound. Receivers with digital decoding capability can also accept a signal that has been digitized, or sampled, at a given rate per second and converted to digital form. Dolby Digital is backward-compatible and supports earlier versions of Dolby such as Pro Logic. Power for Dolby Digital receivers is typically 75 to 150 watts per channel. Price range: $200 to $500 or more.

DTS. A rival to Dolby Digital 5.1, Digital Theater Systems also offers six channels. It's a less common form of digital surround sound that is used in some movie tracks. Both DTS and Dolby Digital are often found on the same receivers. Power for DTS models is typically 75 to 150 watts per channel. Price range: $200 to $500 or more.

THX-certified. The high-end receivers that meet this quality standard include full support for Dolby Pro Logic, Dolby Digital, and DTS. THX Select is the standard for components designed for small and average-sized rooms; THX Ultra is for larger rooms. Power for THX models is typically 100 to 170 watts per channel. Price range: $500 to $2,500 and up.

IMPORTANT FEATURES

Controls should be easy to use. Look for a front panel with displays and controls clearly labeled and grouped by function. **Onscreen display** lets you control the receiver via a TV screen, a squint-free alternative to using the receiver's tiny LED or LCD display. **Switched AC outlets** (expect one or two) let you plug in other components and turn the whole system on and off with one button.

Remote controls are most useful when they have clear labels and buttons that light up for use in dim rooms. It's best if the buttons have different shapes and are color-coded and grouped by function—a goal seldom achieved in receiver remotes. A **learning remote** can receive programming data for other devices via their remotes' infrared signal; on some remotes, the necessary codes for other manufacturers' devices are built-in.

Input/output jacks matter more on a receiver than on perhaps any other component of your home theater. Clear labeling, color-coding, and logical groupings of the many jacks on the rear panel can help avert glitches during setup such as reversed speaker polarities and mixed-up inputs and outputs. Input jacks situated on the front panel make for easy connections to camcorders, video games, MP3 players, digital cameras, MiniDisc players, and PDAs.

A stereo receiver will give you a few audio inputs and no video jacks. Digital-ready receivers with Dolby Pro Logic will have several types of video inputs, including composite and S-video and sometimes component-video. **S-video** and

component-video jacks allow you to route signals from DVD players and other high-quality video sources through the receiver to the TV. Digital-ready receivers also have **audio 5.1 inputs.** These accept input from a DVD player with its own built-in Dolby Digital decoder, an outboard decoder, or other components with multichannel analog signals, such as a DVD-Audio or SACD player. This enables the receiver to convey up to six channels of sound or music to your speakers. Dolby Digital and DTS receivers have the most complete array of audio and video inputs, often with several of a given type to accommodate multiple components.

Tone controls adjust bass and treble, allowing you to correct room acoustics and satisfy your personal preferences. A **graphic equalizer** breaks the sound spectrum into three or more sections, giving you slightly more control over the full audio spectrum. Instead of tone controls, some receivers come with tone styles such as Jazz, Classical, or Rock, each accentuating a different frequency pattern; often you can craft your own styles.

DSP (digital signal processor) modes use a computer chip to duplicate the sound characteristics of a concert hall and other listening environments. A **bass-boost** switch amplifies the deepest sounds, and **midnight mode** reduces loud sounds and amplifies quiet ones in music or soundtracks.

Sometimes called "one touch," a **settings memory** lets you store settings for each source to minimize differences in volume, tone, and other settings when switching between sources. A similar feature, **loudness memory**, is limited to volume settings alone.

Tape monitor lets you either listen to one source as you record a second on a tape deck or listen to the recording as it's being made. **Automatic radio tuning** includes such features as **seek** (automatic searching for the next in-range station) and 20 to 40 **presets** to call up your favorite stations.

To catch stations too weak for the seek mode, most receivers also have a **manual stepping knob** or buttons, best in one-channel increments. But most models creep in half- or quarter-steps, meaning unnecessary button tapping to find the frequency you want. **Direct tuning** of frequencies lets you tune a radio station by entering its frequency on a keypad.

SHOP SMART

For around $200, you can get a basic surround-sound digital receiver that can decode the top channels.

HOW TO CHOOSE

First, don't assume that pricey brands outperform less costly ones. We've found fine performers at all prices. Points to consider:

How many devices do you want to connect? Even low-end receivers generally have enough video and audio inputs for a CD or DVD player, a VCR, and a cable box or satellite receiver. Mid- and high-priced models usually have more inputs, so you can connect additional devices, such as a camcorder, a personal video recorder, or a game system.

The number of inputs isn't the only issue; the type also matters. Composite-video inputs, the most basic type, can be used with everything from an older VCR to a new DVD player. S-video and component-video inputs are used mostly by digital devices such as DVD players and satellite receivers. If you have such digital devices or may add them, get a receiver with a few S-video and/or component-video inputs. Both can provide better video quality than composite-video.

All these video inputs require a companion audio input. The basic left/right audio inputs can be used with almost any device to provide stereo sound. A turntable requires a phono input, which is available on fewer models than in years past.

To get multichannel sound from DVD players, digital-cable boxes, and satellite receivers, you generally use a digital-audio input. With this input, encoded multichannel sound is relayed on one cable to the receiver, which decodes it into separate channels. The input on the receiver must be the same type—either optical, the more common type, or coaxial—as the output on the other device. You usually must buy cables, about $10 and up, for digital-audio, S-video, and component-video connections.

What kind of sound do you want from movies? All new digital receivers support Dolby Digital and DTS, the surround-sound formats used on most movies. Both provide 5.1 channels. Most receivers also support Dolby Pro Logic, Pro Logic II, and Pro Logic IIx. If you want the latest type of surround sound, look for a receiver that supports Dolby Digital EX and DTS-ES. These offer 6.1 or 7.1 channels, subtly enhancing the rear surround. Fairly few movies using these formats are available, but offerings should increase.

What kind of music do you like? Any receiver can reproduce stereo from regular CDs. Most models have digital signal processing (DSP) modes that process a CD's two channels to simulate a sound environment such as a concert hall. DSP modes feed a stereo signal through all the speakers to simulate surround. For multichannel music from SACD or DVD-Audio discs, get a receiver with 5.1 analog inputs.

How big is your room? Make sure a receiver has the oomph to provide adequate volume: at least 50 watts per channel in a typical 12-by-20-foot living room, or 85 watts for a 15-by-25-foot space. A huge room, plush furnishings, or a noisy setting all call for more power.

Is the receiver compatible with your speakers? If you like to blast music for hours on end, get a receiver rated to handle your front speakers' impedance. Most receivers are rated for 6-ohm and 8-ohm speakers. If used with 4-ohm speakers, such a receiver could overheat and shut down.

Is it easy to use? Most receivers have legible displays and well-labeled function buttons. Some add an onscreen menu, which displays settings on your TV screen. An auto-calibration feature adjusts sound levels and balance to improve the surround effect. Models with a test-tone function for setting speaker levels help you balance the sound yourself.

Two tips: When deciding where to place your receiver, allow 4 inches or so of space behind it for cables and at least 2 inches on top for venting to prevent overheating. If setting up a home theater is more than you want to tackle, consider calling in a professional installer. Retailers often offer an installation service or can refer you to one.

Related CR Report: November 2003

SATELLITE TV

Frustration with cable companies has fueled the growth of satellite-TV broadcast systems.

Before you opt for satellite TV, make sure a dish can be mounted on your property with an unobstructed (southern) view of the satellite. Then choose the service provider and the hardware.

If you can get satellite TV, it offers something most cable subscribers don't get—a choice of provider. DirecTV and EchoStar's Dish Network are the dominant providers; their upstart competitors include Voom, which specializes in HD channels. Once renowned for offering hundreds of channels, with the notable exception of local stations, both DirecTV and Dish Network now provide local service in many cities and outlying areas. That's the result of a 1999 federal law that allowed satellite companies to offer so-called local-into-local service. In January 2002 the FCC ruled that if a satellite company offered one local channel, it had to carry all local channels in the markets where local service was offered.

People in an "unserved" household—those living in rural areas where an acceptable signal cannot be received via a rooftop antenna—can pick up local stations (regional affiliates of major networks) from a satellite provider. According to the FCC, you should be able to confirm your status through the satellite provider you've chosen. For much of the country, however, cable remains the only way to receive all local programming, including community and school channels.

WHAT'S AVAILABLE

DirecTV and EchoStar's Dish Network have comparable programming fare, with packages offering up to several hundred channels. The channel lineup is much like that of digital cable: Movie and sports programming is strong, foreign-language programming is available, and both providers carry 30 to 60 commercial-free music services in many genres. Satellite carries all channels digitally, while digital cable is actually a hybrid service, with some channels carried via analog signals. But digital cable still has the edge in HD channels, especially when it comes to passing through HD broadcasts from the major networks.

Typically, the satellite dish and receiver are sold together and will work only with the signal of the chosen provider. Hughes, RCA, and Sony are among the companies that offer DirecTV equipment; JVC and EchoStar offer Dish Network equipment. You can also buy the hardware directly from the service provider.

Satellite dishes are typically 18 or 24 inches. The larger dishes offer increased programming options, such as more channels, pay-per-view movies, HDTV reception, and international programming. Sometimes a second 18-inch dish may be required to receive some of those services.

Receivers accept the signal from the dish, decode it, and send it to your TV. To be able to watch different programs on different TVs at once, you'll need one receiver for each TV. To facilitate this, you need a dish with multiple low-noise block converters (LNBs). Alternatively, the receiver's RF-output jack or an inexpensive splitter may be used to send the same channel to multiple TVs.

For pay-per-view ordering and other services, the satellite-TV receivers must be connected to a telephone line. Typically, you use your existing line.

Price range for programming: Dish Network, $25 to $78 a month for packages with 60 to 180-plus channels; local channels add $5 extra. DirecTV, $37 to $88 for 130 to 210 channels; local channels add $3 extra. Pay-per-view movies cost about $4; special sports packages are available separately. To get high-definition programming, you'll pay another $10 or so per month.

Price range for a dish-receiver package: $100 to more than $1,000 for a system with more features, such as a built-in DVR and HD capability. Extra receivers cost about $100 each and add about $5 apiece to the monthly bill. Some equipment or installation may be free or offered at reduced prices as part of a special promotion.

IMPORTANT FEATURES

On the receiver the number and type of **audio** and **video output jacks** make a difference in the quality of your picture and in what equipment you can connect. The lowest-quality connection is **cable/antenna** or **RF**, the typical antenna-type connector. Better is a **composite-video output;** better still are **S-video outputs,** provided your TV is appropriately equipped with matching inputs, which can take advantage of the higher visual resolution.

SHOP SMART
Go with satellite if your priorities include watching pro teams from across the country.

An **on-screen signal-strength meter** lets you monitor how well the satellite signal is coming in. Satellite receivers with **Dolby Digital audio capability** may have optical or coaxial output for a direct digital connection to a Dolby Digital audio receiver.

Some **remote controls** accompanying the receiver are infrared, like TV or VCR remotes, requiring a direct line of sight to the receiver. Others use a radio-frequency signal, which can pass through walls, allowing the receiver to be placed in an unobtrusive, central location and controlled from anywhere in the house.

Remotes typically include a **program-description button,** which activates an on-screen program-description banner. The **program guide** helps you sort through the hundreds of channels.

A **program guide with picture** lets you continue to watch one program while you scan the onscreen channel guide for another. Some receivers have a **keyword search:** You can enter the full or partial name of a program or performer and search automatically through the listings.

HOW TO CHOOSE

See if you can get reception. You need an unobstructed clear view of the southern horizon and a place to mount a satellite dish. You may be able to get information about service in your area on the providers' sites. Satellite dealers and installers will come out to assess your specific location.

Decide on a service provider. Find out what programming each provider offers in your area, and if local channels are available via satellite. It can be a major inconvenience if local stations are not available in your market. If you have an HDTV, you might consider Voom, the new HD-heavy service. It offers more HD programming than Dish Network or DirecTV.

Pick your hardware. After choosing the service, select hardware that works with that service. Decide if you want HD capability or a built-in DVR to record programming.

Ask about promotions and packages. The providers often have special promotions that offer free hardware, free installation, and special bundles (such as an HDTV plus receiver, dish, and installation for $999).

Be aware that, if you decide to switch providers, you'll need to start all over again.

Related CR report: March 2004

SPEAKERS

Speakers can make or break your audio or video setup. Try to listen to them in a store before buying. And if you can splurge on only part of your system, splurge here.

The best array of audio or video components will let you down if matched with poor-quality speakers. Good speakers don't have to cost a bundle, though it is easy to spend a lot. For a home-theater system, you can start with two or three speakers and add others as need dictates and budget allows. Size is no indication of quality.

WHAT'S AVAILABLE

Among the hundreds of speaker brands available, the major names include Altec, Bose, JBL, KLH, Pioneer, Polk Audio, RCA, Sony, and Yamaha. Speakers are sold through mass merchandisers, audio/video stores, and "boutique" retailers. You can also buy speakers online, but be prepared for shipping charges of up to $100 because speakers can be fairly heavy.

Speakers are sold as pairs for traditional stereo setups, and singly or in sets of three to six for equipping a home theater. To keep a balanced system, buy left and right speakers in pairs, rather than individually. The center-channel speaker should be matched to the front (or main) speakers. For the best effect, the rear speakers should also have a sound similar to the front speakers. The front speakers are used for stereo music playback, and in a home theater set-up, they provide on-screen front left and right sounds. The center (or center-channel) speaker chiefly delivers movie dialog and is usually placed on top of or beneath the TV in a home-theater setup. Rear speakers, sometimes called surround or satellite speakers, deliver rear ambient effects such as crowd noise. A subwoofer carries the lowest tones.

Bookshelf speakers. These are among the smallest, but at 12 to 18 inches tall, many are still too large to fit on a shelf, despite their name. A pair of bookshelf speakers can serve as the sole speakers in a stereo system or as the front or rear duo in a home-theater setup. One can serve as the center-channel unit, provided it's magnetically shielded so it won't interfere with the TV. Small speakers like these have made strides in their ability to handle deep bass without buzzing or distortion. Any bass-handling limitations would be less of a concern in a multispeaker system that uses a subwoofer to reproduce deep bass. Price range: $100 to more than $800.

Floor-standing speakers. Typically about 3 to 4 feet tall, these large speakers can also serve as the sole speakers in a stereo system or as the front pair in a home-theater system. Their big cabinets have the potential to do more justice with deep bass than smaller speakers, but we believe many listeners would be satisfied with smaller speakers that scored well for bass handling. Even if floor models do a bit better, their size and cost may steer buyers toward smaller, cheaper bookshelf models. Price range: $300 to more than $1,000.

Center-channel speaker. In a multichannel setup, the center-channel speaker sits on or below the TV. Because it primarily handles dialog, its frequency range doesn't have to be as full as that of the front pair, but its sound should be similar so all three blend well. Dedicated center-channel speakers are short and wide (6 inches high by 20 inches wide, for instance) so they perch neatly atop a TV. Price range: $100 to more than $500.

Rear-surround speakers. Rear speakers in a multichannel setup carry mostly background sound such as crowd noise. Newer multichannel formats such as Dolby Digital, DTS, DVD-Audio, and SACD make fuller use of these speakers than did earlier formats. You'll get the best blend if the rear pair sounds similar to the front pair. Rear speakers tend to be small and light (often 5 to 10 inches high and 3 to 6 pounds) so they can be wall mounted or placed on a shelf. Price range: $100 to more than $500.

Three-piece sets. Designed to be used as a stand-alone system or integrated with other speakers, these sets combine two bookshelf or satellite speakers for midrange and higher tones with either a center-channel speaker or a subwoofer for bass. Price range: $300 to $800.

Six-piece sets. These systems have four satellites (used for both the front and rear pairs), one center-channel speaker, and a subwoofer. Six-piece sets save you the trouble of matching the distinctive sounds of six speakers. That can be a daunting task at home, and even more of a challenge amidst the din of a store that doesn't have a decent listening room. Price range: $400 to more than $1,000.

TECH TIP

Accuracy is how well a speaker reproduces sound across the range of human hearing. An accurate speaker doesn't overemphasize or underemphasize any frequency.

Other shapes and sizes. A "powertower" is a tower speaker, usually priced above $1,000, with a side-firing, powered subwoofer in its base.

IMPORTANT FEATURES

Lovers of loud sound should pay attention to a speaker's measured **impedance.** The speaker impedance should be the same as recommended in the receiver manual. **Power range** refers to the advertised watts per channel. Speakers placed near a TV set typically have magnetic shielding so they won't distort the picture.

HOW TO CHOOSE

Consider size. Speakers come in all shapes and sizes, so see how they'll fit in your room. Floor-standing speakers might overwhelm smaller spaces. Bookshelf speakers are often a better fit, but they vary greatly in size. Make sure a model you choose will fit the shelf or niche you've earmarked for it. And don't fear that you're giving up quality for compactness. Many small speakers do a fine job. Style may factor into your decision as well. Some speakers are sleekly shaped, with silver finishes. Others are more conventional black boxes.

Focus on accuracy, not advertising. The most critical attribute of any speaker is accuracy—the ability to reproduce sound frequencies without over- or under-emphasizing any part of the audio range. As our tests have shown time and again, some of the lowest-priced speakers are among the most accurate. Ads often tout two-way or three-way drivers and the size of the cone inside a speaker, but you can't judge sound quality by these attributes.

Listen for the differences. Even speakers with comparable accuracy scores can sound quite different. One model may overemphasize treble, while another underemphasizes it. There's no substitute for hearing speakers, so bring a CD with a familiar piece of music to the store. Pay special attention to the front pair, because those speakers do the most work.

Speakers will sound different at home because of your room size, shape, and furnishings, so see if the retailer will allow a home trial or ask about the return policy. If you're torn between two choices, buy the cheaper. Stores may be more open to a return if you want to trade up to a pricier set.

Check impedance. If you like to play music loudly, make sure your receiver is rated to handle the impedance (generally ranging from 4 to 8 ohms) of the front speaker pair.

Related CR Report: November 2003

TV SETS

Conventional TVs, flat screens, rear-projection sets—you have more (and better) viewing choices than before, including HD models, at ever-lower prices.

Conventional TVs with picture tubes, the kind of set you've been watching for years, are still big sellers, and many offer outstanding performance at low prices. But other types of TVs are coming on strong. Want a big picture? Rear-projection TVs have a screen measuring up to 82 inches or so, diagonally, and some new models are much slimmer than the hulking sets you may have seen before. If you'd love a flat screen that's only a few inches thick, an LCD or plasma TV may be right for you. Prices on these models are dropping, although they're still comparatively expensive. Within all these categories there are high-definition (HD) sets, which offer the best picture quality at the highest prices.

WHAT'S AVAILABLE

Among the best-selling brands are Hitachi, JVC, Mitsubishi, Panasonic, Philips, RCA, Samsung, Sanyo, Sharp, Sony, Toshiba, and Zenith. All of the TV types described below are available in standard-definition (analog) and HD (digital) models. Analog TVs can display only standard-definition signals, like those used for most TV broadcasts. This definition is called 480i because images contain up to 480 lines that are drawn onscreen in an interlaced pattern, first odd and then even in each 1⁄60th of a second.

Digital sets can display HD signals with definition of 1080i (1,080 lines with an interlaced scan) or 720p (720 lines scanned progressively, in one sweep). These HD images are sharper and more detailed than standard definition. Enhanced definition (ED), refers to 480p (480 lines scanned progressively). It's better than standard definition but not as good as high definition. Some LCD and plasma TVs are ED sets. These can convert HD signals to a format they can handle, but picture quality won't match that of true HD.

Conventional sets. Most picture-tube TVs have a screen that measures 13 inches to 36 inches diagonally; there are a few 40-inch models. On analog sets, the screens are usually squarish, with an aspect ratio of 4:3, meaning they're four units wide for every three units high. Most HD sets have a 16:9 wide screen with proportions similar to that of a movie-theater screen. There are some 4:3 HD sets as well. Generally, the larger the screen, the higher the price, and the more features and inputs for other video devices. Most sets with screens measuring 27 inches and larger have comb filters, universal remotes, simulated surround sound, and high-quality video inputs. Conventional TVs still offer the best combination of performance and value. Price range: 13-inch sets start at $75 or so; 27-inch sets start at about $250; 32-inch sets start at about $400; 36-inch sets start at $600. HD sets start at several hundred dollars more than analog models.

Rear-projection TVs. Generally measuring 42 to 73 inches diagonally, rear-projection CRT-based TVs are the most affordable jumbo-screen TVs on the market. HD-capable digital sets are becoming the norm as analog models are being phased out. Most have 16:9 screens, but there are some 4:3 models available. These sets use three small CRTs, which makes them big and heavy, sometimes more than 200 pounds. Picture quality can be good and occasionally is very good, but it falls short of most other types of TVs, even with HD programming. Also, the image appears dimmer as your position angles away from the center of the screen. Price range: HD-capable sets start at about $1,500.

Other projection sets, called microdisplays, don't use CRTs. Instead, they create images using LCD, DLP (digital light processing), or LCOS (liquid crystal on silicon) technology. These sets are much slimmer and lighter than CRTs, as well as more expensive. Most are HD-capable digital sets with wide screens measuring 40 to 70 inches or so; LCOS sets are as large as 82 inches. Picture quality of the best microdisplays is better than that of most CRT-based projection sets, but it varies by model. Price range: $2,800 and up.

LCD flat panels. With screens that usually measure between 10 and 46 inches diagonally, LCD TVs are lightweight and only a few inches thick. They can stand on a table or be wall-mounted or suspended under a cabinet. They come in both 4:3 and 16:9 screen shapes and in conventional, ED, and HD models. LCD TVs use the same technology as flat-panel computer monitors. A bright, smooth image is created by a combination of a white backlight and thousands of pixels that open and close like shutters. Slow pixel response may make fast-moving images appear fuzzy, and the image may dim somewhat as you angle away from the center of the screen. Some LCD models have inputs enabling them to serve as both a computer monitor and a TV. Inch for inch, LCD sets are more expensive than other types of TVs, especially in larger sizes. Price range: about $600 and up for 14-inch or 15-inch models.

SHOP SMART

If you want value above all, go with a curved-screen direct-view TV rather than a flat screen.

Plasma flat panels. Also renowned for their thin profile, plasma displays tend to be bigger than LCD models, ranging from about 32 to 63 inches, measured diagonally. They're not as light as LCDs, but you can get special hardware that enables them to be wall-mounted. All are widescreen models; both HD and ED versions are available. Images are created by thousands of pixels containing gas that is converted into plasma by an electrical charge. That results in a bright, colorful display, even in light-filled rooms. Clarity and detail usually aren't quite as sharp as on the best conventional sets, though. Most plasma displays come with a TV tuner and speakers, but with some sets these components must be purchased separately. Price range: about $2,300 and up.

Facts about HD-capable TVs of all types. Within the HD category, there are two types of TV sets. HD-ready sets, also known as HD monitors, can display standard-definition programs on their own. To display HD, they require an external tuner to decode the signals. You can use a special digital cable box or satellite receiver to get HD via cable or satellite; some of those devices can also get HD from a rooftop antenna. To get HD signals without subscribing to cable or satellite, you'll need a separate digital-TV receiver, which costs several hundred dollars, and a rooftop antenna. Depending on your location, an antenna may be able to pull in the major broadcast networks' HD offerings. You don't have to pay to receive the signals, however, as you do with cable and satellite.

Integrated HD sets, also called HDTVs, have a built-in ATSC digital tuner that lets them decode over-the-air HD signals received via a roof antenna. Although they have their own tuner, most of these TVs still require an HD-capable cable box or satellite receiver to get cable or satellite.

Some new models, called digital-cable-ready (DCR) or plug-and-play sets, can receive digital-cable programming, including HD, without using a set-top box. Instead, they have a slot to accept a CableCard provided by the cable company.

WHAT THE NAMES MEAN

Defining definition

What is digital television, exactly? And what does it have to do with high-definition TV? Here's a guide to the terms and how they relate to what you see on the screen.

Digital TV, or DTV, is no more (or less) than the transmission of television images and sound digitally. DTV improves on analog transmission by providing cleaner signals, with less visual "noise" and static. While the current analog-transmission standard has only one level of resolution, and thus one level of picture quality, digital TV offers several levels that provide differing amounts of detail:

Standard definition. The quality level to which we're accustomed. This is used for all analog TV broadcasts and, for the moment, many digital ones. The technical spec is 480i, meaning 480 lines scanned in an interlaced pattern—odd lines first, then even lines—the technique used to "paint" the picture on the screen.

Enhanced definition. A quality level available from progressive-scan DVD players and some DTV broadcasts. It's technically described as 480p, meaning 480 lines scanned progressively, a phrase that may pop up in some ads for TVs. This level provides a smoother, more-detailed picture than 480i.

High definition. Also provided only by DTV transmission, this level offers still-greater resolution: either 720p or 1080i. Details in the image have fewer visible scan lines and are nearly photolike.

To see images in high definition, you must have four elements:

1. High-resolution images

Examples are images converted from cinematic movie cameras or captured by special high-definition video cameras, which are used for a growing body of network prime-time series.

2. High-definition formatting and broadcasts

The source images must remain in HD as they are prepared for broadcast or distribution via cable. If HD content is "down-converted," or reduced in resolution for transmission, you won't receive it as HD.

3. High-definition decoder

Such decoders are built in to some TVs, which are called HDTVs, or integrated HD sets. Other sets, called HD-ready TVs, or HD monitors, require an external decoder. These decoders are contained in HD satellite receivers, HD digital-cable boxes, and set-top boxes that can be used with rabbit-ear or rooftop antennas.

4. A high-definition TV

These sets have a resolution level higher than that of conventional TVs, allowing them to display detail that a regular TV can't handle. If in doubt about a TV's capability, look for references in ads and product materials to 1080i and 720p, the technical terms for the two high-definition modes.

This card enables them to unscramble premium channels, among other things, but doesn't provide all the capability of a cable box, such as an interactive program guide. Integrated sets typically cost more than HD-ready sets.

IMPORTANT FEATURES

A **flat-screen CRT,** a departure from the decades-old curved TV tube, reduces reflections and glare, but doesn't necessarily improve picture quality. A **comb filter,** found on most sets, minimizes minor color flaws at edges within the image and increases picture clarity. Other common features: an **auto-color control,** which can be set to automatically adjust color balance to make flesh tones look natural, and **adjustable color temperature,** which lets you shade the picture toward the blue range ("cooler," better for images with outdoor light) or the red ("warmer," preferred for movie-theater-like realism). **Picture-in-picture** (PIP) lets you watch two channels at once, one in a small picture alongside the full-screen image.

Stereo sound is virtually universal on sets 27 inches or larger, but you'll generally hear little stereo separation from a TV's built-in speakers. For a better stereo effect, route the signals to a sound system. **Ambience sound** is often termed "surround sound," but it isn't true surround like that from a multispeaker home-theater system. It's an effect created by special audio processing. You can turn it off if you don't like it. **Automatic volume leveler** compensates for the volume jumps that often accompany commercials or changes in channel.

Last-channel recall lets you jump to the previously viewed channel. Some models offer an **Extended Data Services (XDS) decoder,** which displays channel and programming information if the station transmits it. **Separate audio program** (SAP) lets you receive a second soundtrack, typically in another language. **Multilingual menus** are also common. **Parental controls** include the V-chip, which blocks specific shows based on their content rating; for access, you must enter a code. A TV with **channel block-out** will block specific channels. Some sets allow you to control use of the audio/video inputs to which video games are connected.

Most TVs have a number of different inputs for connecting other components. **Antenna/cable,** or **radio frequency (RF)** inputs are the most basic; the next step up is **composite video. S-video** inputs let you take advantage of the superior picture quality from a satellite system, a DVD player, or a digital camcorder. **Component-video** inputs offer even better quality, useful with equipment such as most DVD players, high-definition satellite receivers, and cable boxes. Some HD TVs have **DVI** or **HDMI** inputs, which provide a high-quality digital connection to devices such as DVD players, digital-cable boxes, and satellite receivers. These allow the content providers to control your ability to record certain programming.

VGA input lets the TV accept signals from a computer. For a camcorder or video game, a **front-mounted A/V input** is helpful. Audio outputs let you direct a stereo TV's audio signal to a receiver or self-powered speakers. A **headphone jack** lets you watch (and listen) without disturbing others.

Some features are most often found on HD sets and projection TVs. 3:2 pulldown compensation, sometimes referred to by brand-specific names such as CineMotion, can make moving images look less jerky, with less jaggedness around the edges. On 16:9 sets, **stretch and zoom modes** will expand or compress an image to better fill the screen shape. This helps to reduce the dark bands that can appear around images if you watch content formatted for one screen shape on a TV that has the other shape. (The picture may be distorted or cut off a bit in the process of stretching and zooming.) Over time, those bars or any stationary image (such as a ticker or video-game image) can leave residual images on the screens of rear-projection TVs that use CRTs and on plasma sets. Burn-in is not as high a concern with conventional tube-based TVs; LCDs, DLP, and LCOS don't suffer from it at all.

On CRT-based projection sets, **auto convergence** provides a one-touch adjustment to automatically align the three CRTs for a sharp, accurate image. It's much more convenient but perhaps not as thorough as manual convergence, which can be time-consuming.

HOW TO CHOOSE

Choosing the type of TV technology you want is half the battle. The other major decision you'll have to make is whether you want to move up to an HDTV. Consider the following:

Choose the technology. TVs using the familiar picture-tube technology are the least-expensive option, and these still offer the best picture quality. LCD displays are very thin, and they consume less power than other types of TVs. They can be wall-mounted, a consideration if space is an issue. For truly big screens, rear-projection sets and plasma displays are your best bets. CRT-based rear-projection TVs are the lowest-cost way to get a big screen, but they're bulky and heavy. Microdisplays are much thinner but more expensive. Plasma sets are also costly, but they're slimmer still, and they can be wall-mounted. The picture quality characteristics of all these technologies vary, so be sure to view them for yourself to see which you prefer. In general, there's no reason to settle for less than very good picture quality.

Decide on a screen size. TVs with small screens—less than 27 inches—are more likely to come without all the bells and whistles of larger sets. A notable exception: Most LCD sets fall into this size range, and they may be more fully featured. Medium screens—27 to 36 inches—are the most popular in households, so the category has a large number of choices in terms of features, price, and brand. Large screens—40 to 82 inches—are generally plasma or rear-projection models; there are some LCDs and a few direct-view sets around 40 inches. Most big-screen sets are HD-ready. Keep in mind that a jumbo set is likely to look even larger and more overwhelming in your home than it did on a spacious showroom floor.

Decide whether you want HD image quality. Digital HDTVs can display sharper, finer images than conventional analog TVs, whether you're watching HDTV programming, standard TV programming, or DVD movies. Even with standard (non-HD) signals from a good cable connection, a satellite signal, or a DVD player, the picture quality can be better than a conventional set's. But with a poor signal, like the worst channels from cable, an HDTV can make the images look worse. The digital circuitry can't always know how to interpret the noise from the real signal.

While standard-definition TVs can't match HD for picture quality, some offer very good or excellent images that may suit you fine. Only firsthand experience will enable you to decide whether the quality is worth the extra cost. Though HD sets cost less than they used to, they still command a premium—usually hundreds more than a comparable analog set.

Most parts of the U.S. have access to a fair amount of HD content, but offerings vary by locale and the reception method you'll use—antenna, digital cable, or satellite. You can receive programming via an antenna only if you're close enough to the transmitter, with an unobstructed view. Digital cable currently offers more HD content than satellite, but both are constantly adding more programming, so check with your provider.

Decide between an HD-ready set and an integrated HDTV. For the most part, CONSUMER REPORTS thinks HD-ready sets make more sense for most buyers than integrated HDTVs. Integrated sets cost more, and they generally require a cable box or satellite receiver anyway. The new plug-and-play sets have some drawbacks—their one-way CableCards don't offer interactive program guides or video-on-demand via remote control, for instance—so we'd wait till the next generation arrives.

Consider the shape. A regular screen with the familiar 4:3 aspect ratio is a good choice for regular TV programming, which is formatted for this squarish shape. If you watch mostly regular TV programming, a 4:3 screen is probably the better choice for now, although more programming is adopting the widescreen format. Most DVD movies and some HDTV programs are formatted for a 16:9 wide screen.

Related CR Report: November 2004
Ratings: page 311 (LCD), 314 (Plasma)
Reliability: page 335

VIDEO RECORDING

There are a growing number of choices for recording your favorite TV show or movie.

VCRs used to offer the only way to record TV programming at home, and they're still the choice of many consumers. But DVD recorders and digital video recorders (DVRs), sometimes called personal video recorders (PVRs), let you make higher-quality recordings without the hassles of rewinding and fast-forwarding tapes. In addition, there are combination units that pair a DVD player and a VCR, a DVR and a DVD player, or other variations.

Among the various analog and digital recording methods, consider the following:

What kind of picture quality will satisfy you? Digital recording has the edge over analog. A VCR offers decent picture quality, but a DVD recorder or DVR can offer more detail and better images.

Do you want one device that can play movies and record TV programming? Then a stand-alone DVR isn't your best choice. Because it uses a hard drive and has no slot for removable discs or tapes, it can't be used to play prerecorded content as you can with a DVD recorder or VCR.

Do you want permanent recordings for your library? Again, a DVR wouldn't be your best choice because the hard drive has finite storage space. (But you can offload some recordings to a DVD recorder or VCR.) Because they use removable media, a DVD recorder or VCR offers unlimited storage.

How much versatility do you want? DVRs will let you watch the start of a program while you're recording the end, as will DVD recorders when used with some disc formats. Some types of DVRs can also scan TV listings to record shows that match your tastes. Navigation with DVRs and DVD recorders is much more flexible than with a tape-based VCR.

How much do you want to spend? VCRs are by far the cheapest recording option, with prices under $50. DVD recorders start at about $300. DVR prices vary greatly, depending on the hardware you get and the service provider for the programming guide, but the total cost is the highest of the three options.

Is a combination unit best for you? If you want the advantages of several devices—say, the versatility of a DVR plus a DVD's ability to play rentals and swap recordings with friends—a combination unit is worth considering. Decide which capabilities you want to determine which particular combination of devices best suits your needs.

VCRS

Old-hat as they may seem in today's increasingly digital world, VCRs still offer a serviceable way to record your TV programs, as well as to play back prerecorded tapes or to transfer home camcorder movies onto a convenient viewing format.

Both the recorders themselves and blank tapes are inexpensive, and they have the advantages of familiarity and universal compatibility—no format wars here, as you'll find with DVD recordings.

WHAT'S AVAILABLE

Panasonic, Philips Magnavox, RCA, and Sony are among the biggest-selling brands. Most low-end models are VHS; some higher-priced units can record higher-resolution super-VHS, or S-VHS, as well. Hi-fi sound is a common feature, and a desirable one for a home theater setup. Price range: $80 and up for hi-fi models; $45 and up for S-VHS units.

Some TV sets come with built-in VCRs, offering a handy one-stop solution for recording and viewing. VCRs are also being paired with DVD players and DVRs to offer several viewing and recording options in one box.

IMPORTANT FEATURES

VCR Plus, available in several versions, eases the process of programming time-shift recording (taping a program for later viewing) by letting you enter numerical codes from TV listings instead of the program's date, time, duration, and channel.

Index search fast-forwards or rewinds the tape to a specific index point set by the machine at the start of a recorded segment. **Automatic commercial advance** lets the VCR bypass commercials during playback by fast-forwarding past such cues as fade-to-black and changes in sound level. An **onscreen menu** uses the TV to display setup and programming choices.

Some models can automatically switch tapes from SP to EP speed, a feature called **auto speed-switching,** to extend recording time and help ensure that you don't miss a climactic scene because you ran out of tape.

HOW TO CHOOSE

We haven't found many performance differences among VCRs. Most models, even inexpensive ones, are capable of good picture quality. Base your decision more on price and features geared to your needs.

For use in a home-theater, stick with a hi-fi model. These are much better for larger TVs with stereo sound or for connection to a receiver. They can also play surround-sound movies if used with a receiver that decodes the surround-sound information.

For easy programming, look for an onscreen menu and VCR Plus. They'll make setting up timed recordings much easier, letting you avoid fiddling with small buttons and squinting at a tiny display.

Think twice about paying extra for S-VHS. Inexpensive Super VHS models are not much better than common VHS models, but the more expensive models offer a definite improvement in picture quality when playing back S-VHS tapes recorded on the same machine. No S-VHS model will improve picture quality on commercial VHS tapes. If you'll be hooking the recorder up to an S-VHS-C, Hi-8, or digital camcorder, you'll also get some benefit.

If you want to edit recordings, get a model with editing features. Shuttle and jog controls let you scan large segments or move forward or backward a frame at a time to find a precise spot. Audio dub lets you add music or narration. A flying erase head lets you insert a segment without noticeable video glitches.

DVD RECORDERS

While DVD players are playback-only devices, DVD recorders record as well as play. Prices have dropped considerably in the past few years, with entry-level models now selling for less than $300. At the highest-quality record setting, the quality of DVD video recordings is better than that of a VCR. DVD players also offer more ways to navigate recordings, with no need to rewind or fast-forward. With certain disc formats, DVD recorders can perform functions that no VCR can match, such as letting you watch a program from the beginning while recording is already under way. They also offer a way to convert camcorder tapes or home-made VCR recordings to a digital format.

The DVD recorder market is still in its early stages, so it's likely there will be further changes involving disc formats, and prices for machines and for blank storage media may drop further.

WHAT'S AVAILABLE

DVD recorders are available from many of the same manufacturers that make DVD players. Apex Digital, Panasonic, Sony, and Toshiba are among the biggest brands.

In addition to recorders that store content solely on DVDs, some DVD recorders incorporate VHS-tape recording and playback or hard-drive recording. Price range: about $300 and up.

IMPORTANT FEATURES

As with any other video recorder—including digital cameras and DVRs—a recorder's **storage capacity** varies in actual usage. DVD recorders store content at different compression settings and thus at different quality levels. For the best image quality, you have to record programming at the device's lowest level of compression. To get the maximum capacity advertised, you have to use the highest level of compression, which gives the lowest quality.

All **rewritable DVD formats** let you edit, to varying extents, what you've recorded—dropping, hiding, or reordering sections of the recording as needed. DVD-RW and DVD-RAM recorders let you edit more extensively than does DVD+RW.

Besides letting you watch one program while recording another, recorders with **DVD-RAM capability** let you watch an earlier section of a program while you're still recording it.

As with VCRs, DVD recorders may use VCR Plus to ease the setup of time-shift recordings. Some also come with **Gemstar,** a free interactive program guide that gets three days of listings at a time from your TV signal. It offers point-and-click setup of recording events.

In addition to commercial DVD titles, DVD players often support playback or display of numerous other **disc formats**. They include CD-R; the recordable DVD formats DVD+R/RW, DVD-R/RW, and DVD-RAM; Video CD (VCD); and DVD-Audio and Super Audio CD (SACD). They can also play CD-R/RW discs containing MP3 and

Windows Media Audio (WMA) files and JPEG picture files. Make sure a model you're considering plays the discs and formats you use now, or may want to use in the future.

DVD-based movies often come in various formats. **Aspect-ratio control** lets you choose between the 4:3 viewing format of conventional TVs (4 inches wide for every 3 inches high) and the 16:9 ratio of newer, wide-screen sets.

A DVD player gives you all sorts of control over the picture—control you may never have known you needed. **Picture zoom** lets you zoom in on a specific frame. **Black-level adjustment** brings out the detail in dark parts of the screen image. If you've ever wanted to see certain action scenes from different angles, **multi-angle capability** gives you that opportunity. Note that this feature and some others work only with certain discs.

A DVD player enables you to navigate the disc in a number of ways. Unlike a VHS tape, DVDs are sectioned. **Chapter preview** lets you scan the opening seconds of each section or chapter until you find what you want; a related feature, **chapter gallery,** shows thumbnails of section or chapter opening scenes. **Go-to by time** lets you enter how many hours and minutes into the disc you'd like to skip to. **Marker functions** allow easy indexing of specific sections.

To get the most from a DVD player, you need to hook it up to the TV with the best available connection. A **composite-video connection** to the TV can produce a very good picture, but there will be some loss of detail and some color artifacts such as adjacent colors bleeding into each other. Using the **S-video output** can improve picture quality. It keeps the black-and-white and the color portions of the signal separated, producing more picture detail and fewer color defects than standard composite video.

Component video, sometimes not provided on the lowest-end models, improves on S-video by splitting the color signal, resulting in a wider range of color. If you connect a DVD player via an S-video or component connection, don't be surprised if you have to adjust the television-picture setup when you switch to a picture coming from a VCR or a cable box that uses a **radio-frequency** (RF, also called antenna/cable) connection or a composite connection.

Another output, **Digital Video Interface (DVI),** found on some players, is intended for a video connection to digital TVs with DVI inputs. It may be used to pass digital 480p and up-converted higher-resolution video signals. It potentially allows the content providers to control your ability to record the content.

Another benefit of DVD players is the ability to enjoy movies with **multichannel surround sound.** To reap the full sound experience of the audio encoded into DVD titles, you'll need a Dolby Digital receiver and six speakers, including a subwoofer. (For 6.1 and 7.1 soundtracks, you'll need seven or eight speakers.) **Dolby Digital decoding built-in** refers to a DVD player that decodes the multichannel audio before the audio receiver; without the built-in circuitry, you'd need to have the decoder built into the receiver or, in rare instances, use a separate decoder box to take advantage of the audio. (A Dolby Digital receiver will decode an older format, Dolby Pro Logic, as well.) Most players also support **Digital Theater System (DTS)** decoding for titles using the six-channel encoding format. When you're watching DVD-based movies, **dynamic audio-range control** helps keep explosions and other noisy sound effects from seeming too loud.

DVD players also provide features such as **multilingual support,** which lets you choose dialog or subtitles in different languages for a given movie. **Parental control** lets parents "lock out" commercial films by their rating code.

HOW TO CHOOSE

As with DVD players, DVD recorders differ little in commercial DVD picture quality; most are superb. But for the best image quality, you have to record programming at the lowest level of compression. To get the maximum capacity, you have to use the highest level of compression, which gives the lowest quality.

Consider the disc types the recorder uses. Recorders vary in the types of blank discs they can use. That affects what a recorder can do and how readily its discs can be played on other DVD players.

Most recorders on the market record on either DVD-R or DVD+R discs; some record in both. These two disc types provide one-time (write-once) recording, typically with a maximum capacity of six hours. They cost about $2 to $5 apiece. Recorders can also record on at least one type of rewritable disc—DVD-RW, DVD+RW, or DVD-RAM. These rewritable discs cost about $5 to $12 each.

DVD-RAM discs steal a selling point from digital video recorders that record to hard drives: They let you watch a program from the beginning while recording is already under way. You can also view a previously recorded program at the same time you are recording another show on that disc.

Another plus: DVD-RAM discs allow great flexibility in rearranging and editing content. DVD-RW discs recorded in VR mode (rather than video mode) offer similar editing features. But there's a downside: Recordings made on DVD-RAM discs or DVD-RW discs in VR mode will not play back on as many other recorders or players as the other recordable DVD discs. DVD recorders with hard drives allow great flexibility in rearranging and editing content on the hard drive and allow you to burn the final product to DVD that can be played in other machines. Note that editing is not easy to do.

Consider playback capabilities. Virtually all DVD recorders can play commercial DVDs and music CDs, as well as CD-R and CD-RW discs containing CD-audio. Support for MP3, DVD-Audio, SACD, and video CDs varies.

Related CR Report: December 2003

DIGITAL VIDEO RECORDERS

Avid TV watchers are prime candidates for these devices, as are those who'd like to sort programming according to their individual viewing preferences. DVRs are also a good bet for those people who hate sitting through commercials.

DVRs are different from DVDs because they don't have a slot for removable discs or tapes; they record only on the hard drive and can't play prerecorded media. Some combination units pair a DVR with a DVD player or a VCR so you can play removable media. Digital video recorders offer recording capability with the convenience of a program guide. These set-top receivers have a hard drive much like the one in a computer, generally with space for 20 to 80 hours of programming, although some can hold up to 320 hours at lower video quality.

You can get a stand-alone DVR or one that's integrated into a digital-cable box, satellite-TV receiver, off-air digital TV decoder, DVD player/recorder, or VCR. Depending on which provider and plan you choose, you may pay for the service as well as the equipment—either a one-time activation charge or a monthly fee on top of your current cable or satellite-TV bill.

Because they can record and play at the same time, DVRs allow you to pause (and rewind or fast-forward) the current show you're watching, picking up where you left off. If you pause a one-hour show for 10 or 15 minutes at the beginning, you can resume watching it, skip past all the commercials, and catch up to the actual "live" broadcast by the end of the show. Dual-tuner models can record two programs at once, even as you're watching a third recorded program.

Program guides are downloaded via your phone line, generally late at night to avoid tying up the line. These guides are customized according to which broadcast channels are available in your area and to which cable or satellite service you subscribe. A DVR does not replace your usual programming source. You must still get broadcasts via cable, satellite service, or antenna.

WHAT'S AVAILABLE

If you get your DVR functionality in a digital-cable box leased from your cable company, you're typically limited to the cable operator's choice of hardware. For hard-drive recording in a satellite receiver, a few models that work with either DirecTV or Dish Network are available at retail.

For stand-alone DVRs, there are two main service providers: TiVo and ReplayTV. Hardware prices depend mostly on how many hours of programming you can store; service charges vary. The DVRs intended for use with one provider will not work with the other. You can buy TiVo equipment directly from TiVo, Circuit City, and other retailers, or from Hughes or Sony under their brand names. Price range: about $250 to more than $1,000.

TiVo service requires a paid subscription of $13 per month, or $299 for the life of the DVR (transferable if you sell it). You can also get a DirecTV satellite receiver that incorporates TiVo capability. (TiVo service charges still apply.)

ReplayTV offers some models bundled with lifetime service included in the equipment price. With other models, service is separate; you can pay a one-time activation fee of $299 or a monthly charge of $13. In either case, you must buy equipment directly from the company. Price range: $150 to $800.

IMPORTANT FEATURES

Most DVRs resemble VCRs in size and shape but don't have a slot for a tape or disc. (The internal hard drive is not removable.) Combination units that have both a VCR or DVD player or recorder and a DVR will have the requisite media slots. All these units connect to your television like a cable or satellite receiver, using **composite, S-video component,** or possibly **RF antenna outputs** to match the input of your set.

A recorder's hard-drive capacity varies in actual usage. Like digital cameras, DVRs record at different **compression settings** and thus at different quality levels. For the best image quality, you have to record programming at the DVR's lowest level of compression. To get the maximum capacity advertised, you have to use the highest level of compression, which gives the lowest quality. For example, a model that advertises a 30-hour maximum capacity will fit only about nine hours at its best-quality setting.

The **program guide** is an interactive list of the programs that can be recorded by the DVR for the next seven to 14 days. You can use it to select the show currently being broadcast to watch or record—or you can search it by title, artist, or show type for programs you want to record automatically in the future.

Custom channels, available with some models, are individualized groupings of programs that interest you. The feature allows you to set up your own "channel" of your favorites, such as crime dramas or appearances by William Shatner, whether on "Star Trek" or a talk show. A DVR can also record a specified show every time it runs.

A **remote control** is standard. Common features include instant replay, fast-forward, rewind, and pause of either recorded or live programs.

HOW TO CHOOSE

Ultimately, the DVR's picture quality, like the VCR's, depends on the quality of the signal coming in via your cable or satellite provider. A noisy or mediocre signal will produce mediocre digital recordings.

Do you want the most programming features? The services from TiVo and ReplayTV may have more features and functionality than some of the offerings of cable and satellite companies. But you will have to buy another box, deal with another remote, and possibly have another monthly fee.

Would you prefer to have fewer boxes and service providers to contend with? If you have or are considering digital cable, inquire whether a cable box equipped with DVR functionality is available. If satellite service is an option, consider getting a receiver that includes a DVR. Keep in mind that you may have to pay a separate fee for the DVR service. Note that satellite DVRs work only with satellite programming and won't record from cable or an antenna.

Related CR Report: November 2004

KITCHEN & LAUNDRY

Kitchen & Laundry: Cleaned, Cooked, & Cool

Form follows function in the kitchen and laundry areas, where appliances are looking good with new colors and stainless steel. They're smart, too, with sensors to tell you when your food is cooked and your clothes are dry. So now you can add a bit of digital efficiency to household chores.

COOKTOPS & WALL OVENS

Separate appliances give you the flexibility of two cooking areas, with burners placed just about anywhere you want. You also gain the option of cooking with both gas and electricity.

Because about one-third of cooktops and wall ovens are sold as part of a kitchen makeover, style sells. More and more of the appliances have sleek, flush surfaces that are easy to clean or stainless-steel skins that let you easily mix and match brands.

Electric cooktops have added smooth glass cooking surfaces. Some gas models now compete with "gas on glass" designs, which put burners atop a ceramic surface for a sleek look.

Most electric smoothtops now have features such as expandable elements that accommodate pots of various sizes. Many include a "bridge" that spans two burners, useful for griddles and large pots. More and more gas cooktops have continuous grates that let you slide a pot from one burner to another.

Choosing separate appliances doesn't have to take a substantial bite out of your budget. Our tests show that a high level of performance doesn't have to carry a high price. You can bring home a pair of fine performers for about $1,500.

WHAT'S AVAILABLE

GE, Kenmore (sourced from others), Frigidaire, Maytag, and Whirlpool are the leading makers of cooktops and wall ovens. Other major brands include Amana, Jenn-Air, and KitchenAid. Mainstream brands have established high-end offshoots, such as Kenmore Elite, GE Profile, and Whirlpool Gold. High-end, pro-style brands include Bosch, Dacor, DCS, GE Monogram, KitchenAid Pro-Line, Thermador, Viking, and Wolf.

Cooktops. You can install a cooktop on a kitchen island or other location where counter space allows. As with freestanding ranges, cooktops can be electric coil, electric smoothtop, or gas. Cooktops add flexibility since they can be located separately from the oven. Most are 30 inches wide and are made of porcelain-coated steel or ceramic, with four elements or burners. Some are 24 or 36 inches wide, depending on the number of burners.

Modular cooktops let you mix and match parts—removing burners and adding a grill, say—but you pay a premium for that added flexibility. Pre-configured cooktops are less expensive. Price range: electric cooktop, $150 to $1,000; gas cooktop, $200 to $1,500.

Wall ovens. These can be single or double, electric or gas, self-cleaning or manual, with or without a convection setting. Width is typically 24, 27, or 30 inches. They allow you to eliminate bending by installing them at waist or eye level, though you can also nest them beneath a countertop to save space. Price range: $350 to more than $2,500 for double-oven models; figure on about $300 extra for convection.

IMPORTANT FEATURES

On electric cooktops. Consider where the **controls** are located. Slide-in ranges have the dials on the front panel, while freestanding models have them on the backguard. Some models locate controls to the left and right, with oven controls in between, giving you a quick sense of which control operates which element. But controls clustered in the center stay visible when tall pots sit on rear heating elements. On most electric cooktops, controls take up room on the surface. Some models have electronic touchpads, however, allowing the cooktop to be flush with the counter.

Coil elements, the least expensive electric option, are easy to replace if they break.

Spending $200 more will buy you a **smoothtop** model.

Most smoothtops have **expandable elements**—also called **dual elements**—which allow you to switch between a large, high-power element and a small, low-power element contained within it. Some smoothtops also include a **low-wattage element** for warming plates or keeping just-cooked food at the optimal temperature. Some have an elongated "bridge" element that spans two burners—a nicety for accommodating rectangular or odd-shaped cookware. And many have at least **one hot-surface light**—a key safety feature, since the surface can remain hot long after the elements have been turned off. The safest setup includes a dedicated "hot" light for each element.

Many electric cooktops have one large, **higher-wattage element** in front and one in back. An **expanded simmer range** in some smoothtop models lets you fine-tune the simmer setting on one element for, say, melting chocolate or keeping a sauce from getting too hot.

TECH TIP

Most ovens require a 20-amp circuit, but some can require up to 40 amps. So check your wiring before you purchase.

On gas cooktops. Most gas cooktops have four burners in three sizes, measured in British thermal units per hour (Btu/hr.): one or two medium-power burners (about 9,000 Btu/hr.), a small burner (about 5,000 Btu/hr.), and one or two large ones (about 12,500 Btu/hr.). We recommend a model with one or more 12,000 Btu/hr. burners for quick cooktop heating. On a few models, the burners automatically reignite.

For easier cleaning, look for **sealed burners.** Gas ranges typically have **knob controls;** the best rotate 180 degrees or more. Try to avoid knobs that have adjacent "off" and "low" settings and that rotate no more than 90 degrees between High and Low.

Spending more gets you either heavier

grates made of porcelain-coated cast iron or a sleek **ceramic surface**—also called **gas-on-glass**—and **stainless-steel accents,** along with a low-power **simmer burner** with an extra-low setting for delicate sauces (though other burners often are capable of simmering).

On ovens. Electric ovens used to have an edge over gas ovens in roominess, but recently CONSUMER REPORTS has found roomy ovens among both types. Note, though, that an oven's usable capacity may be less than what manufacturers claim, because they don't take protruding broiler elements and other features into account.

A **self-cleaning cycle** uses high heat to burn off spills and splatters. Most ovens have it, although some pro-style gas models still don't. An **automatic door lock,** found on most self-cleaning models, is activated during the cycle, then unlocks when the oven has cooled. Also useful is a **self-cleaning countdown** display, which shows the time left in the cycle.

Higher-priced wall ovens often include **convection,** which uses a fan and, sometimes, an electric element to circulate heated air. CONSUMER REPORTS tests have shown that this mode cut cooking time for a large roast and, in some cases, baked large cookie batches more evenly because of the circulating air. But the fan can take up valuable oven space. A few electric ovens have a low-power **microwave feature** that works with bake and broil elements to speed cooking time further. The GE Advantium over-the-range oven uses a **halogen heating bulb** as well as microwaves. Another cooking technology, Trivection, uses regular thermal heating, convection, and microwave energy to cut cooking time. Trivection is available in some top-of-the-line GE Profile and Monogram ovens and some Kenmore models. Though very good overall, it's very pricey.

A **variable-broil** feature in most electric ovens offers adjustable settings for foods such as fish or thick steaks that need slower or faster cooking. Ovens with **12-hour shutoff** turn off automatically if you leave the oven on for that long. But most models allow you to disable this feature. A **child lockout** allows you to disable oven controls for safety.

Manufacturers are also updating oven controls across the price spectrum. **Electronic touchpad controls** are common. A **digital display** makes it easier to set the precise temperature and keep track of it. A **cook time/delay start** lets you set a time for the oven to start and stop cooking; remember, however, that you shouldn't leave most foods in a cold oven very long. An **automatic oven light** typically comes on when the door opens, although some ovens have a switch-operated light. A **temperature probe,** to be inserted into meat or poultry, indicates when you've obtained a precise internal temperature.

Oven windows come in various sizes. Those without a decorative grid usually offer the clearest view, although some cooks may welcome the grid to hide pots, pans, and other cooking utensils typically stored inside the oven.

HOW TO CHOOSE

Cooktop/wall oven or a range? With a cooktop/wall oven combo, you can put the appliances pretty much anywhere in the kitchen and mount the oven at a convenient height. Choose a range if you want it to be the centerpiece, as a professional-style model would be.

Installing separate appliances is more work. Electric wall ovens and cooktops each need their own electrical circuit and are best installed by a professional.

Gas or electric? If you have gas service, you might want to use both fuels. Electric wall ovens have a larger capacity than gas ones, and they're easier to install. With cooktops, the quick response of a gas flame might better suit your style of cooking. Gas performs very well in our tests. We have found, however, that electric cooktops tend to boil water faster and simmer sauces better.

Consider cleanup and safety. To minimize the parts you need to clean around, check the Ratings for a smooth-surface cooktop and an oven with a covered bottom heating element and smooth touchpad controls.

Cooktops stay hot for a while after you turn off the heat. Since smoothtops blend into the surrounding counter, children and unwary adults could get burned. For safety, smoothtops have lights to signal which element is still hot.

Related CR Report: August 2004
Ratings: page 234

DISHWASHERS

Models selling for as little as $350 or so can excel at washing dishes, but they may not measure up to costlier models in quietness, water and energy usage, or features.

Spend $300 to $400 and you can get a dishwasher that's a little noisy but still does a good job cleaning dirty dishes without prerinsing. To get the best of everything—cleaning prowess plus the quietest operation, convenience features, water and energy efficiency, and designer styling—you'll have to spend $600 or more.

A dirt sensor, once a premium feature, is now becoming standard, even on lower-priced models. Sensors are designed to adjust water level to the amount of soil on dishes. The federal government's EnergyGuide stickers more accurately reflect water and energy usage for sensor models than in the past. Thanks to prodding from Consumers Union, publisher of CONSUMER REPORTS and Consumer Reports.org, and major appliance makers, the Department of Energy recently revised the tests it uses to calculate energy costs, yielding more realistic estimates.

WHAT'S AVAILABLE

Frigidaire, GE, Maytag, and Whirlpool make most dishwashers and sell them under their own names, associated brands, and sometimes the Sears Kenmore label. Whirlpool makes high-end KitchenAid, low-end Roper, and many Kenmore models. Maytag makes the high-end Jenn-Air, midpriced Amana, and low-priced Admiral dishwashers. GE offers a wide range of choices under the GE label and also makes the value-priced Hotpoint. Asko, Bosch, and Miele are high-end European brands; Bosch also makes Siemens models. Haier is an import from China; Fisher & Paykel is from New Zealand.

Most models fit into a 24-inch-wide space under a kitchen countertop and are attached to a hot-water pipe, drain, and an electrical line. Compact models fit into narrower spaces. If you have the room, it's now possible to get a wider, 30-inch dishwasher from Dacor, although you'll pay a hefty premium. Portable models in a finished cabinet can be rolled over to the sink and connected to the faucet. A "dishwasher in a drawer" design from Fisher & Paykel has two stacked drawers that can be used simultaneously or individually, depending upon the number of dishes you need to wash.

Price range: $250 to $1,300 (domestic brands); $400 to $1,800 (foreign-made brands).

IMPORTANT FEATURES

Most models offer a choice of at least three **wash cycles**—Light, Normal, and Heavy (or Pots and Pans)—which should be enough for the typical dishwashing jobs in most households. **Rinse/Hold** lets you rinse dirty dishes before using the dishwasher on a full cycle. Other cycles offered on many models include **Pot Scrubber, Soak/Scrub,** and **China/Crystal,** none of which we consider crucial for most consumers. Dishwashers often spray water from multiple places, or "levels," in the machine. Most models typically offer a choice of **drying** with or without heat.

Some dishwashers use **filters** to keep wash water free of food that can be redistributed on clean dishes. Most such models are self-cleaning: A spray arm cleans residue from the coarse filter during the rinse cycle, and a food-disposal **grinder** cuts up large food particles. Some of the more expensive dishwashers have a filter that you must pull out and clean manually; these are usually quieter than those with grinders. If noise is a concern, see if better **soundproofing**—often in the form of hard, rubbery insulation surrounded by a thick fiberglass blanket—is available as a step-up feature.

SHOP SMART

Often, special wash cycles aren't necessary. The three cycles most dishwashers come with are sufficient.

A **sanitizing wash** or **rinse option** that raises the water temperature above the typical 140° F doesn't necessarily mean improved cleaning. Remember, the moment you touch a dish while taking it out of the dishwasher, it's no longer sanitized.

Most dishwashers have **electronic touchpad controls.** On more expensive ones, controls may be fully or partially hidden, or integrated, in the top edge of the door. The least expensive models have mechanical controls, usually operated by a dial and push buttons. Touchpads are the easiest type of control to clean. **Dials** indicate progress through a cycle. Some electronic models digitally display time left in the wash cycle. Others merely show a "clean" signal. A **delayed-start** control lets you set the dishwasher to start later, for example, at night when utility rates may be lower. Some models offer **child-safety features,** such as locks for the door and controls.

Most dishwashers hold cups and glasses on top, plates on the bottom, and silverware in a basket. **Racks** can sometimes be adjusted to better fit your dishes. On some units, the top rack can be adjusted enough to let you put 10-inch dinner plates on both the top and bottom racks simultaneously, or it can be removed entirely so very tall items will fit on the bottom.

Other features that enhance flexibility include **adjustable** and **removable tines,** which fold down to accommodate bigger dishes, pots, and pans; **slots for silverware** that prevent "nesting"; **removable racks,** which enable loading and unloading outside the dishwasher; **stemware holders,** which steady wine glasses; **clips** to keep light plastic cups from overturning; and **fold-down shelves,** which stack cups in a double-tiered arrangement.

Stainless-steel **tubs** should last virtually forever, but even plastic tubs generally have a warranty of 20 years, much longer than most people keep a dishwasher. Light-colored plastic may discolor, especially from tomato sauce, but there's otherwise no advantage to stainless. Dishwashers with stainless-steel tubs typically cost $550 and up.

If you want a front panel that matches your cabinets, you can buy a kit compatible with many dishwashers. Some higher-priced models are designed to be customized; they come without a front panel so you can choose your own, usually at a cost of several hundred dollars.

HOW TO CHOOSE

Our tests over the years have shown that most new dishwashers will do a great job cleaning even the dirtiest dishes without pre-rinsing, which wastes lots of water. But they differ in appearance, noise, loading, energy efficiency, and features. Here are points to consider when choosing a dishwasher:

Don't settle for drab design. Like other kitchen appliances, dishwashers are becoming more stylish. White is still the dominant color, followed by black and bisque; stainless steel is an increasingly common option. (Keep in mind that stainless, while trendy, often shows fingerprints and smudges.) The least-expensive stainless-finished dishwashers generally cost about $400, but you might find one on sale for closer to $300. Another option: Many models can be fitted with a panel to match your cabinetry so they blend in with the décor.

All but the lowest-cost new models have a one-piece door without a separate bottom panel, creating a clean look that eliminates a dirt trap. Some higher-priced models have most or all controls hidden along the top edge of the door. That makes for a smooth, sleek exterior, but the small labels can be hard to read and the small buttons hard to operate.

Nix the noise. To ensure that the after-dinner cleanup won't drown out the TV or conversation, check the Ratings for a dishwasher judged excellent or very good for noise. You might have to pay $600 or more to get one of the quietest models, which is barely noticeable when running.

Look for loading flexibility. Any dishwasher can fit 10 typical place settings of dishes, glasses, and cutlery, but those with adjustable racks and fold-down tines are better if you want to wash oversized platters or odd-shaped serving pieces. Some top racks adjust enough to hold 10-inch dinner plates on the top and bottom racks simultaneously. In some machines, adjustable parts are color-coded.

Consider the cost of use. Most of the energy a dishwasher uses goes to heating the water. Water usage, and thus the operating costs, vary greatly from model to model. In our latest tests, water usage ranged from about 3½ to 12 gallons a load. Energy costs to heat the water and run the machine could vary by as much as $70 a year for the tested models, depending on rates in your area. Over its lifetime, a more efficient model could be a better buy than a lower-priced model that is less energy-efficient.

Don't get hung up on dirt sensors. Sensors are designed to adjust water use and cycle length to the amount of soil on dishes. Generally, all but the lowest-priced and some of the highest-priced new dishwashers have sensors. In our tests, many sensors couldn't differentiate between slightly and very dirty dishes, so the machines used more water than needed. Also, the cycles on sensor models were about 20 minutes longer than on machines without a sensor. Some Kenmore dishwashers have a second sensor that adjusts the water level to the load size. It cut water usage slightly in our tests.

If speed matters, check cycle time. The normal cycle (including drying time) ranges from about 85 minutes to 150 minutes, but longer cycles don't necessarily clean better. In our tests, models with cycle times of about 100 minutes did just as thorough a job as others that took 145 minutes.

Don't pay more for special cycles. Three basic wash cycles—Light, Normal, and Pots and Pans—are adequate for most chores. Rinse and Hold is handy if you want to delay washing until there is a full load. Settings such as China don't add much, in our opinion. Sanitize settings, usually on high-end models, are pointless: Once you handle the dishes, they are no longer sanitized.

Decide whether a self-cleaning filter is a must. Most dishwashers have self-cleaning filters that grind up food particles and pass them down the drain. The Asko, Bosch, Fisher & Paykel, Haier, Miele, and Siemens models we've tested have filters you clean yourself. That isn't a big deal: You simply remove the filter and rinse it off, typically every week or two. A clogged filter could affect wash performance. Note that a dishwasher with a self-cleaning filter might be noisier than one without it.

Consider the cost of delivery and installation. Installation can run $100 to $200 or more; removing your old dishwasher may cost an extra $25 to $50.

Related CR Reports: January 2004, August 2004
Ratings: page 241
Reliability: page 331

DRYERS

On the whole, clothes dryers do a good job. More sophisticated models dry your laundry with greater finesse.

Dryers are relatively simple. Their major differences are how they heat the air (gas or electricity) and in how they're programmed to shut off once the load is dry (thermostat or moisture sensor). Gas models typically cost about $50 more than electric ones, but they're usually cheaper to operate.

CONSUMER REPORTS has found that dryers with a moisture sensor tend to recognize when laundry is dry more quickly than machines that use a traditional thermostat. Because they don't subject clothing to unnecessary heat, moisture-sensor models are easier on fabrics. And since they shut themselves off when laundry is dry, they use less energy. Sensors are now offered on many dryers, including some relatively low-priced ones. In our most recent tests, some models priced at $300 or so had sensors.

WHAT'S AVAILABLE

The top four brands—GE, Kenmore (Sears), Maytag, and Whirlpool—account for more than 80 percent of dryer sales. Other brands include Amana (made by Maytag), Frigidaire (made by Electrolux), Hotpoint (made by GE), and KitchenAid and Roper (both made by Whirlpool). You may also run across smaller brands such as Crosley, Gibson, and White-Westinghouse, all of which are made by the larger brands. Asko, Bosch, and Miele are European brands. Fisher-Paykel is from New Zealand, LG from Korea, and Haier from China.

Full-sized models. These dryers generally measure between 27 and 29 inches in width—the critical dimension for fitting into cabinetry and closets. Front-mounted controls on some models let you stack the dryer atop a front-loading washer. Full-sized models vary in drum capacity from about 5 to 7½ cubic feet. Most dryers have ample capacity for typical wash loads. A larger drum can more easily handle bulky items such as queen-sized comforters. Price range: electric, $200 to $1,000; gas, $250 to $1,100. Buying a more expensive model may get you more capacity and a few extra conveniences.

Space-saving models. Compacts, exclusively electric, are typically 24 inches wide, with a drum capacity roughly half that of full-sized models—about 3½ cubic feet. Aside from their smaller capacity, they perform much like full-sized machines. They can be stacked atop a companion washer, but shorter people may find it difficult to reach the dryer controls or the inside of the drum. Some dryers operate on 120 volts, others on 240 volts. Price range: $200 to about $1,400.

Another space-saving option is a laundry center, which combines a washer and dryer in a single unit. Laundry centers come with either gas or electric dryers. There are full-sized (27 inches wide) or compact (24 inches wide) models available. The dryer component of a laundry center typically has a somewhat smaller capacity than a full-sized dryer. Models with electric dryers require a dedicated 240-volt power source. Price range: $700 to $1,900.

IMPORTANT FEATURES

Full-sized dryers often have two or three **auto-dry cycles**, which shut off the unit when the clothes reach the desired dryness. Each cycle might have a **More Dry** setting to dry clothes completely, and a **Less Dry** setting to leave clothes damp for ironing. You can set the dryer anywhere in between those two extremes; setting it at the midpoint is a good idea. Manufacturers have refined the way dryers shut themselves off. As clothes tumble past a **moisture sensor**, electrical contacts in the drum sample their conductivity for surface dampness and relay signals to electronic controls. Dryers with a **thermostat** measure moisture indirectly by taking the temperature of exhaust air from the drum (the temperature rises as moisture evaporates).

Most dryers have a separate **temperature control** that allows you to choose a lower heat for delicate fabrics, among other things. An **extended tumble setting**, sometimes called Press Care or Finish Guard, helps to prevent wrinkling when you don't remove clothes immediately. Some models continue to tumble without heat; others cycle on and off. An **express-dry cycle** is meant for drying small loads at high heat in less than a half hour. Large loads will take longer. **Touchpad electronic controls** found in higher-end models tend to be more versatile than mechanical dials and buttons—once you figure them out, that is. Some models allow you to save favorite settings that you use frequently. Some high-end dryers have a display with a progression of **menus** that enable you to program specific settings for recall at any time. Such menus can be time-consuming (and sometimes confusing) to navigate, but they may allow custom programming or offer detailed help information otherwise available only in the manual.

A **top-mounted lint filter** may be somewhat easier to clean than one inside the drum. Some models have a **warning light** that reminds you to clean the lint filter. It's important to clean the lint filter regularly to minimize any fire hazard and to maintain the dryer's efficiency. It's also advisable to use metal ducting (either rigid or flexible) instead of plastic or flexible foil. Plastic or foil ducts can create a fire hazard if they sag and clog with lint, causing lint to build up in the dryer, where it can ignite. You should clean the ducts at least once a year.

Most full-sized models have a **drum light**, making it easy for you to spot stray items that may be hiding in the back. Some models allow you to raise or lower the volume of an **end-of-cycle signal** or shut it off. A **rack** included with many machines attaches inside the drum and is intended to hold sneakers or other items you want to dry without tumbling. Models with **drop-down doors** in front may fit better against a wall, but side-opening doors may make it easier to access the inside of the drum.

HOW TO CHOOSE

Consider gas. Most homes have either the 240-volt outlet that an electric dryer requires or a gas hookup. If you have both, don't rule out a gas dryer because it costs $50 or so more than its electric counterpart. The likely savings in fuel costs should make the gas model cheaper in the long run. Both types perform comparably, our years of testing show. CONSUMER REPORTS tests only electric dryers, which account for about 80 percent of the models sold, but equivalent gas models are listed in the Ratings.

Insist on a moisture sensor. Tumbling around in heated air for longer than necessary can damage or shrink fabrics. You can minimize problems by getting a dryer with a moisture sensor that automatically ends the cycle when laundry reaches the desired level of dryness. Sensors are available on about half the dryers on the market, including some priced at about $300. A thermostat that ends the cycle when the air temperature hits a certain point is a less accurate gauge of when a load is dry. You'll usually find thermostats only on basic models.

Whether a specific model has a sensor or thermostat may not be obvious from labeling or controls. Check the literature, visit the manufacturer's Web site, or pick a highly rated dryer that we've tested.

Don't get hung up on capacity. Manufacturers describe dryer capacity (as they do washer capacity) with terms such as extra large, super, and super plus. The differences aren't meaningful for everyday use. Most full-sized dryers have capacities of about 7 to 7½ cubic feet, which can hold a typical wash load. If you want to dry big, bulky items, capacity matters more.

Set it and forget it. To protect clothes from overdrying and to cut energy consumption, use an automatic setting rather than a timed one. Set the control to the midpoint and raise or lower it as needed. Using "more dry" routinely can overdry or damage clothes and waste energy. Use "less dry" to leave clothing damp for ironing. Don't worry about knowing when an automatic cycle is done: If you don't hear the buzzer, an extended tumble without heat prevents wrinkles if you don't remove clothes immediately.

Don't pay for unnecessary extras. Higher-priced dryers may offer a dozen or so choices, including specialty cycles such as Speed Dry (15 minutes of high heat, for example). These can usually be replicated with standard settings. A choice of heat level, timed and auto-dry, and a few fabric types (regular/cotton and permanent press/delicate) is usually plenty. Touchpads look impressive and may allow you to save custom settings but don't improve performance. Nor do stainless-steel tubs, unlike in washers.

Get a quiet dryer for living areas. If your dryer will be near the kitchen or a bedroom, look for a model judged very good or excellent for noise.

Related CR Report: June 2004
Ratings: page 250
Reliability: page 331

ELECTRIC GRILLS, INDOOR

Once an infomercial novelty, indoor grills have come into their own, with more models, larger sizes, and more features.

There are two basic styles available: contact grills and open grills. Of the former variety, George Foreman's Lean Mean Grilling Machine—and more than a dozen variations made by Salton—have pretty much KO'd the competition, winning nearly 80 percent of sales. Hamilton Beach also markets several contact grill models. Open grills made by DeLonghi, Cuisinart, and T-Fal are also available.

Contact grills sandwich the food between two hot surfaces or grids, like a waffle iron. A drip pan in front or beneath catches any grease. Speed is the key to the cooking clout of this type of grill, which can cook burgers in just 3 to 6 minutes (after a 3- to 10-minute warm-up period). One drawback of contact grills is that they have trouble with items more than an inch thick. Because the food won't fit properly between the grids, cooking will be uneven. Price range: $25 to $100.

Open grills come closer to cooking food in the manner of their outdoor cousins, by grilling meat or other items one side at a time on an open broiler plate. The result is quickly seared food and clearer grill marks, a real draw for some cooks. Grease and juices fall into a drip pan underneath the cooking surface. Not surprisingly, open grills cook more slowly than contact grills, but they are more adept at handling thicker items such as steaks. Indoor grills heat only to 200° to 400°, as opposed to an oven broiler, which should exceed 600°. As a result, grilled foods will turn out much less crispy than what you'd get by putting them under a broiler. Price range: $65 to $100.

HOW TO CHOOSE

First, determine which suits your needs better: a contact or an open grill. The decision will generally hinge on how speedily you want to prepare food, the thickness of the items you grill, and how pronounced you want grill lines to look.

Choose the right size. Almost all grills are large enough to cook four burgers at a time; some can handle as many as eight. Also, remember that the bigger the cooking surface (they range from 38 to 192 square inches), the more counter or storage space you'll need for it.

Ignore extras. Several come with temperature controls; you don't need them. The grills don't heat to much more than 400°, so all foods cook best at the highest temperature. A timer is available on some models—a convenience, but indicator lights work just as well, and you can use a regular kitchen timer to track cooking time.

SHOP SMART

Indoor electric grills tend to take up serious counter space, so you need to decide whether you're willing to give up a lot for a single-use appliance.

Related CR Report: December 2003

FOOD PROCESSORS & MIXERS

Match the machine to the way you prepare foods. But you may find you need more than one.

Which food-prep appliance best suits your style and the foods you prepare? Food processors are versatile machines that can chop, slice, shred, and purée many different foods. Mini-choppers are good for small jobs such as mincing garlic and chopping nuts. Hand mixers can handle light chores such as whipping cream or mixing cake batter. And powerful stand mixers are ideal for cooks who make bread and cookies from scratch.

WHAT'S AVAILABLE

Food processors. Several brands have introduced multifunction models designed to do the job of two or more machines, for instance, an interchangeable food-processor container and a glass blender jar and blade. Either attachment fits on the motorized base.

SHOP SMART
Think small appliances for small jobs, bigger appliances for bigger jobs.

Another design trend is a mini-bowl insert that fits inside the main container for preparing smaller quantities of food. Newer designs tend to be sleek, with rounded corners. Dominant brands are Black & Decker, Cuisinart, and Hamilton Beach. Price range: $30 to $500.

Stand and hand mixers. The big push in mixers is for more power, which is useful for handling heavy dough. You'll find everything from heavy-duty models offering the most power and the largest mixing bowls to light-service machines that are essentially detachable hand mixers resting on a stand. Models vary in power from about 200 to 700 watts. Sales of light-duty, convenient hand mixers have held their own in recent years.

KitchenAid owns about half the stand-mixer market; Hamilton Beach and Sunbeam are the next best-selling brands. Price range: $40 to $400.

Black & Decker, Hamilton Beach, and Sunbeam are the dominant brands among hand mixers. Price range: $10 to $75.

IMPORTANT FEATURES

With food processors: All have a clear plastic **mixing bowl** and lid, an S-shaped metal **chopping blade** (and sometimes a duller version for kneading dough), and a **plastic food pusher** to safely prod food through the feed tube. Some models have a wider tube so you don't have to cut up vegetables—such as potatoes—to fit the opening. One speed is the norm, plus a **pulse setting** to control processing precisely. Bowl capacity ranges from around 3 cups to 14 cups (dry), with most models holding 6 to 11 cups. A **shredding/slicing disk** is standard on full-sized processors. Some come with a juicer attachment. **Touchpad controls** are becoming more commonplace, too.

Mini-choppers look like little food processors, with a capacity of 2 to 3 cups, but they're for small jobs only, like chopping small quantities of nuts or half an onion.

With mixers: Stand mixers generally come with one **bowl,** a **beater** or two, and a **dough hook.** Some mixers offer options such as **splash guards** to prevent flour from spewing out of the bowl, plus **attachments** to make pasta, grind meat, and stuff sausage. Stand mixers generally have 5 to 16 speeds; we think three well-differentiated settings is enough.

You should be able to lock a mixer's power head in the Up position so it won't crash into the bowl when the beaters are weighed down with dough. Conversely, it should lock in the Down position to keep the beaters from kicking back when tackling stiff dough.

Just about any hand mixer is good for nontaxing jobs such as beating egg whites, mashing potatoes, or whipping cream. The slow-start feature on some mixers prevents ingredients from spattering when you start up, but you can achieve the same result by manually stepping through three or so speeds.

An indentation on the underside of the motor housing allows the mixer to sit on the edge of a bowl without taking the beaters out of the batter.

HOW TO CHOOSE

Food processors & choppers

Consider capacity. Food-processor capacity ranges from about 3 to 14 cups. (Those are manufacturers' figures; we've found that processors typically hold a cup or two more or less than claimed.) Choppers, which are designed expressly for small jobs, hold about 1 to 3 cups.

If you regularly cook for a crowd or like to whip up multiple batches of a recipe, you might appreciate the bigger, 11- to 14-cup units. However, they tend to be pricier and heavier than smaller versions and take up more counter space. A midsize (around 7-cup) model is likely fine for most tasks.

Note that even big food processors can handle small jobs such as chopping half an onion. But using a chopper makes cleanup easier.

Don't focus on speeds. Food processors typically have two settings: On and Pulse, which allows you to run the machine in brief bursts for more precise processing control. Choppers typically have one or two Pulse settings (High and Low). Those are really all the speeds you need. Some machines have a few extra speeds (a Dough setting on some high-end processors, for example), but we haven't found that they perform much better.

Note feed-tube size. Some processors have wider feed tubes than others, which can save you the effort of having to cut potatoes, cucumbers, and other big items.

Expect to pay more for kneading prowess and quiet operation. The models we tested that cost $55 or less strained and jumped while kneading dough. They also made quite a racket, where most of the higher-end models we tested were quiet. Choppers can be noisy but are used briefly.

Stand & hand mixers

Decide how much mixer you need. Just about any stand or hand mixer will do for all those simple mixing and whipping chores. But if you're a dedicated baker, you'll probably want to invest in a heavy, powerful stand mixer, because it can knead even two loaves' worth of bread dough with ease.

Downplay wattage and number of speed settings. Manufacturers stress wattage and number of speeds, but neither figure necessarily translates into better performance. For example, some stand mixers have as many as 16 speeds; some hand mixers have 9. We think three well-differentiated speeds are sufficient. The slower the lowest speed, the better; slow speeds prevent spattering.

Speeds should be clearly indicated. With some of the inexpensive hand mixers we tested, the switch you use to select speeds didn't line up well with the speed markings.

Consider size and weight. Hand mixers should feel well balanced and comfortable to hold; most that we tested did. Size and weight can be a concern with stand mixers—some weigh more than 20 pounds—but their heft gives them the stability to handle tough jobs.

All the stand mixers that we tested have heads that tilt up. Make sure that you will have enough clearance if you plan to keep the mixer on a counter below a cupboard.

Consider beater style and motion. Most of the top-performing hand mixers have wire beaters without the thick center post found on traditional-style beaters. The wire beaters performed well and were easier to clean.

Light-duty stand mixers typically have stationary beaters and a bowl that sits on a revolving turntable. The bowl sometimes needs a push to keep spinning.

Related CR Report: December 2003

IRONS

Many new irons are bigger, more colorful, more feature-laden, and more expensive. But you can still get a fine performer for $25 or so.

Casual Fridays at work have meant fewer trips to the dry cleaner and more ironing at home—of casual pants, cotton shirts, and such. Manufacturers are trying to make ironing less of a chore, with features galore on pricey new models. You'll find many irons to choose from, including budget models that should do just fine on those chinos.

WHAT'S AVAILABLE

Familiar names such as Black & Decker, Sunbeam, and Proctor-Silex account for most of the irons sold, but newer players such as GE, Kenmore, and Maytag have entered the market, giving you more choice.

Features once found only on fairly pricey irons are now available on less expensive models. For example, auto shutoff is offered on some models that sell for $20. Other features trickling down include self-cleaning (now available on more than half of new irons), separate steam controls, variable steam output, and vertical steaming. The proliferation of features isn't surprising. About 90 percent of U.S. households have an iron, so manufacturers are offering more features for less money to encourage you to buy a new one.

Price range: $10 for plain vanilla to $150 for top-of-the-line models.

IMPORTANT FEATURES

Steam makes a fabric more pliable, allowing the heat and pressure of the iron to press it flat. Many new irons release more steam than did earlier models. Most produce the best steaming during the first 10 minutes of use and then gradually taper off as the water is used up. A separate steam control lets you adjust the amount of steam or turn it off, but models with **automatic steam** produce more steam at higher temperature settings. A few models won't allow you to use steam at low settings, since the water doesn't get hot enough and simply drips out. An **antidrip** feature, usually on higher-priced irons, is designed to prevent leaks when using steam at lower settings.

Burst of steam, available on most new irons, lets you push a button for an extra blast to tame stubborn wrinkles. If steam isn't enough for something such as a wrinkled linen napkin, dampen it using the **spray function**, available on virtually all irons today. On some models, burst of steam can be used for vertical steaming to remove wrinkles from hanging items.

An iron should have an easy-to-see **fabric guide** with a list of settings for common fabrics. A **temperature control** that's clearly marked and easily accessible, preferably on the front of the handle, is a plus. Most irons have an **indicator light** to show that the power is on; a few also indicate when the iron reaches or exceeds the set temperature.

Automatic shutoff is a must-have safety feature. About half the irons on the market will shut off automatically if they're left motionless in a horizontal or vertical position. Those with three-way shutoff also turn off when tipped on their side. Shutoff times vary from 30 seconds to 60 minutes. Auto shut-off can help prevent a fire, but stored heat can still scorch fabric.

Water reservoirs in general are getting larger. Some are a small, vertical tube; others are a large chamber that spans the saddle area under the handle. Transparent chambers, some brightly colored, make it easy to see the water level.

A growing number of irons have a **hinged** or **sliding cover** on the water-fill hole. The idea is to prevent leaking, but it doesn't always work. Also, the cover may get in the way during filling, or can be awkward to open and close. Most convenient is a **removable tank**. Some irons come with a handy **plastic fill cup**. Nearly all new irons can use tap water, unless the water is very hard. More expensive irons may offer an **anticalcium system**, which is designed to reduce calcium deposits.

Some models now offer a **self-cleaning feature** to flush deposits from vents, but it's not always effective with prolonged use of very hard water. The burst-of-steam feature also cleans vents to some extent.

Many irons have a **soleplate** described as "nonstick." Some other models have a stainless-steel soleplate, while some budget models have an aluminum one. We didn't find any difference in glide among the various types of soleplates when ironing with steam. Nonstick soleplates are generally easier to keep clean, but they may be scratched by something such as a zipper, and a scratch could create drag over time. You should clean the soleplate occasionally to remove residue, especially if you use starch; follow the manufacturer's directions for cleaning.

The power cord on many irons pivots down or to the side during use, which keeps it out of the way. A retractable cord can be convenient, but make sure it doesn't whip when retracted. Cordless irons eliminate fumbling with the cord but must be reheated on the base for a minute or more every couple of minutes, which can be inconvenient and time-consuming.

Weight is more critical to comfort than performance. Managing a heavy iron can be an arm workout you might prefer to have at the gym. Some handles might be too thick for smaller hands; others provide too little clearance for larger hands.

HOW TO CHOOSE

Expect fine performance. The rumpled look doesn't stand a chance with most new irons. We've tested models ranging in price from \$20 to \$150, and almost all have been judged very good or excellent at wrinkle removal and very good overall. As in the past, we found that you don't have to spend a lot to get good results.

While all the irons we tested vanquished creases eventually, the amount of effort required varied. We tested each model with linen, cotton, a cotton-polyester blend, and silk. The fewer passes needed without resorting to bursts of steam or spray, the better an iron scored. Irons differ in a number of ways, including soleplate material, size, weight, and features.

Pick a model that can make ironing less of a drag. The easier it is to move a hot iron across fabric, the less tiring it will be to spruce up garments. All the irons we recently tested, whether they had a metal soleplate or one described as "nonstick," glided smoothly when we ironed damp garments or used steam. With dry fabric and no steam, glide varied much more, but the nonstick soleplates weren't necessarily better than the stainless-steel ones. The nonsticks are easier to clean, though. The bottom line: If you often iron dry fabric without spray or steam, look for a model that we judged very good or better for glide in our Ratings.

Match the iron to your hand. The feel of an iron is a personal preference, so be sure to get a hands-on experience before buying an iron. Some handles don't have enough clearance for bigger hands. Weight is another factor. The tested irons weighed 2¼ to 3¾ pounds without water. Some people might prefer a bit of heft, but others might find heavier irons more than they can manage.

Get enough steam to do the job. If you iron mostly natural fibers such as linen or heavyweight items such as jeans, you'll want lots of steam. Burst-of-steam and spray features will also help smooth out wrinkles. But if you iron mostly synthetic fabrics and blends, a less powerful steamer should be fine.

Find controls you like. Many new irons have dial controls, but there are a few sliders and the occasional digital control. Take your pick. Check whether the controls are easy to see and access, and whether fabric settings are clearly marked.

Decide whether you want to cut the cord. The cordless models we've tested have been excellent for ironing and very good overall, but they were only fair at steaming. Note that the convenience of cord-free ironing is offset by the need to reheat the iron in the base every few minutes for a minute or more, which can be tedious, especially when you're ironing large items like tablecloths.

Related CR Report: September 2004
Ratings: page 266

MICROWAVE OVENS

You'll see larger capacity, sensors that detect doneness, and stylish designs.

Microwave ovens, which built their reputation on speed, are also showing some smarts. Many automatically shut off when a sensor determines that the food is cooked or sufficiently heated. The sensor is also used to automate an array of cooking chores, with buttons labeled for frozen entrées, baked potatoes, popcorn, beverages, and other common items. Design touches include softer edges for less boxy styling, hidden controls for a sleeker look, stainless steel, and, for a few, a translucent finish.

WHAT'S AVAILABLE

GE leads the countertop microwave-oven market with almost 25 percent of sales, followed by Sharp, Panasonic, Emerson, and Kenmore. GE sells the most over-the-range models.

Microwaves come in a variety of sizes, from compact to large. Most sit on the countertop, but a growing number sold—about 20 percent—mount over the range. Several brands offer speed-cooking via halogen bulbs or convection. Speed-cook models promise grilling and browning, though results can vary significantly depending on the food. Manufacturers are working to boost capacity without taking up more space by moving controls to the door and using recessed turntables and smaller electronic components.

Microwave ovens vary in the power of the magnetron, which generates the microwaves. Midsize and large ovens are rated at 900 to 1,350 watts, compact ovens at 600 to 800 watts. A higher wattage may heat food more quickly, but differences of 100 watts are probably inconsequential. Some microwave ovens have a convection feature—a fan and, often, a heating element—which lets you roast and bake, something you don't generally do in a regular microwave.

Price range: $40 to $250 (countertop models); $250 to $500 (over-the-range); $350 to $700 (convection or halogen-bulb countertop or over-the-range).

IMPORTANT FEATURES

On most, a **turntable** rotates the food so it will heat more uniformly, but the center of the dish still tends to be cooler than the rest. With some models, you can turn off the rotation when, for instance, you're using a dish that's too large to rotate. The results won't be as good, however. Some models have replaced the turntable with a rectangular tray that slides from side to side to accept larger dishes. Most turntables are removable for cleaning.

You'll find similarities in **controls** from model to model. A **numeric keypad** is used to set cooking times and power levels. Most ovens have **shortcut keys** for particular foods, and for reheating or defrosting. Some microwaves start immediately when you hit the shortcut key, others make you enter the food quantity or weight. Some models have an **automatic popcorn feature** that takes just one press of a button. Pressing a **1-minute** or **30-second key** runs the oven at full power or extends the current cooking time. Microwave ovens typically have a number of **power levels.** We've found six to be more than adequate.

A **moisture sensor** gauges the steam that food emits when heated and uses that information to determine when the food is cooked. The small premium you pay for a **sensor** (about $10 to $30) is worth it. A few ovens have a **crisper pan** for making bacon or crisping pizza, since microwave cooking without the special pan leaves food hot but not browned or crispy.

Over-the-range ovens vent themselves and the range with a **fan** that has several speed settings. Typically the fan will turn on automatically if it senses excessive heat from the range below. Over-the-range microwaves can be vented to the outside or can just recirculate air in the kitchen. If the oven is venting inside, you'll need a **charcoal filter** (sometimes included). An over-the-range microwave generally doesn't handle ventilation as well as a hood-and-blower ventilation system because it doesn't extend over the front burners.

HOW TO CHOOSE

Despite all the new features and conveniences, most people still use a microwave oven for the same old tasks: reheating and defrosting. So choose a model that meets your needs without encumbering you with more than you need. Some shopping tips:

Consider your kitchen. Particularly if you're remodeling, you'll need to decide whether an over-the-range oven is worth its added cost. Also remember that an over-the-range oven cannot vent steam and smoke from a range's front burners as well as the range hood it replaces—a potential problem if you do lots of cooking.

Choose convenience, not clutter. With sensor-equipped models now available for $100 or less, there's little reason to buy an oven without one. Also look for a model with detailed, onscreen prompts that lead you through the programmed shortcut settings. You may want to avoid an oven with numerous food-specific shortcut and defrost settings if they include foods you or your family don't eat.

TECH TIP

A microwave's wattage shouldn't be the clincher. Small differences aren't likely to produce noticeably faster cooking speed.

Note that sensors do not work with every setting on all models. Check the oven's control panel at the store to be sure that the settings you care about are sensor-controlled to minimize the risk of over- or undercooking.

Don't buy based on wattage or capacity claims. More wattage may sound better. But small differences in wattage aren't likely to provide noticeably faster cooking speed. And you should be wary of oven-capacity claims. Manufacturers tend to tally every cubic inch, including corner spaces, where food on the turntable can't rotate. Our calculation of usable space excludes corners.

Related CR Report: January 2004
Reliability: page 333

RANGES

Choices can be confusing, but you don't have to spend top dollar for impressive performance with high-end touches.

If you're in the market for a range, you're faced with several choices. You can buy a freestanding range that combines a cooktop and oven. The oven can be equipped with a convection feature. If you have access to a gas hookup, you need to decide whether you want gas, electricity, or a combination of the two.

All of these choices bring innovations and upgrades as competition among manufacturers heats up.

Electric ranges now include traditional coil and newer smoothtop models where the heating elements are below a ceramic glass surface. Both types offer quick heating and the ability to maintain low heat levels.

Gas ranges use burners, which typically don't heat as quickly as electric elements, despite increasingly higher power—measured in British thermal units per hour (Btu/hr.). Even the highest-powered burners tend to heat more slowly than the fastest electric coil elements, sometimes because the heavy cast-iron grates that typically come with them slow the process by absorbing some of that heat. But you can see how high or low you are adjusting the flame, and you can instantly shut off the burners.

You'll also see more high-end or "professional-style" gas ranges with beefy knobs; heavy cast-iron grates; thick, stainless-steel construction; and four or more high-powered burners. These high-heat behemoths can easily cost $2,000 or more and typically require a special range hood and blower system, along with special shielding and a reinforced floor in some applications. But because the look is so popular, you'll find a growing number of stoves that include stainless trim and other pro-style perks for far less.

Shared characteristics between electric and gas ranges are also a growing trend. Some gas models have electric warming zones. Convection features are available on both gas and electric ranges. More and more manufacturers are offering dual-fuel gas ranges, which pair a gas cooktop with an electric oven. These cost about $1,000 and up.

WHAT'S AVAILABLE

GE, Kenmore (sourced from others), Frigidaire, Maytag, and Whirlpool are the leading makers of ranges, cooktops, and wall ovens. Other major brands include Amana, Jenn-Air, and KitchenAid. Mainstream brands have established high-end offshoots, such as Kenmore Elite, GE Profile, and Whirlpool Gold. High-end, pro-style brands include Bosch, Dacor, DCS, GE Monogram, KitchenAid Pro-Line, Thermador, Viking, and Wolf.

Freestanding range. These ranges can fit in the middle of a kitchen counter or at the end. Widths are usually 20 to 40 inches, although most are 30 inches wide. They typically have oven controls on the backsplash. Slide-in models eliminate the backsplash and side panels to blend into the countertop, while drop-ins rest atop toe-kick-level cabinetry and typically lack a storage drawer. Most mainstream ranges now include a self-cleaning feature and—for gas models—sealed burners, which keep crumbs from falling beneath the cooktop. Price range: $250 to $1,500.

Pro-style range. Bulkier than freestanding ranges, these gas models can be anywhere from 30 to 60 inches wide. Larger ones include six or eight burners, a grill or griddle, and a double oven. Many have a convection feature, and some have an infrared gas broiler. While you usually don't get a storage drawer, more pro-style stoves now include a self-cleaning oven and sealed burners. Price range: $2,500 to $8,000.

IMPORTANT FEATURES

On all ranges. Look for easy-cleaning features such as a **glass** or **porcelain backguard,** instead of a painted one; **seamless corners and edges,** especially where the cooktop joins the backguard; a **warming drawer** for convenience; six or more **oven-rack positions** for flexibility; and a **raised edge** around the cooktop to contain spills. Note, though, that a range's usable capacity may be less than what manufacturers claim, because they don't take protruding broiler elements and other features into account.

On electric ranges. Consider where the **controls** are located. Slide-in ranges have the dials on the front panel, while freestanding models have them on the backguard. Some models locate controls to the left and right, with oven controls in between, giving you a quick sense of which control operates which element. But controls clustered in the center stay visible when tall pots sit on rear heating elements.

Coil elements, the most common and least expensive electric option, are easy to replace if they break. On an electric range with coil elements, look for a **prop-up top** for easier cleaning, and deep **drip pans** made of porcelain to better contain spills and ease cleaning.

Spending $200 more will buy you a **smoothtop** model; most use radiant heat.

Some smoothtops have **expandable elements**—also called **dual elements**—which allow you to switch between a large, high-power element and a small, low-power element contained within it. Some smoothtops also include a **low-wattage element** for warming plates or keeping just-cooked food at the optimal temperature. Some have an elongated "bridge" element that spans two burners—a nicety for accommodating rectangular or odd-shaped cookware. And many have at least one **hot-surface light**—a key safety feature, since the surface can remain hot long after the elements have been turned off. The safest setup includes a dedicated "hot" light for each element.

SHOP SMART

Some ranges have digital touchpad controls that are easy to clean and easy to use.

Most electric ranges have one large, **higher-wattage element** in front and one in back. An **expanded simmer range** in some electric models lets you fine-tune the simmer setting on one element for, say, melting chocolate or keeping a sauce from getting too hot.

On gas ranges. Most gas ranges have four burners in three sizes, measured in British thermal units per hour (Btu/hr.): one or two medium-power burners (about 9,000 Btu/hr.), a small burner (about 5,000 Btu/hr.), and one or two large ones (about 12,500 Btu/hr.). We recommend a model with one or more 12,000 Btu/hr. burners for quick cooktop heating. On a few models, the burners automatically reignite.

For easier cleaning, look for **sealed**

burners. Gas ranges typically have **knob controls;** the best rotate 180 degrees or more. Try to avoid knobs that have adjacent "off" and "low" settings and that rotate no more than 90 degrees between High and Low.

Spending more gets you either heavier **grates** made of porcelain-coated cast iron or a sleek **ceramic surface**—also called **gas-on-glass**—and **stainless-steel accents,** along with a low-power **simmer burner** with an extra-low setting for delicate sauces (though other burners often are capable of simmering).

On pro-style ranges. These models have six or more brass or cast-iron burners, all of which offer very high output (usually about 15,000 Btu/hr.). The burners are usually non-sealed, with hard-to-clean crevices, though sealed burners are appearing on some models. Large knobs are another typical pro-style feature, as are continuous grates designed for heavy-duty use. The latter, however, can be unwieldy to remove for cleaning.

A **self-cleaning cycle** uses high heat to burn off spills and splatters. Most ranges have it, although many pro-style gas models still don't. An **automatic door lock,** found on most self-cleaning models, is activated during the cycle, then unlocks when the oven has cooled. Also useful is a **self-cleaning countdown** display, which shows the time left in the cycle.

Higher-priced ranges often include **convection,** which uses a fan and, sometimes, an electric element to circulate heated air. Our tests have shown that this mode cut cooking time for a large roast and, in some cases, baked large cookie batches more evenly because of the circulating air. But the fan can take up valuable space. A few electric ovens have a low-power **microwave feature** that works with bake and broil elements to speed cooking time further. Another cooking technology, called Trivection, uses regular thermal heating, convection, and microwave energy to cut cooking time. Trivection is available in some top-of-the-line GE Profile and Monogram ranges and some Kenmore models. Though very good overall, Trivection is very pricey.

A **variable-broil** feature in some ranges offers adjustable settings for foods such as fish or thick steaks that need slower or faster cooking. Ranges with **12-hour shut-off** turn off automatically if you leave the oven on for that long. But most models allow you to disable this feature. A **child lockout** allows you to disable oven controls for safety.

Manufacturers are also updating oven controls across the price spectrum. **Electronic touchpad controls** are common. A **digital display** makes it easier to set the precise temperature and keep track of it. A **cook time/delay start** lets you set a time for the oven to start and stop cooking; remember, however, that you shouldn't leave most foods in a cold oven very long. An **automatic oven light** typically comes on when the door opens, although some ovens have a switch-operated light. A **temperature probe,** to be inserted into meat or poultry, indicates when you've obtained a precise internal temperature.

Oven windows come in various sizes. Those without a decorative grid usually offer the clearest view, although some cooks may welcome the grid to hide pots, pans, and other cooking utensils typically stored inside the oven.

HOW TO CHOOSE

Think about your cooking. If you often cook for a crowd, look for at least one high-powered element or burner and a large oven. Indeed, you'll find more mid-priced gas ranges with the ultrahigh heat once exclusive to pro-style stoves. High-heat burners can be useful for searing, stir-frying, or heating large quantities.

Ranges with convection can speed roasting a little. Models that excelled in broiling produced burgers seared on the outside and cooked quickly and evenly.

Consider the fuel. If you have a choice of electric or gas, decide whether you want the fast response and visual feedback of a gas flame or the simplicity of electric burners. Either type is capable of very good performance. Or you could opt for a dual-fuel range.

Balance convenience and durability. Electric smoothtops are pretty easy to clean, but they require a special cleaner. They can be damaged by a dropped pot or sugary liquids. Coil-tops aren't as susceptible to such harm, but they require more cleaning time.

Keep high-tech in perspective. Ranges with special baking modes may not outperform conventional models. Touchpad oven controls are more precise than knobs. But front-mounted touchpads can be bumped and reset by accident.

Related CR Reports: March 2004, August 2004

Ratings: page 289

Reliability: page 333

REFRIGERATORS

Top-freezer and bottom-freezer fridges generally give you more for your money than their side-by-side siblings—and they cost less to run.

If you're shopping for a new refrigerator, you're probably considering models that are fancier than your current fridge. The trend is toward spacious models with flexible, more-efficiently used storage space. Useful features such as spillproof, slide-out glass shelves and temperature-controlled compartments, once found only in expensive refrigerators, are now practically standard in midpriced models. Stainless-steel doors are stylish, but they add to the cost. Built-in refrigerators appeal to people who want to customize their kitchens and are willing to pay thousands of dollars for the custom look. Some mainstream cabinet-depth models offer a built-in-style look for less.

Replacing an aging refrigerator may save you in electric bills, since refrigerators are more energy-efficient now than they were a decade ago. The Department of Energy toughened its rules in the early 1990s and imposed even stricter requirements in July 2001 for this appliance, which is among the top electricity users in the house.

WHAT'S AVAILABLE

Only a handful of companies actually manufacture refrigerators. The same or very similar units may be sold under several brand names. Frigidaire, General Electric, Kenmore, and Whirlpool account for about three-quarters of top-freezer sales. For side-by-side models, these brands and Maytag account for more than 80 percent of sales. Brands offering bottom-freezers include Amana, Fisher-Paykel, GE, Jenn-Air, Kenmore, KitchenAid, LG, Maytag, Samsung, Sub-Zero, Thermador, and Whirlpool. Mainstream manufacturers have introduced high-end brand lines such as GE Profile and Kenmore Elite.

Six brands cover built-ins: GE Monogram, Jenn-Air, KitchenAid, Sub-Zero, Thermador, and Viking. You can get built-in-style or "cabinet-depth" models from Amana, Electrolux, Frigidaire, GE, Jenn-Air, Kenmore, KitchenAid, LG, Maytag, and Whirlpool. Samsung, a brand known in other product categories, is now selling refrigerators in the U.S. market.

Top-freezer models. Accounting for almost half of models sold, these are generally less expensive to buy and run, and more space efficient, than comparably sized side-by-side models. Widths range from about 24 to 36 inches. The eye-level freezer offers easy access. Fairly wide refrigerator shelves make it easy to reach the back, but you have to bend to reach the bottom shelves and drawers. Claimed, labeled capacity ranges from about 10 to 25 cubic feet. With top-freezers, the usable capacity is typically about 80 percent of its nominal capacity, according to our measurements. Price range: $350 to $2,000, depending on size and features.

SHOP SMART

Measure before you buy. Refrigerators need to fit through your doors and hallways.

Side-by-side models. These are by far the most fully featured fridges, most often equipped with through-the-door ice and water dispensers—among the most requested consumer features—as well as temperature-controlled bins and rapid ice-making cycles. Their narrow doors are handy in tight spaces. High, narrow compartments make finding stray items easy in front (harder in the back), but they may not hold wide items such as a sheet cake or a large turkey. Compared with top- and bottom-freezer models, a higher proportion of capacity goes to freezer space. Side-by-sides are typically large—30 to 36 inches wide, with claimed capacity of 20 to 30 cubic feet. About 65 percent of that space is usable. They're much more expensive than similar-sized top-freezer models and are less efficient in terms of energy use, as well as space. Price range: $800 to $2,600.

Bottom-freezer models. A small but growing part of the market, these put frequently used items at eye level. Fairly wide refrigerator shelves provide easy access. Though you must bend to locate items in the freezer, even with models that have a pull-out drawer, you will probably do less bending overall because the main refrigerated compartment is at eye level. Bottom-freezers are a bit pricier than top-freezers and offer less capacity relative to their external dimensions because of the inefficiency of the pull-out bin. Claimed capacity is up to 25 cubic feet, nominally, and usable space is a bit less than with top-freezers, but more than offered by side-by-sides. Price range: $650 to $2,000.

Built-in models. These are generally side-by-side and bottom-freezer models. They show their commercial heritage, often having fewer standard amenities and less soundproofing than lower-priced "home" models. Usually 25 to 26 inches front to back, they fit nearly flush with cabinets and counters. Their compressor is on top, making them about a foot taller than regular refrigerators—an issue if you have overhead cabinets. Most can accept extra-cost front panels that match the kitchen's décor. Side-by-side models in this style are available in 42-inch and 48-inch widths (vs. the more typical 36-inch width). You can even obtain a built-in pair: a separate refrigerator and freezer mounted together in a 72-inch opening. Price range: $4,000 to more than $6,000.

Built-in-style or cabinet-depth models. These freestanding refrigerators offer the look of a built-in for less money. They are available mostly in side-by-side and bottom-freezer styles, with a few top-freezers. Many accept extra-cost panels for a custom look. Price range: $1,500 to $3,000.

IMPORTANT FEATURES

Interiors are ever more flexible.

Adjustable door bins and **shelves** can be moved to fit tall items. Some shelves can be cranked up and down without removing the contents. Some **split shelves** can be adjusted to different heights independently. With other shelves, the front half of the shelf slides under the rear portion to provide clearance.

Shelf snuggers—sliding brackets on door shelves—secure bottles and jars. A few models have a wine rack that stores a bottle horizontally.

Glass shelves are easier to clean than wire racks. Most glass shelves have a raised, sealed rim to keep spills from dripping over. Some slide out. **Pull-out freezer shelves** or **bins** improve access. An alternative is a bottom-freezer with a sliding drawer.

More models have replaced mechanical controls with **electronic touchpads.** Some have a digital display that shows the temperature setting; a few show the actual temperature, which is more useful.

A **temperature-controlled drawer** can be set to be several degrees cooler than the rest of the interior, useful for storing meat or fish. Crispers have controls to maintain humidity. Our tests have shown that, in general, temperature-controlled drawers work better than plain drawers; results for humidity controls are less clear-cut. See-through drawers let you see at a glance what's inside.

Curved doors give the refrigerator a distinctive profile and retro look. Most manufacturers have at least one curved-door model in their lineups.

Step-up features include a variety of **finishes** and **colors.** Every major manufacturer has a stainless-steel model that typically costs significantly more than one with a standard pebbled finish. Another alternative is a smooth, glass-like finish.

Novel color choices include biscuit, bisque, or linen instead of almond. Several lines include black models, and KitchenAid has colorful finishes, such as cobalt blue, to match its small appliances. Kenmore, LG, Samsung and Whirlpool have models with a stainless-steel-look metallic finish that, unlike stainless, resists fingerprints and accepts magnets.

Most models have an **icemaker** in the freezer or give you the option of installing one yourself. Typically producing several pounds of ice per day (although some produce 10 pounds or more), an icemaker reduces freezer space by about a cubic foot. The ice bin is generally located below the icemaker, but some new models have it on the inside of the freezer door, providing a bit more usable volume. A **through-the-door ice-and-water dispenser** is common in side-by-side refrigerators. Top- and bottom-freezer refrigerators generally don't offer through-the-door ice-and-water dispensers, but some models have water dispensers inside the main compartment.

With many models, the icemaker and/or water dispenser includes a **water filter**, designed to reduce lead, chlorine, and other impurities in ice and/or drinking water. An icemaker or water dispenser will work without one. You can also have a filter installed in the tubing that supplies water to the refrigerator.

Once a refrigerator's **controls** are set, there should be little need to adjust temperature. Still, accessible controls are an added convenience.

HOW TO CHOOSE

Good performance is pretty much a given with new refrigerators. Even the least expensive models keep things cold very well. Top-freezer models give you the most for the money, but kitchen layout or personal preference may necessitate another type. Most built-in models offer no performance or efficiency advantages. New refrigerators are quite energy-efficient as a group. Most cost $30 to $60 a year to run. If you replace a refrigerator bought in 1980 with a similar new model, your energy use should drop about 60 percent. Besides style and type, consider the following points when buying a fridge:

Determine how big a refrigerator you want. Measure the space available before determining the size model you'll buy. Also measure doorways and halls the refrigerator will have to pass through when delivered. If you're fitting a refrigerator into existing cabinetry, you may be limited to the current width; in a remodel, it's easier to go larger. Don't use claimed capacity to compare different types of refrigerators, such as a top-freezer and a side-by-side; consult our Ratings for usable space. You might find that a top-freezer offers more capacity than a larger side-by-side.

Select the features you want. Today's fridges come with lots of bells and whistles. In general, larger refrigerators have more features. Less expensive models usually lack spillproof glass shelves, large bins, and easily arranged shelves. An icemaker adds $50 to $100 to the price; a through-the-door water dispenser adds about $100. While icemakers and ice and water dispensers are handy, they tend to increase the odds of needing a repair.

Consider noise. Your fridge is the one kitchen appliance that runs 24/7. If you value peace and quiet, check the Ratings for a model that doesn't make a racket. Many models are fairly quiet, but some are very quiet.

Check a brand's track record. A refrigerator breakdown is a disaster you don't want to imagine, so consult our brand repair history. Built-ins appear to have higher repair rates than freestanding fridges. Side-by-sides with an icemaker and ice-and-water dispenser tend to require more repairs than top- and bottom-freezers with an icemaker only.

Related CR Reports: February 2004, August 2004
Ratings: page 295
Reliability: page 334

WASHING MACHINES

Front-loaders tend to give you the best of everything, but traditional top-loaders offer the best value.

You'll find more variety in the washing-machine aisle when you visit the local appliance store these days. Traditional top-loaders with agitators still account for most washer purchases, but front-loading washers (which you load the same way you would a dryer) are becoming more popular and more numerous. While front-loaders generally offer the best performance on all counts—washing, water and energy efficiency, gentleness, and noise—many Americans still prefer a top-loading design.

To address this preference, manufacturers are introducing washers that promise the performance advantages of front-loaders in a top-loading design. New top-loading models such as the Calypso from Whirlpool and Kenmore, the GE Harmony, and the Maytag Neptune TL replace the agitator with different types of wash systems. They work somewhat like front-loaders, filling partially with water and spinning at high speeds. That reduces water usage and extracts more water, reducing the time and energy needed for drying.

Washing machines are becoming more energy efficient overall. New, stricter

Department of Energy standards regarding energy and hot-water use and water extraction became effective in January 2004, and standards will become even more stringent in 2007. Many front-loaders and some top-loaders already meet the tougher requirements.

WHAT'S AVAILABLE

The top four brands—GE, Kenmore (Sears), Maytag, and Whirlpool—account for more than 80 percent of washing-machine sales. Other brands include Amana (made by Maytag), Frigidaire (made by Electrolux), Hotpoint (made by GE), and Estate, KitchenAid, and Roper (all made by Whirlpool). You may also run across smaller brands such as Crosley, Gibson, and White-Westinghouse, all of which are made by the larger brands. Asko, Bosch, and Miele are European brands. Fisher-Paykel is imported from New Zealand, LG from Korea, and Haier from China.

Traditional top-loaders. Traditional top-loaders fill the tub with water, then agitate the clothing. They use more water than other types of washers, which requires

CLEANING UP OUR ACT

New, tougher tests

We have updated our tests to better reflect improvements in today's washers and changes in the way you use them.

The Maytag Neptune TL set a new standard for excellence. (But it's expensive, at $1,300, and isn't very gentle.) As a result, we've raised the bar for washing performance, and washers once judged excellent may now score very good.

We've also revised our tests. We've encouraged you to wash full loads and to use only the amount of water needed for smaller loads. We're taking our own advice to heart. In the past, we've washed only 8-pound loads. Now we've added a test with the maximum load each washer can hold (which varies by model). The combination better represents the way you're likely to use a washer.

We've made another change for conventional top-loaders, which require you to set the water level for each load. (Front-loaders and high-efficiency top-loaders automatically adjust water level to load size.) We now use only the amount of water needed for an 8-pound load, rather than the maximum water level. The washing performance score in the Ratings is a 50/50 weighted average of how clean each washer got a full load washed at the maximum water level and an 8-pound load using less water.

Given these changes, overall scores for washing performance were lower than in the past, and we found more variation among models. In general, washing was less thorough when the tub was more crowded and there was less water in which clothing could agitate, especially with maximum loads. The bottom line: Wash full loads, but don't cram top-loaders, especially with very soiled garments.

Lastly, we've made gentleness tests tougher to give you a better idea of which machines will treat your laundry with tender, loving care.

more energy to heat the hot water. They also extract less water during the spin cycle, which results in longer drying time and higher energy costs. Because they need to move the laundry around to ensure thorough cleaning, these machines hold about 12 to 16 pounds, less than front-loaders and top-loaders without agitators in the center of the tub.

On the plus side, top-loaders make it easier to load laundry and to add items midcycle. You can also soak laundry. This type of machine has the shortest cycle times and is the only one that gives the best results with regular detergent. But most top-loaders are noisier than front-loaders, and there's a risk of loads getting unbalanced. Price range: $200 to $650.

TECH TIP

The gentler the washer, the less likely it is to create lint.

High-efficiency top-loaders with new wash systems. The GE Harmony and the Calypso models from Kenmore and Whirlpool have a "wash plate," rather than an agitator, to move clothes around. The Maytag Neptune TL has discs that lift and tumble laundry. Washing performance is usually better than with regular top-loaders, and capacity is generally larger as well. As mentioned, they tend to be more efficient with water and energy than regular top-loaders, but the high spin speeds that reduce drying time (and energy consumption) tend to make clothing more wrinkled. These machines perform best with special low-foaming high-efficiency (HE) detergent. There are few of these detergents on the market, and they tend to be more expensive than regular detergents. Price range: $900 to $1,300.

Front-loaders. Front-loaders get clothes clean by tumbling them in the water. Clothes are lifted to the top of the tub, then dropped into the water below. Their design makes them more efficient with water and energy than regular top-loaders. They can typically handle 12 to 20 pounds of laundry. Like high-efficiency top-loaders, front-loaders wash best with low-sudsing detergent. Many front-loaders can be stacked with a dryer to save floor space. Price range: $600 to $1,600.

Space-saving options. Compact models are typically 24 inches wide or less (compared with about 27 inches for full-sized machines of all types) and they can wash 8 to 12 pounds of laundry. A compact front-loader can be stacked with a compact dryer. Some compact models can be stored in a closet and rolled out to be hooked up to the kitchen sink. Price range: $450 to $1,700.

Washer-dryer laundry centers combine a washer and dryer in one unit, with the dryer located above the washer. These can be full-size (27 inches wide) or compact (24 inches wide). The full-size models hold about 12 to 14 pounds, the compacts a few pounds less. Performance is generally comparable to that of full-sized machines. Price range: $700 to $1,900.

IMPORTANT FEATURES

A **porcelain-coated steel inner tub** can rust if the porcelain is chipped. **Stainless-steel** or **plastic tubs** won't rust. A stainless-steel tub can also withstand higher spin speeds, which extract more water from laundry and speeds drying. A **porcelain top/lid** resists scratching better than a painted metal one.

Controls should be legible, easy to push or turn, and logically arranged. High-end models often have touchpad controls; others have traditional dials. **Touchpad controls** tend to be more versatile; for instance, you may be able to save favorite settings that you use frequently. Some high-end models have a display with a progression of **menus**. Such menus can be time-consuming to navigate, but they may allow custom programming or offer detailed help information otherwise available only in the manual. A plus: **lights** or **signals** that indicate the cycle. On some top-loaders, an **automatic lock** during the spin cycle keeps children from opening the lid. Front-loaders lock at the beginning of a cycle but can usually be opened by interrupting the cycle, although some doors remain shut briefly after the machine stops.

Front-loaders automatically set **wash speed** according to the fabric cycle selected, and some also automatically set the spin speed. Top-loaders typically provide **wash/spin speed combinations**, such as Regular, Permanent Press, and Delicate (or Gentle). A few models also allow an extra rinse or extended spin.

Front-loaders and some top-loaders set **water levels** automatically, ensuring efficient use of water. Some top-loaders can be set for four or more levels; three or four are probably as many as you would need.

Most machines establish wash and rinse temperatures by mixing hot and cold water in preset proportions. For incoming cold water that's especially cold, an **automatic temperature control** adjusts the flow for the correct wash temperature. A **time-delay feature** lets you program the washer to start at a later time, such as at night, when your utility rates are low. Automatic bleach, detergent, and fabric-softener **dispensers** release powder or liquid at the appropriate time. Bleach dispensers also prevent spattering. Some machines offer a hand-washing cycle.

HOW TO CHOOSE

For best high-end performance, go with a front-loader. If you plan to spend $1,000 or so, at this point we'd steer you to a front-loader rather than a high-efficiency top-loader, even though some top-loaders have scored well in our tests. The front-loading design has been around for a while, and Frigidaire, GE, and Kenmore front-loaders have a good track record for reliability.

Get a conventional top-loader for very good performance at a lower price. If you want a less expensive machine that's decent across the board, you have plenty of choices among the conventional top-loaders in our Ratings.

Consider energy usage. Our tests for energy efficiency differ from those used to determine the government's Energy Star eligibility. We give more weight to performance with maximum loads.

The Department of Energy enacted stricter energy standards this year and will make standards tougher still. All washers manufactured after Jan. 1, 2007, must be 17 percent more efficient than required by the 2004 standard.

Decide if noise is an issue. If you plan to install a washer in a laundry room near the kitchen or a bedroom, we strongly recommend one judged very good or excellent for noise. Front-loaders set the standard for quiet operation, but a few top-loaders came close in our tests.

Look for useful features. Stainless-steel tubs can stand up to higher spin speeds than plastic tubs, improving water extraction and shortening drying time. Automatic temperature control mixes hot and cold water to achieve a specific temperature, handy if your incoming water is very cold or if your washer is a long way from the water heater. Automatic dispensers ensure that bleach and detergent are released at the right time in the cycle so they work effectively. An extra rinse option can help if you're sensitive to detergent residue. A porcelain top will resist scratching better than painted metal.

Think twice about pricey extras. The more features a washer has, the more it usually costs. Don't buy an expensive model just to get four or more water levels, dozens of cycle and setting combinations, or dedicated cycles for fabrics such as silk. The basic cycles and settings can handle most washing needs, and you can replicate most special cycles with buttons or dials. An electronic touchpad may allow custom programming, but it can also be more confusing to use, especially at first. Unless you insist on the same style, there's no need to match a washer and a dryer. If your old dryer still works fine, don't think you have to replace it when you buy a new washer.

Use the proper detergent. Any washing machine will do a better job if you use a good detergent. For traditional top-loaders, regular detergent is fine, and that's what we used. With front-loaders and high-efficiency top-loaders, you'll get the cleanest clothes with special low-foaming detergent; that's what we used for these machines. There aren't many on the market, and they tend to be pricey. Figure on paying 25 to 30 cents a load, compared with as little as 12 cents for some very good regular detergents. Consider the cost and convenience of ongoing detergent purchases when you're buying a washer.

Related CR Report: June 2004
Ratings: page 324
Reliability: page 337

HOME & YARD

Home & Yard: Cleaner and Greener

Lower prices, driven by retail competition, have made replacing your old, worn-out tools and household products more practical. Manufacturers have made improvements in product efficiency, safety, and ease of use, meaning there's no excuse not to upgrade your home and yard equipment now.

AIR CLEANERS

Whole-house and room air cleaners can provide some relief from indoor pollution, but they have limitations.

The air inside your home is more polluted than the air on the other side of the window, according to estimates by the U.S. Environmental Protection Agency. But that doesn't mean it's unhealthy and needs to be cleaned. Nor does it mean you need an air cleaner.

Before you buy one, try some commonsense solutions to eliminating and controlling pollutants and ensuring proper ventilation. Ban indoor smoking. If dust is a problem, vacuum with a low-emission vacuum cleaner. Designate pet-free rooms, particularly bedrooms, if pet dander is a problem. A range hood vented outdoors can help rid the kitchen of smoke and odor, while an exhaust fan in the bathroom can help squelch mold, mildew, and odor.

If these measures aren't enough, an air cleaner may help. But only people with respiratory problems are likely to benefit from using one. Even then, experts say, air cleaners may not be consistently effective.

If your house has forced-air heating and cooling, choose an appropriate whole-house cleaner installed by a professional. If your house doesn't have a forced-air system, your only option is a room air cleaner.

WHAT'S AVAILABLE

Whole-house air cleaners. Major brands include American Air Filter, Aprilaire, Honeywell, Lennox, Precisionaire, Purolator, Trane, Trion, and 3M. Whole-house cleaners range from inexpensive fiberglass furnace filters to electronic precipitators, which must be installed professionally in a home's duct system.

Furnace filters range from plain matted-fiberglass (about $1), meant to trap large particles of dust and lint, up to electrostatically charged filters ($10 to $15) designed to attract pollen, lint, pet dander, and dust.

Electronic-precipitator air cleaners impart an electrical charge to particles flowing through them, then collect the particles on oppositely charged metal plates or filters.

These more elaborate systems must be fitted into ductwork and wired into the house's current. Most have a collector-plate assembly that must be removed and washed every one to two months. Price: about $600, plus $200 or more for installation.

Room air cleaners. Sharper Image is the market leader in sales. Other notable brands include Bionaire, Friedrich, Holmes, Honeywell, Hunter, Kenmore, and Whirlpool. Most room air cleaners weigh between 10 and 20 pounds. They can be round or boxy, and can stand on the floor or on a table.

Room air cleaners can work well, even on dust and cigarette-smoke particles, which are much smaller and harder to trap than pollen and mold spores. But they aren't good at trapping dust mites, viruses, and gases like carbon monoxide or radon.

Two technologies predominate. The most common is a filter system in which a high-efficiency particulate air (HEPA) filter mechanically strains the air of fine particles. The other dominant technology uses an electronic precipitator that works like those in some whole-house systems, with a fan to move air through them. Honeywell, Hoover, and Sharper Image sell a type of electrostatic precipitator. It typically has no fan or has one that moves very little air.

The Association of Home Appliance Manufacturers (AHAM), a trade group, tests and rates room air cleaners using a measurement known as clean air delivery rate (CADR), which is determined by how well a filter traps particles and how much air the unit moves. Separate CADRs are listed for dust, tobacco smoke, and pollen. (While most manufacturers participate in this voluntary program, some models do not have an AHAM-certified performance rating.) We've typically found AHAM-certified CADRs to be accurate. If whole-house air cleaners and filters are labeled, they carry a minimum efficiency reporting value (MERV). The higher the MERV, the better for trapping small particles. Price range: $110 to $600. Annual filter cost: $30 to $220.

IMPORTANT FEATURES

Whole-house air cleaners are generally available in a range of standard sizes or can be adapted to fit the space. Some manufacturers say their filters are treated with a special antimicrobial agent, presumably to prevent bacterial growth on the filter. We have not evaluated those claims.

TECH TIP

Air cleaners do not clear gases. Use carbon-monoxide detectors, and be sure that fuel-burning appliances are properly ventilated.

Room air cleaners typically use a **fan** to pull air into the unit for filtration. Some models with an electronic precipitator or a HEPA filter incorporate **ionizing circuitry** that uses powered needles or wires to charge particles, which are then more easily trapped by the filter. But this ionization may also make the particles stick to walls or furnishings, possibly soiling them. An **indicator** in most models let you know when to change the filter.

HEPA filters are supposed to be replaced annually and can cost more than $100—sometimes as much as the room air cleaner itself. **Prefilters,** which are designed to remove larger particles, are generally changed quarterly, while washable prefilters should be cleaned monthly. An electronic precipitator's **collector-plate assembly** must be removed and washed every month or so; it slides out of the cabinet, and you can put it in a dishwasher or rinse it in a sink.

Most room air cleaners have a **handle,** while some heavier models have **wheels.**

Fan speeds usually include low, medium, and high. A few cleaners use a **dust sensor** and an **air-quality monitor** designed to raise or lower the fan speed automatically, depending on conditions.

HOW TO CHOOSE

If you've decided to buy an air cleaner, consider the following:

Choose between the two basic technologies:

• Filter. A fan draws air through a paper or fine-mesh filter. A high-efficiency particulate air (HEPA) filter is used in most room air cleaners.

• Electrostatic precipitator. They draw air through an electrical field. Charged particles are then trapped on oppositely charged collector plates. The best precipitators use a fan to move a large quantity of air.

Precipitators generate small amounts of ozone, which has an odor that may be objectionable. They may also make a crackling sound as they accumulate dirt. In a small, closed room, ozone levels may exceed allowable levels.

Do you have forced-air heating or cooling? If you do, then you're likely to get the best results from a whole-house cleaner even if you need to deal with only one or two rooms. The heating/cooling system circulates so much air that it overwhelms the effects of a room-sized unit.

The least expensive whole-house cleaners are sometimes called furnace filters. They aren't very effective against smoke and other small particles. The more effective filters restrict airflow through the system, which may adversely affect performance of the furnace or air conditioner.

More effective by far for whole-house use are electrostatic precipitators, which remove the smallest particles and restrict airflow much less than filters. HEPA filters are available for central systems, but need special design considerations.

Look for certification. Most room air cleaners are certified by the Association of Home Appliance Manufacturers in a widely accepted voluntary program. The certification label tells you the cleaner's maximum coverage area as well as its clean-air delivery rate (CADR), a measure of the speed of cleaning at its highest fan speed. You may want to select one that's designed to cover an area larger than you need so you can run the cleaner at a lower, and quicker, fan speed and still get adequate cleaning.

If whole-house air cleaners and filters are labeled at all, they carry a minimum efficiency reporting value (MERV) instead of a CADR number. Look for higher MERV numbers for better particle trapping.

Consider operating costs. Most air cleaners require filter replacement, which can be costly. With room air cleaners, electricity costs for the fan can also mount. Products like the Ionic Breeze don't use replaceable filters or a fan, so they rightly claim to cost very little to run.

Related CR Report: October 2003

AIR CONDITIONERS

Falling prices make individual room air conditioners an inexpensive alternative to central-air systems for cooling one or two rooms.

Once a high-priced convenience, relatively precise electronic controls with digital temperature readouts have replaced vague "warmer" and "cooler" settings on a growing number of lower-priced air conditioners. Added efficiency is also trickling down the price scale. No longer do models that use the least electricity cost the most. Most models in our recent tests have a higher Energy Efficiency Rating (EER) than the federal government requires. To have Energy Star status, brands must meet or exceed 10.7 EER. This means a model is at least 10 percent more efficient than the standard. The minimum EER for air conditioners below 8,000 British thermal units per hour (Btu/hr.) is 9.7; the minimum is 9.8 for those with 8,000 to 13,999 Btu/hr.

WHAT'S AVAILABLE

Fedders, GE, Kenmore (Sears), LG, Maytag, and Whirlpool are the leading brands of room air conditioners. You'll find cooling capacities that range from 5,000 Btu/hr. to more than 30,000 Btu/hr. The majority of room air conditioners in stores are small and midsize units from 5,000 to 9,000 Btu/hr. Large models (9,800 to 12,500 Btu/hr.) can also be found. Price range: about $100 to $600 (small to midsize, depending mostly on cooling capacity); $270 to $475 (large).

IMPORTANT FEATURES

An air conditioner's exterior-facing portion contains a **compressor, fan,** and **condenser,** while the part that faces a home's interior contains a fan and an **evaporator.** Most room models are designed to fit double-hung windows, though some are built for casement and slider windows and others for in-wall installation.

Most models have adjustable vertical and horizontal louvers to direct airflow. Many offer a **fresh-air intake** or **exhaust setting** for ventilation, although this feature moves a relatively small amount of air. An **energy-saver setting** on many units stops the fan when the compressor cycles off. **Electronic controls** and **digital temperature readouts** are also common. A **timer** lets you program the unit to switch on (say, half an hour before you get home) or off at a given time. Many models also include a **remote control.** Some models install with a **slide-out chassis**—an outer cabinet that anchors in the window, into which you slide the unit.

HOW TO CHOOSE

These are things to consider:

Assess your room size. A general rule is that 5,000 to 6,000 Btu/hr. models cool rooms 100 to 300 square feet; 7,000 to 8,200 Btu/hr. models cool rooms 250 to 550 square feet; and 9,800 to 12,500 Btu/hr. models cool rooms 350 to 950 square feet. Room construction, climate, and other factors also affect your choice.

> **TECH TIP**
>
> Make sure your circuits can handle the pull of an air conditioner. A dedicated circuit is your best bet.

Consider window location. To direct air to the center of the room for uniform cooling, does the air conditioner need to blow air to the left or right? Most units do a better job directing air in one direction or the other, in part because of the design of the model's internal fan.

Look for third-party certification. When assessing EER, look for a certification sticker from the Association of Home Appliance Manufacturers (AHAM) or the Canadian Standards Association (CSA).

Don't buy features you don't need. Low-profile models take up less space in your window and can direct air up, not just side-to-side, but they are pricier.

Clean it periodically. With any model, clean the filter biweekly or as needed. Where possible, hose off the back of the unit if debris has clogged cooling coils.

Related CR Report: July 2004
Ratings: page 225

CORDLESS DRILLS

Many 14.4-volt drills pack all the power you need for a wide variety of chores. And higher-voltage drills can cost little more than less capable, lower-voltage models.

Battery packs with higher voltage and capacity allow today's cordless drills to run longer and more powerfully per charge. The best can outperform corded drills and handle decks and other big jobs with minimum battery recharging. Recent tests also show that you don't have to spend $200 or more to get very good performance. Models in the 14.4- to 18-volt range that cost as little as $110 perform nearly as well as the most expensive drills.

High value in the 14.4- to 18-volt category means there's little reason to buy a 12- or 9.6-volt drill. You won't save much money, and power and run time are lower.

WHAT'S AVAILABLE

Black & Decker and Craftsman (Sears) are the major brands. Along with Ryobi and Skil, those brands are aimed primarily at do-it-yourselfers. Bosch, DeWalt, Makita, Milwaukee, Ridgid, and Porter-Cable offer pricier drills designed for professionals.

Most 9.6-volt drills cost less than $100. At about three pounds, they weigh half as much as some 18-volt models. But unless you value low weight and cost over performance, you're likely to be disappointed with a 9.6-volt drill. Many 12- and 14.4-volt models also sell for less than $100, and are more capable. Price ranges: Figure on about $40 to $100 for 9.6-volt drills, $50 to $130 for 12-volt drills, $60 to $200 for 14.4-volt models, and about $100 to $270 for 18-volt models.

IMPORTANT FEATURES

A **"smart" charger** recharges a drill's battery in about an hour or less, compared with three to five hours or more for a conventional charger. Smart chargers also extend battery life by adjusting the charge as needed. Most smart chargers switch into a **maintenance** or **"trickle-charge" mode** as the battery approaches full charge. One drill has a **dual charger** that charges two batteries at once.

Most cordless drills 12 volts and more have **two speed ranges**: low for driving screws, high for drilling. Low speed provides more torque, or turning power, than the high-speed setting, which is useful for drilling holes. Most models also have a **variable speed trigger**, which can make starting a hole easier, and an **adjustable clutch**, which lowers maximum torque to avoid driving a screw too far into softwood or wallboard, or mangling its head.

Most drills have a **⅜-inch chuck**, but some higher-voltage models have a **½-inch chuck,** which can accommodate drill bits up to ½ inch. (Large diameter bits with a reduced shank will fit in smaller chucks.) Most of today's models are also **reversible**, letting you more easily remove a screw or back a drill bit out of a hole.

Still other features make some drills easier to use than others. Some models have a **second handle** that attaches onto the side of the drill so you can use two hands for better control when driving screws, for example. All but the least expensive drills come with **two batteries**, letting you use one while the other charges.

Most cordless drills run on **nickel-cadmium (NiCad) batteries**, which can be recharged hundreds of times. Once they're depleted, though, NiCads must be recycled, since cadmium is toxic and can leach out of landfills to contaminate groundwater if disposed of improperly. Incineration can release the substance into the air and pose an even greater hazard. A few models run on **nickel-metal-hydride (NiMH) batteries**, which don't contain cadmium and are friendlier to the environment. In recent tests, CONSUMER REPORTS found that two NiMH-powered models—a 19.2-volt and a 15.6-volt—ran longer than many 18-volt and 14.4-volt NiCad-powered models, yet weighed about the same.

TECH TIP

Longer run time per charge and lower environmental risks are associated with the new nickel-metal-hydride batteries.

Some drills are bundled with other cordless tools and sold as **kits**. The package typically includes a circular saw, a reciprocating saw, and—often—a flashlight and carrying case. Some kits are a relatively good deal. But as our reports have shown, cordless circular saws tend to be far weaker than corded models. And some kits are merely a collection of mediocre tools.

HOW TO CHOOSE

Falling prices for some of the most powerful, 18-volt drills mean you needn't pay a premium for top performance. You'll also find lower-voltage drills that combine ample drilling and screwdriving power for larger household projects without being too heavy for smaller ones.

Determine how much voltage you're likely to need for the drilling and screwdriving tasks you do most. Then ask yourself these questions while you're shopping for a new drill:

Are high-end brands worth it? High voltage isn't the only mark of a capable drill. You can purchase an 18-volt drill with a ½-inch chuck for thicker bits, versus the usual ⅜-inch chuck, letting you drill larger holes. But you may not want to pay the $200 or more typical for most cordless drills with that feature if your home to-do list doesn't include larger projects or heavier-duty drilling.

How much are replacement batteries? A cordless drill's battery can be discharged and recharged roughly 500 times before it must be replaced. While batteries can last five years or more, frequent use can deplete them sooner. At $30 to $80 each for many of the batteries that power drills, replacing them can cost as much as buying a new cordless drill.

Battery replacement may be less of a concern if you're buying a $250 drill you plan to keep for a while. And for models that cost less than $100, simply replacing the drill may make more sense than buying a new pair of batteries. Otherwise, consider battery cost along with the drill.

Are you buying other cordless tools? You're likely to be tempted by multi-tool kits, which cost far less than you'd pay for the tools separately, since the tools in each kit are powered by the same batteries and charger. But these kits can be less of a bargain than they seem; performance of some of the tools they include, particularly circular saws, has been mediocre in our tests, and you may not use all of them.

Related CR Report: May 2004
Ratings: page 246

DECK TREATMENTS

The longest-lasting deck treatments are the ones that are the most like paint. Widely advertised clear finishes don't provide long-term protection.

Lumber, like skin, doesn't fare well when it's left unprotected. The sun's ultraviolet rays are always on the attack. Rain and sun alternately swell and dry wood, eventually causing it to crack and split. Moisture promotes the growth of mold and mildew. Even redwood, cedar, and pressure-treated wood can benefit from a protective coat. Our tests show that many clear deck treatments usually don't offer more than a year of protection.

SHOP SMART

Thoroughly clean your deck and railing before applying a new coating.

WHAT'S AVAILABLE

Major brands include Ace, Akzo Nobel, Behr, Benjamin Moore, Cabot, Flood, Glidden, Olympic, Sears, Sherwin-Williams, Thompson's, True Value, Wolman, and Valspar. There are also many smaller, specialized brands.

Clear finishes are generally water-repellent, but they don't provide protection from ultraviolet and visible light. They let the wood's natural grain show through but allow the wood to turn gray. Semitransparent finishes contain some pigment but still allow the wood grain to show. Opaque stains completely mask wood grain and are also known as solid finishes. Price range: $10 to just over $50 per gallon.

IMPORTANT FEATURES

Deck treatments may be **alkyd-based (solvent)** or **latex-based (water).** Most alkyd-based products require cleanup with mineral spirits, but a few can be cleaned with water. Latex-based products clean up with water. A few products involve a **two-step process,** requiring you to apply a base coat first, and then follow up with a top coat within a year. Linseed oil and tung oil, once common binders in wood coatings, have largely been replaced by synthetic resins. These new formulations are described as **preservatives, protectors, stabilizers, repellents, sealers, cleaners, restorers,** or **rejuvenators.**

HOW TO CHOOSE

Make an opaque treatment your first choice, as it offers the best protection. And because an opaque deck treatment should last for two to three years, it's also more economical in the long run. After several coatings, however, an opaque finish can build up a film layer that may require more extensive preparation—such as sanding—for subsequent coats. Consider a semi-transparent treatment if you want the wood grain to show. Be aware that if you choose a clear deck treatment, you'll likely be doing the job over again within a year.

Related CR Report: July 2004

GRILLS, OUTDOOR

Many people are choosing models that do more than just grill. Go high-end, and you can pay as much as you would for a pro-style kitchen range.

A $15 charcoal hibachi is all it takes to give burgers that outdoorsy barbecue taste. But a gas or electric grill offers flexible controls and spares you the hassle of starting the fire and getting rid of the ashes when you're done. Most grills have extras such as a warming rack for rolls; some have an accessory burner for, say, boiling corn on the cob. Shoppers looking for a backyard statement will find models that cost thousands of dollars and have stainless-steel exteriors and grates, porcelain-coated steel and aluminum lids, separately controlled burners, utensil holders, and other high-end features. You'll also find more modest grills that can serve up flavor and convenience for $200 or so.

WHAT'S AVAILABLE

Char-Broil, Coleman, Kenmore (Sears), and Weber account for more than 60 percent of gas-grill sales. Char-Broil is a mass-market brand. Weber is a high-end brand that also markets its classic dome-top charcoal grills. Sears covers a wide range of gas grills under its Kenmore name.

Gas. These grills are easy to start, warm up quickly, and usually cook predictably, giving meat a full, grilled flavor. Step-up features include shelves and side burners. Better models offer added sturdiness and more even cooking. Price range: $75 to more than $3,000.

Electric. Easy to start, these offer precise temperature control and let you grill with nonstick cookware. But they take a bit longer than gas models to warm up. Price range: about $50 to $300.

Charcoal. These provide an intense, smoky flavor prized by purists. But they don't always light easily (using a chimney-style starter can help). They also burn less cleanly than gas, their heat is harder to regulate, and cleanup can be messy. Price range: usually $100 or less.

IMPORTANT FEATURES

Most cooking **grates** are made of porcelain-coated steel, with others made of the somewhat sturdier porcelain-coated cast iron, bare cast iron, or stainless steel. A porcelain-coated grate is rustproof and easy to clean, but it can eventually chip. Bare cast iron is sturdy and sears beautifully, but you have to season it with cooking oil to fend off rust.

The best of both worlds: Stainless steel is sturdy and resists rust without a porcelain coating. Cooking grates with wide, closely spaced bars tend to provide better searing than grates with thin, round rods, which may allow more food to fall to the bottom of the grill. Both gas and electric grills are mounted on a **cart,** usually made of painted steel tubing assembled with nuts and bolts. Higher-priced grills have welded joints, and some have a cart made of stainless steel. Carts with two wheels and two feet must be lifted at one end to move; better are two large wheels and two casters or four casters, which make moving easier. Wheels with a full axle are better than those bolted to the frame, which can bend over time.

> **TECH TIP**
>
> **Coated cast-iron or stainless-steel grates tend to cook better than grates made of porcelain-coated steel.**

Gas and electric grills generally have one or more **exterior shelves,** which flip up from the front or side or are fixed on the side. Shelves are usually made of plastic, though some are made of cast aluminum or stainless steel, which is more durable. (Wood shelves are the least sturdy and tend to deteriorate over time.) Most grills have **interior racks** for keeping food warm without further cooking. Another plus for gas or electric grills is a **lid** and **firebox** made of stainless steel or porcelain-coated steel, both of which are more durable than cast aluminum.

Still other features help a gas grill start more easily and cook more evenly. An example is the **igniter,** which works via a knob or a push button. Knobs emit two or three sparks per turn, while push buttons emit a single spark per push. Better are **battery-powered electronic igniters,** which produce continuous sparks as long as the button is held down. Also look for **lighting holes** on the side of or beneath the grill, which are handy if the igniter fails and you need to use a wooden match or propane lighter to start the fire.

Most gas grills have steel **burners,** though some are stainless steel, cast iron, or cast brass. Those premium burners typically last longer and carry warranties of 10 years or more. Most grills have two burners, or one with two independent halves. A few have three or four, which can add cooking flexibility. A **side burner,** which resembles a gas-stove burner and has its own heat control, is handy for cooking vegetables or sauce without leaving the grill. Other step-up features include an **electric rotisserie,** a **fuel gauge,** a **smoker drawer,** a **wok,** a **griddle pan,** a **steamer pan,** a **deep fryer,** a **nonstick grill basket,** and one or more high-heat **infrared burners** in place of the conventional type.

Most gas grills also use a cooking medium—a metal plate or metal bars, ceramic or charcoal-like briquettes, or lava rocks—between the burner and grates to distribute heat and vaporize juices, flavoring the food. Our tests have shown that no one type is better at ensuring even heating. But grills with nothing between the burner and the cooking grates typically cook less evenly.

Gas grills sometimes include a **propane tank;** buying a tank separately costs about $25. Some grills can be converted to run on natural gas or come in a natural-gas version. The tank usually sits next to or on the base of the grill and attaches to its gas line with a handwheel. All tanks must now comply with upgraded National Fire Protection Association standards for overfill protection. Noncompliant tanks have a circular or five-lobed valve and aren't refillable, although they can be retrofitted with a three-lobed valve or swapped for a new tank at a hardware store or other refilling facility.

HOW TO CHOOSE

Most of these gas grills should perform at least adequately at your next alfresco feast. But as with indoor ranges, some grills do so with more opulence.

Decide on the style and convenience features you want and the price you're willing to pay. Then use the following shopping criteria to help narrow your choices:

Don't buy more grill than you need. Gas grills fall into three broad size categories based on measured square inches of cooking area. While prices for small and average-sized grills often overlap, you'll typically pay a premium for the largest models.

Check the parts. Burners, which route the gas and create the flames, remain a gas grill's most-replaced part. Look for burners warranted for 10 years or more. Also look for stainless steel or coated cast-iron cooking grates. And check that the rolling cart that supports the firebox and lid is sturdy; it shouldn't rattle when shaken.

Make sure it's safe. Major safety features are easy to spot. Among them are plastic or wooden lid handles, which usually don't get as hot as metal ones. Also look for a drainage system that siphons off grease to help prevent flare-ups.

Related CR Report: June 2004
Ratings: page 256

HUMIDIFIERS

Using a humidifier can help ease dry skin and other problems associated with dry air. But choosing one involves trade-offs among efficiency, cost, noise, and convenience.

Who needs a humidifier? Anyone who suffers from uncomfortably dry or itchy eyes, throat, or skin, or whose asthma is a problem indoors during the heating season. Ideally, the indoor humidity should be 30 to 50 percent. But that level can drop significantly in winter, since cold air holds less moisture, and heating it doesn't change its moisture content.

Humidifiers have improved over some earlier models, which spewed white dust in our tests. But that doesn't mean they all work equally well. What's more, Consumer Reports tests show that manufacturer claims can be a poor guide to how well a humidifier will work; several small tabletop models fell well short of their claimed output and may not raise the humidity to the desired level.

WHAT'S AVAILABLE

Major humidifier brands include Bemis, Bionaire, Emerson, Holmes, Honeywell, Hunter, Kenmore, Lasko, Sunbeam, and Vornado.

Humidifiers come in three major configurations:

Tabletop. These cost the least and are fine for single rooms. Tabletop humidifiers include evaporative models, which use a fan to blow air over a wet wick, and warm-mist models, which use a heating unit to boil water before cooling the steam. However, smaller tanks need to be refilled more frequently. Evaporative models are noisy; warm-mist models are costly to run. Price range: $40 to $80.

Console. With larger tanks that require less refilling, console models are a suitable choice for humidifying multiple rooms. Console humidifiers are also efficient and can be placed unobtrusively. But all use evaporative technology and are relatively noisy. The larger the tank, the more difficult it will be to handle. Price range: $90 to $120.

In-duct. These whole-house humidifiers are convenient, quiet, and efficient, making them the least expensive to operate. Most are evaporative bypass units, which tap into the air supply and return ducts. Some are warm-mist; others are nebulizers, which use a spray technology. In-duct humidifiers can be used only with forced-air heat. While inexpensive to operate, they're the most expensive to buy and often require professional installation. Price range: $90 to $200, plus another $100 to $150 to install.

IMPORTANT FEATURES

A good portable model should offer relatively easy carrying, filling, cleaning, and wick replacement. Also look for easy-to-use controls and tanks that fit beneath faucets. Some portable models can be programmed to turn on automatically, though it's best to maintain a consistent humidity level.

HOW TO CHOOSE

Decide the size you want based on how many rooms you need to humidify. Before buying a portable model, be sure you're willing to take the trouble to clean and disinfect it regularly to prevent mold and mildew. Otherwise, consider an in-duct humidifier, which is plumbed into the water supply and drainpipes, needn't be refilled, and has an easy-to-change filter that requires attention only once or twice a year.

Then keep these considerations in mind as you shop:

Noise level. Consider a warm-mist tabletop if quietness counts. All warm-mist humidifiers were quieter than evaporative models; some made little or no noise beyond mild boiling and hissing sounds. By contrast, comparably sized evaporative humidifiers generated 45 to 50 decibels on low settings—about as much noise as a small air conditioner—and emitted more than 50 decibels on high. At 80 decibels on its high setting, one model proved as raucous as a loud vacuum cleaner.

For larger areas, consider buying a noisier console model and locating it away from sleeping areas; the water vapor travels quickly through the home air and will still benefit remote bedrooms if doors remain open for air exchange. While you could alternatively buy several warm-mist tabletop models, doing so costs more.

Factor in the running costs. In-duct systems and other evaporative models deliver the most energy efficiency. While initially pricey, in-duct humidifiers are likely to cost the least over time; you can easily spend $350 per year to run four tabletop models compared with just $28 for one in-duct model.

Consider your water. Some humidifiers have lower output with hard water. Nonetheless, you'll find tabletop, console, evaporative, and warm-mist humidifiers that perform well under those conditions.

Be sure it has a humidistat. Whether it's dial or digital, a humidistat controls humidity levels and shuts the humidifier off when the set level is reached. Models without a humidistat can allow humidity levels to rise high enough to form condensation on windows and other cold surfaces. Overhumidification can also lead to mold and bacteria growth. Humidistats that display room humidity levels and settings are best.

Also be aware that some humidistats aren't accurate or reliable. And most portable humidifiers won't let you set humidity levels below 30 percent. When outside temperatures drop below 20° F, even a 30-percent indoor humidity level can lead to window condensation. Be sure to lower humidity levels as outdoor temperatures drop.

Related CR Report: October 2004
Ratings: page 264

LAWN MOWERS

Practically any mower will cut your grass. But you'll get better results with less effort if you choose a machine based on your lawn size, mowing preferences, and budget.

Mowing options range anywhere from $100 manual-reel mowers to tractors that cost $4,000 or more. If you have a small yard, a manual-reel or electric walk-behind mower is probably fine. Gasoline-powered walk-behind mowers are appropriate for most lawns up to about a half-acre. If your lawn is larger than that, you might appreciate the ease and speed of a ride-on lawn tractor.

Compared with cars, gasoline-powered lawn mowers produce a disproportionate amount of air pollution. Federal regulations aimed at reducing smog-producing mower emissions have made today's gas-powered mowers cleaner than old ones—something to consider if you're now using an older mower.

WHAT'S AVAILABLE

Manual-reel mowers are still made by a few companies. Major brands of electric mowers include Black & Decker and Craftsman (Sears). Of all brands, Craftsman sells the most gasoline-powered walk-behind mowers. Other less expensive, mass-market brands include Bolens, Murray, Yard Machines, and Yard-Man. Pricier brands, traditionally sold at outdoor power-equipment dealers, include Ariens, Cub Cadet, Honda, Husqvarna, John Deere, Lawn Boy, Snapper, and Toro. Several of those brands are now available at large retailers, including Home Depot and Lowe's.

Which type is best for your lawn? Here are the basics about each to help you decide:

Manual-reel mowers. Pushing these simple mowers turns a series of curved blades that spin with the wheels. Reel mowers are quiet, inexpensive, and nonpolluting. They're also relatively safe to operate and require little maintenance other than periodic blade adjustment and sharpening. On the downside, our tests have shown that cutting performance is typically mediocre, and most can't cut grass higher than 1½ inches or trim closer than 3 inches around obstacles. Some models have cutting swaths just 14 to 18 inches wide—another drawback. Consider them for small, flat lawns a quarter-acre or less. Price range: $100 to about $400.

Electric mowers. These push-type, walk-behind mowers use an electric motor to drive a rotating blade. Both corded and cordless versions start with the push of a button. They produce no exhaust emissions, and, like reel mowers, require little maintenance aside from sharpening. Most offer a side or rear grass catcher, and many can mulch—a process where clippings are recut until they're small enough to hide unobtrusively within the lawn. But electrics are less powerful than gas mowers and less adept at tackling tall or thick grass and weeds. What's more, their narrow, 18- to 19-inch swaths take a smaller bite than most gas-powered mowers at 21 inches.

Both corded and cordless electrics have other significant drawbacks. Corded mowers limit your mowing to within 100 feet of a power outlet—the typical maximum length for extension cords. Cordless versions, while more versatile, weigh up to 30 pounds more than corded models and typically mow just one-quarter to one-third acre before their sealed, lead-acid batteries need recharging. Both types of electrics are mainly suitable for small, flat lawns of a quarter-acre or less. Price range: corded, $125 to $250; cordless, $400 or more.

Gasoline-powered walk-behind mowers. These include push mowers and self-propelled models with driven wheels. Most have a 4.5- to 6.5-hp four-stroke engine and a cutting swath 21 or 22 inches wide, allowing you to cover more ground with each pass, and handle long or thick grass and weeds. All can mow as long as there's fuel in the tank. But gas mowers are relatively noisy and require regular maintenance.

SHOP SMART

If you bag your clippings, rear-wheel drive is better than front-wheel drive.

Most gas mowers provide three cutting modes: bagging, which gathers clippings in a removable catcher; side-discharging, which spews clippings onto the lawn; and mulching, which cuts and recuts clippings until they're small enough to settle and decompose within the lawn.

Consider a push-type model for mowing relatively flat lawns of about a quarter-acre or for trimming larger lawns. Choose a self-propelled model for hilly lawns or lawns of a half-acre or more. You might also choose a self-propelled mower if you mostly bag clippings; a full bag can add 20 or 30 pounds to the mower's weight. Price range: push-type, $150 to $400; self-propelled, $200 to $900.

IMPORTANT FEATURES

For electric mowers. A **sliding clip electric cord keeper (holder)** helps ease turns when using corded mowers by allowing the cord to move from side to side. Some have a **flip-over handle** you move from one end of the mower to the other as you reverse direction, say, at the end of a row.

For gas-powered mowers. Some models have a **blade-brake clutch system** that stops the blade but allows the engine to keep running when you release the handlebar safety bail. This is more convenient than the usual **engine-kill system,** which stops the engine and blade and requires that you restart the engine. An **overhead-valve engine** tends to generate less pollution than a traditional **side-valve engine,** and is often quieter.

With most gas mowers, you press a small rubber bulb called a **primer** to supply extra fuel for cold starting. A manual choke eliminates bending over but requires the additional task to shut off. An **electric starter** is easier to use than a recoil starter, though it typically adds $75 to the price. Most mowers with a **recoil starter** are easier to start than they once were, however. Some models from MTD-made Cub Cadet, White, and Yard-Man now have a spring-powered **self-starter,** which uses energy generated as the engine is shut off to provide push-button starts without a battery or outlet. CONSUMER REPORTS tests have found the device effective.

Some self-propelled mowers have just **one speed,** usually about 2½ mph; others have **several speeds** or a **continuous range,** typically from 1 to 3½ mph. Driven mowers also include **front-drive** and **rear-drive** models. Rear-wheel-drive models tend to have better traction on hills and with a full grass-collection bag. Mowers with **swivel front wheels** offer the most maneuverability by allowing easy 180-degree turns. But on some, each front casterlike wheel must be removed to adjust cutting height.

PROTECTING YOURSELF

Lawn equipment: a greater threat to hearing

We've long recommended hearing protection when using anything that produces noise measuring 90 decibels or more at your ears, based on 30-year-old standards set by the Occupational Safety and Health Administration (OSHA). The Environmental Protection Agency and World Health Organization now recommend significantly lower exposure levels to protect hearing.

OSHA standards don't account for the exposure to other noise typical throughout the day. Because noise exposure is cumulative, accounting for other noise lowers the decibel threshold at which hearing is at risk.

As a result, we now recommend wearing ear protection when exposed to 85 dBA or more—a noise level exceeded by nearly all of the mowers and most of the string trimmers we've tested.

To put those decibel levels in perspective, consider that the sound pressure that threatens your hearing doubles with every 3-dBA increase. Wearing ear protection at 85 dBA rather than 90 dBA significantly reduces the potential for hearing damage.

You'll also find several different deck choices. Most are steel, although some mowers offer **aluminum** or **plastic** decks, which are rustproof; plastic decks also resist dents and cracks. Nearly all mowers now have **tools-free cutting-height adjusters,** which raise and lower the deck with wheel-mounted levers. Some let you adjust cut height with only one or two levers, rather than having to adjust each wheel. Most models also allow you to change mowing modes without tools, although a few still require wrenches and, rarely, a blade change. One model has a **variable-mode lever** that lets you mulch some of the clippings and bag the rest. Some models use a **side-bagging deck** design, where a side-exit chute routes clippings into a side-mounted bag or out onto the lawn—or is blocked with a plate or plug for mulching.

Mowers with a **rear-bagging deck** tend to cost more, but their rear-mounted bag holds more than side bags and eases maneuvering by hanging beneath the handlebar rather than out to the side. The rearward opening is fitted with a chute for side discharging or a plug for mulching.

HOW TO CHOOSE

You'll see lots of competent choices for mowing the typical quarter- to half-acre lawn. All of the gasoline-powered mowers we tested meet stringent new exhaust-emissions limits. You'll also find capable electric models, particularly among those that run on a power cord.

Keep these tips in mind as you shop:

Consider your mowing. Most walk-behind mowers can mulch, bag, or side-discharge clippings. Not all mowers handle all three modes equally well, however. Choose a model that does well in the mode you use most. If you bag most of your clippings, you'll probably prefer a self-propelled mower. Also be aware that you'll probably have to use the messier side-discharge mode on most mowers when clippings are too long or wet to bag or deposit invisibly within the lawn.

Be cautious about cordless models. Plug-in electric mowers can be a good, reasonably priced option if your mowing is within range of a 100-foot power cord. While battery-powered mowers free you from an entangling cord, they're pricey for their performance and short on run time.

Related CR Report: June 2004
Ratings: page 268
Reliability: page 332

LAWN TRACTORS AND RIDING MOWERS

If your lawn is larger than a half-acre, a ride-on lawn tractor could be your best option.

Heated competition among the big-box stores has lowered the price of a well-equipped automatic tractor to as little as $1,350. That's several hundred dollars less than comparable machines from just three years ago.

Big-name brands are also piling on premium features as they trade some of the profit margins they enjoyed at the corner mower shop for the added volume of home centers and large retailers like Sears, which together sell nearly 70 percent of lawn tractors.

WHAT'S AVAILABLE

Lawn tractors have larger engines

mounted in front for better weight distribution. They can accept attachments to plow, tow a cart, or clear snow. That helps explain why lawn tractors have become far more popular than riding mowers. Riding mowers are suitable for lawns that are at least a half-acre. They have the engine in back and tend to be smaller, simpler, and easier to maneuver than tractors. While a riding mower's 28- to 33-inch swath is larger than a walk-behind mower's, it's far smaller than a lawn tractor's 38- to 48-inch swath. Lawn tractors have some drawbacks, however. For example, you'll typically spend another $250 to $400 for a bagging kit, plus another $30 to $180 for a mulching kit.

TECH TIP

A lawn tractor is a better choice than a riding mower.

Also known as zero-turn-radius models, tight-turning riders let you steer by pushing or pulling levers, each controlling a driven rear wheel. The advantage of these tight-turning machines is added maneuverability in tight spots and around obstacles. But you pay a premium for agility.

Price range: riding mowers, $700 to $2,000; lawn tractors, $900 to $2,500; tight-turning riders, $3,000 to $4,000 and beyond.

IMPORTANT FEATURES

Lower-priced models are **gear-driven** and require a lever and combination brake/clutch to change speed. Spending more will buy you a model with a **clutchless automatic drive,** which allows even more convenient, continuously variable speed changes via a hydrostatic transmission. Some models use a foot pedal with a pulley that allows continuously variable speed changes. Most models have a **translucent fuel tank,** making it easy to check fuel level. Some have a **fuel gauge** and **cupholders.** Still others allow you to remove the collection bags without flipping the seat forward.

HOW TO CHOOSE

Wide-swath mowing at a reasonable price makes lawn tractors an appealing choice if you have a half-acre or more of lawn. Falling prices also explain why tractors have eclipsed smaller riding mowers, though riders could be your only option if you have a large lawn and little storage space.

Keep these points in mind as you shop:

Determine the mowing you'll do. All tractors can side-discharge clippings, the mode most people use. Many include a mulching plate that seals the deck so clippings are cut finely and deposited into the lawn rather than on it. But a kit for bagging clippings typically costs hundreds of dollars extra. Before paying more for that bagging, be sure the model you're considering did well in that mode, and that you will use it.

Think twice about added fans. Models with a bagging system route what they cut through a chute and into the rear-mounted bags or bins. An auxiliary fan on some models is designed to help that process along. Such systems tend to improve bagging and leaf vacuuming, but add $200 to $600 to the cost of the bagging kits. Some tractors with a fan perform no better than models without one.

Plan on hearing protection. All of these tractors emitted at least 91 decibels at the operator's ear, more than most walk-behind mowers. Wear ear protection while using any tractor.

Related CR Report: May 2004
Ratings: page 275
Reliability: page 332

PAINT, EXTERIOR

The best paint can improve your home's appearance and protect it from the weather for about nine years.

While a fresh coat of paint on the siding and trim will give your house curb appeal, exterior paint isn't just for show. It provides an important layer of protection against moisture, mildew, and the effects of the sun.

WHAT'S AVAILABLE

Major brands include Ace, Behr (sold at Home Depot), Benjamin Moore, Dutch Boy, Glidden, Sears, Sherwin-Williams, True Value, and Valspar (sold at Lowe's). You'll also see many brands of paint sold regionally.

Exterior paints come in a variety of sheens. The dullest is flat, followed by low-luster (often called eggshell or satin), semi-gloss, and gloss. The flatter finishes are best for siding, with the lowest-sheen variety the best choice if you need to mask imperfections. Glossy paint is most often used for trim because it highlights the details of the woodwork and the paint is easy to clean. Price range: $15 to $40 a gallon.

HOW TO CHOOSE

Our tests of exterior paints are very severe, exposing painted panels on outdoor racks angled to catch the maximum amount of sun. One year of testing is approximately equal to three years of real-life exposure. Generally, most paints will look good for at least three years, and some should look good for about six. Most also do a good job of resisting the buildup of mildew and preventing the wood from cracking. To determine the best paint for your home, consider the following tips:

Buy the best. Our tests have found that the grade of paint matters. "Good" or "economy" grades don't weather as well as top-of-the-line products. Using a cheaper grade of paint means you'll spend more time and money in the long run because you'll need to repaint more often. "Contractor" grades of paint that we've tested in the past also tended to be mediocre.

Consider where you live. Paints of any color accumulate dirt over time. The top-rated paints tended to resist it better than the others; darker colors hide it better. Mildew can be a problem in damp areas, from rainy Seattle to steamy Tampa, or on any house that gets more shade than sun. Baking in bright sun can change even the best-quality pigments. Blues and yellows are the most likely to change.

Don't overlook the prep work. Be sure you scrape, sand, and clean the siding thoroughly before applying the paint. Good preparation makes any paint last longer. And plan to apply two coats.

Related CR Report: June 2004

PAINT, INTERIOR

Plenty of high-quality, durable wall paints are available to brighten your rooms. And you won't need to endure as many fumes as in years past.

A fresh coat of paint is an easy, inexpensive way to freshen a room. Today's paints are significantly better than their predecessors of even a few years ago in several important respects: They spatter less, keep stains at bay, and have ample tolerance for scrubbing. They also resist the buildup of mildew (important if you're painting a kitchen, a bath, or a basement room that tends to be damp). Some are labeled low-VOC (volatile organic compounds).

WHAT'S AVAILABLE

Major brands include Ace, Behr (sold at Home Depot), Benjamin Moore, Dutch Boy, Glidden, Kilz (sold at Wal-Mart), Sears, Sherwin-Williams, True Value, and Valspar (sold at Lowe's). You'll also see designer names such as Martha Stewart and Ralph Lauren, as well as many brands of paint sold regionally.

You'll find several types of paints for interior use. Wall paints can be used in just about any room. Glossier trim enamels are used for windowsills, woodwork, and the like. Kitchen and bath paints are usually fairly glossy and formulated to hold up to water and scrubbing and to release stains. Price range: $15 to $35 per gallon.

IMPORTANT FEATURES

Paint typically comes in a variety of sheens—**flat, low luster,** and **semigloss.** The degree of glossiness can be different from one manufacturer to another. Flat paint, with the dullest finish, is the best at hiding surface imperfections, but it also tends to pick up stains and may be marred by scrubbing. It's well suited for formal living rooms, dining rooms, and other spaces that don't see heavy use.

A low-luster finish (often called eggshell or satin) has a slight sheen and is good for family rooms, kids' rooms, hallways, and the like. Semi-gloss, shinier still, usually works best on kitchen and bathroom walls and on trim because it's generally easier to clean. Low-luster and semigloss paints look best on smooth, well-prepared surfaces, since the paint's shine can accentuate imperfections on the wall.

Most brands come in several tint bases—the uncolored paint that forms the foundation for the specific color you choose. The tint base largely determines the paint's toughness, resistance to dirt and stains, and ability to withstand scrubbing. The colorant determines how much the paint will fade. Whites and browns tend not to fade; reds and blues fade somewhat; bright greens and yellows tend to fade a lot.

HOW TO CHOOSE

Begin with the gloss. The gloss level will affect your perception of the color. Flat paints and textured walls absorb light, so colors seem darker. Glossy paints and smooth surfaces reflect, so colors look brighter.

Then choose a color. Take advantage of the various color-sampling products and computer programs to get the color you think you want. Several manufacturers, including Benjamin Moore and Valspar, now sell small samples of many paint colors, so you can test a paint without having to buy large quantities. Behr and other manufacturers offer large color chips or coupons, which are easier to use than the conventional small swatches. Sunlight and room light can affect your perceptions, so check samples on different walls or at different times of day.

Fluorescent light enhances blues and greens but makes warm reds, oranges, and yellows appear dull. Incandescent light works with warm colors, but might not do much for cool ones. Even natural sunlight changes from day to day, room to room, and morning to night.

Many aspects of paint performance depend on the quality of the base and not on the particular color. We test each brand's pastel and medium bases as well as white. So if you want a medium or dark color, it won't matter whether it's red or blue or something in between. Its performance should track with our findings.

Buy the top of the line. The paints we

test represent the top of each manufacturer's line. Over the years, we have found that lower grades—typically dubbed good, better, or contractor grade—do not perform as well. If a top-line paint will cover all but the darkest colors in two coats, lower-quality paints might need three or four coats. That makes them a poor value. But plan on two coats even with a top-rated paint for best coverage.

Match a paint's strong points to the room's use. Here are the most important considerations:

- Stains are more of a problem with flat paints, which may also get shiny with scrubbing.
- Heavily used rooms need a paint that can stand up to scrubbing. Our tests show that paints in every gloss level can perform well in this regard.
- Mildew can grow in any warm, humid room, not just a bathroom or kitchen. A paint with high mildew resistance won't kill existing mildew (you must clean it off with a bleach solution), but it will slow new growth.
- Sticking can occur with glossier paints long after they've dried. Books seem glued to shelves, and windows become hard to open. Most of the glossy paints we tested did not have that problem.

Related CR Report: September 2004

POWER BLOWERS

The best electric handheld blowers outperform their gas counterparts and cost less. But they aren't any quieter, and the power cord can be a hassle.

These miniature wind machines take some of the effort out of sweeping and cleaning fallen leaves and other small yard and driveway debris. Many can also vacuum and shred what they pick up. But practically all available models still make enough noise to annoy the neighbors. Indeed, some localities have ordinances restricting their use.

WHAT'S AVAILABLE

Mainstream brands include Black & Decker, Craftsman (Sears), Homelite, Ryobi, Toro, and Weed Eater. Pricier brands of gas-powered blowers include Echo, Husqvarna, John Deere, and Stihl. As with other outdoor power tools, gas and electric blowers have their pros and cons. You'll also find variations among gas-powered models. Here are your choices:

Electric handheld blowers. Designed for one-handed maneuvering, these are light (about 7 pounds or less). Many are also relatively quiet, produce no exhaust emissions, and can vacuum and shred. Some perform better than handheld gas-powered models, although mobility and range are limited by the power cord. Price range: $30 to $100.

Gasoline handheld blowers. These perform like the best electrics but aren't restricted by a cord. As with other gas-powered equipment, tougher regulations have reduced emissions. Manufacturers have also quieted some models in response to noise ordinances. But most are still loud enough to warrant hearing protection. Other drawbacks include added weight (most weigh 7 to 12 pounds) and the fuel-and-oil mixing required by the two-stroke engines most gas models use. A few blowers have a four-stroke engine that burns gasoline only, though they tend to be heavy for this group. Price range: $75 to $225.

Gasoline backpack blowers. At 16 to 25 pounds, these are double the weight of handheld blowers, which is why you wear rather than carry them. But the payoff with most is added power and ease of use for extended periods, since your shoulders support their weight. Hearing protection is strongly recommended. Backpack blowers don't vacuum. And they can be expensive. Price range: $300 to $420.

Gasoline wheeled blowers. These offer enough oomph to sweep sizable areas quickly. All use a four-stroke engine that requires no fuel mixing. But these machines are large and heavy, and require some effort to push around. They also cost the most and tend to be hard to maneuver, which can make it difficult to precisely direct leaves and other yard waste. Count on using hearing protection. Price range: $400 to $800.

SHOP SMART

Bigger is better when it comes to fans on wheeled blowers.

IMPORTANT FEATURES

Look for an easy-to-use **on-off switch** and **multiple speeds** on electric blowers, a **variable throttle** you can preset on gasoline-powered models, and a convenient **choke** on gas-powered units. Varying the speed lets you use maximum force for sweeping and minimum force around plants. Blowers that excel at cleaning or loosening debris usually have **round-nozzle blower tubes; oblong** and **rectangular nozzles** are better for moving or sweeping leaves. A bottom-mounted **air intake** is less likely to pull at clothing.

A **control stalk** attached to the blower tube of backpack models improves handling, while an **auxiliary handle** on the engine or motor housing of a handheld blower makes it easier to use—provided the handle is comfortable. Other useful features on gas-powered models include a **wide fuel fill** and a **translucent fuel tank,** which shows the level inside. An **adjustable air deflector,** found on most wheeled blowers, lets you direct airflow forward or to the side.

HOW TO CHOOSE

For sheer power, you can't go wrong with any of the backpack or wheeled blowers and several of the handheld models we tested. There's more to blowers than air power, however. The best in each group also proved easier to handle and control. And some are less noisy than others. Here's what else to think about:

Consider what you'll clear. If it's mostly fallen leaves or grass clippings, choose a model judged very good or excellent in our sweeping tests.

Handheld models that vacuum are also handy for cleaning between shrubs, though their small reduction ratios and bags are impractical for vacuuming larger areas or leaf piles. If embedded leaf fragments are a frequent problem, look for a machine that did well at freeing tenacious debris in our loosening tests.

Consider what you can handle. High performance and low weight at a relatively low price make electric blowers your first choice if arm fatigue or low arm strength is a factor. Backpack blowers put their added weight on your back, not your arms, and provide more air power, though at a much higher price.

Wheeled blowers deliver the most air power, thanks to their larger fans and higher-horsepower engines. But because they lack the drive systems available on mowers, moving these 100-plus-pound machines requires plenty of push, especially uphill. Wheeled blowers also require about 8 square feet of storage space.

Consider your neighbors. While none of these blowers is quiet, several can move lots of debris with a bit less noise.

Regulations typically limit blowers to 65 decibels at 50 feet. About a third of the tested models should meet that standard and were judged very good or excellent in that performance category.

Related CR Report: September 2003
Ratings: page 284

POWER SANDERS

These smooth operators save time and effort. More convenience and safety features for less money help account for their growing popularity.

Some of the latest power sanders can skim off as much wood in 5 minutes as you could in 30 minutes of continuous sanding by hand. Many are easier to use than older models. And nearly all have a dust bag—important considering the health risks of inhaling wood dust.

That and prices as low as $20 help explain why annual sales recently jumped 15 percent to 2.3 million. Homeowners are driving much of that growth as they use power sanders for everything from refinishing a desk to building a picnic table.

WHAT'S AVAILABLE

You'll find four major types of power sanders at the store:

Random-orbit. Best for versatility, these can do some rough sanding and most finish sanding, which helps explain their large share of the market. The round pad moves in a random ellipse to help prevent gouges. Major brands include Craftsman, Dewalt, Makita, Porter Cable, and Ryobi. Price range: about $30 to $100.

Finishing. Best for small to moderate-sized tasks, finishing sanders have squared-off pads that can reach into corners. The most popular type along with random-orbit models, finishing sanders can handle a variety of homeowner tasks. Major brands include Black & Decker, Craftsman, Dewalt, Makita, Porter Cable, and Skil. Price range: about $20 to $90.

Belt. Best for smoothing doors, tabletops, and other large or uneven areas, a belt sander has a pulley-driven loop that removes more wood in less time than other sanders. But it isn't meant for small-area or finish sanding. Major brands include Black & Decker, Makita, Porter Cable, Ryobi, and Skil. Price range: about $50 to $180.

Detail. Best for sanding around chair spindles, moldings, and other tight spots, most detail sanders have triangular pads that are good for corners. Some also come with finger-shaped pads for sanding around slots and grooves. But none are meant for rough-sanding or large areas. Major brands include Craftsman and Ryobi. Price range: $30 to $50.

TECH TIP
Always wear a particulate-filtering mask when using any power sander.

IMPORTANT FEATURES

These help a power sander reduce effort, dust, and cleanup:

Dust bag and vacuum connection. An attached bag captures dust routed into it via holes in the pad, but requires frequent emptying. A vacuum connection lets you attach a wet/dry vac for more thorough dust-collecting, though the hose may hamper maneuverability and handling.

Easy paper changes. Random-orbit and detail sanders use a **hook-and-loop system** to attach the **sanding pad.** Many finishing sanders have a **lever-and-clip system**. And all finishing sanders can be converted to **pressure-sensitive adhesive** pads. All belt sanders use a **flip-out lever** and **tracking control** to lock the sandpaper loop in place.

A place for both hands. Many models of all types can be gripped securely with one or both hands for added ease and stability. A two-handed grip is especially important for a belt sander's heavier-duty rough sanding, as is a **large front grip** that keeps hands well spaced to ease larger jobs.

For belt sanders, easy tracking and trigger locking. Many belt sanders allow you to adjust tracking with a **knob** or **thumbscrew** instead of a screwdriver to move the paper nearer to one edge or the other. Many also have a **trigger lock** that can be locked in the On position with one hand.

A hole puncher for finishing sanders. Most with a dust bag or vacuum connection include a **template** for punching the pattern for the dust-routing holes in replacement sandpaper.

Variable speed. Adds control by letting you sand more slowly and carefully.

Still other power-sander features are nice but not essential:

A long cord. Lets you dispense with an extension cord near an electrical outlet.

A carrying case. Makes storage easier and neater.

Clamp-down capability. Some belt sanders can be secured to a bench with the belt facing upward—convenient for two-handed shaping where you hold the wood against the spinning belt, rather than the belt against the work piece.

HOW TO CHOOSE

Lots of choices for power sanders mean more considerations when shopping. Here are some of the major features you should be thinking about:

Decide how you'll use it. Determine which of the four types of power sanders meets your needs. If you're buying just one sander, you'll probably prefer a random-orbit or a finishing sander, which offer the most versatility.

If you're buying a finishing sander, choose a one-quarter-sheet model for mostly small jobs and a larger, one-third-sheet model for the occasional tabletop.

Consider your strength. A heavier sander tends to remove more wood in less time, since more weight helps the sander contact the wood more effectively. While the added heft isn't an issue with most types of sanders, it could be with belt sanders, some of which weigh 11 pounds or more. Particularly for belt-type sanders, try lifting and holding the sander at the store. Then choose the heaviest model you can handle comfortably.

Check the grip. For added control, especially with larger, harder-working models, make sure the sander is easy to grasp with one or both hands. (Most of the models we tested were.)

Look for a bag and a vac connection. Many sanders now include at least one of these features. But most of the low-cost models lack an attached dust-collection bag, a port for connecting a wet/dry vacuum hose, or both. A vacuum connection is especially important. Besides capturing dust more thoroughly than a bag, attaching a wet/dry vacuum helped speed sanding with several models we tested.

Look for easy paper changes. Even small projects may require that you replace the sandpaper several times. The hook-and-loop pads now common on random-orbit and detail sanders are the easiest to change. Some sanders of other types also make changing the sandpaper relatively convenient.

Related CR Report: January 2004
Ratings: page 287

SNOW THROWERS

Bigger, better, and easier to use describe the latest of these labor-saving machines.

Some of the newest snow throwers are larger and more capable, yet easier to control. Many also cost less, thanks to price pressure from major retailers such as Home Depot, Lowe's, and Sears, which now account for about 60 percent of sales.

Two-stage models are the largest of these machines. Unlike smaller, single-stage models, which rely solely on a rubber-edged auger to move and disperse snow, as well as to provide some pulling power, two-stage models add drive wheels and a fanlike impeller to help disperse what they pick up.

Models from Sears' Craftsman and Troy-Bilt are among those that clear a wide, 30-inch swath, compared with the 24 to 26 inches typical in our 1997 snow-thrower report. Yet at about $1,300, these newest models cost several hundred dollars less than many comparable machines in our last report.

You needn't buy the biggest snow thrower to get competent clearing. Honda and Toro are among the brands with single-stage models that rival some larger machines, yet weigh far less and require less storage space. Manufacturers are designing these more-capable models for homeowners with smaller driveways as well as for women, who make at least part of the buying decisions in more than 30 percent of snow-thrower purchases.

Other advances include easier steering and chute controls. You'll also find easy-handling electric models for smaller driveways.

WHAT'S AVAILABLE

Major brands include Ariens, Craftsman (Sears), Honda, Husqvarna, Simplicity, Toro, Troy-Bilt, Yard Machines, and Yard-Man. While two-stage snow throwers all have a gas engine, single-stage models are sold in both gas and electric versions. Here are the pros and cons of each:

Two-stage gas. Best for long, wide, or hilly driveways, with a typical snowfall over 8 inches. They're essential for gravel driveways, since the auger doesn't contact the ground. All offer electric starting and have driven wheels, an auger that gathers snow, and an impeller to throw it. Some clear a swath 28 to 30 inches wide. But two-stage gas models are relatively heavy, take as much space as some lawn tractors, and require regular engine maintenance. Those without trigger drive releases can be hard to maneuver. Price range: $600 to $2,100.

Single-stage gas. Best for flat, midsize paved driveways and walks, with typical snowfall less than 8 inches. They're lighter and easier to handle, and take up about as much storage space as a mower. Most offer electric starting. But they're a poor choice for gravel, since the auger contacts the surface and can throw stones. Most clear a 20- to 22-inch swath. All lack drive wheels and require engine maintenance. The auger's limited drive action isn't enough for steep hills and can pull from side to side. Price range: $300 to $900.

Single-stage electric. Best for short, flat driveways or decks and walks, with snowfall 4 inches or less. Single-stage electric models are lightest, smallest, and easiest to handle and store. They're also less noisy than gas-powered models, and their electric motors free you from fueling and other engine maintenance. But they're as unsuited to gravel driveways as single-stage gas snow throwers. Their small, 11- to 18-inch swath slows clearing. Electric machines also trade engine fueling and maintenance for the hassle of a power cord. Price range: $100 to $300.

IMPORTANT FEATURES

A **one-handed drive/auger control** on two-stage models lets you engage the drive-wheel and auger-control levers with one hand, leaving the other free to control the chute. A growing number of new two-stage machines use **handlebar-mounted trigger releases** that ease steering by letting you quickly disconnect either or both wheels from the transmission on the fly, rather than having to stop and move a pin or lever at a wheel.

A **dead-man control** is an especially critical safety feature. It stops the spinning auger and, on two-stage models, the impeller when the handlebar-grip controls are released. Also look for a **clearing tool**—typically a plastic stick that is attached to the machine so it's handy for safely clearing clogs in the discharge chute or auger housing. Use a wooden broom handle, never hands or feet, on models without the tool.

Some snow throwers let you quickly change the chute direction and height of thrown snow via a **single-lever joystick** on two-stage machines or a long handle you can reach from the operator's position on single-stage models. That's easier than wrestling with two separate controls on many two-stage snow throwers or the stiff, awkward discharge-chute handle on many single-stage models.

All electric models turn on with a switch, though most gas-powered models now offer **plug-in starting**—handy if you're near an outlet. All two-stage snow throwers have a **four-stroke engine** that requires periodic oil changes. Some single-stage models use a two-stroke engine that requires no oil changes, but entails mixing oil with the fuel. All gas snow throwers must meet the same emissions standards. **Headlights** for night use are an added nicety you'll now find on many two-stage machines.

HOW TO CHOOSE

Snow-throwing may be easier than shoveling, but it's still harder than using a self-propelled mower. Consult a doctor before buying a snow thrower if you have hypertension, diabetes, or heart disease. Also consider having your driveway plowed if it's especially long and two or more cars wide. If a snow thrower meets your needs, match the type to your space and climate and then consider these tips.

Try the controls. Independent dealers and even big-box stores typically have floor samples. Along with trigger releases on two-stage models, look for electric starting. Also be sure you're comfortable with the handle height and the chute adjustment, which you'll use frequently.

Don't get hung up on power claims. You'll find two-stage snow throwers with engines that boast 11 horsepower or more. But higher power claims don't necessarily mean more performance; some less-powerful machines in our most recent tests cleared snow on a par with the highest-horsepower models.

Some manufacturers and retailers are also pushing Briggs & Stratton engines vs. the usual Tecumseh powerplants. We found that the Tecumseh engines on most of these machines performed competently.

Don't get dazzled by drive speeds. Most two-stage machines have five or six forward speeds—useful for going slowly through heavy snow to prevent clogs, or quickly when returning to the garage. While the seven forward speeds on some two-stage models sound like a plus, we found them within the typical range for six-speed models.

Related CR Report: October 2004
Ratings: page 301

STRING TRIMMERS

An electric model can do a good job for many trimming tasks. But for tall grass and weeds, you'll need a gasoline-powered string trimmer.

A string trimmer can pick up where a lawn mower leaves off. It provides the finishing touches, slicing through tufts of grass around trees and flower beds, straightening uneven edges along a driveway, and trimming stretches of lawn your mower or tractor can't reach. Gasoline-powered models can also whisk away tall grass and weeds.

Faster starts, fewer tangles, and easier handling are among the string-trimmer features you'll find as manufacturers improve these bladeless yard tools. Craftsman (Sears) and Troy-Bilt trimmers now start with one or two pulls, thanks to a new starting system. Tangled and jammed-up cutting string can be avoided with a fixed-line head that uses two precut pieces of cutting line; the system is available for Echo and Craftsman models. And trimmers are now more than 1 pound lighter than the ones we tested only a few years ago—they're now 11 pounds, on average.

WHAT'S AVAILABLE

Black & Decker, Craftsman (Sears), Toro, and Weed Eater are the major brands of electric string trimmers, while Craftsman, Homelite, Ryobi, Troy-Bilt, and Weed Eater are the big names in gas-powered models. Leading high-end brands of gas trimmers include Cub Cadet, Echo, Husqvarna, John Deere, and Stihl.

Gasoline-powered trimmers. These are better than electrics at cutting heavy weeds and brush, and are often better at edging—turning the trimmer so its spinning line cuts vertically along a walk or garden border. They also go anywhere, so they're the best choice if you'll be trimming far from a power outlet. On the downside, gas trimmers can be heavy, weighing about 10 to 14 pounds. Most have a two-stroke engine that requires a mixture of gas and oil. These tend to pollute more than a four-stroke engine that uses gasoline only, and entail pull starting and regular maintenance. And gas-powered trimmers are noisy enough to make hearing protection necessary. Price range: less than $85 to more than $300. Most models, however, cost from $100 to $200.

TECH TIP

Use plugs or muffs to protect your ears from damage when using machinery that emits 85 decibels or more.

Electric-corded trimmers. These are the least expensive and lightest; many weigh only about 5 pounds. Some work nearly as well as gas trimmers for most trimming. All are quieter and easier to start than gas trimmers—you simply push a button rather than pulling a starter cord. The power cord does limit your range to about 100 feet from an outlet. Many electrics have the motor at the bottom of the shaft, rather than at the top, making them harder to handle. And even the most powerful models are unlikely to handle the tall grass and weeds that the best gas-powered trimmers can tackle. Price range: $20 to $75.

Electric battery-powered trimmers. Cordless trimmers combine the free range of gas trimmers with the convenience of corded electrics: less noise, easy starting and stopping, no fueling, and no exhaust emissions. But they're weak at cutting and run only about 15 to 20 minutes before the onboard battery needs re-charging, which can take up to a day. They also tend to be pricey and heavy for their size (about 10 pounds). Most models have the motor at the bottom of the shaft, where it can be even harder to handle than the lighter corded versions. Price range: $90 to $100 or more.

IMPORTANT FEATURES

All trimmers have a **shaft** that connects the engine or motor and controls to the trimmer **head**, where the plastic lines revolve. **Curved shafts** are the most common and can be easier to handle when trimming up close. **Straight shafts** tend to be better for reaching beneath bushes and other shrubs, and if you are taller. Some models have a **split shaft** that comes apart so you can replace the trimmer head with a leaf blower, edging blade, or other yard tool, though we've found that most of these attachments aren't very effective.

Gas-powered trimmers have their engine on top, which helps balance the load. Most electric models have their motor on the bottom, at the cutting head, though a few have a **top-mounted motor.**

Most gas-powered trimmers have two **cutting lines**, while most electrics use just one, which means they cut less with each revolution. Most gas and electric trimmers have a **bump-feed line advance** that feeds out more line when you bump the trimmer head on the ground; a blade on the safety shield cuts it to the right length. Models with a **fixed-line head** use two strips of line instead of a spool, which eliminates tangles and jammed line.

Most gasoline models use **two-stroke engines**, which burn lubricating oil with the gasoline. Federal law requires manufacturers to slash exhaust emissions for new gas-powered trimmers by 70 percent by 2005, while California has required that emissions reduction since 2000. Manufacturers predict price increases of $10 to $20 as the cost of meeting emissions restrictions goes up.

Some trimmers use inherently cleaner **four-stroke engines**, but these tend to weigh and cost more. Corded and battery models typically use a 1.8- to 5-amp motor.

To start most gas trimmers, you set a **choke** and push a **primer bulb**, then pull a starter rope. On most models, you have to pull, prime, and adjust the choke several times before the engine starts. But some models have an easy **three-step starting system** that reduces the hassles and starts quicker.

On most gas trimmers, a **centrifugal clutch** allows the engine to idle without spinning the line—safer and more convenient than models where the line continues to turn. On models without a clutch, the string is spinning while the engine is running. Electric-trimmer lines don't spin until you press the switch.

Some models make edging more convenient with a **rotating head** that puts the trimmer head in the vertical position. Heavier-duty models often offer a **shoulder harness**, which can ease handling and reduce fatigue.

Other convenient features include easy-to-reach and easy-to-adjust switches, comfortable handles, and—on gas models—a **translucent fuel tank.**

HOW TO CHOOSE

You don't have to invest in a pricey,

professional-grade trimmer unless you need its metal-blade capability for cutting saplings and other woody waste. Most of the gas trimmers and even some electrics we tested can handle the grass and tall weeds that account for most trimming.

Determine whether a gas-powered or electric trimmer fits your needs. Then keep these points in mind while shopping at the store:

Consider the landscape. Trimmers with a straight shaft can reach beneath shrubs more easily and are less likely than curved-shaft ones to spatter you with clippings. Curved-shaft trimmers trade those benefits for easier maneuvering and, often, less weight—a plus for shorter users and those with less arm strength.

See how it feels. While a lighter trimmer tends to reduce fatigue, weight isn't the whole story. Good balance can be just as critical. To check it, adjust the front handle for comfort and hold the trimmer in the cutting position with both hands. Its weight should feel evenly distributed or slightly heavier at the top.

Also check that all the controls are smooth and easy to reach. If you're left-handed, make sure a gasoline-powered trimmer you're considering has a deflector that routes the hot exhaust gases rearward. Most now include one.

Consider your neighbors. If they're close by, you may want to choose a corded or cordless electric trimmer. Nearly all the ones we tested are significantly less noisy than gasoline-powered models. If you opt for gas, protect your ears with earmuffs or plugs.

Related CR Report: June 2004
Ratings: page 304

VACUUM CLEANERS

Fancy features and a high price don't necessarily mean better cleaning. You'll find plenty of less-flashy performers at a reasonable price.

Which type of vacuum cleaner to buy used to be a no-brainer. Uprights were clearly better for carpets, while canisters were the obvious choice for bare floors. That distinction has blurred somewhat as more upright models clean floors without scattering dust and more canisters do a very good job with carpeting. Central vacuum systems, an increasingly popular third option, add a measure of convenience, along with higher prices.

You'll also see a growing number of features such as dirt sensors and bagless dirt bins, but some of those features may contribute more to price than to function, while other, more essential features may be missing from the least-expensive models. And while cordless and even robotic vacuums have joined your list of choices, neither have been top performers so far.

WHAT'S AVAILABLE

Hoover, the oldest and largest vacuum manufacturer, is a division of Maytag and offers roughly 50 models priced from $50 to $500 as well as central vacuum systems priced higher. Many of Hoover's conventional models are similar, with minor differences in features; the "variety" is mostly in the marketing. Some Hoover machines are made exclusively for retail chain stores. Kenmore is the biggest name for canister models, accounting for about 25 percent of U.S. sales.

Other players include Dirt Devil (made

by Royal Appliance), which sells uprights and canisters as well as stick brooms and hand vacuums; Eureka, which offers low-priced models, central vacs, and high-end Electrolux-branded models; Bissell, a mostly mass-marketed brand; and brands such as Miele, Panasonic, Samsung, Sanyo, Sharp, and Simplicity, which are likely to be sold at specialty stores. Higher-priced Aerus (which also makes central vacs) and Oreck models are sold in their own stores and by direct mail, while upscale Kirby and Rainbow models are still sold door-to-door.

Along with a vacuum's brand, your choices include several types:

Uprights. These tend to be the least expensive. Their one-piece design also makes them easier to store than canister vacs. A top-of-the-line upright might have a wider cleaning path, be self-propelled, and have a HEPA filter, dirt sensor, and full-bag indicator. Price range for most: $75 to $300.

Canister vacuums. These tend to do well on bare floors because they allow you to turn off the brush or use a specialized tool to avoid scattering dirt. Most are quieter than uprights, and their long, flexible hose tends to make them better at cleaning on stairs and in hard-to-reach areas. The added clutter of the loose hose and wand makes canisters somewhat harder to store, however. While canister vacs still tend to cost the most, you'll find a growing number of lower-priced models. Price range for most: $150 to $400.

Central vac systems. They clean like a canister vac without your having to push, pull, or carry the motor and body around. They're also relatively quiet and require less-frequent emptying. But they're the most expensive option, and generally require professional installation. The 35-foot hose can be cumbersome, and there's no place to carry tools while you work. Price range: $500 to $1,250 for the unit including tools, plus $300 to $750 to install.

Stick vacs and hand vacs. Whether corded or cordless, these miniature vacuums typically lack the power of a full-sized vacuum cleaner. But they can be handy for small, quick jobs. Price range: $20 to $75.

IMPORTANT FEATURES

Typical attachments include **crevice** and **upholstery tools.** Most vacuums also include **extension wands** for reaching high places. A **full-bag alert** can be handy, since an overstuffed bag impairs a vacuum's ability to clean.

Lately, many uprights have adopted a **bagless** configuration with a **see-through dirt bin** that replaces the usual bag. Performance has improved for bagless vacs, though emptying their bins can raise enough dust to concern even those without allergies. You'll also find dirt-collection bins on most stick vacs and hand vacs. Some of these have a **revolving brush,** which may help remove surface debris from a carpet. Stick vacs can hang on a hook or, if they're cordless, on a wall-mounted charger base.

Canister vacuums we've tested have a **power nozzle** that cleans carpets more thoroughly than a simple suction nozzle. Look for a **suction-control** feature; found on most canisters and some uprights, it allows you to reduce airflow for drapes and other delicate fabrics. On uprights, also look for an **on/off switch for the brush** if you plan to use attachments. Stopping the brush protects the user from injury, the power cord from damage, and your furnishings from undue wear. Some uprights automatically stop the brush when the handle is in the "up" position.

Most canisters and a few uprights have a **retractable cord** that rewinds with a tug or push of a button—a plus, considering the

20- to 30-foot length for most. Another worthwhile feature is **manual pile-height adjustment,** which can improve cleaning by letting you match the vacuum's height to the carpet pile more effectively than machines that adjust automatically. While a self-propelled mode takes the push out of more and more uprights, it can make them heavier and harder to transport.

Midpriced **accessory kits for central vacs** typically include an electrically powered cleaning head—a must for carpets—as well as a floor brush, crevice tool, upholstery brush, dusting brush, and extension wands. Spending more gets you more tools, a premium powerhead, and a longer hose. A sound-deadening **muffler,** installed in the exhaust air pipe near the central-vac base unit, comes on some models but can be added to any model for about $10 to $25. Most central vacs have a **suction switch** at the wand's handle so you can turn the vacuum unit on and off where you're standing.

Some vacuums have a **dirt sensor** that triggers a light indicator when the concentration of dirt particles in the machine's air stream reaches a certain level. But the sensor signals only that the vacuum is no longer picking up dirt, not whether there's dirt left in your rug. That can result in your vacuuming longer and working harder with little or no more cleanliness.

You'll also hear lots of claims about **microfiltration,** which typically uses a bag with smaller pores or a second, electrostatic filter that supplements the standard motor filter in an attempt to capture fine particles that may pass through the bag or filter and escape into the air through the exhaust. Some vacuums have a **HEPA filter,** which may benefit someone with asthma. But many models without a HEPA filter have performed just as well in CONSUMER REPORTS emissions tests, since the amount of dust emitted depends as much on the design of the entire machine as on its filter.

A vacuum's design can also affect how long it lasts. With some uprights, for example, dirt sucked into the machine passes through the blower fan before entering the bag—a potential problem because most fans are plastic and vulnerable to damage from hard objects. Better systems filter dirt through the bag before it reaches the fan. While hard objects can lodge in the motorized brush, they're unlikely to break the fan.

HOW TO CHOOSE

You'll find upright, canister, and central vacuums that clean capably and are easy to use. While the best of these perform similarly overall, specific strengths vary as much as prices. Determine which type of vacuum cleaner offers the convenience and versatility you want at a price you're willing to pay. Then keep these shopping tips in mind at the store:

Shop central vacs on facts, not hype. Despite what some manufacturers suggest, it's impossible to determine how much a central vacuum system will increase your home's resale value. You're also likely to hear robust claims about cubic feet of air moved per minute and promises of high "air wattage"; neither of these claims correlated with airflow performance in our tests. Instead, consider a central vacuum system if its convenience justifies its cost.

Consider your cleaning. Nearly any vacuum cleans bare floors adequately. But you're likely to prefer a model that scored well in our carpet tests if your home includes kids, pets, and other sources of ground-in carpet dirt.

Strong suction through a hose that can snake beneath furniture and delve into drapes makes canister models and central vacuum systems especially adept with cleaning tools. But unless your home is already plumbed for a central vacuum system, you may find the cost of the unit and its installation prohibitive.

Try any vacuum before buying. A vacuum's weight can be especially critical if your arms aren't strong or your home has more than one level.

Uprights generally range from 16 to 21 pounds, though several we tested weigh as little as 9 pounds. While canister vacuums typically weigh more than upright models, you're moving only the hose and powerhead when cleaning. Insist on lifting and carrying the vacuum and hose and trying out its features before you buy.

Protect your lungs. Choose a vacuum cleaner that scored well in our dust-emissions tests if you're sensitive to dust. If you opt for a bagless vac, be sure to wear a dust mask when emptying its bin, which often creates more dust than with a bag-equipped vacuum.

Related CR Report: July 2004
Ratings: page 317
Reliability: page 337

HOME OFFICE

Home Office: Wireless Workspace

In our increasingly mobile society, your office can be any-where. Phones are portable; laptops, too. And don't forget the king of high-tech portability, the PDA. When it comes time to sit down and do your work, whether you're at home, on the road, or at the beach, technology and equipment are getting better and faster.

CELL PHONES

Complex pricing schemes and incompatible technologies can make it hard to find the right calling plan and handset.

There are now more than 164 million cell-phone subscribers, more than one per household, on average. A small but steadily growing number of people use a cell phone (a.k.a. a mobile phone) as their only phone. Phone manufacturers and wireless-service providers are promoting new generations of equipment that let users do much more than merely make phone calls.

Despite its popularity, wireless service has a reputation for problems: dead zones, where you can't get service; calls that inexplicably end in midconversation; inadequate capacity, so you can't put a call through when you want; hard-to-fathom calling plans; and errors in bills. Problems like those are why one-third of the cell-phone users we've surveyed say they're ready to switch carriers.

Switching is now much easier than ever, thanks to the government mandate on local number portability. However, keep in mind that the phones themselves aren't portable. If you switch carriers, expect to buy a new phone.

WHAT'S AVAILABLE

The cell phone itself is only part of what you need. You also have to sign up for service with a wireless provider and choose a calling plan. You can find phones in many outlets, including independent wireless retailers, electronics stores, and Web sites.

The providers. The major national companies are AT&T Wireless, Cingular, Nextel, Sprint PCS, T-Mobile, and Verizon Wireless. Cingular is acquiring AT&T Wireless and expects to operate under the Cingular brand eventually. (AT&T, the separate long-distance company, has announced plans to enter the wireless market under the AT&T Wireless name, but with service provided by Sprint.) There are also numerous local or regional providers.

You'll often find phones described as tri-mode, dual-band, or multinetwork. Those terms describe the ways a phone can connect to one or more wireless networks. Here are the specifics:

• Tri-mode phones can access digital in two frequency bands and older analog wireless networks.

• Dual-band phones can connect to a digital network, but in two different frequency bands.

• Multinetwork phones are compatible with more than one digital network, often in two frequency bands. Some can also access analog networks.

The calling plans. Most providers offer a range of plans based around a "bucket" of calling time minutes. The more minutes in the bucket, the more the plan costs you each month. However, the total number of minutes isn't the most important figure. Some of those minutes may be good anytime, others available only on nights and weekends; if you exceed the allotment of minutes, you'll be charged 35 to 50 cents per minute, depending on the plan. Cingular, alone among the major carriers, lets customers roll over unused minutes to the next month. Most plans require you to sign a one- or two-year contract and levy a hefty fee if you want to cancel before the contract expires.

Prepaid plans can be a good alternative if you're averse to a long-term contract. Many wireless providers, as well as Virgin Mobile, Liberty Wireless, Metro PCS, and Tracfone, offer prepaid calling. You pay in advance for airtime minutes, which typically last 45 to 60 days before they expire. GoPhone, a service from AT&T, works like the automated highway-toll services. You set up an account with no long-term contract and an opening balance posted to a credit card. Calls debit the account, which is automatically replenished every 30 days or when the balance drops below five dollars. You have 30 days to use the calling time you've bought or replenish the account.

The phones. Some are simple rectangles with a display window and keypad on the front. Others are curvaceous or have a flip-open cover to protect the keys. The major phone manufacturers are Audiovox, Kyocera, LG, Motorola, Nokia, Panasonic, Samsung, Sanyo, and Sony-Ericsson. Light weight is pretty much standard. All the newer phones can send and receive text messages up to 160 characters long to or from any other cell-phone user, and most phones now come with a full-color display. You'll also see phones that can play popular computer games, are integrated with a digital camera, offer wireless Internet access, or that are combined with a personal digital assistant (PDA).

IMPORTANT FEATURES

Some cell-phone makers and service providers are offering so-called **3G service,** which enhances the speed of data transfer. 3G services deliver reasonably fast, secure connections to the Internet and allow you to use the cell phone for playing and downloading audio and video, multimedia messages, and e-mail.

SHOP SMART

Bells and whistles can add lots of fun features—and complexity.

Among basic cell-phone features, look for a **display** that is readable in both low- and bright-light conditions. Be sure it's easy to see the battery-life and signal-strength indicators and the number you're dialing. The **keypad** should be clearly marked and easy to use. **Programmable speed dial** allows you to recall stored names and numbers by pressing one key. **Single-key last-number redial** is useful for dropped calls or when you're having trouble connecting. Most providers offer **caller ID, voice mail**, and **messaging.**

Instead of ringing, most handsets have a **vibrating alert** or a flashing light-emitting diode to let you know about an incoming call, useful when you're in a meeting or at the movies. Handiest is a single-key quiet mode, which switches from ring to vibrate with one key. An **any-key answer** feature lets you answer the phone by pressing any key rather than the Talk or Send key. Many folding phones answer the call when you open the mouthpiece flap.

Some cell-phone models include a **headset.** That capability is sometimes demanded by various local laws for drivers using cell phones. A standard headset connector (also known as a 2.5-mm connector) gives you the widest range of options if you want to buy a different headset.

Phones vary widely in keypad design and readability of screen displays, as well as in the ease of using the function menu or performing such basic tasks as one-button redial and storage of frequently called numbers for speed-dialing later. It's important to handle a phone in the store before you buy, to be sure its design and your fingers are well-matched.

HOW TO CHOOSE

Begin by selecting a service. Finding good service where you want it can be a challenge. The best way is to ask your friends and business associates—people who literally travel the same roads you do—how satisfied they are with their cell-phone service. In addition, keep in mind that Verizon Wireless has consistently come in first in CONSUMER REPORTS satisfaction surveys and so is worth considering first.

Choose a calling plan. You need to determine when and where you'll be using a cell phone most in order to select a plan that's right for you. As a rule, a national calling plan (which typically eliminates extra long-distance charges or fees for "roaming" away from your home calling area) is worth considering first, even if you don't travel often. With a regional plan, roaming charges can be stiff if you make calls too far away from your home.

If two or more family members use cell phones, consider a family plan that lets up to four people share a large monthly pool of minutes for a small additional monthly charge. If you aren't sure how many minutes of phone time you'll use in a month, choose a plan with more minutes than you think you will use. It's often better to let minutes go unused than to have to pay stiff per-minute charges if you exceed your allotment.

Select a phone. You can spend as little as $20 or as much as $600 on a cell phone. You need to begin your selection in the right price tier. Many of the phones we tested fall into the $100-to-$200 tier. Once you've settled on a price range, follow these steps:

- Look first at folding phones. They have two important advantages over other designs, we have found. One, the phone is small between calls but opens to a handy size when in use. Two, the design puts the microphone close to your mouth for better voice performance when talking.
- Be wary of fanciful designs and diminutive keypads. Phones that resemble small sculptures may prove difficult to use. Keys that are small, oddly shaped, or arranged in unusual patterns can be a challenge. Before you settle on a phone, try one at the store to get a feel for its handiness.
- Look for sensible features. These include volume controls on the side, an easy-to-mute ringer, and a standard headset connector.

Related CR Report: February 2004

COMPUTERS,
DESKTOP

Even the least-expensive desktop machines deliver impressive performance.

The desktop computer has become just another appliance you use every day. Replacement sales—not first-time purchases—now drive the computer market. Prices continue to drop. Fully loaded desktops selling for less than $1,000, a novelty a few years ago, are now common, even among established brands.

WHAT'S AVAILABLE

There are dozens of companies vying to put a new desktop in your home. Dell, Gateway, Hewlett-Packard (which merged with Compaq in 2002), IBM, and Sony all make machines that use Microsoft's dominant Windows operating system. Another contender, eMachines, recently merged with Gateway and has a series of budget-priced Windows models. Apple is the sole maker of Macintosh models. Small mail-order and store brands cater to budget-minded buyers. Price range: $400 to $3,000.

IMPORTANT FEATURES

The **processor** houses the "brains" of a computer. Its clock speed, measured in gigahertz (GHz), determines how fast the chip can process information. In general, the higher the clock speed, the faster the computer. But not always, since different families of chips attain different efficiencies. Manufacturers of Windows machines generally use 2.4- to 3.6-GHz processors with one of the following names: Intel's Pentium or Celeron, or AMD's Athlon or Duron. Celeron and Duron are lower-priced processors that are equal to higher-priced chips in many respects. Intel has begun to assign "processor numbers" to its chips, de-emphasizing clock speed. Apple's Macintosh machines use 1.25- to 2.5-GHz PowerPC G4 or G5 processors, which are manufactured by IBM. Apple and AMD have maintained that the system architecture of their chips allows them to be as fast as or faster than Pentiums with higher clock speeds.

All name-brand computers sold today have at least 256 megabytes (MB) of RAM, or **random access memory**, the memory the computer uses while in operation. **Video RAM,** also measured in megabytes, is secondary RAM essential for smooth video imaging and game play.

The **hard drive** is your computer's long-term data storage system. Given the disk-space requirements of today's multimedia games, digital photos, and video files, bigger is better. You'll find hard drives ranging in size from 40 to 300 gigabytes (GB).

A CD-ROM drive has been standard on most desktops for many years. Commonly supplied now is a CD-RW (CD-rewriteable) drive, also known as a "burner" that lets you create backup files or make music compilations on a compact disc. A **DVD-ROM** drive brings full-length movies or action-packed multimedia games with full-motion video to the desktop. It complements the CD-RW drive on midline and higher-end systems, allowing you to copy CDs directly between the two drives. A DVD drive will also play CDs and CD-ROMs. Combo drives combine CD-writing and DVD-playing in a single drive, saving space. The newest in this family is the **DVD-writer,** which lets you transfer home-video footage to a DVD disk. There are three competing, incompatible disk formats: DVD-RW, DVD+RW, and DVD-RAM. Some drives can write to two or all three formats, but all can write a disk that will play on standalone DVD players.

Fast disappearing is the **diskette** drive, where 3.5-inch diskettes are inserted, allowing you to read or store relatively small amounts of data. Apple Macintoshes and a growing number of PCs don't have a diskette drive built in. The traditional capacity of a 3.5-inch diskette is 1.4 MB. That's too small for many purposes today, so many people use a CD-RW as a large "diskette" drive to transport files. You can also get external drives or use a USB memory module that holds much more than a diskette. Many PCs now come with a digital camera memory-card reader that can also serve for file transfer.

The computer's **cathode ray tube** (CRT) or flat-panel **liquid crystal display** (LCD) monitor contains the screen and displays the images sent from the graphics board—internal circuitry that processes the images. Monitors come in sizes (measured diagonally) ranging from 15 to 21 inches and larger. Seventeen-inch monitors are the most common. Apple's eMac and iMac come with built-in monitors. LCD displays are now the most popular, taking less space and using less power than CRTs.

TECH TIP

Assess the technical support each computer maker offers. It can make all the difference if your machine goes on the blink.

The critical components of a desktop computer are usually housed in a case called a **tower**. A **minitower** is the typical configuration. More expensive machines have a **midtower**, which has extra room for upgrades. A **microtower** is a space-saving alternative that is usually less expensive. All-in-one computers, such as the Apple iMac, have no tower; everything but the keyboard and mouse is built into a small case that supports the monitor. Apple's Power Mac line of computers has a tower.

A **mouse**, a small device that fits in your hand and has a "tail" of wire that connects to the computer, moves the cursor (the pointer on the screen) via a rolling ball on its underside. Alternatives include a mouse that replaces the ball with a light sensor; a trackball, which is rolled with the fingers or palm in the direction you want the cursor to go; a pad, which lets you move the cursor by sliding a finger; a tablet, which uses a penlike stylus for input; and a joystick, used to play computer games.

All computers come with a **standard keyboard**, although you can also buy one separately. Many keyboards have **CD (or DVD) controls** to pause playback, change tracks, and so on. Many also have keys to facilitate getting online, starting a search, launching programs, or retrieving e-mail. There are also wireless keyboards that let you move about as you type.

Multimedia computers for home use feature a **high-fidelity sound system** that amplifies music from CDs or downloaded music files, synthesized music, game sounds, and DVD-movie soundtracks. **Speaker systems** with a subwoofer have deeper, more powerful bass. Surround-sound systems can turn a PC into a home theater. Some computers come with a microphone for recording, or one can be added.

PCs come with a modem to allow a dial-up Internet connection. For broadband Internet, there is usually a built-in Ethernet port.

Parallel and **serial ports** are the traditional connection sites for printers and scanners. **Universal Serial Bus** (USB) ports, seen on all new computers, are designed to replace parallel and serial ports. **FireWire** or **IEEE 1394 ports** are used to capture video from digital camcorders and other electronic equipment. An Ethernet or wireless **network** lets you link several computers in the household to share files, a printer, or a broadband connection. An **S-video output jack** lets you run a video cable from the computer to a television, which allows you to use the computer's DVD drive to view a movie on a TV instead of on the computer monitor.

HOW TO CHOOSE

First, decide whether to upgrade your current computer. Upgrading, rather than replacing it, may make sense if your additional needs are modest—a second hard drive, say, because you're running out of room for digital photos. Adding memory or a CD-burner is usually more cost-effective than buying a whole new machine. If your PC has become unreliable, your want list is more demanding, or if there's software you must run that your system is not up to, a new PC is the logical answer.

Consider a laptop. A desktop computer typically costs hundreds less and is easier to upgrade, expand, and repair. It usually offers better ergonomics, such as a more comfortable keyboard, better display, and enhanced audio. But a laptop merits consideration if portability and compactness are priorities.

Pick the right type of desktop. Most manufacturers offer several lines at different price points. Budget computers are the least expensive, yet they are suitable for routine work. Workhorse computers cost a few hundred dollars more, but are faster, more versatile, and upgradable. All-in-one models have most of the components in a single case. And media PCs include TV tuners and software that give them the functions of a DVR (digital video recorder, such as TiVo). They usually provide a remote control for easy operation.

Choose by brand. Our surveys have consistently shown notable differences in reliability and technical support among computer brands. And some brands are generally more expensive than others. Those factors could help you decide which of two similarly equipped computers is the better buy.

Choose between preconfigured and custom built. You can buy a PC off the shelf in a store or via the Web, configured with features and options the manufacturer pitches to average consumers. Or consider purchasing a desktop that you configure to order, either online or in a store. When you configure a computer to order online, onscreen menus typically show you all the options and let you see how a change in one option affects the overall price.

Related CR Reports: June 2004, September 2004

Reliability: page 329

COMPUTERS,
LAPTOP

A longtime companion at work, school, and on the road, the laptop is finally coming home.

Laptop sales outstrip those of desktops for the first time. It's not hard to understand why. Small screens and cramped keyboards have been replaced by bigger displays and more usable key layouts. Processors have caught up in speed, and an innovative new processor provides some real advantages. Fast CD and DVD recording drives are common, as are ample hard drives. And a growing interest in wireless computing plays to the laptop's main strength: its portability. A laptop is the only way to take full advantage of the growing availability of high-speed wireless Internet access at airports, schools, hotels, and even restaurants and coffee shops.

The Centrino technology that's central to Intel's newest laptop processors has wireless capability built in, and delivers considerably longer battery life than comparable chips. The thinnest laptops on the market are less than an inch thick and weigh just 2 to 5 pounds. To get these light, sleek models, however, you'll have to pay a premium and make a few sacrifices.

WHAT'S AVAILABLE

Dell, Gateway, Hewlett-Packard, Compaq (now owned by HP), IBM, Sony, and Toshiba are the leading Windows laptop brands. Macintosh laptops are made by Apple. Laptops can be grouped into several basic configurations:

Budget models. These have slower processors and lower screen quality than others, but are suitable for routine office work. Price range: $800 or less.

TECH TIP

With tablet-style models, you can write on a screen and it will translate into type.

Workhorse models. These have faster processors and built-in drives, so you don't need a lot of external attachments. They're not lightweight or battery-efficient enough for frequent travelers. Price range: $1,000 and up.

Slim-and-light models. These are for travelers. They can be less than an inch thick and weigh as little as two or three pounds. They generally require an external drive to read DVDs or burn CDs. Price range: $1,500 and up.

Tablet-style. These sit in your hands like a clipboard and have handwriting-recognition software. Price range: $1,800 and up. Toshiba makes one that converts to a "normal" laptop with a keyboard.

IMPORTANT FEATURES

A **diskette drive** is becoming a rarity in all computers. As an alternative, you can use a USB memory drive (about $20 and up), which fits on a keychain and holds as much data as numerous diskettes. Or you can save files on a writeable CD or a camera memory card.

Windows laptops generally have a 1.5- to 3.0-GHz **processor.** Pentium 4 processors have the higher speed ratings; the new Pentium M with Centrino technology has a slower rated speed but actually performs on a par with other processors. Macintosh Power PC processors are measured on a different basis altogether. In short, the different types of processors make direct speed comparisons difficult. It doesn't pay to try because any type of processor is likely to deliver all the speed you'll need.

Laptops come with a 30- to 100-gigabyte **hard drive** and 256 megabytes or more of **random access memory (RAM)** and can be upgraded to 512 MB or even 1 gigabyte.

Most of today's laptops use a rechargeable **lithium-ion battery.** In CONSUMER REPORTS tests, batteries provided two to five hours of continuous use when running office applications. (Laptops go into sleep mode when used intermittently, extending the time between charges.) You can extend battery life somewhat by dimming the display as you work and by removing PC cards when they aren't needed. Playing a DVD movie uses more battery power than usual, but any laptop should be able to play a movie through to the end.

A laptop's **keyboard** can be quite different from that of a desktop computer. The keys themselves may be full-sized (generally only lightweight models pare them down), but they may not feel as solid. Some laptops have extra buttons to expedite your access to e-mail or a Web browser or to control DVD playback. You can attach an external keyboard, which you may find easier to use.

A 14- to 15-inch **display**, measured diagonally, should suit most people. A few larger models have a 16- or 17-inch display. A resolution of 1,400x1,050 (SXGA+) pixels (picture elements) or more is better than 1,024x768 (XGA) for viewing the fine detail in photographs or video, but may shrink objects on the screen. You can use settings in Windows to make them larger.

Most laptops use a small **touch-sensitive pad** in place of a mouse—you drag your finger across the pad to move the cursor. You can also program the pad to respond to a "tap" as a "click," or to scroll as you sweep your index finger along the pad's right edge. An alternative pointing system uses a pencil-eraser-sized joystick in the middle of the keyboard. You can attach an external mouse if you prefer.

Laptops include at least one **PC-card slot** for expansion. You might add a **wireless network card** or a **digital-camera memory-card reader,** for example. Many laptops offer a connection for a **docking station,** a $100 or $200 base that makes it easy to connect an external monitor, keyboard, mouse, printer, or phone line. Most laptops let you attach these devices anyway, without the docking station. At least two **USB ports,** for easy hookup of, say, a printer, digital camera, or scanner, is standard. A **wired network (Ethernet) port** is common, as is a **FireWire port** for digital-video transfer. Many models have a standard or optional internal wireless-network adapter. An **infrared** port can be used to synchronize data wirelessly between the computer and a personal digital assistant (PDA).

Laptops typically come with far less software than desktop computers, although almost all are bundled with a basic home-office suite (such as Microsoft Works) and a personal-finance package. The small **speakers** built into laptops often sound tinny, with little bass. Headphones or external speakers deliver much better sound.

HOW TO CHOOSE

Decide if a laptop is right for you. If you're on a very tight budget and aren't cramped for space, a desktop computer may still be OK. Otherwise, consider a laptop.

Windows vs. Macintosh. Many people will choose Windows because it's what they've always used. Apple's hardware will suit you if you're interested in simple photo editing, music, video, and other multimedia applications. The Apple PowerBook and iBook are relatively expensive as laptops go, however.

Buy à la carte. Dell and Gateway pioneered the notion that every computer can be tailored to an individual buyer's needs, much like choosing the options for a car. This configure-to-order model is now common practice for laptops as well as desktops.

You can also purchase a preconfigured computer off the shelf. (You can do the same online if you opt for the default choices of equipment the manufacturer offers.) That's fine if you don't have very strict requirements for how a laptop is outfitted or if you want to take advantage of an attractive sale.

Configure-to-order menus show you all the options and let you see how a change in one affects the overall price. You may decide to use a less-expensive processor, for example, but spend more for wireless capability or better graphics. Configure-to-order will often give you choices you won't get if you buy off the shelf. And configure-to-order means less chance of overlooking important details.

Downplay the processor speed. Speed is no longer the be-all of personal computers. For years, processors have delivered all the speed most people need. That's still very much the case.

A Pentium 4 processor with a speed of 2.4 GHz and a Pentium M at 1.4 GHz earned the same speed score in our tests. The different types of chips now on the market make direct speed comparisons difficult.

Look closely at warranties and insurance. Get the longest manufacturer's warranty you can afford; many offer one or two years above the basic one-year warranty, for a price. If you intend to travel a lot, buy screen insurance from the manufacturer. If you take full advantage of the manufacturer's warranty and insurance, you won't need an extended warranty from the retailer.

Related CR Report: June 2004, September 2004

Reliability: page 329

MONITORS

Prices are dropping for larger CRT monitors, and for flat-panel LCD displays that free up space on your desktop.

Deciding whether to buy a flat-panel LCD or a standard, fairly fat CRT monitor comes down to this: Do you need more space on the surface of your desk or on the screen? If freeing up space on your desk is the priority, an LCD is the clear choice. But since LCDs are costly, you might still opt for a CRT. Despite price drops for both types, the typical 17-inch LCD costs more than $400, more than twice the cost of a CRT whose screen is an inch larger.

Desktop computers and monitors are often sold as a package. Still, some people buying a new desktop decide to hold on to their old monitor. Others choose to buy a new monitor for their existing computer.

WHAT'S AVAILABLE

Apple, Dell, eMachines (which merged with Gateway in 2004), Gateway, Hewlett-Packard (which merged with Compaq in 2002), IBM, and Sony all market their own brands of monitors for their computers. Other brands of monitors, such as CTX, Envision, Mitsubishi, NEC, Philips, Samsung, and ViewSonic are sold separately. Many brands are manufactured on an outsource basis.

CRT monitors. These typically range from 17 to 21 inches. To reduce glare, some CRTs have flattened, squared-off screens (not to be confused with flat-panel LCD screens). The nominal image size—the screen size touted in ads—is generally based on the diagonal measurement of the picture tube. The image you see, called the viewable image size (VIS), is usually an inch smaller. Thus a 17-inch CRT has a 16-inch VIS. As a result of a class-action lawsuit, ads must state a CRT's VIS as well as its nominal image, but you may have to squint at the fine print to find it.

Generally the bigger the screen, the more room a CRT takes up on your desk, with depth roughly matching nominal screen size. "Short-depth" models shave an inch or more off the depth.

A 17-inch monitor, the most frequent choice these days, has almost one-third more viewable area than the 15-inch version now vanishing from the market. The larger size is especially useful when you're using the Internet, playing video games, watching DVD movies, editing photos, or working in several windows.

If you regularly work with graphics or

sprawling spreadsheets, consider getting a 19-inch monitor. Its viewable area is one-fourth larger than a 17-inch model's. A short-depth 19-inch model doesn't take up much more desktop space than a standard 17-inch.

Aimed at graphics professionals, 21- and 22-inch models provide ample viewing area but they gobble up desktop space. Price range: $100 to $200 (17-inch); $175 to $300 (19-inch); $500 to $1,000 (21- to 22-inch).

Flat-panel LCD monitors. These began to outsell CRT monitors in 2003. Because these monitors have a liquid-crystal display rather than a TV-style picture tube, they take up much less desktop space than CRTs. They operate with analog or digital input, or both. Unlike a CRT, the nominal and the viewable image sizes of a flat-panel LCD are the same. Desktop models typically measure 15 inches diagonally and just a few inches deep, and weigh around 15 pounds, compared with 30 to 50 pounds for a CRT. LCDs with a screen 17 inches or larger are available, but they are still somewhat pricey. Wide-screen LCDs with a 17-inch VIS, specially designed for watching wide-format videos, are also available. These screens have an aspect ratio of 16:9, like those found on most digital TVs, and they're also fairly pricey.

Flat-panel displays deliver a very clear image, but they have some inherent quirks. Their range of color is a bit narrower than that of CRT monitors. And you have to view a flat-panel screen straight on; except for wide-screen models, the picture loses contrast as you move off-center. Fine lines may appear grainy. In analog mode you have to tweak the controls in order to get the best picture. Price range: $300 to $450 (15-inch); $300 and up (17- to 18-inch).

IMPORTANT FEATURES

A monitor's **resolution** refers to the number of picture elements, or pixels, that make up an image. More pixels mean finer detail. Most monitors can display at several resolutions, generally ranging from 640x480 to 1,600x1,200, depending on the monitor and the graphics card. An LCD usually displays a sharper image than a CRT of comparable size when both are viewed at identical resolutions. But that's only if the LCD is set to its "native" resolution—1,024x768 pixels for a 15-inch screen; 1,280x1,024 or 1,400x1,050 for a 17-, 18-, or 19-inch model. On both types of monitor, the higher the resolution, the smaller the text and images, so more content fits on the screen. Bigger CRT screens can handle higher resolutions and display more information.

TECH TIP

LCD monitors use less power than the larger CR monitors and quality seems to be just as good.

Dot pitch, measured in millimeters, refers to the spacing between a CRT's pixels. All else being equal, a smaller dot pitch produces a more detailed image, though that's no guarantee of an excellent picture. In general, avoid models with a dot pitch higher than 0.28 mm.

A CRT requires a high **refresh rate** (the number of times per second the image is redrawn on the screen) to avoid annoying image flicker. In general, you'll be more comfortable with a 17-inch monitor with a refresh rate of at least 75 hertz (Hz) at the resolution you want. For a 19-inch monitor, you may need an 85-Hz rate to avoid eyestrain, especially at higher resolutions. While the refresh rate of a flat panel display is 60 or 75 Hz, its native resolution is 1,024x768 unless otherwise specified. Refresh rate isn't an issue with flat-panel displays.

Monitors have controls for **brightness** and **contrast.** Most of them also have controls for **color balance** (usually called color temperature), **distortion,** and such. Buttons activate onscreen controls and menus.

Bigger CRTs use a considerable amount of juice: about 80 watts for a typical 19-inch model, between 65 to 70 watts for a 17-inch model, and about 20 watts for a 15-inch flat-panel LCD, for example. Most monitors have a **sleep mode** that uses less than 3 watts when the computer is on but not in use.

Some monitors include a **microphone,** integrated or separate **speakers,** or **composite-video inputs** for viewing the output of a VCR or camcorder.

Plug-and-play capability makes it relatively simple to add a new monitor to an existing computer.

HOW TO CHOOSE

Decide between LCD and CRT monitors. If your computer's monitor is hogging the top of your desk, you can reclaim much of that space by replacing it with an LCD. But doing so will cost you about $200 to $300 more than if you bought a new CRT monitor. And LCD screens have an inherent shortcoming: The image appears to fade as you move left, right, up, or down. However, most LCD monitors in our recent tests had a wider viewing angle than we've seen in the past. If space isn't an issue but budget is, a CRT monitor is a good choice.

Settle on size. For most people, a 15-inch LCD monitor or a 17-inch CRT is big enough. Larger monitors are best suited for people who need to show photo enlargements or who regularly display multiple windows on the screen.

Consider helpful features. A monitor you can raise or lower can compensate for a desk that's too high or low. It's a feature found on some LCD monitors, but not on CRTs because they're so heavy. Some monitors can be rotated 90 degrees, from a landscape to portrait orientation, with the image automatically adjusting itself. That can be handy for viewing photos and Web pages.

Look for a long warranty. Many monitors, both LCDs and CRTs, come with a three-year warranty on parts and labor. A warranty that long is worth looking for, especially when purchasing a more expensive model.

Related CR Report: June 2004

PDAS

Besides serving as an address book, calendar, and to-do list, many personal digital assistants offer multimedia functions.

PDAs can store thousands of phone numbers, appointments, tasks, and notes. All models can exchange, or synchronize, information with a personal computer. To do this, you connect the PDA to your computer via a cradle or cable. For models that run on rechargeable batteries, the cradle doubles as a charger. Infrared and other wireless technologies let you synchronize your PDA with a computer without the use of wires or a cradle.

Most PDAs can be made to work with both Windows and Macintosh computers, but Macs usually require third-party software. PDAs with Wi-Fi (wireless) capability can access the Internet. Those without can as well with the addition of a separately purchased modem. Some PDAs can record your voice, play videos, display digital photos, or hold maps, city guides, or a novel.

WHAT'S AVAILABLE

Most PDAs on the market are the familiar tablet-with-stylus types that feature a squarish display screen, a design pioneered by Palm Inc. (now called PalmOne). Today the main choices are models that use the Palm operating system (OS)—mostly PalmOne models—and Pocket PC devices from companies such as Dell, Hewlett-Packard, and Toshiba. The latter use a stripped-down version of Microsoft Windows. A few PDAs use a proprietary operating system. Kyocera, Nokia, Samsung, and Sony Ericsson offer units that combine a cell phone and a PDA.

Palm OS systems. Equipped with software to link with Windows and (for PalmOne-brand units) Macintosh computers, PalmOne units and their clones have a simple user interface. You use a stylus to enter data on the units by tapping an onscreen keyboard or writing in a shorthand known as Graffiti. Or you can download data from your computer. Most Palm OS-based PDAs can synchronize with a variety of desktop e-mail programs, such as Outlook Express and Eudora. (PalmOne models with VersaMail software are good at handling e-mails with attachments.) And all include a basic personal-information-management (PIM) application. Palm OS units are easy to use, although navigation between different programs is cumbersome because of the operating system's "single-tasking" nature.

Models with a backlit monochrome display (now scarce) are easy to read under normal lighting conditions and are very easy on batteries. Units that have a color display use a rechargeable lithium-ion battery; some batteries must be recharged after just a few hours of continuous use. Most models make it difficult or impossible to replace the battery yourself. And beyond the warranty period, you can't be sure the manufacturer will do it for you.

The latest Palm OS models typically have expansion slots that let you add memory or attach separately purchased accessories. All Palm OS-based PDAs can be enhanced by adding third-party software applications—the more free memory that a model comes with, the more software it can accommodate. There is a large body of Palm OS-compatible freeware, shareware, and commercial software available for download at such sites as *www.palmgear.com.* Many Palm models come with "Documents to Go"—word-processing and spreadsheet software similar to that used in Pocket PCs but more versatile. Price range: about $100 to $800.

Pocket PC systems. These resemble Palm OS-based models but are more like miniature computers. They have a processor with extra horsepower and come with familiar applications such as a word processor and a spreadsheet. Included is a scaled-down version of Internet Explorer, plus voice-recording and perhaps some financial functions. The included e-mail program handles Word and Excel attachments easily. Also standard is an application that plays MP3 music files, as well as Microsoft Reader, an eBook application.

TECH TIP

Before you buy, assess a PDA's expansion capabilities and wireless connectivity.

As you might expect, all the application software included in a Pocket PC integrates well with the Windows computer environment. You need to purchase third-party software to use a Mac. And you'll need Microsoft Office programs such as Word, Excel, and Outlook on your computer to exchange data with a PDA. Pocket PCs have a color display and rechargeable lithium-ion batteries. Unlike most Palm OS-based PDAs, replacing the battery of most Pocket PCs is usually straightforward. Price range: $200 to $700.

IMPORTANT FEATURES

Whichever operating system your PDA uses, you may need to install programs on your computer to enable the PDA to synchronize with it. This software lets you swap data with leading PIM programs such as Lotus Organizer or Microsoft Outlook.

Most PDAs have the tools for basic tasks: a **calendar** to keep track of your appointments, **contact/address software** for addresses and phone numbers, **tasks/to-do lists** for reminders and keeping track of errands, and a calculator. A **notes/memo function** lets you make quick notes to yourself. Other capabilities include **word-processing, spreadsheet,** and **e-mail functions.** A **voice recorder,** which uses a built-in microphone and speaker, works like a tape recorder. **MP3 playback** lets you listen to digital-music files stored in that format, and a **picture viewer** lets you look at **digital photos.** A few models also include a built-in **digital camera** and **keyboard.**

A PDA's **processor** is the system's brain. In general, the higher the processing speed of this chip, the faster the PDA will execute tasks—and the more expensive the PDA will be. But higher-speed processors may require more battery power and thus deplete batteries more quickly. Processing speeds are 16 to 400 megahertz (MHz), and models typically have 8 to 64 megabytes (MB) of user memory. Even the smallest amount in that range should be more than enough for most people.

Nearly every PDA offers an **expansion slot** for some form of removable memory card: CompactFlash, MultiMediaCard (slots also accept SecureDigital cards), or Memory Stick. Models with two expansion slots can accommodate a **peripheral device,** such as a **Wi-Fi wireless networking card,** as well as removable memory. If you plan to transfer photos from a digital camera to your PDA, make sure the two devices use the same type of card.

Some PDAs offer **wireless connectivity.** Models with a capability known as **Bluetooth** can connect wirelessly over short distances to a properly equipped computer or peripheral such as a printer or modem. Models with Wi-Fi can connect over medium distances to a Wi-Fi-enabled home network or to the Internet at "hotspots" in certain airports, coffee shops, and hotels. A PDA combined with a **cell phone** can make voice calls or directly connect to the Internet via a wireless Internet service provider. It's possible for a single PDA to have more than one of these three types of wireless connectivity.

HOW TO CHOOSE

Consider your ties to a computer. Pocket PCs provide a Windows-like interface that allows simple PC-to-PDA file transfer with drag-and-drop capability. They're also better than Palm OS models for setting up a Wi-Fi (wireless) e-mail connection. Most have replaceable batteries, along with accessible flash memory to which you can back up data.

Palm OS models run a wider range of third-party software applications than do Pocket PCs. For the basics, they're still easier to use.

While all PDAs can sync with Macintoshes, only PalmOne models do so out of the box. Sony units need software such as The Missing Sync (available at *www.markspace.com*). That program and PocketMac (*www.pocketmac.net*) work for Pocket PCs. Both are priced under $50.

Palm OS models: Basic features or innovative design? Differences exist between

PalmOne's and Sony's Palm OS models. Units from PalmOne have more versatile e-mail software, when included, and their straightforward design makes them easier to operate than Sony's.

Sony models offer a wider range of designs for specific uses, such as one-handed operation or the ability to type while the PDA sits on a desktop.

Small size vs. extra features. As a rule, a model with a larger display or physical keyboard won't be the lightest or smallest. A PDA with two slots for memory and peripherals is more expandable, but will tend to be larger.

Related CR Report: July 2004

Ratings: page 280

PRINTERS

New, inexpensive inkjets print color superbly, and they do it faster than ever. Laser printers excel at printing black-and-white text.

Inkjet printers are now the standard for home-computer output. They do an excellent job with color—turning out color photos nearly indistinguishable from photographic prints, along with banners, stickers, transparencies, T-shirt transfers, and greeting cards. Many produce excellent black-and-white text. With some very good models going for less than $200, the vast majority of printers sold for home use are inkjets.

Laser printers still have their place in home offices. If you print reams of black-and-white text documents, you probably need the speed and low per-copy cost of a laser printer.

Printers use a computer's microprocessor and memory to process data. The latest models are so fast partly because computers themselves have become more powerful and contain much more memory than before. Unlike the computers they serve, most home printers can't be upgraded—except for adding memory to laser printers. Most people usually get faster or more detailed output by buying a new printer.

WHAT'S AVAILABLE

The printer market is dominated by a handful of well-established brands. Hewlett-Packard is the market leader. Other brands include Brother, Canon, Dell, Epson, Lexmark, and Samsung.

The type of computer a printer can serve depends on its ports. A Universal Serial Bus (USB) port lets a printer connect to Windows or Macintosh computers. Some models have a parallel port, which lets the printer work with older Windows computers. All these printers lack a serial port, which means they won't work with older Macs.

Inkjet printers. Inkjets use droplets of ink to form letters, graphics, and photos. Some printers have one cartridge that holds the cyan (greenish-blue), magenta, and yellow inks, and a second cartridge for the black ink. Others have an individual cartridge for each ink. For photos, many inkjets also have additional cartridges that contain lighter shades of cyan and magenta inks.

Most inkjets print at 2½ to 9 pages per minute (ppm) for black-and-white text but are much slower for color photos, taking 5 to 22 minutes to print a single 8x10. The cost of printing a black-and-white page with an inkjet varies considerably from model to model—ranging from 3 to 9 cents. The cost of printing a color photo can range from 80 cents to $1.20. Price range: $50 to $700.

Laser printers. These work much like

plain-paper copiers, forming images by transferring toner (powdered ink) to paper passing over an electrically charged drum. The process yields sharp black-and-white text and graphics. Laser printers usually outrun inkjets, cranking out black-and-white text at a rate of 10 to 17 ppm. Black-and-white laser printers generally cost about as much as high-end inkjets, but they're cheaper to operate. Color laser printers are also available. Toner cartridges, about $100, often contain both the toner and the drum and can print thousands of black-and-white pages for a per-page cost of 2 to 4 cents. Price range: $160 to $1,000 (black-and-white); $700 and up (color).

IMPORTANT FEATURES

Printers differ in the fineness of detail they can produce. **Resolution,** expressed in dots per inch (dpi), is often touted as the main measure of print quality. But other factors, such as the way dot patterns are formed by software instructions from the printer driver, count, too. At their default settings—where they're usually expected to run—inkjets currently on the market typically have a resolution of 600x600 dpi. For color photos the dpi can be increased. Some printers go up to 5,760x1,440 dpi. Laser printers for home use typically offer 600 or 1,200 dpi. Printing color inkjet photos on special paper at a higher dpi setting can produce smoother shading of colors but can slow printing significantly.

TECH TIP

For printing color photos, consider the price of supplies like ink when choosing a printer.

Most inkjet printers have an **ink monitor** to warn when you're running low. Generic ink cartridges and refill kits can cut costs, but think twice about using them. A printer's warranty might not cover repairs if an off-brand cartridge damages the machine.

For **double-sided printing,** you can have printers print the odd-numbered pages of a document first, then flip those pages over to print the even-numbered pages on a second pass through the printer. A few printers can automatically print on both sides, but doing so slows down printing.

HOW TO CHOOSE

Be skeptical about advertised speeds. Print speed varies depending on what you're printing and at what quality, but the speeds you see in ads are generally higher than you're likely to achieve in normal use. You can't reliably compare speeds for different brands because each company uses its own methods to measure speed. We run the same tests on all models, printing text pages and photos that are similar to what you might print. As a result, our speeds can be compared across brands.

Don't get hung up on resolution. A printer's resolution, expressed in dots per inch, is another potential source of confusion. All things being equal, the more ink dots a printer puts on the paper, the more detailed the image. But dot size, shape, and placement also affect quality, so don't base a decision solely on resolution.

Consider supply costs as well as a printer's price. High ink costs can make a bargain-priced printer a bad deal in the long run. Shop around for the best ink prices but steer clear of off-brand inks; of those we tested, we found brand-name cartridges to be better overall.

Glossy photo paper costs about 25 to 75 cents a sheet, so use plain paper for works in progress and save the good stuff for the final results. We've gotten the best results using the recommended brand of paper. You may be tempted to buy a cheaper brand, but bear in mind that lower-grade paper can reduce photo quality.

Decide whether you want to print photos without using a computer. Printing without a computer saves you an extra step and a little time. Features such as memory-card support, a cable hookup to the camera, or a wireless interface are generally found on midpriced and high-priced models, so consider whether you want to pay a premium for the convenience.

Weigh convenience features. Most printers make borderless prints like those from a photo developer. This matters most if you're printing to the full size of the paper, as you might with 4x6-inch sheets. Otherwise you can trim the edges.

If you plan to use 4x6-inch paper regularly, look for a printer with a 4x6-inch tray, which makes it easier to feed paper of this size. With smaller sheets, though, the cost per photo may be higher than ganging up a few images on 8½x11-inch paper.

With some models, if you want to use the photo inks to get the best picture quality, you have to remove the black ink cartridge and replace it with the photo-ink cartridge. Then you have to replace the black for text or graphics. This can get tedious. Models that hold all the ink tanks simultaneously eliminate that hassle.

Consider connections. Printers with USB 2.0 ports are showing up; however, they don't enable much faster print speeds than plain USB. All new computers and printers have either USB or USB 2.0 ports, both of which are compatible. Computers more than five years old may have only a parallel port.

Consider an all-in-one printer. Printers that also scan and copy can save space compared with having a separate unit for each.

Most multifunctions are larger than regular printers and require more vertical clearance to lift the lid. But be prepared for trade-offs. In our most recent tests, photo quality from multifunction printers was generally a bit lower than for the regular models. The included scanners, which have resolution ranging from 600 to 2,400 dpi, delivered quality similar to that of the stand-alone scanners in our last tests but were slower. If you decide an all-in-one is right for you, check to see whether it can make copies when the computer is off.

Related CR Reports: May 2004, September 2004

SCANNERS

A scanner is a simple, cheap way to digitize images for printing, editing on your computer, or sending via e-mail.

You don't need a digital camera to take advantage of the computer's ability to edit photos. Images captured on film can be digitized by a photo processor and delivered to you on a CD or via the Web. But if you do more than a modest amount of film photography, having a processor digitize your photos—at $5 to $10 per roll—can quickly create a hefty expense. You're also paying for digitizing outtakes as well as winners. A more cost-effective way to digitize selected photographs is with a scanner, which can capture the image of nearly anything placed on its glass surface—even those old photos you've tucked away in a family album or a shoebox.

Most scanners work basically the same way. As with photocopiers, a bar housing a light source and an array of sensors passes beneath a plate of glass on which the document lies facedown. (In the case of a sheet-fed model, the document passes over the scanner.) The scanner transmits data from the sensor to your computer, typically via a USB port. Driver software, working in concert with the hardware, allows you to scan at certain settings. Once the image is in the computer, software bundled with the scanner (or purchased separately) lets you crop, resize, or otherwise edit the image to suit your needs. From there, you can print it, attach it to e-mail, or post it on the Web.

WHAT'S AVAILABLE

A number of scanners come from companies, including Microtek and Visioneer, that made their name in scanning technology. Other brands include computer makers and photo specialists such as Canon, Epson, Hewlett-Packard, and Nikon.

Which type of scanner you should consider—flatbed, sheet-fed, or film—depends largely on how you will use it. If you're short on space, consider a multifunction device.

Flatbed scanners. More than 90 percent of the scanners on the market are flatbeds. They work well for text, graphics, photos, and anything else that is flat, including a kindergartner's latest drawing. Flatbeds include optical-character-recognition (OCR) software, which converts words on a printed page into a word-processing file in your computer. They also include basic image-editing software. Some stores may throw in a flatbed scanner for free, or for a few dollars extra, when you purchase a desktop computer.

TECH TIP

If you scan at a higher dpi, it will take longer and use more disk space.

A key specification for a scanner is its maximum optical resolution, measured in dots per inch (dpi). You'll pay more for greater resolution. Price range: less than $100 for 600x1,200 dpi; $100 to $500 for models with greater resolution.

Sheet-fed models. Sheet-fed models can automatically scan a stack of loose pages, but they sometimes damage pages that pass through their innards. And they can't scan anything much thicker than a sheet of paper (meaning an old photo might be too thick). This type of scanner is often the one that comes as part of a multifunction device that can also print, send, and receive faxes. An increasing percentage of multifunction devices, however, include a flatbed scanner. Sheet-fed scanners also use OCR software. Price range: $150 to $600.

Film scanners. Serious photographers may want a film-only scanner that scans directly from an original slide (transparency) or negative. These offer a higher maximum resolution than you get from an ordinary flatbed or sheet-fed model. Some can accept small prints as well. Price range: $400 to $800.

IMPORTANT FEATURES

While the quality of images a scanner produces depends in part on the software included with it, there are several hardware features to consider.

You start scanning by running **driver software** that comes with the scanner or by pressing a preprogrammed button. Models with buttons automate routine tasks to let you operate your scanner as you would other office equipment. On some models you can customize the functions of the buttons. Any of these tasks can also be performed through the scanner's software without using buttons. A **copy/print button** initiates a scan and sends a command to print the results on your printer, effectively making the two devices act as a copier. Other button functions found on some models include **scan to a file, scan to a fax modem, scan to e-**

mail, scan to Web, scan to OCR, cancel scan, power save, start scanner software, and **power on/off.**

You can also start the driver software from within an application, such as a word processor, that adheres to an industry standard known as TWAIN. A scanner's driver software allows you to **preview** a scan onscreen and crop it or adjust **contrast** and **brightness.** Once you're satisfied with the edited image, you can perform a final scan and pass the image to a running program or save it on your computer. You can make more extensive changes to an image with specialized **image-editing software.** And to scan text from a book or letter into a word-processing file in your computer, you run **OCR software.**

Many documents combine text with graphic elements, such as photographs and drawings. A handy software feature that's found on many scanners, called **multiple-scan mode,** lets you break down such hybrids into different sections that can be processed separately in a single scan. You can designate, for example, that the sections of a magazine article that are pure text go to the OCR software independently of the article's graphic elements. Other scanners would require a separate scan for each section of the document.

Some flatbed models come with **film adapters** designed to scan film or slides, but if you need to scan from film or slides often, you're better off getting a separate film scanner.

HOW TO CHOOSE

Settle on a resolution. Scanners range in maximum resolution from 600 dots per inch to 4,800 dpi. Just because you can scan at high resolutions, though, doesn't mean you should. The higher the dpi, the slower the scan, and the more disk space the resulting file will need. In our tests, an 8x10-inch color photo scanned at 150 dpi took 8 seconds and made a 5.7-megabyte file; at 600 dpi, the scan took 16 seconds and created a 92MB file. To save disk space you can off-load large, high-resolution images to a CD or DVD, or delete them after printing.

But low-resolution scans may be all you need. For images to be viewed only onscreen, 75 dpi is enough. For most photos, graphics, or text, 150 to 300 dpi is fine. If you want to double an image's size, 600 dpi will yield good results. To enlarge it more, at least 1,200 dpi is preferable.

Consider quality and speed. Quality is a scanner's most critical attribute. All but two of the models we recently tested produced very good or excellent images. For frequent use, pay special attention to speed. The time to scan an 8x10-inch photo at 300 dpi ranged from less than 10 seconds to 40 seconds in our tests.

Will you need to scan negatives or slides? Scanning slides or negatives is more challenging than working with prints or hard copy. That's because film contains more detail than a print, and you might want to perform remedial or restorative work because of scratches, color fading, or other imperfections. Flatbed scanners with adapters can do a decent job for occasional use, but specialized film scanners are better if you'll be scanning slides often or want top quality. Most have resolutions above 2,400 dpi, enabling them to render fine detail.

Don't worry about the software. All the scanners from our recent test are fairly easy to use. Most have image-editing programs—either proprietary software or third-party programs such as Adobe Photoshop Elements, which usually sell for as much as many scanners. In general, image-editing software has gotten smarter, with functions such as photo retouching and automatic color balancing.

Scanners typically come with OCR software for scanning text into word-processing software. Some have software for making digital photo albums or other projects.

Take specs skeptically. If you'll be scanning prints, don't get hung up on color-bit depth, which refers to how many colors a scanner can reproduce. All flatbed scanners have at least 24-bit color—fine for prints. For slides, look for 42-bit or more. Interpolated resolution matters for line art; for photos, optical resolution counts, and 600 dpi will generally do. The lower figure of a spec such as 600x1200 dpi is the one to consider.

Related CR Report: May 2004

TELEPHONES

Corded phones

Today's basic phone is sleeker and more versatile than its boxy predecessor.

For $10 you can now buy a corded phone with such features as volume control and memory-dialing for 10 or more numbers. For $50 or more you get a console with speakerphone or two-line capability, sometimes both.

Every home should have at least one corded phone, if only for emergencies. In an emergency you can't always rely on a cell phone because circuits fill up quickly or because the signal may not reach your house. A cordless phone may not work if you lose electrical power. Because a corded phone draws its power from the phone system, it will operate even if you lose household AC power.

WHAT'S AVAILABLE

AT&T (currently made by VTech) and GE are the dominant brands. When shopping, you'll find these types:

Console models. These are updated versions of the traditional Bell desk phone. Price range: $15 to more than $100.

Trim-style models. These spacesavers have push buttons on the handset, and the base is about half as wide as a console model's. But they can be hard to use when you need to listen and punch buttons at the same time to navigate an unfamiliar voicemail or automated banking menu. Price range: $10 to $30.

Phones with answerers. Combo units can sometimes be less expensive than buying a phone and an answerer separately. Price range: $50 to $150.

IMPORTANT FEATURES

Corded phones tend to be less feature-laden than cordless ones. It's practically standard for any phone to have **handset volume control, last-number redial**, and **memory dialing.** Features such as a **speakerphone, two-line capability,** or **caller ID** add to the price.

HOW TO CHOOSE

Most corded phones should perform quite capably, conveying voices intelligibly under normal conditions. The variations in sound quality that we have found in the past are likely to matter only in very noisy environments.

Since adequate performance is pretty much a given, your main considerations should be features and price. Before you buy, make sure the handset is comfortable in your hand and to your ear. Look for a good-sized, clearly labeled keypad, especially if your eyesight isn't good.

Cordless phones

Two noteworthy trends: Phones use higher frequency bands, and a growing number can handle multiple handsets from a single base.

It's easier than ever to have a phone where you want one. The newest breed of cordless phones lets you put a handset in any room in the house, even if no phone jack is nearby.

However, manufacturers still offer a bewildering array of phones: inexpensive models that offer the basics; multihandset, full-featured phones with a built-in answering machine; single-line and two-line phones; digital and analog phones, and different frequency bands. In many instances, a phone will have a phone-answerer sibling. Many phone-answerers come in a phone-only version. If you have a cordless phone that's several years old, it's probably a 900-MHz phone. Newer phones use higher frequencies, namely 2.4 or 5.8 GHz. They aren't necessarily better than the older ones, but they may provide more calling security and a wider array of useful capabilities and features.

WHAT'S AVAILABLE

AT&T, Bell South, GE, Panasonic, Uniden, and VTech account for more than 70 percent of the market. VTech owns the AT&T Consumer Products Division and now makes phones under the AT&T brand as well as its own name.

MESSAGE CENTERS

Answering machines

Digital answering machines come as stand-alone devices or as part of a phone/answerer combo unit. The main advantage of a combo unit—less clutter—has to be weighed against the loss of one part of the combo if the other goes bad. Answerers usually have standard features and capabilities such as a selectable number of rings and a toll-saver, answerer on/off control, call screening, remote access from a touch-tone phone, and a variety of ways to navigate through your messages. Most have a message day/time stamp, can delete all messages or just individual ones, allow you to adjust the speaker volume, and can retain messages and the greeting after a momentary power outage.

Other answerer features you may want to consider are the number of mailboxes, advanced playback controls, remote handset access, conversation recording, a message counter display that indicates the number of messages received, and a visual indicator or audible message alert that lets you know when you have new messages.

In Consumer Reports tests, most answerers delivered very good voice quality for recorded messages and good quality for the greeting. Phones that let you record your greeting through the handset (i.e., using the remote handset access) usually scored better. Some let you listen to your greeting through the handset, as opposed to listening though the base speaker; that gives you a better indication of how the greeting will sound to the calling party.

Price range: $20 to $80 (stand-alone units); $30 to $240 (combos)

The current trends include phones that support two or more handsets with one base, less expensive 2.4- and 5.8-GHz analog phones, and full-featured 2.4- and 5.8-GHz digital phones. Some of the multiple-handset-capable phones now include an additional handset with a charging cradle. About a third of the cordless phones sold include a digital answering machine.

A main distinction among cordless phones is they way they transmit their signals. Here are some terms that you may see while shopping and what they mean for you:

Analog. These phones are the least expensive type available now. They tend to have better voice quality and enough range to let you chat anywhere in your house and yard, or even a little beyond. They are also unlikely to cause interference to other wireless products. But analog transmission isn't very secure; anyone with an RF scanner or comparable wireless device might be able to listen in. Analog phones are also more likely than digital phones to suffer occasional static and RF interference from other wireless products. Price range: $15 to $100.

Digital. These offer about the same range as analog phones, but with better security and less susceptibility to RF interference. And, like analogs, they are unlikely to cause interference to other wireless products. Price range: $50 to $130.

Digital spread spectrum (DSS). A DSS phone distributes a call across a number of frequencies, providing an added measure of security and more immunity from RF interference. The range may be slightly better than that of analog or digital phones. Note that some DSS phones—usually the 2.4-GHz or the multiple-handset-capable phones with handset-to-handset talk capabilities—use such a wide swath of the spectrum even in standby mode that they may interfere with baby monitors and other wireless products operating in the same frequency band. Price range: $75 to $225 (for multiple handset systems).

Frequency. Cordless phones use one or two of the three available frequency bands:

• 900-MHz. Some manufacturers make inexpensive, 900-MHz phones, usually analog. They are fine for many households, and still account for about one-quarter of the market.

• 2.4-GHz. The band most phones now use. Unfortunately, many other wireless products—baby monitors, wireless computer networks, home security monitors, wireless speakers, microwaves ovens—use the same band. A 2.4-GHz analog phone is inherently susceptible to RF interference from other wireless devices, and a 2.4-GHz DSS phone may cause interference in other products.

• 5.8-GHz. The band that newer phones use. Its main advantage: less chance of RF interference because few other products currently use this band.

Some phones are dual-band, but that only means they transmit between base and handset in one band and receive in another; you can't switch to or choose one band or another.

IMPORTANT FEATURES

Standard features on most cordless phones include **handset earpiece volume control, handset ringer, last-number redial,** a **pager** to locate the handset, a **flash button** to answer call waiting, and a **low-battery indicator.**

Some phones let you support two or more handsets with just one base without the need for extra phone jacks. Additional handsets including the charging cradle are usually sold separately, although more phones are being bundled with an additional handset and charging cradle.

An **LCD screen,** found on many handsets and on some bases, can display a personal phone directory and useful information such as the name and/or number dialed, caller ID, battery strength, or how long you've been connected. **Caller ID** displays the name and number of a caller and the date and time of the call if you use your phone company's caller ID service. If you have caller ID with call waiting, the phone will display data on a second caller when you're already on the phone.

A phone that **supports two lines** can receive calls for two phone numbers—useful if you have, say, a business line and a personal line that you'd like to use from a single phone. Some of the phones have two ringers, each with a distinctive pitch to let you know which line is ringing. The two-line feature also facilitates conferencing two callers in three-way connections. Some two-line phones have an **auxiliary jack data port** to plug in a fax, modem, or other phone device.

A **speakerphone** offers a hands-free way to converse or wait on hold and lets others chime in as well. A base speakerphone lets you answer a call without the handset; a handset speakerphone lets you chat hands-free anywhere in the house as long as you stay within a few feet of the handset.

A **base keypad** supplements the keypad on the handset. It's handy for navigating menu-driven systems, since you don't have to take the phone away from your ear to punch the keys. Some phones have a **lighted keypad** that either glows in the dark or lights up when you press a key, or when the phone rings. This makes the phone easier to use in low-light conditions. All phones have a handset **ringer,** and many phones have a base ringer. Some let you turn them on or off, adjust the volume, or change the auditory tone.

Many cordless phones have a **headset jack** on the handset and include a belt clip for carrying the phone. This allows hands-free conversation anywhere in the house. Some phones have a headset jack on the base, which allows hands-free conversation without any drain on the handset battery. Headsets are usually sold separately for about $20.

Other convenient features include **auto talk,** which lets you lift the handset off the base for an incoming call and start talking without having to press a button, and **any key answer.**

Some phones provide a **battery holder for battery backup**—a compartment in the base to charge a spare handset battery pack or to hold alkaline batteries for base-power backup, either of which can enable the phone to work if you lose household AC power. Still, it's wise to keep a corded phone somewhere in your home.

Some multiple-handset-capable phones allow conversation between handsets in an intercom mode and facilitate **conferencing** handsets with an outside party. In intercom mode, the handsets have to be within range of the base for handset-to-handset use. Others also allow direct communication between handsets, so you can take them with you to use like walkie-talkies. Some phones can register up to eight handsets, for instance, but that doesn't mean you can use all eight at once. You might be able to use two for handset-to-handset intercom, while two others conference with an outside party.

HOW TO CHOOSE

Decide how much hardware you need. The basic options are a stand-alone phone, a phone with a built-in answerer, or a phone that supports multiple handsets from one base. A stand-alone phone is best suited for small families or people in a small apartment, with little need for more than one phone. The built-in answerer, a common choice, adds a big measure of convenience. A multiple-handset phone is good for active families that need phones throughout the house; this type of phone lets you put handsets in a room that doesn't have a phone jack.

Select the technology and frequency band. A 900-MHz phone should suit most users, but that type may be hard to find because 2.4- and 5.8-GHz models dominate. You're likely to find the widest range of models and prices with 2.4-GHz phones. But if you want to minimize problems of interference with other wireless products, look to a 5.8-GHz or 900-MHz phone. Analog phones, apt to be less expensive than digital, are fine for many people. But if privacy is important, choose a DSS or digital phone.

To be sure you're actually getting a DSS or digital phone for its voice-transmission security, check the packaging carefully. Look for wording such as "digital phone" or "phone with voice scrambling." Phrases such as "phone with digital security code," "phone with all-digital answerer," or "spread spectrum technology" (not digital spread spectrum) all denote phones that are less secure.

Phones that use dual-band transmission may indicate the higher frequency in a larger print on the packaging. If you want a true 2.4- or 5.8-GHz phone, check the fine print. If only the frequency is shown on the package, it's probably analog.

Settle on the features you want. You can typically expect caller ID, a headset jack, and a base that can be wall-mounted. But the features don't end there for both stand-alone phones and phone-answerers. Check the box or ask to see an instruction manual to be sure you're getting the capabilities and features that matter to you. As a rule, the more feature-laden the phone, the higher its price.

Performance variations. CONSUMER REPORTS tests show that most new cordless phones have very good overall voice quality. Some are excellent, approaching the voice quality of the best corded phones. In our latest tests, most fully charged nickel-cadmium (NiCad) or nickel-metal hydride (NiMH) batteries handled eight hours of continuous conversation before they needed recharging.

Most manufacturers claim that a fully charged battery will last at least a week in standby mode. When they can no longer hold a charge, a replacement battery, usually proprietary, costs about $10 to $25. Some phones use less-expensive AA or AA rechargeable batteries. (To find a store that will recycle a used battery, call 800-822-8837.)

Give the handset a test drive. In the store, hold the handset to your head to see if it feels comfortable. It should fit the contours of your face. The earpiece should have rounded edges and a recessed center that fits nicely over the middle of your ear. Check the buttons and controls to make sure they're reasonably sized and legible.

Don't discard the corded phone. It's a good idea to keep at least one corded phone in your home, if only for emergencies. A cordless phone may not work if you lose electrical power, and a cell phone won't work if you can't get a signal or the circuits are full. A corded phone draws its power from the phone system and can function without household AC power.

Related CR Report: October 2004
Ratings: page 307

AUTOS

What's New in Autos for 2005

More than 30 new or redesigned vehicles are being introduced for the 2005 model year. They debut against the backdrop of several trends: the automakers continue to mix the attributes of cars, minivans, and SUVs to create models with more versatility; rising gas prices are fueling interest in efficient hybrid and diesel vehicles; and automakers continue to use incentives such as rebates and low-interest loans to help sell their vehicles.

With 260 models now on sale, consumers have a wider choice than ever. The model mix continues to evolve in the direction of versatility. The new Ford Freestyle wagon, for instance, is designed to combine SUV features and all-wheel drive with sedanlike handling. Like many crossover-wagons and car-based SUVs, it shares its platform with a sedan: the new Ford Five Hundred.

Rising fuel costs have helped spur interest in hybrid vehicles. The first hybrid SUV, the Ford Escape Hybrid, went on sale in fall 2004. Two more, the Lexus RX400h and Toyota Highlander, are expected in early 2005. The Honda Accord V6 Hybrid uses a cylinder-deactivation system and electric power to get what Honda claims is the fuel economy of a four-cylinder engine while bettering the performance of a standard Accord V6. These vehicles represent a significant upsizing from early hybrids such as the Toyota Prius and Honda Civic Hybrid.

Diesel vehicles may be on the upstroke as well. Volkswagen already offers diesel versions of the Jetta, Golf, and New Beetle, and it added the Passat and Touareg diesels to its lineup. Jeep joins the fray with its new diesel Liberty, and Mercedes-Benz has introduced a diesel version of the E320.

Diesels are about 30 percent more efficient than gasoline engines, and the modern ones are much cleaner, quieter, and more responsive than their predecessors. However, they produce more nitrogen-oxide (NOx) and particulate emissions than gasoline engines, which prevents them from being sold in five states. That could change after 2006, when government-mandated low-sulfur fuel debuts. This fuel will allow automakers to use new-style catalytic converters, which would otherwise be impaired by sulfur contamination, to clean the exhaust and significantly lower vehicle emissions.

Nearly every auto manufacturer, domestic and foreign, continues to offer incentives, and those are likely to continue. Average incentives have risen five percent since 2003 and total discounts have increased more than 19 percent.

NEW AND NOTEWORTHY

Sedans make a stand. While SUVs and crossovers gather more attention, sedans remain the largest single segment of the automotive market. Manufacturers continue to improve access, revise driving positions, and refine driving dynamics with each generation.

New family sedans for 2005 include the roomy Chrysler 300 and Ford Five Hundred, and the midsize Buick LaCrosse, Pontiac G6, and Subaru Legacy.

The rear-drive 300 has a long hood and a sloping roof. Chrysler's 340-hp Hemi V8 comes in the top-of-the-line 300C. A variable displacement system, which deactivates four cylinders while cruising, is designed to curb the Hemi's thirst for fuel. The rear suspension is patterned on that of the Mercedes-Benz E320. It drives, rides, and handles acceptably but the styling compromises the view out.

The Five Hundred, and its Mercury Montego twin, is larger than the Taurus, a car it may one day replace. It comes with either front- or all-wheel drive and was loosely derived from the current Volvo S80 sedan.

The Buick LaCrosse replaces the reliable but dowdy Century and Regal sedans. It is built on the dated Chevrolet Impala/Pontiac Grand Prix platform, two vehicles near the bottom of our family-sedan ratings.

The G6, on the other hand, shares a platform with the Chevrolet Malibu, a car we were impressed with when we tested it. The Grand Am replacement seems to have an upgraded interior. A sedan comes first, followed by a coupe and a convertible.

GM calls the new Chevrolet Cobalt a "premium small car," but it's unclear what makes this Cavalier replacement "premium" other than its optional heated leather seats. But since it is based on the respected European Opel Astra, it's likely to be a significant improvement. It comes with a choice of four-cylinder engines and will be available as a sedan or coupe.

Subaru has redesigned the competent and reliable Legacy sedan and wagon, and has added a sportier version in the 250-hp turbocharged Legacy GT. The GT is quick, but in our testing it got a lackluster 18 mpg in overall fuel economy.

The look of luxury. On the luxury end, Acura's flagship RL has been redesigned, as have the Audi A6 and Lexus GS. Cadillac has brought out a new car, the STS.

The Acura RL has a 300-hp V6 engine and an all-wheel-drive system that is designed to vary the torque not only front to rear, but also side to side to help improve handling. High-tech gadgets include headlights that turn to illuminate around corners and a navigation system that integrates real-time traffic information to help drivers find the best route around congestion.

The new Audi A6 offers a choice of either a 255-hp V6 or a 335-hp V8 coupled to all-wheel drive. Interior quality should be world-class, but we found the Multi Media Interface multi-control system, which controls the audio, climate, and communications systems, tedious to use.

The Cadillac STS, the replacement for the Seville, is a big, plush performance sedan positioned to compete with BMW and Lexus. The quality of Cadillac's interior materials have never been up to the imports' standard, but if the rear- or all-wheel-drive STS rides and handles as well as the smaller CTS, it has great potential.

The Lexus GS300 comes with a 3.0-liter V6, while the GS430 is powered by a 4.3-liter V8. They are the first Lexus sedans to offer all-wheel drive. That and the six-speed automatic transmission should help it compete more effectively with European luxury marques.

Minivans redux. The minivan remains the most practical choice for hauling both people and cargo, despite its perceived frumpy image. General Motors has refreshed its minivan entries with new sheetmetal and new names, but they're primarily the same as the previous generation. The Buick Terraza, Chevrolet Uplander, Pontiac Montana SV6, and Saturn Relay offer a handy fold-flat third-row seat and optional all-wheel drive, but they use the same seven-year-old platform of the Chevrolet Venture and Pontiac Montana.

The redesigned 2005 Honda Odyssey has a 225-hp V6, and an optional variable displacement system should help fuel economy. The easy-folding third-row seats have a pinch more legroom and the minivan is quieter and seems more refined than the previous Odyssey.

SUVs and wagons. As the SUV market has evolved, car-based models have become mainstream. Added to that, a number of all-wheel-drive SUV-like wagons, called "crossovers," have gained in popularity.

Among the latter is the Ford Freestyle, an all-wheel drive wagon version of the Five Hundred sedan with third-row seats that fold flat. The Subaru Outback, redesigned for 2005, is another SUV-like wagon. With a ground clearance that's one inch higher than the Legacy, on which it's based, the Outback now qualifies as a truck for EPA fuel-economy purposes. The rear-wheel-drive Dodge Magnum, a wagon version of the Chrysler 300, offers all-wheel drive.

New SUVs include the Land Rover LR3, and redesigned versions of the Jeep Grand Cherokee and Nissan Pathfinder and Xterra.

The Land Rover LR3 replaces the Discovery and is a midsized SUV with fully independent suspension, a 4.4-liter V8, and a six-speed automatic transmission. An intriguing "terrain control" system allows the driver to select from several dedicated modes for different driving conditions.

The Grand Cherokee retains its familiar silhouette and it has new engine choices and independent front suspension, but doesn't appear to bring anything new to the SUV market.

The new Pathfinder shares its body-on-frame architecture with the larger Nissan Armada, and now features a fully independent suspension and three rows of seats. The less-refined Xterra should also benefit from that same platform.

Pickup and go. Three midsized pickups have been redesigned: the Dodge Dakota, Nissan Frontier, and Toyota Tacoma. The Dakota has always been on the large end of the midsized spectrum, and has grown larger and more powerful this time around, with a standard 210-hp V6 and two V8 engines. It's based on the large Dodge Durango SUV. The Nissan Frontier shares the same platform as the Pathfinder and has a 265-hp V6. The Toyota Tacoma was also enlarged, and has more interior space, bed volume, and towing capacity. Power comes from a strong V6 engine used in the 4Runner. ABS is standard and stability control is optional. All three models offer extended-cab and crew-cab (four-door) configurations. Dodge and Nissan dropped the regular-cab version, which indicates diminished customer demand for that body style.

FEATURES & OPTIONS

Equipping a vehicle with only the options you want is often a juggling act. If you must have a car quickly, you may have to settle for what's on the dealer's lot. Special or-

dering a car can take weeks or even months, which is fine if you have the time.

Many options are available individually, but particular items often come only as part of an option package, with a name like "convenience group" or "preferred equipment package." If you want most or the entire package's components, then such a package can save you money over buying the options separately. Sometimes you can't get an option you want without buying things you otherwise wouldn't consider.

You can negotiate the price of options. To help, CONSUMER REPORTS offers its New Car Price Report, which includes a complete list of options and packages, with both invoice and retail prices. It also includes CR's equipment recommendations. Call 800-269-1139 or go to *www.ConsumerReports.org* to order the New Car Price Report.

UPGRADES TO CONSIDER

Audio. Many standard audio systems provide good sound and some form of theft protection. Higher-level systems typically improve audio quality and convenience. CD players are usually standard, but you can often upgrade to a multidisc CD changer. Changers mounted in the dash or console are more convenient than changers mounted in the trunk.

Many models now offer audio systems that can receive Sirius or XM satellite digital radio. These are subscriber services that provide high-quality sound, a wide range of channels with music and other formats, and coast-to-coast reception.

Comfort and convenience. From leather upholstery to heated seats, sunroofs, and navigation systems, the list of small and large conveniences can seem endless and maybe irresistible. Be careful, though, because the tally can add up quickly.

A key-fob remote control is a handy addition to power locks. It lets you lock and unlock the doors of the vehicle and, often, turn on interior lights from a distance. That's both a convenience and a security consideration.

Engines. If price and fuel economy are more important to you than performance, a vehicle's base engine is likely to be fine. An engine upgrade usually gets you quicker acceleration, better hill-climbing capability, and quieter operation. Larger engines sometimes increase towing capacity. The trade-off is usually worse fuel economy.

Four- and all-wheel drive. Both maximize traction. Although the terms are often used interchangeably, 4WD systems are generally heavier-duty and equipped with low-range gearing for serious off-road or hazardous-terrain travel. Part-time 4WD systems, the type found on most pickups and less-expensive SUVs, should not be used on dry pavement while in 4WD mode. Full-time 4WD systems are more versatile. All-wheel drive, which usually uses smaller and lighter components, lacks the low-range setting and is intended for all-weather and moderate off-road travel.

Two-wheel drive is enough for most people, especially if the vehicle is front-wheel drive. Modern rear-drive cars (most of which are luxury and high-performance models) can provide reasonable traction in slippery conditions if they're equipped with electronic traction-control and stability-control systems (see "Key Safety Features" on page 154).

Transmission. A manual transmission can provide an edge in fuel economy and acceleration over an automatic, and some drivers prefer the greater control and sporty feel that a stick shift provides. But automatic transmissions have become much smoother and more responsive and are far more popular, particularly among drivers who deal with a lot of traffic congestion.

Tires and wheels. The only parts of a car that actually touch the road, tires can make a big difference in handling, braking, and ride comfort. Upgraded, higher-performance tires improve handling and braking, although they tend to ride more firmly and noisily, and can wear faster. Whatever tires you choose, keeping them inflated to the right pressure optimizes driving dynamics and maximizes tread life.

KEY SAFETY FEATURES

While safety belts remain the most important safety feature, every year new technology shows up to help drivers avoid an accident or help protect passengers during a collision. Here's a rundown of the major features that are available.

Antilock brakes (ABS). Antilock brakes prevent the wheels from locking up during an emergency stop. Locked-up wheels can cause a sideways skid and impede your steering control. ABS can not only help you stop shorter, particularly on slippery surfaces, but it can also help keep the vehicle heading straight. And it allows the driver to retain steering control while braking, so you can steer around an obstacle if necessary. CONSUMER REPORTS strongly recommends ABS when available.

Brake assist. This adjunct to ABS senses the speed or force with which the brake pedal is depressed to determine if the driver is trying to make an emergency stop. If so, it applies greater braking force even if the driver is tentative in pressing the pedal.

Traction control. This system limits wheel-spin during acceleration. It's particularly useful when starting from a standstill in wet or icy conditions. It can serve as a less expensive (though less effective) alternative to all- or four-wheel drive, particularly in rear-wheel-drive cars.

Electronic stability control (ESC). This system helps prevent a vehicle from skidding or sliding in a turn. It's especially helpful in slippery conditions, and can help prevent an SUV from getting into a situation where it could roll over. ESC selectively brakes one or more wheels and, if necessary, cuts back engine power if it detects that the vehicle is beginning to slide or skid. CONSUMER REPORTS strongly recommends ESC, particularly on SUVs.

Front air bags. All new vehicles come with front air bags. Advanced designs use dual-stage deployment, where the bags may not inflate or may inflate with reduced force in a low-level collision. In a higher-speed collision, the bags inflate with full force. Another enhancement on more models: occupant-sensing systems that adjust the deployment of the air bags to fit the size and/or position of the occupant, modifying or preventing deployment as appropriate.

Side air bags. Side air bags for the front seats are now common. Some automakers offer side air bags for the rear seats too. Some models provide occupant-sensing systems for side bags. The system in Acura and Honda models, for instance, deactivates the side bags if a front passenger is leaning too close to the door, to prevent possible air-bag injury.

Head-protection side bags. Head-protection side air bags are an important enhancement. The most common are curtain air bags, which cover both front and rear side windows to prevent occupants from hitting their head or from being ejected through the window.

Pretensioners and force limiters. These features help safety belts work better. Pretensioners retract the belts to remove slack and help place the person in the optimum position for the air bags. Force limiters play the belt back out slightly following the initial impact. That can help prevent chest and internal injuries caused by the belt.

Rollover-detection system. This new system is now available on vehicles such as the Ford Explorer, Expedition, and Freestar; Mercury Mountaineer; Lincoln Aviator and Navigator; Volvo XC90; Lexus LX470; and Toyota Land Cruiser. If sensors determine that the vehicle has leaned beyond a specified angle, indicating that a rollover is imminent, they automatically trigger the side-curtain air bags, and keep them inflated for a time, to help prevent occupants from being injured or ejected.

Child-seat attachments. All new vehicles now must have a LATCH (for Lower Anchors and Tethers for Children) system for attaching compatible child seats. It has anchors for top-tethers and a universal lower mounting system located in the crease between the car's rear-seat backrest and lower cushion.

SMART BUYING OR LEASING

To get the vehicle you want at the best price, do your homework. Think about what you need and like and then follow these steps:

STEP 1: NARROW YOUR CHOICES

Consumer Reports can help you get started. Check out the overall Ratings of models that Consumer Reports has recently tested, starting on page 181. Beginning on page 160 are overviews for all the major 2005 models, including predictions on how reliable the model is likely to be. Models that CR recommends are highlighted. The Reliability History charts that begin on page 195 detail the reliability histories for more than 200 vehicles.

STEP 2: RESEARCH THE DETAILS

Once you have a short list of cars, gather key details on features, prices, safety equipment, and insurance options. Many sources—in both print and online—offer basic information and specifications. The automakers' own brochures and Web sites can be useful for learning about the various features available and how the vehicles come equipped.

STEP 3: BUY OR LEASE?

Most people finance a new vehicle either through a loan or by leasing the vehicle. How you use the car should determine which is best for you.

Leasing generally makes sense only if:

- You don't exceed the annual mileage allowance—typically 12,000 to 15,000 miles per year. Extra miles usually cost 15 to 25 cents each.
- You don't terminate the lease early. You risk thousands of dollars in penalties if you do.
- You keep your vehicle in very good shape. "Excess wear and tear" charges at lease end can run several hundred to a thousand dollars or more.
- You prefer to trade your vehicle in every two or three years. If you keep a car longer, you're probably better off buying it from the start.

STEP 4: NAIL DOWN THE PRICE

The amount of the monthly loan or lease payment hinges on your ability to negotiate the lowest possible price for the vehicle.

Finding the sticker price is easy. It's on the car window and available at many Web sites. You also can find the dealer invoice price on many Web sites and in printed pricing guides.

The dealer-invoice price, however, isn't necessarily what the dealer paid for the vehicle. Behind-the-scenes sales incentives further reduce the dealer's cost. Knowing about these incentives can help you establish an even better place to start your price negotiations. To help you get to the true bottom price, CONSUMER REPORTS provides the CR Wholesale Price. It takes the dealer's invoice price and figures in any sales incentives, holdbacks, and rebates in effect. The CR Wholesale Price is provided as part of the Consumer Reports New Car Price Service.

Typically, models in ample supply sell for 4 to 8 percent over the CR Wholesale Price. Slow-selling models may sell for less than invoice. High-demand vehicles sell for prices closer to the sticker, or in some cases, over the sticker. But most domestic models, even those just introduced, often sell at a discount right away.

STEP 5: SHOP FOR FINANCING

Check online services, local banks, and your credit union for the best rates. Most automakers have finance arms, such as Ford Motor Credit for Ford products or GMAC for General Motors vehicles. They often offer very favorable financing terms, but don't be drawn into a great deal on a car you don't really want.

Here are some tips:

• Review your loan options before you go to the dealership. Often, the quoted rate for a loan from a bank or credit union is better than what a dealership will initially offer. However, dealerships will often come down to match or beat a rate that you were quoted.

• Examine the terms. The most attractive rates, like zero-percent financing, often have limitations. They apply only to short-term loans, or only to people with faultless credit histories, or, often, to cars that aren't selling well.

• Know what's really discounted. Make sure that the "great low rate" is available on the car after you bargain down the price. If it applies only to a car selling for full price, then it may not be such a bargain.

• Avoid needless extras. Pass up extras like credit-life and disability insurance, an extended warranty, rustproofing, paint sealant, and so on.

STEP 6: TAKE SOME TEST DRIVES

This important step lets you see how the car fits you. Seat comfort, visibility, roominess, and the ergonomics of the controls can make a big difference in how happy you'll be with a vehicle over the long term.

List what you like and dislike about your current car, then compare this with your intended purchase. Take a notebook along with you on the test drive, and jot down your impressions.

Don't be rushed; take your time—at least 30 minutes. If possible, take the test drive without a salesperson, so you can better concentrate on the vehicle. Take someone along to give you the passenger's viewpoint. Test drive the exact version of the vehicle you're considering for purchase.

Try to drive along a route that includes different types of road surfaces. A familiar route will let you concentrate on the car rather than where you are going. If the dealership or seller is in an unfamiliar place, scout out a route ahead of time.

Make sure the car fits you. Set the seat in a comfortable driving position and attach the safety belt. Sit at least 10 inches away from the steering wheel but close enough that you can still fully depress all the pedals. Typically, seats fit some bodies better than others, so make sure it feels right for you. Make sure you can reach all the controls without straining, that the controls are easy to use, and the displays easy to see.

As you drive, make sure you can see out well, that you can judge the ends of the car, and that there are no serious blind spots. Pay attention to all of the vehicle's characteristics—how it rides, handles, accelerates, and stops, as well as how quiet it is.

STEP 7: NEGOTIATE SMARTLY

If you can, visit three or four dealers to see how the cars in stock are typically equipped and to gauge which dealers might be willing to accept a smaller profit margin. Then follow this game plan:

Keep the deal simple. Negotiate the price of the new car or of your trade-in first, but don't do both deals at once. It's simplest to negotiate the price of the new vehicle first, and treat it as if it were a straight-out cash deal. When it's concluded, then discuss the possibility of leasing or the price of the trade-in. Make it clear from the outset you're serious about buying soon but won't sign a contract on the spot. Tell the salesperson you are shopping different dealers and whichever offers the lowest price will get your business.

Don't bid against yourself. Bargain up from your lowest figure a little at a time. Once you've made an offer, say nothing until you receive a counteroffer.

Be prepared to walk. Avoid pinning your hopes on one dealer or one car. There will be other good deals on other cars.

Handling the trade-in. Negotiate a trade-in separately from the purchase or lease deal. You're apt to get the best price for your old car if you can sell it privately, but that's too much trouble for some.

Clean the old car thoroughly inside and out, including the trunk and engine bay. Consider fixing small dings or other flaws. Such measures can improve the resale value substantially. To learn what your old car should net as a trade-in, try shopping it around at local new-dealers' used-car departments. That will establish a rock-bottom price. Then check local classified-ad publications and Internet used-car sites to see what dealers and private parties are asking for cars like yours. That establishes the high end of the range. Your trade-in target price is apt to be somewhere in the middle between those extremes.

Special tips for leasing. Proceed with the leasing deal only after you receive a firm price quote for the car. Make sure that the purchase price is the figure used to calculate the lease terms. Other items you can negotiate include the annual mileage limit, the down payment, and the purchase-option price.

Be sure the value of any trade-in is deducted from the "capitalized cost" or selling price, on which the monthly figure is calculated. To figure out what you're really paying in interest, ask the dealer for the "money factor," a four- or five-digit decimal. Multiply that by 2,400 to get an approximate annual interest-rate percentage. For example, a "money factor" of .00375 is about equivalent to a 9 percent annual interest rate (.00375 x 2,400 = 9).

In a typical lease calculation, your monthly payment consists of depreciation, a "lease fee," and applicable taxes. The lease fee is the money factor multiplied by the sum of the capitalized cost and the residual value. Since residual value is already part of the capitalized cost, it may look like it's being counted twice. It isn't. The money factor takes it into account.

Try to avoid a lease that extends past the vehicle's basic warranty. Otherwise you might be saddled with expensive repairs on a vehicle you don't own.

If you might buy the car at lease-end, find out the purchase-option fee and pay it up front. And if you think you'll exceed the annual mileage allowance, buy extra miles up front, too. It's much cheaper that way.

BUYING A USED CAR

Used cars are often the best value. With a used car, the original owner pays for the steepest part of the depreciation curve.

Manufacturer-certified used cars are late-model vehicles that have been pre-screened, inspected, and reconditioned as necessary to ensure top-notch condition. They generally come with a manufacturer's warranty lasting from three months to a year or more, but also cost more than a noncertified car.

Cars from used-car dealers are usually a notch down in price from those available at new-car dealers, but also often a notch down in quality and after-sale care.

You might be able to get the lowest price by buying from a private owner, but you may have little recourse if the car turns out to have problems.

KEY RESEARCH

If buying from a new-car dealer who sells the same make, ask that the car's vehicle identification number (VIN) be run through the dealer's computer and get a printout of any completed warranty repairs. The dealer can also check the status of any federal recalls and service bulletins.

All you need for a good test drive is to rely on your senses and know what to look for. Plan to spend at least 20 minutes behind the wheel, as most problems show up only after a car has warmed up.

Map out your own course beforehand instead of following the salesperson's lead. Often they choose courses with very few challenges like hard cornering, hill climbing, or rough pavement.

White vapor at start-up is likely not a cause for alarm. Black smoke after the car is warm indicates an overly rich air-fuel mixture—due to a dirty air filter or a bad oxygen sensor. Blue smoke indicates oil burning. Billowing white smoke indicates water in the combustion chamber, possibly from a blown head gasket or damaged cylinder head. These are all costly repairs.

At idle, turn the wheel both right and left. You shouldn't feel any play before the tires start to turn on the pavement. The car should quickly respond to your steering input, without the need for constant corrections. If the wheel trembles at highway speed, suspect a problem with wheel balance or front-end alignment, both easily remedied, or with the driveline, suspension, or frame, which may not be as easily fixed.

When accelerating, there shouldn't be appreciable hesitation after depressing the pedal. If so, it can be a sign of transmission or clutch wear—a costly fix.

A clutch should fully engage well before you take your foot off the pedal. If there isn't at least an inch of play the car may need a new clutch.

Listen for knock and pinging while accelerating, which can indicate bad ignition timing, carbon deposits, or the engine beginning to overheat.

On an empty stretch of road apply the brakes hard at about 45 mph. The car should stop quickly, without pulling to one side or vibrating. Pedal feel should be smooth and stopping the car should take little effort. Antilock brakes will rapidly pulse underfoot. Try at least three stops, then park in a safe area and step firmly on the pedal for 30 seconds. If it feels spongy or sinks to the floor, there may be a leak in the brake system.

At a steady speed on a smooth road, note any vibrations. Drive at 30 mph on a bumpy road. If the car bounces and hops on routine bumps it may indicate suspension problems. After you stop, check the suspension by pushing down hard on each fender and then letting go. More than two severe rebounds indicate worn shock absorbers or struts.

Tire wear should be even across the tread and the same on both sides of the car. Over-inflated tires wear more in the middle; under-inflated tires wear more on the sides. Heavy wear on the outside shoulder near the sidewall indicates a car that has been driven hard and may mean that other parts of the car suffer from excessive wear. Tires worn unevenly along the tread's circumference can indicate problems with the steering, suspension, or brakes.

When you find a good prospect, take it to a mechanic for a thorough inspection—well worth the $100 or so that costs. If you're an American Automobile Association member, consider using an AAA-sanctioned garage.

CONSUMER REPORTS can also help. Check the "Best and Worst Used Cars" list starting on page 188. The reliability histories beginning on page 195 give you detailed information about each vehicle's problem areas. To purchase a Used Car Price Report, call the Consumer Reports Used Car Price Service at 800-422-1079.

ONLINE RESEARCH

Using the Web to shop for a car

You can find specs, pictures, and prices online. You can find out what car testers such as CONSUMER REPORTS and others have to say, and what sort of financing is available. You can check insurance and bank rates, lease deals, and look at your credit report. It's getting easier to separate good sites from bad ones. Still, you should treat Web-generated information with caution. When it comes to a car, nothing beats seeing it in person.

If you want to buy or lease a car, various services can get the ball rolling for you by quoting a price (either their set price or one from a participating dealership). Or they can handle the entire deal, from arranging financing to delivery of the car.

With a buying site, you are cued to fill out a detailed questionnaire about the car or cars you are looking for. The service then quotes a price (sometimes instantly, sometimes within hours or days), and searches for a dealer who has the car.

Some buying sites essentially put you in touch with a local dealer who has agreed to sell a car at a specified price. But when you visit the dealer you may be pressured to buy more equipment, extended warranties, or other extras. Other buying sites arrange a final, out-the-door price, and you go to a dealer only to write a check and pick up the car.

Used-car buying sites essentially work like extensive classified-ad publications. After you enter the model in which you're interested, they typically list all vehicles that are available within a specified price and distance from your home. You can use them to find a car or just to get a handle on the going prices, whether you are in the market to sell or buy.

REVIEWS OF THE 2005 MODELS

This rundown of all the major 2005 models can start you on your search for a new car. You'll find a capsule summary of each model, as well as the CONSUMER REPORTS prediction of how reliable the vehicle will be, and how much it's likely to depreciate in value. Model descriptions in this book are based on recent road tests that pertain to this year's models.

Models with a ✔ are recommended by CONSUMER REPORTS. These are models that performed well in CONSUMER REPORTS testing, have average or better reliability according to our latest 2004 annual survey, and performed adequately in crash or rollover tests.

Entries include, where available, the date of the last road test for that model published in CONSUMER REPORTS magazine. These road-test reports are also available to subscribers of our Web site, *www.ConsumerReports.org.*

The 2005 cars, trucks, SUVs & minivans

Predicted reliability is a judgment based on our annual reliability survey data. New or recently redesigned models are marked "New." Depreciation predicts how well a new model will keep its value, based on the difference between the original sticker price of a 2002 model and its current resale value. The average depreciation for all vehicles was 46 percent. Throughout, ✔ indicates a model is recommended by CONSUMER REPORTS; NA means data not available.

Better ⟵⟶ **Worse**

⊜ ⊖ ○ ◒ ●

Model	Predicted reliability	Depreciation	Comments
✔ **Acura MDX**	⊜	⊜	The MDX is a well-designed car-based SUV that can hold seven passengers. Ride and handling are competent. The interior is flexible, with a third-row seat that folds flat into the cargo floor. **Last road test: Sep. 2003**
Acura RL	⊖	NA	Acura's flagship sedan is being redesigned for 2005. The new model will feature a 300-hp V6 engine, available all-wheel drive, headlamps that rotate during turns, and a driver interaction system that seems more intuitive than Audi's MMI and BMW's iDrive. **Last road test: --**
✔ **Acura RSX**	⊜	⊖	The RSX is a two-door coupe with a rear hatch. Two engines are available, with the sportier Type-S using a six-speed manual. Handling is capable but the ride is stiff, choppy, and noisy. The folding seats add versatility, but rear-seat room is tight. **Last road test: Dec. 2001**
✔ **Acura TL**	⊖	⊖	The TL is the highest-scoring car we've tested in its category. Based on the Honda Accord, it provides a near-ideal blend of comfort, convenience, and sportiness. Handling is taut and agile, and the engine delivers very quick acceleration. The ride is firm yet comfortable and quiet. **Last road test: Feb. 2004**

Model	Predicted reliability	Depreciation	Comments
✔ **Acura TSX**	⊖	NA	The TSX is based on the smaller Honda Accord sold in Japan and Europe. This four-door features a smooth-revving engine and slick transmission. Handling is more agile than the Accord's, but the ride is a bit stiff. **Last road test: Nov. 2004**
✔ **Audi A4**	○	⊜	The A4 handles nimbly and accelerates well, though the low speed ride is a bit firm. The interior is polished and luxurious–comfortable in front, cramped in the rear. All-wheel drive is available; a continuously variable transmission is available on front-wheel-drive models. **Last road test: Nov. 2004**
Audi A6/Allroad	◒	⊖	Audi redesigned its midsized sedan for 2005, offering 3.2-liter V6 and a 4.2-liter V8 engines. All-wheel drive is standard. The Allroad wagon continues with the old body style, featuring an adjustable height suspension and 2.7-liter turbo V6 and 4.2-liter V8 engines. **Last road test: July 2001**
Audi A8	NA	NA	Audi's redesigned flagship holds its own with the best. It features a strong V8, AWD, and an aluminum body with a roomy, well-crafted interior. It is quiet and agile, but the ride is unremarkable for a luxury car. A V12 engine is optional. **Last road test: Nov. 2003**
Audi TT	◒	⊖	The stylish TT is available as a convertible or coupe. A nicely detailed interior and available all-wheel drive offset a character that is less sporty than a Porsche Boxster's. The ride is stiff and the engine noisy. A smoother V6 and sequential manual transmission liven up the range. **Last road test: June 2002**
✔ **BMW 3 Series**	○	⊜	The 3 Series models blend comfort, luxury, sportiness, and safety. They are quiet and refined, yet quick and agile. Wagon and all-wheel-drive xi versions are also available, as is a powerful M3 in coupe and convertible bodystyles. **Last road test: May 2001**
BMW 5 Series	●	⊜	The redesigned 5 Series is impressive and frustrating, as well as more expensive. We found the iDrive control system tedious to use. Handling is agile, and the ride is comfortable and quiet. The automatic transmission and engine are smooth. Interior fit and finish is not impressive. **Last road test: June 2004**
BMW 6 Series	NA	NA	The 6 Series shares a platform with the recently redesigned mid-size 5 Series. The standard engine is a smooth and punchy 4.4-liter V8. A convertible version is also available. **Last road test: —**
BMW 7 Series	●	⊜	The stately, quiet, fast, and agile 7 Series misses the mark as a luxury car. The iDrive control system and other ergonomic quirks make it frustrating and annoying instead of comforting and soothing. **Last road test: Nov. 2003**
BMW X3	NA	NA	The X3 is loosely based on the 3 Series wagon, but with a roomier rear seat. The ride is hard and choppy, but handling is agile. All-wheel drive with traction- and stability-control systems endow it with good snow traction. **Last road test: Dec. 2004**
BMW X5	◒	⊜	The X5 delivers an impressive drivetrain and comfortable front seats. But the 3.0i version had moderate tip-ups on runs through our avoidance maneuver. Limited cargo space is a detraction. All engines deliver spirited acceleration. **Last road test: Sep. 2003**

Model	Predicted reliability	Depreciation	Comments
BMW Z4	●	⊖	The Z4 is a sporty two-seat convertible, but not as agile as the Porsche Boxster. The cockpit is roomy and the two inline six-cylinder engines from the previous version power the new one. Electronic stability control and traction control are standard. **Last road test: --**
Buick LaCrosse	NEW	NA	The LaCrosse replaces the Century and Regal. The front-wheel-drive sedan is based on the same platform as the Chevrolet Impala and Pontiac Grand Prix, and offers a choice of V6 engines. The interior ambiance is a step up for a Buick, and will offer five- and six-passenger configurations. **Last road test: --**
✔ **Buick LeSabre**	○	◒	The big LeSabre has a roomy interior and a quiet ride. Handling is reluctant but secure, especially with the Touring suspension, which also makes the ride more settled. The seats are unsupportive. **Last road test: Feb. 2000**
✔ **Buick Park Avenue**	○	◒	Buick's top-of-the-line sedan rides and handles relatively well. Acceleration is effortless in the supercharged Ultra. The interior is roomy and quiet, and the seats are fairly comfortable but interior ambiance is disappointing for a car in this price range. **Last road test: Feb. 2003**
Buick Rainier	◒	NA	The upscale Buick Rainier is a rebadged Oldsmobile Bravada. It comes with a 4.2-liter six-cylinder or a 5.3-liter V8. The permanently engaged AWD system has no low range, making it more suited for slippery roads than for off-roading. **Last road test: --**
✔ **Buick Rendezvous**	○	○	This minivan-based SUV features independent suspension, optional all-wheel drive, and room for seven. The ride is OK, and handling is secure. Good points are offset by so-so acceleration and a cheap-feeling interior. **Last road test: Oct. 2001**
Buick Terraza	NEW	NA	The 2005 Terraza minivan is a freshening of GM's 7-year-old minivans. Power comes from a V6 engine that does a good job in the Chevrolet Malibu. The second-row seats can be folded and removed, while the folding third-row seat stows flat. **Last road test: --**
✔ **Cadillac CTS**	○	NA	This rear-wheel drive, German-style sports sedan feels agile and taut, but has pesky oversights and relatively poor reliability. Power is provided by a smooth 3.6-liter V6. A 400-hp V8 powers the sporty CTS-V. Acceleration is quick and the transmission is very smooth. **Last road test: July 2003**
Cadillac DeVille	◒	◒	This big, plush freeway cruiser handles well for such a large car. It offers plenty of power, a very comfortable ride, and generous rear-seat room. Well-thought-out details festoon the interior. **Last road test: Nov. 2000**
Cadillac Escalade	○	⊖	Essentially a Chevrolet Tahoe, this SUV features powerful engines and a smooth transmission. Though spacious, the interior isn't very flexible and the third seat is uncomfortable. Luxury details mix with cheap plastic materials. The EXT is a plush version of the Avalanche; the ESV is based on the Suburban. **Last road test: --**
Cadillac SRX	●	NA	The upscale SRX is the first car-based SUV from Cadillac. This tall wagon is powered by a smooth V8 or a V6. Handling is agile and secure. The ride is taut, yet supple. The optional power-folding third-row seat operates slowly. **Last road test: Mar. 2004**

Model	Predicted reliability	Depreciation	Comments
Cadillac STS	NEW	NA	The 2005 STS arrives this fall, replacing the Seville nameplate. Based on the new Sigma rear-wheel-drive platform, it will feature Cadillac's contemporary styling. Power will come from a standard 225-hp V6 or optional 320-hp Northstar V8. All-wheel drive will be optional. **Last road test: —**
Cadillac XLR	NA	NA	The XLR is based on the C6 Corvette, but is powered by a sophisticated, smooth Northstar V8 and mated to a five speed automatic. It is quick and handles quite well, but doesn't feel as sporty as a Mercedes-Benz SL or a Porsche 911. **Last road test: —**
Chevrolet Astro	●	●	The Astro is seriously outclassed by all modern minivans. Handling is ponderous, and the ride is uncomfortable. It can haul lots of cargo or tow a heavy trailer. AWD is optional. **Last road test: —**
✔ Chevrolet Avalanche	○	⊖	Essentially a crew-cab pickup version of the Suburban, this truck has an innovative "midgate" that allows long items to extend into the rear-passenger compartment. The ride is comfortable. The four-wheel-drive system can remain engaged indefinitely—a plus. **Last road test: Sep. 2002**
Chevrolet Aveo	NA	NA	The Aveo is a Daewoo rebadged as a Chevrolet. Available in sedan and hatchback body styles, the Aveo handles clumsily, but is ultimately secure. Acceleration and fuel economy are unimpressive. Fit and finish is commendable. **Last road test: Aug. 2004**
Chevrolet Cobalt	NEW	NA	The Cobalt is the successor to the aged Cavalier, and shares its standard 2.2-liter four-cylinder with the Malibu. A more powerful 2.4-liter and a supercharged 2.0-liter will be offered. ABS and traction control are available on uplevel trim lines, but unfortunately not in the Base model. **Last road test: —**
Chevrolet Colorado	⊖	NA	The Colorado replaces the S-10 compact pickup truck, and is a twin of the GMC Canyon. The engines are noisy four- or five-cylinders. The truck is fairly quiet and ride and handling are more accomplished than in other compact pickups. **Last road test: —**
Chevrolet Corvette	NEW	NA	The redesigned 2005 Corvette is slightly smaller than the outgoing model. Power comes from a revised 6.0-liter, 400-hp V8. A six-speed manual is standard, with a four-speed automatic optional. Interior trim and materials appear to be improved compared to the outgoing model. **Last road test: —**
Chevrolet Equinox	NEW	NA	The Equinox has a roomy rear seat that can move fore and aft to increase passenger or cargo room. Interior quality is subpar and the V6 is noisy and unrefined. Access is easy. Handling is clumsy but secure. **Last road test: Oct. 2004**
✔ Chevrolet Impala	⊖	◒	The Impala handles fairly well and its V6 provides very good acceleration. Fuel economy is an unimpressive 20 mpg overall. The ride is absorbent but road noise is pronounced. The front bench seats lack support, and the rear is too low and short. Crash-test results are impressive. **Last road test: Jan. 2004**
Chevrolet Malibu	◒	NA	The Malibu is a well-rounded sedan that scores very well. The spacious interior offers easy access and a comfortable ride. The V6 delivers quick acceleration and a commendable 26 mpg overall. The Malibu Maxx is a four-door hatchback with an extended wheelbase for more rear seat room. **Last road test: Jan. 2004**

Model	Predicted reliability	Depreciation	Comments
Chevrolet Monte Carlo	⊖	○	A coupe version of the Impala, the Monte Carlo accelerates well, but road noise is pronounced and rear access is a chore. Overall, it offers an underwhelming driving experience. **Last road test: —**
Chevrolet S-10	●	○	The S-10 has a quiet cabin and torquey but coarse-sounding V6. Less impressive is the ride. Handling is far from nimble and the 4WD system can't be used on dry roads. The four-door crew-cab model with a V6 and four-wheel drive is the only version available. The Colorado replaced the S-10. **Last road test: Aug. 2001**
Chevrolet SSR	NA	NA	The SSR (Super Sport Roadster) is a pickup truck with a retractable hardtop. The V8 engine gained more power for 2005. Evoking the styling of Chevy trucks from the 1950s, this two-seater is about nostalgia and open-topped motoring. **Last road test: —**
✔ **Chevrolet Silverado 1500**	○	⊖	The Silverado, a full-sized pickup, is beginning to lose ground to newer competitors. The optional four-wheel drive is a selectable full-time system, a plus. Quadrasteer is a handy four-wheel-steering option. Extended-cab versions have a usable rear seat, a rarity in this class. **Last road test: July 2004**
Chevrolet Suburban	○	⊖	One of the largest SUVs, the Suburban can seat nine people, hold their luggage, and still tow a heavy trailer. Handling is commendable for such a large vehicle, but the turning circle is wide. Seating is comfortable, and the ride is quiet and well-controlled. Third-row access is a bit tough. The standard V8 is powerful but not fuel efficient. **Last road test: —**
Chevrolet Tahoe	○	⊖	This SUV is similar to the Suburban, but with less cargo room. Eight can ride, but those in the third seat will be very uncomfortable. It (and the similar GMC Yukon) boasts an impressive towing capability. The steering is vague and the brakes are so-so. A tip-up in NHTSA's rollover tests is cause for concern, and we can no longer recommend the Tahoe and its GMC Yukon twin. **Last road test: Nov. 2002**
Chevrolet TrailBlazer	●	○	This SUV is quiet and spacious, with a compliant low-speed ride. The vehicle falls short due to sloppy handling, uncomfortable seats, ill-fitting trim, and too much wind noise. A longer EXT model has a third-row seat. The annoying seat-mounted front safety belts can pull down uncomfortably and are hard to reach. **Last road test: Aug. 2003**
Chevrolet Uplander	NEW	NA	The Uplander minivan features some SUV styling details in the front, but can't disguise the fact that it is just a freshening of a seven-year-old design. The second-row seats can be folded and removed, while the folding third-row seat stows flat when not in use. **Last road test: —**
Chrysler 300	NEW	NA	The retro-styled, rear-wheel-drive 300 is based on Mercedes-Benz architecture. Power is delivered by two V6 engines in the lower-priced trims, or a V8 in the 300C. All-wheel drive is optional. Visibility is limited. **Last road test: —**
Chrysler Crossfire	NA	NA	This German-built rear-drive two-seater is based on the old Mercedes-Benz SLK. The engine is strong, but handling lacks finesse. The ride is stiff, visibility is poor, and there's too much wind noise. A convertible and a supercharged SRT-6 are available. **Last road test: Dec. 2003**

Model	Predicted reliability	Depreciation	Comments
✔ **Chrysler PT Cruiser**	⊖	○	Though classed as a truck, the PT Cruiser is really a tall front-drive wagon. It offers a versatile interior and secure handling. The two turbocharged engines rectify the sluggish acceleration. Other drawbacks include a somewhat stiff ride and a noisy cabin, although fit and finish is good. A convertible version with a power-operated top is available. **Last road test: Oct. 2000**
Chrysler Pacifica	NEW	NA	The Pacifica combines the characteristics of an SUV, a minivan, and a wagon in an all-wheel-drive package that seats six. Ride and handling are capable, but the powertrain falls a bit short. Access is easy, and the third row folds flat when not needed. A five-passenger version arrives for 2005. **Last road test: Aug. 2003**
Chrysler Sebring	◒	◒	The Sebring is available in sedan, coupe, and convertible forms. The coupe is derived from the mediocre Mitsubishi Eclipse. The sedan is quick enough with a V6, but it lacks agility and doesn't ride comfortably. The four-cylinder is slow and noisy. **Last road test: June 2001**
✔ **Chrysler Town & Country**	○	◒	This cousin of the Dodge Grand Caravan has a roomy interior and is pleasant to drive, but is falling behind the competition. 2005 models have optional flat-folding second- and third-row seats. AWD isn't available in long-wheelbase models. The minivan rides well enough with a light load and handles securely. **Last road test: Oct. 2003**
✔ **Dodge Caravan/ Grand Caravan**	○	◒	The Grand Caravan we tested had a roomy interior and was pleasant to drive, but is falling behind the competition. 2005 models have optional flat-folding second- and third-row seats. AWD is not available for the long-wheelbase model. The Grand Caravan rides well enough with a light load and handles securely. **Last road test: Oct. 2003**
Dodge Dakota	NEW	NA	Redesigned for 2005, the new Dakota is based on the Durango SUV. It should be an improvement. A 210-hp V6 is standard, and the 4.7-liter V8 engine is optional. Full-time four-wheel drive is available. **Last road test: —**
✔ **Dodge Durango**	○	NA	The Durango straddles the midsized and large SUV classes. The body-on-frame SUV handles soundly and securely, and the ride is compliant. The cabin is fairly quiet, but the engine is a bit noisy. The third-row seat is more usable than in the previous generation. Fit and finish falls a bit short of the mark. **Last road test: Mar. 2004**
Dodge Magnum	NEW	NA	The Dodge Magnum is a wagon version of the Chrysler 300 sedan. Power is delivered by two V6 engines in the lower-priced trims, or a V8 in the RT model. The retro-styled Magnum features rear-wheel drive relying on Mercedes-Benz architecture. All-wheel drive is optional. Visibility is wanting. **Last road test: Dec. 2004**
Dodge Neon	○	●	This small sedan handles securely, brakes well, and has a relatively roomy interior. But the ride is stiff and uncomfortable and the cabin noisy. The four-speed automatic is mediocre. **Last road test: Mar. 2003**
Dodge Ram 1500	○	⊜	The Ram falls short of the competition, with a jittery ride and cumbersome handling. The engines are strong, but noisy and thirsty. The crew-cab version has less rear-seat room than the competition. The SRT-10 has a V10 and six-speed manual. **Last road test: July 2004**

Model	Predicted reliability	Depreciation	Comments
Dodge Stratus	◒	●	The Stratus, available as a sedan or coupe, feels a bit rough and underdeveloped. The sedan offers quick acceleration with the V6, but ride and handling fall short. The four-cylinder is slow, noisy, and thirsty. The cabin is noisy and access is difficult. **Last road test: May 2004**
Ford Crown Victoria	○	◒	A big, old-fashioned sedan, the Crown Victoria's jiggly ride and engine noise reveal how dated the car is. Braking and emergency handling are fairly good. Rear leg room is skimpier than you might expect. **Last road test: Feb. 2003**
Ford Escape	⊖	○	The Escape (and Mazda Tribute and Mercury Mariner siblings) has a roomy interior and a spacious rear bench. Handling is relatively nimble, and the brakes are strong. Fuel economy is disappointing. Interior trim, comfort, and noise suppression have been improved for 2005. A tip-up in the gov't rollover test is a concern. Therefore we can't recommend these models. **Last road test: Oct. 2004**
Ford Excursion	●	○	Designed to be the largest SUV on the road, the Excursion is a clumsy, fuel-guzzling behemoth with a noisy engine, atrocious fuel economy, an uncomfortable ride, and marginal brakes. **Last road test: --**
Ford Expedition	●	○	This large SUV has a well-designed interior with flexible seating and a handy fold-down split third seat. Ride and handling are commendable, but the available engines are slow and thirsty. **Last road test: Nov. 2002**
✔ **Ford Explorer**	○	○	The fully-independent suspension improves the ride, handling, and access. An available third-row seat brings passenger capacity to seven. The base V6 is noisy and unrefined, but provides adequate acceleration; a V8 is optional. A 2WD version tipped up in the gov't rollover test. Therefore we only recommend the 4WD version. **Last road test: Sep. 2001**
✔ **Ford Explorer Sport Trac**	○	⊜	This crew-cab truck is based on the previous Ford Explorer and features a truncated pickup bed and five-person cabin. The ride is stiff and choppy. Handling is secure and relatively responsive, but the 2WD Sport Track tipped up in the gov't rollover test. Therefore we only recommend the 4WD version. **Last road test: Aug. 2001**
Ford F-150	◒	NA	Ford significantly improved the redesigned F-150 full-sized pickup, including crashworthiness and the towing and payload capacities. The rear gate is relatively light. The part-time four-wheel-drive system can't be used on dry pavement. The F-150 is quieter now, steers better, and rides more comfortably than the old model, but the engine is noisy. **Last road test: July 2004**
Ford Five Hundred	NEW	NA	The Ford Five Hundred (and its Mercury Montego twin) is a large sedan with elevated seating positions to improve outward vision and access. The V6 engine is mated to either a six-speed automatic or a continuously variable transmission (CVT). Front-wheel drive is standard, with AWD optional. **Last road test: --**
✔ **Ford Focus**	○	◒	All versions of the Focus tested very well–it's agile, spacious, and fun to drive. Reliability has finally improved. It is also available in wagon and hatchback models. **Last road test: Aug. 2002**

Model	Predicted reliability	Depre-ciation	Comments
✔ Ford Freestar	○	NA	The Freestar is a freshened version of the Windstar minivan. Like its competitors, it features a flat-folding third-row seat. The two V6 engines are still noisy and road noise is pronounced. Handling is more responsive, but the ride is unsettled. Fit and finish is unimpressive. **Last road test: Mar. 2004**
Ford Freestyle	NEW	NA	This is a wagon version of the Ford Five Hundred. Second- and third-row seats fold flat and offer room for six or seven, depending on the version. Front-wheel-drive models come with a six-speed automatic, while the AWD models use a CVT. **Last road test: —**
Ford Mustang	NEW	NA	The new Mustang brings the look of Mustangs past to the showroom. Styled like the original, the 2005 Mustang is slightly bigger than the model it replaces. Power comes from a standard V6 or optional V8. The suspension still features a live rear axle rather than an independent rear set-up. **Last road test: —**
Ford Ranger	○	○	The Ranger and similar Mazda B-Series are long in the tooth. The ride is stiff and choppy. The Explorer Sport Trac is a crew-cab version of the Ranger. Minor cosmetic interior and exterior changes arrived for 2004. **Last road test: —**
✔ Ford Taurus	○	●	The Taurus is roomy and comfortable but showing its age. It has a decent ride and a spacious rear seat. Handling is sound but not agile. The optional V6 performs well but isn't as responsive or quiet as those from competitors. The wagon offers seven-passenger capacity. **Last road test: Jan. 2004**
✔ Ford Thunderbird	○	⊖	The T-Bird is a retro-revival two-seater. While the car accelerates quickly and steers well, it isn't particularly sporty. The ride is supple but slightly floaty, and body flex is pronounced. Head room is meager. The soft top is power operated; a removable hard top is also available. **Last road test: June 2002**
GMC Envoy	●	○	This midsized SUV, twin of the Chevrolet TrailBlazer, is spacious, with a fairly comfortable ride and a spirited inline-Six. Handling is a bit ponderous and can be tricky at the limit. Wind noise is pronounced. The longer XL model has a third seat, and the XUV features a retractable top. **Last road test: Sep. 2001**
✔ GMC Sierra 1500	○	○	The Sierra is a full-sized pickup like the Chevrolet Silverado. The optional four-wheel drive is a selectable full-time system. The Denali version has a handy four-wheel-steering option. Extended-cab versions have a usable rear seat, a rarity in this class. **Last road test: July 2004**
GMC Yukon	○	⊖	This SUV is a twin of the Chevrolet Tahoe. The XL model is similar to the Chevrolet Suburban. Eight can ride, but those in the third seat will be very tight. It boasts an impressive towing capability. Seating is comfortable, and the ride is quiet. A tip-up in NHTSA's rollover test for the regular Tahoe is cause for concern, and we no longer recommend the Yukon. **Last road test: Nov. 2002**
✔ Honda Accord	⊖	⊖	The Accord features agile handling and a steady, compliant ride. The cabin is roomy and controls are intuitive. The five-speed automatic shifts very smoothly and responsively. The four-cylinder engine is smooth and the V6 is relatively fuel efficient. A hybrid V6 arrives for 2005. **Last road test: May 2003**

Model	Predicted reliability	Depre-ciation	Comments
✔ **Honda CR-V**	⊜	⊜	One of the better car-based SUVs, the CR-V has a supple and controlled ride. The rear seat is roomy. Road noise is pronounced. Crash-test results are impressive. 2005 models receive standard ABS and electronic stability control. **Last road test: May 2002**
✔ **Honda Civic**	⊜	○	One of the best small sedans, the Civic handles well and gets good fuel economy, though its ride is a bit nervous. The interior is well finished, and controls are excellent. The sporty Si version doesn't feel very sporty. The gasoline/electric Hybrid averaged 36 mpg overall in CR tests. **Last road test: Dec. 2002**
✔ **Honda Element**	⊜	NA	This small SUV is based on Honda's very good CR-V. Styling is boxy, with rear doors that are hinged at the rear and no middle roof pillar. This creates a huge loading port. The rear seat folds away to create a big cargo area. **Last road test: June 2003**
Honda Insight	NA	⊖	This lightweight two-seater has a three-cylinder engine and a 13-hp electric motor that assists the gas engine. Handling is secure but not nimble. A stiff, uncomfortable ride and intrusive interior noise are major trade-offs for the car's excellent economy. **Last road test: Dec. 2000**
Honda Odyssey	⊖	NA	The outgoing Odyssey was one of our top-rated minivans with dual sliding rear door, and a flat-folding third row. A 2005 redesign is quieter and has impressive interior quality. The second row seats don't fold flat. **Last road test: --**
✔ **Honda Pilot**	⊖	NA	The Pilot is a well-designed car-based SUV that can hold eight passengers. Ride and handling are competent. The interior is flexible, with a third-row seat that folds flat into the cargo floor. Although quiet overall, road noise is pronounced. For 2005 the EX-L trim level gets standard stability control. **Last road test: Nov. 2002**
Honda S2000	○	⊖	The S2000 is a pure sports car that delivers impressive acceleration, handling, and braking. But it's noisy and hard riding, and feels a bit ordinary in normal driving. A glass rear window is now standard. **Last road test: --**
Hummer H2	●	NA	The H2 is based on the Chevy Tahoe and has a more usable interior than the grossly impractical H1. Ride and handling are fairly civilized, with exceptional off-road ability. The short windshield and wide roof pillars make the view out wanting. The H2 SUT is a pickup version. **Last road test: --**
Hyundai Accent	○	●	The Accent offers basic transportation in sedan or a two-door hatchback form. The ride is choppy but relatively quiet. It is now powered by a 1.6-liter four-cylinder engine. Antilock brakes are now available on 2005 models. **Last road test: Mar. 2003**
Hyundai Elantra	⊖	◒	The spacious Elantra rides well and handles securely, making it competitive with other good small sedans. Seats are firm and supportive. A four-door hatchback is also available. Models with the optional antilock brakes are hard to find. The Elantra did poorly in an IIHS offset-crash test. **Last road test: Feb. 2001**
✔ **Hyundai Santa Fe**	⊖	⊖	This car-based SUV has a supple, quiet ride and handles securely, if not nimbly. Acceleration and fuel economy are not impressive. Fit and finish are good. A steeply raked windshield makes the cockpit feel a bit confining. **Last road test: Mar. 2001**

Model	Predicted reliability	Depreciation	Comments
✔ **Hyundai Sonata**	⊜	○	The Sonata with an automatic shifts smoothly, and the brakes perform well. The ride becomes a bit unsettled on a rough highway. Handling is less than nimble, though ultimately secure. **Last road test: June 2001**
Hyundai Tiburon	●	NA	The GT V6 version of this sporty coupe delivers refined power, but handling is not so agile. The ride is stiff. Even average-height drivers will have to duck under the low roof. **Last road test: Oct. 2002**
Hyundai Tucson	NEW	NA	The Elantra-based Tucson is smaller than the Santa Fe. The standard four-cylinder engine comes with a five-speed manual or optional four-speed automatic. A V6 and front- and all-wheel-drive models are available. **Last road test: —**
✔ **Hyundai XG350**	○	◒	This quiet, roomy sedan, a little larger than the Sonata, comes with many standard features, including automatic climate control. Handling is short on agility, and the ride floats a bit at highway speeds. **Last road test: May 2003**
✔ **Infiniti FX**	⊖	NA	The FX drives more like a sports sedan than an SUV. The FX45 has a V8, but even the V6 FX35 is quick. Handling is nimble. The stiff ride transmits bumps and pavement flaws to the passengers. The cabin feels snug, partly because of the high doorsills and low roof. **Last road test: Sep. 2003**
✔ **Infiniti G35**	⊖	NA	The G35 is available with four or two doors. The 3.5-liter V6 provides abundant power. The firm and steady ride provides capable handling. Many controls are not intuitive. The AWD G35X is available only as a sedan. **Last road test: July 2003**
Infiniti M35/M45	NEW	NA	The outgoing M45 has a strong V8 and many luxury appointments, though the interior is quite tight. A redesign will arrive in 2005 with a 3.5-liter V6 as well as optional all-wheel drive. **Last road test: —**
Infiniti Q45	○	⊖	Nissan's flagship sedan competes against the Lexus LS430. The engine is smooth and quiet. But ride and handling aren't very impressive, and rear-seat room is tight. The many high-tech gadgets take some practice to master. **Last road test: —**
Infiniti QX56	NA	NA	This is Infiniti's version of the Nissan Armada. The V8 in our tested Armada was smooth and powerful, linked to a slick five-speed automatic. Handling was quite responsive. The ride was quite stiff and engine noise was pronounced. **Last road test: —**
Isuzu Ascender	NA	NA	This midsized SUV is essentially a rebadged Chevrolet Trailblazer/GMC Envoy, and the only remaining Isuzu model in the U.S. The TrailBlazer we tested was spacious, with a comfortable low-speed ride and a spirited inline six-cylinder, but emergency handling was sloppy and braking mediocre. **Last road test: —**
Jaguar S-Type	●	○	The S-Type shares a platform with the Lincoln LS. The V8 is strong and smooth, the V6 much less so. The interior is cramped, and the trunk is small. The overall experience is more run-of-the-mill than luxurious. A mild face-lift marks the 2005 model. **Last road test: June 2004**
Jaguar X-Type	●	○	Based on the European Ford Mondeo, this entry-level Jag comes with standard all-wheel drive and a choice of two V6 engines. It targets the BMW 3 Series and Audi A4, but lacks their refinement and driving enjoyment. **Last road test: Mar. 2002**

Model	Predicted reliability	Depre-ciation	Comments
Jaguar XJ8	NA	NA	The XJ8 features an aluminum body and offers a bit more interior room. The classy styling remains. The powertrain is strong but the ride isn't luxurious. Handling is nimble, but steering is light. A long-wheelbase model arrives for 2005. **Last road test: Nov. 2003**
Jeep Grand Cherokee	NEW	NA	The outgoing model was cramped and rough riding, with imprecise handling and a noisy six-cylinder engine. A 2005 redesign arrives this fall with an independent front suspension and better steering, but lacking a third-row seat. **Last road test: --**
✔ **Jeep Liberty**	○	⊜	The Liberty replaced the Cherokee. It has independent front suspension and a modern rack-and-pinion steering setup for more precise handling on and off road, but the ride is still jittery. The cockpit is narrow, and access is awkward. **Last road test: May 2002**
Jeep Wrangler	○	⊜	The Wrangler is the smallest and crudest Jeep. The ride is hard and noisy, handling is primitive, and the driving position is unpleasant. Nevertheless, it remains popular with off-road enthusiasts. The long-wheelbase Unlimited model improves seating room. **Last road test: --**
Kia Amanti	NA	NA	The Amanti is based on the Hyundai XG350. Kia hopes it can compete with the Buick LeSabre and Toyota Avalon, while offering a luxurious appearance with a host of standard features for a family sedan price. **Last road test: --**
Kia Optima	NA	●	The Optima provides a lot of features for a competitive price. It has a comfortable ride and a quiet cabin. The V6 performs smoothly, but averaged just 20 mpg overall. Handling is not the Optima's forte. Antilock brakes aren't offered on four-cylinder models. **Last road test: Jan. 2004**
Kia Rio	NA	●	The Rio sedan is one of the lowest-priced cars sold in the U.S. Expect to get what you pay for. It's based on the dreadful Ford Aspire, which was made for Ford by Kia in the mid-1990s. A wagon, the Cinco, is also available. **Last road test: --**
Kia Sedona	◒	○	The Sedona is relatively refined, with good fit and finish. It isn't very nimble and corners reluctantly. The ride is stiff and jiggly, and the van's heavy weight hinders acceleration and fuel economy. **Last road test: Oct. 2003**
✔ **Kia Sorento**	○	NA	This body-on-frame SUV competes with the Jeep Liberty. On road the stiff and unsettled ride is annoying and fatiguing. Handling is clumsy, though ultimately secure. **Last road test: June 2004**
Kia Spectra	NA	NA	The new Spectra is based on the Hyundai Elantra and is available as a sedan or a hatchback. It is relatively comfortable and quiet, but lacks agility. **Last road test: Aug. 2004**
Kia Sportage	NEW	NA	The Sportage name returns in a new vehicle based on the Hyundai Tucson, a small, car-based SUV. **Last road test: --**
Land Rover Freelander	●	○	The Freelander offers full-time AWD and fully independent suspension for capable off-road performance. But it's noisy, thirsty, and not very quick. Ride and handling are commendable. **Last road test: May 2002**
Land Rover LR3	NEW	NA	The LR3 is a redesign of the Discovery. It has a contemporary four-wheel independent suspension and should retain its off-road capability. Interior room is increased. The V8 is from Jaguar. **Last road test: --**

Model	Predicted reliability	Depre-ciation	Comments
Land Rover Range Rover	NA	NA	The Range Rover delivers smooth, strong acceleration, mechanical refinement, and a very comfortable ride, although handling isn't quite BMW X5 agile. It also features a height-adjustable air suspension and luxury amenities. **Last road test: --**
✔ Lexus ES330	⊖	⊜	The ES330 is a quiet, comfortable, easy-going car with a nicely trimmed interior. The 3.3-liter V6 is smooth and powerful. Handling is lackluster, with pronounced body lean in corners. **Last road test: Feb. 2004**
Lexus GS300/ GS430	⊖	NA	The GS is sportier and less expensive than Lexus' LS430 flagship. Ride and handling are competent, but unexceptional. Seating is comfortable, but the rear is tight for three. The redesigned 2006 model will feature V6 and V8 engines, and optional all-wheel drive. **Last road test: --**
✔ Lexus GX470	○	NA	The GX470 is based on the Toyota 4Runner, and combines comfort, luxury, and off-road capability. It is a bit smaller than the huge LX470, but offers a third seat. The ride is comfortable and quiet, but it gets unsettled. Cornering is less than agile, though ultimately secure. **Last road test: Mar. 2004**
✔ Lexus IS300	⊜	⊖	This rear-drive sedan has a smooth, powerful six-cylinder, and handles and brakes very capably. The ride is firm and a bit jittery, and it lacks the compliance found in its German competitors. The trunk is small and the rear seat tight. **Last road test: May 2001**
✔ Lexus LS430	⊜	⊜	Lexus' flagship is one of the world's finest luxury sedans. The engine and transmission are extremely smooth, and passengers are pampered with every imaginable convenience. The ride is smooth, supple, and quiet. **Last road test: Nov. 2003**
Lexus LX470	⊜	⊜	This luxury SUV, based on the Toyota Land Cruiser, features a height-adjustable suspension and a well-equipped interior. Like the Cruiser, it has a smooth engine and transmission, full-time four-wheel drive, and a comfortable, quiet ride. It's capable off-road and civilized on pavement. **Last road test: --**
✔ Lexus RX330	○	⊜	Our top-rated SUV, the RX330 has a comfortable and quiet ride, and AWD traction for bad weather and light off-road use. The V6 is smooth and responsive, and handling is secure. Attention to detail is impressive. The 400h hybrid arrives this fall. **Last road test: Sep. 2003**
Lexus SC430	⊜	⊜	This convertible features an electrically operated hard top. Power comes from the potent and refined V8 in the LS430. Handling isn't as sporty as some of its competitors. **Last road test: --**
Lincoln Aviator	◒	NA	The Aviator is Lincoln's version of the Ford Explorer. It has a smooth and strong V8, many luxury features, and is styled like the Lincoln Navigator. A standard third row expands seating to seven and folds flat into the floor. **Last road test: --**
Lincoln LS	◒	◒	The LS is a capable rear-drive sedan with a smooth powertrain, agile handling, and a firm, comfortable ride. Some recent tweaks yielded much needed storage space and better finishing touches. **Last road test: July 2003**

Model	Predicted reliability	Depre-ciation	Comments
Lincoln Navigator	●	○	The Navigator features a fully independent suspension and a comfortable, power-operated split third-row seat that folds flat into the floor. The cabin is quiet, steering is responsive, and ride and handling are improved over the old version. **Last road test: —**
✔ **Lincoln Town Car**	○	◒	The Town Car is the last of the domestic rear-wheel-drive luxury cruisers. The ride is smooth, and handling is OK. The front seats are soft and poorly shaped. The rear seats three with ease, and the trunk is very large. **Last road test: Feb. 2003**
Lotus Elise	NEW	NA	This mid-engined roadster is super-quick due to its light weight. Power comes from a high-revving four-cylinder from Toyota. The Elise features legendary Lotus race-car handling, a spartan driver-focused interior, and difficult cabin access. **Last road test: —**
Mazda B-Series	○	○	This compact pickup is a Ford Ranger with a Mazda nameplate. Handling is quite good for a truck, but the ride is stiff and jiggly. The 4.0-liter SOHC V6 is a welcome option. The rear seats in the extended-cab version are tight. **Last road test: —**
Mazda MPV	●	○	The MPV minivan is smaller and narrower than most competitors, but has some clever interior details, such as a fold-flat third-row seat. It rides stiffly but handles securely. The engine is a bit lackluster. **Last road test: Oct. 2003**
Mazda MX-5 Miata	⊖	○	The latest version rides marginally better than older Miatas. The engine is responsive and the stubby shifter is a joy to use. A glass rear window is standard. The interior is cramped for tall people. A Mazdaspeed turbo version was new for 2004. **Last road test: —**
Mazda RX-8	●	NA	The RX-8 revived the rotary-engine in Mazda sports cars. It is an agile and fun coupe that revs exceptionally smoothly and the ride is more than tolerable. The rear-hinged rear doors make backseat access relatively easy. **Last road test: Dec. 2003**
Mazda Tribute	⊖	⊖	The car-based Tribute is a twin of the Ford Escape. The 2005 freshening made it a bit quieter, and interior ambience improved. A tip-up in the gov't rollover test prevents us from recommending these models. **Last road test: Oct. 2004**
✔ **Mazda3**	⊜	NA	The Mazda3 has a standard 2.0-liter, four-cylinder engine that is relatively quick and sparing with fuel; the 2.3-liter version is strong and refined. Handling is precise and sporty. Interior quality is very good. **Last road test: Aug. 2004**
Mazda6	◒	NA	The Mazda6 offers nimble handling and a firm, but compliant ride. A five-speed automatic transmission is available only with the V6. The four-cylinder doesn't feel as punchy or refined as those in the Accord or Camry. Wagon and hatchback versions are also available. **Last road test: May 2003**
Mercedes-Benz C-Class	◒	⊖	The entry-level C-Class comes in sedan, coupe, and wagon body styles. They offer quick acceleration, a quiet, comfortable ride, and agile, secure handling. The seats are comfortable and supportive, but the rear is tight. **Last road test: May 2001**
Mercedes-Benz CLK	●	⊜	The coupe version of the C-Class accelerates quickly, handles well, and rides comfortably. The available engines are powerful. Rear seating is reasonably hospitable. A convertible is available. Steering feel has improved with a new design. **Last road test: —**

Model	Predicted reliability	Depre-ciation	Comments
Mercedes-Benz E-Class	●	⊖	The E-Class was redesigned for 2003, combining agile handling with a supremely comfortable ride. Seat comfort and driving position are first-class. Wagon and all-wheel-drive 4Matic models were added in 2004. **Last road test: June 2004**
Mercedes-Benz M-Class	●	⊖	This SUV is showing its age and due for a redesign. Both the V6 and V8 engines are smooth and powerful. The cabin is spacious, and the seats are comfortable. Noise suppression and ride comfort are falling behind the class leaders. **Last road test: —**
Mercedes-Benz S-Class	●	⊖	The S-Class is stately and advanced. The V8 and V12 engines are smooth, powerful, and refined. The S-Class handles with surprising agility and the cushy ride is extremely comfortable. The sumptuous rear is roomy. All-wheel drive is optional. **Last road test: Nov. 2003**
Mercedes-Benz SLK	NEW	NA	This two-seat convertible with a retractable hardtop has been redesigned for 2005. The new model feels more sporty and precise, due to a different steering system, and it's longer and wider than the old model. **Last road test: —**
Mercury Grand Marquis	○	◒	A big, old-fashioned sedan, the Grand Marquis' ride is jiggly and engine noise is pronounced. Braking and emergency handling are fairly good. Rear leg room is skimpier than you might expect. **Last road test: Feb. 2003**
Mercury Mariner	NEW	NA	The Mariner is a rebadged twin of the Ford Escape. The Escape's handling is relatively nimble, and the rear seat is roomy. The interior trim was upgraded for 2005 and it is now quieter and more comfortable. An Escape tipped-up in the gov't rollover test, so we don't recommend these SUVs. **Last road test: —**
Mercury Montego	NEW	NA	The Mercury Montego (and its Ford Five Hundred twin) is a large sedan with elevated seating positions to improve outward vision and access. The V6 engine is mated to either a six-speed automatic or a continuously variable transmission (CVT). Front-wheel drive is standard, with AWD optional. **Last road test: —**
✔ Mercury Monterey	○	NA	This is an upscale version of the Ford Freestar with a standard, but noisy, 4.2-liter V6. It features a flat-folding third-row seat. The side-curtain air-bag system protects occupants in all three rows in the event of a rollover. **Last road test: Mar. 2004**
Mercury Mountaineer	○	○	The much-improved Mountaineer has an independent suspension, an optional third-row seat, and up-to-date safety gear. The all-wheel-drive system is permanent and lacks a low range, differentiating it from the Explorer A tip-up of the 2WD version in the gov't rollover test is a cause for concern. **Last road test: —**
✔ Mercury Sable	○	●	The Sable is roomy and comfortable but showing its age. It has a decent ride and a spacious rear seat. Handling is sound but not agile. The optional V6 performs well but isn't as responsive or quiet as those from competitors. **Last road test: Jan. 2004**
Mini Cooper	◒	⊜	The diminutive Mini, from BMW, features extremely agile handling and is fun to drive, but the ride is choppy. Even tall people will find the cockpit adequately roomy, but the rear is very tight. A convertible is available, as is a supercharged version. **Last road test: Oct. 2002**

Model	Predicted reliability	Depreciation	Comments
Mitsubishi Eclipse	○	◒	A powerful engine in the GT trim is this coupe's major appeal. The cockpit is cramped. Handling and braking are nothing special. The ride is stiff and busy. A redesign is due shortly. **Last road test: —**
✔ **Mitsubishi Endeavor**	⊜	NA	The Endeavor is a midsized car-based SUV. Power comes from a 3.8-liter V6. Front-wheel-drive and all-wheel-drive versions are available. The Endeavor rides reasonably well, but cornering isn't particularly agile. **Last road test: Aug. 2003**
Mitsubishi Galant	NA	NA	The redesigned Galant arrived for 2004. Engine choices include a four-cylinder and a V6. The ride is not very comfortable. Handling is secure, but not particularly agile. The interior is roomy but bland, with disappointing fit and finish. **Last road test: May 2004**
Mitsubishi Lancer	⊜	●	Mitsubishi's small sedan falls short of the competition–and offers no price advantage, either. Handling is clumsy, the ride unsettled, and the interior noisy. The racy all-wheel-drive Evolution competes with the Subaru WRX STi. **Last road test: July 2002**
Mitsubishi Montero	NA	◒	The Montero is a pleasant SUV that's marred by clumsy and disconcerting handling. With the help of its standard stability-control system, it performed measurably better in our avoidance-maneuver tests compared with that of the 2001 Limited model, which earned a "Not Acceptable" rating. Therefore, the 2003 Montero moved to a poor rating in our emergency-handling tests. **Last road test: Aug. 2003**
Mitsubishi Outlander	⊖	NA	The Outlander is based on the Lancer. Available with either front- or all-wheel drive, it's powered by a 2.4-liter four-cylinder. The ride is reasonably comfortable and secure, but with pronounced body lean. Cargo volume is relatively small. **Last road test: June 2003**
✔ **Nissan 350Z**	○	NA	The 350Z is a two-seat coupe that shares underpinnings with the Infiniti G35. The engine is a smooth-revving 3.5-liter V6. The manual gearbox feels slightly notchy. Handling is fairly agile, but the stiff ride is uncomfortable. A convertible with a power-operated top is available. **Last road test: Dec. 2003**
✔ **Nissan Altima**	○	⊖	The Altima is roomy, with strong engines and secure handling, but a stiff and jittery ride. The front seats are fairly comfortable, but the rear seat is too low to provide much support. A freshening for 2005 has improved interior fit and finish. A wide turning circle hampers maneuverability. **Last road test: Feb. 2002**
Nissan Armada	●	NA	The Armada is a large SUV with seating for eight passengers. Power comes from a 5.6-liter V8 engine with a five-speed automatic. Two- and four-wheel drive versions are available and it features an independent-rear suspension. **Last road test: Mar. 2004**
Nissan Frontier	NEW	NA	The outgoing Frontier was crude, with cumbersome handling and an awful ride. A redesign goes on sale this fall with a strong V6, a much improved structure, and available crew- and extended-cab bodystyles. **Last road test: —**
✔ **Nissan Maxima**	○	○	The Maxima is very quick. The spacious, airy cabin and handling are improved from the previous model, though the ride is stiff and the automatic isn't as smooth. The wide turning circle is a nuisance. **Last road test: July 2003**

Model	Predicted reliability	Depre-ciation	Comments
Nissan Murano	⊖	NA	The Murano is a car-based SUV that competes with the Honda Pilot and Toyota Highlander, but doesn't offer a third-row seat. The spring-loaded rear seat can be folded by flipping a lever. The V6 delivers strong performance. Handling is fairly nimble, but the ride is stiff and noisy. **Last road test: Aug. 2003**
Nissan Pathfinder	NEW	NA	A redesigned Pathfinder goes on sale this fall with independent rear suspension, a third-row seat, full-time four-wheel drive, and a 4.0-liter V6. It shares the same platform as the new Frontier and Xterra. **Last road test: —**
Nissan Quest	●	NA	The Nissan Quest is a capable, competitively priced minivan powered by a 240-hp, 3.5-liter V6. Both the second- and third-row seats fold flat into the floor. Ride and handling are good. The center-mounted gauges are a nuisance. **Last road test: Oct. 2003**
Nissan Sentra	◒	○	The Sentra is a solid small sedan with a refined, efficient powertrain, decent handling, and a well-designed interior. But ride comfort, braking, and rear-seat room fall a bit short. **Last road test: Sep. 2000**
✔ **Nissan Titan**	○	NA	The Titan more than holds its own next to the competition. It is quick and roomy. The engine is a bit noisy and the ride jittery. Extended-cab models feature a rear door that opens flat against the body. **Last road test: July 2004**
Nissan Xterra	NEW	NA	The outgoing Xterra suffered from clumsy handling, an uncomfortable ride, leisurely acceleration, and poor fuel economy. A 2005 redesign goes on sale this fall and should be an improvement. It remains one of the few affordable SUVs with real off-road ability. **Last road test: —**
Pontiac Aztek	◒	◒	The minivan-derived Aztek includes some innovative interior touches and lots of neat little storage nooks. The rear seat is too low, the rear gate is a nuisance, and the engine is slow and thirsty. The Aztek also lacks a rear wiper, which exacerbates poor visibility in inclement weather. **Last road test: June 2003**
Pontiac Bonneville	◒	◒	Pontiac's flagship offers lots of gadgets and frills. The SE has a supple, well-controlled ride. Handling is taut though not sporty. The front seats lack support, and the seat-mounted shoulder belts may be uncomfortable for some. The rear seat is too low and soft. **Last road test: Feb. 2000**
Pontiac G6	NEW	NA	The G6 debuts this fall, replacing the Grand Am. The sedan arrives first, with a coupe and a convertible following. The V6 from the Chevrolet Malibu will be standard. A four-cylinder and more-powerful V6 will be available as well. **Last road test: —**
Pontiac GTO	NA	NA	The new Pontiac GTO is a slightly modified Holden Monaro, a car produced by GM's Australian subsidiary. For 2005 the four-passenger, rear drive coupe features a 400-hp version of the Corvette's 6.0-liter V8. The shifter and handling detract from the driving experience. **Last road test: Sep. 2004**
Pontiac Grand Prix	⊜	NA	The Grand Prix is a mediocre sedan. Its ride, rear seat comfort, and 20 mpg overall fuel economy aren't up to the levels of most competing sedans. The V6 is fairly quick but noisy. Taller drivers may find headroom insufficient. The rear seats are very cramped. **Last road test: Jan. 2004**

Model	Predicted reliability	Depreciation	Comments
Pontiac Montana SV6	NEW	NA	The Montana SV6 minivan is a freshening of GM's 7-year-old minivans. Power comes from a V6 engine that does a good job in the Chevrolet Malibu. The second-row seats can be folded and removed; the third-row seat folds flat. **Last road test: —**
Pontiac Sunfire	○	●	The Sunfire, cousin of the Chevrolet Cavalier, is basic transportation only—crude and outdated. The ride is noisy and hard. Seats are uncomfortable, and interior fit and finish are subpar. ABS is no longer standard. **Last road test: —**
✔ **Pontiac Vibe**	⊖	NA	The Vibe, cousin of the Toyota Matrix, is a roomy small wagon that's easy to get people and cargo in and out of. Handling and ride are OK, but the engine is noisy and the driving position is not ideal. All-wheel drive is optional. **Last road test: Aug. 2002**
✔ **Porsche Boxster**	○	⊖	This roadster is everything a sports car should be. The front and rear storage compartments almost make it practical. Handling and braking are superb, and the ride is firm but not punishing. Lowering the top, which features a glass rear window, is very easy. **Last road test: June 2002**
Porsche Cayenne	●	NA	The Cayenne, Porsche's first SUV, is a midsized, luxury-car-based design with all-wheel drive. Made mainly for road use, low-range gearing and advanced electronics promise some off-road capability. It comes with a choice of three engines and adjustable ride height in the turbo. **Last road test: —**
Saab 9-2X	NEW	NA	This thinly disguised Subaru Impreza wagon has a traditional Saab nose but the rest of the vehicle is virtually identical to the Impreza. All-wheel drive and the Subaru's adequate four-cylinder are standard. The WRX's turbo engine comes in the Aero trim line. **Last road test: —**
Saab 9-3	●	○	The 9-3 sedan is available with two turbocharged engines. Handling was significantly improved with the 2003 redesign, with quick, direct steering and taut body control. The rear seat is cramped and the ride is stiff. A convertible is now available. **Last road test: July 2003**
✔ **Saab 9-5**	⊖	○	The 9-5 is losing ground to newer competitors. Ride and handling are unimpressive. Front seats are comfortable, and the rear is relatively roomy. The wagon is competent and well designed but lacks a third-seat option. **Last road test: Feb. 2004**
Saab 9-7X	NEW	NA	This is an interim SUV based on the Chevrolet TrailBlazer, but featuring some unique Saab exterior and interior styling cues. **Last road test: —**
Saturn Ion	◒	NA	The Ion replaces Saturn's long-running S-series. Roomier and with a more refined engine, it's still a fairly plain small car. The coupe version has rear-hinged back doors for easier access. **Last road test: Mar. 2003**
Saturn Relay	NEW	NA	The 2005 Relay minivan is a freshening of GM's 7-year-old minivans. Power comes from a V6 engine that does a good job in the Chevrolet Malibu. The second-row seats can be folded and removed, while the folding third-row seat stows flat. **Last road test: —**

Model	Predicted reliability	Depreciation	Comments
Saturn Vue	●	⊖	The Vue uses a unibody platform. Handling is secure, but the steering is too light at low speeds and the AWD system is slow to respond. Interior fit and finish are subpar, the front seats lack support, and the rear bench is too low. A tip-up in the gov't rollover test is a cause for concern. **Last road test: Oct. 2004**
Scion tC	NEW	NA	The tC coupe is the third Scion model. Power comes from a 160-hp, 2.4-liter four-cylinder engine, with the choice of a five-speed manual or four-speed automatic. Rear seat room is generous for a coupe, and interior quality is very good. **Last road test: —**
Scion xA	NA	NA	The xA is a small four-door hatchback powered by a 1.5-liter, 108-hp four-cylinder engine. Standard amenities include antilock brakes and air conditioning. Handling is nimble, but the ride is stiff. The 60/40-split rear seat folds to increase cargo room. **Last road test: Aug. 2004**
✔ Scion xB	⊖	NA	The xB is a small, tall, slab-sided wagon powered a 1.5-liter, 108-hp Four. It offers an enormous amount of room. Antilock brakes and stability control are standard. The xB is noisy and has a stiff ride. **Last road test: Aug. 2004**
✔ Subaru Baja	⊖	NA	The Baja is essentially a previous-generation Subaru Legacy with a rear roof section chopped off to form a small pickup with four full-sized doors. A removable partition between cabin and cargo bed adds to its versatility. A 210-hp turbocharged model is available. **Last road test: June 2003**
✔ Subaru Forester	⊖	⊖	Our top-rated small SUV, the Forester has a tall and roomy cargo area and a controlled, compliant ride. Handling is relatively responsive, and acceleration and rear seat room have improved. **Last road test: June 2003**
✔ Subaru Impreza	⊖	⊖	The small Impreza delivers good handling and a quiet, comfortable ride. The line includes an Outback Sport, a small wagon, and the sporty WRX, available as sedan or wagon as well as in 300-hp STI trim. **Last road test: Dec. 2001**
✔ Subaru Legacy/ Outback	⊖	NA	The 2005 model improves acceleration with the 250-hp turbo engine, and interior quality is significantly upgraded. The Outback is a wagon with added ground clearance and more-rugged styling. The mainstream models retain the underpowered 168 hp four-cylinder. **Last road test: Nov. 2004**
Suzuki Aerio	○	●	The Aerio replaced the unimpressive Esteem and the small Swift. It features a tall roofline designed to increase head room and improve outward visibility. It's available in sedan and four-door wagon/hatchback versions. **Last road test: Mar. 2003**
Suzuki Forenza	NA	NA	This small sedan is the successor to the Daewoo Nubira, marketed as Suzuki. Ride, handling, the powertrain, and noise suppression are behind the times. It falls short of most competitors. The Reno is the new hatchback version. **Last road test: Aug. 2004**
Suzuki Verona	NA	NA	The Verona offers a lot of equipment for a low price. Handling is reluctant with vague steering, but the ride is fairly comfortable. Power comes from a quiet but lackluster six-cylinder engine. The automatic transmission is hesitant to downshift, blunting performance. **Last road test: May 2004**

Model	Predicted reliability	Depreciation	Comments
✔ **Suzuki Grand Vitara/XL-7**	○	◓	This truck-based SUV is hampered by a crude, unresponsive automatic and a stiff ride. Handling is vague but secure. The driver's seat lacks support, and the cockpit feels narrow. The extended-length XL-7 has a small third-row seat. **Last road test: May 2002**
✔ **Toyota 4Runner**	⊖	⊜	The 4Runner is roomy and comes with an optional third-row seat. V8 and V6 engines are available. The driving position and cabin access are markedly improved. This credible off-roader offers hill-descent control and a system that prevents roll-back on slow, steep ascents. **Last road test: Aug. 2003**
✔ **Toyota Avalon**	⊜	⊖	The Avalon is an upscale Camry with an extra-roomy rear seat and trunk. It features interior ambiance similar to that of a Lexus, a powerful V6, and a quiet cabin. A redesign arrives in early 2005. **Last road test: Feb. 2003**
✔ **Toyota Camry**	⊜	⊖	The Camry remains an excellent sedan—quiet, refined, and roomy. Both the four-cylinder and V6 are smooth and responsive. Cabin controls are logical, with plenty of storage. So-so front-seat thigh support and a lack of a telescoping wheel makes finding a comfortable driving position difficult for some. **Last road test: Feb. 2002**
Toyota Camry Solara	○	NA	The Solara is based on the current Camry. The standard engine is a four-cylinder. The optional V6 is smooth and refined, and mated to an automatic gearbox that has a manual-shift mode. A convertible arrived in 2004. **Last road test: —**
✔ **Toyota Celica**	⊜	⊖	The Celica is a fun-to-drive sporty coupe that handles nimbly. The ride is relatively good. The budget-minded may prefer the plain GT, which isn't as quick or agile as the high-revving GT-S, but is about $4,500 cheaper. 2005 is the last year for the Celica. **Last road test: Aug. 2000**
✔ **Toyota Corolla**	⊜	○	The Corolla is a solid small car, with a roomy, high-quality interior. It handles and rides better than the previous version. The standard engine delivers both responsive performance and excellent fuel economy, though it sounds a bit boomy. **Last road test: July 2002**
✔ **Toyota Echo**	⊜	⊖	The Echo is a surprisingly roomy small runabout. The driving position is fairly high, and it's easy to get in and out. The 1.5-liter engine provides good fuel economy. Handling is fairly responsive and secure, but body roll is pronounced. **Last road test: Dec. 2000**
✔ **Toyota Highlander**	⊜	⊜	This Camry-derived all-wheel-drive SUV has a punchy V6 powertrain. It is roomy, quiet, comfortable, and well designed. It's conceptually similar to the Lexus RX330 but less expensive. A small third-row seat is optional and a hybrid arrives for 2005. **Last road test: Dec. 2004**
✔ **Toyota Land Cruiser**	⊜	⊖	This big, expensive SUV sports a smooth, quiet 4.7-liter V8 and rides smoothly. The interior offers lots of room and a third seat. It combines plushness and quality with off-road ability. **Last road test: Mar. 2001**
✔ **Toyota MR2**	⊜	⊖	Think of the mid-engine MR2 as a small Porsche Boxster at a Mazda Miata price. It offers impressive steering and acceleration, precise shifting, and excellent brakes, but luggage space is close to zero. 2005 is the last year for the MR2. **Last road test: Aug. 2000**

Model	Predicted reliability	Depreciation	Comments
✔ **Toyota Matrix**	⊖	NA	The Matrix is a roomy small wagon that's easy to get people and cargo in and out of. Handling and ride are acceptable, but the engine is noisy and the driving position is not ideal. All-wheel drive is optional. **Last road test: Aug. 2002**
✔ **Toyota Prius**	⊜	NA	Toyota's second-generation hybrid couples a small gasoline engine with an electric motor, and returned an excellent 44 mpg in our tests. Acceleration is comparable to any conventional family sedan. Access is easy and the interior is well put together. The unusual controls and displays take some getting used to. **Last road test: May 2004**
✔ **Toyota RAV4**	⊜	⊜	The RAV4 is one of our highest-rated small SUVs. It has a flexible interior layout, easy access, nimble handling, and standard stability control. There's still no V6, but the improved four-cylinder accelerates adequately. **Last road test: Oct. 2004**
✔ **Toyota Sequoia**	⊖	⊜	The Sequoia competes against the Nissan Armada, Ford Expedition, and Chevrolet Tahoe. It is roomier than the Land Cruiser, but doesn't ride as comfortably. It boasts a V8 powertrain and a third-row seat. **Last road test: Nov. 2002**
✔ **Toyota Sienna**	○	⊖	The redesigned Sienna is our top-rated minivan, and rides very comfortably and quietly. The spacious interior features a third seat that folds flat into the floor. The sliding doors have windows that can be opened. **Last road test: Oct. 2003**
Toyota Tacoma	⊖	NA	The outgoing Tacoma pickup was a super off-roader, but rode uncomfortably and handled ponderously. The 2005 redesign gets improved interior quality, a better driving position, and more responsive handling. **Last road test: —**
✔ **Toyota Tundra**	⊜	⊜	The Tundra is among the better full-sized pickups. The V8 is smooth and powerful, the cabin is quiet, and the ride is pleasant. The rear seat in extended-cab versions is very cramped. **Last road test: July 2004**
Volkswagen Golf	◒	○	The Golf's responsive but noisy 2.0-liter four-cylinder and easy-shifting manual perform well together. You can also get a smooth, powerful V6, a 1.8-liter turbo four-cylinder, or a diesel engine. The ride is supple. The front seats offer good, firm support, but the rear is cramped. A redesign is around the corner. **Last road test: —**
Volkswagen Jetta	◒	⊖	The Jetta shares underpinnings with the Golf and boasts many thoughtful details, a comfortable ride, and responsive handling. The front seats are supportive; the rear is cramped. The standard 2.0-liter four-cylinder is noisy and the diesel is economical. A redesign arrives shortly. **Last road test: Aug. 2002**
Volkswagen New Beetle	◒	○	The modern, well-equipped New Beetle rides and handles well. The front seats are supportive, but the rear is cramped. A 180-hp Turbo S model is quick but not very sporty. A convertible is available. **Last road test: Oct. 2002**
✔ **Volkswagen Passat**	○	⊖	Our top-rated family sedan is roomy and comfortable. The Passat handles precisely and delivers a firm yet supple ride. The interior appointments have a high-quality feel. All-wheel drive is available. The economical diesel engine returned 28 mpg overall, but was a bit noisy. **Last road test: May 2003**

Model	Predicted reliability	Depre-ciation	Comments
Volkswagen Phaeton	NA	NA	The Phaeton is Volkswagen's first large, premium-luxury cruiser. Engines include a 4.2-liter V8 and an optional 6.0-liter 12-cylinder. All-wheel drive is standard. This heavy and plush sedan rides on an adjustable air suspension. **Last road test: —**
Volkswagen Touareg	●	NA	Volkswagen's first SUV has features such as low-range gearing and a locking center differential, making it one of the few car-based SUVs that's capable off road. The V6 is thirsty and underpowered, and the V8 is stronger but expensive. A V10 diesel is available. The interior is elegant but not so roomy. **Last road test: Sep. 2003**
Volvo S40/V50	NEW	NA	The new S40 shares its platform with the Mazda3. Handling is fairly nimble, but the ride is stiff and the engine is noisy. Nice interior details contribute to a good ambiance. The rear is cramped. The V50 is a wagon version. All-wheel drive is available. **Last road test: Nov. 2004**
✔ Volvo S60	○	⊖	The S60 is neither luxurious nor sporty. The interior is fairly quiet and the front seats are comfortable. The ride is stiff and handling is secure, but not particularly agile. The rear seat is cramped. The confusing radio controls have been improved. **Last road test: Feb. 2004**
Volvo S80	◒	○	Volvo's front- or all-wheel-drive flagship performs well. It's roomy, quiet, and comfortable. The base engine is a lively straight Six; the turbocharged T6 version offers effortless acceleration. **Last road test: June 2004**
✔ Volvo V70/XC70	○	⊖	The V70 is spacious, with comfortable seats. The all-wheel-drive XC70 Cross Country model is an SUV alternative that rides and handles more roughly than the V70. AWD is also available on the V70. **Last road test: July 2001**
Volvo XC90	●	NA	This seven-seater SUV has all-wheel drive and a third row that folds flat. It features a stability-control system that detects a rollover and helps a driver maintain control. The ride is more comfortable than in the XC70. Power comes from either a five- or six-cylinder engine. **Last road test: Sep. 2003**

RATING THE 2005 MODELS

Which cars are the best? This section can give you a head start in answering that question. Included here are overall Ratings on 185 vehicles from CONSUMER REPORTS' extensive testing program. Though most tests were conducted on 2004 or earlier models, results still apply unless there was a redesign since. Recommended models are indicated with a ✔. This means that the model performed well in our tests; they should have at least average reliability; and they have performed adequately if crash tested or included in a government rollover test. Twins (similar models sold under different nameplates) are grouped together in the charts and marked with ■ symbols when only one version has been tested. Overall MPG is based on our tests in a range of mixed highway and city driving conditions.

Recommendations are based on results from our latest 2004 reliability survey.

Model	Overall score	Overall mpg	Tested model
	P F G VG E		
SMALL CARS (AUTO TRANS.)			
✔ Mazda3		27	i 2.0 4-cyl.; four-speed automatic
✔ Ford Focus		25	ZTS 2.0 4-cyl.; four-speed automatic
✔ Honda Civic		29	EX 1.7 4-cyl.; four-speed automatic
✔ Toyota Prius		44	1.5 4-cyl.; CVT
✔ Honda Civic		36	Hybrid 1.3 4-cyl.; CVT
✔ Toyota Corolla		29	LE 1.8 4-cyl.; four-speed automatic
Volkswagen Jetta		32	GLS 1.9 4-cyl. turbodiesel; four-speed auto.
Hyundai Elantra		25	GLS 2.0 4-cyl.; four-speed automatic
Kia Spectra		25	EX 2.0 4-cyl.; four-speed automatic
✔ Subaru Impreza		22	2.5 RS 2.5 4-cyl.; four-speed automatic
Nissan Sentra		26	GXE 1.8 4-cyl.; four-speed automatic
✔ Scion xB		30	1.5 4-cyl.; four-speed automatic
Suzuki Aerio		25	GS 2.0 4-cyl.; four-speed automatic
Mitsubishi Lancer		26	LS 2.0 4-cyl.; four-speed automatic
Scion xA		30	1.5 4-cyl.; four-speed automatic
Suzuki Forenza		24	S 2.0 4-cyl.; four-speed automatic
Hyundai Accent		26	GL 1.6 4-cyl.; four-speed automatic
Chevrolet Aveo		28	LS 1.6 4-cyl.; four-speed automatic
Saturn Ion		24	3 2.2 4-cyl.; five-speed automatic

Model	Overall score (P F G VG E)	Overall mpg	Tested model
SMALL CARS (AUTO TRANS.) *continued*			
Dodge Neon		24	SXT 2.0 4-cyl.; four-speed automatic
Chevrolet Cavalier		26	LS 2.2 4-cyl.; four-speed automatic
SMALL CARS (MANUAL TRANS.)			
✔ Mazda3		30	i 2.0 4-cyl.; five-speed manual
✔ Toyota Echo		38	1.5 4-cyl.; five-speed manual
Kia Spectra		28	EX 2.0 4-cyl.; five-speed manual
✔ Scion xB		32	1.5 4-cyl.; five-speed manual
Scion xA		31	1.5 4-cyl.; five-speed manual
Suzuki Forenza		27	S 2.0 4-cyl.; five-speed manual
Honda Insight		51	1.0 3-cyl.; five-speed manual
Chevrolet Aveo		27	LS 1.6 4-cyl.; five-speed manual
FUEL EFFICIENT CARS			
✔ Toyota Prius		44	1.5 4-cyl.; CVT
✔ Honda Civic		36	Hybrid 1.3 4-cyl.; CVT
Volkswagen Jetta		32	GLS 1.9 4-cyl. turbodiesel; four-speed auto.
✔ Toyota Echo		38	1.5 4-cyl.; five-speed manual
Honda Insight		51	1.0 3-cyl.; five-speed manual
FAMILY SEDANS			
✔ Volkswagen Passat		21	GLX 2.8 V6; five-speed automatic
✔ Toyota Camry		20	XLE 3.0 V6; four-speed automatic
✔ Honda Accord		23	EX 3.0 V6; five-speed automatic
✔ Honda Accord		24	EX 2.4 4-cyl.; five-speed automatic
✔ Volkswagen Passat		23	GLS 1.8 4-cyl. turbo; five-speed automatic
✔ Toyota Camry		24	LE 2.4 4-cyl.; four-speed automatic
✔ Subaru Legacy		18	GT Limited 2.5 4-cyl. turbo; five-speed automatic
✔ Nissan Maxima		21	3.5 SE 3.5 V6; five-speed automatic
✔ Nissan Altima		20	3.5 SE 3.5 V6; four-speed automatic
Volkswagen Passat		28	GLS TDI 2.0 4-cyl. turbodiesel; five-speed auto.
Mazda6		23	i 2.3 4-cyl.; four-speed automatic
Chevrolet Malibu		26	LS 3.5 V6; four-speed automatic
Mazda6		20	s 3.0 V6; five-speed automatic
✔ Toyota Prius		44	1.5 4-cyl.; CVT
Chevrolet Malibu		24	Base 2.2 4-cyl.; four-speed automatic
✔ Nissan Altima		22	2.5 S 2.5 4-cyl.; four-speed automatic
✔ Hyundai Sonata		21	GLS-L 2.5 V6; four-speed automatic

Model	Overall score (P F G VG E)	Overall mpg	Tested model
FAMILY SEDANS *continued*			
Volvo S40		23	2.4i 2.4 Five; five-speed automatic
Mitsubishi Galant		23	ES 2.4 4-cyl.; four-speed automatic
✔ Hyundai XG350		19	L 3.5 V6; five-speed automatic
Kia Optima		20	EX 2.7 V6; four-speed automatic
✔ ■ Ford Taurus		22	SES 3.0 V6; four-speed automatic
✔ ■ Mercury Sable		22	Ford Taurus SES 3.0 V6; four-speed automatic
■ Chrysler Sebring		21	LX 2.7 V6; four-speed automatic
■ Dodge Stratus		21	Chrysler Sebring LX 2.7 V6; four-speed auto
✔ Chevrolet Impala		20	LS 3.8 V6; four-speed automatic
Suzuki Verona		20	LX 2.5 6-cyl.; four-speed automatic
Pontiac Grand Prix		20	GT2 3.8 V6; four-speed automatic
■ Chrysler Sebring		21	Dodge Stratus SXT 2.4 4-cyl.; four-speed auto
■ Dodge Stratus		21	SXT 2.4 4-cyl.; four-speed automatic
UPSCALE SEDANS			
✔ Acura TL		23	3.2 V6; five-speed automatic
✔ BMW 3 Series		22	330i 3.0 6-cyl.; five-speed automatic
✔ Lexus IS300		21	3.0 6-cyl.; five-speed automatic
✔ Lexus ES330		22	3.3 V6; five-speed automatic
Mercedes-Benz C-Class		21	C320 3.2 V6; five-speed automatic
Lincoln LS		19	Premium 3.0 V6; five-speed automatic
✔ Acura TSX		23	2.0 4-cyl.; five-speed automatic
✔ Audi A4		24	1.8T 1.8 4-cyl. turbo; CVT
✔ Audi A4		20	Quattro 3.0 V6; five-speed automatic
✔ Cadillac CTS		20	3.2 V6; five-speed automatic
Saab 9-3		21	Vector 2.0 4-cyl. turbo; five-speed auto.
✔ Infiniti G35		20	3.5 V6; five-speed automatic
Jaguar X-Type		19	3.0 3.0 V6; five-speed automatic
✔ Saab 9-5		21	Arc 2.3 4-cyl. turbo; five-speed automatic
✔ Volvo S60		22	2.5T 2.5 Five turbo; five-speed automatic
LUXURY SEDANS			
✔ Lexus LS430		19	4.3 V8; five-speed automatic
Mercedes-Benz S-Class		18	S430 4.3 V8; five-speed automatic
Mercedes-Benz E-Class		20	E320 3.2 V6; five-speed automatic
BMW 5 Series		20	530i 3.0 6-cyl.; six-speed automatic
Cadillac DeVille		19	DHS 4.6 V8; four-speed automatic

Model	Overall score P F G VG E	Overall mpg	Tested model
LUXURY SEDANS *continued*			
Audi A8		17	L 4.2 V8; six-speed automatic
Jaguar S-Type		19	4.2 V8; six-speed automatic
Jaguar XJ8		19	Vanden Plas 4.2 V8; six-speed automatic
Volvo S80		19	T6 2.9 6-cyl. twin-turbo; four-speed automatic
BMW 7 Series		18	745Li 4.4 V8; six-speed automatic
LARGE SEDANS			
✔ Toyota Avalon		21	XLS 3.0 V6; four-speed automatic
✔ Buick Park Avenue		21	Ultra 3.8 V6 supercharged; four-speed auto.
✔ Lincoln Town Car		17	Signature 4.6 V8; four-speed automatic
Pontiac Bonneville		20	SE 3.8 V6; four-speed automatic
✔ Buick LeSabre		20	Limited 3.8 V6; four-speed automatic
■ Ford Crown Victoria		16	Mercury Grand Marquis LSE 4.6 V8; four-spd. auto.
■ Mercury Grand Marquis		16	LSE 4.6 V8; four-speed automatic
SPORTS/SPORTY CARS			
✔ Audi A4		20	S4 4.2 V8; six-speed manual
✔ BMW 3 Series		19	M3 3.2 6-cyl.; six-speed manual
✔ Subaru Impreza		20	WRX STi 2.5 4-cyl. turbo; six-speed manual
Mazda RX-8		18	1.3 rotary; six-speed manual
✔ Cadillac CTS		17	CTS-V 5.7 V8; six-speed manual
Mitsubishi Lancer		20	Evolution 2.0 4-cyl. turbo; five-speed manual
✔ Subaru Impreza		21	WRX 2.0 4-cyl. turbo; five-speed manual
✔ Toyota Celica		28	GT-S 1.8 4-cyl.; six-speed manual
Volkswagen New Beetle		25	Turbo S 1.8 4-cyl. turbo; six-speed manual
Mini Cooper		30	Base 1.6 4-cyl.; five-speed manual
✔ Honda Civic		26	Si 2.0 4-cyl.; five-speed manual
✔ Nissan 350Z		22	Touring 3.5 V6; six-speed manual
✔ Acura RSX		26	Type-S 2.0 4-cyl.; six-speed manual
Pontiac GTO		17	5.7 V8; six-speed manual
Chrysler Crossfire		22	3.2 V6; six-speed manual
Hyundai Tiburon		22	GT V6 2.7 V6; six-speed manual
Mitsubishi Eclipse		24	GT 3.0 V6; five-speed manual
ROADSTERS			
✔ Porsche Boxster		22	Base 2.7 6-cyl.; five-speed manual
✔ Toyota MR2		31	1.8 4-cyl.; five-speed manual
Audi TT		22	Conv. AWD 1.8 4-cyl. turbo; six-speed manual

Model	Overall score P F G VG E	Overall mpg	Tested model
ROADSTERS *continued*			
✔ Ford Thunderbird		17	Premium 3.9 V8; five-speed automatic
MINIVANS			
✔ Toyota Sienna		21	LE 3.3 V6; five-speed automatic
Mazda MPV		19	ES 3.0 V6; five-speed automatic
Nissan Quest		18	3.5 SL 3.5 V6; four-speed automatic
✔ ■ Chrysler Town & Country		17	Dodge Grand Caravan eX 3.8 V6; four-speed auto.
✔ ■ Dodge Grand Caravan		17	eX 3.8 V6; four-speed automatic
✔ ■ Ford Freestar		17	SEL 4.2 V6; four-speed automatic
✔ ■ Mercury Monterey		17	Ford Freestar SEL 4.2 V6; four-speed auto.
Kia Sedona		16	EX 3.5 V6; five-speed automatic
WAGONS & HATCHBACKS			
Volkswagen Passat		18	GLX 4Motion 2.8 V6; five-speed automatic
Audi Allroad		16	2.7 V6 turbo; five-speed automatic
✔ Ford Focus		23	SE 2.0 4-cyl.; four-speed automatic
Volkswagen Jetta		23	GLS 1.8 4-cyl. turbo; five-speed automatic
✔ Volvo XC70		18	XC 2.4 Five turbo; five-speed automatic
✔ Pontiac Vibe		26	Base 1.8 4-cyl.; four-speed automatic
✔ Toyota Matrix		24	XR AWD 1.8 4-cyl.; four-speed automatic
✔ Ford Focus hatchback		24	ZX5 2.0 4-cyl.; four-speed automatic
✔ Chrysler PT Cruiser		18	Limited 2.4 4-cyl.; four-speed automatic
✔ Subaru Impreza		22	Outback Sport 2.5 4-cyl.; four-speed automatic
✔ Scion xB		30	1.5 4-cyl.; four-speed automatic
SMALL SPORT-UTILITY VEHICLES			
✔ Subaru Forester		21	2.5 X 2.5 4-cyl.; four-speed automatic
✔ Toyota RAV4		21	2.4 4-cyl.; four-speed automatic
✔ ■ Pontiac Vibe		24	Toyota Matrix XR AWD 1.6 4-cyl.; four-speed auto.
✔ ■ Toyota Matrix		24	XR AWD 1.6 4-cyl.; four-speed automatic
✔ Subaru Baja		20	Base 2.5 4-cyl.; four-speed automatic
✔ Honda CR-V		21	EX 2.4 4-cyl.; four-speed automatic
■ Ford Escape		18	XLT 3.0 V6; four-speed automatic
■ Mazda Tribute		18	Ford Escape XLT 3.0 V6; four-speed automatic
✔ Honda Element		20	EX 2.4 4-cyl.; four-speed automatic
✔ Hyundai Santa Fe		18	GLS 2.7 V6; four-speed automatic
✔ Mitsubishi Outlander		20	XLS 2.4 4-cyl.; four-speed automatic
Saturn Vue		19	V6 3.5 V6; five-speed automatic

Model	Overall score (P F G VG E)	Overall mpg	Tested model
SMALL SPORT-UTILITY VEHICLES *continued*			
Chevrolet Equinox		17	LT 3.4 V6; five-speed automatic
✔ Suzuki XL-7		17	Touring 2.7 V6; four-speed automatic
✔ Kia Sorento		15	LX 3.5 V6; four-speed automatic
Land Rover Freelander		17	SE 2.5 V6; five-speed automatic
✔ Jeep Liberty		15	Sport 3.7 V6; four-speed automatic
Pontiac Aztek		17	3.4 V6; four-speed automatic
MIDSIZED SPORT-UTILITY VEHICLES			
Audi Allroad		16	2.7 V6 turbo; five-speed automatic
✔ Lexus RX330		18	3.3 V6; five-speed automatic
✔ Honda Pilot		19	EX 3.5 V6; five-speed automatic
Nissan Murano		19	SL 3.5 V6; CVT
✔ Toyota Highlander		18	Limited 3.0 V6; four-speed automatic
Cadillac SRX		16	V8 4.6 V8; five-speed automatic
✔ Volvo XC70		18	XC 2.4 Five turbo; five-speed automatic
✔ Acura MDX		17	Touring 3.5 V6; five-speed automatic
✔ Infiniti FX		18	FX35 3.5 V6; five-speed automatic
BMW X5		17	3.0i 3.0 6-cyl.; five-speed automatic
✔ Lexus GX470		15	4.7 V8; five-speed automatic
✔ Mitsubishi Endeavor		17	XLS 3.8 V6; four-speed automatic
✔ Toyota 4Runner		16	SR5 4.0 V6; four-speed automatic
Chrysler Pacifica		16	3.5 V6; four-speed automatic
Volvo XC90		15	T6 2.9 6-cyl. twin-turbo; four-speed automatic
Volkswagen Touareg		15	V6 3.2 V6; six-speed automatic
✔ Ford Explorer		16	XLT 4.6 V6; five-speed automatic
✔ Dodge Durango		12	Limited 5.7 V8; five-speed automatic
✔ Buick Rendezvous		16	CXL 3.4 V6; four-speed automatic
Mitsubishi Montero		14	Limited 3.8 V6; five-speed automatic
▪ Chevrolet TrailBlazer		15	GMC Envoy SLE 4.2 6-cyl.; four-speed automatic
▪ GMC Envoy		15	SLE 4.2 6-cyl.; four-speed automatic
▪ Chevrolet TrailBlazer		13	EXT LT 4.2 6-cyl.; four-speed automatic
▪ GMC Envoy		13	Chevrolet TrailBlazer EXT LT 4.2 Six; four-spd. auto.
LARGE SPORT-UTILITY VEHICLES			
✔ Toyota Land Cruiser		14	4.7 V8; four-speed automatic
Nissan Armada		13	LE 5.6 V8; five-speed automatic
✔ Toyota Sequoia		15	Limited 4.7 V8; four-speed automatic

Model	Overall score	Overall mpg	Tested model
	P F G VG E		
LARGE SPORT-UTILITY VEHICLES ***continued***			
Ford Expedition		12	Eddie Bauer 5.4 V8; four-speed automatic
✔ Dodge Durango		12	Limited 5.7 V8; five-speed automatic
■ Chevrolet Tahoe		13	LT 5.3 V8; four-speed automatic
■ GMC Yukon		13	Chevrolet Tahoe LT 5.3 V8; four-speed auto.
COMPACT PICKUP TRUCKS - CREW CAB 4WD V6			
✔ Ford Explorer Sport Trac		15	4.6 V6; five-speed automatic
■ Chevrolet S-10		15	LS 4.3 V6; four-speed automatic
■ GMC Sonoma		15	Chevrolet S-10 LS 4.3 V6; four-speed auto.
FULL-SIZED PICKUP TRUCKS - CREW CAB 4WD V8			
✔ Toyota Tundra		14	SR5 4.7 V8; four-speed automatic
✔ Chevrolet Avalanche		13	5.3 V8; four-speed automatic
Ford F-150		14	XLT 5.4 V8; four-speed automatic
✔ Nissan Titan		13	SE 5.6 V8; five-speed automatic
✔ ■ Chevrolet Silverado 1500		14	Z71 5.3 V8; four-speed automatic
✔ ■ GMC Sierra 1500		14	Chevrolet Silverado 1500 Z71 5.3 V8; four-spd. auto.
Dodge Ram 1500		11	SLT 5.7 V8; five-speed automatic
Dodge Ram 1500		12	SLT 4.7 V8; four-speed automatic

THE BEST AND WORST USED CARS

A great way to reduce the uncertainty in buying a used car is to shop for cars with proven reliability. The lists on these pages can guide you to the best and help you steer clear of the worst.

CONSUMER REPORTS annually surveys its more than 5 million magazine and online subscribers. They're asked to list any serious problems they've had with their vehicles during the past 12 months. The 2003 survey garnered about 675,000 responses, allowing CR to publish the most comprehensive reliability information available.

The results detail how 1996 through 2003 vehicles are holding up. To see reliability ratings in 14 trouble areas, refer to the Reliability History charts beginning on page 195. On these pages we look at the overall reliability and separate the models into lists that highlight the best and worst.

CR Good Bets (below) are the best of the best; they have performed well in our road tests and have been consistently better than average in overall reliability. The complete list of **Reliable Used Cars** (pages 189-190) includes all the models that have had above-average reliability, according to our survey, and divides models by price category, make, and model year.

Used Cars to Avoid (pages 191-192) shows you all models, by manufacturer and year, that have had below-average reliability, according to our 2003 survey. **Repeat Offenders** (page 191) are models that are especially risky buys. They have exhibited several years of poor overall reliability.

CR GOOD BET

These models represent the best of both worlds

They have performed well in CONSUMER REPORTS tests over the years and have had much-better-than-average reliability for multiple years. They are listed alphabetically.

Acura Integra
Acura MDX
Acura RL
Acura TL
Buick Regal
Chevrolet/Geo Prizm
Chrysler PT Cruiser
Ford Escort
Honda Accord
Honda Civic
Honda CR-V
Honda Odyssey
Honda Prelude
Honda S2000
Infiniti G20
Infiniti I30, I35
Infiniti QX4
Isuzu Oasis
Lexus ES300
Lexus GS300/GS400, GS430
Lexus LS400, LS430
Lexus RX300
Lincoln Town Car (except '03)
Mazda 626
Mazda MPV
Mazda MX-5 Miata
Mazda Millenia
Mazda Protegé
Mercury Tracer
Nissan Altima
Nissan Maxima
Nissan Pathfinder
Subaru Forester
Subaru Impreza
Subaru Legacy
Subaru Outback
Toyota 4Runner
Toyota Avalon
Toyota Camry
Toyota Camry Solara
Toyota Celica
Toyota Corolla
Toyota Echo
Toyota Highlander
Toyota Land Cruiser
Toyota RAV4
Toyota Sequoia
Toyota Sienna
Toyota Tundra

Reliable used cars

These models showed better-than-average reliability in our latest survey; they are listed alphabetically by price range and model year. All prices are rounded to the nearest $1,000. The price ranges are what you'd pay for a typically equipped vehicle with average mileage.

LESS THAN $6,000

Buick Century '97-98
Chevrolet Prizm '98-00
Ford Crown Victoria '97, **Escort** '97-01, **F-150 (2WD)** '96, **Ranger (2WD)** '96-98
Geo Prizm '96-97, **Tracker** '96-97
Honda Civic '96-97
Mazda 626 '98, **B-Series (2WD)** '96-98, **Protegé** '96-00
Mercury Grand Marquis '97, **Tracer** '97-99
Nissan Altima '96-98, **Frontier** '98, **Pickup** '96-97, **Sentra** '96-99
Saturn S-Series '96, '98-99
Subaru Impreza '96-97
Suzuki Sidekick '96-97
Toyota Corolla '96-99, **Echo** '00, **Tercel** '96-97

$6,000-$8,000

Acura Integra '96-97
Buick Century '00-01, **Regal** '99
Chevrolet Prizm '01-02
Ford Crown Victoria '98-99, **Escort** '02, **F-150 (2WD)** '97, **Mustang** '98, **Ranger (2WD)** '99-00
Honda Accord '96-97, **Civic** '98-99, **Prelude** '96
Hyundai Elantra '02
Infiniti G20 '96, **I30** '96
Isuzu Oasis '96
Lincoln Continental '98
Mazda 626 '99-00, **B-Series (2WD)** '99-00, **Millenia** '96-97, **MX-5 Miata** '96-97, **Protegé** '01
Mercury Grand Marquis '98-99
Nissan Altima '99, **Maxima** '96-97, **Sentra** '00-01
Saturn S-Series '01
Subaru Impreza '98-99, **Legacy/Outback** '96-98
Toyota Avalon '96, **Camry** '96-98 , **Celica** '96, **Corolla** '00-01, **Echo** '01-02, **RAV4** '96-98, **T100** '96, **Tacoma** '96-97

$8,000-$10,000

Acura CL '97-98, **Integra** '98-99, **TL** '96
Buick Century '02, **Regal** '00
Chrysler PT Cruiser '01
Ford Crown Victoria '00, **F-150 (2WD)** '98-99, **F-150 (4WD)** '97, **Mustang** '99-00
Honda Accord '98-99, **Civic** '00-01, **CR-V** '97-99, **Odyssey** '96-97, **Prelude** '97
Infiniti G20 '99, **I30** '97-98
Isuzu Oasis '97-98
Lincoln Continental '99, **Town Car** '96-97
Mazda 626 '01, **Millenia** '98-99, **MX-5 Miata** '99, **Protegé** '02
Mercury Grand Marquis '00
Mitsubishi Eclipse '00
Nissan Altima '00-01, **Frontier** '99, **Maxima** '98-99, **Pathfinder** '96-97
Saturn S-Series '02
Subaru Forester '98, **Impreza** '00, **Legacy/Outback** '99
Toyota 4Runner '96, **Avalon** '97-98, **Camry** '99, **Camry Solara** '99, **Celica** '97-98, **Corolla** '02, **Previa** '96, **RAV4** '99, **T100** '97-98, **Tacoma** '98-99

$10,000-$12,000

Acura CL '99, **Integra** '00, **RL** '96, **TL** '97-98
Buick Century '03, **Regal** '01
Chevrolet Impala '02
Chrysler PT Cruiser '02
Ford F-150 (2WD) '00, **F-150 (4WD)** '98
Honda Accord '00, **Civic** '02, **Odyssey** '98, **Prelude** '98-99
Hyundai Elantra '03
Infiniti G20 '00, **I30** '99, **Q45** '96, **QX4** '97-98
Lexus ES300 '96-98
Lincoln Town Car '98-99
Mazda 626 '02, **Millenia** '00, **MPV** '00, **MX-5 Miata** '00, **Protegé** '03
Mercedes-Benz C-Class '96-97
Mitsubishi Eclipse '01
Nissan Frontier '00, **Pathfinder** '98-99
Subaru Forester '00, **Impreza** '01, **Legacy/Outback** '00
Toyota 4Runner '97-98, **Camry** '00, **Celica** '99-00, **RAV4** '00, **Sienna** '98-99, **Tacoma** '00

$12,000-$14,000

Acura Integra '01, **RL** '97-98, **TL** '99
BMW 3 Series '97, **Z3** '97
Buick Regal '02
Chevrolet Silverado 1500 (2WD) '00
Ford F-150 (2WD) '01
Honda Accord '01, **Civic** '03, **CR-V** '00, **Prelude** '00
Infiniti G20 '01, **I30** '00, **Q45** '97
Lexus ES300 '99
Lincoln Continental '00, **Town Car** '00
Mazda Millenia '01, **MPV** '01,

MX-5 Miata '01
Nissan Maxima '00, **Xterra** '00-01
Subaru Legacy/Outback '01
Toyota Avalon '99, **Camry** '01, **Camry Solara** '00, **Celica** '01, **Corolla** '03, **Sienna** '00

$14,000-$16,000

Acura RL '99, **TL** '00
BMW 3 Series '99, **Z3** '98-99
Buick LeSabre '02, **Regal** '03
Chevrolet Impala '03, **Silverado 1500 (2WD)** '01
Ford F-150 (2WD) '02, **F-150 (4WD)** '00
GMC Sierra 1500 (2WD) '00
Honda Accord '02, **CR-V** '01, **Prelude** '01
Hyundai Santa Fe '02
Infiniti G20 '02, **Q45** '98, **QX4** '99
Lexus GS300/GS400 '96, **LS400** '96, **SC400** '96-97
Mazda MPV '02, **MX-5 Miata** '02
Nissan Maxima '01, **Pathfinder** '00
Pontiac Vibe '03
Subaru Forester '01, **Impreza** '02
Toyota 4Runner '99, **Avalon** '00, **Camry** '02, **Camry Solara** '01, **Celica** '02, **Land Cruiser** '96, **Prius** '01, **RAV4** '01, **Tacoma** '01, **Tundra** '00

$16,000-$18,000

Acura CL '01, **RL** '00, **RSX** '02, **TL** '01
Buick LeSabre '03
Ford F-150 (2WD) '03
GMC Sierra 1500 (2WD) '01
Honda CR-V '02, **Element** '03, **Odyssey** '00
Infiniti I30 '01, **Q45** '99, **QX4** '00
Lexus ES300 '00, **GS300/GS400** '98, **LS400** '97-98
Lincoln Town Car '01
Mazda Millenia '02, **MX-5 Miata** '03, **6** '03
Nissan Altima '03, **Frontier** '03, **Maxima** '02, **Pathfinder** '01
Toyota 4Runner '00, **Avalon** '01, **Camry Solara** '02, **Celica** '03, **Land Cruiser** '97, **Prius** '02, **RAV4** '02, **Sienna** '01, **Tacoma** '02, **Tundra** '01

$18,000-$20,000

Acura CL '02, **RSX** '03
BMW Z3 '00
Honda Accord '03, **CR-V** '03, **Odyssey** '01, **S2000** '00
Hyundai Santa Fe '03
Lexus GS300/GS400 '99, **IS300** '01, **RX300** '99
Nissan Maxima '03, **Pathfinder** '02, **Xterra** '03
Subaru Forester '03
Toyota Camry '03, **Camry Solara** '03, **Highlander** '01, **Land Cruiser** '98, **Prius** '03, **RAV4** '03, **Sienna** '02, **Tacoma** '03, **Tundra** '02

$20,000-$22,000

BMW 5 Series '99, **Z3** '01
Ford F-150 (4WD) '03
Infiniti I35 '02, **QX4** '01
Lexus ES300 '01, **LS400** '99, **RX300** '00
Toyota 4Runner '01, **Avalon** '02, **Highlander** '02, **Sienna** '03

$22,000-$26,000

Acura RL '01
BMW 5 Series '00
Honda Odyssey '02-03, **S2000** '02-03
Infiniti I35 '03, **Q45** '01, **QX4** '02
Lexus GS300/GS400 '00, **IS300** '02, **LS400** '00, **RX300** '01
Lincoln Town Car '02
Nissan 350Z '03, **Pathfinder** '03
Porsche Boxster '00
Toyota 4Runner '02, **Avalon** '03, **Highlander** '03, **Land Cruiser** '99, **Tundra** '03

$26,000-$30,000

Acura MDX '01, **RL** '02
BMW 3 Series '02
Honda Pilot '03
Infiniti G35 '03
Lexus ES300 '02, **GS300/GS430** '01, **IS300** '03, **LX470** '99, **RX300** '02
Nissan Murano '03
Saab 9-5 '03
Toyota Land Cruiser '00, **Sequoia** '01

$30,000 AND UP

Acura MDX '02-03
BMW 5 Series '01-03
Infiniti FX '03, **Q45** '02
Lexus ES300 '03, **GS300/GS430** '02-03, **LS430** '01-03, **LX470** '00-03, **RX300** '03, **SC430** '02
Toyota Land Cruiser '01-02, **Sequoia** '02

About these lists

The lists in this report are distilled from reliability data on 1996 through 2003 models.

CR Good Bets and **Repeat Offenders** include only models for which we have sufficient data for at least three model years. Models that were new in 2002-2004 do not appear. Problems with the engine, cooling system, transmission, and drive system were weighted more heavily than other problems. 2WD, 4WD, and AWD stand for two-, four-, and all-wheel drive, respectively.

REPEAT OFFENDERS

Be careful when considering these models

They have shown several years of much-worse-than-average overall reliability. They are listed alphabetically.

Audi A6
BMW 7 Series
Cadillac Seville
Chevrolet Astro
Chevrolet Blazer
Chevrolet S-10 (4WD)
Chrysler Town & Country (AWD)
Dodge Grand Caravan (AWD)
Dodge Neon
GMC Jimmy
GMC Safari
GMC Sonoma (4WD)
Jaguar S-Type
Jeep Grand Cherokee
Mercedes-Benz M-Class
Oldsmobile Bravada
Oldsmobile Cutlass
Plymouth Neon
Volkswagen Golf
Volkswagen Jetta
Volkswagen New Beetle

Used cars to avoid

These models showed below-average reliability in our latest survey. They are listed alphabetically by make, model, and year.

Audi A4 (4-cyl.) '97-98, '01-02; **A4 (V6)** '96-98, '02; **A6 (V6)** '98-00, '02-03; **A6 (V6 Turbo)** '00-01; **TT** '01-02

BMW 7 Series '97-99, '02-03; **X5** '00-02

Buick Park Avenue '97-98, '01; **Roadmaster** '96; **Skylark** '96-97

Cadillac Catera '97-01; **CTS** '03; **DeVille** '96-98, '00-01, '03; **Escalade** '02-03; **Seville** '96-98, '00-03

Chevrolet Astro '96-03; **Blazer** '96-03; **C1500** '97-98; **Camaro** '97-99, '01; **Caprice** '96; **Cavalier** '96; **Corsica, Beretta** '96; **Corvette** '98, '00-03; **Express 1500** '96-03; **K1500** '96-98; **Malibu** '97-01; **S-10** '96-03; **Silverado 1500 (4WD)** '99-00, '02-03; **Suburban** '96-00, '03; **Tahoe** '96-99, '03; **TrailBlazer** '02-03; **Venture** '97-00; **Venture (AWD)** '02

Chrysler 300M '99, '03; **Cirrus**, '96; **Concorde** '96-99; **New Yorker, LHS** '96, '99; **Sebring Convertible** '96-97, '01; **Town & Country** '96-97, '99-02; **Voyager (4-cyl.)** '02; **Voyager** 01, '03

Dodge Caravan '96-01, '03; **Caravan (4-cyl.)** '02; **Dakota (2WD)** '97-98; **Dakota (4WD)** '96, '98-01; **Durango** '98-00; **Grand Caravan** '96-97, '99-02; **Intrepid** '96-99; **Neon** '96-00; **Ram 1500** '96-99, '01-02; **Ram 1500 (2WD)** '00; **Ram Van/Wagon 1500** '96, '98-00; **Stratus** '96; **Stratus (4-cyl.)** '97-99

Ford Contour (4-cyl.) '97-98; **Contour (V6)** '96, '98, '00; **Crown Victoria** '03; **Econoline Van 150** '96, '01-03; **Escape** '01; **Excursion** '01; **Expedition** '03; **Explorer** '00, '02; **Explorer (4WD)** '98-99, '01; **Explorer Sport Trac** '03; **Focus** '00-01; **Mustang** '03; **Ranger (4WD)** '00-02; **Taurus Wagon** '02; **Windstar** '96-01

GMC Envoy '02-03; **Jimmy** '96-01; **S-15 Sonoma** '96-03; **Safari** '96-03; **Savana Van 1500** '96-03; **Sierra 1500 (2WD)** '97-98; **Sierra 1500 (4WD)** '96-00, '02-03; **Suburban** '96-99; **Yukon** '96-99, '03; **Yukon XL** '00, '03

Honda Passport '98-99

Hummer H2 '03

Hyundai Santa Fe '01; **Sonata** '01; **XG350** '02

Isuzu Rodeo '98-99

Jaguar S-Type '00-03; **XJ8** '99-00; **X-Type** '02-03

Jeep Grand Cherokee '96-03
Kia Sedona '02
Land Rover Discovery '00-01; **Freelander** '02
Lincoln Navigator '03; **Town Car** '03
Mazda B-Series (4WD) '00-02; **Tribute** '01
Mercedes-Benz C-Class '01-03; **CLK** '02; **E-Class** '03; **E-Class (AWD)** '00-01; **M-Class** '98-02; **S-Class** '00, '02; **SLK** '02
Mercury Cougar '99-01; **Grand Marquis** '03; **Mountaineer** '00, '02; **Mountaineer (4WD)** '98-99, '01; **Mystique (4-cyl.)** '97-98; **Mystique (V6)** '96, '98, '00; **Sable Wagon** '02
Mini Cooper '02-03
Mitsubishi Eclipse '03; **Galant** '96, '02
Nissan Sentra '03
Oldsmobile 88 '97-98; **Alero** '99-01; **Aurora** '96, '01; **Bravada** '97-03; **Cutlass** '97-99; **Cutlass Ciera** '96; **Silhouette** '97-00; **Silhouette (AWD)** '02
Plymouth Breeze '96-99; **Grand Voyager** '96-97, '99-00; **Neon** '96-00; **Voyager** '96-00
Pontiac Aztek '01, '03; **Bonneville** '97-98, '00-03; **Firebird** '97, '99-01; **Grand Am** '96-97, '99-01; **Grand Prix** '97-98; **Montana** '00; **Montana (AWD)** '02; **Sunfire** '96; **TransSport, Montana** '97-99
Saturn L-Series (V6) '00-02; **SW** '00; **Vue** '02-03
Subaru Baja '03; **Legacy Outback (6-cyl.)** '03
Toyota 4Runner (V6) '03
Volkswagen Golf '96-03; **Jetta** '96-03; **New Beetle** '98-03; **Passat** '98-00; **Passat (4-cyl.)** '02; **Passat (V6)** '96-97
Volvo S90/V90 '97-98; **S40/V40** '00; **S80** '99-00; **V70/Cross Country** '98-01; **XC90** '03

DETAILED RELIABILITY

In the following pages, CR provides you with reliability information on more than 200 models. Based on 675,000 responses to our 2003 annual subscriber survey, these charts show you how 1996 through 2003 models are holding up in 14 trouble spots.

To check a model's overall reliability, look at the Reliability Verdict. A key is included below and at the top of all even-numbered pages in this section. To identify the most reliable models, look for those with a ✔, which means they had above-average reliability overall. Be wary of models with an ✘—they showed below-average reliability overall.

The Reliability Verdict is calculated from the problem rates for the 14 trouble spots and compared with the average for that model year. Extra weight is given to the engine, cooling system, transmission, and drive system ratings.

To assess a model in more detail, look at the individual ratings for each of the 14 trouble spots. Refer to the "Trouble-Spot Ratings" key, below, to see model's strengths and weaknesses.

What's normal? To see whether a model's problems are unusually high or the result of normal aging, compare its trouble-spot ratings with those for an average model in the chart below. You'll see that older models generally have more problems than newer ones, and some trouble spots pose more problems than others.

2003 models were generally less than six months old at the time of the survey, with an average of about 3,000 miles. New

How to read the charts

RELIABILITY VERDICTS

Black check ✔
Better-than-average overall reliability.

Black dash –
Average overall reliability.

Black ✘
Below-average overall reliability.

Reliability History

TROUBLE SPOTS	The Average Model 96	97	98	99	00	01	02	03
Engine	○	○	○	⊖	⊖	⊜	⊜	⊜
Cooling	○	○	⊖	⊖	⊖	⊜	⊜	⊜
Fuel	○	○	○	○	⊖	⊖	⊖	⊜
Ignition	⊖	⊖	⊖	⊖	⊜	⊜	⊜	⊜
Transmission	○	○	⊖	⊖	⊖	⊖	⊜	⊜
Electrical	◒	◒	◒	○	○	○	⊖	⊜
Air conditioning	◒	○	○	⊖	⊖	⊖	⊜	⊜
Suspension	○	○	○	⊖	⊖	⊖	⊜	⊜
Brakes	◒	◒	◒	○	○	○	⊖	⊜
Exhaust	⊖	⊖	⊖	⊜	⊜	⊜	⊜	⊜
Paint/trim/rust	○	⊖	⊖	⊖	⊖	⊖	⊜	⊜
Body Integrity	○	○	○	○	○	○	○	⊖
Power equipment	○	○	○	○	○	○	⊖	⊜
Body hardware	○	○	○	○	○	⊖	⊖	⊜
RELIABILITY VERDICT	–	–	–	–	–	–	–	–

TROUBLE-SPOT RATINGS

Scores for the individual trouble spots represent the percentage of survey respondents who reported problems occurring in the 12 months from April 1, 2002, through March 31, 2003, that were deemed serious because of cost, failure, compromised safety, or downtime.

- ⊜ 2.0% or less
- ⊖ 2.0% to 5.0%
- ○ 5.0% to 9.3%
- ◒ 9.3% to 14.8%
- ● More than 14.8%

vehicles should have few problems, so a score of ⊖ or worse is below average for most. A ○ may be cause for concern. With older vehicles, a ○ can be average; scores of ◒ or ● may not be unusual in categories such as electrical, brakes, and air conditioning.

What the trouble spots include

ENGINE: Pistons, rings, valves, block, heads, bearings, camshafts, gaskets, supercharger, turbocharger, cam belts and chains, oil pumps.

COOLING: Radiator, heater core, water pump, thermostat, hoses, intercooler, and plumbing.

FUEL: Fuel injection, computer and sensors, fuel pump, tank, emissions controls, check-engine light.

IGNITION: Spark plugs, coil, distributor, electronic ignition, sensors and modules, timing.

TRANSMISSION: Transaxle, gear selector and linkage, coolers, and lines. (We no longer provide separate data for manual transmissions, since survey responses in this area are so few.)

ELECTRICAL: Starter, alternator, battery, horn, gauges, lights, wiring, and wiper motor.

AIR CONDITIONING: Compressor, condenser, evaporator, expansion valves, hoses, dryer, fans, electronics.

SUSPENSION: Steering linkage, power-steering gear, pump, coolers and lines, alignment and balance, springs and torsion bars, ball joints, bushings, shocks and struts, electronic or air suspension.

BRAKES: Hydraulic system, linings, rotors and drums, power boost, antilock system, parking brake, and linkage.

EXHAUST: Manifold, muffler, catalytic converter, pipes.

PAINT/TRIM/RUST: Fading, discoloring, chalking, peeling, cracking paint; loose exterior trim or moldings; rust.

BODY INTEGRITY: Seals, weather stripping, air and water leaks, wind noise, rattles and squeaks.

POWER EQUIPMENT: Electronically operated accessories such as mirrors, sunroof, windows, door locks and seats, cruise control, audio system, navigational system.

BODY HARDWARE: Manual mirrors, sunroof; window, door, and seat mechanisms; locks; safety belts; loose interior trim; glass defects.

Why does it look reliable but get an ✘?

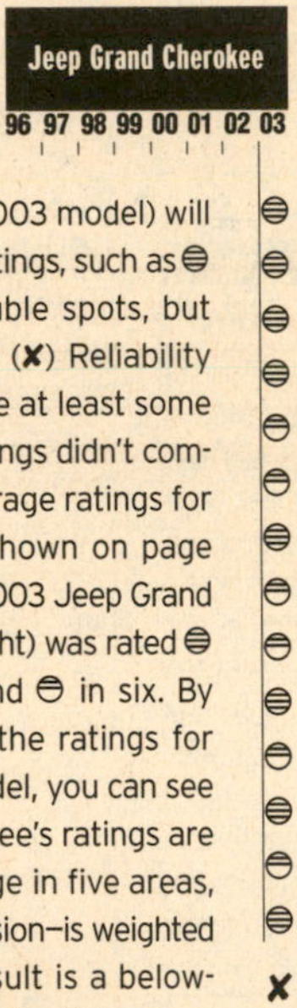

This is a frequently asked question about our reliability charts. Sometimes a newer vehicle (especially a 2003 model) will have seemingly high ratings, such as ⊜ and ⊖, in the 14 trouble spots, but gets a below-average (✘) Reliability Verdict. That's because at least some of the trouble-spot ratings didn't compare well with the average ratings for that model year, as shown on page 193. For instance, the 2003 Jeep Grand Cherokee (shown at right) was rated ⊜ in eight categories and ⊖ in six. By comparing that with the ratings for the average 2003 model, you can see that the Grand Cherokee's ratings are worse than the average in five areas, one of which—transmission—is weighted more heavily. The result is a below-average (✘) Reliability Verdict.

Acura CL

Trouble spots	96	97	98	99	00	01	02	03
Engine		⊖	⊖	⊖		⊖	⊖	⊖
Cooling		⊖	⊖	⊖		⊖	⊖	⊖
Fuel		⊖	⊖	⊖		⊖	⊖	⊖
Ignition		⊖	⊖	⊖		⊖	⊖	⊖
Transmission		⊖	⊖	⊖		○	○	⊖
Electrical		○	○	⊖		⊖	⊖	⊖
A/C		⊖	⊖	⊖		⊖	⊖	⊖
Suspension		⊖	⊖	⊖		⊖	⊖	⊖
Brakes		○	○	○		○	⊖	⊖
Exhaust		⊖	⊖	⊖		⊖	⊖	⊖
Power equip.		◒	◒	○		⊖	⊖	⊖
Paint/trim/rust		⊖	⊖	⊖		⊖	⊖	⊖
Integrity		⊖	⊖	⊖		○	⊖	⊖
Hardware		⊖	⊖	⊖		⊖	⊖	⊖
RELIABILITY VERDICT		✔	✔	✔		-	✔	-

Acura Integra, RSX

Trouble spots	96	97	98	99	00	01	02	03
Engine	⊖	⊖	⊖	⊖	⊖	⊖	⊖	⊖
Cooling	○	○	⊖	⊖	⊖	⊖	⊖	⊖
Fuel	⊖	⊖	⊖	⊖	⊖	⊖	⊖	⊖
Ignition	⊖	⊖	⊖	⊖	⊖	⊖	⊖	⊖
Transmission	⊖	⊖	⊖	⊖	⊖	⊖	⊖	⊖
Electrical	⊖	⊖	⊖	⊖	⊖	⊖	⊖	⊖
A/C	⊖	⊖	⊖	⊖	⊖	⊖	⊖	⊖
Suspension	⊖	⊖	⊖	⊖	⊖	⊖	⊖	⊖
Brakes	○	○	○	○	⊖	⊖	⊖	⊖
Exhaust	⊖	⊖	⊖	⊖	⊖	⊖	⊖	⊖
Power equip.	⊖	⊖	⊖	○	⊖	⊖	⊖	⊖
Paint/trim/rust	○	○	○	⊖	⊖	⊖	⊖	⊖
Integrity	○	○	○	⊖	○	⊖	⊖	⊖
Hardware	⊖	⊖	○	○	⊖	⊖	⊖	⊖
RELIABILITY VERDICT	✔	✔	✔	✔	✔	✔	✔	✔

Acura MDX

Trouble spots	96	97	98	99	00	01	02	03
Engine						⊖	⊖	⊖
Cooling						⊖	⊖	⊖
Fuel						⊖	⊖	⊖
Ignition						⊖	⊖	⊖
Transmission						⊖	⊖	⊖
Electrical						⊖	⊖	⊖
A/C						⊖	⊖	⊖
Suspension						⊖	⊖	⊖
Brakes						⊖	⊖	⊖
Exhaust						⊖	⊖	⊖
Power equip.						⊖	⊖	⊖
Paint/trim/rust						⊖	⊖	⊖
Integrity						⊖	⊖	⊖
Hardware						⊖	⊖	⊖
RELIABILITY VERDICT						✔	✔	✔

Acura RL

Trouble spots	96	97	98	99	00	01	02
Engine	⊖	⊖	⊖	⊖	⊖	Insufficient data	⊖
Cooling	⊖	⊖	⊖	⊖	⊖		⊖
Fuel	⊖	⊖	⊖	⊖	⊖		⊖
Ignition	⊖	⊖	⊖	⊖	⊖		⊖
Transmission	⊖	○	⊖	⊖	⊖		⊖
Electrical	○	⊖	⊖	⊖	⊖		⊖
A/C	⊖	⊖	⊖	⊖	⊖		⊖
Suspension	⊖	○	⊖	⊖	⊖		⊖
Brakes	●	○	○	⊖	⊖		⊖
Exhaust	⊖	⊖	⊖	⊖	⊖		⊖
Power equip.	◒	○	○	⊖	⊖		⊖
Paint/trim/rust	⊖	⊖	⊖	⊖	⊖		⊖
Integrity	⊖	⊖	⊖	⊖	⊖		⊖
Hardware	⊖	⊖	⊖	⊖	⊖		⊖
RELIABILITY VERDICT	✔	✔	✔	✔	✔		✔

Acura TL

Trouble spots	96	97	98	99	00	01	02	03
Engine	⊖	⊖	⊖	⊖	⊖	⊖	⊖	⊖
Cooling	⊖	○	⊖	⊖	⊖	⊖	⊖	⊖
Fuel	⊖	⊖	⊖	⊖	⊖	⊖	⊖	⊖
Ignition	⊖	⊖	⊖	⊖	⊖	⊖	⊖	⊖
Transmission	⊖	⊖	⊖	⊖	⊖	○	○	⊖
Electrical	○	◒	⊖	⊖	⊖	⊖	⊖	⊖
A/C	⊖	⊖	⊖	⊖	⊖	⊖	⊖	⊖
Suspension	⊖	⊖	⊖	⊖	⊖	⊖	⊖	⊖
Brakes	◒	○	⊖	⊖	○	⊖	⊖	⊖
Exhaust	◒	⊖	○	⊖	⊖	⊖	⊖	⊖
Power equip.	○	⊖	○	⊖	⊖	⊖	⊖	⊖
Paint/trim/rust	⊖	⊖	⊖	⊖	⊖	⊖	⊖	⊖
Integrity	⊖	○	⊖	⊖	⊖	⊖	⊖	⊖
Hardware	⊖	⊖	⊖	⊖	⊖	⊖	⊖	⊖
RELIABILITY VERDICT	✔	✔	✔	✔	✔	✔	-	-

Audi A4 4-cyl.

Trouble spots	96	97	98	99	00	01	02	03
Engine	Insufficient data	●	◒	○	⊖	○	○	⊖
Cooling		◒	⊖	⊖	⊖	⊖	⊖	⊖
Fuel		○	⊖	⊖	◒	○	⊖	⊖
Ignition		⊖	○	○	⊖	◒	●	⊖
Transmission		⊖	⊖	⊖	⊖	⊖	⊖	⊖
Electrical		◒	○	◒	◒	◒	○	⊖
A/C		⊖	⊖	⊖	⊖	⊖	⊖	⊖
Suspension		○	○	⊖	⊖	⊖	⊖	⊖
Brakes		○	●	○	⊖	⊖	⊖	⊖
Exhaust		⊖	⊖	⊖	⊖	⊖	⊖	⊖
Power equip.		○	○	⊖	◒	○	○	⊖
Paint/trim/rust		○	○	⊖	⊖	⊖	⊖	⊖
Integrity		○	○	○	○	⊖	⊖	⊖
Hardware		○	⊖	⊖	⊖	⊖	⊖	⊖
RELIABILITY VERDICT		✘	✘	-	-	✘	✘	-

Audi A6 V6

Trouble spots	96	97	98	99	00	01	02	03
Engine	○	⊖	●	◒	○	○	⊖	⊖
Cooling	◒	◒	○	○	⊖	⊖	⊖	⊖
Fuel	○	⊖	●	◒	◒	○	⊖	⊖
Ignition	○	⊖	⊖	⊖	⊖	⊖	○	⊖
Transmission	○	○	⊖	⊖	⊖	⊖	⊖	⊖
Electrical	●	●	●	●	◒	○	○	⊖
A/C	○	⊖	⊖	⊖	⊖	⊖	⊖	⊖
Suspension	○	◒	◒	◒	⊖	⊖	⊖	⊖
Brakes	○	◒	●	◒	○	○	○	⊖
Exhaust	⊖	⊖	⊖	⊖	⊖	⊖	⊖	⊖
Power equip.	●	○	◒	●	●	○	○	○
Paint/trim/rust	⊖	⊖	○	○	⊖	⊖	⊖	⊖
Integrity	○	⊖	○	○	○	○	⊖	⊖
Hardware	○	⊖	◒	◒	○	○	⊖	⊖
RELIABILITY VERDICT	-	-	✘	✘	✘	-	✘	✘

Audi TT

Trouble spots	96	97	98	99	00	01	02	03
Engine					⊖	⊖	⊖	Insufficient data
Cooling					⊖	⊖	⊖	
Fuel					◒	○	⊖	
Ignition					⊖	⊖	⊖	
Transmission					⊖	⊖	⊖	
Electrical					●	●	○	
A/C					⊖	⊖	⊖	
Suspension					⊖	⊖	⊖	
Brakes					⊖	⊖	⊖	
Exhaust					⊖	⊖	⊖	
Power equip.					○	◒	○	
Paint/trim/rust					⊖	⊖	⊖	
Integrity					○	○	⊖	
Hardware					○	○	⊖	
RELIABILITY VERDICT					-	✘	✘	

TROUBLE SPOTS	BMW 3-Series 96	97	98	99	00	01	02	03
Engine	⊖	⊖	⊜	⊜	⊜	⊜	⊜	⊜
Cooling	●	◒	○	⊖	⊖	⊖	⊜	⊜
Fuel	○	○	○	⊜	⊖	⊖	⊜	⊜
Ignition	⊜	⊖	⊜	⊜	⊜	⊜	⊜	⊜
Transmission	⊜	⊜	⊖	⊜	⊜	⊜	⊜	⊜
Electrical	●	●	◒	◒	◒	○	⊖	⊖
A/C	○	○	○	○	○	⊖	⊜	⊜
Suspension	⊖	○	○	○	⊖	⊜	⊜	⊜
Brakes	○	⊖	○	○	○	⊖	⊜	⊜
Exhaust	○	⊜	⊖	⊜	⊜	⊜	⊜	⊜
Power equip.	◒	◒	◒	◒	◒	○	⊖	⊖
Paint/trim/rust	⊖	⊜	⊖	⊜	⊖	⊖	⊜	⊜
Integrity	○	○	○	○	○	○	○	⊖
Hardware	⊖	⊖	○	○	○	○	⊖	⊖
RELIABILITY VERDICT	-	✓	-	✓	-	-	✓	-

TROUBLE SPOTS	BMW 5-Series 96	97	98	99	00	01	02	03
Engine		○	⊖	⊜	⊖	⊜	⊜	⊜
Cooling		●	◒	○	⊖	⊜	⊜	⊜
Fuel		⊖	⊖	⊖	⊖	⊖	⊜	⊜
Ignition		⊜	⊜	⊜	⊜	⊜	⊜	⊜
Transmission		⊖	⊜	⊖	⊜	⊜	⊜	⊜
Electrical		◒	◒	◒	○	◒	○	⊖
A/C		○	⊖	⊖	○	○	⊜	⊜
Suspension		⊖	⊖	⊖	⊜	⊜	⊜	⊜
Brakes		○	○	⊖	⊖	⊖	⊜	⊜
Exhaust		⊖	⊖	⊜	⊜	⊜	⊜	⊜
Power equip.		◒	◒	○	○	⊖	⊖	⊖
Paint/trim/rust		⊖	⊜	⊜	⊜	⊜	⊜	⊜
Integrity		○	○	○	⊖	○	⊖	⊜
Hardware		○	◒	○	⊖	⊖	⊖	⊖
RELIABILITY VERDICT		-	-	✓	✓	✓	✓	✓

TROUBLE SPOTS	BMW 7-Series 96	97	98	99	00	01	02	03
Engine	Insufficient data	◒	◒	Insufficient data	⊖	⊜	⊖	⊜
Cooling		●	●		◒	⊜	⊜	⊜
Fuel		⊖	○		⊖	⊜	○	⊖
Ignition		⊜	⊖		⊜	⊜	○	⊖
Transmission		⊖	⊖		⊜	⊜	○	⊖
Electrical		◒	●		◒	○	●	◒
A/C		⊖	◒		⊖	○	⊜	⊜
Suspension		○	◒		⊖	⊖	⊖	⊜
Brakes		○	○		⊖	⊖	⊜	⊜
Exhaust		◒	◒		⊜	⊜	⊜	⊜
Power equip.		○	◒		◒	⊖	●	◒
Paint/trim/rust		⊖	⊖		⊜	⊖	⊜	⊜
Integrity		○	◒		⊖	○	⊖	⊖
Hardware		○	◒		○	○	○	⊖
RELIABILITY VERDICT		✗	✗		-	-	✗	✗

TROUBLE SPOTS	BMW X5 96	97	98	99	00	01	02	03
Engine					Insufficient data	⊜	⊜	⊜
Cooling						⊖	⊜	⊜
Fuel						⊖	⊖	⊖
Ignition						⊜	⊜	⊜
Transmission						⊖	⊖	⊜
Electrical						◒	○	⊖
A/C						○	⊜	⊜
Suspension						⊖	⊜	⊜
Brakes						○	⊜	⊜
Exhaust						⊜	⊜	⊜
Power equip.						●	◒	⊖
Paint/trim/rust						⊖	⊖	⊜
Integrity						◒	○	⊖
Hardware						◒	○	⊖
RELIABILITY VERDICT						✗	✗	-

TROUBLE SPOTS	BMW Z3, Z4 96	97	98	99	00	01	02	03
Engine	Insufficient data	⊜	⊖	Insufficient data	⊜	⊜	Insufficient data	⊜
Cooling		○	⊖		⊖	⊜		⊖
Fuel		⊖	⊖		⊖	⊖		⊜
Ignition		⊜	⊜		⊖	⊜		⊜
Transmission		⊜	⊖		⊜	⊜		⊜
Electrical		○	○		○	⊖		⊜
A/C		○	⊖		⊜	⊜		⊜
Suspension		○	⊜		⊜	⊜		⊜
Brakes		⊖	⊜		⊜	⊖		⊜
Exhaust		⊖	⊜		⊜	⊜		⊜
Power equip.		⊖	○		⊖	⊖		⊖
Paint/trim/rust		○	○		⊜	⊜		⊜
Integrity		●	◒		○	○		○
Hardware		●	⊖		○	○		⊜
RELIABILITY VERDICT		✓	✓		✓	✓		-

TROUBLE SPOTS	Buick Century 96	97	98	99	00	01	02	03
Engine	○	○	⊖	○	⊖	⊖	⊜	⊜
Cooling	◒	○	○	○	⊜	⊜	⊜	⊜
Fuel	◒	○	○	○	⊜	⊖	⊜	⊜
Ignition	⊖	⊖	⊜	⊖	⊜	⊜	⊜	⊜
Transmission	⊖	⊖	⊜	⊜	○	⊖	⊜	⊜
Electrical	●	●	◒	◒	○	○	⊖	⊜
A/C	⊖	○	⊖	⊖	⊜	⊜	⊜	⊜
Suspension	○	○	⊖	⊖	⊖	⊖	⊜	⊜
Brakes	●	○	◒	○	○	⊖	⊜	⊜
Exhaust	⊖	⊜	⊜	⊜	⊜	⊜	⊜	⊜
Power equip.	●	○	◒	◒	⊖	⊖	⊜	⊜
Paint/trim/rust	◒	⊖	⊖	⊖	⊜	⊜	⊜	⊜
Integrity	◒	○	○	○	⊖	⊖	⊖	⊖
Hardware	○	⊜	⊖	⊖	⊖	⊖	⊜	⊜
RELIABILITY VERDICT	-	✓	-	-	✓	✓	✓	✓

TROUBLE SPOTS	Buick LeSabre 96	97	98	99	00	01	02	03
Engine	◒	○	◒	⊖	⊖	⊜	⊜	⊜
Cooling	◒	◒	○	○	⊖	⊖	⊜	⊜
Fuel	○	◒	◒	○	○	⊖	⊜	⊜
Ignition	⊖	⊖	⊖	⊖	⊖	⊜	⊜	⊜
Transmission	⊖	◒	○	○	⊖	⊖	⊜	⊜
Electrical	◒	●	◒	○	◒	○	⊖	⊜
A/C	◒	○	⊖	⊖	⊜	⊜	⊜	⊜
Suspension	○	○	⊜	⊖	○	⊖	⊜	⊜
Brakes	◒	◒	◒	◒	○	⊖	⊖	⊜
Exhaust	⊜	⊖	⊜	⊜	⊜	⊜	⊜	⊜
Power equip.	○	○	○	○	●	○	⊖	⊜
Paint/trim/rust	⊖	⊖	⊖	⊖	⊜	⊜	⊜	⊜
Integrity	○	○	○	○	○	◒	○	⊖
Hardware	⊖	⊖	⊖	⊖	⊖	⊖	⊜	⊜
RELIABILITY VERDICT	-	-	-	-	-	-	✓	✓

TROUBLE SPOTS	Buick Park Avenue 96	97	98	99	00	01	02	03
Engine	⊖	◒	◒	⊖	⊜	⊜	⊜	⊜
Cooling	○	◒	○	⊖	⊖	⊜	⊜	⊜
Fuel	○	◒	○	⊖	⊖	⊜	⊜	⊜
Ignition	⊖	⊖	⊖	⊖	⊜	⊜	⊜	⊜
Transmission	○	○	○	⊖	⊖	⊖	⊜	⊖
Electrical	◒	●	●	◒	◒	◒	○	⊖
A/C	◒	○	⊖	⊖	⊜	⊜	⊜	⊜
Suspension	○	○	○	○	○	◒	⊜	⊜
Brakes	◒	◒	●	○	○	○	⊜	⊜
Exhaust	⊜	⊜	⊜	⊜	⊜	⊜	⊜	⊜
Power equip.	◒	◒	◒	○	○	○	○	⊖
Paint/trim/rust	⊖	○	⊖	⊜	⊖	⊜	⊜	⊜
Integrity	○	◒	○	⊖	⊖	○	⊖	⊖
Hardware	⊖	◒	◒	◒	○	○	⊖	⊖
RELIABILITY VERDICT	✓	✗	✗	-	-	✗	-	-

Buick Regal

TROUBLE SPOTS	96	97	98	99	00	01	02	03
Engine	◒	◒	◒	⊖	⊖	⊜	⊜	⊜
Cooling	◒	●	⊖	⊜	⊖	⊜	⊜	⊜
Fuel	○	○	⊖	⊖	⊖	⊖	⊜	⊜
Ignition	⊖	⊖	⊖	⊜	⊜	⊜	⊜	⊜
Transmission	⊖	○	⊖	⊖	⊜	⊖	⊜	⊜
Electrical	◒	◒	◒	◒	○	○	⊜	⊖
A/C	○	○	⊖	⊖	⊜	⊜	⊜	⊜
Suspension	○	○	⊖	⊖	⊖	⊖	⊜	⊜
Brakes	●	○	○	○	○	⊖	⊖	⊜
Exhaust	⊜	⊜	⊜	⊜	⊜	⊜	⊜	⊜
Power equip.	○	○	◒	◒	○	⊖	⊜	⊜
Paint/trim/rust	○	○	⊖	⊜	⊖	⊜	⊜	⊜
Integrity	○	◒	○	○	○	⊖	⊜	⊜
Hardware	○	○	○	⊖	⊖	⊜	⊜	⊜
RELIABILITY VERDICT	–	–	–	✔	–	✔	✔	✔

Buick Rendezvous

TROUBLE SPOTS	96	97	98	99	00	01	02	03
Engine							⊜	⊜
Cooling							⊜	⊜
Fuel							⊜	⊜
Ignition							⊜	⊜
Transmission							⊖	⊜
Electrical							○	⊖
A/C							⊜	⊜
Suspension							⊜	⊜
Brakes							⊜	⊜
Exhaust							⊜	⊜
Power equip.							○	⊜
Paint/trim/rust							⊜	⊜
Integrity							⊖	⊖
Hardware							⊖	⊜
RELIABILITY VERDICT							–	–

Cadillac Catera, CTS

TROUBLE SPOTS	96	97	98	99	00	01	02	03
Engine		●	●	Insufficient data	Insufficient data	Insufficient data		⊖
Cooling		●	●	Insufficient data	Insufficient data	Insufficient data		⊜
Fuel		◒	⊖	Insufficient data	Insufficient data	Insufficient data		⊜
Ignition		◒	⊖	Insufficient data	Insufficient data	Insufficient data		⊜
Transmission		○	○	Insufficient data	Insufficient data	Insufficient data		⊜
Electrical		●	●	Insufficient data	Insufficient data	Insufficient data		⊖
A/C		◒	○	Insufficient data	Insufficient data	Insufficient data		⊜
Suspension		○	◒	Insufficient data	Insufficient data	Insufficient data		○
Brakes		◒	◒	Insufficient data	Insufficient data	Insufficient data		⊜
Exhaust		⊜	⊜	Insufficient data	Insufficient data	Insufficient data		⊜
Power equip.		◒	●	Insufficient data	Insufficient data	Insufficient data		⊖
Paint/trim/rust		○	⊖	Insufficient data	Insufficient data	Insufficient data		⊜
Integrity		○	○	Insufficient data	Insufficient data	Insufficient data		⊖
Hardware		◒	◒	Insufficient data	Insufficient data	Insufficient data		⊜
RELIABILITY VERDICT		✗	✗					✗

Cadillac DeVille

TROUBLE SPOTS	96	97	98	99	00	01	02	03
Engine	◒	●	○	⊖	○	○	⊜	⊜
Cooling	○	◒	⊖	⊖	○	⊖	⊜	⊜
Fuel	●	◒	○	○	○	⊖	⊖	⊜
Ignition	○	◒	⊖	⊖	○	⊖	⊜	⊜
Transmission	◒	⊜	⊖	⊖	⊖	⊜	⊜	⊜
Electrical	●	●	●	◒	◒	○	○	⊖
A/C	●	●	◒	⊖	⊖	⊖	⊜	⊜
Suspension	○	○	○	○	○	◒	⊖	⊜
Brakes	◒	◒	●	◒	○	⊖	⊖	⊜
Exhaust	⊖	⊜	⊜	⊜	⊜	⊜	⊜	⊜
Power equip.	◒	◒	◒	○	◒	○	⊖	⊖
Paint/trim/rust	⊖	⊖	○	⊖	⊜	⊜	⊜	⊜
Integrity	○	○	○	○	○	⊖	⊖	⊜
Hardware	○	○	○	⊖	○	○	⊖	⊖
RELIABILITY VERDICT	✗	✗	✗	–	✗	✗	–	✗

Cadillac Escalade

TROUBLE SPOTS	96	97	98	99	00	01	02	03
Engine				Insufficient data	Insufficient data		⊖	⊜
Cooling				Insufficient data	Insufficient data		⊜	⊜
Fuel				Insufficient data	Insufficient data		⊜	⊜
Ignition				Insufficient data	Insufficient data		⊜	⊜
Transmission				Insufficient data	Insufficient data		⊜	⊜
Electrical				Insufficient data	Insufficient data		⊖	○
A/C				Insufficient data	Insufficient data		⊜	⊜
Suspension				Insufficient data	Insufficient data		⊖	⊜
Brakes				Insufficient data	Insufficient data		⊜	⊜
Exhaust				Insufficient data	Insufficient data		⊜	⊜
Power equip.				Insufficient data	Insufficient data		⊖	⊖
Paint/trim/rust				Insufficient data	Insufficient data		⊖	⊜
Integrity				Insufficient data	Insufficient data		○	⊖
Hardware				Insufficient data	Insufficient data		○	⊖
RELIABILITY VERDICT							✗	✗

Cadillac Seville

TROUBLE SPOTS	96	97	98	99	00	01	02	03
Engine	◒	●	◒	○	○	○	⊜	Insufficient data
Cooling	◒	◒	◒	○	⊖	⊖	⊜	Insufficient data
Fuel	◒	◒	○	⊖	○	○	⊖	Insufficient data
Ignition	○	○	⊖	⊖	⊖	⊖	⊜	Insufficient data
Transmission	⊖	⊖	⊖	⊖	⊖	⊜	⊜	Insufficient data
Electrical	●	●	●	◒	○	●	○	Insufficient data
A/C	●	●	○	⊜	⊖	⊖	⊜	Insufficient data
Suspension	◒	●	○	◒	◒	◒	○	Insufficient data
Brakes	○	●	◒	○	○	○	⊜	Insufficient data
Exhaust	⊖	⊜	⊜	⊜	⊜	⊜	⊖	Insufficient data
Power equip.	●	◒	◒	◒	○	◒	○	Insufficient data
Paint/trim/rust	⊖	⊖	⊖	⊖	○	⊖	⊖	Insufficient data
Integrity	○	○	○	○	◒	◒	○	Insufficient data
Hardware	○	⊖	○	◒	○	○	⊖	Insufficient data
RELIABILITY VERDICT	✗	✗	✗	–	✗	✗	✗	

Chevrolet Astro

TROUBLE SPOTS	96	97	98	99	00	01	02	03
Engine	◒	○	○	⊖	⊖	⊜	⊜	Insufficient data
Cooling	●	○	○	⊖	⊜	⊜	⊜	Insufficient data
Fuel	●	●	○	◒	⊖	⊖	⊖	Insufficient data
Ignition	⊖	⊖	⊖	⊜	⊖	⊖	⊜	Insufficient data
Transmission	○	◒	◒	○	○	⊜	⊜	Insufficient data
Electrical	●	●	●	◒	◒	○	○	Insufficient data
A/C	●	●	◒	○	⊖	⊖	⊖	Insufficient data
Suspension	○	◒	○	○	○	⊜	⊖	Insufficient data
Brakes	●	●	●	◒	◒	○	◒	Insufficient data
Exhaust	○	⊖	⊖	⊖	⊖	⊖	⊖	Insufficient data
Power equip.	●	●	●	●	◒	◒	○	Insufficient data
Paint/trim/rust	◒	○	○	○	⊜	⊖	⊜	Insufficient data
Integrity	●	●	◒	◒	●	◒	◒	Insufficient data
Hardware	●	●	●	◒	◒	◒	⊖	Insufficient data
RELIABILITY VERDICT	✗	✗	✗	✗	✗	✗	✗	

Chevrolet Avalanche

TROUBLE SPOTS	96	97	98	99	00	01	02	03
Engine							⊜	⊜
Cooling							⊜	⊜
Fuel							⊜	⊜
Ignition							⊜	⊜
Transmission							⊜	⊜
Electrical							⊖	⊖
A/C							⊜	⊜
Suspension							⊜	⊜
Brakes							⊖	⊜
Exhaust							⊜	⊜
Power equip.							⊖	⊖
Paint/trim/rust							⊖	⊜
Integrity							○	⊖
Hardware							⊖	⊜
RELIABILITY VERDICT							–	✗

TROUBLE SPOTS	Chevrolet Blazer 96	97	98	99	00	01	02	03 (Insufficient data)
Engine	●	◒	○	○	○	⊜	⊖	
Cooling	●	●	◒	○	⊜	⊜	⊜	
Fuel	◒	●	○	⊖	○	○	⊖	
Ignition	⊖	○	⊖	⊖	⊖	⊖	⊜	
Transmission	◒	◒	○	○	⊖	○	⊖	
Electrical	●	●	●	●	●	●	○	
A/C	●	●	○	○	⊖	⊖	⊜	
Suspension	◒	◒	○	○	○	○	⊖	
Brakes	●	●	○	○	○	○	⊜	
Exhaust	⊖	⊜	⊜	⊖	⊖	⊜	⊜	
Power equip.	○	◒	◒	○	○	○	⊖	
Paint/trim/rust	○	○	⊖	⊖	○	⊖	○	
Integrity	◒	●	◒	●	◒	◒	◒	
Hardware	○	◒	◒	◒	○	○	⊖	
RELIABILITY VERDICT	✗	✗	✗	✗	✗	✗	✗	

TROUBLE SPOTS	Chevrolet C1500, Silverado 2WD 96	97	98	99	00	01	02	03
Engine	○	○	⊖	⊜	⊖	⊜	⊜	⊜
Cooling	◒	◒	◒	⊜	⊜	⊜	⊜	⊜
Fuel	●	◒	○	○	○	⊖	⊜	⊜
Ignition	⊖	⊖	⊖	⊜	⊜	⊜	⊜	⊜
Transmission	○	◒	○	⊖	⊖	⊜	⊖	⊜
Electrical	●	●	●	○	○	⊖	⊖	⊜
A/C	●	◒	○	⊖	⊜	⊜	⊜	⊖
Suspension	⊖	◒	○	⊖	○	○	⊖	⊜
Brakes	◒	○	◒	●	○	⊖	⊜	⊜
Exhaust	○	⊖	⊜	⊜	⊜	⊜	⊜	⊜
Power equip.	⊖	⊖	⊖	◒	⊖	⊖	⊜	⊖
Paint/trim/rust	⊖	⊖	⊖	⊖	⊜	⊜	⊜	⊜
Integrity	○	⊖	○	◒	○	⊖	○	⊖
Hardware	○	○	○	○	⊖	⊖	⊖	⊜
RELIABILITY VERDICT	-	✗	✗	-	✓	✓	-	-

TROUBLE SPOTS	Chevrolet Camaro 96	97	98	99	00	01	02	03
Engine	○	◒	○	○	⊖	○	⊜	
Cooling	●	◒	⊖	⊜	⊖	⊜	⊜	
Fuel	○	◒	⊖	⊖	⊖	⊖	⊜	
Ignition	○	○	⊜	○	⊜	⊖	⊜	
Transmission	○	○	⊖	○	⊖	⊖	⊜	
Electrical	●	●	●	●	◒	○	⊜	
A/C	○	⊜	⊖	⊖	⊖	⊖	⊜	
Suspension	○	○	⊖	⊖	⊜	⊖	⊖	
Brakes	○	○	◒	◒	●	◒	○	
Exhaust	⊖	⊖	⊜	⊖	○	○	⊜	
Power equip.	◒	●	○	◒	◒	○	⊖	
Paint/trim/rust	○	○	⊜	⊖	⊖	⊜	⊖	
Integrity	◒	●	○	◒	●	○	◒	
Hardware	○	◒	⊖	○	○	⊖	⊖	
RELIABILITY VERDICT	-	✗	-	✗	✗	✗	-	

TROUBLE SPOTS	Chevrolet Cavalier Sedan 96	97	98	99	00	01	02	03 (Insufficient data)
Engine	◒	⊖	⊖	⊖	⊖	⊖	⊜	
Cooling	●	◒	○	⊖	⊖	⊜	⊜	
Fuel	◒	⊖	⊖	⊖	○	○	⊖	
Ignition	○	⊖	⊜	⊖	⊜	⊖	⊜	
Transmission	○	⊜	⊜	⊖	⊜	⊜	⊜	
Electrical	●	●	◒	○	○	⊖	⊖	
A/C	●	○	⊖	⊖	⊖	⊜	⊜	
Suspension	○	◒	○	⊖	⊖	○	⊜	
Brakes	◒	◒	●	◒	●	◒	⊖	
Exhaust	⊖	⊜	⊖	⊜	⊜	⊜	⊜	
Power equip.	○	○	⊜	○	⊖	⊖	⊜	
Paint/trim/rust	◒	⊖	⊖	○	⊖	⊜	⊜	
Integrity	◒	○	○	○	○	◒	⊖	
Hardware	○	○	⊖	⊖	○	⊖	⊖	
RELIABILITY VERDICT	✗	-	-	-	-	-	✓	

TROUBLE SPOTS	Chevrolet Corvette 96 (Insufficient data)	97 (Insufficient data)	98	99	00	01	02	03
Engine			⊜	⊜	⊜	○	⊜	⊜
Cooling			○	⊜	⊜	⊜	⊜	⊖
Fuel			○	○	◒	○	⊖	⊜
Ignition			⊖	⊜	⊖	⊜	⊖	⊜
Transmission			○	⊜	○	⊖	⊖	⊖
Electrical			●	◒	●	●	◒	⊜
A/C			○	⊖	⊜	⊖	⊜	⊜
Suspension			○	○	⊖	⊜	⊖	⊖
Brakes			◒	◒	○	⊖	⊖	⊜
Exhaust			○	⊖	⊜	⊜	⊜	⊜
Power equip.			●	●	●	◒	⊖	⊜
Paint/trim/rust			○	⊜	⊜	⊜	⊖	⊜
Integrity			◒	○	◒	⊖	◒	⊜
Hardware			◒	⊜	◒	⊖	○	⊜
RELIABILITY VERDICT			✗	✓	✗	✗	✗	✗

TROUBLE SPOTS	Chevrolet Impala 96	97	98	99	00	01	02	03
Engine					⊖	⊜	⊜	⊜
Cooling					⊖	○	⊜	⊜
Fuel					○	⊖	⊜	⊜
Ignition					⊜	⊜	⊜	⊜
Transmission					⊖	⊖	⊜	⊜
Electrical					○	○	○	⊜
A/C					⊖	⊜	⊜	⊜
Suspension					◒	○	⊜	⊜
Brakes					◒	○	⊖	⊜
Exhaust					⊜	⊜	⊜	⊜
Power equip.					○	⊖	⊜	⊜
Paint/trim/rust					⊖	⊖	⊜	⊖
Integrity					○	○	⊖	⊖
Hardware					⊖	⊖	⊜	⊜
RELIABILITY VERDICT					✗	-	✓	✓

TROUBLE SPOTS	Chevrolet Lumina 96	97	98	99	00	01	02	03
Engine	◒	○	○	◒				
Cooling	◒	○	⊖	○				
Fuel	◒	◒	○	○				
Ignition	⊖	⊖	⊜	⊜				
Transmission	⊖	⊖	⊖	⊖				
Electrical	●	●	◒	○				
A/C	◒	○	⊖	⊖				
Suspension	⊖	⊖	⊖	⊖				
Brakes	●	◒	◒	◒				
Exhaust	⊖	⊜	⊜	⊜				
Power equip.	○	○	⊖	⊖				
Paint/trim/rust	○	○	⊖	⊖				
Integrity	○	○	⊖	○				
Hardware	⊖	⊖	○	⊖				
RELIABILITY VERDICT	-	-	✓	-				

TROUBLE SPOTS	Chevrolet Malibu 96	97	98	99	00	01	02	03
Engine		◒	◒	◒	○	○	⊜	⊜
Cooling		●	◒	◒	○	⊜	⊜	⊜
Fuel		◒	○	○	○	○	⊖	⊜
Ignition		○	⊖	⊜	⊖	⊖	⊜	⊜
Transmission		⊖	⊖	⊖	⊜	⊜	⊜	⊜
Electrical		●	●	●	◒	◒	⊖	⊜
A/C		◒	●	◒	◒	⊖	⊜	⊜
Suspension		○	○	○	○	⊖	⊖	⊜
Brakes		●	●	●	●	●	○	⊜
Exhaust		⊜	⊜	⊜	⊜	⊜	⊜	⊜
Power equip.		○	○	○	⊖	⊜	⊖	⊜
Paint/trim/rust		○	⊖	○	⊜	⊖	⊜	⊜
Integrity		◒	◒	○	○	⊖	⊖	⊖
Hardware		○	○	○	⊖	⊖	⊜	⊜
RELIABILITY VERDICT		✗	✗	✗	✗	✗	-	✓

Chevrolet Monte Carlo

Trouble spots	96	97	98	99	00	01	02	03
Engine	Insufficient data	○	○	○	⊜	⊖	⊜	⊜
Cooling		◒	⊜	○	○	⊜	⊜	⊜
Fuel		●	⊖	⊖	⊖	⊖	⊜	⊜
Ignition		○	⊖	⊜	⊜	⊜	⊜	⊜
Transmission		○	⊜	⊖	⊖	⊜	⊜	⊜
Electrical		◒	○	◒	○	◒	○	⊜
A/C		○	⊖	⊖	⊖	⊜	⊜	⊜
Suspension		○	⊖	⊖	◒	○	⊜	⊜
Brakes		◒	●	◒	○	○	⊖	⊜
Exhaust		⊜	⊜	⊜	⊜	⊜	⊜	⊜
Power equip.		◒	○	○	◒	⊖	⊜	⊜
Paint/trim/rust		⊖	⊖	○	⊖	⊜	⊖	⊜
Integrity		○	○	◒	○	○	⊖	⊜
Hardware		◒	○	○	⊖	○	⊖	⊜
RELIABILITY VERDICT		-	-	✗	-	-	-	✓

Chevrolet S-10 V6 2WD

Trouble spots	96	97	98	99	00	01	02	03
Engine	○	⊖	⊖	⊖	○	○	⊖	⊜
Cooling	●	○	○	○	⊖	⊜	⊜	⊜
Fuel	◒	◒	⊖	⊖	⊖	○	⊖	⊜
Ignition	⊖	○	⊖	⊜	⊜	⊜	⊜	⊜
Transmission	○	◒	○	⊖	⊖	⊖	⊖	⊜
Electrical	●	●	◒	◒	◒	○	⊖	⊖
A/C	●	●	○	⊖	⊖	⊖	⊜	⊜
Suspension	○	⊖	○	⊖	⊖	⊖	○	⊜
Brakes	◒	◒	○	○	◒	○	⊖	⊜
Exhaust	⊖	⊖	⊖	⊖	⊜	⊜	⊜	⊜
Power equip.	⊖	⊖	⊖	⊜	⊜	⊜	⊜	⊜
Paint/trim/rust	○	○	⊖	⊖	○	⊖	⊜	⊜
Integrity	◒	◒	●	○	◒	○	◒	◒
Hardware	◒	◒	●	●	◒	○	○	○
RELIABILITY VERDICT	✗	✗	-	-	✗	-	✗	✗

Chevrolet Suburban

Trouble spots	96	97	98	99	00	01	02	03
Engine	◒	○	◒	○	⊜	⊖	⊜	⊜
Cooling	◒	◒	◒	○	⊜	⊜	⊜	⊜
Fuel	◒	○	○	○	○	⊖	⊖	⊜
Ignition	⊖	⊖	⊜	⊖	⊜	⊜	⊜	⊜
Transmission	◒	●	○	○	⊖	⊖	⊜	⊜
Electrical	●	●	●	●	◒	○	⊖	⊖
A/C	●	◒	◒	○	⊜	⊖	⊖	⊜
Suspension	○	◒	◒	○	○	⊜	⊜	⊜
Brakes	●	●	●	●	○	⊖	⊜	⊜
Exhaust	⊖	⊖	⊜	⊖	⊜	⊜	⊜	⊜
Power equip.	○	○	○	●	●	○	⊜	⊖
Paint/trim/rust	⊖	⊖	⊜	⊜	⊜	⊜	⊜	⊜
Integrity	○	○	○	○	◒	○	○	⊜
Hardware	◒	○	○	○	○	○	⊜	⊜
RELIABILITY VERDICT	✗	✗	✗	✗	✗	-	-	✗

Chevrolet Tahoe

Trouble spots	96	97	98	99	00	01	02	03
Engine	◒	◒	○	⊖	⊜	⊜	⊜	⊜
Cooling	◒	◒	◒	⊖	⊜	⊜	⊜	⊜
Fuel	◒	◒	○	○	⊖	⊜	⊜	⊜
Ignition	⊖	⊜	⊜	⊖	⊜	⊜	⊜	⊜
Transmission	○	◒	○	⊖	⊜	⊜	⊜	⊜
Electrical	●	●	●	◒	◒	○	⊖	○
A/C	●	○	○	⊖	⊖	⊖	⊜	⊖
Suspension	○	◒	○	⊖	○	⊖	⊖	⊜
Brakes	●	●	●	●	○	⊖	⊜	⊜
Exhaust	⊖	⊜	⊜	⊜	⊜	⊜	⊜	⊜
Power equip.	○	⊖	⊖	○	◒	○	⊜	⊖
Paint/trim/rust	⊖	⊖	⊖	⊜	⊖	⊜	⊜	⊜
Integrity	○	○	○	○	◒	○	○	⊜
Hardware	○	○	⊜	○	○	○	⊜	⊜
RELIABILITY VERDICT	✗	✗	✗	✗	-	-	-	✗

Chevrolet TrailBlazer

Trouble spots	96	97	98	99	00	01	02	03
Engine							⊖	⊜
Cooling							⊜	⊜
Fuel							⊖	⊜
Ignition							⊜	⊜
Transmission							⊖	⊜
Electrical							◒	⊖
A/C							⊖	⊖
Suspension							⊖	⊜
Brakes							⊜	⊜
Exhaust							⊜	⊜
Power equip.							○	⊜
Paint/trim/rust							⊖	⊜
Integrity							◒	⊖
Hardware							○	⊜
RELIABILITY VERDICT							✗	✗

Chevrolet Venture (ext.)

Trouble spots	96	97	98	99	00	01	02	03
Engine		◒	◒	◒	○	⊜	⊜	⊜
Cooling		◒	○	◒	○	⊖	⊜	⊜
Fuel		○	○	○	○	⊖	⊖	⊜
Ignition		⊜	⊜	⊜	⊜	⊜	⊜	⊜
Transmission		○	⊜	○	○	⊖	⊜	⊜
Electrical		●	●	◒	●	○	⊖	⊖
A/C		○	⊖	⊖	⊖	⊖	⊜	⊜
Suspension		●	○	⊖	⊖	⊖	⊜	⊜
Brakes		●	◒	◒	○	⊖	⊖	⊜
Exhaust		⊜	⊜	⊜	⊜	⊜	⊜	⊜
Power equip.		●	●	●	●	◒	○	⊖
Paint/trim/rust		○	⊖	⊖	⊖	⊖	⊖	⊜
Integrity		●	◒	◒	◒	◒	○	⊜
Hardware		●	◒	◒	●	○	⊖	⊖
RELIABILITY VERDICT		✗	✗	✗	✗	-	-	-

Chevrolet Venture (reg.)

Trouble spots	96	97	98	99	00	01	02	03
Engine		◒	○	○	○	⊖	⊜	Insufficient data
Cooling		●	○	◒	○	⊖	⊜	
Fuel		○	○	○	○	⊖	⊖	
Ignition		⊜	⊜	⊜	⊜	⊜	⊜	
Transmission		○	⊜	○	⊖	⊖	⊜	
Electrical		●	●	◒	◒	○	○	
A/C		○	⊖	⊖	⊖	⊖	⊜	
Suspension		●	○	○	⊖	⊖	⊖	
Brakes		◒	◒	◒	○	○	⊖	
Exhaust		⊜	⊜	⊜	⊜	⊜	⊜	
Power equip.		●	●	◒	◒	⊖	○	
Paint/trim/rust		⊖	⊖	⊜	⊖	⊜	⊜	
Integrity		○	◒	○	○	⊖	○	
Hardware		◒	◒	⊖	◒	⊖	⊖	
RELIABILITY VERDICT		✗	-	✗	✗	-	-	

Chevrolet/Geo Prizm

Trouble spots	96	97	98	99	00	01	02	03
Engine	⊜	⊜	⊜	⊜	⊖	⊜	⊜	
Cooling	⊜	⊜	⊜	⊜	⊜	⊜	⊜	
Fuel	⊜	⊜	⊖	⊜	○	⊜	⊜	
Ignition	⊜	⊜	⊜	⊜	⊜	⊜	⊜	
Transmission	⊜	⊜	⊜	⊜	⊜	⊜	⊜	
Electrical	○	○	○	⊜	⊜	⊜	⊜	
A/C	⊖	⊖	⊖	⊖	⊜	⊜	⊜	
Suspension	⊖	⊖	⊖	⊖	⊖	⊜	⊜	
Brakes	○	⊖	⊖	⊖	⊖	⊜	⊜	
Exhaust	⊜	⊜	⊜	⊜	⊜	⊜	⊜	
Power equip.	⊜	⊜	⊜	⊜	⊜	⊜	⊜	
Paint/trim/rust	○	⊜	⊖	⊖	⊖	⊜	⊜	
Integrity	⊖	⊖	⊖	○	⊖	⊖	⊖	
Hardware	○	○	○	⊖	⊖	⊜	⊜	
RELIABILITY VERDICT	✓	✓	✓	✓	✓	✓	✓	

Chevrolet/Geo Tracker

Trouble spots	96	97	98	99	00	01	02	03
Engine	⊖	○	Insufficient data	⊖	○	⊜	⊜	Insufficient data
Cooling	⊖	⊜		⊜	⊜	⊜	⊜	
Fuel	●	◒		⊖	⊖	⊜	⊜	
Ignition	⊖	⊖		⊖	⊜	⊜	⊜	
Transmission	⊜	⊖		○	⊜	⊖	⊜	
Electrical	◒	○		○	⊖	⊖	⊜	
A/C	●	◒		◒	○	⊖	⊖	
Suspension	⊖	⊖		⊖	⊖	⊖	⊖	
Brakes	○	○		○	○	⊜	⊖	
Exhaust	○	⊖		⊖	⊖	⊜	⊜	
Power equip.	⊜	⊜		○	⊜	⊖	⊜	
Paint/trim/rust	⊖	⊖		○	⊖	⊖	⊖	
Integrity	◒	◒		◒	◒	○	⊖	
Hardware	○	◒		⊖	○	⊖	⊜	
RELIABILITY VERDICT	✔	✔		✘	–	–	–	

Chrysler 300M

Trouble spots	96	97	98	99	00	01	02	03
Engine				⊜	⊜	⊜	⊖	⊜
Cooling				⊖	⊜	⊜	⊜	⊜
Fuel				⊖	⊖	⊜	⊜	⊜
Ignition				⊖	⊜	⊜	⊜	⊖
Transmission				◒	⊖	⊜	⊖	⊖
Electrical				◒	○	⊖	○	⊖
A/C				◒	⊖	⊖	⊜	⊜
Suspension				○	⊖	⊖	⊜	⊜
Brakes				○	○	⊖	⊖	⊖
Exhaust				⊜	⊜	⊜	⊜	⊜
Power equip.				●	◒	○	○	⊖
Paint/trim/rust				⊖	⊖	⊖	⊜	⊖
Integrity				○	○	○	○	⊖
Hardware				○	○	⊖	⊜	⊜
RELIABILITY VERDICT				✘	✔	✔	–	✘

Chrysler Cirrus

Trouble spots	96	97	98	99	00	01	02	03
Engine	◒	◒	⊖	⊖	⊜			
Cooling	○	○	⊖	⊜	⊖			
Fuel	○	○	⊖	○	○			
Ignition	○	⊖	⊜	⊖	⊜			
Transmission	●	○	○	◒	○			
Electrical	○	⊖	⊖	○	⊖			
A/C	●	○	○	⊖	⊖			
Suspension	◒	◒	○	⊖	⊖			
Brakes	●	●	●	◒	◒			
Exhaust	○	⊜	⊜	⊜	⊜			
Power equip.	○	○	◒	○	⊖			
Paint/trim/rust	○	⊖	⊖	○	⊖			
Integrity	◒	○	○	○	○			
Hardware	○	⊖	⊖	⊖	⊖			
RELIABILITY VERDICT	✘	–	–	–	–			

Chrysler Concorde

Trouble spots	96	97	98	99	00	01	02	03
Engine	○	○	⊜	⊖	⊖	⊜	⊜	Insufficient data
Cooling	●	●	⊖	⊖	⊜	⊜	⊜	
Fuel	○	○	⊖	⊖	⊜	⊖	○	
Ignition	○	⊖	⊜	⊖	⊜	⊜	⊖	
Transmission	◒	○	○	◒	⊖	⊖	⊖	
Electrical	○	○	◒	◒	○	○	⊜	
A/C	●	●	○	◒	○	⊜	⊜	
Suspension	●	○	○	○	⊖	⊜	⊖	
Brakes	◒	◒	◒	○	⊖	⊖	⊜	
Exhaust	⊜	⊜	⊜	⊜	⊜	⊜	⊜	
Power equip.	○	⊖	●	●	◒	⊖	⊖	
Paint/trim/rust	◒	○	◒	○	⊖	⊜	⊜	
Integrity	○	◒	●	◒	◒	○	⊖	
Hardware	○	○	○	◒	○	⊖	⊜	
RELIABILITY VERDICT	✘	✘	✘	✘	–	✔	–	

Chrysler New Yorker, LHS

Trouble spots	96	97	98	99	00	01	02	03
Engine	◒	○		⊖	⊜	Insufficient data		
Cooling	●	◒		⊖	⊜			
Fuel	◒	⊖		⊖	⊜			
Ignition	○	⊖		⊖	⊖			
Transmission	◒	○		○	⊖			
Electrical	○	○		◒	○			
A/C	●	●		◒	○			
Suspension	●	◒		○	○			
Brakes	◒	○		○	⊖			
Exhaust	⊜	⊜		⊜	⊜			
Power equip.	○	○		●	●			
Paint/trim/rust	⊖	⊖		○	○			
Integrity	○	◒		◒	●			
Hardware	⊖	○		○	◒			
RELIABILITY VERDICT	✘	–		✘	–			

Chrysler PT Cruiser

Trouble spots	96	97	98	99	00	01	02	03
Engine						⊜	⊜	⊜
Cooling						⊜	⊜	⊖
Fuel						⊖	⊖	⊜
Ignition						⊜	⊜	⊖
Transmission						⊜	⊜	⊜
Electrical						⊖	⊖	⊖
A/C						⊜	⊜	⊖
Suspension						○	⊜	⊜
Brakes						○	⊜	⊜
Exhaust						⊜	⊜	⊜
Power equip.						⊖	⊜	⊜
Paint/trim/rust						⊖	⊜	⊖
Integrity						⊖	⊖	⊜
Hardware						⊖	⊜	⊜
RELIABILITY VERDICT						✔	✔	–

Chrysler Sebring Convertible

Trouble spots	96	97	98	99	00	01	02	03
Engine	○	○	⊖	⊜	⊜	⊖	⊜	Insufficient data
Cooling	⊖	◒	⊖	⊖	⊖	⊜	⊖	
Fuel	◒	○	⊖	⊖	⊖	⊜	⊜	
Ignition	⊖	○	⊖	⊖	⊖	⊜	⊜	
Transmission	◒	○	⊖	◒	○	⊖	⊖	
Electrical	●	●	●	○	○	○	○	
A/C	◒	○	○	○	⊖	⊖	⊜	
Suspension	◒	○	○	⊖	⊖	○	⊜	
Brakes	●	●	◒	●	◒	○	⊜	
Exhaust	⊖	⊜	⊜	⊜	⊜	⊜	⊜	
Power equip.	◒	◒	○	○	○	◒	⊖	
Paint/trim/rust	◒	◒	○	⊜	⊖	⊖	⊖	
Integrity	●	●	●	◒	◒	●	◒	
Hardware	◒	○	○	○	⊖	○	⊖	
RELIABILITY VERDICT	✘	✘	–	–	–	✘	–	

Chrysler Sebring Sedan

Trouble spots	96	97	98	99	00	01	02	03
Engine						⊜	⊜	Insufficient data
Cooling						⊜	⊜	
Fuel						⊜	⊜	
Ignition						⊜	⊜	
Transmission						⊖	⊖	
Electrical						○	⊖	
A/C						⊖	⊜	
Suspension						○	⊜	
Brakes						○	⊖	
Exhaust						⊜	⊜	
Power equip.						⊖	⊜	
Paint/trim/rust						⊖	⊖	
Integrity						○	⊖	
Hardware						⊖	⊖	
RELIABILITY VERDICT						–	–	

Chrysler Town & Country (ext.) 2WD	96	97	98	99	00	01	02	03
Engine	◒	○	◒	⊖	⊖	⊜	⊜	⊜
Cooling	◒	◒	⊖	⊖	⊖	⊜	⊜	⊜
Fuel	◒	◒	⊖	⊖	⊖	⊖	○	⊜
Ignition	⊖	⊖	⊖	⊖	⊜	⊜	⊜	⊜
Transmission	●	◒	○	◒	●	⊖	⊖	⊜
Electrical	●	●	◒	○	○	○	⊖	⊜
A/C	●	◒	○	○	⊖	○	⊖	⊜
Suspension	○	○	○	⊜	⊖	○	⊖	⊜
Brakes	●	◒	◒	◒	◒	◒	⊖	⊜
Exhaust	⊜	⊜	⊜	⊜	⊜	⊜	⊜	⊜
Power equip.	●	◒	○	○	○	●	○	⊖
Paint/trim/rust	○	⊖	⊖	⊖	⊖	⊖	⊜	⊜
Integrity	◒	◒	○	○	○	◒	⊖	⊖
Hardware	◒	○	⊖	⊖	⊖	○	⊖	⊜
RELIABILITY VERDICT	✗	✗	–	✗	✗	✗	✗	–

Chrysler Town & Country ~~AWD~~	96	97	98	99	00	01	02	03
Engine	Insufficient data	○	○	○	○	⊖	⊜	⊜
Cooling		○	⊜	○	◒	⊜	⊜	⊜
Fuel		○	⊖	⊖	⊖	⊖	⊖	⊜
Ignition		⊖	⊜	⊖	⊖	⊜	⊜	⊜
Transmission		◒	◒	◒	◒	○	⊜	⊜
Electrical		●	◒	○	◒	◒	⊖	○
A/C		◒	⊖	⊖	⊖	○	⊜	⊜
Suspension		○	○	○	○	○	⊖	⊜
Brakes		◒	●	●	●	◒	⊜	⊜
Exhaust		⊜	⊖	⊜	⊜	⊜	⊜	⊜
Power equip.		○	○	○	◒	●	⊖	⊜
Paint/trim/rust		⊖	⊖	⊖	⊖	○	⊜	⊜
Integrity		○	○	○	◒	◒	○	⊖
Hardware		○	⊖	○	◒	◒	⊖	⊜
RELIABILITY VERDICT		✗	–	✗	✗	✗	–	–

Dodge Caravan V6	96	97	98	99	00	01	02	03
Engine	◒	◒	◒	○	⊖	⊜	⊜	⊜
Cooling	◒	○	⊖	⊖	⊖	⊜	⊜	⊜
Fuel	◒	○	⊖	⊖	⊜	⊜	⊜	⊜
Ignition	⊖	⊖	⊖	⊖	⊜	⊜	⊜	⊜
Transmission	●	◒	○	●	●	⊖	⊖	⊖
Electrical	●	●	◒	○	○	○	⊖	⊖
A/C	●	●	◒	○	⊖	⊖	⊖	⊜
Suspension	○	○	○	⊖	⊖	○	○	⊜
Brakes	●	●	◒	◒	◒	◒	⊖	⊖
Exhaust	⊜	⊜	⊜	⊜	⊜	⊜	⊜	⊜
Power equip.	◒	○	○	○	⊖	○	⊖	⊜
Paint/trim/rust	○	○	⊖	⊖	⊖	⊖	⊜	⊜
Integrity	◒	◒	○	○	○	○	○	⊖
Hardware	◒	◒	○	○	○	○	⊖	⊜
RELIABILITY VERDICT	✗	✗	–	✗	✗	✗	–	✗

Dodge Dakota 2WD	96	97	98	99	00	01	02	03
Engine	○	○	⊖	○	⊜	⊜	⊜	⊜
Cooling	●	◒	◒	○	⊖	⊜	⊜	⊜
Fuel	○	○	○	⊖	⊖	⊖	⊜	⊖
Ignition	⊖	⊖	⊖	⊖	⊜	⊖	⊜	⊜
Transmission	○	◒	○	⊖	⊖	⊖	⊜	⊜
Electrical	◒	○	◒	◒	○	⊖	⊖	⊖
A/C	●	●	◒	○	⊖	⊖	⊖	⊜
Suspension	○	○	○	⊖	⊖	⊖	⊖	⊜
Brakes	◒	◒	◒	◒	◒	○	⊖	⊖
Exhaust	○	◒	◒	○	⊜	⊜	⊜	⊜
Power equip.	⊖	⊖	⊖	⊖	○	⊖	⊜	⊜
Paint/trim/rust	◒	◒	○	⊖	⊖	⊖	⊖	⊜
Integrity	◒	⊖	○	⊖	⊖	⊖	⊖	⊜
Hardware	○	○	○	⊖	⊖	⊖	⊜	⊜
RELIABILITY VERDICT	–	✗	✗	–	–	–	✓	–

Dodge Dakota 4WD	96	97	98	99	00	01	02	03
Engine	Insufficient data	⊖	○	○	⊖	⊖	⊜	⊜
Cooling		○	○	◒	⊖	⊖	⊜	⊜
Fuel		◒	○	⊖	○	⊖	⊜	⊜
Ignition		○	⊜	⊖	⊜	⊜	⊜	⊜
Transmission		○	◒	○	○	○	⊖	⊖
Electrical		○	○	○	⊖	⊖	⊖	⊜
A/C		◒	◒	⊜	⊜	⊖	⊖	⊜
Suspension		◒	◒	◒	○	⊖	⊜	⊜
Brakes		◒	◒	○	●	◒	⊖	⊜
Exhaust		○	○	○	⊜	⊜	⊜	⊜
Power equip.		⊜	⊖	⊖	⊖	⊖	⊜	⊜
Paint/trim/rust		○	○	⊜	⊖	⊜	⊜	⊜
Integrity		⊖	○	⊖	⊖	⊖	⊖	⊖
Hardware		⊖	⊖	⊖	⊖	⊖	⊜	⊜
RELIABILITY VERDICT		–	✗	✗	✗	✗	–	–

Dodge Durango	96	97	98	99	00	01	02	03
Engine			○	○	⊜	⊜	⊜	⊜
Cooling			◒	○	⊖	⊜	⊜	⊜
Fuel			○	○	⊖	⊜	⊜	⊜
Ignition			⊜	⊖	⊜	⊜	⊜	⊜
Transmission			◒	◒	○	⊖	⊖	⊖
Electrical			○	◒	○	⊖	⊖	⊖
A/C			◒	⊖	⊖	⊖	⊜	⊜
Suspension			○	◒	◒	⊖	⊜	⊖
Brakes			◒	◒	◒	○	⊖	⊜
Exhaust			⊜	⊜	⊜	⊜	⊜	⊜
Power equip.			●	●	◒	⊖	⊜	⊜
Paint/trim/rust			○	⊖	⊖	⊖	⊖	⊜
Integrity			○	⊖	○	○	⊖	⊜
Hardware			○	○	◒	⊖	⊖	⊜
RELIABILITY VERDICT			✗	✗	✗	–	–	–

Dodge Grand Caravan 2WD	96	97	98	99	00	01	02	03
Engine	◒	○	◒	⊖	⊖	⊜	⊜	⊜
Cooling	◒	◒	⊖	⊖	⊖	⊜	⊜	⊜
Fuel	◒	◒	⊖	⊖	⊖	⊖	○	⊜
Ignition	⊖	⊖	⊖	⊖	⊜	⊜	⊜	⊜
Transmission	●	◒	○	◒	●	⊜	⊜	⊜
Electrical	●	●	◒	○	○	○	⊖	⊜
A/C	●	◒	○	○	⊖	○	⊖	⊜
Suspension	○	○	○	⊖	⊖	○	⊖	⊜
Brakes	●	◒	◒	◒	◒	◒	⊖	⊜
Exhaust	⊜	⊜	⊜	⊜	⊜	⊜	⊜	⊜
Power equip.	●	◒	○	○	○	●	○	⊖
Paint/trim/rust	○	⊖	⊖	⊖	⊖	⊖	⊜	⊜
Integrity	◒	◒	○	○	○	◒	⊖	⊖
Hardware	◒	○	⊖	⊖	⊖	○	⊖	⊜
RELIABILITY VERDICT	✗	✗	–	✗	✗	✗	✗	–

Dodge Intrepid	96	97	98	99	00	01	02	03
Engine	◒	◒	⊖	⊖	⊜	⊜	⊜	Insufficient data
Cooling	●	◒	⊖	⊖	⊜	⊜	⊜	
Fuel	○	◒	⊖	○	⊖	⊖	⊖	
Ignition	⊖	⊖	⊖	⊖	⊜	⊜	⊖	
Transmission	◒	○	◒	◒	⊖	⊖	⊖	
Electrical	◒	◒	●	◒	○	○	○	
A/C	●	◒	◒	◒	⊖	⊖	⊖	
Suspension	●	◒	◒	⊖	⊖	⊖	⊜	
Brakes	●	◒	◒	○	⊖	⊖	⊖	
Exhaust	⊜	⊜	⊖	⊜	⊜	⊜	⊜	
Power equip.	○	○	◒	●	◒	⊖	⊖	
Paint/trim/rust	●	◒	○	⊖	⊖	⊖	⊖	
Integrity	◒	●	◒	○	◒	⊖	⊖	
Hardware	○	⊖	⊖	○	○	⊖	⊜	
RELIABILITY VERDICT	✗	✗	✗	✗	–	✓	–	

Dodge Ram 1500 2WD

TROUBLE SPOTS	96	97	98	99	00	01	02	03
Engine	○	○	⊖	○	⊜	⊖	⊜	⊜
Cooling	○	○	⊖	○	○	⊜	⊜	⊜
Fuel	◒	○	○	⊖	○	⊖	⊖	⊜
Ignition	⊖	⊖	⊖	⊖	⊜	⊖	⊜	⊜
Transmission	●	◒	○	○	◒	○	⊖	⊜
Electrical	◒	○	○	○	⊖	⊖	⊖	⊜
A/C	●	◒	○	○	⊖	⊖	⊖	⊜
Suspension	○	○	⊖	⊖	○	⊖	⊖	⊜
Brakes	○	○	◒	◒	○	⊖	⊜	⊜
Exhaust	◒	○	⊖	⊖	⊜	⊜	⊜	⊜
Power equip.	○	○	⊖	⊖	⊖	⊜	⊖	⊜
Paint/trim/rust	◒	◒	⊖	⊖	⊖	⊖	⊜	⊜
Integrity	○	○	⊖	○	○	○	○	⊖
Hardware	○	○	⊖	⊖	⊖	⊖	○	⊖
RELIABILITY VERDICT	✗	-	-	✗	✗	-	✗	-

Dodge Ram 1500 4WD

TROUBLE SPOTS	96	97	98	99	00	01	02	03
Engine	○	○	○	◒	⊜	⊖	⊜	⊜
Cooling	○	○	⊖	⊖	⊖	⊜	⊖	⊜
Fuel	○	○	○	○	⊜	⊖	⊖	⊜
Ignition	⊖	⊖	⊖	⊖	⊖	⊖	⊜	⊜
Transmission	●	◒	◒	◒	○	○	⊖	⊜
Electrical	◒	○	⊖	⊖	⊖	⊖	⊖	⊖
A/C	◒	○	⊖	○	⊖	⊜	⊖	⊜
Suspension	○	◒	○	○	○	○	○	⊜
Brakes	◒	◒	◒	◒	○	⊖	⊖	⊜
Exhaust	◒	⊖	⊖	⊖	⊜	⊜	⊜	⊜
Power equip.	⊖	○	⊖	⊖	⊖	⊖	⊖	⊜
Paint/trim/rust	◒	◒	⊖	⊖	○	⊖	⊜	⊜
Integrity	○	○	○	○	○	○	○	⊜
Hardware	⊖	○	⊖	⊖	⊖	⊖	⊖	⊜
RELIABILITY VERDICT	✗	✗	✗	✗	-	✗	✗	-

Dodge Stratus Sedan V6

TROUBLE SPOTS	96	97	98	99	00	01	02	03
Engine	◒	◒	⊖	⊖	⊜	⊜	⊜	Insufficient data
Cooling	○	○	⊖	⊜	⊖	⊜	⊜	
Fuel	○	○	⊜	○	○	⊜	⊜	
Ignition	○	⊖	⊜	⊖	⊜	⊜	⊜	
Transmission	●	○	○	◒	○	⊖	⊖	
Electrical	○	⊖	⊖	○	⊖	○	⊖	
A/C	●	○	○	⊖	⊖	⊖	⊜	
Suspension	◒	◒	○	⊜	⊖	○	⊜	
Brakes	●	●	●	◒	◒	○	⊖	
Exhaust	○	⊜	⊜	⊜	⊜	⊜	⊜	
Power equip.	○	○	◒	○	⊜	⊜	⊜	
Paint/trim/rust	○	⊖	⊖	○	⊖	⊜	⊖	
Integrity	◒	○	○	○	○	○	⊖	
Hardware	○	⊖	⊖	⊖	⊖	⊖	⊖	
RELIABILITY VERDICT	✗	-	-	-	-	-	-	

Dodge/Plymouth Neon

TROUBLE SPOTS	96	97	98	99	00	01	02	03
Engine	●	●	●	●	⊖	⊖	⊖	Insufficient data
Cooling	◒	◒	○	⊖	○	⊜	⊜	
Fuel	◒	○	○	◒	⊜	⊖	⊜	
Ignition	○	○	⊖	○	⊜	⊜	⊜	
Transmission	○	○	○	○	⊖	⊜	⊜	
Electrical	●	●	○	◒	◒	◒	⊖	
A/C	●	●	◒	○	○	⊖	⊜	
Suspension	○	○	⊖	⊖	○	⊖	⊜	
Brakes	●	◒	◒	○	◒	○	⊖	
Exhaust	⊖	⊖	⊖	⊜	⊜	⊜	⊜	
Power equip.	⊖	⊖	◒	○	◒	◒	⊖	
Paint/trim/rust	●	◒	○	○	⊖	⊜	⊜	
Integrity	●	●	●	◒	◒	○	○	
Hardware	○	○	○	◒	○	○	⊜	
RELIABILITY VERDICT	✗	✗	✗	✗	✗	-	✓	

Ford Contour 4-cyl.

TROUBLE SPOTS	96	97	98	99	00	01	02	03
Engine	◒	○	○	⊜				
Cooling	◒	○	○	⊜				
Fuel	◒	◒	◒	○				
Ignition	○	⊖	⊖	⊖				
Transmission	◒	○	○	⊖				
Electrical	●	◒	◒	○				
A/C	○	○	○	⊖				
Suspension	○	◒	○	⊖				
Brakes	◒	◒	◒	○				
Exhaust	⊖	⊖	⊖	⊜				
Power equip.	○	○	○	○				
Paint/trim/rust	○	○	○	⊖				
Integrity	◒	◒	◒	●				
Hardware	○	◒	○	○				
RELIABILITY VERDICT	-	✗	✗	-				

Ford Crown Victoria

TROUBLE SPOTS	96	97	98	99	00	01	02	03
Engine	○	⊖	⊜	⊜	⊜	⊖	⊜	⊜
Cooling	○	⊖	⊜	⊜	⊜	⊜	⊜	⊜
Fuel	◒	○	⊖	⊖	⊖	○	⊜	⊜
Ignition	○	⊖	⊜	⊖	⊖	⊖	⊜	⊜
Transmission	⊖	⊖	⊖	⊜	⊖	⊜	⊜	⊜
Electrical	◒	○	○	○	○	○	⊖	⊖
A/C	○	⊖	⊜	⊖	⊖	⊖	⊜	⊜
Suspension	○	○	○	⊖	⊖	⊖	⊖	⊖
Brakes	◒	◒	○	○	⊖	⊖	⊜	⊜
Exhaust	○	⊖	⊜	⊜	⊜	⊜	⊜	⊜
Power equip.	●	◒	⊖	○	○	○	⊖	⊖
Paint/trim/rust	⊖	⊖	⊖	⊖	⊖	⊖	⊖	⊜
Integrity	○	○	⊖	○	◒	◒	○	○
Hardware	○	⊖	⊜	⊖	○	○	⊖	⊖
RELIABILITY VERDICT	-	✓	✓	✓	✓	-	-	✗

Ford Escape

TROUBLE SPOTS	96	97	98	99	00	01	02	03
Engine						⊖	⊜	⊜
Cooling						⊖	⊜	⊜
Fuel						○	⊖	⊜
Ignition						⊜	⊜	⊜
Transmission						⊖	⊜	⊜
Electrical						○	⊖	⊜
A/C						⊜	⊜	⊜
Suspension						⊖	⊜	⊜
Brakes						○	⊜	⊜
Exhaust						⊜	⊜	⊜
Power equip.						⊖	⊖	⊜
Paint/trim/rust						⊖	⊜	⊜
Integrity						◒	○	⊖
Hardware						⊖	⊖	⊜
RELIABILITY VERDICT						✗	-	✓

Ford Escort, ZX2

TROUBLE SPOTS	96	97	98	99	00	01	02	03
Engine	◒	⊖	⊖	⊖	⊖	⊖	⊜	Insufficient data
Cooling	◒	◒	○	⊜	⊜	⊜	⊜	
Fuel	○	○	⊖	⊖	⊖	⊜	⊖	
Ignition	○	⊜	⊜	⊖	⊖	⊜	⊜	
Transmission	⊖	⊖	⊜	⊖	⊜	⊖	⊖	
Electrical	◒	○	⊖	○	○	⊜	⊖	
A/C	○	○	⊖	⊖	⊖	⊜	⊜	
Suspension	○	◒	○	⊖	○	⊜	⊜	
Brakes	◒	◒	○	○	○	⊖	⊜	
Exhaust	○	⊖	⊜	⊜	⊜	⊜	⊜	
Power equip.	⊖	⊜	⊖	⊖	⊖	⊜	⊜	
Paint/trim/rust	◒	⊖	⊖	⊖	⊖	⊜	⊜	
Integrity	○	○	○	⊖	○	○	○	
Hardware	◒	⊜	⊜	⊖	⊖	⊖	⊜	
RELIABILITY VERDICT	-	-	✓	✓	✓	✓	✓	

Ford Excursion	96	97	98	99	00	01	02	03
Engine					⊖	⊖	⊖	Insufficient data
Cooling					⊜	⊜	⊜	
Fuel					⊖	⊖	⊜	
Ignition					⊖	⊜	⊜	
Transmission					⊜	⊖	⊜	
Electrical					○	⊖	○	
A/C					⊖	⊖	⊜	
Suspension					○	⊖	⊖	
Brakes					◒	◒	⊖	
Exhaust					⊜	⊜	⊜	
Power equip.					◒	○	⊖	
Paint/trim/rust					⊖	⊜	⊜	
Integrity					○	○	○	
Hardware					◒	○	⊖	
RELIABILITY VERDICT					-	✗	-	

Ford Expedition	96	97	98	99	00	01	02	03
Engine		⊖	⊖	○	⊜	⊖	⊜	⊜
Cooling		⊜	⊖	⊜	⊜	⊜	⊜	⊜
Fuel		⊖	⊖	⊖	⊖	⊖	⊜	⊜
Ignition		⊖	○	⊖	⊜	⊜	⊜	⊜
Transmission		⊖	⊖	⊖	⊖	⊖	⊖	⊜
Electrical		◒	◒	◒	○	○	⊖	⊖
A/C		⊖	⊖	⊖	⊖	⊜	⊜	⊜
Suspension		○	○	⊖	○	⊖	⊜	⊜
Brakes		◒	○	○	○	⊖	⊜	⊜
Exhaust		⊜	⊜	⊜	⊜	⊜	⊜	⊜
Power equip.		○	○	○	○	○	○	○
Paint/trim/rust		⊖	⊖	⊖	⊖	⊖	⊖	⊜
Integrity		○	⊖	○	○	○	⊖	○
Hardware		○	○	○	⊖	○	⊖	⊖
RELIABILITY VERDICT		✓	-	-	-	-	-	✗

Ford Explorer 2WD	96	97	98	99	00	01	02	03
Engine	⊖	⊖	⊖	⊖	⊖	⊜	⊜	⊜
Cooling	○	○	○	⊖	○	⊖	⊜	⊜
Fuel	◒	○	○	◒	○	○	⊖	⊜
Ignition	⊜	⊖	⊖	⊖	⊖	⊜	⊜	⊜
Transmission	○	⊖	⊖	⊖	⊖	⊖	⊖	⊜
Electrical	◒	◒	●	●	●	◒	⊜	⊜
A/C	○	●	◒	⊖	⊖	⊖	⊖	⊜
Suspension	○	○	○	⊖	⊖	⊖	⊜	⊜
Brakes	○	○	○	○	○	⊖	⊜	⊜
Exhaust	⊖	⊖	⊜	⊜	⊜	⊜	⊜	⊜
Power equip.	○	○	◒	○	○	○	⊖	⊜
Paint/trim/rust	○	○	⊖	⊖	⊖	⊖	⊖	⊜
Integrity	○	○	○	○	○	○	○	⊖
Hardware	○	○	○	○	◒	○	○	⊖
RELIABILITY VERDICT	✓	-	-	-	✗	-	✗	-

Ford Explorer 4WD	96	97	98	99	00	01	02	03
Engine	⊖	○	○	⊖	⊖	⊖	⊜	⊜
Cooling	○	○	○	⊖	○	⊜	⊜	⊜
Fuel	◒	○	○	○	○	⊖	⊜	⊜
Ignition	⊜	⊖	⊖	⊖	⊖	⊜	⊜	⊜
Transmission	○	○	○	⊖	○	⊖	⊖	⊜
Electrical	○	○	◒	◒	◒	○	⊖	⊖
A/C	○	◒	○	⊖	⊜	⊖	⊜	⊜
Suspension	○	○	○	○	⊖	⊖	⊖	⊜
Brakes	◒	◒	○	◒	○	⊖	⊜	⊖
Exhaust	⊖	⊖	⊜	⊜	⊜	⊜	⊜	⊜
Power equip.	○	○	◒	○	○	⊖	⊖	⊜
Paint/trim/rust	○	○	⊖	⊖	⊖	⊖	⊖	⊜
Integrity	○	○	○	○	○	○	○	⊜
Hardware	○	○	○	○	⊖	○	○	⊖
RELIABILITY VERDICT	-	-	✗	✗	✗	✗	✗	-

Ford Explorer Sport Trac	96	97	98	99	00	01	02	03
Engine						⊖	⊜	⊜
Cooling						⊖	⊜	⊜
Fuel						○	⊖	⊖
Ignition						⊜	⊜	⊜
Transmission						⊜	⊜	⊜
Electrical						⊖	⊖	⊖
A/C						⊜	⊜	⊜
Suspension						⊖	⊜	⊜
Brakes						○	⊖	⊜
Exhaust						⊜	⊜	⊜
Power equip.						⊖	⊖	⊖
Paint/trim/rust						○	⊜	⊜
Integrity						○	○	○
Hardware						⊖	○	⊖
RELIABILITY VERDICT						-	-	✗

Ford F-150 2WD	96	97	98	99	00	01	02	03
Engine	⊖	⊖	⊜	⊖	⊜	⊜	⊜	⊜
Cooling	⊖	⊖	⊜	⊜	⊜	⊜	⊜	⊜
Fuel	◒	○	⊖	⊖	⊖	⊖	⊜	⊜
Ignition	⊖	⊖	⊖	⊖	⊖	⊜	⊜	⊜
Transmission	○	⊖	⊖	⊖	⊖	⊖	⊜	⊜
Electrical	○	◒	○	○	⊖	⊖	⊜	⊜
A/C	⊖	⊖	⊖	⊖	⊖	⊜	⊜	⊜
Suspension	○	○	⊖	⊜	⊖	⊜	⊜	⊜
Brakes	○	○	○	○	⊖	⊜	⊜	⊖
Exhaust	⊖	⊜	⊜	⊜	⊜	⊜	⊜	⊜
Power equip.	⊖	○	○	⊖	⊖	⊖	⊜	⊖
Paint/trim/rust	⊖	⊖	⊖	⊜	⊖	⊜	⊖	⊖
Integrity	○	○	○	○	⊖	⊖	⊖	⊜
Hardware	⊖	⊖	⊖	⊖	⊖	⊖	⊖	⊜
RELIABILITY VERDICT	✓	✓	✓	✓	✓	✓	✓	✓

Ford F-150 4WD	96	97	98	99	00	01	02	03
Engine	⊖	⊖	⊖	○	⊖	⊖	⊜	⊜
Cooling	⊖	⊜	⊜	⊜	⊜	⊜	⊜	⊜
Fuel	◒	○	⊖	⊖	⊜	⊖	⊜	⊜
Ignition	○	⊜	⊜	⊜	⊜	⊜	⊜	⊜
Transmission	⊖	⊖	⊖	⊖	⊖	⊖	⊜	⊜
Electrical	○	◒	◒	○	⊖	⊖	⊜	⊜
A/C	⊜	⊖	⊖	⊖	⊖	⊜	⊜	⊜
Suspension	◒	○	○	⊖	⊖	⊖	⊜	⊜
Brakes	○	◒	○	◒	◒	⊖	⊜	⊜
Exhaust	○	⊜	⊜	⊜	⊜	⊜	⊜	⊜
Power equip.	⊖	○	⊖	○	⊖	⊖	⊖	⊜
Paint/trim/rust	⊖	⊖	⊖	⊖	⊖	⊜	⊜	⊜
Integrity	○	○	○	○	⊖	○	○	⊖
Hardware	⊖	⊖	⊖	⊖	⊖	⊖	⊖	⊜
RELIABILITY VERDICT	-	✓	✓	-	✓	-	-	✓

Ford Focus	96	97	98	99	00	01	02	03
Engine					⊖	⊖	⊜	⊜
Cooling					⊜	⊜	⊜	⊜
Fuel					◒	◒	⊖	⊜
Ignition					⊖	⊖	⊜	⊜
Transmission					○	⊜	⊜	⊜
Electrical					●	○	⊖	⊜
A/C					⊖	⊖	⊜	⊜
Suspension					◒	○	⊖	⊖
Brakes					●	◒	⊖	⊜
Exhaust					⊜	⊜	⊜	⊜
Power equip.					○	⊖	⊖	⊜
Paint/trim/rust					⊖	⊖	⊜	⊜
Integrity					◒	○	○	⊖
Hardware					◒	⊖	⊖	⊜
RELIABILITY VERDICT					✗	✗	-	✓

TROUBLE SPOTS

Ford Mustang

Trouble spots	96	97	98	99	00	01	02	03
Engine	○	⊖	⊖	⊖	⊜	⊖	⊜	⊜
Cooling	●	◒	⊖	⊜	⊜	⊖	⊜	⊜
Fuel	○	⊖	○	⊖	⊖	⊖	⊜	⊜
Ignition	○	⊖	⊖	⊖	⊜	⊜	⊜	⊜
Transmission	○	○	○	⊖	⊖	⊖	⊜	⊜
Electrical	◒	○	⊖	⊖	⊖	⊖	⊖	⊜
A/C	⊖	○	⊖	⊜	⊜	⊜	⊜	⊜
Suspension	○	⊖	⊖	⊖	⊜	⊜	⊜	⊜
Brakes	○	○	○	○	○	⊖	⊜	⊜
Exhaust	⊖	⊜	⊜	⊜	⊜	⊜	⊜	⊜
Power equip.	⊖	○	⊖	⊖	⊖	○	○	⊜
Paint/trim/rust	○	○	⊖	⊖	⊖	⊖	⊖	⊖
Integrity	○	○	○	◒	○	○	○	○
Hardware	○	○	⊖	○	○	⊖	⊖	⊖
RELIABILITY VERDICT	-	-	✔	✔	✔	-	-	✘

Ford Ranger 2WD

Trouble spots	96	97	98	99	00	01	02	03
Engine	⊖	⊖	⊖	⊖	⊖	⊖	⊜	⊜
Cooling	⊖	⊖	⊖	⊜	⊜	⊜	⊜	⊜
Fuel	◒	○	○	○	⊖	⊖	⊖	⊜
Ignition	⊖	⊜	⊖	⊖	⊖	⊜	⊜	⊜
Transmission	⊖	⊖	⊖	⊖	⊖	⊖	⊖	⊜
Electrical	●	●	●	◒	○	○	⊖	⊜
A/C	○	◒	○	⊖	⊖	⊖	⊜	⊜
Suspension	⊖	⊜	○	⊖	⊖	⊖	⊖	⊜
Brakes	○	○	○	○	⊖	○	⊖	⊜
Exhaust	⊜	⊜	⊜	⊜	⊜	⊜	⊜	⊜
Power equip.	⊖	⊖	⊖	⊖	⊖	⊖	⊖	⊜
Paint/trim/rust	⊖	⊖	⊖	⊜	⊜	⊜	⊜	⊜
Integrity	⊖	⊖	⊖	⊖	⊖	○	⊖	⊖
Hardware	⊖	○	○	⊖	⊖	○	⊖	⊖
RELIABILITY VERDICT	✔	✔	✔	✔	✔	-	-	-

Ford Ranger 4WD

Trouble spots	96	97	98	99	00	01	02	03
Engine	⊖	⊖	⊖	⊖	⊖	⊜	⊜	⊜
Cooling	○	○	○	⊖	⊖	⊜	⊜	⊜
Fuel	○	○	○	⊖	⊖	⊖	⊖	⊜
Ignition	⊖	⊖	⊖	⊖	⊜	⊖	⊜	⊜
Transmission	○	⊖	○	⊖	○	⊖	○	⊜
Electrical	◒	●	●	◒	○	○	⊖	○
A/C	○	◒	⊖	⊜	⊖	⊖	⊜	⊜
Suspension	⊖	⊖	○	○	⊖	⊖	⊖	⊜
Brakes	◒	○	◒	◒	◒	⊖	⊜	⊜
Exhaust	⊜	⊜	⊜	⊜	⊜	⊜	⊜	⊜
Power equip.	○	○	○	⊖	○	⊖	⊖	⊜
Paint/trim/rust	⊖	⊖	⊜	⊖	⊖	⊖	⊖	⊖
Integrity	○	○	○	⊖	○	○	○	⊖
Hardware	⊖	⊖	○	⊖	○	○	⊖	⊖
RELIABILITY VERDICT	-	-	-	-	✘	✘	✘	-

Ford Taurus

Trouble spots	96	97	98	99	00	01	02	03
Engine	○	○	⊖	⊖	⊖	⊜	⊜	⊜
Cooling	◒	○	⊖	⊖	⊜	⊜	⊜	⊜
Fuel	◒	○	○	○	○	○	⊖	⊜
Ignition	⊖	⊖	⊖	⊜	⊖	⊖	⊜	⊜
Transmission	◒	○	○	○	⊖	⊖	⊖	⊜
Electrical	◒	●	●	◒	◒	○	⊖	⊖
A/C	○	○	⊖	⊖	⊖	⊖	⊜	⊜
Suspension	◒	○	○	○	○	○	⊖	⊜
Brakes	◒	◒	●	◒	◒	○	⊖	⊜
Exhaust	⊖	⊖	⊜	⊜	⊜	⊜	⊜	⊜
Power equip.	○	◒	○	○	⊖	⊖	⊖	⊜
Paint/trim/rust	○	⊖	⊖	⊖	⊖	⊜	⊜	⊜
Integrity	◒	○	○	○	○	○	○	⊖
Hardware	○	○	○	⊖	⊖	⊖	⊖	⊜
RELIABILITY VERDICT	-	-	-	-	-	-	-	-

TROUBLE SPOTS

Ford Thunderbird

Trouble spots	96	97	98	99	00	01	02	03
Engine	○	○					⊜	Insufficient data
Cooling	●	◒					⊜	
Fuel	◒	○					⊖	
Ignition	○	⊖					⊜	
Transmission	◒	○					⊜	
Electrical	◒	◒					○	
A/C	○	⊖					⊜	
Suspension	○	⊖					⊜	
Brakes	◒	○					⊖	
Exhaust	⊖	⊖					⊜	
Power equip.	○	○					⊜	
Paint/trim/rust	⊖	○					⊜	
Integrity	○	⊖					○	
Hardware	○	⊖					⊖	
RELIABILITY VERDICT	-	-					-	

Ford Windstar

Trouble spots	96	97	98	99	00	01	02	03
Engine	●	◒	⊖	◒	○	⊜	⊜	⊜
Cooling	◒	○	⊖	⊜	⊜	⊜	⊜	⊜
Fuel	◒	◒	○	◒	○	○	⊖	⊜
Ignition	○	○	⊖	⊖	⊖	⊜	⊜	⊜
Transmission	◒	○	◒	◒	○	⊖	⊜	⊜
Electrical	●	●	●	●	◒	◒	○	⊖
A/C	○	○	○	⊖	⊖	⊖	⊜	⊜
Suspension	◒	●	●	◒	○	⊖	⊖	⊜
Brakes	●	●	●	○	○	⊖	⊜	⊜
Exhaust	⊖	⊜	⊜	⊜	⊜	⊜	⊜	⊜
Power equip.	●	◒	●	◒	◒	◒	○	⊖
Paint/trim/rust	○	○	○	○	○	⊖	⊜	⊜
Integrity	◒	◒	○	○	◒	◒	○	⊖
Hardware	◒	●	◒	○	◒	○	○	⊖
RELIABILITY VERDICT	✘	✘	✘	✘	✘	✘	-	-

GMC Envoy XL

Trouble spots	96	97	98	99	00	01	02	03
Engine							⊜	⊜
Cooling							⊜	⊜
Fuel							○	⊜
Ignition							⊜	⊜
Transmission							⊜	⊜
Electrical							◒	⊖
A/C							○	⊜
Suspension							⊖	⊜
Brakes							⊖	⊜
Exhaust							⊜	⊜
Power equip.							◒	⊖
Paint/trim/rust							⊖	⊜
Integrity							◒	○
Hardware							○	⊖
RELIABILITY VERDICT							✘	✘

GMC Jimmy

Trouble spots	96	97	98	99	00	01	02	03
Engine	●	◒	○	○	○	⊖		
Cooling	●	●	◒	○	⊜	⊖		
Fuel	◒	●	○	⊖	○	○		
Ignition	⊖	○	⊖	⊖	⊖	⊖		
Transmission	◒	◒	○	○	⊖	○		
Electrical	●	●	●	●	●	●		
A/C	●	●	○	○	⊖	⊖		
Suspension	◒	◒	○	○	○	○		
Brakes	●	●	○	○	○	○		
Exhaust	⊖	⊜	⊜	⊖	⊖	⊜		
Power equip.	○	◒	◒	○	○	○		
Paint/trim/rust	○	○	⊖	⊖	○	⊖		
Integrity	◒	●	◒	●	◒	◒		
Hardware	○	◒	◒	◒	○	○		
RELIABILITY VERDICT	✘	✘	✘	✘	✘	✘		

GMC S-15 Sonoma V6 4WD

Trouble spots	96	97	98	99	00	01	02	03
Engine	Insufficient data	Insufficient data	●	Insufficient data	○	⊖	⊜	⊜
Cooling			○		⊖	⊜	⊜	⊜
Fuel			○		○	○	⊖	⊖
Ignition			⊖		⊖	⊖	⊜	⊜
Transmission			◒		○	⊖	⊜	⊜
Electrical			●		○	○	⊜	⊖
A/C			◒		⊖	⊜	⊜	⊜
Suspension			○		○	○	⊖	⊜
Brakes			◒		○	⊜	⊜	⊜
Exhaust			○		○	⊜	⊜	⊜
Power equip.			○		○	⊖	⊜	⊜
Paint/trim/rust			○		⊜	⊖	⊖	⊖
Integrity			◒		◒	◒	◒	○
Hardware			●		◒	○	○	⊖
RELIABILITY VERDICT			✗		✗	✗	✗	✗

GMC Safari

Trouble spots	96	97	98	99	00	01	02	03
Engine	◒	○	○	⊖	⊖	⊜	⊜	Insufficient data
Cooling	●	○	○	⊖	⊜	⊜	⊜	
Fuel	●	●	○	◒	⊖	⊖	⊖	
Ignition	⊖	⊖	⊖	⊜	⊖	⊖	⊜	
Transmission	○	◒	◒	○	○	⊖	⊜	
Electrical	●	●	●	◒	◒	○	○	
A/C	●	●	◒	○	⊖	⊖	⊖	
Suspension	○	◒	○	○	○	⊖	⊖	
Brakes	●	●	●	◒	◒	○	◒	
Exhaust	○	⊖	⊖	⊖	⊖	⊜	⊖	
Power equip.	●	●	●	●	◒	◒	○	
Paint/trim/rust	◒	○	○	○	⊜	⊖	⊜	
Integrity	●	●	◒	◒	●	◒	◒	
Hardware	●	●	●	◒	◒	◒	⊖	
RELIABILITY VERDICT	✗	✗	✗	✗	✗	✗	✗	

GMC Sierra 1500 4WD

Trouble spots	96	97	98	99	00	01	02	03
Engine	◒	○	○	⊖	⊖	⊖	⊜	⊜
Cooling	◒	◒	◒	⊜	⊜	⊜	⊜	⊜
Fuel	●	◒	○	○	○	⊖	⊜	⊜
Ignition	⊖	⊜	⊜	⊖	⊜	⊜	⊜	⊜
Transmission	○	◒	○	○	⊖	⊖	⊖	⊜
Electrical	●	●	◒	◒	○	⊖	⊖	⊜
A/C	◒	○	⊖	⊜	⊜	⊜	⊜	⊜
Suspension	⊖	◒	○	○	○	⊖	⊖	⊜
Brakes	●	●	●	●	◒	⊖	⊜	⊜
Exhaust	⊖	⊖	⊜	⊜	⊜	⊜	⊜	⊜
Power equip.	⊖	⊖	⊖	◒	⊜	⊖	⊖	⊖
Paint/trim/rust	⊖	⊜	⊜	⊜	⊜	⊜	⊜	⊜
Integrity	○	○	○	●	◒	○	○	○
Hardware	○	○	○	◒	○	⊖	⊖	⊜
RELIABILITY VERDICT	✗	✗	✗	✗	✗	-	✗	✗

GMC Suburban, Yukon XL

Trouble spots	96	97	98	99	00	01	02	03
Engine	◒	○	◒	○	⊜	⊖	⊜	⊜
Cooling	◒	◒	◒	○	⊜	⊜	⊜	⊜
Fuel	◒	○	○	○	○	⊖	⊖	⊜
Ignition	⊖	⊖	⊜	⊖	⊜	⊜	⊜	⊜
Transmission	◒	●	○	○	⊖	⊖	⊜	⊜
Electrical	●	●	●	●	◒	○	⊖	⊖
A/C	●	◒	◒	○	⊖	⊖	⊖	⊜
Suspension	○	◒	◒	○	○	⊖	⊖	⊜
Brakes	●	●	●	●	○	⊖	⊜	⊜
Exhaust	⊖	⊖	⊜	⊖	⊜	⊜	⊜	⊜
Power equip.	○	○	○	●	●	○	⊖	⊖
Paint/trim/rust	⊖	⊖	⊜	⊜	⊜	⊜	⊜	⊜
Integrity	○	○	○	○	◒	○	○	⊖
Hardware	◒	○	○	○	○	○	⊖	⊖
RELIABILITY VERDICT	✗	✗	✗	✗	✗	-	-	✗

GMC Yukon

Trouble spots	96	97	98	99	00	01	02	03
Engine	◒	◒	○	⊖	⊜	⊜	⊜	⊜
Cooling	◒	◒	◒	⊖	⊜	⊜	⊜	⊜
Fuel	◒	◒	○	○	⊜	⊜	⊜	⊜
Ignition	⊖	⊜	⊜	⊖	⊜	⊜	⊜	⊜
Transmission	○	◒	○	⊖	⊜	⊜	⊜	⊜
Electrical	●	●	●	◒	◒	○	⊖	○
A/C	●	○	○	⊖	⊖	⊖	⊜	⊖
Suspension	○	◒	○	⊖	○	⊖	⊖	⊜
Brakes	●	●	●	●	○	⊖	⊜	⊜
Exhaust	⊖	⊜	⊜	⊜	⊜	⊜	⊜	⊜
Power equip.	○	⊖	⊖	○	◒	○	⊖	⊖
Paint/trim/rust	⊖	⊖	⊖	⊜	⊖	⊜	⊜	⊜
Integrity	○	○	○	○	◒	○	○	⊖
Hardware	○	○	⊖	○	○	○	⊖	⊜
RELIABILITY VERDICT	✗	✗	✗	✗	-	-	-	✗

Honda Accord

Trouble spots	96	97	98	99	00	01	02	03
Engine	⊖	⊖	⊜	⊜	⊜	⊜	⊜	⊜
Cooling	⊖	⊜	⊜	⊜	⊜	⊜	⊜	⊜
Fuel	⊜	⊜	○	⊖	⊖	⊜	⊜	⊜
Ignition	⊜	⊖	⊜	⊖	⊜	⊜	⊜	⊜
Transmission	⊜	⊜	⊖	⊜	⊖	⊖	⊜	⊜
Electrical	○	○	○	⊖	⊖	⊜	⊜	⊜
A/C	○	○	⊜	⊜	⊜	⊜	⊜	⊜
Suspension	⊖	⊜	⊜	⊜	⊜	⊜	⊜	⊜
Brakes	○	⊖	⊖	⊖	⊖	⊖	⊜	⊜
Exhaust	○	⊖	⊖	⊜	⊜	⊜	⊜	⊜
Power equip.	○	◒	⊖	⊖	⊜	⊜	⊜	⊜
Paint/trim/rust	⊖	⊖	⊖	⊖	⊖	⊜	⊜	⊜
Integrity	⊖	⊖	⊖	⊖	⊖	⊖	⊖	⊖
Hardware	⊖	⊖	⊖	⊖	⊖	⊖	⊜	⊜
RELIABILITY VERDICT	✓	✓	✓	✓	✓	✓	✓	✓

Honda CR-V

Trouble spots	96	97	98	99	00	01	02	03
Engine		⊜	⊜	⊜	⊜	⊜	⊜	⊜
Cooling		⊜	⊜	⊜	⊜	⊜	⊜	⊜
Fuel		⊜	⊜	⊜	⊜	⊜	⊖	⊜
Ignition		⊖	⊜	⊜	⊜	⊜	⊜	⊜
Transmission		⊜	⊜	⊜	⊜	⊜	⊜	⊜
Electrical		⊜	⊖	⊜	⊜	⊜	⊜	⊜
A/C		⊖	⊜	⊜	⊜	⊜	⊜	⊜
Suspension		⊖	⊜	⊜	⊜	⊜	⊜	⊜
Brakes		⊖	⊖	⊜	⊜	⊜	⊖	⊜
Exhaust		⊜	⊜	⊜	⊜	⊜	⊜	⊜
Power equip.		⊖	⊜	⊖	⊜	⊜	⊜	⊜
Paint/trim/rust		⊜	⊖	⊜	⊜	⊜	⊜	⊜
Integrity		⊖	⊖	⊜	⊖	⊖	⊖	⊜
Hardware		⊜	⊖	⊖	⊖	⊜	⊖	⊜
RELIABILITY VERDICT		✓	✓	✓	✓	✓	✓	✓

Honda Civic

Trouble spots	96	97	98	99	00	01	02	03
Engine	⊜	⊜	⊜	⊜	⊜	⊜	⊜	⊜
Cooling	⊜	⊜	⊜	⊜	⊜	⊜	⊜	⊜
Fuel	⊖	⊖	⊖	⊜	⊜	⊜	⊜	⊜
Ignition	⊜	⊜	⊜	⊜	⊜	⊜	⊜	⊜
Transmission	⊜	⊜	⊖	⊜	⊜	⊜	⊜	⊜
Electrical	⊖	⊖	⊖	⊖	⊜	⊖	⊜	⊜
A/C	⊖	⊖	⊖	⊜	⊜	⊜	⊜	⊜
Suspension	⊖	⊜	⊜	⊜	⊜	⊖	⊖	⊜
Brakes	⊖	⊖	⊖	⊖	⊖	⊜	⊜	⊜
Exhaust	○	○	○	⊖	⊜	⊜	⊜	⊜
Power equip.	⊖	○	⊜	⊜	⊜	⊜	⊜	⊜
Paint/trim/rust	⊖	⊖	⊖	⊜	⊖	⊖	⊖	⊜
Integrity	○	○	⊜	⊜	⊖	○	○	⊖
Hardware	⊖	⊜	⊖	⊖	⊜	⊖	⊖	⊜
RELIABILITY VERDICT	✓	✓	✓	✓	✓	✓	✓	✓

Honda Element (TROUBLE SPOTS)	96	97	98	99	00	01	02	03
Engine								⊜
Cooling								⊜
Fuel								⊜
Ignition								⊜
Transmission								⊜
Electrical								⊜
A/C								⊜
Suspension								⊜
Brakes								⊜
Exhaust								⊜
Power equip.								⊜
Paint/trim/rust								⊜
Integrity								○
Hardware								⊜
RELIABILITY VERDICT								✔

Honda Odyssey (TROUBLE SPOTS)	96	97	98	99	00	01	02	03
Engine	○	⊜	⊜	⊜	⊜	⊜	⊜	⊜
Cooling	⊜	⊜	⊜	⊜	⊜	⊖	⊜	⊜
Fuel	⊜	⊜	⊖	⊖	⊖	⊜	⊜	⊜
Ignition	⊜	⊖	⊖	⊜	⊜	⊜	⊜	⊜
Transmission	⊜	⊜	○	○	⊖	⊖	⊜	⊜
Electrical	⊖	⊖	⊖	○	⊖	⊖	⊖	⊜
A/C	⊖	⊜	⊜	⊜	⊜	⊜	⊜	⊜
Suspension	⊜	⊜	⊜	⊜	⊜	⊜	⊜	⊜
Brakes	●	○	○	○	⊖	⊖	⊜	⊜
Exhaust	⊖	⊜	⊜	⊖	⊜	⊜	⊜	⊜
Power equip.	⊖	⊜	⊜	●	◒	○	⊖	⊜
Paint/trim/rust	⊖	⊜	⊜	⊖	⊜	⊜	⊜	⊜
Integrity	⊖	⊜	⊖	○	○	○	○	⊖
Hardware	○	⊖	⊜	◒	◒	○	⊖	⊜
RELIABILITY VERDICT	✔	✔	✔	-	✔	✔	✔	✔

Honda Passport (TROUBLE SPOTS)	96	97	98	99	00	01	02	03
Engine	◒	◒	◒	◒	⊖	⊖	⊜	
Cooling	⊖	⊖	⊖	⊜	⊜	⊜	⊜	
Fuel	○	○	○	●	◒	⊖	⊜	
Ignition	⊖	○	⊜	⊖	⊜	⊖	⊜	
Transmission	⊖	○	⊖	○	⊜	⊜	⊜	
Electrical	●	●	◒	○	○	○	⊖	
A/C	⊖	○	○	○	⊜	⊜	⊜	
Suspension	⊖	⊖	○	⊖	⊖	⊖	⊖	
Brakes	○	◒	●	●	○	⊖	⊖	
Exhaust	⊜	⊖	⊜	⊖	⊜	⊜	⊖	
Power equip.	●	○	⊖	○	○	⊖	⊖	
Paint/trim/rust	◒	○	○	⊖	○	⊖	⊜	
Integrity	◒	●	◒	○	◒	◒	○	
Hardware	◒	○	○	○	○	⊖	⊜	
RELIABILITY VERDICT	-	-	✗	✗	-	-	✔	

Honda Pilot (TROUBLE SPOTS)	96	97	98	99	00	01	02	03
Engine								⊜
Cooling								⊜
Fuel								⊜
Ignition								⊜
Transmission								⊜
Electrical								⊜
A/C								⊜
Suspension								⊜
Brakes								⊜
Exhaust								⊜
Power equip.								⊜
Paint/trim/rust								⊜
Integrity								⊖
Hardware								⊜
RELIABILITY VERDICT								✔

Honda Prelude (TROUBLE SPOTS)	96	97	98	99	00	01	02	03
Engine	Insufficient data	⊖	⊖	Insufficient data	Insufficient data	⊖		
Cooling		⊖	⊜			⊜		
Fuel		⊜	⊖			⊖		
Ignition		⊜	○			⊜		
Transmission		○	⊜			⊖		
Electrical		⊜	⊜			⊜		
A/C		⊖	⊜			⊜		
Suspension		⊜	⊖			⊜		
Brakes		⊖	⊖			⊜		
Exhaust		⊜	⊜			⊜		
Power equip.		⊜	⊜			○		
Paint/trim/rust		○	⊜			⊖		
Integrity		⊖	⊖			○		
Hardware		⊖	⊜			○		
RELIABILITY VERDICT		✔	✔			✔		

Honda S2000 (TROUBLE SPOTS)	96	97	98	99	00	01	02	03
Engine					⊖	⊜	⊜	Insufficient data
Cooling					⊜	⊜	⊜	
Fuel					⊖	⊜	⊜	
Ignition					⊜	⊜	⊜	
Transmission					○	○	⊜	
Electrical					⊜	⊜	⊜	
A/C					⊜	⊜	⊜	
Suspension					⊜	⊖	⊜	
Brakes					⊜	⊜	⊜	
Exhaust					⊖	⊜	⊜	
Power equip.					⊖	○	⊖	
Paint/trim/rust					⊖	⊜	⊜	
Integrity					⊖	◒	⊖	
Hardware					⊖	○	⊜	
RELIABILITY VERDICT					✔	-	✔	

Hummer H2 (TROUBLE SPOTS)	96	97	98	99	00	01	02	03
Engine								⊜
Cooling								⊜
Fuel								⊜
Ignition								⊜
Transmission								⊜
Electrical								⊜
A/C								⊜
Suspension								⊖
Brakes								⊜
Exhaust								⊜
Power equip.								⊖
Paint/trim/rust								⊜
Integrity								⊖
Hardware								○
RELIABILITY VERDICT								✗

Hyundai Elantra (TROUBLE SPOTS)	96	97	98	99	00	01	02	03
Engine	Insufficient data	Insufficient data	Insufficient data	⊖	⊖	⊜	⊜	⊜
Cooling				⊖	⊖	⊜	⊜	⊜
Fuel				◒	○	⊖	⊖	⊜
Ignition				○	○	⊜	⊜	⊜
Transmission				◒	○	⊖	⊖	⊜
Electrical				◒	◒	◒	⊖	⊜
A/C				⊜	⊖	⊜	⊜	⊜
Suspension				⊖	⊜	⊖	⊜	⊜
Brakes				⊖	⊖	⊖	⊜	⊜
Exhaust				⊖	⊜	⊜	⊜	⊜
Power equip.				○	◒	⊖	⊜	⊜
Paint/trim/rust				○	○	○	⊖	⊜
Integrity				○	○	○	○	⊖
Hardware				○	○	⊖	⊖	⊜
RELIABILITY VERDICT				-	-	-	✔	✔

Hyundai Santa Fe

TROUBLE SPOTS	96	97	98	99	00	01	02	03
Engine						⊖	⊜	⊜
Cooling						⊜	⊜	⊜
Fuel						○	⊜	⊜
Ignition						○	⊜	⊜
Transmission						○	⊜	⊜
Electrical						◒	⊖	⊜
A/C						⊜	⊜	⊜
Suspension						○	⊜	⊜
Brakes						⊖	⊜	⊜
Exhaust						⊜	⊜	⊜
Power equip.						⊖	⊜	⊜
Paint/trim/rust						⊖	⊜	⊜
Integrity						○	⊜	⊖
Hardware						⊜	⊜	⊜
RELIABILITY VERDICT						✗	✔	✔

Hyundai Sonata

TROUBLE SPOTS	96	97	98	99	00	01	02	03
Engine	Insufficient data	Insufficient data	Insufficient data	Insufficient data	⊜	⊖	⊜	⊜
Cooling					⊜	⊜	⊜	⊜
Fuel					○	⊖	⊖	⊜
Ignition					⊖	⊜	⊜	⊜
Transmission					⊖	⊖	⊜	⊜
Electrical					◒	○	⊖	⊜
A/C					⊜	⊖	⊖	⊜
Suspension					⊖	⊜	⊜	⊜
Brakes					○	○	⊖	⊜
Exhaust					⊜	⊜	⊜	⊜
Power equip.					●	◒	○	⊖
Paint/trim/rust					○	◒	⊜	⊖
Integrity					⊖	○	⊖	⊖
Hardware					○	◒	⊖	⊜
RELIABILITY VERDICT					–	✗	–	–

Hyundai XG300, XG350

TROUBLE SPOTS	96	97	98	99	00	01	02	03
Engine						⊜	⊜	Insufficient data
Cooling						⊜	⊜	
Fuel						○	○	
Ignition						⊜	⊜	
Transmission						○	⊖	
Electrical						○	○	
A/C						⊜	⊜	
Suspension						⊜	⊜	
Brakes						⊜	⊖	
Exhaust						⊜	⊜	
Power equip.						○	⊖	
Paint/trim/rust						○	⊜	
Integrity						⊖	⊖	
Hardware						○	⊖	
RELIABILITY VERDICT						–	✗	

Infiniti FX

TROUBLE SPOTS	96	97	98	99	00	01	02	03
Engine								⊜
Cooling								⊜
Fuel								⊜
Ignition								⊜
Transmission								⊜
Electrical								⊜
A/C								⊜
Suspension								⊜
Brakes								⊜
Exhaust								⊜
Power equip.								⊜
Paint/trim/rust								⊜
Integrity								⊖
Hardware								⊜
RELIABILITY VERDICT								✔

Infiniti G20

TROUBLE SPOTS	96	97	98	99	00	01	02	03
Engine	⊖			⊜	⊜	Insufficient data	⊜	
Cooling	⊖			⊜	⊜		⊜	
Fuel	⊖			⊖	⊖		⊜	
Ignition	⊖			⊜	⊜		⊜	
Transmission	⊖			⊜	⊜		⊜	
Electrical	○			⊖	○		⊜	
A/C	⊜			⊜	⊜		⊜	
Suspension	○			⊖	⊜		⊜	
Brakes	○			⊜	⊖		⊜	
Exhaust	⊖			⊜	⊖		⊜	
Power equip.	○			⊜	○		⊜	
Paint/trim/rust	⊜			⊜	⊜		⊜	
Integrity	⊖			⊖	⊖		⊖	
Hardware	⊖			⊜	⊜		⊜	
RELIABILITY VERDICT	✔			✔	✔		✔	

Infiniti G35

TROUBLE SPOTS	96	97	98	99	00	01	02	03
Engine								⊜
Cooling								⊜
Fuel								⊜
Ignition								⊜
Transmission								⊜
Electrical								⊜
A/C								⊜
Suspension								⊜
Brakes								⊜
Exhaust								⊜
Power equip.								⊖
Paint/trim/rust								⊜
Integrity								⊖
Hardware								⊜
RELIABILITY VERDICT								✔

Infiniti I30, I35

TROUBLE SPOTS	96	97	98	99	00	01	02	03
Engine	⊜	⊖	⊜	⊜	⊜	⊜	⊜	⊜
Cooling	⊜	⊜	⊜	⊜	⊜	⊜	⊜	⊜
Fuel	○	⊖	⊖	⊜	⊖	⊖	⊜	⊜
Ignition	⊜	⊜	⊜	⊖	⊖	⊜	⊜	⊜
Transmission	⊖	⊖	⊜	⊜	⊜	⊜	⊜	⊜
Electrical	◒	○	○	⊖	⊖	⊜	⊜	⊜
A/C	○	⊖	⊜	⊜	⊜	⊜	⊜	⊜
Suspension	⊖	⊖	⊖	⊜	⊜	⊜	⊖	⊜
Brakes	○	○	○	○	○	⊖	⊜	⊜
Exhaust	⊜	⊖	⊜	⊜	⊜	⊜	⊜	⊜
Power equip.	⊖	⊖	⊖	⊜	⊖	⊖	⊖	⊖
Paint/trim/rust	⊖	⊖	⊖	⊜	⊜	⊜	⊜	⊜
Integrity	⊜	⊖	⊖	⊖	⊖	⊖	⊖	⊜
Hardware	⊖	⊜	⊜	⊜	⊖	⊜	⊜	⊖
RELIABILITY VERDICT	✔	✔	✔	✔	✔	✔	✔	✔

Infiniti QX4

TROUBLE SPOTS	96	97	98	99	00	01	02	03
Engine		Insufficient data	⊜	⊜	Insufficient data	⊜	⊜	Insufficient data
Cooling			⊖	⊜		⊜	⊜	
Fuel			⊖	⊜		⊜	⊜	
Ignition			⊜	⊜		⊜	⊜	
Transmission			⊖	⊜		⊜	⊜	
Electrical			⊖	⊖		⊜	⊜	
A/C			⊜	⊖		⊜	⊜	
Suspension			⊖	⊜		⊜	⊜	
Brakes			⊜	⊜		⊖	⊖	
Exhaust			⊖	⊜		⊜	⊜	
Power equip.			⊜	⊜		⊖	⊖	
Paint/trim/rust			⊜	⊜		⊜	⊜	
Integrity			○	○		⊜	⊖	
Hardware			⊜	⊜		⊜	⊜	
RELIABILITY VERDICT			✔	✔		✔	✔	

Isuzu Rodeo	96	97	98	99	00	01	02	03
Engine	◒	◒	◒	◒	⊖	⊖	⊜	Insufficient data
Cooling	⊖	⊖	⊖	⊜	⊜	⊜	⊜	
Fuel	○	○	○	●	◒	⊖	⊜	
Ignition	⊖	○	⊜	⊖	⊖	⊖	⊜	
Transmission	⊖	○	⊖	○	⊖	⊜	⊜	
Electrical	●	●	◒	○	○	○	⊖	
A/C	⊖	○	○	○	⊜	⊜	⊜	
Suspension	⊖	⊖	○	⊖	⊖	⊖	⊖	
Brakes	○	◒	●	●	○	⊖	⊖	
Exhaust	⊜	⊖	⊖	⊖	⊜	⊜	⊖	
Power equip.	●	○	⊖	○	○	⊖	⊖	
Paint/trim/rust	◒	○	○	⊜	○	⊖	⊜	
Integrity	◒	●	◒	○	◒	◒	○	
Hardware	◒	○	○	○	○	⊖	⊜	
RELIABILITY VERDICT	-	-	✗	✗	-	-	✓	

Jaguar S-Type	96	97	98	99	00	01	02	03
Engine					⊖	⊖	Insufficient data	⊜
Cooling					○	⊖		⊜
Fuel					⊜	⊖		⊜
Ignition					⊖	⊜		⊜
Transmission					○	○		○
Electrical					◒	○		○
A/C					⊖	⊜		⊖
Suspension					○	○		⊜
Brakes					⊖	○		⊜
Exhaust					⊜	⊜		⊜
Power equip.					◒	◒		◒
Paint/trim/rust					⊖	⊜		⊜
Integrity					○	○		⊖
Hardware					○	⊖		⊜
RELIABILITY VERDICT					✗	✗		✗

Jaguar X-Type	96	97	98	99	00	01	02	03
Engine							⊖	⊜
Cooling							○	⊜
Fuel							○	⊖
Ignition							⊖	⊜
Transmission							○	⊖
Electrical							◒	⊜
A/C							⊖	⊜
Suspension							⊖	⊜
Brakes							⊖	⊜
Exhaust							⊜	⊜
Power equip.							◒	⊖
Paint/trim/rust							⊜	⊜
Integrity							◒	⊖
Hardware							◒	⊖
RELIABILITY VERDICT							✗	✗

Jaguar XJ6, XJ8, XJR	96	97	98	99	00	01	02	03
Engine	Insufficient data	Insufficient data	⊖	○	⊖	Insufficient data	Insufficient data	Insufficient data
Cooling			◒	◒	○			
Fuel			○	⊖	◒			
Ignition			⊖	⊖	○			
Transmission			⊖	⊖	○			
Electrical			◒	◒	◒			
A/C			⊜	⊜	⊜			
Suspension			⊖	○	●			
Brakes			⊖	○	○			
Exhaust			⊜	⊜	⊖			
Power equip.			◒	○	⊜			
Paint/trim/rust			⊜	⊜	⊜			
Integrity			⊖	○	⊖			
Hardware			⊖	⊜	⊖			
RELIABILITY VERDICT			-	✗	✗			

Jeep Cherokee	96	97	98	99	00	01	02	03
Engine	⊖	⊖	⊖	⊜	⊜	⊖		
Cooling	◒	◒	⊖	⊜	⊖	⊜		
Fuel	○	◒	⊖	⊖	⊖	⊖		
Ignition	⊖	⊖	⊜	⊜	⊜	⊖		
Transmission	⊖	⊖	⊖	⊖	⊖	⊜		
Electrical	○	◒	○	○	○	⊖		
A/C	○	●	◒	⊖	⊖	⊜		
Suspension	○	⊖	⊖	⊖	⊖	⊖		
Brakes	○	●	◒	◒	◒	◒		
Exhaust	○	⊖	⊜	⊜	⊖	⊜		
Power equip.	○	○	◒	●	○	⊖		
Paint/trim/rust	◒	○	○	○	⊖	⊖		
Integrity	◒	◒	○	○	○	○		
Hardware	○	○	⊖	○	○	⊜		
RELIABILITY VERDICT	-	-	-	-	-	-		

Jeep Grand Cherokee	96	97	98	99	00	01	02	03
Engine	○	○	⊖	⊖	⊖	⊖	⊜	⊜
Cooling	◒	○	○	○	⊖	⊜	⊜	⊜
Fuel	○	◒	○	○	⊖	⊖	⊖	⊜
Ignition	⊖	⊖	⊜	⊖	⊖	⊜	⊜	⊜
Transmission	◒	◒	◒	◒	○	○	⊜	⊖
Electrical	●	◒	◒	◒	○	○	⊖	⊖
A/C	●	◒	◒	○	⊖	⊖	⊜	⊜
Suspension	○	○	◒	○	○	○	⊖	⊖
Brakes	◒	●	●	●	●	●	◒	⊖
Exhaust	○	○	⊖	⊜	⊜	⊜	⊜	⊜
Power equip.	◒	○	○	●	○	◒	⊖	⊖
Paint/trim/rust	⊖	⊖	⊖	⊖	⊜	⊜	⊜	⊜
Integrity	◒	○	◒	◒	○	○	○	⊖
Hardware	○	○	○	○	○	⊖	⊜	⊜
RELIABILITY VERDICT	✗	✗	✗	✗	✗	✗	✗	✗

Jeep Liberty	96	97	98	99	00	01	02	03
Engine							⊜	⊜
Cooling							⊜	⊜
Fuel							⊜	⊜
Ignition							⊜	⊜
Transmission							⊖	⊜
Electrical							⊖	⊜
A/C							⊜	⊜
Suspension							⊖	⊜
Brakes							⊖	⊜
Exhaust							⊜	⊜
Power equip.							⊖	⊜
Paint/trim/rust							⊜	⊜
Integrity							⊖	⊖
Hardware							⊖	⊖
RELIABILITY VERDICT							-	✓

Jeep Wrangler	96	97	98	99	00	01	02	03
Engine		⊖	⊜	⊜	⊜	⊜	⊜	⊜
Cooling		○	○	⊖	⊖	⊖	⊜	⊜
Fuel		◒	⊖	⊖	⊖	⊖	⊖	⊜
Ignition		⊖	⊜	⊜	⊜	⊜	⊜	⊜
Transmission		⊖	○	○	⊖	⊖	⊜	⊖
Electrical		○	●	●	○	⊖	⊖	⊖
A/C		●	○	⊖	⊜	⊜	⊜	⊜
Suspension		○	○	⊖	⊖	⊜	⊜	⊜
Brakes		○	○	⊖	⊖	⊖	⊜	⊜
Exhaust		●	○	○	⊜	⊜	⊜	⊜
Power equip.		⊜	⊜	⊜	⊜	⊜	⊜	⊜
Paint/trim/rust		○	◒	○	◒	○	○	⊜
Integrity		◒	○	○	○	○	○	⊜
Hardware		○	○	⊜	○	⊖	⊖	⊜
RELIABILITY VERDICT		-	-	-	-	-	-	-

Kia Sedona 96	97	98	99	00	01	02	03	TROUBLE SPOTS	Kia Sorento 96	97	98	99	00	01	02	03
						⊜	⊜	Engine								⊜
						⊜	⊜	Cooling								⊜
						⊜	⊜	Fuel								⊜
						⊜	⊜	Ignition								⊜
						⊜	⊜	Transmission								⊜
						○	⊜	Electrical								⊖
						○	⊖	A/C								⊜
						⊖	⊜	Suspension								⊜
						⊖	⊜	Brakes								⊜
						⊜	⊜	Exhaust								⊜
						○	⊜	Power equip.								⊖
						○	⊜	Paint/trim/rust								⊖
						◒	⊜	Integrity								⊜
						◒	⊜	Hardware								⊖
						✗	–	RELIABILITY VERDICT								–

TROUBLE SPOTS	Land Rover Discovery 96	97	98	99	00	01	02	03	Land Rover Freelander 96	97	98	99	00	01	02	03
Engine	Insufficient data	Insufficient data	Insufficient data	Insufficient data	●	⊖	Insufficient data	Insufficient data							⊖	Insufficient data
Cooling					●	⊖									⊜	
Fuel					⊖	⊖									⊜	
Ignition					⊜	⊜									⊜	
Transmission					⊖	⊖									⊖	
Electrical					◒	◒									○	
A/C					⊖	⊜									○	
Suspension					⊖	⊜									⊖	
Brakes					◒	○									⊖	
Exhaust					⊜	⊜									⊜	
Power equip.					◒	○									●	
Paint/trim/rust					⊖	⊜									⊖	
Integrity					◒	◒									○	
Hardware					◒	◒									⊖	
RELIABILITY VERDICT					✗	✗									✗	

Lexus ES300 96	97	98	99	00	01	02	03	TROUBLE SPOTS	Lexus GS300/GS400, GS430 96	97	98	99	00	01	02	03
○	⊖	⊜	⊜	⊜	⊜	⊜	⊜	Engine	Insufficient data	Insufficient data	⊜	⊜	⊜	⊜	⊜	⊜
⊜	⊜	⊜	⊜	⊜	⊜	⊜	⊜	Cooling			⊜	⊜	⊜	⊜	⊜	⊜
⊜	⊖	⊖	⊖	⊜	⊜	⊜	⊜	Fuel			⊖	⊖	⊜	⊜	⊜	⊜
⊜	⊜	⊜	⊜	⊜	⊜	⊜	⊜	Ignition			⊜	⊜	⊜	⊜	⊜	⊜
⊖	⊜	⊜	⊜	⊜	⊜	⊖	⊜	Transmission			⊜	⊜	⊜	⊜	⊜	⊜
○	⊖	⊖	○	⊖	⊜	⊜	⊜	Electrical			⊖	⊖	⊖	⊖	⊜	⊜
⊜	⊜	⊜	⊜	⊜	⊜	⊜	⊜	A/C			⊜	⊜	⊜	⊜	⊜	⊜
⊖	⊖	⊖	⊜	⊜	⊜	⊜	⊜	Suspension			⊖	⊜	⊜	⊖	⊜	⊜
○	⊖	⊜	⊜	⊖	⊖	◒	⊜	Brakes			⊖	⊖	⊖	⊖	⊜	⊜
⊜	⊜	⊜	⊜	⊜	⊜	⊜	⊜	Exhaust			⊜	⊜	⊜	⊜	⊜	⊜
○	⊖	⊖	⊜	⊜	⊖	⊖	⊜	Power equip.			○	○	⊜	⊜	⊜	⊜
⊖	⊖	⊜	⊜	⊖	⊖	⊜	⊜	Paint/trim/rust			⊖	⊜	⊜	⊖	⊜	⊜
⊖	⊖	⊖	⊖	⊖	⊖	⊖	⊖	Integrity			⊖	⊖	⊖	○	⊖	⊜
⊖	⊖	⊖	⊖	⊜	⊖	⊜	⊜	Hardware			⊜	⊜	⊜	⊜	⊜	⊜
✓	✓	✓	✓	✓	✓	–	✓	RELIABILITY VERDICT			✓	✓	✓	✓	✓	✓

TROUBLE SPOTS	Lexus GX470 96	97	98	99	00	01	02	03	Lexus IS300 96	97	98	99	00	01	02	03
Engine								⊜						⊜	⊜	Insufficient data
Cooling								⊜						⊜	⊜	
Fuel								⊜						⊖	⊜	
Ignition								⊜						⊜	⊜	
Transmission								⊜						⊖	⊜	
Electrical								⊖						⊖	⊖	
A/C								⊖						⊜	⊜	
Suspension								⊜						⊖	⊖	
Brakes								⊖						⊜	⊜	
Exhaust								⊜						⊜	⊜	
Power equip.								⊜						⊖	⊜	
Paint/trim/rust								⊜						⊖	⊜	
Integrity								⊜						⊖	○	
Hardware								⊖						⊖	⊖	
RELIABILITY VERDICT								–						✓	✓	

Lexus LS400, LS430

TROUBLE SPOTS	96	97	98	99	00	01	02	03
Engine	⊜	⊜	⊜	⊜	⊜	⊜	⊜	⊜
Cooling	⊜	⊜	⊜	⊜	⊜	⊜	⊜	⊜
Fuel	⊜	⊜	⊜	⊜	⊜	⊜	⊜	⊜
Ignition	⊜	⊜	⊜	⊜	⊜	⊜	⊜	⊜
Transmission	⊜	⊜	⊜	⊜	⊜	⊜	⊜	⊜
Electrical	⊖	⊖	⊖	⊖	⊖	⊖	⊖	⊜
A/C	⊖	⊜	⊜	⊜	⊜	⊜	⊜	⊜
Suspension	○	○	⊖	⊖	⊜	⊖	⊜	⊜
Brakes	○	⊜	⊜	⊖	⊜	⊖	⊖	⊜
Exhaust	⊜	⊜	⊜	⊜	⊜	⊜	⊜	⊜
Power equip.	○	⊖	⊜	⊖	⊖	○	⊜	⊜
Paint/trim/rust	⊜	⊜	⊜	⊜	⊜	⊜	⊜	⊜
Integrity	⊜	⊜	⊜	⊜	⊖	⊜	⊖	⊜
Hardware	⊖	⊜	⊜	⊜	⊜	⊖	⊜	⊜
RELIABILITY VERDICT	✔	✔	✔	✔	✔	✔	✔	✔

Lexus RX300

TROUBLE SPOTS	96	97	98	99	00	01	02	03
Engine				⊖	⊜	⊜	⊜	⊜
Cooling				⊜	⊜	⊜	⊜	⊜
Fuel				⊖	⊜	⊜	⊜	⊜
Ignition				⊜	⊜	⊜	⊜	⊜
Transmission				⊖	⊜	⊜	⊜	⊜
Electrical				○	⊖	⊜	⊜	⊜
A/C				⊜	⊜	⊜	⊜	⊜
Suspension				⊖	⊜	⊜	⊜	⊜
Brakes				⊖	⊖	⊜	⊜	⊜
Exhaust				⊖	⊜	⊜	⊜	⊜
Power equip.				⊖	⊜	⊜	⊜	⊜
Paint/trim/rust				⊖	⊜	⊜	⊜	⊜
Integrity				⊖	⊖	⊖	⊖	⊜
Hardware				⊖	⊖	⊜	⊜	⊜
RELIABILITY VERDICT				✔	✔	✔	✔	✔

Lexus SC300/SC400, SC430

TROUBLE SPOTS	96	97	98	99	00	01	02	03
Engine	Insufficient data	Insufficient data	Insufficient data	Insufficient data	Insufficient data		⊜	Insufficient data
Cooling							⊜	
Fuel							⊜	
Ignition							⊜	
Transmission							⊜	
Electrical							⊖	
A/C							⊜	
Suspension							⊖	
Brakes							⊜	
Exhaust							⊜	
Power equip.							⊖	
Paint/trim/rust							⊖	
Integrity							⊖	
Hardware							⊖	
RELIABILITY VERDICT							✔	

Lincoln Continental

TROUBLE SPOTS	96	97	98	99	00	01	02	03
Engine	⊜	⊖	⊜	⊜	⊜	⊖	⊜	
Cooling	⊖	⊖	⊖	⊜	⊜	⊜	⊜	
Fuel	○	○	⊖	⊖	⊖	⊜	⊜	
Ignition	◒	⊖	⊖	⊖	⊜	⊜	⊜	
Transmission	◒	○	⊖	⊖	⊜	⊜	⊜	
Electrical	●	●	○	○	○	○	⊖	
A/C	⊖	○	⊖	⊖	⊜	⊖	⊖	
Suspension	●	●	○	◒	⊖	⊖	⊖	
Brakes	○	○	○	◒	○	○	⊖	
Exhaust	⊜	⊜	⊜	⊜	⊜	⊜	⊜	
Power equip.	◒	◒	○	○	◒	◒	⊖	
Paint/trim/rust	⊖	○	⊜	⊜	⊖	⊖	⊜	
Integrity	●	○	⊖	⊖	⊖	○	○	
Hardware	●	○	⊖	○	○	⊖	⊖	
RELIABILITY VERDICT	-	-	✔	✔	✔	-	-	

Lincoln LS

TROUBLE SPOTS	96	97	98	99	00	01	02	03
Engine					⊜	⊖	⊜	Insufficient data
Cooling					⊖	⊜	⊜	
Fuel					⊖	⊖	⊖	
Ignition					⊜	⊖	⊜	
Transmission					⊖	⊜	⊜	
Electrical					○	○	⊖	
A/C					⊖	⊖	⊜	
Suspension					⊖	⊜	⊖	
Brakes					⊖	⊜	⊖	
Exhaust					⊜	⊜	⊜	
Power equip.					●	○	○	
Paint/trim/rust					⊖	⊖	⊜	
Integrity					◒	○	○	
Hardware					○	○	⊖	
RELIABILITY VERDICT					-	-	-	

Lincoln Navigator

TROUBLE SPOTS	96	97	98	99	00	01	02	03
Engine			⊜	⊖	⊜	⊜	Insufficient data	⊜
Cooling			⊜	⊜	⊜	⊜		⊜
Fuel			⊖	⊖	⊖	⊜		⊜
Ignition			⊖	⊜	⊜	⊖		⊖
Transmission			○	⊖	⊜	⊜		⊜
Electrical			◒	◒	⊖	○		○
A/C			⊜	⊖	⊖	⊜		⊜
Suspension			◒	○	○	⊖		⊖
Brakes			◒	○	○	⊖		⊖
Exhaust			⊖	⊜	⊜	⊜		⊜
Power equip.			○	◒	○	◒		◒
Paint/trim/rust			⊖	○	⊖	○		⊖
Integrity			◒	◒	○	◒		⊖
Hardware			⊖	○	○	◒		⊖
RELIABILITY VERDICT			-	-	✔	-		✘

Lincoln Town Car

TROUBLE SPOTS	96	97	98	99	00	01	02	03
Engine	⊖	⊖	⊜	⊜	⊖	⊜	⊜	⊜
Cooling	⊖	⊖	⊜	⊜	⊜	⊜	⊜	⊜
Fuel	○	○	⊜	⊖	⊖	⊖	⊜	⊜
Ignition	⊖	⊖	⊜	⊖	⊖	⊖	⊜	⊜
Transmission	⊖	⊖	⊜	⊜	⊖	⊜	⊜	⊜
Electrical	○	◒	○	○	○	○	⊜	⊖
A/C	○	○	○	⊖	⊖	⊜	⊜	⊜
Suspension	◒	○	○	⊖	⊖	⊜	⊜	⊜
Brakes	◒	◒	○	○	○	⊖	⊜	⊜
Exhaust	⊖	⊖	⊜	⊜	⊜	⊜	⊜	⊜
Power equip.	◒	◒	●	◒	○	○	⊖	⊖
Paint/trim/rust	○	⊖	⊖	⊖	⊖	⊖	⊖	⊖
Integrity	○	○	○	○	⊖	○	⊖	○
Hardware	○	○	○	○	⊜	⊖	⊜	⊜
RELIABILITY VERDICT	✔	✔	✔	✔	✔	✔	✔	✘

Mazda 626, Mazda6

TROUBLE SPOTS	96	97	98	99	00	01	02	03
Engine	○	○	⊖	⊜	⊜	⊜	⊜	⊜
Cooling	◒	◒	⊖	⊖	⊜	⊜	⊜	⊜
Fuel	◒	◒	○	⊖	⊖	⊜	⊜	⊖
Ignition	⊖	⊖	⊖	⊖	⊜	⊜	⊜	⊜
Transmission	◒	○	○	○	⊖	⊖	⊜	⊜
Electrical	◒	○	○	○	⊖	○	⊖	⊜
A/C	⊖	⊜	⊜	⊖	○	⊖	⊖	⊜
Suspension	○	○	⊜	⊖	⊖	⊖	⊖	⊜
Brakes	○	○	○	○	⊖	⊖	⊖	⊜
Exhaust	◒	◒	⊖	⊜	⊜	⊜	⊜	⊜
Power equip.	⊖	⊖	⊖	⊖	⊖	⊖	⊖	⊖
Paint/trim/rust	○	⊜	⊖	⊖	⊖	⊖	⊜	⊜
Integrity	○	⊖	○	○	○	⊜	○	⊜
Hardware	○	⊜	⊖	⊖	⊖	⊖	⊖	⊜
RELIABILITY VERDICT	-	-	✔	✔	✔	✔	✔	✔

Mazda B-Series 4WD								TROUBLE SPOTS	Mazda MPV							
96	97	98	99	00	01	02	03		96	97	98	99	00	01	02	03
⊖	⊖	⊖	⊖	⊖	⊜	⊜	⊜	Engine	Insufficient data	Insufficient data	Insufficient data		⊖	⊜	⊜	⊜
○	○	○	⊖	⊖	⊜	⊜	⊜	Cooling					⊜	⊜	⊜	⊜
○	○	○	⊖	⊖	⊖	⊖	⊜	Fuel					⊖	⊖	⊖	⊜
⊖	⊖	⊖	⊖	⊜	⊖	⊜	⊜	Ignition					⊜	⊜	⊜	⊜
○	⊖	○	⊖	○	⊖	○	⊜	Transmission					⊜	⊜	⊖	⊖
◒	●	●	◒	○	○	⊖	○	Electrical					⊖	⊜	⊖	⊜
○	◒	⊖	⊜	⊖	⊖	⊜	⊜	A/C					⊜	⊜	⊜	⊜
⊖	⊖	○	○	⊖	⊖	⊖	⊜	Suspension					⊖	⊜	⊖	⊜
◒	○	◒	◒	◒	⊖	⊜	⊜	Brakes					⊜	⊖	⊜	⊜
⊜	⊜	⊜	⊜	⊜	⊜	⊜	⊜	Exhaust					⊜	⊜	⊖	⊜
○	○	○	⊖	○	⊖	⊖	⊜	Power equip.					⊖	⊖	⊜	⊜
⊖	⊖	⊜	⊖	⊖	⊖	⊖	⊖	Paint/trim/rust					⊜	⊜	⊜	⊜
○	○	○	⊖	○	○	○	⊖	Integrity					○	⊖	⊖	⊜
⊖	⊖	○	⊖	○	○	⊖	⊖	Hardware					○	⊖	⊜	⊜
-	-	-	-	✗	✗	✗	-	RELIABILITY VERDICT					✓	✓	✓	-

Mazda MX-5 Miata								TROUBLE SPOTS	Mazda Millenia							
96	97	98	99	00	01	02	03		96	97	98	99	00	01	02	03
⊜	⊖		⊜	⊜	⊜	⊜	Insufficient data	Engine	Insufficient data	Insufficient data	⊖	⊜	⊜	⊖	⊜	
⊖	⊖		⊜	⊜	⊜	⊜		Cooling			⊜	⊜	⊜	⊜	⊜	
⊖	⊜		○	⊖	⊜	⊜		Fuel			◒	◒	○	⊖	⊖	
⊜	⊜		⊜	⊖	⊜	⊜		Ignition			⊖	⊜	⊖	⊜	⊜	
⊖	⊜		⊜	⊖	⊜	⊖		Transmission			⊜	⊜	⊜	⊖	⊜	
⊖	○		⊖	⊜	⊜	⊜		Electrical			○	⊜	⊜	⊜	⊜	
⊖	○		⊖	⊜	⊜	⊖		A/C			⊖	⊖	⊜	⊜	⊜	
⊖	⊜		⊜	⊜	⊜	⊜		Suspension			⊖	○	⊜	⊖	⊜	
⊜	⊖		⊜	⊜	⊜	⊜		Brakes			⊜	⊜	⊜	⊖	⊜	
⊜	⊜		⊜	⊜	⊜	⊜		Exhaust			⊖	⊖	⊖	⊜	⊜	
○	○		⊖	⊜	⊜	⊖		Power equip.			○	○	⊖	⊖	⊜	
⊖	○		⊜	⊜	⊜	⊜		Paint/trim/rust			⊖	⊜	⊖	⊜	⊜	
○	⊖		⊖	○	⊖	⊖		Integrity			⊖	⊖	○	⊖	⊖	
⊖	⊜		⊖	⊖	⊖	⊜		Hardware			⊖	⊜	⊖	⊖	⊜	
✓	✓		✓	✓	✓	✓		RELIABILITY VERDICT			✓	✓	✓	✓	✓	

Mazda Protege								TROUBLE SPOTS	Mazda Tribute							
96	97	98	99	00	01	02	03		96	97	98	99	00	01	02	03
⊖	⊜	⊖	⊖	⊜	⊜	⊜	⊜	Engine						⊖	⊜	⊜
○	⊖	⊜	⊜	⊜	⊜	⊜	⊜	Cooling						⊖	⊜	⊜
○	○	○	○	⊖	⊜	⊜	⊜	Fuel						○	⊖	⊜
⊖	⊜	⊜	⊖	⊖	⊜	⊜	⊜	Ignition						⊜	⊜	⊜
⊖	⊖	⊖	⊖	⊜	⊜	⊜	⊜	Transmission						⊖	⊜	⊜
○	○	⊖	⊖	⊖	⊖	⊜	⊜	Electrical						○	⊖	⊜
◒	○	⊖	⊜	⊜	⊜	⊜	⊜	A/C						⊜	⊜	⊜
⊖	⊜	⊜	⊖	⊜	⊜	⊜	⊜	Suspension						⊖	⊜	⊜
◒	◒	○	⊖	⊖	⊜	⊜	⊜	Brakes						○	⊜	⊜
◒	○	○	⊜	⊖	⊜	⊜	⊜	Exhaust						⊜	⊜	⊜
⊖	⊖	⊖	⊖	○	○	⊜	⊜	Power equip.						⊖	⊖	⊜
○	⊖	⊖	⊖	⊜	⊖	⊜	⊜	Paint/trim/rust						⊖	⊜	⊜
○	○	○	○	○	⊖	⊖	⊜	Integrity						◒	○	⊖
⊖	○	◒	⊖	⊖	⊖	⊖	⊜	Hardware						⊖	⊖	⊜
✓	✓	✓	✓	✓	✓	✓	✓	RELIABILITY VERDICT						✗	-	✓

Mercedes-Benz C-Class								TROUBLE SPOTS	Mercedes-Benz CLK							
96	97	98	99	00	01	02	03		96	97	98	99	00	01	02	03
○	○	⊖	⊖	⊖	⊖	⊜	⊜	Engine			Insufficient data	○	⊖	⊜	⊜	Insufficient data
⊖	⊜	⊜	⊜	⊜	⊖	⊜	⊜	Cooling				⊜	⊜	⊜	⊜	
◒	◒	◒	○	○	○	○	⊜	Fuel				◒	⊖	⊖	⊖	
⊖	⊖	⊖	⊜	⊜	⊖	⊖	⊜	Ignition				○	⊖	⊜	⊜	
⊖	○	○	⊜	⊖	⊖	⊜	⊜	Transmission				⊖	○	⊜	⊖	
●	◒	◒	◒	◒	●	◒	⊖	Electrical				●	◒	○	○	
○	◒	○	○	⊖	⊖	⊖	⊜	A/C				○	◒	○	⊖	
○	○	⊖	○	⊖	○	⊖	⊜	Suspension				⊖	⊖	⊜	⊜	
○	○	⊖	⊖	⊖	⊖	⊖	⊜	Brakes				○	○	⊖	⊜	
⊜	⊜	⊜	⊜	⊖	⊜	⊜	⊜	Exhaust				⊜	⊖	⊖	⊖	
○	⊖	○	○	○	●	◒	⊖	Power equip.				◒	◒	●	◒	
⊜	⊜	⊜	⊜	⊖	⊖	⊜	⊜	Paint/trim/rust				⊜	⊖	⊜	⊜	
○	⊜	⊖	○	○	◒	⊖	⊜	Integrity				◒	⊖	○	○	
⊖	⊜	○	○	⊖	◒	○	⊖	Hardware				●	○	○	⊖	
✓	✓	-	-	-	✗	✗	✗	RELIABILITY VERDICT				-	-	-	✗	

Mercedes-Benz E-Class

TROUBLE SPOTS	96	97	98	99	00	01	02	03
Engine	◒	○	○	○	⊖	⊜	⊜	⊜
Cooling	⊖	⊖	⊜	⊖	⊜	⊜	⊜	⊜
Fuel	○	○	○	○	○	⊖	⊖	⊖
Ignition	○	⊖	⊖	⊖	⊜	⊜	⊜	⊜
Transmission	⊜	○	○	○	⊖	⊖	⊜	⊜
Electrical	●	●	●	●	●	◒	○	○
A/C	◒	◒	○	⊖	○	◒	○	⊜
Suspension	◒	○	⊖	⊖	⊖	○	⊜	⊜
Brakes	○	○	⊖	○	○	⊖	⊖	⊖
Exhaust	⊖	⊜	⊖	⊜	⊜	⊜	⊖	⊜
Power equip.	◒	◒	●	●	◒	◒	⊖	◒
Paint/trim/rust	○	⊖	⊜	⊖	⊜	⊜	⊜	⊜
Integrity	⊖	⊖	⊖	○	○	⊖	⊜	⊜
Hardware	○	○	○	○	○	○	⊖	⊜
RELIABILITY VERDICT	-	-	-	-	-	-	-	✗

Mercedes-Benz M-Class

TROUBLE SPOTS	96	97	98	99	00	01	02	03
Engine			○	⊖	⊖	⊖	⊜	⊜
Cooling			⊖	⊜	⊖	⊖	○	⊜
Fuel			●	◒	◒	○	⊖	⊜
Ignition			⊖	⊖	⊖	⊖	⊜	⊜
Transmission			○	⊖	⊖	⊖	⊖	⊜
Electrical			●	◒	●	●	◒	⊖
A/C			○	⊖	⊖	⊖	⊜	⊜
Suspension			○	○	◒	◒	⊖	⊜
Brakes			○	○	●	◒	○	⊜
Exhaust			⊖	⊜	⊖	⊜	⊜	⊜
Power equip.			●	●	●	●	◒	○
Paint/trim/rust			○	⊖	○	○	⊖	⊖
Integrity			●	●	●	●	○	⊜
Hardware			●	●	●	◒	○	⊜
RELIABILITY VERDICT			✗	✗	✗	✗	✗	-

Mercedes-Benz S-Class

TROUBLE SPOTS	96	97	98	99	00	01	02	03
Engine	Insufficient data	Insufficient data	Insufficient data	Insufficient data	⊜	⊜	⊖	Insufficient data
Cooling					⊜	⊖	⊜	
Fuel					⊖	⊖	⊖	
Ignition					⊜	⊜	⊜	
Transmission					⊖	⊜	⊖	
Electrical					●	◒	○	
A/C					◒	⊜	⊖	
Suspension					◒	⊖	⊖	
Brakes					◒	○	⊖	
Exhaust					⊜	⊜	⊜	
Power equip.					●	◒	◒	
Paint/trim/rust					⊖	⊜	⊜	
Integrity					○	⊖	⊖	
Hardware					○	⊖	⊜	
RELIABILITY VERDICT					✗	-	✗	

Mercedes-Benz SLK

TROUBLE SPOTS	96	97	98	99	00	01	02	03
Engine			⊖	⊖	Insufficient data	⊜	⊜	Insufficient data
Cooling			⊜	⊜		⊖	⊜	
Fuel			◒	⊖		○	⊖	
Ignition			⊜	⊜		⊜	⊖	
Transmission			⊜	⊜		⊖	⊜	
Electrical			●	●		○	⊖	
A/C			⊜	⊜		⊜	○	
Suspension			⊖	⊖		⊖	⊖	
Brakes			⊜	⊖		⊜	⊜	
Exhaust			⊜	⊖		⊖	⊖	
Power equip.			⊖	◒		○	○	
Paint/trim/rust			⊜	⊖		⊜	⊖	
Integrity			○	○		◒	◒	
Hardware			⊖	○		○	◒	
RELIABILITY VERDICT			✓	-		-	✗	

Mercury Cougar

TROUBLE SPOTS	96	97	98	99	00	01	02	03
Engine	○	○		○	○	Insufficient data	⊜	
Cooling	●	◒		⊖	⊖		⊜	
Fuel	◒	○		◒	●		⊖	
Ignition	○	⊖		⊖	⊖		⊜	
Transmission	◒	○		⊖	⊖		⊜	
Electrical	◒	◒		●	◒		○	
A/C	○	⊜		○	⊖		⊜	
Suspension	○	⊖		⊖	⊖		⊜	
Brakes	◒	○		●	○		⊖	
Exhaust	⊖	⊖		⊖	⊜		⊜	
Power equip.	○	○		◒	○		⊜	
Paint/trim/rust	⊜	○		○	⊖		⊜	
Integrity	○	⊜		◒	●		○	
Hardware	○	⊖		◒	⊖		⊖	
RELIABILITY VERDICT	-	-		✗	✗		-	

Mercury Grand Marquis

TROUBLE SPOTS	96	97	98	99	00	01	02	03
Engine	○	⊖	⊜	⊜	⊜	⊖	⊜	⊜
Cooling	○	⊖	⊜	⊜	⊜	⊜	⊜	⊜
Fuel	◒	○	⊖	⊖	⊖	○	⊜	⊜
Ignition	○	⊖	⊜	⊖	⊖	⊖	⊜	⊜
Transmission	⊖	⊖	⊖	⊜	⊖	⊜	⊜	⊜
Electrical	◒	○	○	○	○	○	⊖	⊖
A/C	○	⊖	⊜	⊖	⊖	⊖	⊜	⊜
Suspension	○	○	○	⊖	⊖	⊖	⊖	⊖
Brakes	◒	◒	○	○	⊖	⊖	⊜	⊜
Exhaust	○	⊖	⊜	⊜	⊜	⊜	⊜	⊜
Power equip.	●	◒	⊖	○	○	○	⊖	⊖
Paint/trim/rust	⊖	⊖	⊖	⊖	⊖	⊖	⊖	⊖
Integrity	○	○	⊖	○	◒	◒	○	○
Hardware	○	⊖	⊜	⊖	○	○	⊖	⊖
RELIABILITY VERDICT	-	✓	✓	✓	✓	-	-	✗

Mercury Mountaineer 4WD

TROUBLE SPOTS	96	97	98	99	00	01	02	03
Engine		○	○	⊖	⊖	⊖	⊜	⊜
Cooling		○	○	⊖	○	⊜	⊜	⊜
Fuel		○	○	○	○	⊖	⊜	⊜
Ignition		⊖	⊖	⊖	⊖	⊜	⊜	⊜
Transmission		○	○	⊖	○	⊖	⊜	⊜
Electrical		○	◒	◒	◒	○	⊖	⊖
A/C		◒	○	⊖	⊜	⊖	⊜	⊜
Suspension		○	○	○	⊜	⊜	⊜	⊜
Brakes		◒	○	◒	○	⊖	⊜	⊜
Exhaust		⊖	⊜	⊜	⊜	⊜	⊜	⊜
Power equip.		○	◒	○	○	⊖	⊖	⊜
Paint/trim/rust		○	⊖	⊖	⊖	⊖	⊖	⊜
Integrity		○	○	○	○	○	○	⊜
Hardware		○	○	○	⊖	○	○	⊖
RELIABILITY VERDICT		-	✗	✗	✗	✗	✗	-

Mercury Mystique V6

TROUBLE SPOTS	96	97	98	99	00	01	02	03
Engine	◒	Insufficient data	⊖	○	⊖			
Cooling	●		○	⊜	⊜			
Fuel	●		◒	◒	●			
Ignition	○		⊖	⊜	⊖			
Transmission	○		○	⊖	⊖			
Electrical	◒		◒	◒	○			
A/C	○		○	○	⊖			
Suspension	○		◒	⊖	⊖			
Brakes	◒		◒	◒	○			
Exhaust	◒		○	⊖	⊜			
Power equip.	◒		○	⊖	⊖			
Paint/trim/rust	⊖		⊖	⊜	⊖			
Integrity	○		○	●	●			
Hardware	⊖		○	○	◒			
RELIABILITY VERDICT	✗		✗	-	✗			

Mercury Sable

TROUBLE SPOTS	96	97	98	99	00	01	02	03
Engine	○	○	⊖	⊖	⊖	⊜	⊜	⊜
Cooling	◒	○	⊖	⊖	⊜	⊜	⊜	⊜
Fuel	◒	○	○	○	○	○	⊖	⊜
Ignition	⊖	⊖	⊖	⊜	⊖	⊖	⊜	⊜
Transmission	◒	○	○	○	⊖	⊖	⊖	⊜
Electrical	◒	●	●	◒	◒	○	⊖	⊖
A/C	○	○	⊖	⊖	⊖	⊖	⊜	⊜
Suspension	◒	○	○	○	○	○	⊖	⊜
Brakes	◒	◒	●	◒	◒	○	⊖	⊜
Exhaust	⊖	⊖	⊜	⊜	⊜	⊜	⊜	⊜
Power equip.	○	◒	○	○	⊖	⊖	⊖	⊜
Paint/trim/rust	○	⊖	⊖	⊖	⊖	⊜	⊜	⊜
Integrity	◒	○	○	○	○	○	○	⊖
Hardware	○	○	○	⊖	⊖	⊖	⊖	⊜
RELIABILITY VERDICT	-	-	-	-	-	-	-	-

Mercury Tracer

TROUBLE SPOTS	96	97	98	99	00	01	02	03
Engine	◒	⊖	⊖	⊖				
Cooling	◒	◒	○	⊜				
Fuel	○	○	⊖	⊖				
Ignition	○	⊜	⊜	⊖				
Transmission	⊖	⊖	⊖	⊖				
Electrical	◒	○	⊖	○				
A/C	○	○	⊖	⊖				
Suspension	○	◒	○	⊖				
Brakes	◒	◒	○	○				
Exhaust	○	⊖	⊜	⊜				
Power equip.	⊖	⊜	⊖	⊖				
Paint/trim/rust	◒	⊖	⊖	⊖				
Integrity	○	○	○	⊖				
Hardware	◒	⊖	⊖	⊖				
RELIABILITY VERDICT	-	-	✓	✓				

Mercury Villager

TROUBLE SPOTS	96	97	98	99	00	01	02	03
Engine	⊖	⊜	⊖	⊖	⊜	⊜	⊜	
Cooling	○	⊖	⊜	⊜	⊜	⊜	⊜	
Fuel	◒	◒	⊖	○	⊖	⊜	⊜	
Ignition	⊖	⊖	⊜	⊜	⊜	⊜	⊜	
Transmission	⊖	⊜	⊜	⊜	⊜	⊜	⊜	
Electrical	●	◒	○	◒	○	○	⊖	
A/C	◒	◒	○	⊖	⊖	⊖	⊜	
Suspension	○	○	○	○	⊖	⊖	⊖	
Brakes	◒	◒	◒	○	○	⊖	⊖	
Exhaust	⊖	⊖	⊜	⊜	⊜	⊜	⊜	
Power equip.	●	●	●	◒	○	◒	⊖	
Paint/trim/rust	○	○	⊖	⊖	⊖	⊖	⊜	
Integrity	◒	○	◒	◒	○	◒	◒	
Hardware	●	●	◒	○	○	◒	○	
RELIABILITY VERDICT	-	-	-	-	✓	-	-	

Mini Cooper

TROUBLE SPOTS	96	97	98	99	00	01	02	03
Engine							⊜	⊜
Cooling							○	⊖
Fuel							⊖	⊜
Ignition							⊖	⊜
Transmission							○	⊖
Electrical							○	⊖
A/C							⊜	⊜
Suspension							⊖	⊜
Brakes							⊜	⊜
Exhaust							⊜	⊜
Power equip.							⊖	⊖
Paint/trim/rust							⊜	⊜
Integrity							◒	⊖
Hardware							◒	⊖
RELIABILITY VERDICT							✗	✗

Mitsubishi Eclipse

TROUBLE SPOTS	96	97	98	99	00	01	02	03
Engine	Insufficient data	Insufficient data	Insufficient data	Insufficient data	⊜	⊜	⊜	⊜
Cooling					⊜	⊜	⊜	⊜
Fuel					⊜	⊖	⊜	⊖
Ignition					⊜	⊜	⊜	⊜
Transmission					⊜	⊜	⊖	⊜
Electrical					⊖	⊖	⊖	⊖
A/C					⊖	⊜	⊜	⊜
Suspension					⊖	⊜	⊜	⊜
Brakes					⊖	⊖	⊖	⊜
Exhaust					⊜	⊜	⊜	⊜
Power equip.					○	○	⊖	⊜
Paint/trim/rust					⊖	⊖	⊖	⊜
Integrity					○	○	⊖	○
Hardware					○	○	◒	⊖
RELIABILITY VERDICT					✓	✓	-	✗

Mitsubishi Galant

TROUBLE SPOTS	96	97	98	99	00	01	02	03
Engine	◒	Insufficient data	Insufficient data	⊖	⊜	⊜	⊖	Insufficient data
Cooling	○			⊖	⊜	⊜	⊜	
Fuel	⊜			⊖	⊜	⊜	⊖	
Ignition	⊖			⊖	⊜	⊜	⊜	
Transmission	●			⊖	⊜	⊜	⊜	
Electrical	◒			○	○	⊖	○	
A/C	●			⊖	⊜	⊜	⊖	
Suspension	○			○	⊖	⊖	⊖	
Brakes	○			●	○	○	○	
Exhaust	⊖			⊜	⊜	⊖	⊖	
Power equip.	◒			⊖	⊜	⊖	⊜	
Paint/trim/rust	◒			○	○	⊖	⊜	
Integrity	◒			◒	○	◒	⊖	
Hardware	○			○	⊖	⊖	⊖	
RELIABILITY VERDICT	✗			-	✓	-	✗	

Nissan 350Z

TROUBLE SPOTS	96	97	98	99	00	01	02	03
Engine								⊜
Cooling								⊜
Fuel								⊜
Ignition								⊜
Transmission								⊜
Electrical								⊜
A/C								⊜
Suspension								⊖
Brakes								⊜
Exhaust								⊜
Power equip.								⊖
Paint/trim/rust								⊜
Integrity								⊖
Hardware								⊜
RELIABILITY VERDICT								✓

Nissan Altima 4-cyl.

TROUBLE SPOTS	96	97	98	99	00	01	02	03
Engine	○	○	⊖	⊜	⊜	⊜	⊜	⊜
Cooling	⊖	⊖	⊖	⊜	⊜	⊜	⊜	⊜
Fuel	○	⊖	⊖	⊜	⊜	⊜	⊜	⊜
Ignition	⊖	⊖	⊜	⊜	⊜	⊜	⊖	⊜
Transmission	⊖	⊖	⊜	⊜	⊜	⊜	⊜	⊜
Electrical	◒	◒	⊖	⊖	○	⊜	⊖	⊜
A/C	⊖	⊖	⊖	⊖	⊖	⊜	⊜	⊜
Suspension	⊖	⊖	⊖	⊖	⊖	⊖	⊖	⊜
Brakes	○	○	○	○	⊖	⊖	⊜	⊜
Exhaust	○	⊖	⊜	⊜	⊜	⊜	⊜	⊜
Power equip.	⊖	○	⊖	⊖	○	○	⊖	⊜
Paint/trim/rust	○	◒	⊖	⊖	⊖	⊖	⊜	⊜
Integrity	◒	◒	○	⊖	○	○	○	⊜
Hardware	○	○	⊖	⊖	⊖	⊖	⊖	⊜
RELIABILITY VERDICT	✓	✓	✓	✓	✓	✓	-	✓

Nissan Maxima

TROUBLE SPOTS	96	97	98	99	00	01	02	03
Engine	⊜	⊜	⊜	⊜	⊜	⊜	⊜	⊜
Cooling	⊜	⊜	⊜	⊜	⊜	⊜	⊜	⊜
Fuel	○	○	⊖	⊖	⊖	⊖	⊜	⊜
Ignition	⊖	⊖	⊖	○	⊖	⊜	⊜	⊜
Transmission	⊜	⊜	⊜	⊜	⊜	⊜	⊜	⊜
Electrical	○	◒	○	○	⊖	⊜	⊖	⊜
A/C	⊖	⊖	⊜	⊜	⊜	⊜	⊜	⊜
Suspension	⊖	⊖	⊖	⊜	⊜	⊜	⊖	⊜
Brakes	○	○	○	◒	○	○	⊖	⊜
Exhaust	⊜	⊜	⊜	⊜	⊜	⊜	⊜	⊜
Power equip.	⊖	⊜	⊜	⊜	⊖	⊖	⊖	⊜
Paint/trim/rust	⊖	⊖	⊖	⊜	⊖	⊖	⊖	⊜
Integrity	⊖	⊖	⊖	⊖	⊜	⊜	○	⊖
Hardware	⊖	⊜	⊜	⊜	⊜	⊜	⊖	⊜
RELIABILITY VERDICT	✔	✔	✔	✔	✔	✔	✔	✔

Nissan Murano

TROUBLE SPOTS	96	97	98	99	00	01	02	03
Engine								⊜
Cooling								⊜
Fuel								⊜
Ignition								⊜
Transmission								⊜
Electrical								⊜
A/C								⊜
Suspension								⊜
Brakes								⊜
Exhaust								⊜
Power equip.								⊜
Paint/trim/rust								⊜
Integrity								⊖
Hardware								⊖
RELIABILITY VERDICT								✔

Nissan Pathfinder

TROUBLE SPOTS	96	97	98	99	00	01	02	03
Engine	⊖	⊖	⊜	⊜	⊜	⊜	⊜	⊜
Cooling	⊜	⊜	⊜	⊜	⊜	⊜	⊜	⊜
Fuel	○	○	⊖	⊜	⊜	⊖	⊜	⊜
Ignition	⊜	⊜	⊖	⊖	⊜	⊜	⊜	⊜
Transmission	⊖	⊜	⊖	⊜	⊜	⊜	⊜	⊜
Electrical	⊖	○	⊜	⊖	⊖	⊖	⊜	⊜
A/C	⊖	⊖	⊖	⊖	⊜	⊜	⊜	⊜
Suspension	○	◒	○	⊖	⊜	⊜	⊜	⊜
Brakes	○	○	○	○	⊜	⊜	⊜	⊜
Exhaust	●	●	⊖	⊖	⊜	⊜	⊜	⊜
Power equip.	○	⊜	⊜	⊖	⊖	○	⊜	⊜
Paint/trim/rust	⊖	⊖	⊜	⊖	⊜	⊜	⊜	⊜
Integrity	○	○	⊖	⊜	⊜	⊜	⊜	⊜
Hardware	⊖	⊖	⊖	⊖	⊜	⊖	⊜	⊜
RELIABILITY VERDICT	✔	✔	✔	✔	✔	✔	✔	✔

Nissan Pickup, Frontier

TROUBLE SPOTS	96	97	98	99	00	01	02	03
Engine	⊖	⊖	⊜	⊜	⊜	⊖	⊜	Insufficient data
Cooling	⊜	⊜	⊜	⊖	⊜	⊜	⊜	
Fuel	◒	○	⊖	⊜	⊜	⊖	⊖	
Ignition	⊖	⊖	⊖	⊜	⊜	⊜	⊜	
Transmission	⊖	⊜	⊜	⊜	⊜	⊜	⊜	
Electrical	○	○	○	⊖	○	⊖	⊖	
A/C	⊖	⊖	○	⊖	○	⊖	⊖	
Suspension	⊜	⊜	⊖	⊖	⊖	⊖	⊜	
Brakes	○	⊖	⊖	⊖	⊖	⊖	○	
Exhaust	⊖	⊜	⊖	⊖	⊜	⊜	⊜	
Power equip.	⊜	⊜	⊜	⊜	⊖	⊖	⊖	
Paint/trim/rust	⊖	⊖	⊖	⊖	⊖	⊜	⊜	
Integrity	○	○	○	⊖	○	○	○	
Hardware	⊖	⊖	⊖	⊜	⊖	○	⊖	
RELIABILITY VERDICT	✔	✔	✔	✔	✔	-	-	

Nissan Quest

TROUBLE SPOTS	96	97	98	99	00	01	02	03
Engine	⊖	⊜	⊖	⊖	⊜	⊜	⊜	
Cooling	○	⊖	⊜	⊜	⊜	⊜	⊜	
Fuel	◒	◒	⊖	○	⊖	⊜	⊜	
Ignition	⊖	⊖	⊜	⊜	⊜	⊜	⊜	
Transmission	⊖	⊜	⊜	⊜	⊜	⊜	⊜	
Electrical	●	◒	○	◒	○	○	⊖	
A/C	◒	◒	○	⊖	⊖	⊖	⊜	
Suspension	○	○	○	○	⊜	⊖	⊖	
Brakes	◒	◒	◒	○	○	⊖	⊖	
Exhaust	⊖	⊖	⊜	⊜	⊜	⊜	⊜	
Power equip.	●	●	●	◒	○	◒	⊖	
Paint/trim/rust	○	○	⊖	⊖	⊖	⊖	⊜	
Integrity	◒	○	◒	◒	○	◒	◒	
Hardware	●	●	◒	○	○	◒	○	
RELIABILITY VERDICT	-	-	-	-	✔	-	-	

Nissan Sentra

TROUBLE SPOTS	96	97	98	99	00	01	02	03
Engine	○	⊖	⊖	⊖	⊖	⊜	⊖	⊜
Cooling	⊜	⊜	⊖	⊜	⊜	⊜	⊜	⊜
Fuel	⊖	○	○	⊜	○	⊖	⊜	⊜
Ignition	⊖	⊖	⊜	⊜	⊖	⊜	⊜	⊜
Transmission	⊖	⊜	⊜	⊖	⊜	⊜	⊜	⊜
Electrical	●	●	○	○	◒	○	⊖	⊖
A/C	○	○	⊖	⊜	⊖	⊜	⊖	⊜
Suspension	⊖	⊖	○	⊖	⊖	⊖	⊜	⊖
Brakes	◒	◒	◒	○	○	⊖	⊜	⊜
Exhaust	⊖	⊖	⊖	⊜	⊜	⊜	⊜	⊜
Power equip.	○	⊖	○	⊖	⊖	⊖	⊖	⊜
Paint/trim/rust	○	○	○	○	⊖	⊖	⊖	⊖
Integrity	◒	○	○	◒	◒	○	⊖	○
Hardware	⊖	○	○	⊖	⊖	⊖	⊖	⊖
RELIABILITY VERDICT	✔	✔	✔	✔	-	✔	-	✘

Nissan Xterra

TROUBLE SPOTS	96	97	98	99	00	01	02	03
Engine					⊖	⊜	⊖	Insufficient data
Cooling					⊖	⊜	⊜	
Fuel					⊜	⊖	⊖	
Ignition					⊜	⊜	⊜	
Transmission					⊜	⊜	⊜	
Electrical					○	⊖	⊖	
A/C					○	⊜	⊜	
Suspension					⊖	⊜	⊖	
Brakes					⊖	⊜	⊖	
Exhaust					⊖	⊜	⊜	
Power equip.					⊖	○	⊖	
Paint/trim/rust					○	⊖	⊖	
Integrity					○	○	⊖	
Hardware					⊖	⊖	⊖	
RELIABILITY VERDICT					✔	✔	-	

Oldsmobile 88

TROUBLE SPOTS	96	97	98	99	00	01	02	03
Engine	○	○	◒	⊖				
Cooling	◒	●	○	○				
Fuel	○	◒	◒	○				
Ignition	⊖	○	⊖	○				
Transmission	○	○	○	○				
Electrical	○	●	◒	◒				
A/C	○	○	⊖	⊜				
Suspension	⊖	○	⊖	⊜				
Brakes	◒	◒	○	◒				
Exhaust	⊜	⊜	⊜	⊜				
Power equip.	○	○	○	○				
Paint/trim/rust	⊖	⊖	⊖	⊖				
Integrity	○	◒	◒	○				
Hardware	○	○	⊖	⊖				
RELIABILITY VERDICT	✔	✘	✘	-				

Oldsmobile Alero

Trouble spots	96	97	98	99	00	01	02	03 (Insufficient data)
Engine				○	⊖	⊖	⊜	
Cooling				○	⊖	⊖	⊜	
Fuel				○	⊖	○	⊖	
Ignition				⊖	⊜	⊖	⊜	
Transmission				⊜	⊜	⊜	⊜	
Electrical				●	●	◒	○	
A/C				○	⊖	⊖	⊜	
Suspension				○	○	⊖	⊜	
Brakes				●	●	●	○	
Exhaust				⊜	⊜	⊜	⊜	
Power equip.				◒	◒	○	⊖	
Paint/trim/rust				○	⊖	⊖	⊜	
Integrity				●	◒	○	⊖	
Hardware				◒	○	⊖	⊖	
RELIABILITY VERDICT				✗	✗	✗	-	

Oldsmobile Aurora

Trouble spots	96	97	98	99 (Insufficient data)	00	01	02	03 (Insufficient data)
Engine	○	○	⊖			⊖	⊖	
Cooling	●	◒	○			⊖	⊜	
Fuel	●	◒	⊖			⊖	⊜	
Ignition	⊖	○	⊖			⊖	⊜	
Transmission	○	⊜	⊖			⊖	⊜	
Electrical	◒	●	●			○	⊖	
A/C	●	○	◒			⊖	⊖	
Suspension	○	○	⊖			●	○	
Brakes	●	◒	◒			○	⊜	
Exhaust	⊜	⊜	⊜			⊜	⊜	
Power equip.	◒	◒	○			○	⊖	
Paint/trim/rust	○	○	○			⊖	⊜	
Integrity	◒	○	○			○	○	
Hardware	○	○	⊖			⊖	⊖	
RELIABILITY VERDICT	✗	-	-			✗	-	

Oldsmobile Bravada

Trouble spots	96 (Insufficient data)	97 (Insufficient data)	98	99	00	01 (Insufficient data)	02	03 (Insufficient data)
Engine			○	○	⊜		⊜	
Cooling			◒	○	⊜		⊜	
Fuel			○	⊖	⊖		⊖	
Ignition			○	⊖	⊖		⊖	
Transmission			●	◒	⊜		⊖	
Electrical			●	◒	◒		◒	
A/C			○	○	⊖		⊖	
Suspension			○	◒	○		○	
Brakes			◒	⊖	○		⊖	
Exhaust			⊖	⊜	○		⊜	
Power equip.			○	○	○		●	
Paint/trim/rust			○	◒	⊜		⊜	
Integrity			◒	◒	◒		◒	
Hardware			◒	○	○		○	
RELIABILITY VERDICT			✗	✗	-		✗	

Oldsmobile Ciera, Cutlass

Trouble spots	96	97	98	99	00	01	02	03
Engine	◒	◒	◒	◒				
Cooling	●	●	◒	◒				
Fuel	◒	◒	○	○				
Ignition	⊖	○	⊜	⊜				
Transmission	○	⊖	⊖	⊖				
Electrical	●	●	●	●				
A/C	◒	◒	●	◒				
Suspension	⊖	○	○	○				
Brakes	●	●	●	●				
Exhaust	⊖	⊜	⊜	⊜				
Power equip.	◒	○	○	○				
Paint/trim/rust	◒	○	⊖	○				
Integrity	○	◒	◒	○				
Hardware	◒	○	○	○				
RELIABILITY VERDICT	✗	✗	✗	✗				

Oldsmobile Cutlass Supreme, Intrigue

Trouble spots	96	97	98	99	00	01	02	03
Engine	○	◒	○	⊜	⊖	⊜	⊜	
Cooling	◒	○	○	⊜	⊖	⊜	⊜	
Fuel	◒	⊜	⊜	○	○	⊖	⊜	
Ignition	⊖	⊜	⊜	○	⊖	⊜	⊜	
Transmission	⊜	⊜	⊖	⊖	⊖	○	⊜	
Electrical	●	●	◒	◒	◒	◒	○	
A/C	○	○	○	⊜	⊜	⊜	⊜	
Suspension	○	○	○	○	◒	○	⊖	
Brakes	◒	●	◒	○	○	⊜	⊜	
Exhaust	⊜	⊜	⊜	⊜	⊜	⊜	⊜	
Power equip.	◒	⊖	◒	◒	○	○	⊜	
Paint/trim/rust	◒	○	⊖	⊜	⊜	⊖	⊜	
Integrity	●	○	○	◒	○	○	⊜	
Hardware	○	○	⊖	○	⊖	⊜	⊖	
RELIABILITY VERDICT	-	-	-	-	-	-	✓	

Oldsmobile Silhouette (ext.)

Trouble spots	96	97	98	99	00	01	02	03
Engine		◒	◒	◒	○	⊜	⊜	⊜
Cooling		◒	○	◒	○	⊖	⊜	⊜
Fuel		○	○	○	○	⊖	⊖	⊜
Ignition		⊜	⊜	⊜	⊜	⊜	⊜	⊜
Transmission		○	⊖	○	○	⊖	⊜	⊜
Electrical		●	●	◒	●	○	⊜	⊖
A/C		○	⊖	⊖	⊖	⊖	⊜	⊜
Suspension		●	○	⊖	⊖	⊖	⊜	⊜
Brakes		●	◒	◒	○	⊖	⊖	⊜
Exhaust		⊜	⊜	⊜	⊜	⊜	⊜	⊜
Power equip.		●	●	●	●	◒	○	⊖
Paint/trim/rust		○	⊖	⊖	⊖	⊖	⊖	⊜
Integrity		●	◒	◒	◒	◒	○	⊜
Hardware		●	◒	◒	●	○	⊖	⊖
RELIABILITY VERDICT		✗	✗	✗	✗	-	-	-

Plymouth Breeze

Trouble spots	96	97	98	99	00	01	02	03
Engine	●	●	●	◒	⊖			
Cooling	○	◒	⊖	⊖	⊜			
Fuel	◒	◒	⊖	⊖	⊖			
Ignition	⊖	⊖	⊖	⊜	⊜			
Transmission	●	○	⊖	○	○			
Electrical	◒	○	○	○	○			
A/C	○	○	⊖	⊖	⊖			
Suspension	◒	◒	○	⊖	⊖			
Brakes	●	●	●	◒	◒			
Exhaust	⊖	⊖	⊜	⊜	⊜			
Power equip.	○	⊖	○	○	⊖			
Paint/trim/rust	◒	⊖	⊖	○	⊖			
Integrity	○	⊖	○	○	○			
Hardware	⊖	⊖	⊖	⊖	⊖			
RELIABILITY VERDICT	✗	✗	✗	✗	-			

Plymouth Grand Voyager V6

Trouble spots	96	97	98	99	00	01	02	03
Engine	◒	○	◒	⊖	⊖			
Cooling	◒	◒	⊖	⊖	⊖			
Fuel	◒	◒	⊖	⊖	⊖			
Ignition	⊖	⊖	⊖	⊖	⊜			
Transmission	●	◒	○	◒	●			
Electrical	●	●	◒	○	○			
A/C	●	◒	○	○	⊖			
Suspension	○	○	○	⊖	⊖			
Brakes	●	◒	◒	◒	◒			
Exhaust	⊜	⊜	⊜	⊜	⊜			
Power equip.	●	◒	○	○	○			
Paint/trim/rust	○	⊖	⊖	⊖	⊖			
Integrity	◒	◒	○	○	○			
Hardware	◒	○	⊖	⊖	⊖			
RELIABILITY VERDICT	✗	✗	-	✗	✗			

Pontiac Aztek	96	97	98	99	00	01	02	03
Engine						⊖	⊜	Insufficient data
Cooling						⊖	⊜	
Fuel						⊖	⊖	
Ignition						⊖	⊜	
Transmission						⊖	⊜	
Electrical						◒	⊖	
A/C						◒	⊜	
Suspension						⊖	⊜	
Brakes						⊖	⊖	
Exhaust						⊜	⊜	
Power equip.						○	◒	
Paint/trim/rust						⊖	⊜	
Integrity						○	○	
Hardware						○	○	
RELIABILITY VERDICT						✗	-	

Pontiac Bonneville	96	97	98	99	00	01	02	03
Engine	◒	●	●	○	⊖	⊖	⊜	⊜
Cooling	●	●	◒	⊖	⊖	○	⊖	⊜
Fuel	◒	◒	◒	○	⊖	⊖	⊜	⊜
Ignition	⊖	⊖	⊖	⊖	⊖	⊜	⊜	⊜
Transmission	○	◒	⊖	⊖	⊖	⊖	⊜	⊜
Electrical	◒	●	◒	◒	◒	○	○	⊜
A/C	◒	○	⊖	⊜	⊖	⊖	⊜	⊜
Suspension	○	○	⊖	⊖	●	◒	○	⊜
Brakes	◒	◒	◒	○	○	⊖	⊜	⊖
Exhaust	⊜	⊜	⊜	⊜	⊜	⊜	⊜	⊜
Power equip.	○	○	○	○	●	○	○	⊖
Paint/trim/rust	○	⊖	⊖	○	⊖	⊖	⊖	⊜
Integrity	◒	○	◒	◒	●	◒	◒	◒
Hardware	○	⊖	⊖	⊖	◒	○	⊖	⊖
RELIABILITY VERDICT	-	✗	✗	-	✗	✗	✗	✗

Pontiac Firebird	96	97	98	99	00	01	02	03
Engine	○	◒	○	○	⊖	○	⊜	
Cooling	●	◒	⊖	⊜	⊖	⊜	⊜	
Fuel	○	◒	⊖	⊖	⊖	⊖	⊜	
Ignition	○	○	⊜	○	⊜	⊖	⊜	
Transmission	○	○	⊖	○	⊜	⊖	⊜	
Electrical	●	●	●	●	◒	○	⊜	
A/C	○	⊖	⊖	⊖	⊖	⊖	⊜	
Suspension	○	○	⊜	⊖	⊜	⊖	⊖	
Brakes	○	○	◒	◒	●	◒	○	
Exhaust	⊖	⊖	⊜	⊖	○	○	⊜	
Power equip.	◒	●	○	◒	◒	○	⊖	
Paint/trim/rust	○	○	⊜	⊖	⊖	⊜	⊖	
Integrity	◒	●	○	◒	●	○	◒	
Hardware	○	◒	⊖	○	○	⊖	⊖	
RELIABILITY VERDICT	-	✗	-	✗	✗	✗	-	

Pontiac Grand Am	96	97	98	99	00	01	02	03
Engine	○	◒	⊖	◒	⊖	⊜	⊜	⊜
Cooling	●	●	○	◒	○	⊖	⊜	⊜
Fuel	◒	◒	○	○	◒	⊖	⊜	⊜
Ignition	○	○	⊖	⊖	⊜	⊖	⊜	⊜
Transmission	○	○	⊖	⊖	⊜	⊖	⊜	⊜
Electrical	●	●	●	●	●	◒	⊖	⊜
A/C	●	○	⊖	⊖	⊖	⊖	⊜	⊜
Suspension	◒	◒	⊖	○	⊖	⊖	⊜	⊜
Brakes	●	●	●	●	●	●	⊖	⊜
Exhaust	○	⊖	⊖	⊜	⊜	⊜	⊜	⊜
Power equip.	●	●	○	◒	●	○	⊖	⊜
Paint/trim/rust	◒	○	○	○	⊖	⊖	⊖	⊜
Integrity	◒	●	○	◒	◒	◒	○	⊜
Hardware	●	◒	○	○	◒	○	⊖	⊜
RELIABILITY VERDICT	✗	✗	-	✗	✗	✗	-	✓

Pontiac Grand Prix	96	97	98	99	00	01	02	03
Engine	○	◒	○	⊖	⊖	⊜	⊜	⊜
Cooling	◒	◒	○	⊖	⊖	⊖	⊜	⊜
Fuel	○	○	⊖	⊖	⊖	⊖	⊜	⊜
Ignition	○	⊖	⊜	⊜	⊜	⊜	⊜	⊜
Transmission	◒	⊖	○	○	⊖	⊖	⊜	⊜
Electrical	●	●	●	◒	○	○	⊖	⊜
A/C	○	◒	○	○	○	⊖	⊜	⊜
Suspension	○	●	◒	⊖	⊖	⊖	⊜	⊜
Brakes	●	○	○	○	○	⊖	⊜	⊜
Exhaust	⊖	⊜	⊜	⊜	⊜	⊜	⊜	⊜
Power equip.	◒	●	●	◒	○	○	⊖	⊜
Paint/trim/rust	◒	○	○	⊖	⊖	⊖	⊖	⊖
Integrity	◒	◒	◒	◒	○	○	⊖	⊖
Hardware	◒	○	○	⊖	⊖	⊖	⊖	⊖
RELIABILITY VERDICT	-	✗	✗	-	-	-	✓	-

Pontiac Sunfire Coupe & Conv.	96	97	98	99	00	01	02	03
Engine	◒	○	○	○	⊜	⊖	⊜	Insufficient data
Cooling	●	◒	○	⊖	⊖	⊖	⊜	
Fuel	◒	◒	⊖	⊖	○	○	⊜	
Ignition	○	○	○	⊖	⊜	⊜	⊜	
Transmission	○	⊖	⊜	⊜	⊜	⊖	⊜	
Electrical	●	●	◒	◒	◒	⊖	⊖	
A/C	●	◒	⊖	⊜	⊖	⊖	⊜	
Suspension	○	◒	⊖	○	⊖	⊖	⊖	
Brakes	◒	○	◒	●	●	○	⊖	
Exhaust	⊖	⊜	⊖	⊜	⊜	⊜	⊜	
Power equip.	○	○	○	○	○	○	⊖	
Paint/trim/rust	○	⊖	○	○	○	⊜	⊜	
Integrity	●	●	◒	◒	◒	○	○	
Hardware	◒	○	○	◒	○	⊖	⊖	
RELIABILITY VERDICT	✗	-	-	-	-	-	-	

Pontiac Trans Sport, Montana (ext.)	96	97	98	99	00	01	02	03
Engine		◒	◒	◒	○	⊜	⊜	⊜
Cooling		◒	○	◒	○	⊖	⊜	⊜
Fuel		○	○	○	○	⊖	⊖	⊜
Ignition		⊜	⊜	⊜	⊜	⊜	⊜	⊜
Transmission		○	⊖	○	○	⊖	⊜	⊜
Electrical		●	●	◒	●	○	⊖	⊖
A/C		○	⊖	⊖	⊖	⊖	⊜	⊜
Suspension		●	○	⊖	⊖	⊖	⊜	⊜
Brakes		●	◒	◒	○	⊖	⊖	⊜
Exhaust		⊜	⊜	⊜	⊜	⊜	⊜	⊜
Power equip.		●	●	●	●	◒	○	⊖
Paint/trim/rust		○	⊖	⊖	⊖	⊖	⊖	⊜
Integrity		●	◒	◒	◒	◒	○	⊜
Hardware		●	◒	◒	●	○	⊜	⊖
RELIABILITY VERDICT		✗	✗	✗	✗	-	-	-

Pontiac Vibe	96	97	98	99	00	01	02	03
Engine								⊜
Cooling								⊜
Fuel								⊜
Ignition								⊜
Transmission								⊜
Electrical								⊜
A/C								⊜
Suspension								⊜
Brakes								⊜
Exhaust								⊜
Power equip.								⊜
Paint/trim/rust								⊜
Integrity								⊖
Hardware								⊜
RELIABILITY VERDICT								✓

Porsche Boxster

Trouble spots	96	97	98	99	00	01	02	03
Engine	Insufficient data	Insufficient data		⊖	○	○	Insufficient data	Insufficient data
Cooling				◒	⊜	⊜		
Fuel				○	⊖	⊜		
Ignition				⊜	⊖	⊜		
Transmission				⊜	⊜	⊜		
Electrical				○	⊜	○		
A/C				⊖	◒	⊜		
Suspension				⊜	⊜	⊜		
Brakes				⊖	⊖	⊜		
Exhaust				⊜	⊜	⊜		
Power equip.				⊖	⊖	⊖		
Paint/trim/rust				⊜	⊜	⊜		
Integrity				⊖	○	○		
Hardware				◒	⊜	⊜		
RELIABILITY VERDICT				–	✔	–		

Saab 9-5

Trouble spots	96	97	98	99	00	01	02	03
Engine				○	○	⊖	⊖	⊜
Cooling				⊖	⊖	⊖	⊜	⊜
Fuel				○	⊖	⊖	⊜	⊜
Ignition				○	⊖	⊖	⊜	⊜
Transmission				⊜	⊜	⊜	⊜	⊜
Electrical				●	●	◒	○	⊜
A/C				○	⊖	⊖	⊖	⊜
Suspension				⊜	⊖	⊖	⊜	⊜
Brakes				⊖	⊖	⊖	⊖	⊖
Exhaust				⊖	⊜	⊜	⊜	⊜
Power equip.				○	○	⊖	⊖	⊜
Paint/trim/rust				⊖	⊜	⊜	⊖	⊜
Integrity				⊖	⊖	○	⊖	⊜
Hardware				⊖	○	⊖	⊖	⊜
RELIABILITY VERDICT				–	–	–	–	✔

Saab 900, 9-3

Trouble spots	96	97	98	99	00	01	02	03
Engine	◒	●	○	⊖	⊖	⊖	⊜	⊜
Cooling	◒	○	⊖	⊜	⊜	⊜	⊖	⊜
Fuel	◒	⊖	○	⊖	⊖	○	⊜	⊜
Ignition	○	○	⊖	⊜	⊜	⊖	⊜	⊜
Transmission	○	○	⊜	⊜	⊖	⊜	⊜	⊜
Electrical	●	●	●	◒	○	○	⊖	⊖
A/C	◒	○	○	○	⊖	⊜	⊜	⊜
Suspension	○	⊖	⊖	○	⊜	⊜	⊖	⊜
Brakes	○	○	○	⊖	○	⊖	⊖	⊖
Exhaust	◒	○	○	⊖	⊜	⊜	⊜	⊜
Power equip.	◒	○	◒	◒	○	○	⊖	⊖
Paint/trim/rust	⊖	⊖	⊖	⊖	○	⊖	⊖	⊜
Integrity	○	○	○	◒	◒	⊖	○	⊜
Hardware	○	⊖	○	◒	○	○	⊖	⊖
RELIABILITY VERDICT	–	–	–	–	–	–	–	–

Saturn L-Series 4-cyl.

Trouble spots	96	97	98	99	00	01	02	03
Engine					⊖	⊜	⊜	⊜
Cooling					⊖	⊜	⊜	⊜
Fuel					⊖	⊖	⊖	⊜
Ignition					⊖	⊖	⊖	⊜
Transmission					⊜	⊖	⊜	⊜
Electrical					◒	○	○	⊜
A/C					⊖	⊖	⊜	⊜
Suspension					○	○	⊖	⊜
Brakes					○	⊖	⊖	⊖
Exhaust					⊜	⊜	⊜	⊜
Power equip.					○	○	⊖	⊖
Paint/trim/rust					⊖	⊜	⊜	⊜
Integrity					○	○	○	⊜
Hardware					○	○	⊖	⊜
RELIABILITY VERDICT					–	–	–	✔

Saturn SL, Ion

Trouble spots	96	97	98	99	00	01	02	03
Engine	◒	○	○	⊖	⊖	⊖	⊜	⊜
Cooling	○	○	○	⊖	⊖	⊖	⊜	⊜
Fuel	○	◒	○	○	⊜	⊜	⊜	⊜
Ignition	○	○	⊖	⊖	⊖	⊜	⊜	⊜
Transmission	⊖	⊖	⊖	⊖	⊖	⊖	⊜	⊜
Electrical	●	●	○	○	○	⊖	⊖	⊖
A/C	⊖	⊖	⊖	⊖	⊜	⊜	⊜	⊜
Suspension	⊖	⊖	⊜	⊜	⊖	⊜	⊜	⊜
Brakes	○	○	○	⊖	○	⊖	⊖	⊜
Exhaust	⊖	⊖	○	○	⊖	⊜	⊜	⊜
Power equip.	○	○	○	○	○	⊖	⊜	⊜
Paint/trim/rust	○	⊖	⊖	⊖	⊖	⊜	⊜	⊜
Integrity	◒	◒	◒	○	○	⊜	○	⊖
Hardware	○	○	○	⊖	○	⊖	⊖	⊜
RELIABILITY VERDICT	–	–	–	✔	–	✔	✔	✔

Saturn VUE

Trouble spots	96	97	98	99	00	01	02	03
Engine							⊜	⊜
Cooling							⊖	⊜
Fuel							○	⊖
Ignition							⊜	⊜
Transmission							⊖	⊜
Electrical							○	⊖
A/C							⊖	⊜
Suspension							○	⊖
Brakes							⊖	⊜
Exhaust							⊜	⊜
Power equip.							⊖	⊜
Paint/trim/rust							⊖	⊜
Integrity							◒	⊖
Hardware							○	⊜
RELIABILITY VERDICT							✘	✘

Subaru Baja

Trouble spots	96	97	98	99	00	01	02	03
Engine								⊜
Cooling								⊜
Fuel								⊜
Ignition								⊜
Transmission								⊜
Electrical								⊖
A/C								⊖
Suspension								⊜
Brakes								⊖
Exhaust								⊜
Power equip.								⊖
Paint/trim/rust								⊜
Integrity								○
Hardware								⊜
RELIABILITY VERDICT								✘

Subaru Forester

Trouble spots	96	97	98	99	00	01	02	03
Engine			○	○	⊖	⊜	⊜	⊜
Cooling			⊜	⊜	⊜	⊜	⊜	⊜
Fuel			⊖	○	⊖	⊖	⊖	⊜
Ignition			⊜	⊜	⊜	⊜	⊜	⊜
Transmission			⊖	⊖	⊜	⊜	⊖	⊜
Electrical			⊖	⊖	⊖	⊖	⊜	⊜
A/C			⊜	⊖	⊜	⊜	⊜	⊜
Suspension			⊜	⊜	⊜	⊜	⊜	⊜
Brakes			○	○	⊖	⊜	⊖	⊜
Exhaust			⊜	⊜	⊖	⊜	⊜	⊜
Power equip.			⊜	⊖	⊜	⊜	⊜	⊜
Paint/trim/rust			⊖	⊜	⊖	⊖	⊜	⊜
Integrity			⊖	⊖	⊖	⊖	⊖	⊜
Hardware			⊖	⊜	⊖	⊖	⊖	⊜
RELIABILITY VERDICT			✔	–	✔	✔	–	✔

Subaru Impreza

TROUBLE SPOTS	96	97	98	99	00	01	02	03
Engine	○	○	○	⊜	⊖	⊜	⊜	⊜
Cooling	⊖	⊖	⊜	⊜	⊜	⊜	⊜	⊜
Fuel	⊖	⊜	⊜	○	⊖	○	⊖	⊜
Ignition	⊖	⊜	⊜	⊜	⊜	⊜	⊜	⊖
Transmission	⊜	⊜	⊜	⊖	⊖	⊜	⊖	⊖
Electrical	○	○	○	⊜	⊖	⊖	⊜	⊜
A/C	⊖	○	⊖	⊜	⊖	⊜	⊜	⊜
Suspension	○	⊖	⊜	⊖	⊜	⊜	⊜	⊜
Brakes	○	⊖	⊖	○	⊖	○	⊖	⊖
Exhaust	⊜	⊖	⊜	⊜	⊜	⊖	⊜	⊜
Power equip.	⊖	⊖	⊜	⊖	⊖	⊖	⊖	⊜
Paint/trim/rust	⊖	⊖	⊖	⊖	⊖	⊖	⊜	⊜
Integrity	○	⊖	○	○	○	○	⊖	⊜
Hardware	⊜	⊜	⊖	⊜	⊜	⊜	⊖	⊜
RELIABILITY VERDICT	✔	✔	✔	✔	-	✔	✔	-

Subaru Impreza WRX

TROUBLE SPOTS	96	97	98	99	00	01	02	03
Engine							⊜	⊜
Cooling							⊜	⊜
Fuel							⊖	⊜
Ignition							⊜	⊜
Transmission							⊜	⊜
Electrical							⊜	⊜
A/C							⊜	⊜
Suspension							⊜	⊜
Brakes							⊜	⊜
Exhaust							⊜	⊜
Power equip.							⊜	⊜
Paint/trim/rust							⊖	⊖
Integrity							⊖	⊖
Hardware							⊜	⊜
RELIABILITY VERDICT							-	-

Subaru Legacy/Outback 4-cyl.

TROUBLE SPOTS	96	97	98	99	00	01	02	03
Engine	●	◒	◒	○	⊖	⊜	⊜	⊜
Cooling	⊖	⊖	⊜	⊜	⊖	⊜	⊜	⊜
Fuel	○	⊜	⊜	⊖	⊖	⊖	⊖	⊜
Ignition	⊖	⊜	⊜	⊜	⊜	⊜	⊜	⊜
Transmission	⊖	⊜	⊖	⊖	⊜	⊜	⊖	⊖
Electrical	◒	◒	○	⊜	⊖	⊜	⊜	⊜
A/C	⊖	⊖	⊖	⊜	⊜	⊜	⊜	⊜
Suspension	⊖	⊖	⊜	⊜	⊜	⊜	⊜	⊜
Brakes	○	○	○	○	⊖	○	○	⊜
Exhaust	⊖	⊜	⊜	⊜	⊜	⊜	⊜	⊜
Power equip.	○	⊖	⊖	⊖	⊖	⊜	⊜	⊜
Paint/trim/rust	○	⊜	⊖	⊖	⊖	⊜	⊜	⊜
Integrity	⊖	⊖	⊖	⊖	○	○	○	⊖
Hardware	○	⊖	⊖	⊖	⊖	⊖	⊜	⊖
RELIABILITY VERDICT	✔	✔	✔	✔	✔	✔	-	-

Suzuki Sidekick, Vitara/XL-7

TROUBLE SPOTS	96	97	98	99	00	01	02	03
Engine	⊖	○	Insufficient data	⊜	○	⊜	⊜	Insufficient data
Cooling	⊖	⊜		⊜	⊜	⊜	⊜	
Fuel	●	◒		⊖	⊖	⊜	⊜	
Ignition	⊖	⊖		⊖	⊜	⊜	⊜	
Transmission	⊜	⊖		○	⊜	⊖	⊜	
Electrical	◒	○		○	⊖	⊖	⊜	
A/C	●	◒		◒	○	⊖	⊖	
Suspension	⊖	⊖		⊖	⊖	⊖	⊖	
Brakes	○	○		○	○	⊖	⊖	
Exhaust	○	⊜		⊜	⊖	⊜	⊜	
Power equip.	⊜	⊜		○	⊖	⊖	⊜	
Paint/trim/rust	⊖	⊖		○	⊖	⊖	⊖	
Integrity	◒	◒		◒	◒	○	⊖	
Hardware	○	◒		⊖	○	⊖	⊜	
RELIABILITY VERDICT	✔	✔		✘	-	-	-	

Toyota 4Runner V6

TROUBLE SPOTS	96	97	98	99	00	01	02	03
Engine	○	⊜	⊜	⊜	⊜	⊜	⊜	⊜
Cooling	⊜	⊜	⊜	⊜	⊜	⊜	⊜	⊜
Fuel	⊖	⊜	⊜	⊖	⊖	⊜	⊜	⊖
Ignition	⊜	⊜	⊜	⊜	⊜	⊜	⊜	⊜
Transmission	⊜	⊜	⊜	⊜	⊜	⊜	⊜	⊜
Electrical	⊖	○	⊖	⊖	⊖	⊜	⊜	⊜
A/C	⊜	⊜	⊜	⊜	⊜	⊜	⊜	⊜
Suspension	○	⊖	⊜	⊜	⊜	⊜	⊜	⊜
Brakes	○	○	○	⊖	⊖	⊖	⊜	⊜
Exhaust	⊜	⊜	⊜	⊜	⊜	⊜	⊜	⊜
Power equip.	⊖	○	○	⊖	⊜	⊜	⊜	⊜
Paint/trim/rust	⊖	⊖	⊜	⊜	⊖	⊜	⊜	⊖
Integrity	⊜	⊖	⊖	⊖	⊖	⊖	○	⊖
Hardware	⊖	⊖	⊜	⊜	⊖	⊜	⊜	⊜
RELIABILITY VERDICT	✔	✔	✔	✔	✔	✔	✔	✘

Toyota 4Runner V8

TROUBLE SPOTS	96	97	98	99	00	01	02	03
Engine								⊜
Cooling								⊜
Fuel								⊜
Ignition								⊜
Transmission								⊜
Electrical								⊜
A/C								⊜
Suspension								⊜
Brakes								⊜
Exhaust								⊜
Power equip.								⊜
Paint/trim/rust								⊜
Integrity								⊖
Hardware								⊜
RELIABILITY VERDICT								✔

Toyota Avalon

TROUBLE SPOTS	96	97	98	99	00	01	02	03
Engine	⊖	⊖	⊜	⊜	⊜	⊜	⊜	⊜
Cooling	⊜	⊜	⊜	⊜	⊜	⊜	⊜	⊜
Fuel	⊜	⊖	⊖	⊖	⊖	⊜	⊜	⊜
Ignition	⊜	⊜	⊜	⊜	⊜	⊜	⊜	⊜
Transmission	⊜	⊜	⊜	⊜	⊜	⊜	⊜	⊜
Electrical	○	⊖	○	⊖	⊖	⊖	⊜	⊜
A/C	⊖	⊖	○	⊜	⊜	⊜	⊜	⊜
Suspension	◒	●	◒	◒	⊖	⊜	⊜	⊜
Brakes	○	⊖	⊖	⊖	⊖	⊜	⊜	⊜
Exhaust	⊜	⊜	⊜	⊜	⊜	⊜	⊜	⊜
Power equip.	○	⊖	⊖	⊖	⊜	⊜	⊜	⊜
Paint/trim/rust	⊖	⊖	⊖	⊖	⊜	⊜	⊜	⊜
Integrity	○	○	○	○	⊖	⊖	⊖	⊜
Hardware	⊖	⊖	⊖	⊖	⊜	⊜	⊖	⊜
RELIABILITY VERDICT	✔	✔	✔	✔	✔	✔	✔	✔

Toyota Camry

TROUBLE SPOTS	96	97	98	99	00	01	02	03
Engine	○	○	⊖	⊖	⊜	⊜	⊜	⊜
Cooling	⊖	⊜	⊜	⊖	⊜	⊜	⊜	⊜
Fuel	⊖	⊖	⊖	⊖	⊜	⊖	⊜	⊜
Ignition	⊜	⊜	⊜	⊜	⊜	⊜	⊜	⊜
Transmission	⊜	⊜	⊜	⊜	⊜	⊜	⊜	⊜
Electrical	○	○	⊖	⊖	⊜	⊜	⊜	⊜
A/C	⊖	⊜	⊜	⊜	⊜	⊜	⊜	⊜
Suspension	○	◒	○	○	⊜	⊜	⊖	⊜
Brakes	○	○	○	○	⊖	⊖	⊖	⊜
Exhaust	⊖	⊜	⊜	⊜	⊜	⊜	⊜	⊜
Power equip.	○	⊜	⊜	⊖	⊜	⊜	⊜	⊜
Paint/trim/rust	⊖	⊖	⊖	⊖	⊜	⊜	⊖	⊜
Integrity	⊖	⊖	⊖	⊖	⊖	⊖	○	⊖
Hardware	⊖	⊖	⊖	⊖	⊖	⊖	⊖	⊜
RELIABILITY VERDICT	✔	✔	✔	✔	✔	✔	✔	✔

TROUBLE SPOTS	Toyota Camry Solara 96	97	98	99	00	01	02	03
Engine				⊜	⊜	⊜	⊜	⊜
Cooling				⊜	⊜	⊜	⊜	⊜
Fuel				⊜	⊜	⊜	⊜	⊜
Ignition				⊜	⊜	⊜	⊜	⊜
Transmission				⊜	⊜	⊜	⊜	⊜
Electrical				⊜	⊜	⊜	⊜	⊜
A/C				⊜	⊜	⊜	⊜	⊜
Suspension				◒	⊜	⊜	⊜	⊜
Brakes				⊜	⊜	⊜	⊜	⊜
Exhaust				⊜	⊜	⊜	⊜	⊜
Power equip.				⊜	⊜	⊜	⊜	⊜
Paint/trim/rust				⊜	⊜	⊜	⊜	⊜
Integrity				○	○	○	⊜	⊜
Hardware				⊜	⊜	⊜	⊜	⊜
RELIABILITY VERDICT				✔	✔	✔	✔	✔

TROUBLE SPOTS	Toyota Celica 96	97	98	99	00	01	02	03
Engine	⊜	○	Insufficient data	Insufficient data	○	⊜	⊜	Insufficient data
Cooling	⊜	⊜			⊜	⊜	⊜	
Fuel	⊜	⊜			⊜	⊜	○	
Ignition	⊜	⊜			⊜	⊜	⊜	
Transmission	⊜	⊜			⊜	⊜	⊜	
Electrical	⊜	⊜			⊜	⊜	⊜	
A/C	⊜	⊜			⊜	⊜	⊜	
Suspension	⊜	⊜			⊜	⊜	⊜	
Brakes	⊜	⊜			⊜	⊜	⊜	
Exhaust	⊜	⊜			⊜	⊜	⊜	
Power equip.	○	○			⊜	⊜	⊜	
Paint/trim/rust	⊜	⊜			⊜	⊜	⊜	
Integrity	○	○			○	○	○	
Hardware	⊜	⊜			⊜	⊜	⊜	
RELIABILITY VERDICT	✔	✔			✔	✔	✔	

TROUBLE SPOTS	Toyota Corolla 96	97	98	99	00	01	02	03
Engine	⊜	⊜	⊜	⊜	⊜	⊜	⊜	⊜
Cooling	⊜	⊜	⊜	⊜	⊜	⊜	⊜	⊜
Fuel	⊜	⊜	⊜	⊜	⊜	⊜	⊜	⊜
Ignition	⊜	⊜	⊜	⊜	⊜	⊜	⊜	⊜
Transmission	⊜	⊜	⊜	⊜	⊜	⊜	⊜	⊜
Electrical	○	○	⊜	⊜	⊜	⊜	⊜	⊜
A/C	⊜	⊜	⊜	⊜	⊜	⊜	⊜	⊜
Suspension	⊜	⊜	⊜	⊜	⊜	⊜	⊜	⊜
Brakes	○	⊜	⊜	⊜	⊜	⊜	⊜	⊜
Exhaust	⊜	⊜	⊜	⊜	⊜	⊜	⊜	⊜
Power equip.	⊜	⊜	⊜	⊜	⊜	⊜	⊜	⊜
Paint/trim/rust	⊜	⊜	⊜	⊜	⊜	⊜	⊜	⊜
Integrity	⊜	⊜	⊜	⊜	⊜	⊜	⊜	⊜
Hardware	⊜	○	○	⊜	⊜	⊜	⊜	⊜
RELIABILITY VERDICT	✔	✔	✔	✔	✔	✔	✔	✔

TROUBLE SPOTS	Toyota Echo 96	97	98	99	00	01	02	03
Engine					⊜	⊜	⊜	⊜
Cooling					⊜	⊜	⊜	⊜
Fuel					⊜	⊜	⊜	⊜
Ignition					⊜	⊜	⊜	⊜
Transmission					⊜	⊜	⊜	⊜
Electrical					⊜	⊜	⊜	⊜
A/C					⊜	⊜	⊜	⊜
Suspension					⊜	⊜	⊜	⊜
Brakes					⊜	⊜	⊜	⊜
Exhaust					⊜	⊜	⊜	⊜
Power equip.					⊜	⊜	⊜	⊜
Paint/trim/rust					⊜	⊜	⊜	⊜
Integrity					⊜	⊜	⊜	⊜
Hardware					⊜	⊜	⊜	⊜
RELIABILITY VERDICT					✔	✔	✔	–

TROUBLE SPOTS	Toyota Highlander 96	97	98	99	00	01	02	03
Engine						⊜	⊜	⊜
Cooling						⊜	⊜	⊜
Fuel						⊜	⊜	⊜
Ignition						⊜	⊜	⊜
Transmission						⊜	⊜	⊜
Electrical						⊜	⊜	⊜
A/C						⊜	⊜	⊜
Suspension						⊜	⊜	⊜
Brakes						⊜	⊜	⊜
Exhaust						⊜	⊜	⊜
Power equip.						⊜	⊜	⊜
Paint/trim/rust						⊜	⊜	⊜
Integrity						○	⊜	⊜
Hardware						⊜	⊜	⊜
RELIABILITY VERDICT						✔	✔	✔

TROUBLE SPOTS	Toyota Land Cruiser 96	97	98	99	00	01	02	03
Engine	Insufficient data	○	Insufficient data	⊜	⊜	⊜	Insufficient data	Insufficient data
Cooling		⊜		⊜	⊜	⊜		
Fuel		⊜		⊜	⊜	⊜		
Ignition		⊜		⊜	⊜	⊜		
Transmission		⊜		⊜	⊜	⊜		
Electrical		◒		⊜	⊜	⊜		
A/C		⊜		⊜	⊜	⊜		
Suspension		⊜		⊜	⊜	⊜		
Brakes		●		⊜	○	⊜		
Exhaust		⊜		⊜	⊜	⊜		
Power equip.		○		○	⊜	⊜		
Paint/trim/rust		⊜		⊜	⊜	⊜		
Integrity		⊜		⊜	⊜	⊜		
Hardware		⊜		⊜	⊜	⊜		
RELIABILITY VERDICT		✔		✔	✔	✔		

TROUBLE SPOTS	Toyota Matrix 96	97	98	99	00	01	02	03
Engine								⊜
Cooling								⊜
Fuel								⊜
Ignition								⊜
Transmission								⊜
Electrical								⊜
A/C								⊜
Suspension								⊜
Brakes								⊜
Exhaust								⊜
Power equip.								⊜
Paint/trim/rust								⊜
Integrity								⊜
Hardware								⊜
RELIABILITY VERDICT								–

TROUBLE SPOTS	Toyota Prius 96	97	98	99	00	01	02	03
Engine						⊜	⊜	⊜
Cooling						⊜	⊜	⊜
Fuel						○	⊜	⊜
Ignition						⊜	⊜	⊜
Transmission						⊜	⊜	⊜
Electrical						○	⊜	⊜
A/C						⊜	⊜	⊜
Suspension						⊜	⊜	⊜
Brakes						⊜	⊜	⊜
Exhaust						⊜	⊜	⊜
Power equip.						⊜	⊜	⊜
Paint/trim/rust						⊜	⊜	⊜
Integrity						⊜	⊜	⊜
Hardware						⊜	⊜	⊜
RELIABILITY VERDICT						✔	✔	✔

Toyota RAV4

TROUBLE SPOTS	96	97	98	99	00	01	02	03
Engine	⊖	⊖	⊜	⊜	⊜	⊜	⊜	⊜
Cooling	⊜	⊜	⊜	⊜	⊜	⊜	⊜	⊜
Fuel	⊖	⊖	⊖	⊖	⊜	⊖	⊜	⊜
Ignition	⊜	⊜	⊜	⊜	⊜	⊜	⊜	⊜
Transmission	⊜	⊖	⊖	⊜	⊜	⊜	⊜	⊜
Electrical	⊖	⊖	⊖	⊖	⊜	⊜	⊜	⊜
A/C	⊖	⊖	⊜	⊜	⊜	⊜	⊜	⊜
Suspension	⊖	⊜	⊜	⊜	⊜	⊜	⊜	⊜
Brakes	◒	◒	○	⊖	⊖	○	⊜	⊜
Exhaust	⊖	⊖	⊜	⊜	⊜	⊖	⊜	⊜
Power equip.	⊖	⊜	⊖	⊜	⊜	⊜	⊜	⊜
Paint/trim/rust	⊖	⊜	⊜	⊜	⊜	⊖	⊜	⊜
Integrity	○	○	⊖	⊖	⊖	◒	○	⊖
Hardware	○	⊖	⊖	⊖	⊜	⊜	⊖	⊜
RELIABILITY VERDICT	✓	✓	✓	✓	✓	✓	✓	✓

Toyota Sequoia

TROUBLE SPOTS	96	97	98	99	00	01	02	03
Engine						⊜	⊜	⊜
Cooling						⊜	⊜	⊜
Fuel						⊖	⊜	⊜
Ignition						⊜	⊜	⊜
Transmission						⊜	⊜	⊜
Electrical						⊖	⊜	⊜
A/C						⊖	⊖	⊜
Suspension						⊜	⊜	⊜
Brakes						◒	⊖	⊜
Exhaust						⊜	⊜	⊜
Power equip.						⊖	⊖	⊖
Paint/trim/rust						⊖	⊜	⊜
Integrity						⊖	⊖	⊜
Hardware						⊖	⊜	⊜
RELIABILITY VERDICT						✓	✓	-

Toyota Sienna

TROUBLE SPOTS	96	97	98	99	00	01	02	03
Engine			⊖	⊖	⊜	⊜	⊜	⊜
Cooling			⊜	⊜	⊜	⊜	⊜	⊜
Fuel			⊜	⊜	⊜	⊜	⊜	⊜
Ignition			⊜	⊜	⊜	⊜	⊜	⊜
Transmission			⊖	⊜	⊖	⊜	⊜	⊜
Electrical			⊖	⊖	⊖	⊖	⊜	⊜
A/C			⊖	⊜	⊜	⊜	⊜	⊜
Suspension			⊖	⊖	⊜	⊜	⊜	⊜
Brakes			○	○	⊖	⊖	⊖	⊜
Exhaust			⊜	⊜	⊜	⊜	⊜	⊜
Power equip.			⊖	○	○	○	⊖	⊜
Paint/trim/rust			⊜	⊜	⊜	⊜	⊜	⊜
Integrity			◒	○	⊖	⊖	⊖	⊜
Hardware			●	◒	○	⊖	○	⊜
RELIABILITY VERDICT			✓	✓	✓	✓	✓	✓

Toyota T100, Tundra

TROUBLE SPOTS	96	97	98	99	00	01	02	03
Engine	⊜	⊜			⊜	⊜	⊜	⊜
Cooling	⊜	⊜			⊜	⊜	⊜	⊜
Fuel	⊖	⊖			⊖	⊖	⊜	⊜
Ignition	⊜	⊖			⊜	⊜	⊜	⊜
Transmission	⊜	⊜			⊜	⊜	⊜	⊜
Electrical	⊖	○			⊖	⊜	⊜	⊜
A/C	⊖	⊖			⊜	⊜	⊜	⊜
Suspension	⊖	⊜			⊜	⊜	⊜	⊜
Brakes	⊖	⊖			◒	○	⊖	⊜
Exhaust	⊜	⊜			⊜	⊜	⊜	⊜
Power equip.	⊖	⊜			⊜	⊜	⊜	⊜
Paint/trim/rust	⊜	⊜			⊖	⊜	⊜	⊜
Integrity	⊖	⊖			⊖	⊖	⊜	⊜
Hardware	○	⊖			⊖	⊖	⊜	⊜
RELIABILITY VERDICT	✓	✓			✓	✓	✓	✓

Insufficient data

Toyota Tacoma

TROUBLE SPOTS	96	97	98	99	00	01	02	03
Engine	⊖	⊜	⊜	⊜	⊜	⊜	⊜	⊜
Cooling	⊖	⊜	⊜	⊜	⊜	⊜	⊜	⊜
Fuel	⊖	⊖	⊖	⊜	⊖	⊜	⊜	⊜
Ignition	⊜	⊜	⊜	⊜	⊜	⊜	⊜	⊜
Transmission	⊜	⊜	⊜	⊜	⊜	⊜	⊜	⊜
Electrical	○	⊖	⊖	⊖	⊜	⊜	⊜	⊜
A/C	⊖	⊖	⊜	⊜	⊜	⊜	⊜	⊜
Suspension	○	⊖	⊖	⊖	⊜	⊖	⊜	⊜
Brakes	○	⊖	⊖	⊖	⊖	⊖	⊜	⊜
Exhaust	⊖	⊖	⊜	⊜	⊜	⊜	⊜	⊜
Power equip.	⊜	⊜	⊜	⊜	⊜	⊜	⊜	⊜
Paint/trim/rust	⊖	⊖	⊖	⊜	⊜	○	⊖	⊜
Integrity	⊖	⊖	⊖	⊖	⊖	○	○	⊖
Hardware	⊖	⊖	⊖	⊖	⊖	⊖	⊜	⊜
RELIABILITY VERDICT	✓	✓	✓	✓	✓	✓	✓	✓

Volkswagen Golf 4-cyl.

TROUBLE SPOTS	96	97	98	99	00	01	02	03
Engine	○	⊖	⊖	○	○	○	⊖	⊜
Cooling	○	○	⊖	⊖	⊖	⊜	⊜	⊜
Fuel	●	○	○	●	◒	○	⊖	⊜
Ignition	◒	○	○	⊖	⊖	⊖	⊜	⊜
Transmission	◒	○	⊖	⊖	⊖	⊖	⊖	⊜
Electrical	●	●	●	●	◒	◒	○	⊜
A/C	○	◒	○	○	⊖	⊜	⊜	⊜
Suspension	⊖	⊖	⊖	⊖	⊜	⊜	⊜	⊜
Brakes	◒	◒	○	◒	◒	◒	⊖	⊜
Exhaust	●	◒	◒	○	⊖	⊜	⊜	⊜
Power equip.	◒	◒	●	●	●	◒	●	⊜
Paint/trim/rust	●	●	●	○	○	⊜	⊜	⊜
Integrity	●	●	●	●	●	○	○	⊖
Hardware	●	◒	○	●	◒	○	○	⊜
RELIABILITY VERDICT	✗	✗	✗	✗	✗	✗	✗	-

Volkswagen Jetta 4-cyl. Turbo

TROUBLE SPOTS	96	97	98	99	00	01	02	03
Engine					⊖	⊖	○	⊖
Cooling					○	⊖	⊜	⊜
Fuel					●	○	⊖	⊖
Ignition					○	◒	●	○
Transmission					⊜	⊖	⊖	⊜
Electrical					◒	◒	○	⊖
A/C					⊜	⊖	⊜	⊜
Suspension					⊖	⊜	⊜	⊜
Brakes					○	○	⊜	⊜
Exhaust					⊖	⊜	⊜	⊜
Power equip.					●	●	◒	⊜
Paint/trim/rust					⊜	⊖	⊜	⊜
Integrity					◒	○	○	⊖
Hardware					●	◒	○	⊖
RELIABILITY VERDICT					✗	✗	✗	✗

Volkswagen New Beetle

TROUBLE SPOTS	96	97	98	99	00	01	02	03
Engine			◒	○	○	⊖	⊖	⊜
Cooling			○	⊖	⊖	⊜	⊜	⊜
Fuel			○	◒	●	○	⊖	⊖
Ignition			⊖	⊖	⊖	⊖	○	⊖
Transmission			⊖	⊖	⊖	⊖	⊖	⊜
Electrical			●	●	●	●	◒	⊜
A/C			◒	◒	⊖	⊖	⊜	⊜
Suspension			⊜	⊜	⊜	⊜	⊜	⊜
Brakes			⊖	○	◒	○	⊖	⊜
Exhaust			⊖	⊖	⊖	⊜	⊜	⊜
Power equip.			●	●	●	◒	○	⊜
Paint/trim/rust			⊖	⊖	⊖	⊖	⊜	⊖
Integrity			●	◒	○	○	○	⊖
Hardware			●	●	●	◒	○	⊖
RELIABILITY VERDICT			✗	✗	✗	✗	✗	✗

Chrysler Town & Country (ext.) 2WD

Trouble spots	96	97	98	99	00	01	02	03
Engine	◒	○	◒	⊖	⊖	⊜	⊜	⊜
Cooling	◒	◒	⊖	⊖	⊖	⊜	⊜	⊜
Fuel	◒	◒	⊖	⊖	⊖	⊖	○	⊜
Ignition	⊖	⊖	⊖	⊖	⊜	⊜	⊜	⊜
Transmission	●	◒	○	◒	●	⊖	⊖	⊜
Electrical	●	●	◒	○	○	○	⊖	⊜
A/C	●	◒	○	○	⊖	○	⊖	⊜
Suspension	○	○	○	⊖	⊖	○	⊖	⊜
Brakes	●	◒	◒	◒	◒	◒	⊖	⊜
Exhaust	⊜	⊜	⊜	⊜	⊜	⊜	⊜	⊜
Power equip.	●	◒	○	○	○	●	○	⊖
Paint/trim/rust	○	⊖	⊜	⊜	⊜	⊜	⊜	⊜
Integrity	◒	◒	○	○	○	◒	⊜	⊜
Hardware	◒	○	⊖	⊖	⊖	○	⊖	⊜
RELIABILITY VERDICT	✗	✗	-	✗	✗	✗	✗	-

Chrysler Town & Country ~~AWD~~

Trouble spots	96	97	98	99	00	01	02	03
Engine	Insufficient data	○	○	○	○	⊖	⊜	⊜
Cooling		○	⊜	○	◒	⊜	⊜	⊜
Fuel		○	⊖	⊖	⊖	⊖	⊖	⊜
Ignition		⊖	⊜	⊜	⊖	⊜	⊜	⊜
Transmission		◒	◒	◒	◒	○	⊜	⊜
Electrical		●	◒	○	◒	◒	⊖	○
A/C		◒	⊖	⊖	⊖	○	⊜	⊜
Suspension		○	○	○	○	○	⊖	⊜
Brakes		◒	●	●	●	◒	⊜	⊜
Exhaust		⊜	⊖	⊜	⊜	⊜	⊜	⊜
Power equip.		○	○	○	◒	●	⊖	⊜
Paint/trim/rust		⊖	⊖	⊖	⊖	○	⊜	⊜
Integrity		○	○	○	◒	◒	○	⊜
Hardware		○	⊖	○	◒	◒	⊖	⊜
RELIABILITY VERDICT		✗	-	✗	✗	✗	-	-

Dodge Caravan V6

Trouble spots	96	97	98	99	00	01	02	03
Engine	◒	◒	◒	○	⊖	⊜	⊜	⊜
Cooling	◒	○	⊖	⊖	⊖	⊜	⊜	⊜
Fuel	◒	○	⊖	⊖	⊜	⊜	⊜	⊜
Ignition	⊖	⊖	⊖	⊖	⊜	⊜	⊜	⊜
Transmission	●	◒	○	●	●	⊖	⊖	⊖
Electrical	●	●	◒	○	○	○	⊖	⊖
A/C	●	●	◒	○	⊖	⊖	⊖	⊜
Suspension	○	○	○	⊜	⊖	○	○	⊜
Brakes	●	●	◒	◒	◒	◒	⊖	⊖
Exhaust	⊜	⊜	⊜	⊜	⊜	⊜	⊜	⊜
Power equip.	◒	○	○	○	⊖	○	⊖	⊜
Paint/trim/rust	○	○	⊖	⊖	⊖	⊖	⊜	⊜
Integrity	◒	◒	○	○	○	○	○	⊖
Hardware	◒	◒	○	○	○	○	⊖	⊜
RELIABILITY VERDICT	✗	✗	-	✗	✗	✗	-	✗

Dodge Dakota 2WD

Trouble spots	96	97	98	99	00	01	02	03
Engine	○	○	⊖	○	⊜	⊜	⊜	⊜
Cooling	●	◒	◒	○	⊖	⊜	⊜	⊜
Fuel	○	○	○	⊖	⊖	⊖	⊜	⊖
Ignition	⊖	⊖	⊖	⊖	⊜	⊖	⊜	⊜
Transmission	○	◒	○	⊖	⊖	⊖	⊜	⊜
Electrical	◒	○	◒	◒	○	⊖	⊖	⊖
A/C	●	●	◒	○	⊖	⊖	⊖	⊜
Suspension	○	○	○	⊖	⊖	⊖	⊖	⊜
Brakes	◒	◒	◒	◒	◒	○	⊖	⊖
Exhaust	○	◒	◒	○	⊜	⊜	⊜	⊜
Power equip.	⊖	⊖	⊖	⊖	○	⊖	⊜	⊜
Paint/trim/rust	◒	◒	○	⊖	⊖	⊖	⊖	⊜
Integrity	◒	⊖	○	⊖	⊖	⊖	⊖	⊜
Hardware	○	○	○	⊖	⊖	⊖	⊜	⊜
RELIABILITY VERDICT	-	✗	✗	-	-	-	✓	-

Dodge Dakota 4WD

Trouble spots	96	97	98	99	00	01	02	03
Engine	Insufficient data	⊖	○	○	⊖	⊖	⊜	⊜
Cooling		○	○	◒	⊖	⊖	⊜	⊜
Fuel		◒	○	⊖	○	⊖	⊜	⊜
Ignition		○	⊜	⊖	⊜	⊜	⊜	⊜
Transmission		○	◒	○	○	○	⊖	⊖
Electrical		○	○	○	⊖	⊖	⊖	⊜
A/C		◒	◒	⊜	⊜	⊖	⊖	⊜
Suspension		◒	◒	◒	○	⊖	⊜	⊜
Brakes		◒	◒	○	●	◒	⊖	⊜
Exhaust		○	○	○	⊜	⊜	⊜	⊜
Power equip.		⊜	⊖	⊖	⊖	⊖	⊜	⊜
Paint/trim/rust		○	○	⊜	⊖	⊜	⊜	⊜
Integrity		⊖	○	⊖	⊖	⊖	⊖	⊖
Hardware		⊖	⊖	⊖	⊖	⊖	⊜	⊜
RELIABILITY VERDICT		-	✗	✗	✗	✗	-	-

Dodge Durango

Trouble spots	96	97	98	99	00	01	02	03
Engine			○	○	⊜	⊜	⊜	⊜
Cooling			◒	○	⊖	⊜	⊜	⊜
Fuel			○	○	⊖	⊜	⊜	⊜
Ignition			⊜	⊖	⊜	⊜	⊜	⊜
Transmission			◒	◒	○	⊖	⊖	⊖
Electrical			○	◒	○	⊖	⊖	⊖
A/C			◒	⊖	⊖	⊖	⊜	⊜
Suspension			○	◒	◒	⊖	⊜	⊖
Brakes			◒	◒	◒	○	⊖	⊜
Exhaust			⊜	⊜	⊜	⊜	⊜	⊜
Power equip.			●	●	◒	⊖	⊜	⊜
Paint/trim/rust			○	⊖	⊖	⊖	⊖	⊜
Integrity			○	⊖	○	○	⊖	⊜
Hardware			○	○	◒	⊖	⊖	⊜
RELIABILITY VERDICT			✗	✗	✗	-	-	-

Dodge Grand Caravan 2WD

Trouble spots	96	97	98	99	00	01	02	03
Engine	◒	○	◒	⊖	⊖	⊜	⊜	⊜
Cooling	◒	◒	⊖	⊖	⊖	⊜	⊜	⊜
Fuel	◒	◒	⊖	⊜	⊖	⊖	○	⊜
Ignition	⊖	⊖	⊖	⊖	⊜	⊜	⊜	⊜
Transmission	●	◒	○	◒	●	⊖	⊖	⊜
Electrical	●	●	◒	○	○	○	⊖	⊜
A/C	●	◒	○	○	⊖	○	⊖	⊜
Suspension	○	○	○	⊖	⊖	○	⊖	⊜
Brakes	●	◒	◒	◒	◒	◒	⊖	⊜
Exhaust	⊜	⊜	⊜	⊜	⊜	⊜	⊜	⊜
Power equip.	●	◒	○	○	○	●	○	⊖
Paint/trim/rust	○	⊖	⊖	⊖	⊖	⊖	⊜	⊜
Integrity	◒	◒	○	○	○	◒	⊖	⊖
Hardware	◒	○	⊖	⊖	⊖	○	⊜	⊜
RELIABILITY VERDICT	✗	✗	-	✗	✗	✗	✗	-

Dodge Intrepid

Trouble spots	96	97	98	99	00	01	02	03
Engine	◒	◒	⊖	⊖	⊜	⊜	⊜	Insufficient data
Cooling	●	◒	⊖	⊖	⊜	⊜	⊜	
Fuel	○	◒	⊖	○	⊖	⊖	⊖	
Ignition	⊖	⊖	⊖	⊖	⊜	⊜	⊖	
Transmission	◒	○	◒	◒	⊖	⊖	⊖	
Electrical	◒	◒	●	◒	○	○	○	
A/C	●	◒	◒	◒	⊖	⊖	⊖	
Suspension	●	◒	◒	⊖	⊖	⊖	⊜	
Brakes	●	◒	◒	○	⊖	⊖	⊖	
Exhaust	⊜	⊜	⊖	⊜	⊜	⊜	⊜	
Power equip.	○	○	◒	●	◒	⊖	⊖	
Paint/trim/rust	●	◒	○	⊖	⊖	⊖	⊖	
Integrity	◒	●	◒	○	◒	⊖	⊖	
Hardware	○	⊖	⊖	○	○	⊖	⊜	
RELIABILITY VERDICT	✗	✗	✗	✗	-	✓	-	

Dodge Ram 1500 2WD 96	97	98	99	00	01	02	03	Dodge Ram 1500 4WD 96	97	98	99	00	01	02	03	TROUBLE SPOTS
○	○	⊖	○	⊜	⊖	⊜	⊜	○	○	○	◒	⊜	⊖	⊜	⊜	Engine
○	○	⊖	○	○	⊜	⊜	⊜	○	○	⊖	⊖	⊖	⊜	⊖	⊜	Cooling
◒	○	○	⊖	○	⊖	⊖	⊜	○	○	○	○	⊜	⊖	⊖	⊜	Fuel
⊖	⊖	⊖	⊖	⊜	⊖	⊜	⊜	⊖	⊖	⊖	⊖	⊖	⊖	⊜	⊜	Ignition
●	◒	○	○	◒	○	⊖	⊜	●	◒	◒	◒	○	○	⊖	⊜	Transmission
◒	○	○	○	⊖	⊖	⊖	⊜	◒	○	⊖	⊖	⊖	⊖	⊖	⊖	Electrical
●	◒	○	○	⊖	⊖	⊖	⊜	◒	○	⊖	○	⊖	⊜	⊖	⊜	A/C
○	○	⊖	⊖	○	⊖	⊖	⊜	○	◒	○	○	○	○	○	⊜	Suspension
○	○	◒	◒	○	⊖	⊜	⊜	◒	◒	◒	◒	○	⊖	⊖	⊜	Brakes
◒	○	⊖	⊖	⊜	⊜	⊜	⊜	◒	⊖	⊖	⊖	⊜	⊜	⊜	⊜	Exhaust
○	○	⊖	⊖	⊖	⊜	⊖	⊜	⊖	○	⊖	⊖	⊖	⊖	⊖	⊜	Power equip.
◒	◒	⊖	⊖	⊖	⊖	⊜	⊜	◒	◒	⊖	⊖	○	⊖	⊜	⊜	Paint/trim/rust
○	○	⊖	○	○	○	○	⊖	○	○	○	○	○	○	○	⊜	Integrity
○	○	⊖	⊖	⊖	⊖	○	⊜	⊖	○	⊖	⊖	⊖	⊖	⊖	⊜	Hardware
✗	–	–	✗	✗	–	✗	–	✗	✗	✗	✗	–	✗	✗	–	RELIABILITY VERDICT

TROUBLE SPOTS	Dodge Stratus Sedan V6 96	97	98	99	00	01	02	03	Dodge/Plymouth Neon 96	97	98	99	00	01	02	03
Engine	◒	◒	⊖	⊖	⊜	⊜	⊜	Insufficient data	●	●	●	●	⊖	⊖	⊖	Insufficient data
Cooling	○	○	⊖	⊜	⊖	⊜	⊜		◒	◒	○	⊖	○	⊜	⊜	
Fuel	○	○	⊜	○	○	⊜	⊜		◒	○	○	◒	⊖	⊖	⊜	
Ignition	○	⊖	⊜	⊖	⊜	⊜	⊜		○	○	⊖	○	⊖	⊜	⊜	
Transmission	●	○	○	◒	○	⊖	⊖		○	○	○	○	⊖	⊜	⊜	
Electrical	○	⊖	⊖	○	⊖	○	⊖		●	●	○	◒	◒	◒	⊖	
A/C	●	○	○	⊖	⊜	⊖	⊜		●	●	◒	○	○	⊖	⊜	
Suspension	◒	◒	○	⊜	⊜	○	⊜		○	○	⊖	⊖	○	⊖	⊜	
Brakes	●	●	●	◒	◒	○	⊖		●	◒	◒	○	◒	○	⊖	
Exhaust	○	⊜	⊜	⊜	⊜	⊜	⊜		⊖	⊖	⊖	⊜	⊜	⊜	⊜	
Power equip.	○	○	◒	○	⊖	⊖	⊜		⊖	⊖	◒	○	◒	◒	⊖	
Paint/trim/rust	○	⊖	⊖	○	⊖	⊖	⊖		●	◒	○	○	⊖	⊖	⊜	
Integrity	◒	○	○	○	○	○	⊖		●	●	●	◒	◒	○	○	
Hardware	○	⊖	⊖	⊖	⊖	⊖	⊖		○	○	○	◒	○	○	⊜	
RELIABILITY VERDICT	✗	–	–	–	–	–	–		✗	✗	✗	✗	✗	–	✓	

Ford Contour 4-cyl. 96	97	98	99	00	01	02	03	Ford Crown Victoria 96	97	98	99	00	01	02	03	TROUBLE SPOTS
◒	○	○	⊜					○	⊖	⊜	⊜	⊜	⊖	⊜	⊜	Engine
◒	○	○	⊜					○	⊖	⊜	⊜	⊜	⊜	⊜	⊜	Cooling
◒	◒	◒	○					◒	○	⊖	⊖	⊖	○	⊜	⊜	Fuel
○	⊖	⊖	⊖					○	⊖	⊜	⊖	⊜	⊖	⊜	⊜	Ignition
◒	○	○	⊖					⊖	⊖	⊖	⊜	⊖	⊜	⊜	⊜	Transmission
●	◒	◒	○					◒	○	○	○	○	○	⊖	⊖	Electrical
○	○	○	⊖					○	⊖	⊜	⊖	⊖	⊖	⊜	⊜	A/C
○	◒	○	⊖					○	○	○	⊖	⊖	⊖	⊖	⊖	Suspension
◒	◒	◒	○					◒	◒	○	○	⊖	⊖	⊜	⊜	Brakes
⊖	⊖	⊖	⊜					○	⊖	⊜	⊜	⊜	⊜	⊜	⊜	Exhaust
○	○	○	○					●	◒	⊖	○	○	○	⊖	⊖	Power equip.
○	○	○	⊖					⊖	⊖	⊖	⊖	⊖	⊖	⊖	⊜	Paint/trim/rust
◒	◒	◒	●					○	○	⊖	○	◒	◒	○	○	Integrity
○	◒	○	○					○	⊖	⊜	⊖	○	○	⊖	⊖	Hardware
–	✗	✗	–					–	✓	✓	✓	✓	–	–	✗	RELIABILITY VERDICT

TROUBLE SPOTS	Ford Escape 96	97	98	99	00	01	02	03	Ford Escort, ZX2 96	97	98	99	00	01	02	03
Engine						⊖	⊜	⊜	◒	⊖	⊖	⊖	⊖	⊖	⊜	Insufficient data
Cooling						⊖	⊜	⊜	◒	◒	○	⊜	⊜	⊜	⊜	
Fuel						○	⊖	⊜	○	○	⊖	⊖	⊖	⊜	⊖	
Ignition						⊜	⊜	⊜	○	⊜	⊜	⊖	⊖	⊜	⊜	
Transmission						⊖	⊜	⊜	⊖	⊖	⊖	⊖	⊜	⊖	⊖	
Electrical						○	⊖	⊜	◒	○	⊖	○	○	⊜	⊖	
A/C						⊜	⊜	⊜	○	○	⊖	⊖	⊖	⊜	⊜	
Suspension						⊖	⊜	⊜	○	◒	○	⊖	○	⊜	⊜	
Brakes						○	⊜	⊜	◒	◒	○	○	○	⊖	⊜	
Exhaust						⊜	⊜	⊜	○	⊖	⊜	⊜	⊜	⊜	⊜	
Power equip.						⊖	⊖	⊜	⊖	⊜	⊖	⊖	⊖	⊜	⊜	
Paint/trim/rust						⊖	⊜	⊜	◒	⊖	⊖	⊖	⊖	⊜	⊜	
Integrity						◒	○	⊖	○	○	○	⊖	○	○	○	
Hardware						⊖	⊖	⊜	◒	⊜	⊜	⊖	⊖	⊖	⊜	
RELIABILITY VERDICT						✗	–	✓	–	–	✓	✓	✓	✓	✓	

Ford Excursion

TROUBLE SPOTS	96	97	98	99	00	01	02	03
Engine					⊖	⊖	⊖	Insufficient data
Cooling					⊜	⊜	⊜	
Fuel					⊖	⊖	⊜	
Ignition					⊖	⊜	⊜	
Transmission					⊜	⊖	⊜	
Electrical					○	⊖	○	
A/C					⊜	⊖	⊜	
Suspension					○	⊖	⊖	
Brakes					◒	◒	⊖	
Exhaust					⊜	⊜	⊜	
Power equip.					◒	○	⊜	
Paint/trim/rust					⊖	⊜	⊜	
Integrity					○	○	○	
Hardware					◒	○	⊜	
RELIABILITY VERDICT					–	✗	–	

Ford Expedition

TROUBLE SPOTS	96	97	98	99	00	01	02	03
Engine		⊖	⊖	○	⊜	⊖	⊜	⊜
Cooling		⊜	⊖	⊜	⊜	⊜	⊜	⊜
Fuel		⊖	⊖	⊖	⊖	⊖	⊜	⊜
Ignition		⊖	○	⊖	⊜	⊜	⊜	⊜
Transmission		⊖	⊖	⊖	⊖	⊖	⊖	⊜
Electrical		◒	◒	◒	○	○	⊜	⊖
A/C		⊖	⊖	⊖	⊖	⊜	⊜	⊜
Suspension		○	○	⊜	○	⊖	⊜	⊜
Brakes		◒	○	○	○	⊖	⊜	⊜
Exhaust		⊜	⊜	⊜	⊜	⊜	⊜	⊜
Power equip.		○	○	○	○	○	○	○
Paint/trim/rust		⊜	⊖	⊖	⊖	⊖	⊖	⊜
Integrity		○	⊜	○	○	○	⊖	○
Hardware		○	○	○	⊜	○	⊜	⊜
RELIABILITY VERDICT		✓	–	–	–	–	–	✗

Ford Explorer 2WD

TROUBLE SPOTS	96	97	98	99	00	01	02	03
Engine	⊖	⊖	⊖	⊖	⊖	⊜	⊜	⊜
Cooling	○	○	○	⊖	○	⊖	⊜	⊜
Fuel	◒	○	○	◒	○	○	⊖	⊜
Ignition	⊜	⊖	⊖	⊖	⊖	⊜	⊜	⊜
Transmission	○	⊖	⊖	⊖	⊖	⊖	⊖	⊜
Electrical	◒	◒	●	●	●	◒	⊜	⊜
A/C	○	●	◒	⊖	⊖	⊖	⊖	⊜
Suspension	○	○	○	⊖	⊖	⊖	⊜	⊜
Brakes	○	○	○	○	○	⊖	⊜	⊜
Exhaust	⊖	⊖	⊜	⊜	⊜	⊜	⊜	⊜
Power equip.	○	○	◒	○	○	○	⊖	⊜
Paint/trim/rust	○	○	⊖	⊖	⊜	⊖	⊜	⊜
Integrity	○	○	○	○	○	○	○	⊜
Hardware	○	○	○	○	◒	○	○	⊖
RELIABILITY VERDICT	✓	–	–	–	✗	–	✗	–

Ford Explorer 4WD

TROUBLE SPOTS	96	97	98	99	00	01	02	03
Engine	⊖	○	○	⊖	⊖	⊖	⊜	⊜
Cooling	○	○	○	⊖	○	⊜	⊜	⊜
Fuel	◒	○	○	○	○	⊖	⊜	⊜
Ignition	⊖	⊖	⊖	⊖	⊖	⊜	⊜	⊜
Transmission	○	○	○	⊖	○	⊖	⊖	⊜
Electrical	○	○	◒	◒	◒	○	⊜	⊖
A/C	○	◒	○	⊖	⊜	⊖	⊜	⊜
Suspension	○	○	○	○	⊖	⊖	⊖	⊜
Brakes	◒	◒	○	◒	○	⊖	⊜	⊜
Exhaust	⊖	⊖	⊜	⊜	⊜	⊜	⊜	⊜
Power equip.	○	○	◒	○	○	⊖	⊖	⊜
Paint/trim/rust	○	○	⊖	⊖	⊖	⊖	⊖	⊜
Integrity	○	○	○	○	○	○	○	⊜
Hardware	○	○	○	○	⊜	○	○	⊖
RELIABILITY VERDICT	–	–	✗	✗	✗	✗	✗	–

Ford Explorer Sport Trac

TROUBLE SPOTS	96	97	98	99	00	01	02	03
Engine						⊖	⊜	⊜
Cooling						⊖	⊜	⊜
Fuel						○	⊜	⊜
Ignition						⊜	⊜	⊜
Transmission						⊜	⊜	⊜
Electrical						⊖	⊖	⊖
A/C						⊜	⊜	⊜
Suspension						⊜	⊜	⊜
Brakes						○	⊖	⊜
Exhaust						⊜	⊜	⊜
Power equip.						⊖	⊖	⊖
Paint/trim/rust						○	⊜	⊜
Integrity						○	○	○
Hardware						⊖	○	⊖
RELIABILITY VERDICT						–	–	✗

Ford F-150 2WD

TROUBLE SPOTS	96	97	98	99	00	01	02	03
Engine	⊖	⊖	⊜	⊖	⊜	⊜	⊜	⊜
Cooling	⊖	⊖	⊜	⊜	⊜	⊜	⊜	⊜
Fuel	◒	○	⊜	⊖	⊖	⊖	⊜	⊜
Ignition	⊖	⊖	⊖	⊖	⊖	⊜	⊜	⊜
Transmission	○	⊜	⊖	⊖	⊖	⊖	⊜	⊜
Electrical	○	◒	○	○	⊖	⊖	⊖	⊖
A/C	⊜	⊖	⊖	⊖	⊖	⊜	⊜	⊜
Suspension	○	○	⊖	⊜	⊖	⊜	⊜	⊜
Brakes	○	○	○	○	⊖	⊜	⊜	⊜
Exhaust	⊖	⊜	⊜	⊜	⊜	⊜	⊜	⊜
Power equip.	⊖	○	○	⊖	⊖	⊖	⊜	⊜
Paint/trim/rust	⊖	⊖	⊖	⊜	⊖	⊜	⊖	⊜
Integrity	○	○	○	○	⊖	⊖	⊖	⊜
Hardware	⊖	⊖	⊖	⊖	⊖	⊖	⊖	⊜
RELIABILITY VERDICT	✓	✓	✓	✓	✓	✓	✓	✓

Ford F-150 4WD

TROUBLE SPOTS	96	97	98	99	00	01	02	03
Engine	⊖	⊖	⊖	○	⊖	⊖	⊜	⊜
Cooling	⊖	⊜	⊜	⊜	⊜	⊜	⊜	⊜
Fuel	◒	○	⊖	⊖	⊜	⊖	⊜	⊜
Ignition	○	⊜	⊖	⊖	⊜	⊖	⊜	⊜
Transmission	⊜	⊜	⊜	⊜	⊜	⊜	⊜	⊜
Electrical	○	◒	◒	○	⊖	⊖	⊜	⊜
A/C	⊜	⊜	⊖	⊖	⊖	⊜	⊜	⊜
Suspension	◒	○	○	⊖	⊖	⊖	⊜	⊜
Brakes	○	◒	○	◒	◒	⊖	⊜	⊜
Exhaust	○	⊜	⊜	⊜	⊜	⊜	⊜	⊜
Power equip.	⊖	○	⊖	○	⊖	⊖	⊖	⊜
Paint/trim/rust	⊖	⊖	⊖	⊖	⊖	⊜	⊜	⊜
Integrity	○	○	○	○	⊖	○	○	⊖
Hardware	⊖	⊖	⊖	⊖	⊖	⊖	⊖	⊜
RELIABILITY VERDICT	–	✓	✓	–	✓	–	–	✓

Ford Focus

TROUBLE SPOTS	96	97	98	99	00	01	02	03
Engine					⊖	⊖	⊜	⊜
Cooling					⊜	⊜	⊜	⊜
Fuel					◒	◒	⊖	⊜
Ignition					⊖	⊖	⊜	⊜
Transmission					○	⊜	⊜	⊜
Electrical					●	○	⊖	⊖
A/C					⊖	⊖	⊜	⊜
Suspension					◒	○	⊖	⊖
Brakes					●	◒	⊖	⊜
Exhaust					⊜	⊜	⊜	⊜
Power equip.					○	⊖	⊖	⊜
Paint/trim/rust					⊖	⊖	⊜	⊜
Integrity					◒	○	○	⊖
Hardware					◒	⊖	⊖	⊜
RELIABILITY VERDICT					✗	✗	–	✓

Ford Mustang

TROUBLE SPOTS	96	97	98	99	00	01	02	03
Engine	○	⊖	⊖	⊖	⊜	⊖	⊜	⊜
Cooling	●	◒	⊖	⊖	⊖	⊖	⊜	⊜
Fuel	○	⊖	○	⊖	⊖	⊖	⊜	⊜
Ignition	○	⊖	⊖	⊖	⊜	⊜	⊜	⊜
Transmission	○	○	○	⊖	⊖	⊖	⊜	⊜
Electrical	◒	○	⊖	⊖	⊖	⊖	⊖	⊜
A/C	⊖	○	⊖	⊜	⊜	⊜	⊜	⊜
Suspension	○	⊖	⊖	⊖	⊜	⊜	⊜	⊜
Brakes	○	○	○	○	○	⊖	⊜	⊜
Exhaust	⊖	⊜	⊜	⊜	⊜	⊜	⊜	⊜
Power equip.	⊖	○	⊖	⊖	⊖	○	○	⊜
Paint/trim/rust	○	○	⊖	⊖	⊖	⊖	⊖	⊖
Integrity	○	○	○	◒	○	○	○	○
Hardware	○	○	⊖	○	○	⊖	⊖	⊖
RELIABILITY VERDICT	-	-	✓	✓	✓	-	-	✗

Ford Ranger 2WD

TROUBLE SPOTS	96	97	98	99	00	01	02	03
Engine	⊖	⊖	⊖	⊖	⊖	⊖	⊜	⊜
Cooling	⊖	⊖	⊖	⊜	⊜	⊜	⊜	⊜
Fuel	◒	○	○	○	⊖	⊖	⊖	⊜
Ignition	⊖	⊜	⊖	⊖	⊖	⊜	⊜	⊜
Transmission	⊖	⊖	⊖	⊖	⊖	⊖	⊖	⊜
Electrical	●	●	●	◒	○	○	⊖	⊜
A/C	○	◒	○	⊖	⊖	⊖	⊜	⊜
Suspension	⊖	⊜	○	⊖	⊖	⊖	⊖	⊜
Brakes	○	○	○	○	⊖	○	⊖	⊜
Exhaust	⊜	⊜	⊜	⊜	⊜	⊜	⊜	⊜
Power equip.	⊖	⊖	⊖	⊖	⊖	⊖	⊖	⊜
Paint/trim/rust	⊖	⊖	⊖	⊖	⊜	⊜	⊜	⊜
Integrity	⊖	⊖	⊖	⊖	⊖	○	⊖	⊖
Hardware	⊖	○	○	⊖	⊖	○	⊖	⊖
RELIABILITY VERDICT	✓	✓	✓	✓	✓	-	-	-

Ford Ranger 4WD

TROUBLE SPOTS	96	97	98	99	00	01	02	03
Engine	⊖	⊖	⊖	⊖	⊖	⊜	⊜	⊜
Cooling	○	○	○	⊖	⊖	⊜	⊜	⊜
Fuel	○	○	○	⊖	⊖	⊖	⊖	⊜
Ignition	⊖	⊖	⊖	⊖	⊜	⊖	⊜	⊜
Transmission	○	⊖	○	⊖	○	⊖	○	⊜
Electrical	◒	●	●	◒	○	○	⊖	○
A/C	○	◒	⊖	⊜	⊖	⊖	⊜	⊜
Suspension	⊖	⊖	○	○	⊖	⊖	⊖	⊜
Brakes	◒	○	◒	◒	◒	⊖	⊜	⊜
Exhaust	⊜	⊜	⊜	⊜	⊜	⊜	⊜	⊜
Power equip.	○	○	○	⊖	○	⊖	⊖	⊜
Paint/trim/rust	⊖	⊖	⊜	⊖	⊖	⊖	⊖	⊖
Integrity	○	○	○	⊖	○	○	○	⊖
Hardware	⊖	⊖	○	⊖	○	○	⊖	⊖
RELIABILITY VERDICT	-	-	-	-	✗	✗	✗	-

Ford Taurus

TROUBLE SPOTS	96	97	98	99	00	01	02	03
Engine	○	○	⊖	⊖	⊖	⊜	⊜	⊜
Cooling	◒	○	⊖	⊖	⊜	⊜	⊜	⊜
Fuel	◒	○	○	○	○	○	⊖	⊜
Ignition	⊖	⊖	⊖	⊜	⊖	⊖	⊜	⊜
Transmission	◒	○	○	○	⊖	⊖	⊖	⊜
Electrical	◒	●	●	◒	◒	○	⊖	⊖
A/C	○	○	⊖	⊖	⊜	⊖	⊜	⊜
Suspension	◒	○	○	○	○	○	⊖	⊜
Brakes	◒	◒	●	◒	◒	○	⊖	⊜
Exhaust	⊖	⊖	⊜	⊜	⊜	⊜	⊜	⊜
Power equip.	○	◒	○	○	⊖	⊖	⊖	⊜
Paint/trim/rust	○	⊖	⊖	⊖	⊖	⊜	⊜	⊜
Integrity	◒	○	○	○	○	○	○	⊖
Hardware	○	○	○	⊖	⊖	⊖	⊖	⊜
RELIABILITY VERDICT	-	-	-	-	-	-	-	-

Ford Thunderbird

TROUBLE SPOTS	96	97	98	99	00	01	02	03
Engine	○	○					⊜	Insufficient data
Cooling	●	◒					⊜	
Fuel	◒	○					⊖	
Ignition	○	⊖					⊜	
Transmission	◒	○					⊜	
Electrical	◒	◒					○	
A/C	○	⊖					⊜	
Suspension	○	⊖					⊜	
Brakes	◒	○					⊖	
Exhaust	⊖	⊖					⊜	
Power equip.	○	○					⊜	
Paint/trim/rust	⊖	○					⊜	
Integrity	○	⊖					○	
Hardware	○	⊖					⊖	
RELIABILITY VERDICT	-	-					-	

Ford Windstar

TROUBLE SPOTS	96	97	98	99	00	01	02	03
Engine	●	◒	⊖	◒	○	⊜	⊜	⊜
Cooling	◒	○	⊖	⊜	⊜	⊜	⊜	⊜
Fuel	◒	◒	○	◒	○	○	⊖	⊜
Ignition	○	○	⊖	⊖	⊖	⊜	⊜	⊜
Transmission	◒	○	◒	◒	○	⊖	⊜	⊜
Electrical	●	●	●	●	◒	◒	○	⊖
A/C	○	○	○	⊖	⊖	⊖	⊜	⊜
Suspension	◒	●	●	◒	○	⊖	⊖	⊜
Brakes	●	●	●	○	○	⊖	⊜	⊜
Exhaust	⊖	⊜	⊜	⊜	⊜	⊜	⊜	⊜
Power equip.	●	◒	●	◒	◒	◒	○	⊖
Paint/trim/rust	○	○	○	○	○	⊖	⊜	⊜
Integrity	◒	◒	○	○	◒	◒	○	⊖
Hardware	◒	●	◒	○	◒	○	○	⊖
RELIABILITY VERDICT	✗	✗	✗	✗	✗	✗	-	-

GMC Envoy XL

TROUBLE SPOTS	96	97	98	99	00	01	02	03
Engine							⊜	⊜
Cooling							⊜	⊜
Fuel							○	⊜
Ignition							⊜	⊜
Transmission							⊜	⊜
Electrical							◒	⊖
A/C							○	⊜
Suspension							⊖	⊜
Brakes							⊖	⊜
Exhaust							⊜	⊜
Power equip.							◒	⊖
Paint/trim/rust							⊖	⊜
Integrity							◒	○
Hardware							○	⊖
RELIABILITY VERDICT							✗	✗

GMC Jimmy

TROUBLE SPOTS	96	97	98	99	00	01	02	03
Engine	●	◒	○	○	○	⊖		
Cooling	●	●	◒	○	⊜	⊖		
Fuel	◒	●	○	⊖	○	○		
Ignition	⊖	○	⊖	⊖	⊖	⊖		
Transmission	◒	◒	○	○	⊖	○		
Electrical	●	●	●	●	●	●		
A/C	●	●	○	○	⊖	⊖		
Suspension	◒	◒	○	○	○	○		
Brakes	●	●	○	○	○	○		
Exhaust	⊖	⊜	⊜	⊖	⊖	⊜		
Power equip.	○	◒	◒	○	○	○		
Paint/trim/rust	○	○	⊖	⊖	○	⊖		
Integrity	◒	●	◒	●	◒	◒		
Hardware	○	◒	◒	◒	○	○		
RELIABILITY VERDICT	✗	✗	✗	✗	✗	✗		

GMC S-15 Sonoma V6 4WD

TROUBLE SPOTS	96	97	98	99	00	01	02	03
Engine	Insufficient data	Insufficient data	●	Insufficient data	○	⊖	⊜	⊜
Cooling			○		⊖	⊜	⊜	⊜
Fuel			○		○	○	⊖	⊖
Ignition			⊖		⊖	⊖	⊜	⊜
Transmission			◒		○	⊖	⊜	⊜
Electrical			●		○	○	⊖	⊖
A/C			◒		⊖	⊜	⊜	⊖
Suspension			○		○	○	⊖	⊜
Brakes			◒		○	⊜	⊜	⊜
Exhaust			○		○	⊜	⊜	⊜
Power equip.			○		○	⊖	⊖	⊜
Paint/trim/rust			○		⊜	⊖	⊖	⊖
Integrity			◒		◒	◒	◒	○
Hardware			●		◒	○	○	⊖
RELIABILITY VERDICT			✗		✗	✗	✗	✗

GMC Safari

TROUBLE SPOTS	96	97	98	99	00	01	02	03
Engine	◒	○	○	⊖	⊖	⊜	⊜	Insufficient data
Cooling	●	○	○	⊖	⊜	⊜	⊜	
Fuel	●	●	○	◒	⊖	⊖	⊖	
Ignition	⊖	⊖	⊖	⊜	⊖	⊖	⊜	
Transmission	○	◒	◒	○	○	⊖	⊜	
Electrical	●	●	●	◒	◒	○	○	
A/C	●	●	◒	○	⊖	⊖	⊖	
Suspension	○	◒	○	○	○	⊖	⊖	
Brakes	●	●	●	◒	◒	○	◒	
Exhaust	○	⊖	⊖	⊖	⊜	⊖	⊖	
Power equip.	●	●	●	●	◒	◒	○	
Paint/trim/rust	◒	○	○	○	⊜	⊖	⊜	
Integrity	●	●	◒	◒	●	◒	◒	
Hardware	●	●	●	◒	◒	◒	⊖	
RELIABILITY VERDICT	✗	✗	✗	✗	✗	✗	✗	

GMC Sierra 1500 4WD

TROUBLE SPOTS	96	97	98	99	00	01	02	03
Engine	◒	○	○	⊖	⊖	⊖	⊜	⊜
Cooling	◒	◒	◒	⊜	⊜	⊜	⊜	⊜
Fuel	●	◒	○	○	○	⊖	⊜	⊖
Ignition	⊖	⊜	⊜	⊖	⊜	⊜	⊜	⊜
Transmission	○	◒	○	○	⊖	⊖	⊜	⊜
Electrical	●	●	◒	◒	○	⊖	⊖	⊜
A/C	◒	○	⊖	⊜	⊜	⊜	⊜	⊜
Suspension	⊖	◒	○	○	○	⊖	⊖	⊜
Brakes	●	●	●	●	◒	⊖	⊜	⊜
Exhaust	⊖	⊖	⊜	⊜	⊜	⊜	⊜	⊜
Power equip.	⊖	⊖	⊖	◒	⊖	⊖	⊜	⊖
Paint/trim/rust	⊖	⊖	⊖	⊜	⊜	⊜	⊜	⊜
Integrity	○	○	○	●	◒	○	○	○
Hardware	○	○	○	◒	○	⊖	⊖	⊜
RELIABILITY VERDICT	✗	✗	✗	✗	✗	–	✗	✗

GMC Suburban, Yukon XL

TROUBLE SPOTS	96	97	98	99	00	01	02	03
Engine	◒	○	◒	○	⊜	⊖	⊜	⊜
Cooling	◒	◒	◒	○	⊜	⊜	⊜	⊜
Fuel	◒	○	○	○	○	⊖	⊖	⊜
Ignition	⊖	⊖	⊜	⊖	⊜	⊜	⊜	⊜
Transmission	◒	●	○	○	⊖	⊖	⊜	⊜
Electrical	●	●	●	●	◒	○	⊖	⊖
A/C	●	◒	◒	○	⊖	⊖	⊖	⊜
Suspension	○	◒	◒	○	○	⊖	⊜	⊜
Brakes	●	●	●	●	○	⊖	⊜	⊜
Exhaust	⊖	⊖	⊜	⊖	⊜	⊜	⊜	⊜
Power equip.	○	○	○	●	●	○	⊖	⊖
Paint/trim/rust	⊖	⊖	⊜	⊜	⊜	⊜	⊜	⊜
Integrity	○	○	○	○	◒	○	○	⊜
Hardware	◒	○	○	○	○	○	⊜	⊜
RELIABILITY VERDICT	✗	✗	✗	✗	✗	–	–	✗

GMC Yukon

TROUBLE SPOTS	96	97	98	99	00	01	02	03
Engine	◒	◒	○	⊖	⊜	⊜	⊜	⊜
Cooling	◒	◒	◒	⊖	⊜	⊜	⊜	⊜
Fuel	◒	◒	○	○	⊖	⊜	⊜	⊜
Ignition	⊖	⊜	⊜	⊖	⊜	⊜	⊜	⊜
Transmission	○	◒	○	⊖	⊜	⊜	⊜	⊜
Electrical	●	●	●	◒	◒	○	⊖	○
A/C	●	○	○	⊖	⊖	⊖	⊜	⊖
Suspension	○	◒	○	⊖	○	⊖	⊖	⊜
Brakes	●	●	●	●	○	⊖	⊜	⊜
Exhaust	⊖	⊜	⊜	⊜	⊜	⊜	⊜	⊜
Power equip.	○	⊖	⊖	○	◒	○	⊖	⊖
Paint/trim/rust	⊖	⊖	⊖	⊜	⊜	⊜	⊜	⊜
Integrity	○	○	○	○	◒	○	○	⊖
Hardware	○	○	⊜	○	○	○	⊜	⊜
RELIABILITY VERDICT	✗	✗	✗	✗	–	–	–	✗

Honda Accord

TROUBLE SPOTS	96	97	98	99	00	01	02	03
Engine	⊖	⊖	⊜	⊜	⊜	⊜	⊜	⊜
Cooling	⊖	⊜	⊜	⊜	⊜	⊜	⊜	⊜
Fuel	⊜	⊜	○	⊖	⊖	⊜	⊜	⊜
Ignition	⊜	⊖	⊜	⊖	⊜	⊜	⊜	⊖
Transmission	⊜	⊜	⊖	⊜	⊖	⊖	⊜	⊜
Electrical	○	○	○	⊖	⊖	⊜	⊜	⊜
A/C	○	○	⊜	⊜	⊜	⊜	⊜	⊜
Suspension	⊖	⊜	⊜	⊜	⊜	⊜	⊜	⊜
Brakes	○	⊖	⊖	⊜	⊖	⊖	⊜	⊜
Exhaust	○	⊖	⊖	⊜	⊜	⊜	⊖	⊜
Power equip.	○	◒	⊖	⊖	⊜	⊜	⊜	⊜
Paint/trim/rust	⊖	⊖	⊖	⊖	⊖	⊜	⊜	⊜
Integrity	⊖	⊖	⊖	⊖	⊖	⊖	⊖	⊖
Hardware	⊖	⊖	⊖	⊖	⊖	⊖	⊜	⊜
RELIABILITY VERDICT	✓	✓	✓	✓	✓	✓	✓	✓

Honda CR-V

TROUBLE SPOTS	96	97	98	99	00	01	02	03
Engine		⊜	⊜	⊜	⊜	⊜	⊜	⊜
Cooling		⊜	⊜	⊜	⊜	⊜	⊜	⊜
Fuel		⊜	⊜	⊜	⊜	⊜	⊖	⊜
Ignition		⊖	⊜	⊜	⊜	⊜	⊜	⊜
Transmission		⊜	⊜	⊜	⊜	⊜	⊜	⊜
Electrical		⊖	⊖	⊖	⊖	⊜	⊜	⊜
A/C		⊖	⊜	⊜	⊜	⊜	⊜	⊜
Suspension		⊖	⊜	⊜	⊜	⊜	⊜	⊜
Brakes		⊖	⊖	⊜	⊜	⊜	⊖	⊜
Exhaust		⊜	⊜	⊜	⊜	⊜	⊜	⊜
Power equip.		⊖	⊜	⊖	⊜	⊜	⊜	⊜
Paint/trim/rust		⊜	⊖	⊜	⊜	⊜	⊜	⊜
Integrity		⊖	⊖	⊜	⊖	⊖	⊖	⊜
Hardware		⊜	⊖	⊖	⊖	⊜	⊖	⊜
RELIABILITY VERDICT		✓	✓	✓	✓	✓	✓	✓

Honda Civic

TROUBLE SPOTS	96	97	98	99	00	01	02	03
Engine	⊜	⊜	⊜	⊜	⊜	⊜	⊜	⊜
Cooling	⊜	⊜	⊜	⊜	⊜	⊜	⊜	⊜
Fuel	⊖	⊖	⊖	⊜	⊜	⊜	⊜	⊜
Ignition	⊖	⊖	⊖	⊖	⊜	⊜	⊜	⊜
Transmission	⊜	⊜	⊖	⊜	⊜	⊜	⊜	⊜
Electrical	⊖	⊖	⊖	⊖	⊜	⊖	⊖	⊖
A/C	⊖	⊖	⊖	⊜	⊜	⊜	⊜	⊜
Suspension	⊖	⊜	⊜	⊜	⊜	⊖	⊖	⊜
Brakes	⊖	⊖	⊖	⊖	⊖	⊜	⊜	⊜
Exhaust	○	○	○	⊖	⊜	⊜	⊜	⊜
Power equip.	⊖	○	⊖	⊖	⊜	⊖	⊜	⊜
Paint/trim/rust	⊖	⊜	⊖	⊜	⊜	⊖	⊖	⊜
Integrity	○	○	⊖	⊖	⊖	○	○	⊖
Hardware	⊖	⊖	⊖	⊖	⊜	⊖	⊖	⊜
RELIABILITY VERDICT	✓	✓	✓	✓	✓	✓	✓	✓

Honda Element

TROUBLE SPOTS	96	97	98	99	00	01	02	03
Engine								⊜
Cooling								⊜
Fuel								⊜
Ignition								⊜
Transmission								⊜
Electrical								⊜
A/C								⊜
Suspension								⊜
Brakes								⊜
Exhaust								⊜
Power equip.								⊜
Paint/trim/rust								⊜
Integrity								○
Hardware								⊜
RELIABILITY VERDICT								✓

Honda Odyssey

TROUBLE SPOTS	96	97	98	99	00	01	02	03
Engine	○	⊜	⊜	⊜	⊜	⊜	⊜	⊜
Cooling	⊜	⊜	⊜	⊜	⊜	⊜	⊜	⊜
Fuel	⊜	⊜	⊖	⊖	⊖	⊜	⊜	⊜
Ignition	⊜	⊖	⊖	⊜	⊜	⊜	⊜	⊜
Transmission	⊜	⊜	○	○	⊖	⊖	⊜	⊜
Electrical	⊖	⊖	⊖	○	⊖	⊖	⊖	⊜
A/C	⊖	⊜	⊜	⊜	⊜	⊜	⊜	⊜
Suspension	⊜	⊜	⊜	⊜	⊜	⊜	⊜	⊜
Brakes	●	○	○	○	⊖	⊖	⊜	⊜
Exhaust	⊖	⊜	⊜	⊖	⊜	⊜	⊜	⊜
Power equip.	⊖	⊖	⊜	●	◒	○	⊖	⊜
Paint/trim/rust	⊖	⊜	⊜	⊖	⊜	⊜	⊜	⊜
Integrity	⊖	⊜	⊖	○	○	○	○	⊖
Hardware	○	⊖	⊜	◒	◒	○	⊖	⊜
RELIABILITY VERDICT	✓	✓	✓	-	✓	✓	✓	✓

Honda Passport

TROUBLE SPOTS	96	97	98	99	00	01	02	03
Engine	◒	◒	◒	◒	⊖	⊖	⊜	
Cooling	⊖	⊖	⊖	⊜	⊜	⊜	⊜	
Fuel	○	○	○	●	◒	⊖	⊜	
Ignition	⊖	○	⊜	⊖	⊖	⊖	⊜	
Transmission	⊖	○	⊖	○	⊖	⊜	⊜	
Electrical	●	●	◒	○	○	○	⊖	
A/C	⊖	○	○	○	⊜	⊜	⊜	
Suspension	⊖	⊖	○	⊖	⊖	⊖	⊖	
Brakes	○	◒	●	●	○	⊖	⊖	
Exhaust	⊜	⊖	⊖	⊖	⊜	⊜	⊖	
Power equip.	●	○	⊖	○	○	⊖	⊖	
Paint/trim/rust	◒	○	○	⊖	○	⊖	⊜	
Integrity	◒	●	◒	○	◒	◒	○	
Hardware	◒	○	○	○	○	⊖	⊜	
RELIABILITY VERDICT	-	-	✗	✗	-	-	✓	

Honda Pilot

TROUBLE SPOTS	96	97	98	99	00	01	02	03
Engine								⊜
Cooling								⊜
Fuel								⊜
Ignition								⊜
Transmission								⊜
Electrical								⊜
A/C								⊜
Suspension								⊜
Brakes								⊜
Exhaust								⊜
Power equip.								⊜
Paint/trim/rust								⊜
Integrity								⊖
Hardware								⊜
RELIABILITY VERDICT								✓

Honda Prelude

TROUBLE SPOTS	96	97	98	99	00	01	02	03
Engine	Insufficient data	⊖	⊖	Insufficient data	Insufficient data	⊖		
Cooling		⊖	⊜			⊜		
Fuel		⊜	⊖			⊖		
Ignition		⊜	○			⊜		
Transmission		○	⊜			⊖		
Electrical		⊜	⊜			⊜		
A/C		⊖	⊜			⊜		
Suspension		⊜	⊖			⊜		
Brakes		⊖	⊖			⊜		
Exhaust		⊜	⊜			⊜		
Power equip.		⊜	⊜			○		
Paint/trim/rust		○	⊜			⊜		
Integrity		⊜	⊖			○		
Hardware		⊖	⊜			○		
RELIABILITY VERDICT		✓	✓			✓		

Honda S2000

TROUBLE SPOTS	96	97	98	99	00	01	02	03
Engine					⊖	⊜	⊜	Insufficient data
Cooling					⊜	⊜	⊜	
Fuel					⊖	⊜	⊜	
Ignition					⊜	⊜	⊜	
Transmission					○	○	⊜	
Electrical					⊜	⊜	⊜	
A/C					⊜	⊜	⊜	
Suspension					⊜	⊖	⊜	
Brakes					⊜	⊜	⊜	
Exhaust					⊖	⊜	⊜	
Power equip.					⊖	○	⊖	
Paint/trim/rust					⊖	⊜	⊜	
Integrity					⊜	◒	⊜	
Hardware					⊖	○	⊜	
RELIABILITY VERDICT					✓	-	✓	

Hummer H2

TROUBLE SPOTS	96	97	98	99	00	01	02	03
Engine								⊜
Cooling								⊜
Fuel								⊜
Ignition								⊜
Transmission								⊜
Electrical								⊜
A/C								⊜
Suspension								⊖
Brakes								⊜
Exhaust								⊜
Power equip.								⊖
Paint/trim/rust								⊜
Integrity								⊜
Hardware								○
RELIABILITY VERDICT								✗

Hyundai Elantra

TROUBLE SPOTS	96	97	98	99	00	01	02	03
Engine	Insufficient data	Insufficient data	Insufficient data	⊖	⊖	⊜	⊜	⊜
Cooling				⊖	⊖	⊜	⊜	⊜
Fuel				◒	○	⊖	⊖	⊜
Ignition				○	○	⊜	⊜	⊜
Transmission				◒	○	⊖	⊖	⊜
Electrical				◒	◒	◒	⊖	⊜
A/C				⊜	⊖	⊜	⊜	⊜
Suspension				⊖	⊜	⊖	⊜	⊜
Brakes				⊖	⊖	⊖	⊜	⊜
Exhaust				⊖	⊜	⊜	⊜	⊜
Power equip.				○	◒	⊖	⊜	⊜
Paint/trim/rust				○	○	○	⊖	⊜
Integrity				○	○	○	○	⊖
Hardware				○	○	⊖	⊖	⊜
RELIABILITY VERDICT				-	-	-	✓	✓

Hyundai Santa Fe

TROUBLE SPOTS	96	97	98	99	00	01	02	03
Engine						⊖	⊜	⊜
Cooling						⊜	⊜	⊜
Fuel						○	⊜	⊜
Ignition						○	⊜	⊜
Transmission						○	⊜	⊜
Electrical						◒	⊖	⊜
A/C						⊜	⊜	⊜
Suspension						○	⊜	⊜
Brakes						⊖	⊜	⊜
Exhaust						⊜	⊜	⊜
Power equip.						⊖	⊜	⊜
Paint/trim/rust						⊖	⊜	⊜
Integrity						○	⊜	⊖
Hardware						⊖	⊜	⊜
RELIABILITY VERDICT						✗	✓	✓

Hyundai Sonata

TROUBLE SPOTS	96	97	98	99	00	01	02	03
Engine	Insufficient data	Insufficient data	Insufficient data	Insufficient data	⊜	⊖	⊜	⊜
Cooling					⊜	⊜	⊜	⊜
Fuel					○	⊖	⊖	⊜
Ignition					⊖	⊜	⊜	⊜
Transmission					⊖	⊖	⊜	⊜
Electrical					◒	○	⊖	⊜
A/C					⊜	⊖	⊖	⊜
Suspension					⊖	⊜	⊜	⊜
Brakes					○	○	⊖	⊜
Exhaust					⊜	⊜	⊜	⊜
Power equip.					●	◒	○	⊖
Paint/trim/rust					○	◒	⊖	⊖
Integrity					⊖	○	⊖	⊖
Hardware					○	◒	⊖	⊜
RELIABILITY VERDICT					-	✗	-	-

Hyundai XG300, XG350

TROUBLE SPOTS	96	97	98	99	00	01	02	03
Engine						⊜	⊜	Insufficient data
Cooling						⊜	⊜	
Fuel						○	○	
Ignition						⊜	⊜	
Transmission						○	⊖	
Electrical						○	○	
A/C						⊜	⊜	
Suspension						⊜	⊜	
Brakes						⊜	⊖	
Exhaust						⊜	⊜	
Power equip.						○	⊜	
Paint/trim/rust						○	⊜	
Integrity						⊖	⊖	
Hardware						○	⊖	
RELIABILITY VERDICT						-	✗	

Infiniti FX

TROUBLE SPOTS	96	97	98	99	00	01	02	03
Engine								⊜
Cooling								⊜
Fuel								⊜
Ignition								⊜
Transmission								⊜
Electrical								⊜
A/C								⊜
Suspension								⊜
Brakes								⊜
Exhaust								⊜
Power equip.								⊜
Paint/trim/rust								⊜
Integrity								⊖
Hardware								⊜
RELIABILITY VERDICT								✓

Infiniti G20

TROUBLE SPOTS	96	97	98	99	00	01	02	03
Engine	⊜			⊜	⊜	Insufficient data	⊜	
Cooling	⊜			⊜	⊜		⊜	
Fuel	⊖			⊖	⊖		⊜	
Ignition	⊜			⊜	⊜		⊜	
Transmission	⊜			⊜	⊜		⊜	
Electrical	○			⊖	○		⊜	
A/C	⊜			⊜	⊜		⊜	
Suspension	○			⊖	⊜		⊜	
Brakes	○			⊜	⊖		⊜	
Exhaust	⊜			⊜	⊖		⊜	
Power equip.	○			⊜	○		⊜	
Paint/trim/rust	⊜			⊜	⊜		⊜	
Integrity	⊖			⊖	⊖		⊖	
Hardware	⊖			⊜	⊜		⊜	
RELIABILITY VERDICT	✓			✓	✓		✓	

Infiniti G35

TROUBLE SPOTS	96	97	98	99	00	01	02	03
Engine								⊜
Cooling								⊜
Fuel								⊜
Ignition								⊜
Transmission								⊜
Electrical								⊜
A/C								⊜
Suspension								⊜
Brakes								⊜
Exhaust								⊜
Power equip.								⊖
Paint/trim/rust								⊜
Integrity								⊖
Hardware								⊜
RELIABILITY VERDICT								✓

Infiniti I30, I35

TROUBLE SPOTS	96	97	98	99	00	01	02	03
Engine	⊜	⊖	⊜	⊜	⊜	⊜	⊜	⊜
Cooling	⊜	⊜	⊜	⊜	⊜	⊜	⊜	⊜
Fuel	○	⊖	⊖	⊜	⊖	⊖	⊜	⊜
Ignition	⊜	⊜	⊜	⊖	⊖	⊜	⊜	⊜
Transmission	⊖	⊖	⊜	⊜	⊜	⊜	⊜	⊜
Electrical	◒	○	○	⊖	⊖	⊜	⊜	⊜
A/C	○	⊜	⊜	⊜	⊜	⊜	⊜	⊜
Suspension	⊖	⊖	⊖	⊜	⊜	⊜	⊖	⊜
Brakes	○	○	○	○	○	⊖	⊜	⊜
Exhaust	⊜	⊖	⊜	⊜	⊜	⊜	⊜	⊜
Power equip.	⊖	⊖	⊖	⊜	⊖	⊖	⊖	⊖
Paint/trim/rust	⊖	⊖	⊖	⊜	⊜	⊜	⊜	⊜
Integrity	⊜	⊖	⊖	⊖	⊖	⊖	⊖	⊜
Hardware	⊖	⊜	⊜	⊜	⊖	⊜	⊜	⊖
RELIABILITY VERDICT	✓	✓	✓	✓	✓	✓	✓	✓

Infiniti QX4

TROUBLE SPOTS	96	97	98	99	00	01	02	03
Engine		Insufficient data	⊜	⊜	Insufficient data	⊜	⊜	Insufficient data
Cooling			⊖	⊜		⊜	⊜	
Fuel			⊖	⊜		⊖	⊖	
Ignition			⊜	⊜		⊜	⊜	
Transmission			⊖	⊜		⊜	⊜	
Electrical			⊖	⊖		⊜	⊜	
A/C			⊜	⊖		⊜	⊜	
Suspension			⊖	⊜		⊜	⊜	
Brakes			⊜	⊜		⊖	⊖	
Exhaust			⊖	⊜		⊜	⊜	
Power equip.			⊜	⊜		⊖	⊖	
Paint/trim/rust			⊜	⊜		⊜	⊜	
Integrity			○	○		⊖	⊖	
Hardware			⊜	⊜		⊜	⊜	
RELIABILITY VERDICT			✓	✓		✓	✓	

Isuzu Rodeo

TROUBLE SPOTS	96	97	98	99	00	01	02	03
Engine	◒	◒	◒	◒	⊖	⊖	⊜	Insufficient data
Cooling	⊖	⊖	⊖	⊜	⊜	⊜	⊜	
Fuel	○	○	○	●	◒	⊖	⊜	
Ignition	⊖	○	⊜	⊖	⊖	⊖	⊜	
Transmission	⊖	○	⊖	○	⊖	⊜	⊜	
Electrical	●	●	◒	○	○	○	⊖	
A/C	⊖	○	○	○	⊜	⊜	⊜	
Suspension	⊖	⊖	○	⊖	⊖	⊖	⊖	
Brakes	○	◒	●	●	○	⊖	⊖	
Exhaust	⊜	⊖	⊖	⊖	⊜	⊜	⊖	
Power equip.	●	○	⊖	○	○	⊖	⊖	
Paint/trim/rust	◒	○	○	⊖	○	⊖	⊜	
Integrity	◒	●	◒	○	◒	◒	○	
Hardware	◒	○	○	○	○	⊜	⊜	
RELIABILITY VERDICT	-	-	✗	✗	-	-	✓	

Jaguar S-Type

TROUBLE SPOTS	96	97	98	99	00	01	02	03
Engine					⊖	⊖	Insufficient data	⊜
Cooling					○	⊖		⊜
Fuel					⊜	⊖		⊜
Ignition					⊖	⊜		⊜
Transmission					○	○		○
Electrical					◒	○		○
A/C					⊖	⊜		⊖
Suspension					○	○		⊜
Brakes					⊖	○		⊜
Exhaust					⊜	⊜		⊜
Power equip.					◒	◒		◒
Paint/trim/rust					⊖	⊜		⊜
Integrity					○	○		⊖
Hardware					○	⊖		⊜
RELIABILITY VERDICT					✗	✗		✗

Jaguar X-Type

TROUBLE SPOTS	96	97	98	99	00	01	02	03
Engine							⊖	⊜
Cooling							○	⊜
Fuel							○	⊖
Ignition							⊖	⊜
Transmission							○	⊖
Electrical							◒	⊜
A/C							⊖	⊜
Suspension							⊖	⊜
Brakes							⊖	⊜
Exhaust							⊜	⊜
Power equip.							◒	⊖
Paint/trim/rust							⊜	⊜
Integrity							◒	⊖
Hardware							◒	⊖
RELIABILITY VERDICT							✗	✗

Jaguar XJ6, XJ8, XJR

TROUBLE SPOTS	96	97	98	99	00	01	02	03
Engine	Insufficient data	Insufficient data	⊖	○	⊖	Insufficient data	Insufficient data	Insufficient data
Cooling			◒	◒	○			
Fuel			○	⊖	◒			
Ignition			⊖	⊖	○			
Transmission			⊖	⊖	○			
Electrical			◒	◒	◒			
A/C			⊜	⊜	⊜			
Suspension			⊖	○	●			
Brakes			⊖	○	○			
Exhaust			⊜	⊜	⊖			
Power equip.			◒	○	⊜			
Paint/trim/rust			⊜	⊜	⊜			
Integrity			⊖	○	⊖			
Hardware			⊖	⊜	⊖			
RELIABILITY VERDICT			-	✗	✗			

Jeep Cherokee

TROUBLE SPOTS	96	97	98	99	00	01	02	03
Engine	⊖	⊖	⊖	⊜	⊜	⊖		
Cooling	◒	◒	⊖	⊜	⊖	⊜		
Fuel	○	◒	⊖	⊖	⊖	⊖		
Ignition	⊖	⊖	⊜	⊜	⊜	⊖		
Transmission	⊖	⊖	⊖	⊖	⊖	⊜		
Electrical	○	◒	○	○	○	⊖		
A/C	○	●	◒	⊖	⊖	⊜		
Suspension	○	⊖	⊖	⊖	⊖	⊖		
Brakes	○	●	◒	◒	◒	◒		
Exhaust	○	⊖	⊜	⊜	⊖	⊜		
Power equip.	○	○	◒	●	○	⊜		
Paint/trim/rust	◒	○	○	○	⊖	⊖		
Integrity	◒	◒	○	○	○	○		
Hardware	○	○	⊖	○	○	⊜		
RELIABILITY VERDICT	-	-	-	-	-	-		

Jeep Grand Cherokee

TROUBLE SPOTS	96	97	98	99	00	01	02	03
Engine	○	○	⊖	⊖	⊖	⊖	⊜	⊜
Cooling	◒	○	○	○	⊖	⊜	⊜	⊜
Fuel	○	◒	○	○	⊖	⊖	⊖	⊜
Ignition	⊖	⊖	⊜	⊖	⊖	⊜	⊜	⊜
Transmission	◒	◒	◒	◒	○	○	⊖	⊖
Electrical	●	◒	◒	◒	○	○	⊖	⊖
A/C	●	◒	◒	○	⊖	⊖	⊜	⊜
Suspension	○	○	◒	○	○	○	⊖	⊖
Brakes	◒	●	●	●	●	●	◒	⊖
Exhaust	○	○	⊖	⊜	⊜	⊜	⊜	⊜
Power equip.	◒	○	○	●	○	◒	⊖	⊖
Paint/trim/rust	⊖	⊖	⊖	⊖	⊜	⊜	⊜	⊜
Integrity	◒	○	◒	◒	○	○	○	⊖
Hardware	○	○	○	○	○	⊖	⊖	⊜
RELIABILITY VERDICT	✗	✗	✗	✗	✗	✗	✗	✗

Jeep Liberty

TROUBLE SPOTS	96	97	98	99	00	01	02	03
Engine							⊜	⊜
Cooling							⊜	⊜
Fuel							⊜	⊜
Ignition							⊜	⊜
Transmission							⊖	⊜
Electrical							⊖	⊜
A/C							⊜	⊜
Suspension							⊖	⊜
Brakes							⊖	⊜
Exhaust							⊜	⊜
Power equip.							⊖	⊜
Paint/trim/rust							⊜	⊜
Integrity							⊖	⊖
Hardware							⊖	⊖
RELIABILITY VERDICT							-	✓

Jeep Wrangler

TROUBLE SPOTS	96	97	98	99	00	01	02	03
Engine		⊖	⊜	⊜	⊜	⊜	⊜	⊜
Cooling		○	○	⊖	⊖	⊖	⊜	⊜
Fuel		◒	⊖	⊖	⊖	⊖	⊖	⊜
Ignition		⊖	⊜	⊜	⊜	⊜	⊜	⊜
Transmission		⊖	○	○	⊖	⊖	⊜	⊖
Electrical		○	●	●	○	⊖	⊖	⊖
A/C		●	○	⊖	⊜	⊜	⊜	⊜
Suspension		○	○	⊖	⊖	⊜	⊜	⊜
Brakes		○	○	⊖	⊖	⊖	⊜	⊜
Exhaust		●	○	○	⊜	⊜	⊜	⊜
Power equip.		⊜	⊜	⊜	⊜	⊜	⊜	⊜
Paint/trim/rust		○	◒	○	◒	○	○	⊜
Integrity		◒	○	○	○	○	○	⊜
Hardware		○	○	⊖	○	⊖	⊖	⊜
RELIABILITY VERDICT		-	-	-	-	-	-	-

Kia Sedona

TROUBLE SPOTS	96	97	98	99	00	01	02	03
Engine							⊜	⊜
Cooling							⊜	⊜
Fuel							⊜	⊜
Ignition							⊜	⊜
Transmission							⊜	⊜
Electrical							○	⊜
A/C							○	◓
Suspension							◓	⊜
Brakes							◓	⊜
Exhaust							⊜	⊜
Power equip.							○	⊜
Paint/trim/rust							○	⊜
Integrity							◒	◓
Hardware							◒	◓
RELIABILITY VERDICT							✘	-

Kia Sorento

TROUBLE SPOTS	96	97	98	99	00	01	02	03
Engine								⊜
Cooling								⊜
Fuel								⊜
Ignition								⊜
Transmission								⊜
Electrical								◓
A/C								⊜
Suspension								⊜
Brakes								⊜
Exhaust								⊜
Power equip.								◓
Paint/trim/rust								◓
Integrity								⊜
Hardware								◓
RELIABILITY VERDICT								-

Land Rover Discovery

TROUBLE SPOTS	96	97	98	99	00	01	02	03
Engine	Insufficient data	Insufficient data	Insufficient data	Insufficient data	●	◓	Insufficient data	Insufficient data
Cooling					●	◓		
Fuel					◓	◓		
Ignition					⊜	⊜		
Transmission					◓	◓		
Electrical					◒	◒		
A/C					◓	⊜		
Suspension					◓	⊜		
Brakes					◒	○		
Exhaust					⊜	⊜		
Power equip.					◒	○		
Paint/trim/rust					◓	⊜		
Integrity					◒	◒		
Hardware					◒	◒		
RELIABILITY VERDICT					✘	✘		

Land Rover Freelander

TROUBLE SPOTS	96	97	98	99	00	01	02	03
Engine							◓	Insufficient data
Cooling							⊜	
Fuel							⊜	
Ignition							⊜	
Transmission							◓	
Electrical							○	
A/C							○	
Suspension							◓	
Brakes							◓	
Exhaust							⊜	
Power equip.							●	
Paint/trim/rust							◓	
Integrity							○	
Hardware							◓	
RELIABILITY VERDICT							✘	

Lexus ES300

TROUBLE SPOTS	96	97	98	99	00	01	02	03
Engine	○	◓	⊜	⊜	⊜	⊜	⊜	⊜
Cooling	⊜	⊜	⊜	⊜	⊜	⊜	⊜	⊜
Fuel	⊜	◓	◓	◓	⊜	⊜	⊜	⊜
Ignition	⊜	⊜	⊜	⊜	⊜	⊜	⊜	⊜
Transmission	◓	⊜	⊜	⊜	⊜	⊜	◓	⊜
Electrical	○	◓	◓	○	◓	⊜	⊜	⊜
A/C	◓	⊜	⊜	⊜	⊜	⊜	⊜	⊜
Suspension	◓	◓	◓	⊜	⊜	⊜	⊜	⊜
Brakes	○	◓	⊜	⊜	◓	◓	◒	⊜
Exhaust	⊜	⊜	⊜	⊜	⊜	⊜	⊜	⊜
Power equip.	○	◓	◓	⊜	⊜	◓	◓	⊜
Paint/trim/rust	◓	◓	⊜	⊜	◓	◓	⊜	⊜
Integrity	◓	◓	◓	◓	◓	◓	◓	◓
Hardware	◓	◓	◓	◓	⊜	◓	⊜	⊜
RELIABILITY VERDICT	✔	✔	✔	✔	✔	✔	-	✔

Lexus GS300/GS400, GS430

TROUBLE SPOTS	96	97	98	99	00	01	02	03
Engine	Insufficient data	Insufficient data	⊜	⊜	⊜	⊜	⊜	⊜
Cooling			⊜	⊜	⊜	⊜	⊜	⊜
Fuel			◓	◓	⊜	⊜	⊜	⊜
Ignition			⊜	⊜	⊜	⊜	⊜	⊜
Transmission			⊜	⊜	⊜	⊜	⊜	⊜
Electrical			◓	◓	◓	◓	⊜	⊜
A/C			⊜	⊜	⊜	⊜	⊜	⊜
Suspension			◓	⊜	⊜	◓	⊜	⊜
Brakes			◓	◓	◓	◓	⊜	⊜
Exhaust			⊜	⊜	⊜	⊜	⊜	⊜
Power equip.			○	○	◓	◓	⊜	⊜
Paint/trim/rust			◓	⊜	⊜	◓	⊜	⊜
Integrity			◓	◓	◓	○	◓	⊜
Hardware			⊜	⊜	⊜	⊜	⊜	⊜
RELIABILITY VERDICT			✔	✔	✔	✔	✔	✔

Lexus GX470

TROUBLE SPOTS	96	97	98	99	00	01	02	03
Engine								⊜
Cooling								⊜
Fuel								⊜
Ignition								⊜
Transmission								⊜
Electrical								◓
A/C								◓
Suspension								⊜
Brakes								◓
Exhaust								⊜
Power equip.								⊜
Paint/trim/rust								⊜
Integrity								⊜
Hardware								◓
RELIABILITY VERDICT								-

Lexus IS300

TROUBLE SPOTS	96	97	98	99	00	01	02	03
Engine						⊜	⊜	Insufficient data
Cooling						⊜	⊜	
Fuel						◓	⊜	
Ignition						⊜	⊜	
Transmission						⊜	⊜	
Electrical						◓	◓	
A/C						⊜	⊜	
Suspension						◓	◓	
Brakes						⊜	⊜	
Exhaust						⊜	⊜	
Power equip.						◓	⊜	
Paint/trim/rust						◓	⊜	
Integrity						◓	○	
Hardware						◓	◓	
RELIABILITY VERDICT						✔	✔	

TROUBLE SPOTS	Lexus LS400, LS430 96	97	98	99	00	01	02	03
Engine	⊜	⊜	⊜	⊜	⊜	⊜	⊜	⊜
Cooling	⊜	⊜	⊜	⊜	⊜	⊜	⊜	⊜
Fuel	⊜	⊜	⊜	⊜	⊜	⊜	⊜	⊜
Ignition	⊜	⊜	⊜	⊜	⊜	⊜	⊜	⊜
Transmission	⊜	⊜	⊜	⊜	⊜	⊜	⊜	⊜
Electrical	⊖	⊖	⊖	⊖	⊖	⊖	⊖	⊜
A/C	⊖	⊜	⊜	⊜	⊜	⊜	⊜	⊜
Suspension	○	○	⊖	⊖	⊜	⊖	⊜	⊜
Brakes	○	⊜	⊜	⊖	⊜	⊖	⊖	⊜
Exhaust	⊜	⊜	⊜	⊜	⊜	⊜	⊜	⊜
Power equip.	○	⊖	⊜	⊖	⊖	○	⊜	⊜
Paint/trim/rust	⊜	⊜	⊜	⊜	⊜	⊜	⊜	⊜
Integrity	⊜	⊜	⊜	⊜	⊖	⊜	⊖	⊜
Hardware	⊖	⊜	⊜	⊜	⊜	⊖	⊜	⊜
RELIABILITY VERDICT	✔	✔	✔	✔	✔	✔	✔	✔

TROUBLE SPOTS	Lexus RX300 96	97	98	99	00	01	02	03
Engine				⊖	⊜	⊜	⊜	⊜
Cooling				⊜	⊜	⊜	⊜	⊜
Fuel				⊖	⊜	⊜	⊜	⊜
Ignition				⊜	⊜	⊜	⊜	⊜
Transmission				⊖	⊜	⊜	⊜	⊜
Electrical				○	⊖	⊜	⊜	⊜
A/C				⊜	⊜	⊜	⊜	⊜
Suspension				⊖	⊜	⊜	⊜	⊜
Brakes				⊖	⊖	⊜	⊜	⊜
Exhaust				⊖	⊜	⊜	⊜	⊜
Power equip.				⊖	⊜	⊜	⊜	⊜
Paint/trim/rust				⊖	⊜	⊜	⊜	⊜
Integrity				⊖	⊖	⊖	⊖	⊜
Hardware				⊖	⊖	⊜	⊜	⊜
RELIABILITY VERDICT				✔	✔	✔	✔	✔

TROUBLE SPOTS	Lexus SC300/SC400, SC430 96	97	98	99	00	01	02	03
	Insufficient data	Insufficient data	Insufficient data	Insufficient data	Insufficient data	Insufficient data		Insufficient data
Engine							⊜	
Cooling							⊜	
Fuel							⊜	
Ignition							⊜	
Transmission							⊜	
Electrical							⊖	
A/C							⊜	
Suspension							⊖	
Brakes							⊜	
Exhaust							⊜	
Power equip.							⊖	
Paint/trim/rust							⊜	
Integrity							⊖	
Hardware							⊖	
RELIABILITY VERDICT							✔	

TROUBLE SPOTS	Lincoln Continental 96	97	98	99	00	01	02	03
Engine	⊜	⊖	⊜	⊜	⊜	⊖	⊜	
Cooling	⊖	⊖	⊖	⊜	⊜	⊜	⊜	
Fuel	○	○	⊖	⊖	⊖	⊜	⊜	
Ignition	◒	⊖	⊖	⊖	⊜	⊜	⊜	
Transmission	◒	○	⊖	⊖	⊜	⊜	⊜	
Electrical	●	●	○	○	○	○	⊖	
A/C	⊖	○	⊜	⊖	⊜	⊖	⊖	
Suspension	●	●	○	◒	⊖	⊖	⊖	
Brakes	○	○	○	◒	○	○	⊖	
Exhaust	⊜	⊜	⊜	⊜	⊜	⊜	⊜	
Power equip.	◒	◒	○	○	◒	◒	⊖	
Paint/trim/rust	⊖	○	⊜	⊜	⊖	⊖	⊜	
Integrity	●	○	⊖	⊖	⊖	○	○	
Hardware	●	○	⊖	○	○	⊖	⊖	
RELIABILITY VERDICT	–	–	✔	✔	✔	–	–	

TROUBLE SPOTS	Lincoln LS 96	97	98	99	00	01	02	03
								Insufficient data
Engine					⊜	⊖	⊜	
Cooling					⊖	⊜	⊜	
Fuel					⊖	⊜	⊖	
Ignition					⊜	⊖	⊜	
Transmission					⊖	⊜	⊜	
Electrical					○	○	⊖	
A/C					⊖	⊖	⊜	
Suspension					⊖	⊜	⊖	
Brakes					⊖	⊜	⊖	
Exhaust					⊜	⊜	⊜	
Power equip.					●	○	○	
Paint/trim/rust					⊖	⊖	⊜	
Integrity					◒	○	○	
Hardware					○	○	⊖	
RELIABILITY VERDICT					–	–	–	

TROUBLE SPOTS	Lincoln Navigator 96	97	98	99	00	01	02	03
							Insufficient data	
Engine			⊜	⊖	⊜	⊜		⊜
Cooling			⊜	⊜	⊜	⊜		⊜
Fuel			⊖	⊖	⊖	⊜		⊜
Ignition			⊖	⊜	⊜	⊖		⊖
Transmission			○	⊖	⊜	⊜		⊜
Electrical			◒	◒	⊖	○		○
A/C			⊜	⊖	⊖	⊜		⊜
Suspension			◒	○	○	⊖		⊖
Brakes			◒	○	○	⊖		⊖
Exhaust			⊖	⊜	⊜	⊜		⊜
Power equip.			○	◒	○	◒		◒
Paint/trim/rust			⊖	○	⊖	○		⊖
Integrity			◒	◒	○	◒		⊖
Hardware			⊖	○	○	◒		⊖
RELIABILITY VERDICT			–	–	✔	–		✘

TROUBLE SPOTS	Lincoln Town Car 96	97	98	99	00	01	02	03
Engine	⊖	⊖	⊜	⊜	⊖	⊜	⊜	⊜
Cooling	⊖	⊖	⊜	⊜	⊜	⊜	⊜	⊜
Fuel	○	○	⊜	⊖	⊖	⊖	⊜	⊜
Ignition	⊖	⊖	⊜	⊖	⊖	⊖	⊜	⊜
Transmission	⊖	⊖	⊜	⊜	⊖	⊜	⊜	⊜
Electrical	○	◒	○	○	○	○	⊜	⊖
A/C	○	○	○	⊜	⊖	⊜	⊜	⊜
Suspension	◒	○	○	⊜	⊖	⊜	⊜	⊜
Brakes	◒	◒	○	○	○	⊖	⊜	⊜
Exhaust	⊖	⊖	⊜	⊜	⊜	⊜	⊜	⊜
Power equip.	◒	◒	●	◒	○	○	⊖	⊖
Paint/trim/rust	○	⊖	⊖	⊖	⊖	⊖	⊖	⊖
Integrity	○	○	○	○	⊖	○	⊖	○
Hardware	○	○	○	○	⊖	⊖	⊜	⊜
RELIABILITY VERDICT	✔	✔	✔	✔	✔	✔	✔	✘

TROUBLE SPOTS	Mazda 626, Mazda6 96	97	98	99	00	01	02	03
Engine	○	○	⊖	⊜	⊜	⊜	⊜	⊜
Cooling	◒	◒	⊖	⊖	⊜	⊜	⊜	⊜
Fuel	◒	◒	○	⊖	⊖	⊜	⊜	⊖
Ignition	⊖	⊖	⊖	⊖	⊜	⊜	⊜	⊜
Transmission	◒	○	○	○	⊖	⊖	⊜	⊜
Electrical	◒	○	○	○	⊖	○	⊖	⊜
A/C	⊖	⊜	⊜	⊖	○	⊖	⊖	⊜
Suspension	○	○	⊜	⊖	⊖	⊖	⊖	⊜
Brakes	○	○	○	○	⊖	⊖	⊖	⊜
Exhaust	◒	◒	⊖	⊜	⊜	⊜	⊜	⊜
Power equip.	⊖	⊖	⊖	⊖	⊖	⊖	⊖	⊖
Paint/trim/rust	○	⊖	⊖	⊖	⊖	⊖	⊜	⊜
Integrity	○	⊖	○	○	○	⊜	○	⊜
Hardware	○	⊜	⊖	⊖	⊖	⊖	⊖	⊜
RELIABILITY VERDICT	–	–	✔	✔	✔	✔	✔	✔

Mazda B-Series 4WD

TROUBLE SPOTS	96	97	98	99	00	01	02	03
Engine	⊜	⊜	⊜	⊜	⊜	⊜	⊜	⊜
Cooling	○	○	○	⊜	⊜	⊜	⊜	⊜
Fuel	○	○	○	⊜	⊜	⊜	⊜	⊜
Ignition	⊜	⊜	⊜	⊜	⊜	⊜	⊜	⊜
Transmission	○	⊜	○	⊜	○	⊜	○	⊜
Electrical	◒	●	●	◒	○	○	⊜	○
A/C	○	◒	⊜	⊜	⊜	⊜	⊜	⊜
Suspension	⊜	⊜	○	○	⊜	⊜	⊜	⊜
Brakes	◒	○	◒	◒	◒	⊜	⊜	⊜
Exhaust	⊜	⊜	⊜	⊜	⊜	⊜	⊜	⊜
Power equip.	○	○	○	⊜	○	⊜	⊜	⊜
Paint/trim/rust	⊜	⊜	⊜	⊜	⊜	⊜	⊜	⊜
Integrity	○	○	○	⊜	○	○	○	⊜
Hardware	⊜	⊜	○	⊜	○	○	⊜	⊜
RELIABILITY VERDICT	-	-	-	-	✘	✘	✘	-

Mazda MPV

TROUBLE SPOTS	96	97	98	99	00	01	02	03
Engine	Insufficient data	Insufficient data	Insufficient data		⊜	⊜	⊜	⊜
Cooling					⊜	⊜	⊜	⊜
Fuel					⊜	⊜	⊜	⊜
Ignition					⊜	⊜	⊜	⊜
Transmission					⊜	⊜	⊜	⊜
Electrical					⊜	⊜	⊜	⊜
A/C					⊜	⊜	⊜	⊜
Suspension					⊜	⊜	⊜	⊜
Brakes					⊜	⊜	⊜	⊜
Exhaust					⊜	⊜	⊜	⊜
Power equip.					⊜	⊜	⊜	⊜
Paint/trim/rust					⊜	⊜	⊜	⊜
Integrity					○	⊜	⊜	⊜
Hardware					○	⊜	⊜	⊜
RELIABILITY VERDICT					✔	✔	✔	-

Mazda MX-5 Miata

TROUBLE SPOTS	96	97	98	99	00	01	02	03
Engine	⊜	⊜		⊜	⊜	⊜	⊜	Insufficient data
Cooling	⊜	⊜		⊜	⊜	⊜	⊜	
Fuel	⊜	⊜		○	⊜	⊜	⊜	
Ignition	⊜	⊜		⊜	⊜	⊜	⊜	
Transmission	⊜	⊜		⊜	⊜	⊜	⊜	
Electrical	⊜	○		⊜	⊜	⊜	⊜	
A/C	⊜	○		⊜	⊜	⊜	⊜	
Suspension	⊜	⊜		⊜	⊜	⊜	⊜	
Brakes	⊜	⊜		⊜	⊜	⊜	⊜	
Exhaust	⊜	⊜		⊜	⊜	⊜	⊜	
Power equip.	○	○		⊜	⊜	⊜	⊜	
Paint/trim/rust	⊜	○		⊜	⊜	⊜	⊜	
Integrity	○	⊜		⊜	○	⊜	⊜	
Hardware	⊜	⊜		⊜	⊜	⊜	⊜	
RELIABILITY VERDICT	✔	✔		✔	✔	✔	✔	

Mazda Millenia

TROUBLE SPOTS	96	97	98	99	00	01	02	03
Engine	Insufficient data	Insufficient data	⊜	⊜	⊜	⊜	⊜	
Cooling			⊜	⊜	⊜	⊜	⊜	
Fuel			◒	◒	○	⊜	⊜	
Ignition			⊜	⊜	⊜	⊜	⊜	
Transmission			⊜	⊜	⊜	⊜	⊜	
Electrical			○	⊜	⊜	⊜	⊜	
A/C			⊜	⊜	⊜	⊜	⊜	
Suspension			⊜	○	⊜	⊜	⊜	
Brakes			⊜	⊜	⊜	⊜	⊜	
Exhaust			⊜	⊜	⊜	⊜	⊜	
Power equip.			○	○	⊜	⊜	⊜	
Paint/trim/rust			⊜	⊜	⊜	⊜	⊜	
Integrity			⊜	⊜	○	⊜	⊜	
Hardware			⊜	⊜	⊜	⊜	⊜	
RELIABILITY VERDICT			✔	✔	✔	✔	✔	

Mazda Protege

TROUBLE SPOTS	96	97	98	99	00	01	02	03
Engine	⊜	⊜	⊜	⊜	⊜	⊜	⊜	⊜
Cooling	○	⊜	⊜	⊜	⊜	⊜	⊜	⊜
Fuel	○	○	○	○	⊜	⊜	⊜	⊜
Ignition	⊜	⊜	⊜	⊜	⊜	⊜	⊜	⊜
Transmission	⊜	⊜	⊜	⊜	⊜	⊜	⊜	⊜
Electrical	○	○	⊜	⊜	⊜	⊜	⊜	⊜
A/C	◒	○	⊜	⊜	⊜	⊜	⊜	⊜
Suspension	⊜	⊜	⊜	⊜	⊜	⊜	⊜	⊜
Brakes	◒	◒	○	⊜	⊜	⊜	⊜	⊜
Exhaust	◒	○	○	⊜	⊜	⊜	⊜	⊜
Power equip.	⊜	⊜	⊜	⊜	○	○	⊜	⊜
Paint/trim/rust	○	⊜	⊜	⊜	⊜	⊜	⊜	⊜
Integrity	○	○	○	○	○	⊜	⊜	⊜
Hardware	⊜	○	◒	⊜	⊜	⊜	⊜	⊜
RELIABILITY VERDICT	✔	✔	✔	✔	✔	✔	✔	✔

Mazda Tribute

TROUBLE SPOTS	96	97	98	99	00	01	02	03
Engine						⊜	⊜	⊜
Cooling						⊜	⊜	⊜
Fuel						○	⊜	⊜
Ignition						⊜	⊜	⊜
Transmission						⊜	⊜	⊜
Electrical						○	⊜	⊜
A/C						⊜	⊜	⊜
Suspension						⊜	⊜	⊜
Brakes						○	⊜	⊜
Exhaust						⊜	⊜	⊜
Power equip.						⊜	⊜	⊜
Paint/trim/rust						⊜	⊜	⊜
Integrity						◒	○	⊜
Hardware						⊜	⊜	⊜
RELIABILITY VERDICT						✘	-	✔

Mercedes-Benz C-Class

TROUBLE SPOTS	96	97	98	99	00	01	02	03
Engine	○	○	⊜	⊜	⊜	⊜	⊜	⊜
Cooling	⊜	⊜	⊜	⊜	⊜	⊜	⊜	⊜
Fuel	◒	◒	◒	○	○	○	○	⊜
Ignition	⊜	⊜	⊜	⊜	⊜	⊜	⊜	⊜
Transmission	⊜	○	○	⊜	⊜	⊜	⊜	⊜
Electrical	●	◒	◒	◒	◒	●	◒	⊜
A/C	○	◒	○	○	⊜	⊜	⊜	⊜
Suspension	○	○	⊜	○	⊜	○	⊜	⊜
Brakes	○	○	⊜	⊜	⊜	⊜	⊜	⊜
Exhaust	⊜	⊜	⊜	⊜	⊜	⊜	⊜	⊜
Power equip.	○	⊜	○	○	○	●	◒	⊜
Paint/trim/rust	⊜	⊜	⊜	⊜	⊜	⊜	⊜	⊜
Integrity	○	⊜	⊜	○	○	◒	⊜	⊜
Hardware	⊜	⊜	○	○	⊜	◒	○	⊜
RELIABILITY VERDICT	✔	✔	-	-	-	✘	✘	✘

Mercedes-Benz CLK

TROUBLE SPOTS	96	97	98	99	00	01	02	03
Engine			Insufficient data	○	⊜	⊜	⊜	Insufficient data
Cooling				⊜	⊜	⊜	⊜	
Fuel				◒	⊜	⊜	⊜	
Ignition				○	⊜	⊜	⊜	
Transmission				⊜	○	⊜	⊜	
Electrical				●	◒	○	○	
A/C				○	◒	○	⊜	
Suspension				⊜	⊜	⊜	⊜	
Brakes				○	○	⊜	⊜	
Exhaust				⊜	⊜	⊜	⊜	
Power equip.				◒	◒	●	◒	
Paint/trim/rust				⊜	⊜	⊜	⊜	
Integrity				◒	⊜	○	○	
Hardware				●	○	○	⊜	
RELIABILITY VERDICT				-	-	-	✘	

Mercedes-Benz E-Class

TROUBLE SPOTS	96	97	98	99	00	01	02	03
Engine	◒	○	○	○	⊖	⊜	⊜	⊜
Cooling	⊖	⊖	⊜	⊖	⊜	⊜	⊜	⊜
Fuel	○	○	○	○	○	⊖	⊖	⊖
Ignition	○	⊖	⊖	⊖	⊜	⊜	⊜	⊜
Transmission	⊜	○	○	○	⊖	⊖	⊜	⊜
Electrical	●	●	●	●	●	◒	○	○
A/C	◒	◒	○	⊖	○	◒	○	⊜
Suspension	◒	○	⊖	⊖	⊖	○	⊜	⊜
Brakes	○	○	⊖	○	○	⊖	⊖	⊖
Exhaust	⊖	⊜	⊖	⊜	⊜	⊜	⊖	⊜
Power equip.	◒	◒	●	●	◒	◒	⊖	◒
Paint/trim/rust	○	⊖	⊜	⊖	⊜	⊜	⊜	⊜
Integrity	⊖	⊖	⊖	○	○	⊖	⊜	⊜
Hardware	○	○	○	○	○	○	⊖	⊜
RELIABILITY VERDICT	-	-	-	-	-	-	-	✗

Mercedes-Benz M-Class

TROUBLE SPOTS	96	97	98	99	00	01	02	03
Engine			○	⊖	⊖	⊖	⊜	⊜
Cooling			⊖	⊜	⊖	⊖	○	⊜
Fuel			●	◒	◒	○	⊖	⊜
Ignition			⊖	⊖	⊖	⊖	⊜	⊜
Transmission			○	⊖	⊖	⊖	⊖	⊜
Electrical			●	◒	●	●	◒	⊖
A/C			○	⊖	⊖	⊖	⊜	⊜
Suspension			○	○	◒	◒	⊖	⊜
Brakes			○	○	●	◒	○	⊜
Exhaust			⊖	⊜	⊖	⊜	⊜	⊜
Power equip.			●	●	●	●	◒	○
Paint/trim/rust			○	⊖	○	○	⊖	⊜
Integrity			●	●	●	●	○	⊜
Hardware			●	●	●	◒	○	⊜
RELIABILITY VERDICT			✗	✗	✗	✗	✗	-

Mercedes-Benz S-Class

TROUBLE SPOTS	96	97	98	99	00	01	02	03
Engine	Insufficient data	Insufficient data	Insufficient data	Insufficient data	⊜	⊜	⊖	Insufficient data
Cooling					⊜	⊖	⊜	
Fuel					⊖	⊖	⊖	
Ignition					⊜	⊜	⊜	
Transmission					⊖	⊜	⊖	
Electrical					●	◒	○	
A/C					◒	⊜	⊖	
Suspension					◒	⊖	⊖	
Brakes					◒	○	⊖	
Exhaust					⊜	⊜	⊜	
Power equip.					●	◒	◒	
Paint/trim/rust					⊖	⊜	⊜	
Integrity					○	⊖	⊖	
Hardware					○	⊖	⊖	
RELIABILITY VERDICT					✗	-	✗	

Mercedes-Benz SLK

TROUBLE SPOTS	96	97	98	99	00	01	02	03
Engine			⊖	⊖	Insufficient data	⊜	⊜	Insufficient data
Cooling			⊜	⊜		⊖	⊜	
Fuel			◒	⊖		○	⊖	
Ignition			⊜	⊜		⊜	⊖	
Transmission			⊜	⊜		⊖	⊜	
Electrical			●	●		○	⊖	
A/C			⊜	⊜		⊜	○	
Suspension			⊖	⊖		⊖	⊖	
Brakes			⊜	⊖		⊜	⊜	
Exhaust			⊜	⊜		⊖	⊖	
Power equip.			⊖	◒		○	○	
Paint/trim/rust			⊜	⊖		⊜	⊖	
Integrity			○	○		◒	◒	
Hardware			⊖	○		○	◒	
RELIABILITY VERDICT			✓	-		-	✗	

Mercury Cougar

TROUBLE SPOTS	96	97	98	99	00	01	02	03
Engine	○	○		○	○	Insufficient data	⊜	
Cooling	●	◒		⊖	⊖		⊜	
Fuel	◒	○		◒	●		⊖	
Ignition	○	⊖		⊖	⊖		⊜	
Transmission	◒	○		⊖	⊖		⊜	
Electrical	◒	◒		●	◒		○	
A/C	○	⊖		○	⊖		⊜	
Suspension	○	⊖		⊖	⊖		⊜	
Brakes	◒	○		●	○		⊖	
Exhaust	⊖	⊖		⊖	⊜		⊜	
Power equip.	○	○		◒	○		⊜	
Paint/trim/rust	⊖	○		○	⊖		⊜	
Integrity	○	⊖		◒	●		○	
Hardware	○	⊖		◒	⊖		⊖	
RELIABILITY VERDICT	-	-		✗	✗		-	

Mercury Grand Marquis

TROUBLE SPOTS	96	97	98	99	00	01	02	03
Engine	○	⊖	⊜	⊜	⊜	⊖	⊜	⊜
Cooling	○	⊖	⊜	⊜	⊜	⊜	⊜	⊜
Fuel	◒	○	⊖	⊖	⊖	○	⊜	⊜
Ignition	○	⊖	⊜	⊖	⊖	⊖	⊜	⊜
Transmission	⊖	⊖	⊖	⊜	⊖	⊜	⊜	⊜
Electrical	◒	○	○	○	○	○	⊖	⊖
A/C	○	⊖	⊜	⊖	⊖	⊖	⊜	⊜
Suspension	○	○	○	⊖	⊖	⊖	⊖	⊖
Brakes	◒	◒	○	○	⊖	⊖	⊜	⊜
Exhaust	○	⊖	⊜	⊜	⊜	⊜	⊜	⊜
Power equip.	●	◒	⊖	○	○	○	⊖	⊖
Paint/trim/rust	⊖	⊖	⊖	⊖	⊖	⊖	⊖	⊜
Integrity	○	○	⊖	○	◒	◒	○	○
Hardware	○	⊖	⊜	⊖	○	○	⊖	⊖
RELIABILITY VERDICT	-	✓	✓	✓	✓	-	-	✗

Mercury Mountaineer 4WD

TROUBLE SPOTS	96	97	98	99	00	01	02	03
Engine		○	○	⊖	⊖	⊖	⊜	⊜
Cooling		○	○	⊖	○	⊜	⊜	⊜
Fuel		○	○	○	○	⊖	⊜	⊜
Ignition		⊖	⊖	⊖	⊖	⊜	⊜	⊜
Transmission		○	○	⊜	○	⊖	⊖	⊜
Electrical		○	◒	◒	◒	○	⊖	⊖
A/C		◒	○	⊖	⊜	⊖	⊜	⊜
Suspension		○	○	○	⊖	⊖	⊖	⊜
Brakes		◒	○	◒	○	⊖	⊜	⊜
Exhaust		⊖	⊜	⊜	⊜	⊜	⊜	⊜
Power equip.		○	◒	○	○	⊖	⊖	⊜
Paint/trim/rust		○	⊖	⊖	⊖	⊖	⊖	⊜
Integrity		○	○	○	○	○	○	⊜
Hardware		○	○	○	⊖	○	○	⊖
RELIABILITY VERDICT		-	✗	✗	✗	✗	✗	-

Mercury Mystique V6

TROUBLE SPOTS	96	97	98	99	00	01	02	03
Engine	◒	Insufficient data	⊖	○	⊖			
Cooling	●		○	⊜	⊜			
Fuel	●		◒	◒	●			
Ignition	○		⊖	⊜	⊖			
Transmission	○		○	⊖	⊖			
Electrical	◒		◒	◒	○			
A/C	○		○	○	⊖			
Suspension	○		◒	⊖	⊖			
Brakes	◒		◒	◒	○			
Exhaust	◒		○	⊖	⊜			
Power equip.	◒		○	⊖	⊖			
Paint/trim/rust	⊖		⊖	⊜	⊖			
Integrity	○		○	●	●			
Hardware	⊖		○	○	◒			
RELIABILITY VERDICT	✗		✗	-	✗			

Mercury Sable

TROUBLE SPOTS	96	97	98	99	00	01	02	03
Engine	○	○	⊖	⊖	⊖	⊜	⊜	⊜
Cooling	◒	○	⊖	⊖	⊜	⊜	⊜	⊜
Fuel	◒	○	○	○	○	○	⊖	⊜
Ignition	⊖	⊖	⊖	⊜	⊖	⊖	⊜	⊜
Transmission	◒	○	○	○	⊖	⊖	⊖	⊜
Electrical	◒	●	●	◒	◒	○	⊖	⊖
A/C	○	○	⊖	⊖	⊖	⊖	⊜	⊜
Suspension	◒	○	○	○	○	○	⊖	⊜
Brakes	◒	◒	●	◒	◒	○	⊖	⊜
Exhaust	⊖	⊖	⊜	⊜	⊜	⊜	⊜	⊜
Power equip.	○	◒	○	○	⊖	⊖	⊖	⊜
Paint/trim/rust	○	⊖	⊖	⊖	⊖	⊜	⊜	⊜
Integrity	◒	○	○	○	○	○	○	⊖
Hardware	○	○	○	⊖	⊖	⊖	⊖	⊜
RELIABILITY VERDICT	–	–	–	–	–	–	–	–

Mercury Tracer

TROUBLE SPOTS	96	97	98	99	00	01	02	03
Engine	◒	⊖	⊖	⊖				
Cooling	◒	◒	○	⊜				
Fuel	○	○	⊖	⊖				
Ignition	○	⊜	⊜	⊖				
Transmission	⊖	⊖	⊖	⊖				
Electrical	◒	○	⊖	○				
A/C	○	○	⊖	⊖				
Suspension	○	◒	○	⊖				
Brakes	◒	◒	○	○				
Exhaust	○	⊖	⊜	⊜				
Power equip.	⊖	⊜	⊖	⊖				
Paint/trim/rust	◒	⊖	⊖	⊖				
Integrity	○	○	○	⊖				
Hardware	◒	⊜	⊜	⊖				
RELIABILITY VERDICT	–	–	✓	✓				

Mercury Villager

TROUBLE SPOTS	96	97	98	99	00	01	02	03
Engine	⊖	⊜	⊖	⊖	⊜	⊜	⊜	
Cooling	○	⊖	⊜	⊜	⊜	⊜	⊜	
Fuel	◒	◒	⊖	○	⊖	⊜	⊜	
Ignition	⊖	⊖	⊜	⊜	⊜	⊜	⊜	
Transmission	⊖	⊜	⊜	⊜	⊜	⊜	⊜	
Electrical	●	◒	○	◒	○	○	⊖	
A/C	◒	◒	○	⊖	⊖	⊖	⊜	
Suspension	○	○	○	○	⊖	⊖	⊖	
Brakes	◒	◒	◒	○	○	⊖	⊖	
Exhaust	⊖	⊖	⊜	⊜	⊜	⊜	⊜	
Power equip.	●	●	●	◒	○	◒	⊖	
Paint/trim/rust	○	○	⊖	⊖	⊖	⊖	⊜	
Integrity	◒	○	◒	◒	○	◒	◒	
Hardware	●	●	◒	○	○	◒	○	
RELIABILITY VERDICT	–	–	–	–	✓	–	–	

Mini Cooper

TROUBLE SPOTS	96	97	98	99	00	01	02	03
Engine							⊜	⊜
Cooling							○	⊖
Fuel							⊖	⊜
Ignition							⊖	⊜
Transmission							○	⊖
Electrical							○	⊖
A/C							⊜	⊜
Suspension							⊖	⊜
Brakes							⊜	⊜
Exhaust							⊜	⊜
Power equip.							⊖	⊖
Paint/trim/rust							⊜	⊜
Integrity							◒	⊖
Hardware							◒	⊖
RELIABILITY VERDICT							✗	✗

Mitsubishi Eclipse

TROUBLE SPOTS	96	97	98	99	00	01	02	03
Engine	Insufficient data	Insufficient data	Insufficient data	Insufficient data	⊜	⊜	⊜	⊜
Cooling					⊜	⊜	⊜	⊜
Fuel					⊜	⊖	⊜	⊖
Ignition					⊜	⊜	⊜	⊜
Transmission					⊜	⊜	⊖	⊜
Electrical					⊖	⊖	⊜	⊖
A/C					⊖	⊜	⊜	⊜
Suspension					⊖	⊜	⊜	⊜
Brakes					⊖	⊖	⊖	⊜
Exhaust					⊜	⊜	⊜	⊜
Power equip.					○	○	⊖	⊜
Paint/trim/rust					⊖	⊖	⊖	⊜
Integrity					○	○	⊖	○
Hardware					○	○	◒	⊖
RELIABILITY VERDICT					✓	✓	–	✗

Mitsubishi Galant

TROUBLE SPOTS	96	97	98	99	00	01	02	03
Engine	◒	Insufficient data	Insufficient data	⊖	⊜	⊜	⊖	Insufficient data
Cooling	○			⊖	⊜	⊜	⊜	
Fuel	⊜			⊖	⊜	⊜	⊖	
Ignition	⊖			⊖	⊜	⊜	⊜	
Transmission	●			⊖	⊜	⊜	⊜	
Electrical	◒			○	○	⊖	○	
A/C	●			⊜	⊜	⊜	⊖	
Suspension	○			○	⊜	⊖	⊖	
Brakes	○			●	○	○	○	
Exhaust	⊖			⊜	⊜	⊖	⊖	
Power equip.	◒			⊜	⊜	⊖	⊜	
Paint/trim/rust	◒			○	○	⊖	⊜	
Integrity	◒			◒	○	◒	⊖	
Hardware	○			○	⊖	⊖	⊖	
RELIABILITY VERDICT	✗			–	✓	–	✗	

Nissan 350Z

TROUBLE SPOTS	96	97	98	99	00	01	02	03
Engine								⊜
Cooling								⊜
Fuel								⊜
Ignition								⊜
Transmission								⊜
Electrical								⊜
A/C								⊜
Suspension								⊖
Brakes								⊜
Exhaust								⊜
Power equip.								⊖
Paint/trim/rust								⊜
Integrity								⊖
Hardware								⊜
RELIABILITY VERDICT								✓

Nissan Altima 4-cyl.

TROUBLE SPOTS	96	97	98	99	00	01	02	03
Engine	○	○	⊖	⊜	⊜	⊜	⊜	⊜
Cooling	⊖	⊖	⊖	⊜	⊜	⊜	⊜	⊜
Fuel	○	⊖	⊖	⊜	⊜	⊜	⊖	⊜
Ignition	⊖	⊖	⊜	⊜	⊜	⊜	⊖	⊜
Transmission	⊖	⊖	⊜	⊜	⊜	⊜	⊜	⊜
Electrical	◒	◒	⊖	⊖	○	⊜	⊖	⊜
A/C	⊖	⊖	⊖	⊖	⊖	⊜	⊜	⊜
Suspension	⊖	⊖	⊖	⊖	⊖	⊖	⊖	⊜
Brakes	○	○	○	○	⊖	⊖	⊜	⊜
Exhaust	○	⊖	⊜	⊜	⊜	⊜	⊜	⊜
Power equip.	⊖	○	⊖	⊖	○	○	⊖	⊜
Paint/trim/rust	○	◒	⊖	⊖	⊖	⊖	⊜	⊜
Integrity	◒	◒	○	⊖	○	○	○	⊜
Hardware	○	○	⊖	⊖	⊖	⊜	⊖	⊜
RELIABILITY VERDICT	✓	✓	✓	✓	✓	✓	–	✓

Nissan Maxima

TROUBLE SPOTS	96	97	98	99	00	01	02	03
Engine	⊜	⊜	⊜	⊜	⊜	⊜	⊜	⊜
Cooling	⊜	⊜	⊜	⊜	⊜	⊜	⊜	⊜
Fuel	○	○	⊖	⊖	⊖	⊖	⊜	⊜
Ignition	⊖	⊖	⊖	○	⊖	⊜	⊜	⊜
Transmission	⊜	⊜	⊜	⊜	⊜	⊜	⊜	⊜
Electrical	○	◒	○	○	⊖	⊜	⊖	⊜
A/C	⊖	⊖	⊜	⊜	⊜	⊜	⊜	⊜
Suspension	⊖	⊖	⊖	⊜	⊜	⊜	⊖	⊜
Brakes	○	○	○	◒	○	○	⊖	⊜
Exhaust	⊜	⊜	⊜	⊜	⊜	⊜	⊜	⊜
Power equip.	⊖	⊖	⊖	⊖	⊖	⊖	⊖	⊜
Paint/trim/rust	⊖	⊖	⊖	⊜	⊖	⊖	⊖	⊜
Integrity	⊖	⊖	⊖	⊖	⊖	⊖	○	⊖
Hardware	⊖	⊜	⊜	⊜	⊜	⊜	⊖	⊜
RELIABILITY VERDICT	✔	✔	✔	✔	✔	✔	✔	✔

Nissan Murano

TROUBLE SPOTS	96	97	98	99	00	01	02	03
Engine								⊜
Cooling								⊜
Fuel								⊜
Ignition								⊜
Transmission								⊜
Electrical								⊜
A/C								⊜
Suspension								⊜
Brakes								⊜
Exhaust								⊜
Power equip.								⊜
Paint/trim/rust								⊜
Integrity								⊖
Hardware								⊖
RELIABILITY VERDICT								✔

Nissan Pathfinder

TROUBLE SPOTS	96	97	98	99	00	01	02	03
Engine	⊖	⊖	⊜	⊜	⊜	⊜	⊜	⊜
Cooling	⊜	⊜	⊜	⊜	⊜	⊜	⊜	⊜
Fuel	○	○	⊖	⊜	⊜	⊖	⊜	⊜
Ignition	⊜	⊜	⊖	⊖	⊜	⊜	⊜	⊜
Transmission	⊖	⊜	⊖	⊜	⊜	⊜	⊜	⊜
Electrical	⊖	○	⊖	⊖	⊖	⊖	⊜	⊜
A/C	⊖	⊖	⊖	⊖	⊜	⊜	⊜	⊜
Suspension	○	◒	○	⊖	⊖	⊜	⊜	⊜
Brakes	○	○	○	○	⊖	⊖	⊜	⊜
Exhaust	●	●	⊖	⊖	⊜	⊜	⊜	⊜
Power equip.	○	⊖	⊖	⊖	⊖	○	⊖	⊜
Paint/trim/rust	⊖	⊖	⊜	⊖	⊜	⊜	⊜	⊜
Integrity	○	○	⊖	⊖	⊖	⊜	⊖	⊜
Hardware	⊖	⊖	⊖	⊖	⊜	⊖	⊜	⊜
RELIABILITY VERDICT	✔	✔	✔	✔	✔	✔	✔	✔

Nissan Pickup, Frontier

TROUBLE SPOTS	96	97	98	99	00	01	02	03
Engine	⊖	⊖	⊜	⊜	⊜	⊖	⊜	Insufficient data
Cooling	⊜	⊜	⊜	⊖	⊜	⊜	⊜	
Fuel	◒	○	⊖	⊜	⊜	⊖	⊖	
Ignition	⊖	⊖	⊖	⊜	⊜	⊜	⊜	
Transmission	⊖	⊜	⊜	⊜	⊜	⊜	⊜	
Electrical	○	○	○	⊖	○	⊖	⊖	
A/C	⊖	⊖	○	⊖	○	⊖	⊖	
Suspension	⊜	⊜	⊖	⊖	⊖	⊖	⊜	
Brakes	○	⊖	⊖	⊖	⊖	⊖	○	
Exhaust	⊖	⊜	⊖	⊖	⊜	⊜	⊜	
Power equip.	⊜	⊜	⊜	⊜	⊖	⊖	⊖	
Paint/trim/rust	⊖	⊖	⊖	⊖	⊖	⊖	⊜	
Integrity	○	○	○	⊜	○	○	○	
Hardware	⊖	⊖	⊖	⊜	⊖	○	⊖	
RELIABILITY VERDICT	✔	✔	✔	✔	✔	-	-	

Nissan Quest

TROUBLE SPOTS	96	97	98	99	00	01	02	03
Engine	⊖	⊜	⊖	⊖	⊜	⊜	⊜	
Cooling	○	⊖	⊜	⊜	⊜	⊜	⊜	
Fuel	◒	◒	⊖	○	⊜	⊜	⊜	
Ignition	⊖	⊖	⊜	⊜	⊜	⊜	⊜	
Transmission	⊖	⊜	⊜	⊜	⊜	⊜	⊜	
Electrical	●	◒	○	◒	○	○	⊖	
A/C	◒	◒	○	⊖	⊖	⊖	⊜	
Suspension	○	○	○	○	⊖	⊖	⊖	
Brakes	◒	◒	◒	○	○	⊜	⊖	
Exhaust	⊖	⊖	⊜	⊜	⊜	⊜	⊜	
Power equip.	●	●	●	◒	○	◒	⊖	
Paint/trim/rust	○	○	⊖	⊖	⊖	⊖	⊜	
Integrity	◒	○	◒	◒	○	◒	◒	
Hardware	●	●	◒	○	○	◒	○	
RELIABILITY VERDICT	-	-	-	-	✔	-	-	

Nissan Sentra

TROUBLE SPOTS	96	97	98	99	00	01	02	03
Engine	○	⊖	⊖	⊖	⊖	⊜	⊖	⊜
Cooling	⊜	⊜	⊖	⊜	⊜	⊜	⊜	⊜
Fuel	⊖	○	○	⊜	○	⊖	⊜	⊜
Ignition	⊖	⊖	⊖	⊜	⊖	⊜	⊜	⊜
Transmission	⊖	⊜	⊜	⊖	⊜	⊜	⊜	⊜
Electrical	●	●	○	○	◒	○	⊖	⊖
A/C	○	○	⊖	⊜	⊖	⊜	⊖	⊜
Suspension	⊖	⊖	○	⊖	⊖	⊖	⊜	⊖
Brakes	◒	◒	◒	○	○	⊖	⊜	⊜
Exhaust	⊖	⊖	⊖	⊜	⊜	⊜	⊜	⊜
Power equip.	○	⊖	○	⊖	⊖	⊖	⊖	⊜
Paint/trim/rust	○	○	○	○	⊖	⊖	⊖	⊖
Integrity	◒	○	○	◒	◒	○	⊖	○
Hardware	⊖	○	○	⊖	⊖	⊖	⊖	⊖
RELIABILITY VERDICT	✔	✔	✔	✔	-	✔	-	✘

Nissan Xterra

TROUBLE SPOTS	96	97	98	99	00	01	02	03
Engine					⊖	⊜	⊖	Insufficient data
Cooling					⊖	⊜	⊜	
Fuel					⊜	⊖	⊖	
Ignition					⊜	⊜	⊜	
Transmission					⊜	⊜	⊜	
Electrical					○	⊖	⊖	
A/C					○	⊜	⊜	
Suspension					⊖	⊜	⊖	
Brakes					⊖	⊜	⊖	
Exhaust					⊖	⊜	⊜	
Power equip.					⊖	○	⊖	
Paint/trim/rust					○	⊖	⊖	
Integrity					○	○	⊖	
Hardware					⊖	⊖	⊖	
RELIABILITY VERDICT					✔	✔	-	

Oldsmobile 88

TROUBLE SPOTS	96	97	98	99	00	01	02	03
Engine	○	○	◒	⊖				
Cooling	◒	●	○	○				
Fuel	○	◒	◒	○				
Ignition	⊖	○	⊖	○				
Transmission	○	○	○	○				
Electrical	○	●	◒	◒				
A/C	○	○	⊖	⊜				
Suspension	⊖	○	⊖	⊜				
Brakes	◒	◒	○	◒				
Exhaust	⊜	⊜	⊜	⊜				
Power equip.	○	○	○	○				
Paint/trim/rust	⊖	⊖	⊖	⊖				
Integrity	○	◒	◒	○				
Hardware	○	○	⊖	⊖				
RELIABILITY VERDICT	✔	✘	✘	-				

Oldsmobile Alero

TROUBLE SPOTS	96	97	98	99	00	01	02	03
Engine				○	⊖	⊖	⊜	Insufficient data
Cooling				○	⊖	⊖	⊜	
Fuel				○	⊖	○	⊖	
Ignition				⊖	⊜	⊖	⊜	
Transmission				⊜	⊜	⊜	⊜	
Electrical				●	●	◒	○	
A/C				○	⊖	⊖	⊜	
Suspension				○	○	⊖	⊜	
Brakes				●	●	●	○	
Exhaust				⊜	⊜	⊜	⊜	
Power equip.				◒	◒	○	⊖	
Paint/trim/rust				○	⊖	⊖	⊜	
Integrity				●	◒	○	⊖	
Hardware				◒	○	⊖	⊖	
RELIABILITY VERDICT				✗	✗	✗	–	

Oldsmobile Aurora

TROUBLE SPOTS	96	97	98	99	00	01	02	03
Engine	○	○	⊖	Insufficient data		⊖	⊖	Insufficient data
Cooling	●	◒	○			⊖	⊜	
Fuel	●	◒	⊖			⊖	⊜	
Ignition	⊖	○	⊖			⊖	⊜	
Transmission	○	⊜	⊖			⊖	⊜	
Electrical	◒	●	●			○	⊖	
A/C	●	○	◒			⊖	⊖	
Suspension	○	○	⊖			●	○	
Brakes	●	◒	◒			○	⊜	
Exhaust	⊜	⊜	⊜			⊜	⊜	
Power equip.	◒	◒	○			○	⊖	
Paint/trim/rust	○	○	○			⊖	⊜	
Integrity	◒	○	○			○	○	
Hardware	○	○	⊖			⊖	⊖	
RELIABILITY VERDICT	✗	–	–			✗	–	

Oldsmobile Bravada

TROUBLE SPOTS	96	97	98	99	00	01	02	03
Engine	Insufficient data	Insufficient data	○	○	⊜	Insufficient data	⊜	Insufficient data
Cooling			◒	○	⊜		⊜	
Fuel			○	⊖	⊖		⊖	
Ignition			○	⊜	⊖		⊖	
Transmission			●	◒	⊖		⊖	
Electrical			●	◒	◒		◒	
A/C			○	○	⊖		⊖	
Suspension			○	◒	○		○	
Brakes			◒	⊖	○		⊖	
Exhaust			⊖	⊜	○		⊜	
Power equip.			○	○	○		●	
Paint/trim/rust			○	◒	⊖		⊖	
Integrity			◒	◒	◒		◒	
Hardware			◒	○	○		○	
RELIABILITY VERDICT			✗	✗	–		✗	

Oldsmobile Ciera, Cutlass

TROUBLE SPOTS	96	97	98	99	00	01	02	03
Engine	◒	◒	◒	◒				
Cooling	●	●	◒	◒				
Fuel	◒	◒	○	○				
Ignition	⊖	○	⊖	⊜				
Transmission	○	⊖	⊖	⊖				
Electrical	●	●	●	●				
A/C	◒	◒	●	◒				
Suspension	⊖	○	○	○				
Brakes	●	●	●	●				
Exhaust	⊖	⊜	⊜	⊜				
Power equip.	◒	○	○	○				
Paint/trim/rust	◒	○	⊖	○				
Integrity	○	◒	◒	○				
Hardware	◒	○	○	○				
RELIABILITY VERDICT	✗	✗	✗	✗				

Oldsmobile Cutlass Supreme, Intrigue

TROUBLE SPOTS	96	97	98	99	00	01	02	03
Engine	○	◒	○	⊖	⊖	⊜	⊜	
Cooling	◒	○	○	⊜	⊖	⊜	⊜	
Fuel	◒	⊖	⊜	○	○	⊖	⊜	
Ignition	⊖	⊜	⊜	○	⊖	⊜	⊜	
Transmission	⊖	⊖	⊖	⊖	⊖	○	⊜	
Electrical	●	●	◒	◒	◒	◒	○	
A/C	○	○	○	⊖	⊖	⊜	⊜	
Suspension	○	○	○	○	◒	○	⊖	
Brakes	◒	●	◒	○	○	⊖	⊜	
Exhaust	⊜	⊜	⊜	⊜	⊜	⊜	⊜	
Power equip.	◒	⊖	◒	◒	○	○	⊜	
Paint/trim/rust	◒	○	⊖	⊖	⊖	⊖	⊜	
Integrity	●	○	○	◒	○	○	⊖	
Hardware	○	○	⊖	○	⊖	⊖	⊖	
RELIABILITY VERDICT	–	–	–	–	–	–	✓	

Oldsmobile Silhouette (ext.)

TROUBLE SPOTS	96	97	98	99	00	01	02	03
Engine		◒	◒	◒	○	⊜	⊜	⊜
Cooling		◒	○	◒	○	⊖	⊜	⊜
Fuel		○	○	○	○	⊖	⊖	⊜
Ignition		⊜	⊜	⊜	⊜	⊜	⊜	⊜
Transmission		○	⊖	○	○	⊖	⊜	⊜
Electrical		●	●	◒	●	○	⊖	⊖
A/C		○	⊖	⊖	⊖	⊖	⊜	⊜
Suspension		●	○	⊖	⊖	⊖	⊜	⊜
Brakes		●	◒	◒	○	⊖	⊖	⊜
Exhaust		⊜	⊜	⊜	⊜	⊜	⊜	⊜
Power equip.		●	●	●	●	◒	○	⊖
Paint/trim/rust		○	⊖	⊖	⊖	⊖	⊖	⊜
Integrity		●	◒	◒	◒	◒	○	⊜
Hardware		●	◒	◒	●	○	⊖	⊖
RELIABILITY VERDICT		✗	✗	✗	✗	–	–	–

Plymouth Breeze

TROUBLE SPOTS	96	97	98	99	00	01	02	03
Engine	●	●	●	◒	⊖			
Cooling	○	◒	⊖	⊖	⊜			
Fuel	◒	◒	⊖	⊖	⊖			
Ignition	⊖	⊖	⊖	⊜	⊜			
Transmission	●	○	⊖	○	○			
Electrical	◒	○	○	○	○			
A/C	○	○	⊖	⊖	⊖			
Suspension	◒	◒	○	⊖	⊖			
Brakes	●	●	●	◒	◒			
Exhaust	⊖	⊖	⊜	⊜	⊜			
Power equip.	○	⊖	○	○	⊖			
Paint/trim/rust	◒	⊖	⊖	○	⊖			
Integrity	○	⊖	○	○	○			
Hardware	⊖	⊖	⊖	⊖	⊖			
RELIABILITY VERDICT	✗	✗	✗	✗	–			

Plymouth Grand Voyager V6

TROUBLE SPOTS	96	97	98	99	00	01	02	03
Engine	◒	○	◒	⊖	⊖			
Cooling	◒	◒	⊖	⊖	⊖			
Fuel	◒	◒	⊖	⊖	⊖			
Ignition	⊖	⊖	⊖	⊖	⊜			
Transmission	●	◒	○	◒	●			
Electrical	●	●	◒	○	○			
A/C	●	◒	○	○	⊖			
Suspension	○	○	○	⊖	⊖			
Brakes	●	◒	◒	◒	◒			
Exhaust	⊜	⊜	⊜	⊜	⊜			
Power equip.	●	◒	○	○	○			
Paint/trim/rust	○	⊖	⊖	⊖	⊖			
Integrity	◒	◒	○	○	○			
Hardware	◒	○	⊖	⊖	⊖			
RELIABILITY VERDICT	✗	✗	–	✗	✗			

Pontiac Aztek

Trouble spots	96	97	98	99	00	01	02	03
Engine						⊖	⊜	
Cooling						⊖	⊜	
Fuel						⊖	⊖	
Ignition						⊖	⊜	
Transmission						⊖	⊜	
Electrical						◒	⊖	
A/C						◒	⊜	
Suspension						⊖	⊜	
Brakes						⊖	⊖	
Exhaust						⊜	⊜	
Power equip.						○	◒	
Paint/trim/rust						⊜	⊜	
Integrity						○	○	
Hardware						○	○	
RELIABILITY VERDICT						✗	-	

Insufficient data

Pontiac Bonneville

Trouble spots	96	97	98	99	00	01	02	03
Engine	◒	●	●	○	⊖	⊖	⊜	⊜
Cooling	●	●	◒	⊖	⊖	○	⊖	⊜
Fuel	◒	◒	◒	○	⊖	⊖	⊜	⊜
Ignition	⊖	⊖	⊖	⊖	⊖	⊜	⊜	⊜
Transmission	○	◒	⊖	⊖	⊖	⊖	⊜	⊜
Electrical	◒	●	◒	◒	◒	○	○	⊜
A/C	◒	○	⊖	⊜	⊖	⊖	⊜	⊜
Suspension	○	○	⊖	⊖	●	◒	○	⊜
Brakes	◒	◒	◒	○	○	⊖	⊜	⊖
Exhaust	⊜	⊜	⊜	⊜	⊜	⊜	⊜	⊜
Power equip.	○	○	○	○	●	○	○	⊖
Paint/trim/rust	○	⊖	⊖	○	⊖	⊖	⊖	⊜
Integrity	◒	○	◒	◒	●	◒	◒	◒
Hardware	○	⊖	⊖	⊖	◒	○	⊖	⊖
RELIABILITY VERDICT	-	✗	✗	-	✗	✗	✗	✗

Pontiac Firebird

Trouble spots	96	97	98	99	00	01	02	03
Engine	○	◒	○	○	⊖	○	⊜	
Cooling	●	◒	⊖	⊜	⊖	⊜	⊜	
Fuel	○	◒	⊜	⊖	⊜	⊖	⊜	
Ignition	○	○	⊜	○	⊜	⊖	⊜	
Transmission	○	○	⊜	○	⊜	⊖	⊜	
Electrical	●	●	●	●	◒	○	⊜	
A/C	○	⊖	⊖	⊖	⊖	⊖	⊜	
Suspension	○	○	⊖	⊖	⊜	⊖	⊖	
Brakes	○	○	◒	◒	●	◒	○	
Exhaust	⊖	⊖	⊜	⊖	○	○	⊜	
Power equip.	◒	●	○	◒	◒	○	⊖	
Paint/trim/rust	○	○	⊜	⊖	⊖	⊜	⊖	
Integrity	◒	●	○	◒	●	○	◒	
Hardware	○	◒	⊖	○	○	⊖	⊖	
RELIABILITY VERDICT	-	✗	-	✗	✗	✗	-	

Pontiac Grand Am

Trouble spots	96	97	98	99	00	01	02	03
Engine	○	◒	⊖	◒	⊖	⊜	⊜	⊜
Cooling	●	●	○	◒	○	⊖	⊜	⊜
Fuel	◒	◒	○	○	◒	⊖	⊜	⊜
Ignition	○	○	⊖	⊖	⊜	⊖	⊜	⊜
Transmission	○	○	⊖	⊖	⊜	⊖	⊜	⊜
Electrical	●	●	●	●	●	◒	⊖	⊜
A/C	●	○	⊖	⊖	⊖	⊖	⊜	⊜
Suspension	◒	◒	⊖	○	⊖	⊖	⊜	⊜
Brakes	●	●	●	●	●	●	⊖	⊜
Exhaust	○	⊖	⊖	⊜	⊜	⊜	⊜	⊜
Power equip.	●	●	○	◒	●	○	⊖	⊜
Paint/trim/rust	◒	○	○	○	⊖	⊖	⊖	⊜
Integrity	◒	●	○	◒	◒	◒	○	⊜
Hardware	●	◒	○	○	◒	○	⊖	⊜
RELIABILITY VERDICT	✗	✗	-	✗	✗	✗	-	✓

Pontiac Grand Prix

Trouble spots	96	97	98	99	00	01	02	03
Engine	○	◒	○	⊖	⊖	⊜	⊜	⊜
Cooling	◒	◒	○	⊖	⊖	⊖	⊜	⊜
Fuel	○	○	⊖	⊖	⊖	⊖	⊜	⊜
Ignition	○	⊖	⊜	⊜	⊜	⊜	⊜	⊜
Transmission	◒	⊖	○	○	⊖	⊖	⊜	⊜
Electrical	●	●	●	◒	○	○	⊖	⊜
A/C	○	◒	○	○	○	⊖	⊜	⊜
Suspension	○	●	◒	⊖	⊖	⊖	⊜	⊜
Brakes	●	○	○	○	○	⊖	⊜	⊜
Exhaust	⊖	⊜	⊜	⊜	⊜	⊜	⊜	⊜
Power equip.	◒	●	●	◒	○	○	⊖	⊜
Paint/trim/rust	◒	○	○	⊖	⊖	⊖	⊖	⊖
Integrity	◒	◒	◒	◒	○	○	⊖	⊖
Hardware	◒	○	○	⊖	⊖	⊖	⊜	⊖
RELIABILITY VERDICT	-	✗	✗	-	-	-	✓	-

Pontiac Sunfire Coupe & Conv.

Trouble spots	96	97	98	99	00	01	02	03
Engine	◒	○	○	○	⊜	⊖	⊜	
Cooling	●	◒	○	⊖	⊖	⊖	⊜	
Fuel	◒	◒	⊖	⊖	○	○	⊜	
Ignition	○	○	○	⊖	⊜	⊜	⊜	
Transmission	○	⊖	⊜	⊖	⊜	⊖	⊜	
Electrical	●	●	◒	◒	◒	⊖	⊖	
A/C	●	◒	⊖	⊜	⊖	⊖	⊜	
Suspension	○	◒	⊖	○	⊖	⊖	⊖	
Brakes	◒	○	◒	●	●	○	⊖	
Exhaust	⊖	⊜	⊖	⊜	⊜	⊜	⊜	
Power equip.	○	○	○	○	○	○	⊖	
Paint/trim/rust	○	⊖	○	○	○	⊜	⊜	
Integrity	●	●	◒	◒	◒	○	○	
Hardware	◒	○	○	◒	○	⊖	⊖	
RELIABILITY VERDICT	✗	-	-	-	-	-	-	

Insufficient data

Pontiac Trans Sport, Montana (ext.)

Trouble spots	96	97	98	99	00	01	02	03
Engine		◒	◒	◒	○	⊜	⊜	⊜
Cooling		◒	○	◒	○	⊖	⊜	⊜
Fuel		○	○	○	○	⊖	⊖	⊜
Ignition		⊜	⊜	⊜	⊜	⊜	⊜	⊜
Transmission		○	⊖	○	○	⊖	⊜	⊜
Electrical		●	●	◒	●	○	⊖	⊖
A/C		○	⊖	⊖	⊖	⊖	⊜	⊜
Suspension		●	○	⊖	⊖	⊖	⊜	⊜
Brakes		●	◒	◒	○	⊖	⊖	⊜
Exhaust		⊜	⊜	⊜	⊜	⊜	⊜	⊜
Power equip.		●	●	●	●	◒	○	⊖
Paint/trim/rust		○	⊖	⊖	⊖	⊖	⊖	⊜
Integrity		●	◒	◒	◒	◒	○	⊜
Hardware		●	◒	◒	●	○	⊖	⊖
RELIABILITY VERDICT		✗	✗	✗	✗	-	-	-

Pontiac Vibe

Trouble spots	96	97	98	99	00	01	02	03
Engine								⊜
Cooling								⊜
Fuel								⊜
Ignition								⊜
Transmission								⊜
Electrical								⊜
A/C								⊜
Suspension								⊜
Brakes								⊜
Exhaust								⊜
Power equip.								⊜
Paint/trim/rust								⊜
Integrity								⊖
Hardware								⊜
RELIABILITY VERDICT								✓

Porsche Boxster

TROUBLE SPOTS	96	97	98	99	00	01	02	03
Engine	Insufficient data	Insufficient data		⊜	○	○	Insufficient data	Insufficient data
Cooling				◒	⊜	⊜		
Fuel				○	⊜	⊜		
Ignition				⊜	⊜	⊜		
Transmission				⊜	⊜	⊜		
Electrical				○	⊜	○		
A/C				⊜	◒	⊜		
Suspension				⊜	⊜	⊜		
Brakes				⊜	⊜	⊜		
Exhaust				⊜	⊜	⊜		
Power equip.				⊜	⊜	⊜		
Paint/trim/rust				⊜	⊜	⊜		
Integrity				⊜	○	○		
Hardware				◒	⊜	⊜		
RELIABILITY VERDICT				–	✔	–		

Saab 9-5

TROUBLE SPOTS	96	97	98	99	00	01	02	03
Engine				○	○	⊜	⊜	⊜
Cooling				⊜	⊜	⊜	⊜	⊜
Fuel				○	⊜	⊜	⊜	⊜
Ignition				○	⊜	⊜	⊜	⊜
Transmission				⊜	⊜	⊜	⊜	⊜
Electrical				●	●	◒	○	⊜
A/C				○	⊜	⊜	⊜	⊜
Suspension				⊜	⊜	⊜	⊜	⊜
Brakes				⊜	⊜	⊜	⊜	⊜
Exhaust				⊜	⊜	⊜	⊜	⊜
Power equip.				○	○	⊜	⊜	⊜
Paint/trim/rust				⊜	⊜	⊜	⊜	⊜
Integrity				⊜	⊜	○	⊜	⊜
Hardware				⊜	○	⊜	⊜	⊜
RELIABILITY VERDICT				–	–	–	–	✔

Saab 900, 9-3

TROUBLE SPOTS	96	97	98	99	00	01	02	03
Engine	◒	●	○	⊜	⊜	⊜	⊜	⊜
Cooling	◒	○	⊜	⊜	⊜	⊜	⊜	⊜
Fuel	◒	⊜	○	⊜	⊜	○	⊜	⊜
Ignition	○	○	⊜	⊜	⊜	⊜	⊜	⊜
Transmission	○	○	⊜	⊜	⊜	⊜	⊜	⊜
Electrical	●	●	●	◒	○	○	⊜	⊜
A/C	◒	○	○	○	⊜	⊜	⊜	⊜
Suspension	○	⊜	⊜	○	⊜	⊜	⊜	⊜
Brakes	○	○	○	⊜	○	⊜	⊜	⊜
Exhaust	◒	○	○	⊜	⊜	⊜	⊜	⊜
Power equip.	◒	○	◒	◒	○	○	⊜	⊜
Paint/trim/rust	⊜	⊜	⊜	⊜	○	⊜	⊜	⊜
Integrity	○	○	○	◒	◒	⊜	○	⊜
Hardware	○	⊜	○	◒	○	○	⊜	⊜
RELIABILITY VERDICT	–	–	–	–	–	–	–	–

Saturn L-Series 4-cyl.

TROUBLE SPOTS	96	97	98	99	00	01	02	03
Engine					⊜	⊜	⊜	⊜
Cooling					⊜	⊜	⊜	⊜
Fuel					⊜	⊜	⊜	⊜
Ignition					⊜	⊜	⊜	⊜
Transmission					⊜	⊜	⊜	⊜
Electrical					◒	○	○	⊜
A/C					⊜	⊜	⊜	⊜
Suspension					○	○	⊜	⊜
Brakes					○	⊜	⊜	⊜
Exhaust					⊜	⊜	⊜	⊜
Power equip.					○	○	⊜	⊜
Paint/trim/rust					⊜	⊜	⊜	⊜
Integrity					○	○	○	⊜
Hardware					○	○	⊜	⊜
RELIABILITY VERDICT					–	–	–	✔

Saturn SL, Ion

TROUBLE SPOTS	96	97	98	99	00	01	02	03
Engine	◒	○	○	⊜	⊜	⊜	⊜	⊜
Cooling	○	○	○	⊜	⊜	⊜	⊜	⊜
Fuel	○	◒	○	○	⊜	⊜	⊜	⊜
Ignition	○	○	⊜	⊜	⊜	⊜	⊜	⊜
Transmission	⊜	⊜	⊜	⊜	⊜	⊜	⊜	⊜
Electrical	●	●	○	○	○	⊜	⊜	⊜
A/C	⊜	⊜	⊜	⊜	⊜	⊜	⊜	⊜
Suspension	⊜	⊜	⊜	⊜	⊜	⊜	⊜	⊜
Brakes	○	○	○	⊜	○	⊜	⊜	⊜
Exhaust	⊜	⊜	○	○	⊜	⊜	⊜	⊜
Power equip.	○	○	○	○	○	⊜	⊜	⊜
Paint/trim/rust	○	⊜	⊜	⊜	⊜	⊜	⊜	⊜
Integrity	◒	◒	◒	○	○	⊜	○	⊜
Hardware	○	○	○	⊜	○	⊜	⊜	⊜
RELIABILITY VERDICT	–	–	–	✔	–	✔	✔	✔

Saturn VUE

TROUBLE SPOTS	96	97	98	99	00	01	02	03
Engine							⊜	⊜
Cooling							⊜	⊜
Fuel							○	⊜
Ignition							⊜	⊜
Transmission							⊜	⊜
Electrical							○	⊜
A/C							⊜	⊜
Suspension							○	⊜
Brakes							⊜	⊜
Exhaust							⊜	⊜
Power equip.							⊜	⊜
Paint/trim/rust							⊜	⊜
Integrity							◒	⊜
Hardware							○	⊜
RELIABILITY VERDICT							✘	✘

Subaru Baja

TROUBLE SPOTS	96	97	98	99	00	01	02	03
Engine								⊜
Cooling								⊜
Fuel								⊜
Ignition								⊜
Transmission								⊜
Electrical								⊜
A/C								⊜
Suspension								⊜
Brakes								⊜
Exhaust								⊜
Power equip.								⊜
Paint/trim/rust								⊜
Integrity								○
Hardware								⊜
RELIABILITY VERDICT								✘

Subaru Forester

TROUBLE SPOTS	96	97	98	99	00	01	02	03
Engine			○	○	⊜	⊜	⊜	⊜
Cooling			⊜	⊜	⊜	⊜	⊜	⊜
Fuel			⊜	○	⊜	⊜	⊜	⊜
Ignition			⊜	⊜	⊜	⊜	⊜	⊜
Transmission			⊜	⊜	⊜	⊜	⊜	⊜
Electrical			⊜	⊜	⊜	⊜	⊜	⊜
A/C			⊜	⊜	⊜	⊜	⊜	⊜
Suspension			⊜	⊜	⊜	⊜	⊜	⊜
Brakes			○	○	⊜	⊜	⊜	⊜
Exhaust			⊜	⊜	⊜	⊜	⊜	⊜
Power equip.			⊜	⊜	⊜	⊜	⊜	⊜
Paint/trim/rust			⊜	⊜	⊜	⊜	⊜	⊜
Integrity			⊜	⊜	⊜	⊜	⊜	⊜
Hardware			⊜	⊜	⊜	⊜	⊜	⊜
RELIABILITY VERDICT			✔	–	✔	✔	–	✔

Trouble spots	Subaru Impreza 96	97	98	99	00	01	02	03	Subaru Impreza WRX 96	97	98	99	00	01	02	03
Engine	○	○	○	⊜	⊖	⊜	⊜	⊜							⊜	⊜
Cooling	⊖	⊖	⊜	⊜	⊜	⊜	⊜	⊜							⊜	⊜
Fuel	⊖	⊜	⊜	○	⊖	○	⊖	⊜							⊖	⊜
Ignition	⊖	⊜	⊜	⊜	⊜	⊜	⊜	⊖							⊜	⊜
Transmission	⊜	⊜	⊜	⊖	⊖	⊜	⊖	⊖							⊜	⊜
Electrical	○	○	○	⊖	⊖	⊖	⊜	⊜							⊜	⊜
A/C	⊖	○	⊖	⊜	⊖	⊜	⊜	⊜							⊜	⊜
Suspension	○	⊖	⊜	⊖	⊜	⊜	⊜	⊜							⊜	⊜
Brakes	○	⊖	⊖	○	⊖	○	⊖	⊖							⊜	⊜
Exhaust	⊜	⊖	⊜	⊜	⊜	⊖	⊜	⊜							⊜	⊜
Power equip.	⊖	⊖	⊜	⊖	⊖	⊖	⊖	⊜							⊜	⊜
Paint/trim/rust	⊖	⊖	⊖	⊖	⊖	⊖	⊜	⊜							⊖	⊖
Integrity	○	⊖	○	○	○	○	⊖	⊜							⊖	⊖
Hardware	⊜	⊜	⊖	⊜	⊜	⊜	⊖	⊜							⊜	⊜
RELIABILITY VERDICT	✓	✓	✓	✓	–	✓	✓	–							–	–

Trouble spots	Subaru Legacy/Outback 4-cyl. 96	97	98	99	00	01	02	03	Suzuki Sidekick, Vitara/XL-7 96	97	98	99	00	01	02	03
Engine	●	◒	◒	○	⊖	⊜	⊜	⊜	⊖	○	Insufficient data	⊖	○	⊜	⊜	Insufficient data
Cooling	⊖	⊖	⊜	⊜	⊖	⊜	⊜	⊜	⊖	⊜		⊜	⊜	⊜	⊜	
Fuel	○	⊜	⊜	⊖	⊖	⊖	⊖	⊜	●	◒		⊖	⊖	⊜	⊜	
Ignition	⊖	⊜	⊜	⊜	⊜	⊜	⊜	⊜	⊖	⊖		⊖	⊜	⊜	⊜	
Transmission	⊖	⊜	⊖	⊖	⊜	⊜	⊖	⊖	⊜	⊖		○	⊜	⊖	⊜	
Electrical	◒	◒	○	⊖	⊖	⊜	⊜	⊜	◒	○		○	⊖	⊖	⊜	
A/C	⊖	⊖	⊖	⊜	⊜	⊜	⊜	⊜	●	◒		◒	○	⊖	⊖	
Suspension	⊖	⊖	⊜	⊜	⊜	⊜	⊜	⊜	⊖	⊖		⊖	⊖	⊖	⊖	
Brakes	○	○	○	○	⊖	○	○	⊜	○	○		○	○	⊖	⊖	
Exhaust	⊖	⊜	⊜	⊜	⊜	⊜	⊜	⊜	○	⊖		⊖	⊖	⊜	⊜	
Power equip.	○	⊖	⊖	⊖	⊖	⊜	⊜	⊜	⊜	⊜		○	⊖	⊖	⊜	
Paint/trim/rust	○	⊜	⊖	⊖	⊖	⊜	⊜	⊜	⊖	⊖		○	⊖	⊖	⊖	
Integrity	⊖	⊖	⊖	⊖	○	○	○	⊖	◒	◒		◒	◒	○	⊖	
Hardware	○	⊖	⊖	⊖	⊖	⊖	⊜	⊖	○	◒		⊖	○	⊖	⊜	
RELIABILITY VERDICT	✓	✓	✓	✓	✓	✓	–	–	✓	✓		✗	–	–	–	

Trouble spots	Toyota 4Runner V6 96	97	98	99	00	01	02	03	Toyota 4Runner V8 96	97	98	99	00	01	02	03
Engine	○	⊜	⊜	⊜	⊜	⊜	⊜	⊜								⊜
Cooling	⊜	⊜	⊜	⊜	⊜	⊜	⊜	⊜								⊜
Fuel	⊖	⊜	⊜	⊖	⊖	⊜	⊜	⊖								⊜
Ignition	⊜	⊜	⊜	⊜	⊜	⊜	⊜	⊜								⊜
Transmission	⊜	⊜	⊜	⊜	⊜	⊜	⊜	⊜								⊜
Electrical	⊖	○	⊖	⊖	⊖	⊜	⊜	⊜								⊜
A/C	⊜	⊜	⊜	⊜	⊜	⊜	⊜	⊜								⊜
Suspension	○	⊖	⊜	⊜	⊜	⊜	⊜	⊜								⊜
Brakes	○	○	○	⊖	⊖	⊖	⊜	⊜								⊜
Exhaust	⊜	⊜	⊜	⊜	⊜	⊜	⊜	⊜								⊜
Power equip.	⊖	○	○	⊖	⊖	⊜	⊜	⊜								⊜
Paint/trim/rust	⊖	⊖	⊜	⊜	⊖	⊜	⊜	⊖								⊜
Integrity	⊜	⊖	⊖	⊖	⊖	⊖	○	⊖								⊖
Hardware	⊖	⊖	⊜	⊜	⊖	⊜	⊜	⊜								⊜
RELIABILITY VERDICT	✓	✓	✓	✓	✓	✓	✓	✗								✓

Trouble spots	Toyota Avalon 96	97	98	99	00	01	02	03	Toyota Camry 96	97	98	99	00	01	02	03
Engine	⊖	⊖	⊜	⊜	⊜	⊜	⊜	⊜	○	○	⊖	⊖	⊜	⊜	⊜	⊜
Cooling	⊜	⊜	⊜	⊜	⊜	⊜	⊜	⊜	⊖	⊜	⊜	⊖	⊜	⊜	⊜	⊜
Fuel	⊜	⊖	⊖	⊖	⊖	⊜	⊜	⊜	⊖	⊖	⊖	⊖	⊜	⊖	⊜	⊜
Ignition	⊜	⊜	⊜	⊜	⊜	⊜	⊜	⊜	⊜	⊜	⊜	⊜	⊜	⊜	⊜	⊜
Transmission	⊜	⊜	⊜	⊜	⊜	⊜	⊜	⊜	⊜	⊜	⊜	⊜	⊜	⊜	⊜	⊜
Electrical	○	⊖	○	⊖	⊖	⊖	⊜	⊜	○	○	⊖	⊖	⊜	⊜	⊜	⊜
A/C	⊖	⊖	○	⊜	⊜	⊜	⊜	⊜	⊖	⊜	⊜	⊜	⊜	⊜	⊜	⊜
Suspension	◒	●	◒	◒	⊖	⊜	⊜	⊜	○	◒	○	○	⊜	⊜	⊖	⊜
Brakes	○	⊖	⊖	⊖	⊖	⊜	⊜	⊜	○	○	○	○	⊖	⊖	⊖	⊜
Exhaust	⊜	⊜	⊜	⊜	⊜	⊜	⊜	⊜	⊖	⊜	⊜	⊜	⊜	⊜	⊜	⊜
Power equip.	○	⊖	⊖	⊖	⊜	⊜	⊜	⊜	○	⊖	⊖	⊖	⊜	⊜	⊜	⊜
Paint/trim/rust	⊖	⊖	⊖	⊖	⊜	⊜	⊜	⊜	⊖	⊖	⊖	⊖	⊜	⊜	⊖	⊜
Integrity	○	○	○	○	⊖	⊖	⊖	⊜	⊖	⊖	⊖	⊖	⊖	⊖	○	⊖
Hardware	⊖	⊖	⊖	⊖	⊜	⊜	⊖	⊜	⊖	⊖	⊖	⊖	⊖	⊖	⊖	⊜
RELIABILITY VERDICT	✓	✓	✓	✓	✓	✓	✓	✓	✓	✓	✓	✓	✓	✓	✓	✓

Toyota Camry Solara

TROUBLE SPOTS	96	97	98	99	00	01	02	03
Engine				⊜	⊜	⊜	⊜	⊜
Cooling				⊜	⊜	⊜	⊜	⊜
Fuel				◓	◓	◓	⊜	⊜
Ignition				⊜	⊜	⊜	⊜	⊜
Transmission				⊜	⊜	⊜	⊜	⊜
Electrical				◓	◓	◓	⊜	⊜
A/C				⊜	⊜	⊜	⊜	⊜
Suspension				◒	◓	◓	⊜	◓
Brakes				◓	◓	◓	⊜	⊜
Exhaust				⊜	⊜	⊜	⊜	⊜
Power equip.				◓	◓	⊜	◓	⊜
Paint/trim/rust				◓	⊜	◓	⊜	⊜
Integrity				○	○	○	◓	⊜
Hardware				◓	◓	◓	◓	⊜
RELIABILITY VERDICT				✔	✔	✔	✔	✔

Toyota Celica

TROUBLE SPOTS	96	97	98	99	00	01	02	03
Engine	◓	○	Insufficient data	Insufficient data	○	⊜	⊜	Insufficient data
Cooling	⊜	⊜			⊜	⊜	⊜	
Fuel	◓	⊜			◓	⊜	○	
Ignition	⊜	⊜			⊜	⊜	⊜	
Transmission	◓	◓			⊜	⊜	⊜	
Electrical	◓	◓			⊜	◓	⊜	
A/C	◓	◓			⊜	⊜	⊜	
Suspension	⊜	⊜			⊜	⊜	⊜	
Brakes	◓	⊜			⊜	⊜	◓	
Exhaust	◓	⊜			⊜	⊜	⊜	
Power equip.	○	○			◓	⊜	◓	
Paint/trim/rust	◓	◓			◓	◓	◓	
Integrity	○	○			○	○	○	
Hardware	◓	◓			◓	◓	◓	
RELIABILITY VERDICT	✔	✔			✔	✔	✔	

Toyota Corolla

TROUBLE SPOTS	96	97	98	99	00	01	02	03
Engine	◓	⊜	◓	⊜	⊜	⊜	⊜	⊜
Cooling	⊜	⊜	⊜	⊜	⊜	⊜	⊜	⊜
Fuel	◓	⊜	◓	⊜	⊜	⊜	⊜	⊜
Ignition	⊜	⊜	⊜	⊜	⊜	⊜	⊜	⊜
Transmission	⊜	⊜	⊜	⊜	⊜	⊜	⊜	⊜
Electrical	○	○	⊜	◓	◓	⊜	◓	⊜
A/C	◓	⊜	⊜	⊜	⊜	⊜	⊜	⊜
Suspension	◓	⊜	◓	◓	◓	⊜	⊜	⊜
Brakes	○	◓	◓	◓	◓	◓	◓	◓
Exhaust	⊜	⊜	⊜	⊜	⊜	⊜	⊜	⊜
Power equip.	◓	◓	◓	◓	◓	⊜	⊜	⊜
Paint/trim/rust	◓	◓	◓	⊜	⊜	⊜	⊜	⊜
Integrity	◓	◓	◓	◓	◓	◓	◓	◓
Hardware	◓	○	○	◓	⊜	⊜	◓	⊜
RELIABILITY VERDICT	✔	✔	✔	✔	✔	✔	✔	✔

Toyota Echo

TROUBLE SPOTS	96	97	98	99	00	01	02	03
Engine					⊜	⊜	⊜	⊜
Cooling					⊜	⊜	⊜	⊜
Fuel					⊜	⊜	⊜	⊜
Ignition					⊜	⊜	⊜	⊜
Transmission					⊜	⊜	⊜	⊜
Electrical					⊜	⊜	⊜	⊜
A/C					⊜	⊜	⊜	⊜
Suspension					⊜	⊜	⊜	⊜
Brakes					◓	◓	◓	⊜
Exhaust					⊜	⊜	⊜	⊜
Power equip.					⊜	⊜	⊜	⊜
Paint/trim/rust					◓	◓	⊜	⊜
Integrity					◓	◓	◓	◓
Hardware					⊜	◓	⊜	◓
RELIABILITY VERDICT					✔	✔	✔	–

Toyota Highlander

TROUBLE SPOTS	96	97	98	99	00	01	02	03
Engine						⊜	⊜	⊜
Cooling						⊜	⊜	⊜
Fuel						⊜	⊜	⊜
Ignition						⊜	⊜	⊜
Transmission						⊜	⊜	⊜
Electrical						⊜	⊜	⊜
A/C						⊜	⊜	⊜
Suspension						⊜	⊜	⊜
Brakes						◓	⊜	⊜
Exhaust						⊜	⊜	⊜
Power equip.						⊜	⊜	⊜
Paint/trim/rust						⊜	⊜	⊜
Integrity						○	◓	⊜
Hardware						⊜	⊜	⊜
RELIABILITY VERDICT						✔	✔	✔

Toyota Land Cruiser

TROUBLE SPOTS	96	97	98	99	00	01	02	03
Engine	Insufficient data	○	Insufficient data	◓	⊜	⊜	Insufficient data	Insufficient data
Cooling		◓		⊜	⊜	⊜		
Fuel		⊜		◓	⊜	⊜		
Ignition		⊜		⊜	⊜	⊜		
Transmission		⊜		⊜	⊜	⊜		
Electrical		◒		◓	◓	⊜		
A/C		⊜		◓	⊜	⊜		
Suspension		⊜		⊜	⊜	⊜		
Brakes		●		◓	○	◓		
Exhaust		⊜		⊜	⊜	⊜		
Power equip.		○		○	⊜	⊜		
Paint/trim/rust		◓		⊜	⊜	◓		
Integrity		◓		⊜	◓	◓		
Hardware		⊜		◓	◓	⊜		
RELIABILITY VERDICT		✔		✔	✔	✔		

Toyota Matrix

TROUBLE SPOTS	96	97	98	99	00	01	02	03
Engine								⊜
Cooling								⊜
Fuel								⊜
Ignition								⊜
Transmission								⊜
Electrical								⊜
A/C								⊜
Suspension								⊜
Brakes								⊜
Exhaust								⊜
Power equip.								⊜
Paint/trim/rust								⊜
Integrity								◓
Hardware								⊜
RELIABILITY VERDICT								–

Toyota Prius

TROUBLE SPOTS	96	97	98	99	00	01	02	03
Engine						⊜	⊜	⊜
Cooling						⊜	⊜	⊜
Fuel						○	⊜	⊜
Ignition						⊜	⊜	⊜
Transmission						⊜	⊜	⊜
Electrical						○	◓	⊜
A/C						⊜	⊜	⊜
Suspension						◓	◓	⊜
Brakes						⊜	⊜	⊜
Exhaust						⊜	⊜	⊜
Power equip.						⊜	⊜	⊜
Paint/trim/rust						⊜	⊜	⊜
Integrity						⊜	⊜	⊜
Hardware						⊜	⊜	⊜
RELIABILITY VERDICT						✔	✔	✔

TROUBLE SPOTS	Toyota RAV4 96	97	98	99	00	01	02	03
Engine	⊖	⊖	⊜	⊜	⊜	⊜	⊜	⊜
Cooling	⊜	⊜	⊜	⊜	⊜	⊜	⊜	⊜
Fuel	⊖	⊖	⊖	⊖	⊜	⊖	⊜	⊜
Ignition	⊜	⊜	⊜	⊜	⊜	⊜	⊜	⊜
Transmission	⊜	⊖	⊖	⊜	⊜	⊜	⊜	⊜
Electrical	⊖	⊖	⊖	⊖	⊜	⊜	⊜	⊜
A/C	⊖	⊖	⊜	⊜	⊜	⊜	⊜	⊜
Suspension	⊖	⊜	⊜	⊜	⊜	⊜	⊜	⊜
Brakes	◒	◒	○	⊖	⊖	○	⊜	⊜
Exhaust	⊜	⊖	⊜	⊜	⊜	⊖	⊜	⊜
Power equip.	⊖	⊜	⊖	⊜	⊜	⊜	⊜	⊜
Paint/trim/rust	⊖	⊜	⊜	⊜	⊜	⊖	⊜	⊜
Integrity	○	○	⊜	⊖	⊖	◒	○	⊖
Hardware	○	⊖	⊜	⊖	⊜	⊜	⊖	⊜
RELIABILITY VERDICT	✓	✓	✓	✓	✓	✓	✓	✓

TROUBLE SPOTS	Toyota Sequoia 96	97	98	99	00	01	02	03
Engine						⊜	⊜	⊜
Cooling						⊜	⊜	⊜
Fuel						⊖	⊜	⊜
Ignition						⊜	⊜	⊜
Transmission						⊜	⊜	⊜
Electrical						⊖	⊜	⊜
A/C						⊖	⊖	⊜
Suspension						⊜	⊜	⊜
Brakes						◒	⊖	⊜
Exhaust						⊜	⊜	⊜
Power equip.						⊖	⊖	⊖
Paint/trim/rust						⊖	⊜	⊜
Integrity						⊖	⊖	⊜
Hardware						⊖	⊜	⊜
RELIABILITY VERDICT						✓	✓	-

TROUBLE SPOTS	Toyota Sienna 96	97	98	99	00	01	02	03
Engine			⊖	⊖	⊜	⊜	⊜	⊜
Cooling			⊜	⊜	⊜	⊜	⊜	⊜
Fuel			⊜	⊜	⊜	⊜	⊜	⊜
Ignition			⊜	⊜	⊜	⊜	⊜	⊜
Transmission			⊖	⊜	⊖	⊜	⊜	⊜
Electrical			⊖	⊖	⊖	⊖	⊜	⊜
A/C			⊖	⊜	⊜	⊜	⊜	⊜
Suspension			⊖	⊖	⊜	⊜	⊜	⊜
Brakes			○	○	⊖	⊖	⊖	⊜
Exhaust			⊜	⊜	⊜	⊜	⊜	⊜
Power equip.			⊖	○	○	○	⊖	⊜
Paint/trim/rust			⊜	⊜	⊜	⊜	⊜	⊜
Integrity			◒	○	⊖	⊖	⊖	⊜
Hardware			●	◒	○	⊖	○	⊜
RELIABILITY VERDICT			✓	✓	✓	✓	✓	✓

TROUBLE SPOTS	Toyota T100, Tundra 96	97	98	99	00	01	02	03
Engine	⊜	⊜	Insufficient data		⊜	⊜	⊜	⊜
Cooling	⊜	⊜			⊜	⊜	⊜	⊜
Fuel	⊖	⊖			⊖	⊖	⊜	⊜
Ignition	⊜	⊖			⊜	⊜	⊜	⊜
Transmission	⊜	⊜			⊜	⊜	⊜	⊜
Electrical	⊖	○			⊖	⊜	⊜	⊜
A/C	⊖	⊖			⊜	⊜	⊜	⊜
Suspension	⊖	⊜			⊜	⊜	⊜	⊜
Brakes	⊖	⊖			◒	○	⊖	⊜
Exhaust	⊜	⊜			⊜	⊜	⊜	⊜
Power equip.	⊖	⊜			⊜	⊜	⊜	⊜
Paint/trim/rust	⊜	⊜			⊖	⊜	⊜	⊜
Integrity	⊖	⊖			⊖	⊖	⊜	⊜
Hardware	○	⊖			⊖	⊖	⊜	⊜
RELIABILITY VERDICT	✓	✓			✓	✓	✓	✓

TROUBLE SPOTS	Toyota Tacoma 96	97	98	99	00	01	02	03
Engine	⊖	⊜	⊜	⊜	⊜	⊜	⊜	⊜
Cooling	⊖	⊜	⊜	⊜	⊜	⊜	⊜	⊜
Fuel	⊖	⊖	⊖	⊜	⊖	⊜	⊜	⊜
Ignition	⊜	⊜	⊜	⊜	⊜	⊜	⊜	⊜
Transmission	⊜	⊜	⊜	⊜	⊜	⊜	⊜	⊜
Electrical	○	⊖	⊖	⊖	⊜	⊜	⊜	⊜
A/C	⊖	⊖	⊜	⊜	⊜	⊜	⊜	⊜
Suspension	○	⊖	⊜	⊖	⊜	⊖	⊜	⊜
Brakes	○	⊖	⊖	⊖	⊖	⊖	⊜	⊜
Exhaust	⊖	⊖	⊜	⊜	⊜	⊜	⊜	⊜
Power equip.	⊜	⊜	⊜	⊜	⊜	⊜	⊜	⊜
Paint/trim/rust	⊖	⊖	⊖	⊜	⊜	○	⊖	⊜
Integrity	⊖	⊖	⊖	⊖	⊖	○	○	⊖
Hardware	⊖	⊖	⊖	⊖	⊖	⊖	⊜	⊜
RELIABILITY VERDICT	✓	✓	✓	✓	✓	✓	✓	✓

TROUBLE SPOTS	Volkswagen Golf 4-cyl. 96	97	98	99	00	01	02	03
Engine	○	⊖	⊖	○	○	○	⊖	⊜
Cooling	○	○	⊖	⊖	⊖	⊜	⊜	⊜
Fuel	●	○	○	●	◒	○	⊖	⊜
Ignition	◒	○	○	⊖	⊖	⊖	⊜	⊜
Transmission	◒	○	⊖	⊖	⊜	⊖	⊖	⊜
Electrical	●	●	●	●	◒	◒	○	⊜
A/C	○	◒	○	○	⊖	⊜	⊜	⊜
Suspension	⊖	⊖	⊖	⊖	⊜	⊜	⊜	⊜
Brakes	◒	◒	○	◒	◒	◒	⊖	⊜
Exhaust	●	◒	◒	○	⊖	⊜	⊜	⊜
Power equip.	◒	◒	●	●	●	◒	●	⊜
Paint/trim/rust	●	●	●	○	○	⊜	⊜	⊜
Integrity	●	●	●	●	●	○	○	⊖
Hardware	●	◒	○	●	◒	○	○	⊜
RELIABILITY VERDICT	✗	✗	✗	✗	✗	✗	✗	-

TROUBLE SPOTS	Volkswagen Jetta 4-cyl. Turbo 96	97	98	99	00	01	02	03
Engine					⊖	⊖	○	⊖
Cooling					○	⊖	⊜	⊜
Fuel					●	○	⊖	⊖
Ignition					○	◒	●	○
Transmission					⊜	⊖	⊖	⊜
Electrical					◒	◒	○	⊖
A/C					⊜	⊖	⊜	⊜
Suspension					⊖	⊜	⊜	⊜
Brakes					○	○	⊖	⊜
Exhaust					⊖	⊜	⊜	⊜
Power equip.					●	●	◒	⊜
Paint/trim/rust					⊜	⊖	⊜	⊜
Integrity					◒	○	○	⊖
Hardware					●	◒	○	⊖
RELIABILITY VERDICT					✗	✗	✗	✗

TROUBLE SPOTS	Volkswagen New Beetle 96	97	98	99	00	01	02	03
Engine			◒	○	○	⊖	⊖	⊜
Cooling			○	⊖	⊖	⊜	⊜	⊜
Fuel			○	◒	●	○	⊖	⊖
Ignition			⊖	⊖	⊖	⊖	○	⊖
Transmission			⊖	⊖	⊖	⊖	⊖	⊜
Electrical			●	●	●	●	◒	⊜
A/C			◒	◒	⊖	⊖	⊜	⊜
Suspension			⊜	⊜	⊜	⊜	⊜	⊜
Brakes			⊖	○	◒	○	⊖	⊜
Exhaust			⊖	⊖	⊖	⊜	⊜	⊜
Power equip.			●	●	●	◒	○	⊜
Paint/trim/rust			⊖	⊖	⊖	⊖	⊜	⊖
Integrity			●	◒	○	○	○	⊖
Hardware			●	●	●	◒	○	⊖
RELIABILITY VERDICT			✗	✗	✗	✗	✗	✗

Volkswagen Passat 4-cyl.

TROUBLE SPOTS	96	97	98	99	00	01	02	03
Engine	Insufficient data	Insufficient data	◒	○	○	⊖	⊖	⊜
Cooling			⊖	⊖	○	⊜	⊜	⊜
Fuel			○	○	●	⊖	⊖	⊜
Ignition			○	○	⊖	◒	●	⊖
Transmission			⊜	⊜	⊜	⊜	⊜	⊜
Electrical			●	◒	◒	○	◒	⊖
A/C			⊖	⊜	⊜	⊜	⊜	⊜
Suspension			◒	○	⊖	⊜	⊜	⊜
Brakes			○	○	⊖	⊖	⊜	⊜
Exhaust			⊜	⊜	⊖	⊜	⊜	⊜
Power equip.			●	◒	○	○	○	⊜
Paint/trim/rust			⊜	⊖	⊜	⊜	⊜	⊜
Integrity			○	○	○	○	⊖	⊜
Hardware			◒	○	○	○	⊖	⊜
RELIABILITY VERDICT			✗	✗	✗	-	✗	-

Volkswagen Passat V6

TROUBLE SPOTS	96	97	98	99	00	01	02	03
Engine	○	○	Insufficient data	◒	○	⊖	⊜	⊜
Cooling	○	◒		○	○	⊖	⊜	⊜
Fuel	◒	◒		○	○	⊖	⊖	⊜
Ignition	●	○		⊖	⊖	⊖	⊜	⊜
Transmission	◒	◒		⊖	⊜	⊜	⊜	⊜
Electrical	●	●		◒	◒	◒	○	⊜
A/C	◒	●		⊜	⊜	⊜	⊜	⊜
Suspension	◒	○		○	⊜	⊜	⊜	⊜
Brakes	◒	◒		◒	⊖	⊖	⊜	⊜
Exhaust	⊖	⊖		⊜	⊖	⊜	⊜	⊜
Power equip.	●	●		◒	○	○	○	⊖
Paint/trim/rust	○	○		⊖	⊖	⊜	⊜	⊜
Integrity	●	◒		○	○	⊖	⊖	⊜
Hardware	●	●		○	○	○	⊖	⊜
RELIABILITY VERDICT	✗	✗		✗	✗	-	-	-

Volvo 960, S90/V90

TROUBLE SPOTS	96	97	98	99	00	01	02	03
Engine	○	⊖	⊜					
Cooling	●	◒	○					
Fuel	○	⊜	⊖					
Ignition	⊖	⊖	⊖					
Transmission	⊖	◒	○					
Electrical	◒	◒	◒					
A/C	●	●	●					
Suspension	◒	◒	◒					
Brakes	◒	●	●					
Exhaust	⊖	⊖	⊜					
Power equip.	◒	●	●					
Paint/trim/rust	⊖	⊖	⊖					
Integrity	◒	◒	◒					
Hardware	○	●	●					
RELIABILITY VERDICT	-	✗	✗					

Volvo S40/V40

TROUBLE SPOTS	96	97	98	99	00	01	02	03
Engine					⊖	⊖	⊜	Insufficient data
Cooling					⊖	⊜	⊜	
Fuel					○	○	⊜	
Ignition					⊖	⊖	⊜	
Transmission					⊜	⊖	⊜	
Electrical					●	◒	○	
A/C					⊖	⊖	⊖	
Suspension					○	⊖	⊜	
Brakes					●	◒	○	
Exhaust					⊜	⊜	⊜	
Power equip.					⊖	○	○	
Paint/trim/rust					⊖	⊖	⊖	
Integrity					○	⊖	⊖	
Hardware					○	○	⊖	
RELIABILITY VERDICT					✗	-	-	

Volvo S70, S60

TROUBLE SPOTS	96	97	98	99	00	01	02	03
Engine			⊖	⊖	⊜	⊜	⊜	⊜
Cooling			⊖	⊖	⊜	⊜	⊜	⊜
Fuel			○	○	⊖	⊖	⊖	⊜
Ignition			⊖	⊖	⊖	⊜	⊜	⊜
Transmission			⊜	⊜	⊜	⊖	⊜	⊜
Electrical			●	●	●	○	○	⊖
A/C			○	⊖	⊖	⊖	⊜	⊜
Suspension			⊖	⊖	⊖	⊖	⊜	⊜
Brakes			◒	○	○	⊜	⊜	⊜
Exhaust			⊜	⊜	⊜	⊜	⊜	⊜
Power equip.			◒	○	○	○	⊖	⊜
Paint/trim/rust			⊖	⊖	⊖	⊖	⊜	⊜
Integrity			◒	○	○	○	⊖	⊜
Hardware			◒	○	⊖	⊖	⊖	⊜
RELIABILITY VERDICT			-	-	-	-	-	-

Volvo S80

TROUBLE SPOTS	96	97	98	99	00	01	02	03
Engine				○	○	⊖	⊜	Insufficient data
Cooling				⊖	○	⊖	⊜	
Fuel				◒	◒	⊜	⊖	
Ignition				⊖	⊖	⊜	⊜	
Transmission				◒	○	⊖	⊖	
Electrical				●	◒	◒	○	
A/C				⊖	⊖	⊜	⊜	
Suspension				◒	●	○	⊖	
Brakes				○	○	⊖	⊖	
Exhaust				⊜	⊜	⊜	⊜	
Power equip.				◒	◒	◒	○	
Paint/trim/rust				⊖	⊖	⊖	⊖	
Integrity				◒	○	○	○	
Hardware				◒	○	⊖	○	
RELIABILITY VERDICT				✗	✗	-	-	

Volvo V70 Cross Country, XC70

TROUBLE SPOTS	96	97	98	99	00	01	02	03
Engine			○	○	⊖	⊖	⊜	⊜
Cooling			○	⊖	⊜	⊜	⊜	⊜
Fuel			◒	●	◒	⊖	⊜	⊜
Ignition			⊜	⊖	⊖	⊜	⊜	⊜
Transmission			⊖	⊖	⊖	○	⊜	⊜
Electrical			●	●	●	◒	○	⊖
A/C			◒	⊖	⊖	⊜	⊜	⊜
Suspension			○	◒	○	⊖	⊜	⊖
Brakes			●	○	○	⊖	⊜	⊜
Exhaust			⊖	⊜	⊜	⊜	⊜	⊜
Power equip.			●	◒	◒	◒	○	⊖
Paint/trim/rust			⊖	⊜	⊖	⊖	⊜	⊜
Integrity			◒	○	⊖	○	⊖	⊜
Hardware			◒	⊖	⊖	○	⊖	⊜
RELIABILITY VERDICT			✗	✗	✗	✗	-	✓

Volvo XC90

TROUBLE SPOTS	96	97	98	99	00	01	02	03
Engine								⊜
Cooling								⊜
Fuel								⊜
Ignition								⊜
Transmission								⊜
Electrical								⊖
A/C								⊖
Suspension								⊖
Brakes								⊖
Exhaust								⊜
Power equip.								○
Paint/trim/rust								⊖
Integrity								⊖
Hardware								⊖
RELIABILITY VERDICT								✗

REFERENCE

PRODUCT RATINGS

How to use the Ratings listed here? First, read the general buying advice for the product you're interested in. The page numbers for these reports are noted on each Ratings page. The Ratings chart gives the big picture in terms of performance. The Quick Picks highlight the best models for most people plus models that may be especially suited to your family's needs. The Recommendations provide additional detail on features and performance for individual models. Use the key numbers to move easily between the charts and the other information. CONSUMER REPORTS checked the availability for most products for this book. Some tested models may no longer be available. Models similar to the tested models, when they exist, are also listed. Such models differ in features, not essential performance, according to the manufacturers.

QUICK GUIDE

AIR CONDITIONERS

All 35 air conditioners in our tests should keep you cool. Top-scoring models perform the most efficiently and quietly; several also offer the best value.

The Ratings rank models by overall performance within size groups. Once you determine the size you need, think about the placement of your window and focus on the "air directing" column. The more off-center your window, the more it matters that the unit adequately blow air where you need it (to the left or right, facing the unit). Buy the highest-rated model within your budget that meets this need and that has other attributes you may favor, such as a very good score for noise.

Excellent ⊜ Very good ⊖ Good ○ Fair ◒ Poor ●

Within types, in performance order. Gray **key numbers indicate Quick Picks.**

Key number	Brand & model	Price	Overall score (0–100: P F G VG E)	Specifications: Btu/hr.	EER	Test results: Comfort	Noise	Ease of use	Air directing	Fit (in.)
	SMALL: 5,000 TO 6,000 BTU/HR.									
1	**Kenmore** 72059 **A CR Best Buy**	$180		5,700	11.2	Excellent	Very good	Very good	L	23-34
2	**Friedrich** X Star XQ05J10A	400		5,400	10.7	Excellent	Very good	Good	L	25-42
3	**LG** LW5200ER	180		5,200	10.8	Excellent	Very good	Very good	L	22-33
4	**GE** Deluxe Series AGM06LCG	200		5,950	10.8	Excellent	Very good	Fair	-	22-34
5	**Frigidaire** Electrolux FAA065N7A	170		6,000	10.7	Excellent	Good	Good	R	22-36
6	**Whirlpool** ACQ068MP	175		6,000	11.0	Excellent	Very good	Very good	L	26-39
7	**Carrier** Solaire ACA051T	200		5,400	11.2	Excellent	Good	Very good	-	23-37
8	**Kenmore** 72056	130		5,300	10.8	Excellent	Very good	Very good	L	23-34
9	**LG** LP6000ER	370		6,000	10.7	Excellent	Very good	Good	-	25-41
10	**LG** LW5200E	150		5,200	10.8	Excellent	Very good	Very good	L	22-33
11	**Kenmore** 73069	220		6,000	10.7	Excellent	Good	Good	L	25-40
12	**Panasonic** Deluxe CW-XC54HU	185		5,200	10.8	Excellent	Good	Very good	L	23-36
13	**Goldstar** R5050	100		5,050	9.7	Excellent	Very good	Very good	L	22-33
14	**Fedders** X Series A6X06F2A	170		6,000	9.7	Excellent	Good	Very good	L	24-38
15	**Fedders** X Series A6X05F2B	120		5,200	9.7	Excellent	Fair	Excellent	L	24-37
16	**Haier** Preference Plus HWR06XCA	190		6,000	9.7	Excellent	Good	Very good	R	23-33

Excellent ⊜ Very good ⊖ Good ○ Fair ◒ Poor ●

Within types, in performance order. Gray key numbers indicate Quick Picks.

Key number	Brand & model	Price	Overall score (0–100; P F G VG E)	Specifications: Btu/hr.	Specifications: EER	Test results: Comfort	Test results: Noise	Test results: Ease of use	Test results: Air directing	Fit (in.)
	SMALL: 5,000 TO 6,000 BTU/HR. *Continued*									
17	**Amana** Touch Cooling AAC061STA	240		6,000	9.7	Excellent	Good	Very good	R	23-33
	MIDSIZED: 7,800 TO 8,200 BTU/HR.									
18	**LG** LW8000ER **A CR Best Buy**	260		8,200	10.9	Excellent	Very good	Very good	R	23-38
19	**Fedders** Q Series A7Q08F2A	230		8,000	10.8	Excellent	Good	Very good	L,R	24-36
20	**Friedrich** Quietmaster Electronic SS08J10R	600		8,200	11	Very good	Fair	Good	L	26-43
21	**GE** Deluxe Series AGM08FD	240		8,000	10.8	Excellent	Fair	Fair	-	22-34
22	**Whirlpool** ACQ088XP	210		8,000	10.8	Excellent	Fair	Very good	L	26-40
23	**Panasonic** Deluxe CW-XC84HU	280		7,800	10.8	Excellent	Good	Fair	-	22-36
	LARGE: 9,800 TO 12,300 BTU/HR.									
24	**Kenmore** 74107 **A CR Best Buy**	300		10,000	10.8	Excellent	Very good	Good	R	27-39
25	**Panasonic** Deluxe CW-XC104HU	330		9,800	10.8	Excellent	Very good	Fair	R	27-39
26	**LG** LW1000ER **A CR Best Buy**	300		10,000	11	Excellent	Very good	Good	L,R	28-39
27	**Kenmore** 76129	370		12,300	10.8	Excellent	Good	Very good	R	28-41
28	**GE** Deluxe Series AGM12AC	350		12,000	10.8	Excellent	Very good	Fair	-	27-39
29	**Carrier** XC-Series XCD121D	420		12,000	10	Very good	Very good	Fair	L	33-46
30	**Amana** Touch Cooling AAC101STA	370		10,800	9.8	Excellent	Good	Very good	L,R	25-35
31	**Fedders** Y Series A6Y12F2A	270		12,000	9.8	Excellent	Fair	Very good	L,R	27-43
32	**Frigidaire** Electrolux FAC106N1A	250		10,000	10.8	Excellent	Fair	Good	L	24-37
33	**Fedders** Q Series A6Q10F2A	240		10,000	9.8	Excellent	Poor	Fair	L,R	24-38
34	**Whirlpool** ACQ128XP	310		11,600	10.8	Very good	Fair	Very good	L	30-46
35	**Kenmore** 74131	300		12,000	9.8	Very good	Fair	Good	L	23-37

See report, page 98. Based on tests published in Consumer Reports in July 2004, with updated prices and availability.

Guide to the Ratings

Overall score is based mainly on comfort, noise, and energy efficiency. **Btu/hr.** (British thermal units per hour) is the manufacturer's rating of cooling capacity. **EER** is the maker's energy-efficiency rating; higher is better. **Comfort** is temperature and humidity control on low-cool. **Noise** reflects judgments and instrument readings on low-cool. **Ease of use** includes controls, adjusting the louvers, and changing the filter. **Air directing** shows which better direct air to the left (L) or right (R) facing the unit; notation of both L and R means good air flow in both directions; a dash means directional control in both directions was limited. **Fit** is the range of window widths the unit will fit. **Price** is approximate retail. **All models:** Require a 3-wire, 15-amp outlet protected by a time-delay fuse or circuit breaker. Are made for double-hung windows. Have a removable air filter. Have at least a 1-year parts-and-labor warranty. Should be installed by two people.

Quick Picks

Best value; efficient and quiet:

1 Kenmore $180 (small), CR Best Buy
18 LG $260 (midsized), CR Best Buy
24 Kenmore $300 (large), CR Best Buy

If you need air blown to the left:

1 Kenmore $180 (small), CR Best Buy
19 Fedders $230 (midsized)
26 LG $300 (large), CR Best Buy

If you need air blown to the right:

5 Frigidaire $170 (small)
18 LG $260 (midsized), CR Best Buy
24 Kenmore $300 (large), CR Best Buy

The Frigidaire is noisier than others of its size. If your window is only slightly off-center, you may want to consider noise more than air flow.

Recommendations

SMALL: 5,000 TO 6,000 BTU/HR.

1 KENMORE 72059 **A CR Best Buy Very good.** Exterior support bracket with leveling provision. Digital temperature readout (also indicates that power is on in energy-saver mode). Built-in timer. Has remote control. Up/down louver control. Minor drawbacks: No vent. Not certified by the Association of Home Appliance Manufacturers (AHAM) for capacity or efficiency.

2 FRIEDRICH X Star XQ05J10 **Very good.** Up/down louver control.

3 LG LW5200ER **Very good.** Digital temperature readout (also indicates that power is on in energy-saver mode). Minor drawbacks: Only 2 fan speeds on cool. No vent. Must manually turn on when power has been interrupted.

4 GE Deluxe Series AGM06LCG **Very good.** Slide-out chassis. Exterior support bracket with leveling provision. Digital temperature readout (also indicates power is on in energy-saver mode). Built-in timer. Has remote control up/down louver control.

5 FRIGIDAIRE Electrolux FAA065N7A **Very good.** Digital temperature readout (also

Recommendations

indicates that power is on in energy-saver mode). Built-in timer. Auto-fan speed. Dirty filter indicator. Has remote control up/down louver control. Minor drawback: No vent.

6 WHIRLPOOL ACQ068MP **Very good.** Digital temperature readout (also indicates that power is on in energy-saver mode). Built-in timer. Has remote control. Up/down louver control. Minor drawbacks: No vent. Not certified by the Association of Home Appliance Manufacturers (AHAM) for capacity or efficiency.

7 CARRIER Solaire ACA051T **Very good.** Digital temperature readout (also indicates that power is on in energy-saver mode). Up/down louver control.

8 KENMORE 72056 **Very good.** Exterior support bracket with leveling provision. Digital temperature readout (also indicates that power is on in energy-saver mode). Built-in timer. Has remote control. Up/down louver control. Minor drawbacks: Only 2 fan speeds on cool. No vent. Not certified by the Association of Home Appliance Manufacturers (AHAM) for capacity or efficiency. Must manually turn on when power has been interrupted.

9 LG LP6000ER **Very good.** Low profile design. Exterior support bracket with leveling provision. Has handles to ease carrying. Digital temperature readout (also indicates that power is on in energy-saver mode). Built-in timer. Has remote control. Up/down louver control. Minor drawbacks: No vent. Not certified by the Association of Home Appliance Manufacturers (AHAM) for capacity or efficiency. Similar: LG BP6000ER, LG GP6000ER.

10 LG LW5200E **Very good.** Minor drawbacks: Only 2 fan speeds on cool. No vent. Must manually turn on when power has been interrupted.

11 KENMORE 73069 **Very good.** Low profile design. Exterior support bracket with leveling provision. Handles to ease carrying. Digital temperature readout (also indicates that power is on in energy-saver mode). Built-in timer. Has remote control. Up/down louver control. Minor drawbacks: No vent. Not certified by the Association of Home Appliance Manufacturers (AHAM) for capacity or efficiency.

12 PANASONIC Deluxe CW-XC54HU **Very good.** Exterior support bracket with leveling provision. Digital temperature readout (also indicates that power is on in energy-saver mode). Built-in timer. Has remote control. Minor drawbacks: Only 2 fan speeds on cool. No vent.

13 GOLDSTAR R5050 **Very good.** Minor drawbacks: Only 2 fan speeds on cool. No vent. Not certified by the Association of Home Appliance Manufacturers (AHAM) for capacity or efficiency.

14 FEDDERS X Series A6X06F2A **Very good.** Digital temperature readout (also indicates that power is on in energy-saver mode). 2-yr. parts-only warranty on fan motor. Minor drawbacks: No upper sash lock. Only 2 fan speeds on cool. No vent. Not certified by the Association of Home Appliance Manufacturers (AHAM) for capacity or efficiency. Must manually turn on when power has been interrupted. Similar: Maytag M6X06F2A.

15 FEDDERS X Series A6X05F2B **Very good.** Digital temperature readout (also indicates that power is on in energy-saver mode). 2-yr. parts-only warranty on fan motor. Minor drawbacks: No upper sash lock. Only 2 fan speeds on cool. No vent. Not certified by the Association of Home

Recommendations

Appliance Manufacturers (AHAM) for capacity or efficiency. Must manually turn on when power has been interrupted.

16 HAIER Preference Plus HWR06XCA **Very good.** Through-the-wall installation instructions provided. Digital temperature readout (also indicates that power is on in energy-saver mode). Up/down louver control. Minor drawback: No vent.

17 AMANA Touch Cooling AAC061STA **Very good.** Through-the-wall installation instructions provided. Digital temperature readout (also indicates that power is on in energy-saver mode). Up/down louver control. Minor drawbacks: No vent. Must manually turn on when power has been interrupted.

MIDSIZED: 7,000 TO 8,200 BTU/HR.

18 LG LW8000ER **A CR Best Buy Very good.** 2-yr. parts-only warranty on fan motor. Minor drawback: Harder to install. Similar: LB8000ER

19 FEDDERS Q Series A7Q08F2A **Very good.** Auto-fan speed Dirty filter indicator 2-yr. parts-only warranty on fan motor. Minor drawbacks: Harder to install. No upper sash lock. Not certified by the Association of Home Appliance Manufacturers (AHAM) for capacity or efficiency. Must manually turn on when power has been interrupted. No slide-out chassis. Similar: Maytag M7Q08F2A

20 FRIEDRICH Quietmaster Electronic SS08J10R **Very good.** Through-the-wall installation instructions provided. Up/down louver control. Minor drawbacks: Harder to install. No upper sash lock.

21 GE Deluxe Series AGM08FD **Very good.** Minor drawback: Harder to install.

22 WHIRLPOOL ACQ088XP **Very good.** Auto-fan speed. Minor drawbacks: No exterior support bracket. No vent. Not certified by the Association of Home Appliance Manufacturers (AHAM) for capacity or efficiency.

23 PANASONIC Deluxe CW-XC84HU **Very good.** Minor drawback: Harder to install.

LARGE: 9,800 TO 12,300 BTU/HR.

24 KENMORE 74107 **A CR Best Buy Very good.** Digital temperature readout (also indicates that power is on in energy-saver mode). Built-in timer. Has remote control. Up/down louver control.

25 PANASONIC Deluxe CW-XC104HU **Very good.** Digital temperature readout (also indicates that power is on in energy-saver mode). Built-in timer. Has remote control. Up/down louver control.

26 LG LW1000ER A CR Best Buy. **Very good.** Digital temperature readout (also indicates that power is on in energy-saver mode). Built-in timer. Has remote control. Up/down louver control.

27 KENMORE 76129 **Very good.** Digital temperature readout (also indicates that power is on in energy-saver mode). Built-in timer. Has remote control. Up/down louver control.

28 GE Deluxe Series AGM12AC **Very good.** Minor drawback: Harder to install.

29 CARRIER XC Series XCD121D **Very good.** Through-the-wall installation instructions provided. Minor drawbacks: No upper sash lock. Only 1 fan-only setting. Shorter power cord than most.

30 AMANA Touch Cooling AAC101STA **Very good.** Through-the-wall installation instructions provided. Digital temperature readout (also indicates that power is on in energy-saver mode). 2-yr. parts-only warranty on fan motor.

31 FEDDERS Y Series A6Y12F2A **Very good.** Through-the-wall installation instructions provided. Digital temperature readout (also indicates that power is on in energy-saver mode). Minor drawbacks: No upper sash lock. Not certified by the Association of Home Appliance Manufacturers (AHAM) for capacity or efficiency. Must manually turn on when power has been interrupted. Similar: Maytag M6Y12F2A.

32 FRIGIDAIRE Electrolux FAC106N1A **Very good.** Digital temperature readout (also indicates that power is on in energy-saver mode). Built-in timer. Auto-fan speed. Dirty filter indicator. Has remote control Up/down louver control. Minor drawbacks: No slide-out chassis. No exterior support bracket.

33 FEDDERS Q Series A6Q10F2A **Very good.** Digital temperature readout (also indicates that power is on in energy-saver mode) Built-in timer. Auto-fan speed. Dirty filter indicator. Has remote control. 2-yr. parts-only warranty on fan motor. Minor drawbacks: No upper sash lock. Not certified by the Association of Home Appliance Manufacturers (AHAM) for capacity or efficiency. Must manually turn on when power has been interrupted. No slide-out chassis. Similar: Maytag M6Q10F2A.

34 WHIRLPOOL ACQ128XP **Very good.** Digital temperature readout (also indicates that power is on in energy-saver mode). Built-in timer. Auto-fan speed. Has remote control. Up/down louver control. Minor drawbacks: No vent. Not certified by the Association of Home Appliance Manufacturers (AHAM) for capacity or efficiency. Shorter power cord than most.

35 KENMORE 74131 **Very good.** Digital temperature readout (also indicates that power is on in energy-saver mode). Built-in timer. Auto-fan speed. Dirty filter indicator. Has remote control. Up/down louver control. Minor drawback: No exterior support bracket.

CAMCORDERS

You can expect a digital camcorder to deliver very good video. Digital camcorders that record directly onto small DVD discs topped the Ratings. However, that doesn't automatically make them the best choice. As the Ratings show, most DVD models were not markedly better than many camcorders using MiniDV tape. The MiniDV camcorders win on price, making them the type that most people should consider first. The DVD models are for people who want ease of playback above all else.

Most camcorders weigh about a pound, give or take a few ounces. As camcorders get smaller and lighter, image-stabilization features become more important. A lightweight camcorder is harder to hold steady than a heavy one. Fortunately, most did an excellent job of minimizing the shakes.

Nearly all these camcorders turned in fair or poor performance when we tested them in low light. The Canon (11) and Sony (12) were better than the rest.

Analog camcorders are a dying breed. We tested two this time, neither in the same league as the digitals. Their picture quality is only fair, comparable with that of a rental tape.

The Ratings rank models strictly on performance. Quick Picks considers other factors such as features, reliability, and value.

Excellent / Very good / Good / Fair / Poor

Within types, in performance order. Gray key numbers indicate Quick Picks.

Key number	Brand & model (Similar models, in small type, comparable to tested model.)	Price	Format	Overall score (0–100; P F G VG E)	Test results: Picture quality	Ease of use	Image stabilizer	Audio quality	Features: Weight (lb.)	Optical zoom	LCD size (in.)
	DIGITAL MODELS										
1	**Panasonic** VDR-M70	$850	DVD-RAM, -R		Excellent	Good	Excellent	Very good	1.2	10	2.5
2	**Hitachi** DZ-MV550A	700	DVD-RAM, -R		Very good	Very good	Excellent	Good	1.2	18	2.5
3	**Panasonic** VDR-M50	800	DVD-RAM, -R		Very good	Good	Excellent	Very good	1.4	18	2.5
4	**Hitachi** DZ-MV580A	800	DVD-RAM, -R		Very good	Very good	Excellent	Very good	1.4	10	2.5
5	**Panasonic** PV-GS200	1,000	MiniDV		Very good	Good	Excellent	Very good	1.2	10	2.5
6	**Canon** Optura 30 Optura 40	900	MiniDV		Very good	Very good	Excellent	Good	1.4	12	2.5
7	**Sony** DCR-HC20 DCR-HC30	500	MiniDV		Very good	Good	Excellent	Fair	1	10	2.5
8	**Sony** DCR-HC40	700	MiniDV		Very good	Good	Excellent	Very good	1	10	2.5

Excellent ⊜ | Very good ⊖ | Good ○ | Fair ◒ | Poor ●

Within types, in performance order. Gray key numbers indicate Quick Picks.

Key number	Brand & model (Similar models, in small type, comparable to tested model.)	Price	Format	Overall score (0–100; P F G VG E)	Test results: Picture quality	Test results: Ease of use	Test results: Image stabilizer	Test results: Audio quality	Features: Weight (lb.)	Features: Optical zoom	Features: LCD size (in.)
	DIGITAL MODELS *Continued*										
9	**Sony** DCR-IP1	$1,200	MicroMV		Very good	Good	Excellent	Good	0.6	10	2
10	**Sony** DCR-HC85	1,000	MiniDV		Very good	Good	Excellent	Fair	1.6	10	3.5
11	**Canon** Elura 60 Elura 65	600	MiniDV		Good	Very good	Excellent	Fair	1.2	14	2.5
12	**Sony** DCR-TRV260 **A CR Best Buy** DCR-TRV460	350	D8		Very good	Good	Good	Very good	2	20	2.5
13	**Panasonic** PV-GS55 PV-GS33	600	MiniDV		Very good	Good	Very good	Very good	0.8	10	2.5
14	**Panasonic** PV-GS120	700	MiniDV		Good	Good	Good	Very good	1.2	10	2.5
15	**Sony** DCR-DVD201	1,000	DVD-RAM, -R		Good	Good	Excellent	Fair	1.2	10	2.5
16	**Sony** DCR-PC109	900	MiniDV		Very good	Good	Excellent	Good	1	10	2.5
17	**JVC** GR-D33US GR-D72S	350	MiniDV		Very good	Very good	Good	Fair	1.2	16	2.5
18	**JVC** GR-D93US	550	MiniDV		Very good	Good	Good	Fair	1.4	10	2.5
19	**Canon** Elura 70	800	MiniDV		Good	Very good	Excellent	Good	1.4	18	2.5
20	**Canon** ZR85 ZR90	500	MiniDV		Good	Very good	Good	Fair	1.2	20	2.5
21	**JVC** GR-D230US	580	MiniDV		Good	Good	Very good	Fair	1.2	10	2.5
22	**Samsung** SC-D103	330	MiniDV		Good	Good	Fair	Very good	1.2	18	2.5
23	**Sony** DCR-DVD101	900	DVD-RAM, -R		Good	Good	Excellent	Good	1.2	10	2.5
24	**Canon** ZR80	400	MiniDV		Good	Very good	Good	Fair	1.2	18	2.5
25	**JVC** GR-DX77US GR-DX97US	475	MiniDV		Good	Good	Excellent	Good	1.2	12	2.5
26	**Panasonic** PV-GS9 PV-GS2, PV-GS12, PV-GS14, PV-GS15	350	MiniDV		Good	Good	Very good	Poor	1	20	2.5
	ANALOG MODELS										
27	**Sony** CCD-TRV128 CCD-TRV328	290	Hi8		Fair	Good	NA	Very good	2	20	2.5
28	**Panasonic** PV-L354D PV-L454D	230	VHS-C		Fair	Very good	Very good	Poor	2.4	20	2.5

See report, page 30. Based on tests published in Consumer Reports in November 2004.

Guide to the Ratings

Overall score is based mainly on picture quality; ease of use, image stabilizing, and audio quality carried less weight. **Picture quality** is based on the judgments of trained panelists who viewed static images shot in good light at standard speed (SP) for tape and "fine" mode for DVDs. **Ease of use** takes into account ergonomics, weight, how accurately the viewfinder frames scenes, and contrast in the LCD viewer. **Image stabilizer** indicates how well that circuitry worked. **Audio quality** represents accuracy using the built-in microphone, plus freedom from noise and flutter. **Weight** includes battery and tape or disk. **Optical zoom range** is as stated by the manufacturer. **Price** is approximate retail.

Expect these camcorders to have: Tape counter. Backlight-compensation switch. Manual aperture control. High-speed manual shutter. Manual white balance. Simple switch for manual focus. Audio dub. Tape-position memory. Audio fade. Transitional effects. S-video signal out. Video fade.

Quick Picks

Best values in digital tape:

7 Sony $500

12 Sony $350, CR Best Buy

Sony has been a reliable brand of camcorder. The (7) weighs just a pound and is among the lowest-priced digital camcorders we tested. Although very good overall, its sound quality was only fair; that may not matter much for recording speech, but you may notice it with music. The (12), a CR Best Buy, has much better audio and a lower price. Moreover, it's the only model we tested that can use and play 8mm and Hi8 tapes, a consideration if you already have a library of those. However, it's also the heaviest digital we tested.

Best value in a DVD camcorder:

2 Hitachi $700

This is the least expensive DVD camcorder we tested; its straightforward controls also made it one of the easiest to use. We don't have enough data to judge the reliability of DVD camcorders.

COOKTOPS & WALL OVENS

It's hard to choose a bad electric cooktop or wall oven; we've found wider performance differences among gas cooktops. In our tests, most cooktops produce lots of heat for fast cooking and also do well at providing low heat for simmering.

Wall ovens generally perform very well overall, and most are large enough to handle a Thanksgiving dinner or lots of hot hors d'oeuvres.

Note, due to a major line change, the Kenmore models we tested for this report are no longer available and do not appear in the Ratings below.

The Ratings list products strictly on performance. Quick Picks considers factors such as features and value.

ELECTRIC COOKTOPS

Excellent · Very good · Good · Fair · Poor

Within types, in performance order. Gray key numbers indicate Quick Picks.

Key number	Brand & model	Price	Overall score (0–100: P F G VG E)	Test results: Heating, high	Test results: Heating, low	Features: Elements, high	Features: Elements, medium	Features: Elements, low	Features: Bridge element	Features: Touch controls
	Similar models, in small type, comparable to tested model except it is 36 inches wide, has an extra element or warming zone, and costs about $100 more.									
1	**Jenn-Air** JEC9530AD[W]	$700		Excellent	Excellent	1	1	2		
2	**Frigidaire** Gallery GLEC30S8C[S] **CR Best Buy** GLEC36S8C[ ]	500		Very good	Excellent	1	2	1	•	
3	**GE** Profile JP930TC[WW] JP960TC[ ]	750		Very good	Excellent	1	2	1	•	
4	**GE** Profile JP939BH[BB]	1,200		Very good	Excellent	2		2		•
5	**Jenn-Air** JEC8430AD[W]	580		Very good	Excellent	1	2	1		
6	**KitchenAid** KECC508M[SS]	900		Very good	Excellent	1	1	2		•
7	**Thermador** CEP304Z[B]	1,300		Very good	Excellent	2		2		•
8	**Whirlpool** Gold GJC3034L[P] GJC3634L[ ]	570		Very good	Excellent	1	1	2		
9	**Whirlpool** RCC3024L[Q]	480		Excellent	Excellent	1	1	2		
10	**Bosch** NES73[2] NES93[ ]	950		Very good	Excellent	1	1	2		•
11	**Maytag** MEC5430BD[B]	450		Very good	Excellent	1	2	1		
12	**Amana** AKT3040[WW] AKT3650[ ]	550		Very good	Very good	1	1	2		
13	**KitchenAid** KECC502G[WH]	650		Very good	Good	1	1	2		

See report, page 68. Based on tests published in Consumer Reports in August 2004, with updated prices and availability.

GAS COOKTOPS

Key number	Brand & model	Price	Overall score	Test results: Heating high	Test results: Heating low	Features: Burners, high	Features: Burners, medium	Features: Burners, low	Style options: Stainless-steel	Style options: Glass	Style options: Porcelain enamel	Style options: Continuous grates
	Similar models, in small type, comparable to tested model except it is 30 inches wide, has only 4 burners, and costs about $120 less.		0–100 (P F G VG E)									
14	**GE** Monogram ZGU375NSD[SS] ZGU375LSD[SS] (propane)	$1,400		⊖	⊜	1	4		•			•
15	**Jenn-Air** JGC8536AD[S] **A CR Best Buy**	800		⊜	⊖	2	1	2	•			•
16	**Maytag** MGC6536BD[W] **A CR Best Buy** MGC6430BD[ ]	650		○	⊜	1	3	1		•		•
17	**Thermador** SGSX365Z[S]	1,400		⊖	⊖	1	4		•			•
18	**Jenn-Air** JGC9536AD[B]	800		⊜	○	2	1	2		•		•
19	**KitchenAid** Pro Line KGCV465M[SS]	1,900		⊖	○	3		2	•		•	•
20	**GE** Profile JGP962TEC[WW]	1,100		⊖	○	1	2	2		•		•
21	**Magic Chef** CGC2536AD[W]	330		○	⊖	1	4				•	
22	**Amana** AKS3640[SS]	550		○	⊖	1	4		•			•
23	**KitchenAid** KGCC566H[WH]	860		⊖	⊖	2	1	2		•		•
24	**Bosch** NGT93[5]	925		⊖	◒	1	3	1	•			•
25	**Whirlpool** Gold GLT3615L[B]	700		◒	○	1	2	2		•		
26	**Viking** VGSU161-6B[SS]	1,600		○	◒	4	1	1	•			•

30-INCH ELECTRIC WALL OVENS

Key number	Brand & model	Price	Overall score	Test results: Capacity	Test results: Bake	Test results: Broil	Features: Covered element	Features: Convection cooking
	Similar models, in small type, comparable to tested model.		0–100 (P F G VG E)					
1	**Jenn-Air** JJW8530DD[W]	$1,110		⊖	⊖	⊖	•	
2	**Jenn-Air** JJW9530DD[S]	1,600		⊖	⊖	⊖	•	•
3	**GE** Profile JT915WF[WW]	1,500		○	⊖	⊖	•	•
4	**Maytag** MEW6530DD[W]	1,100		○	⊖	⊖		•
5	**GE** JTP20WF[WW]	850		⊖	○	⊖		
6	**Frigidaire** Gallery GLEB30S8C[S] PLEB30S8C[ ]	750		◒	⊜	○		•
7	**KitchenAid** Superba KEBC107K[WH]	1,450		⊖	⊖	⊖	•	•
8	**Whirlpool** Gold GBS307PD[Q]	1,160		⊖	⊖	◒		•
9	**Bosch** HBL74[2]	1,600		◒	○	○	•	•

Guide to the Ratings

Overall score for cooktops covers high- and low-heating performance; for wall ovens, score includes capacity, cooking performance, self-cleaning. **Heating, high,** for cooktops, denotes how quickly the highest-powered element heated 6⅓ quarts of water to a near-boil. **Heating, low** shows how well the least-powerful element melted and held chocolate without scorching and whether the most powerful, set to low, held tomato sauce below a boil. **Capacity,** for wall ovens, is usable space. **Bake** shows evenness for cakes and cookies. **Broil** shows cooking evenness and searing for a tray of burgers. **Price** is the approximate retail. Under brand & model, brackets show a tested model's color code. **For cooktops:** Number of elements or burners cover the following categories. **High:** more than 2,000 watts for electric, 11,000 Btu/hr. for gas. **Medium:** over 1,500 up to 2,000 watts for electric, over 6,500 up to 11,000 Btu/hr. for gas. **Low:** 1,500 watts or less for electric, 6,500 Btu/hr. or less for gas.

Quick Picks

COOKTOPS

Best for most cooking:

2 Frigidaire, $500
16 Maytag, $650
21 Magic Chef, $330

The electric Frigidaire (2) has a bridge element, useful when you're using a griddle. Among gas cooktops, the Maytag (16) excelled at low-heat simmering. Both are CR Best Buys. Consider the Magic Chef (21) if you can trade style and features for a very low price; it has a porcelain-enamel-on-steel surface.

If fast cooking matters most:

1 Jenn-Air, $700
15 Jenn-Air, $800
18 Jenn-Air, $800

Three Jenn-Air models (1, 15, 18) excelled at high-heat settings. The Jenn-Air (15) is a CR Best Buy. The gas models have continuous grates, for sliding pots from burner to burner.

WALL OVENS

Best for most cooking:

5 GE, $850
6 Frigidaire, $750

The GE (5) has generous capacity and broils very well. The Frigidaire (6), though small, has a convection feature and is excellent at baking.

If you want an easy-to-clean oven:

1 Jenn-Air, $1,110

The Jenn-Air (1) has a covered bottom element, which makes for easy cleanup of drips and spills. It's also excellent at self-cleaning.

DIGITAL CAMERAS

All the cameras produced uncropped 8x10 prints that are very good or excellent—a quality difference that's subtle. However, higher-megapixel models would have a clear edge with heavily cropped or even larger prints.

Note that battery life and next-shot delay vary widely within megapixel ranges. So does price, with the most expensive models in each category typically having a long zoom range and manual controls.

Excellent ⊜ Very good ⊖ Good ○ Fair ◒ Poor ●

Within types, in performance order. Gray key numbers indicate Quick Picks.

Key number	Brand & model	Price	Overall score (0–100; P F G VG E)	Test results: Print quality	Camera size	Weight (oz.)	Flash range (ft.)	Battery life (shots)	Next-shot delay (sec.)	Optical zoom	Features: Manual controls	Secure grip	Charger	AA batteries	Direct printing
	2- TO 3-MEGAPIXEL CAMERAS *For printing everyday snapshots*														
1	**Olympus** Camedia C-740 Ultra Zoom	$280		⊜	M	13	15	65	3	10x	●			●	
2	**Canon** PowerShot S1IS	360		⊜	M	17	14	180	3	10x	●	●		●	●
3	**Canon** PowerShot A75	210		⊜	M	11	14	520	2	3x	●	●		●	●
4	**Fujifilm** FinePix F700	325		⊖	M	7	16	180	1	3x	●		●		
5	**Canon** PowerShot A70	225		⊖	M	11	14	280	2	3x	●	●		●	
6	**Sony** Cyber-Shot DSC P8	280		⊖	C	7	11	95	2	3x			●		
7	**Olympus** Stylus 300	230		⊖	C	7	12	170	2	3x			●		
8	**Canon** PowerShot SD110	235		⊖	C	7	10	380	2	2x			●		●
9	**Konica Minolta** DiMage Xg	225		⊖	S	5	6	280	4	3x			●		●
10	**Olympus** D-540 Zoom	165		⊖	C	7	11	460	5	3x				●	●
11	**Nikon** Coolpix 2200 **A CR Best Buy**	125		⊖	C	7	10	340	2	3x		●			●
12	**Sony** Cyber-Shot DSC P72	230		⊖	M	9	12	260	3	3x			●	●	
13	**Hewlett-Packard** Photosmart 735	215		⊖	M	10	10	35	3	3x	●			●	
14	**Canon** PowerShot A60	135		⊖	M	11	14	360	2	3x	●	●		●	
15	**Panasonic** Lumix DMC-F1-S	355		⊖	C	6	8	95	2	3x			●		
16	**Fujifilm** FinePix A330 **A CR Best Buy**	130		⊖	C	7	11	380	4	3x				●	●
17	**Pentax** Optio 33L	230		⊖	M	8	16	35	6	3x					
18	**Canon** PowerShot A310	130		⊜	C	8	7	420	3	None				●	●

Within types, in performance order. Gray key numbers indicate Quick Picks.

Key number	Brand & model	Price	Overall score (P F G VG E, 0–100)	Print quality	Camera size	Weight (oz.)	Flash range (ft.)	Battery life (shots)	Next-shot delay (sec.)	Optical zoom	Manual controls	Secure grip	Charger	AA batteries	Direct printing
	2- TO 3-MEGAPIXEL CAMERAS *Continued*														
19	**Panasonic** Lumix DMC-LC33	175		⊖	M	7	8	80	2	3x		•		•	
20	**Pentax** Optio S	290		⊖	C	4	11	60	8	3x			•		
21	**Sony** Cyber-Shot DSC-P52	230		⊖	M	10	11	160	1	2x			•	•	
22	**Sony** CD Mavica MVC-CD350	370		⊖	L	18	8	120	2	3x		•	•		
23	**Minolta** Dimage E223	185		⊖	M	9	8	25	16	3x				•	
24	**Kodak** EasyShare CX7300	120		⊖	C	7	8	240	2	None				•	
25	**Canon** PowerShot A300	175		⊖	M	8	7	60	2	None				•	
26	**Sony** Cyber-Shot DSC-U60	235		⊖	C	6	6	65	3	None		•	•		
	4- TO 5-MEGAPIXEL CAMERAS *For making 8x10s from cropped photos*														
27	**Kodak** EasyShare DX 6490	400		⊜	L	14	16	60	2	10x	•	•	•		
28	**Olympus** C-765 Ultra Zoom	400		⊜	M	11	15	130	2	10x	•		•		•
29	**Olympus** C-750 Ultra Zoom	475		⊜	M	15	15	120	3	10x	•		•	•	
30	**Olympus** C-770 Ultra Zoom	425		⊜	M	12	15	120	3	10x	•		•		•
31	**Nikon** Coolpix 5700	615		⊜	L	19	13	100	3	8x	•	•	•	•	
32	**Sony** Cyber-Shot DSC-F717	575		⊜	L	24	15	200	2	5x	•	•	•		
33	**Olympus** Stylus 410	235		⊜	C	7	12	360	2	3x			•		•
34	**Olympus** C-5060 Zoom	520		⊜	M	18	12	560	2	4x	•	•			
35	**Kodak** EasyShare CX7430	220		⊜	C	8	12	520	2	3x				•	
36	**Canon** PowerShot G5	530		⊜	M	18	16	750	3	4x	•	•	•		
37	**Nikon** Coolpix 5400	470		⊜	M	14	15	240	2	4x	•	•	•		
38	**Hewlett-Packard** PhotoSmart 945	375		⊜	L	17	8	60	2	8x	•	•		•	
39	**Canon** PowerShot S410	310		⊜	C	8	11	380	2	3x			•		•
40	**Kodak** Easy Share LS753	255		⊜	C	6	10	400	1	2.8x			•		
41	**Konica Minolta** DiMage Z2	365		⊖	M	14	10	280	3	10x	•	•		•	•
42	**Nikon** Coolpix 4300	315		⊜	M	10	12	360	3	3x	•	•	•		
43	**Kodak** EasyShare LS743	300		⊜	C	6	10	400	2	2.8x			•		
44	**Sony** Cyber-Shot DSC-P100	325		⊜	C	7	11	460	3	3x	•		•		•
45	**Olympus** D-580 Zoom	220		⊜	C	8	11	600	2	3x				•	•
46	**Hewlett-Packard** PhotoSmart R707 **A CR Best Buy**	280		⊜	C	7	9	320	3	3x	•		•		•
47	**Panasonic** Lumix DMC-LC1	1,150		⊜	L	27	16	320	4	3x	•	•	•		•

Key number	Brand & model	Price	Overall score (0–100; P F G VG E)	Print quality	Camera size	Weight (oz.)	Flash range (ft.)	Battery life (shots)	Next-shot delay (sec.)	Optical zoom	Manual controls	Secure grip	Charger	AA batteries	Direct printing
4- TO 5-MEGAPIXEL CAMERAS *Continued*															
48	**Panasonic** Lumix DMC-LC70	245		◓	C	8	16	320	2	3x		●		●	●
49	**Canon** PowerShot S500	385		●	C	8	11	320	3	3x			●		●
50	**Sony** Cyber-Shot DSC-P73	250		●	C	8	11	560	4	3x	●		●	●	●
51	**Canon** PowerShot A80	285		◓	M	12	14	360	3	3x	●	●		●	
52	**Olympus** Camedia C-5000	320		◓	M	10	12	40	3	3x	●	●	●		
53	**Pentax** S40 Optio	215		◓	C	6	19	95	5	3x				●	●
54	**Pentax** S4i Optio	295		◓	S	4	11	150	3	3x			●		●
55	**Hewlett-Packard** Photosmart 935	335		●	M	9	8	50	2	3x	●	●		●	
56	**Sony** Cyber-Shot DSC-T1	380		●	S	6	5	120	4	3x			●		●
57	**Sony** Cyber-Shot DSC-W1	325		◓	M	9	11	240	4	3x	●		●	●	●
58	**Nikon** Coolpix 5200	395		◓	S	6	15	120	3	3x		●	●		●
59	**Canon** PowerShot SD10	320		●	S	4	7	110	2	None			●		●
60	**Olympus** Stylus 400	275		◓	C	6	12	150	4	3x			●		
61	**Sony** Cyber-Shot DSC-V1	420		◓	M	10	9	120	2	4x	●		●		
62	**Fujifilm** FinePix A340	180		◓	C	7	11	340	4	3x				●	●
63	**Kyocera** Contax TVS Digital	650		◓	M	9	10	45	7	3x	●		●		
64	**Sony** CD Mavica MVC-CD500	525		◓	L	21	16	55	2	3x	●	●	●		
65	**Sony** Cyber-Shot DSC-P92	310		◓	M	9	12	260	2	3x			●	●	
66	**Vivitar** Vivicam 3826	200		◓	M	9	0	120	6	3x				●	
67	**Kyocera** Finecam SL400R	330		◓	S	5	8	45	6	3x	●		●		
6- TO 8-MEGAPIXEL CAMERAS *For maximum flexibility in cropping and enlarging*															
68	**Nikon** Coolpix 8700	760		●	L	19	13	140	3	8x	●	●	●		●
69	**Olympus** Camedia C-8080	755		●	L	27	19	120	3	5x	●	●	●		●
70	**Fujifilm** FinePix S7000	465		●	L	21	28	60	2	6x	●	●		●	
71	**Canon** PowerShot Pro1	775		●	L	23	16	110	3	7x	●	●	●		●
72	**Kodak** EasyShare DX7630 **A CR Best Buy**	340		●	C	10	14	400	3	3x	●	●	●		
73	**Olympus** Camedia C-60 **A CR Best Buy**	310		●	M	8	11	400	2	3x	●		●		●
74	**Konica Minolta** Dimage A2	785		●	L	24	8	160	1	7x	●	●	●		●
75	**Sony** Cyber-shot DSC-F828	810		●	L	33	15	110	4	7x	●	●	●		●
76	**Casio** EX-P600	475		◓	M	9	10	260	4	4x	●		●		●

See report, page 33. Based on tests published in Consumer Reports in November 2004.

Guide to the Ratings

Overall score is based mainly on print quality, weight, and the presence of useful features. **Print quality** is based on expert judgments using 8x10-inch prints made with each camera's best resolution and compression settings and printed on a high-rated inkjet printer. **Camera size** denotes small (S), compact (C), medium (M), and large (L) cameras. **Weight** includes battery and memory card. **Flash range** is the maximum claimed range for a well-lighted subject. **Battery life** is the number of high-resolution photos taken with the batteries supplied; half the shots used flash, and the zoom lens was racked in and out. **Next-shot delay** is the time the camera needs to ready itself for the next photo. **Optical zoom** refers to the range of focal lengths. A 3x zoom means the subject appears about three times closer than it is. **Price** is approximate retail, to nearest $5.

Quick Picks

Best values for simple snapshots:

- **2** Canon $360
- **3** Canon $210
- **11** Nikon $125, CR Best Buy
- **14** Canon $135
- **16** Fujifilm $130, CR Best Buy

Unlike the Olympus (1), these 2- and 3-megapixel models all have a long battery life. The Canons have manual controls; (2) costs more because it has a 10x zoom, image stabilization, and other features, while (3) has the longest battery life in this group. The Canon (14) is the only one of this group that can't print directly to a Pictbridge-enabled printer, but prints directly to a Canon printer. The inexpensive Nikon (11) is small enough to fit in a pocket and has excellent battery life, but no manual controls. The inexpensive Fujifilm (16) also fits in a pocket, but has a longer next-shot delay than the others and no manual controls.

Best values if you'll often edit shots:

- **28** Olympus $400
- **33** Olympus $235
- **35** Kodak $220
- **41** Konica Minolta $365
- **45** Olympus $220
- **46** HP $280, CR Best Buy

All are 4- to 5-megapixel models. The Olympus (28) has a 10x zoom, manual controls, and very good battery life, but no image stabilization. The Olympus (33), Kodak (35), Olympus (45), and HP (46) are all small enough to fit in a pocket and have excellent battery life, but only the HP (46) has manual controls. The Konica (41) has a 10x zoom and manual controls, but lacks image stabilization and takes 3 seconds between shots.

Best values for extensive editing of casual photos; both are CR Best Buys:

- **72** Kodak $340
- **73** Olympus $310

As 6-megapixel models, these give you more flexibility than 4- and 5-megapixel cameras to enlarge and manipulate images. But their 3x zoom lenses make them better suited to casual photography than more serious shooting. The Kodak (72) is smaller; the Olympus (73) can print directly to a printer.

Best choices for serious photography:

- **68** Nikon $760
- **74** Konica Minolta $785

These 8-megapixel cameras are suitable if you routinely make jumbo prints of enlarged images and take ambitious photos that require the maximum amount of photographic control. They have manual controls and long zoom-lens ranges of 5x to 8x. Both come with a charger and can print directly to Pictbridge-enabled printers. But they're also large and, at about a pound (the Nikon) and a pound and a half (Konica Minolta), very heavy.

DISHWASHERS

All but a few of the models we tested will clean dishes well, so your choice may hinge on style, energy efficiency, noise, or brand reliability.

The Ratings rank models by performance. The Quick Picks highlight models you might want to consider based on how they scored and on factors such as reliability, features, and price.

Excellent · Very good · Good · Fair · Poor

Within types, in performance order. Gray key numbers indicate Quick Picks.

Key	Brand & model	Price	Overall score (0–100; P F G VG E)	Washing	Energy use	Noise	Loading flexibility	Ease of use	Cycle time (hr:min)	Sensor	Self-cleaning filter	Stainless-steel tub	Stainless finish available	Hidden controls
1	**Bosch** SHU66C0[2]	$850		Excellent	Very good	Excellent	Very good	Very good	1:45	●		●	●	
2	**Bosch** SHU43C0[2]	580		Excellent	Very good	Excellent	Very good	Good	1:45	●		●	●	
3	**Siemens** SL84A305UC	850		Excellent	Very good	Excellent	Very good	Good	1:50	●		●	●	●
4	**Kenmore** (Sears) 1637[2]	520		Excellent	Very good	Very good	Excellent	Excellent	2:15	●	●		●	
5	**Kenmore** (Sears) Elite 1648[2]	870		Excellent	Very good	Excellent	Excellent	Excellent	2:25	●	●	●	●	●
6	**KitchenAid** KUDI01IL[BL]	650		Excellent	Very good	Very good	Good	Very good	2:10		●	●	●	
7	**Miele** G894SC	1,350		Excellent	Very good	Very good	Very good	Very good	2:15			●	●	
8	**Amana** ADB1200AW[W] **A CR Best Buy**	350		Excellent	Good	Good	Good	Excellent	2:05	●	●		●	
9	**Kenmore** (Sears) 1638[2]	570		Excellent	Very good	Very good	Good	Excellent	2:25	●	●	●		
10	**KitchenAid** KUDP01DL[WH]	830		Excellent	Very good	Very good	Very good	Very good	2:10	●	●	●	●	●
11	**KitchenAid** Superba KUDS01FL[SS]	1,200		Excellent	Very good	Very good	Excellent	Very good	2:10	●	●	●	●	●
12	**Maytag** MDB8600AW[W]	550		Excellent	Good	Very good	Very good	Excellent	1:50	●	●		●	
13	**Maytag** MDB7600AW[W]	480		Excellent	Good	Very good	Excellent	Excellent	2:00	●	●		●	
14	**GE** Profile PDW9200J[WW]	770		Excellent	Good	Good	Very good	Excellent	2:00	●	●	●	●	●
15	**GE** Profile PDW8200J[WW]	650		Excellent	Good	Very good	Very good	Excellent	2:00	●	●	●	●	

Excellent ⊜ Very good ⊖ Good ○ Fair ◒ Poor ●

Within types, in performance order. Gray key numbers indicate Quick Picks.

	Brand & model	Price	Overall score (0–100; P F G VG E)	Test results: Washing	Energy use	Noise	Loading flexibility	Ease of use	Cycle time (hr:min)	Features: Sensor	Self-cleaning filter	Stainless-steel tub	Stainless finish available	Hidden controls
16	**Maytag** MDB5600AW[W]	410		⊜	○	⊖	⊖	⊜	2:15	•	•		•	
17	**Fisher & Paykel** DD603[W]	1,200		⊜	⊖	⊖	⊖	⊖	1:55				•	•
18	**GE** GSD6900J[WW]	500		⊜	○	○	⊜	⊜	2:00	•	•		•	
19	**GE** Profile PDW8600J[WW]	850		⊜	○	⊖	⊜	⊜	2:00	•	•	•	•	
20	**GE** GSD6600G[WW]	450		⊜	○	○	⊖	⊜	2:00	•	•		•	
21	**Maytag** MDB8750AW[W]	600		⊜	◒	○	⊖	⊜	2:25	•	•	•	•	
22	**GE** GSD5500G[WW]	380		⊜	○	○	◒	⊜	1:35	•	•		•	
23	**Jenn-Air** JDB2150AWP	1,000		⊜	◒	○	⊖	⊜	2:30	•	•	•	•	
24	**Maytag** Performa PDB4600AW[W]	300		⊜	⊖	◒	○	⊜	1:30		•			
25	**Admiral** DWB1000A	270		⊖	⊖	○	○	⊖	1:35		•			
26	**Frigidaire** FDB2310L[C]	365		○	⊖	○	○	⊜	1:40		•		•	
27	**Hotpoint** HDA3700G[WW]	280		⊖	⊖	◒	◒	⊖	1:35		•			
28	**Haier** ESD200	420		◒	⊜	○	○	○	1:40			•		
29	**Frigidaire** FDB710L[C]	240		◒	⊖	○	○	⊖	1:25		•			

See report, page 71. Based on tests posted to ConsumerReports.org in July 2004, with updated prices and availability.

Guide to the Ratings

Overall score is based mainly on washing but also factors in noise, energy and water use, loading, and more. **Washing** judges results with a full load of very dirty dishes, glasses, and flatware. **Energy use** is for the normal cycle. **Noise** was judged by listeners, aided by sound-level measurements. **Loading** reflects ability to hold extra place settings and oversized items. **Cycle time** (rounded to the nearest 5 minutes) is for the normal cycle, including heated dry, if available. **Ease of use** considers controls and other factors. Under **Brand & model,** a bracketed letter or number is the color code. Model 11 is priced with a stainless-steel finish. All other prices are for black or white; a stainless exterior adds $60 to $200 to the price.

Quick Picks

A great value if you don't need all the bells and whistles:

8 Amana, $350, CR Best Buy

The Amana ADB1200AW[W] (8) offers excellent washing from a reliable brand, making it a CR Best Buy. It has a clean design with a one-piece door and touchpad controls, but lacks niceties such as adjustable tines and flatware slots. You can get it with a stainless-steel exterior for $450.

For stainless steel at a modest price:

6 KitchenAid, $650

Many new models are available with a exterior, so find one you like and see what it costs in stainless. Besides the Amana ADB1200AW[W] (8), we'd highlight the KitchenAid KUDI01IL[BL] (6), with a stainless exterior and a stainless tub.

If you're willing to pay more for style, quiet operation, and flexible loading:

5 Kenmore (Sears), $870

10, 11 KitchenAid, $830-$1200

Fine choices include the Kenmore (Sears) Elite 1648[2] (5), available with stainless exterior for $950; KitchenAid KUDP01DL[WH] (10), $900 with stainless exterior; and KitchenAid Superba KUDS01FL[SS] (11), $1,200 with stainless exterior. All three have stainless tubs. The KitchenAid KUDS01FL[SS], has totally hidden controls; on the Kenmore (Sears) Elite 1648[2] (5) and KitchenAid KUDP01DL[WH] (10), the controls are partially hidden.

For flexible loading at a modest price:

4 Kenmore (Sears), $520

13 Maytag, $480

18 GE, $500

The Kenmore (Sears) 1637[2] (4) was among the best on all counts, but it has a long, 135-minute cycle. The Maytag MDB7600AW[W] (13) and GE GSD6900J[WW] (18) were faster but used more energy. The GE is a bit noisier than both.

For excellent performance, a modest price, and low operating costs:

9 Kenmore (Sears), $570

Two Kenmore models were among the most frugal with water and energy without compromising wash performance. Besides the Kenmore 1637[2] (4), consider its brandmate: the Kenmore 1638[2] (9).

Recommendations

1 BOSCH SHU66C0[2] **Excellent, but pricey.** Among the quietest models tested. But among the more repair-prone brands. Uses about 7 gallons of water in the normal cycle. Hidden or partially hidden controls are available on higher-priced similar models. Has stainless tub. Stainless finish available. Similar: SHI66A0[ ], SHV66A0[ ], SHY66C0[ ].

2 BOSCH SHU43C0[2] **Excellent.** Among the quietest models tested. But among the more repair-prone brands. Has an adjustable upper rack. Uses about 7 gallons of water in the normal cycle. Stainless finish available. Similar: SHU53A0[ ].

3 SIEMENS SL84A305UC **Excellent, but pricey.** Among the quietest dishwashers tested. Uses about 7 gallons of water in the normal cycle. Hidden controls. stainless-steel tub. Removable top rack. Stainless finish available. Similar: Bosch SHV46C0[ ], SHX46B0[ ], SHX46A0[ ].

Recommendations

4 KENMORE (SEARS) 1637[2] **Excellent.** Has an adjustable upper rack. Long cycle time. Uses about 7 gallons of water in the normal cycle. Stainless finish available. Similar: 1636[ ], 1736[ ], 1737[ ].

5 KENMORE (SEARS) Elite 1648[2] **Excellent.** Among the quietest models tested. Long cycle time. Uses about 7 gallons of water in the normal cycle. Stainless tub. Removable top rack. Partially hidden controls. Stainless finish available. Similar: 1649[ ], 1748[ ].

6 KITCHENAID KUDI01IL[BL] **Excellent.** Long cycle time. Uses about 7 gallons of water in the normal cycle. Hidden or partially hidden controls are available on higher-priced similar models. Stainless tub. Stainless finish available. Similar: KUDI01DL[ ], KUDI01FL[ ].

7 MIELE G894SC **Excellent, but pricey.** Cycle time longer than most. Has adjustable top rack and stainless-steel tub. Long cycle time. Uses about 6 gallons of water in the normal cycle. Removable top rack. Similar: G694SC.

8 AMANA ADB1200AW[W] **A CR Best Buy Very good and low-priced.** Uses about 7 gallons of water in the normal cycle. Has a removable top rack. Stainless finish available. Similar: ADB2200AW[ ].

9 KENMORE (SEARS) 1638[2] **Very good.** Long cycle time. Uses about 7 gallons of water in the normal cycle. Has stainless-steel tub. Similar: 1647[ ], 1746[ ], 1646[ ], 1747[ ], 1738[ ].

10 KITCHENAID KUDP01DL[WH] **Very good, but pricey.** Long cycle time. Uses about 8 gallons of water in the normal cycle. Hidden controls are available on higher-priced similar models. Stainless tub. Stainless finish available. Similar: KUDP01IL[ ], KUDP01FL[ ].

11 KITCHENAID Superba KUDS01FL[SS] **Very good, but pricey.** Adjustable upper rack. Hidden controls. Long cycle time. Uses about 8 gal. of water in the normal cycle. Stainless tub. Stainless finish available. Similar: KUDS01IL[ ], KUDS01DL[ ].

12 MAYTAG MDB8600AW[W] **Very good, but pricey.** Has third rack at bottom, which allows loading of oversized items such as mixing bowls and platters. Center rack is adjustable. Uses about 8 gallons of water in the normal cycle. Removable top rack. Stainless finish available. Similar: MDB9600AW[ ].

13 MAYTAG MDB7600AW[W] **Very good.** Has adjustable upper rack. Uses about 9 gallons of water in the normal cycle. Removable top rack. Stainless finish available. Similar: MDBH970AW[ ], MDBTT79AW[ ], MDBF750AW[ ].

14 GE Profile PDW9200J[WW] **Very good.** Uses about 9 gallons of water in the normal cycle. Hidden controls. Stainless-steel tub. Removable top rack. Stainless finish.

15 GE Profile PDW8200J[WW] **Very good.** Has an adjustable and removable upper rack and a stainless-steel tub. Uses more water than most, about 10 gallons of water in the normal cycle. Stainless finish available. Similar: PDW8480J[ ], PDW8400J[ ], PDW8280J[ ].

16 MAYTAG MDB5600AW[W] **Very good.** Long cycle time. Uses about 6 gallons of water in the normal cycle. Removable top rack. Stainless finish available. Similar: MDB6600AW[ ], MDBF550AW[ ], MDBTT59AW[ ], MDBH950AW[ ].

17 FISHER & PAYKEL DD603[W] **Very good, but pricey, with two independent**

Recommendations

drawers. Has partially hidden controls. No heated-dry option. Uses about 8 gallons of water in the normal cycle. Stainless finish available. Our most recent repair data give us concern about this brand's reliability.

18 GE GSD6900J[WW] **Very good.** Uses more water than most, about 10 gallons of water in the normal cycle. Stainless finish available. Similar: GSD6860J[ ].

19 GE Profile PDW8600J[WW] **Very good, but pricey.** Has an adjustable upper rack and a stainless-steel tub. Uses more water than most, about 11 gallons of water in the normal cycle. Stainless finish available. Discontinued, but similar PDW8800J[ ] is available.

20 GE GSD6600G[WW] **Very good.** Uses more water than most, about 10 gallons of water in the normal cycle. Stainless finish available. Similar: GSD6200J[ ], GSD6260J[ ], GSD6660G[ ].

21 MAYTAG MDB8750AW[W] **Very good.** Uses more water than most, about 11 gallons in the normal cycle. Less energy-efficient than most. Cycle time is longer than most. Stainless-steel tub. Removable top rack. Stainless finish available.

22 GE GSD5500G[WW] **Very good.** Uses more water than most, about 10 gallons in the normal cycle. Cycle time is shorter than most. Stainless finish available.

23 JENN-AIR JDB2150AWP **Very good, but pricey.** Uses more water than most, about 12 gallons in the normal cycle. Less energy-efficient than most. Cycle time is longer than most. Pro-style look; in stainless exterior finish. Stainless-steel tub. Removable top rack.

24 MAYTAG Performa PDB4600AW[W] **Very good and low-priced.** Noisier than most. Uses about 9 gallons of water in the normal cycle. Removable top rack.

25 ADMIRAL DWB1000A **Very good and low-priced.** Uses about 9 gallons of water in the normal cycle. Has a removable top rack.

26 FRIGIDAIRE FDB2310L[C] **Very good.** Uses less water than most, about 6 gallons in the normal cycle. Cycle time is shorter than most. Removable top rack. Stainless finish available.

27 HOTPOINT HDA3700G[WW] **Very good and low-priced.** Uses about 7 gallons of water in the normal cycle. Cycle time is shorter than most. Noisier than most.

28 HAIER ESD200 **Good overall, but wash score only fair.** Among the most energy-efficient models tested. Uses less water than most, about 4 gallons in the normal cycle. Cycle time is shorter than most. Has an adjustable upper rack and stainless-steel tub.

29 FRIGIDAIRE FDB710L[C] **Good and low-priced.** Only fair wash score. Has a short cycle time. Uses less water than most, about 6 gallons in the normal cycle. Similar: FDB750R[ ], FDB510L[ ].

DRILLS, CORDLESS

Top-rated cordless drills blend ample power and run time with quick recharging in an hour or less. Most of the best we tested cost more than $200 and deliver at least 18 volts of drilling power, though you'll find notable exceptions.

More features for less is another welcome development. But as the features columns in the Ratings reveal, those that count most tend to disappear as you move down the price scale, especially among the lowest-voltage models. Our run-time scores also show that you tend to get less of it as the voltage goes down.

Pricier replacement batteries for pricier drills is yet another pattern you'll see. Many cost $30 to $60. But a few cells—including those for the Panasonic (1, 11), DeWalt (2), Milwaukee (3), Porter-Cable (4), Craftsman (5), Bosch (6, 15), and Ridgid (12, 13)—cost $70 to $100 each.

The Ratings rank models by overall score. See Quick Picks for drills with the attributes you want at a price you're willing to pay.

Excellent | Very good | Good | Fair | Poor

Within types, in performance order. Gray key numbers indicate Quick Picks.

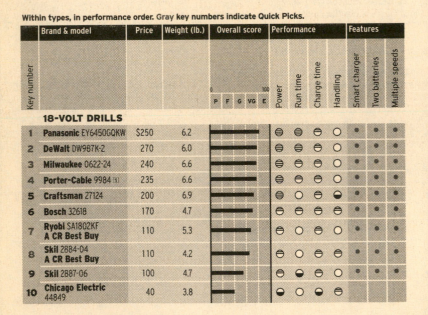

Key number	Brand & model	Price	Weight (lb.)	Overall score (0–100; P F G VG E)	Performance: Power	Run time	Charge time	Handling	Features: Smart charger	Two batteries	Multiple speeds
	18-VOLT DRILLS										
1	**Panasonic** EY6450GQKW	$250	6.2		Excellent	Excellent	Very good	Good	•	•	•
2	**DeWalt** DW987K-2	270	6.0		Excellent	Excellent	Very good	Good	•	•	•
3	**Milwaukee** 0622-24	240	6.6		Excellent	Very good	Very good	Good	•	•	•
4	**Porter-Cable** 9984 [1]	235	6.6		Excellent	Very good	Very good	Good	•	•	•
5	**Craftsman** 27124	200	6.9		Excellent	Good	Very good	Fair	•	•	•
6	**Bosch** 32618	170	4.7		Very good	Very good	Very good	Very good	•	•	•
7	**Ryobi** SA1802KF **A CR Best Buy**	110	5.3		Very good	Good	Very good	Good	•	•	•
8	**Skil** 2884-04 **A CR Best Buy**	110	4.2		Very good	Good	Very good	Very good	•	•	•
9	**Skil** 2887-06	100	4.7		Very good	Fair	Very good	Good	•	•	•
10	**Chicago Electric** 44849	40	3.8		Fair	Good	Fair	Very good			

Key number	Brand & model	Price	Weight (lb.)	Overall score (0–100; P F G VG E)	Performance: Power	Performance: Run time	Performance: Charge time	Performance: Handling	Features: Smart charger	Features: Two batteries	Features: Multiple speeds
	14.4-VOLT DRILLS										
11	**Panasonic** EY6432GQKW [2]	200	4.8		⊖	⊜	⊖	⊖	•	•	•
12	**Ridgid** R83015	200	6.6		⊜	◒	⊜	◒	•	•	•
13	**Ridgid** R83001	170	5.0		⊖	◒	⊜	○	•	•	•
14	**DeWalt** DW928K-2	170	4.3		⊖	◒	⊖	⊖	•	•	•
15	**Bosch** 32614	150	4.3		⊖	○	⊖	⊖	•	•	•
16	**Porter-Cable** 9978	180	5.7		⊖	◒	⊖	○	•	•	•
17	**Milwaukee** 0612-22	180	4.7		⊖	◒	⊖	○	•	•	•
18	**Skil** 2584-04	70	3.9		⊖	◒	⊖	⊖	•	•	•
19	**Hitachi** DS 14DVB	180	4.6		⊖	○	○	◒	•	•	•
20	**Ryobi** SA14402KF	90	4.5		○	◒	⊖	○	•	•	•
21	**Makita** 6228DWAE	160	3.8		○	○	⊖	⊜	•	•	•
22	**Craftsman** 11453	90	4.1		○	●	⊖	○	•	•	•
23	**Skil** 2567-03	60	3.4		◒	◒	◒	⊖			
24	**Black & Decker** CD14GSF-2	60	3.4		◒	●	◒	⊖		•	
	12-VOLT DRILLS										
25	**Ridgid** R82001	130	4.3		⊖	●	⊜	⊖	•	•	•
26	**DeWalt** DW927K-2	130	4.0		⊖	●	⊖	⊖	•	•	•
27	**Makita** 6227DWE	130	3.4		○	◒	⊖	⊜	•	•	•
28	**Craftsman** 11443	60	3.9		○	●	◒	⊖		•	•
29	**Skil** 2468-02	50	3.2		◒	●	○	⊖			
30	**Black & Decker** XD1200K	50	2.9		◒	●	◒	○			
	9.6-VOLT DRILLS										
31	**DeWalt** DW926K-2	100	3.4		◒	●	⊖	⊜	•	•	•
32	**Ryobi** SA960BK	40	3.1		◒	●	◒	⊜			
33	**Black & Decker** CD9600K	40	2.9		◒	●	●	⊖			

See report, page 100. *Based on tests published in Consumer Reports in May 2004, with updated prices and availability.*

Guide to the Ratings

Weight is to the nearest tenth of a pound for the drill, battery pack, and detachable second handle, if applicable. **Overall score** is based on power, run time, charge time, and handling. **Power** denotes speed of drilling and driving screws as well as torque, or twisting force. **Run time** reflects work per battery charge, measured on a dynamometer. **Charge time** is how much time it took to completely recharge a fully discharged battery. **Handling** includes weight, balance, and effort needed to position the head. **Price** is approximate retail. **All tested drills have:** A keyless chuck. A reversible drive. **Most have:** A trigger lockout for safety. Bit storage. A carrying case. A one-year warranty.

Quick Picks

Best for most; ample performance at a low price:

7 Ryobi $110 (18v), CR Best Buy
8 Skil $110 (18v), CR Best Buy

The Ryobi (7) comes with a heavier-duty, ½-inch chuck, while the Skil (8) is lighter and easier to use. It also performs comparably to pricier lightweights—a plus for those with less arm strength.

For larger projects:

1 Panasonic $250 (18v)
2 DeWalt $270 (18v)
3 Milwaukee $240 (18v)
4 Porter-Cable $235 (19.2v)
11 Panasonic $200 (15.6v)

The Panasonic (1) and DeWalt (2) weigh less than the Milwaukee (3) and Porter-Cable (4) and deliver longer run time. Consider the Panasonic (11) if you don't mind trading some power for even less weight. Also be aware that replacement batteries for these relatively high-priced drills cost more than for most models.

For small jobs or occasional use:

18 Skil $70 (14.4v)
27 Makita $130 (12v)

Impressive power for its weight and price makes the Skil (18) a fine choice. Consider the Makita (27) or the less-capable, lower-priced Ryobi (32) if you simply want an easy-to-handle drill for quick repairs.

Recommendations

18-VOLT AND 19.2-VOLT DRILLS

1 **PANASONIC** EY6450GQKW **Powerful.** Second handle. Nickel-metal-hydride battery. Half-inch chuck.

2 **DEWALT** DW987K-2 **Powerful and well-equipped.** Three speed ranges.

3 **MILWAUKEE** 0622-24 **Powerful, but heavy.** Second handle. Half-inch chuck.

4 **PORTER-CABLE** 9984 **Powerful, but among the heaviest in this group.** 19.2 volts. Second handle. Half-inch chuck.

5 **CRAFTSMAN (SEARS)** Professional 27124 **Capable and well-equipped, but heavy.**

6 **BOSCH** 32618 **Very good overall and among the lightest in this group.**

7 **RYOBI** SA1802KF **A CR Best Buy Lots of power for the money.** Half-inch chuck.

8 **SKIL** 2884-04 **Capable and light, but has limited clutch settings.** ⅜-inch chuck. Magnetic screw holder. Clutch slipped in torque tests. 2-year warranty.

Recommendations

9 SKIL 2887-06 **OK, but shorter run time than others.** Second handle.

10 CHICAGO ELECTRIC 44849 **There are better choices.** Only one battery. Charging takes 5 to 7 hours.

14.4-VOLT AND 15.6-VOLT DRILLS

11 PANASONIC EY6432GQKW **The clear choice in this group.** 15.6-volt nickel-metal-hydride battery. Half-inch chuck.

12 RIDGID R83015 **Capable but heavy.** 20- to 30-minute charging; can charge two batteries at the same time. Second handle. Half-inch chuck.

13 RIDGID R83001 **Capable.** 20- to 30-minute charging. Second handle.

14 DEWALT DW928K-2 **Capable overall.**

15 BOSCH 32614 **Capable overall.**

16 PORTER-CABLE 9978 **Capable overall.**

17 MILWAUKEE 0612-22 **Capable overall.** Half-inch chuck.

18 SKIL 2584-04 **Inexpensive and light, but has limited clutch settings.** Magnetic screw holder. Clutch slipped in torque tests. 2-year warranty.

19 HITACHI DS 14DVB **Capable overall, but there are better values.** Half-inch chuck.

20 RYOBI SA14402KF **There are better choices.**

21 MAKITA 6228DWAE **Light and well-balanced.** No bit storage.

22 CRAFTSMAN (SEARS) 11453 **There are better choices.** Relatively short run time.

23 SKIL 2567-03 **There are better choices.** Built-in stud finder. Only one battery; one speed range. Charging takes 3 to 5 hours.

24 BLACK & DECKER CD14GSF-2 **There are better choices.** Includes stud finder. Only one speed range. Charging takes 3 to 5 hours.

12-VOLT DRILLS

25 RIDGID R82001 **Capable overall.** 20-minute charging.

26 DEWALT DW927K-2 **Power offset by relatively short run time.**

27 MAKITA 6227DWE **Light and well-balanced, but otherwise unimpressive.** No bit storage.

28 CRAFTSMAN (SEARS) 11443 **There are better choices.**

29 SKIL 2468-02 **There are better choices.** Only one battery. Charging takes 3 to 5 hours. Discontinued, but replaced by the 2467-02.

30 BLACK & DECKER XD1200K **There are better choices.** Only one battery. Only one speed range. Charging takes 3 to 5 hours.

9.6-VOLT DRILLS

31 DEWALT DW926K-2 **Best of an unimpressive group.** Well-balanced and well-equipped.

32 RYOBI SA960BK **There are better choices.** Only one battery. Only one speed range. Charging takes 3 to 5 hours.

33 BLACK & DECKER CD9600K **There are better choices.** Only one battery. Charging takes 16 hours.

DRYERS

Most of the dryers we tested were very good or excellent performers with ample capacity. Models judged excellent for drying were noticeably better than lower-rated units at leaving a load damp for ironing and for drying delicates at low heat. All except Estate by Whirlpool (30), Hotpoint (31), Amana (35), Admiral (36), Roper (37), and Asko (38) have moisture sensors; those six have thermostats, which we've found to be less effective than sensors at determining when laundry is dry.

Buying a pricier dryer may get you fancier styling, touchpad controls, a porcelain top, a stainless-steel drum, and extras such as programmability and numerous cycles—none essential in our view. All the tested models except the low-priced Roper (37) offer extended tumble, which is a useful feature for minimizing wrinkles.

The Ratings rank models by performance. Quick Picks highlights models you might want to consider based on how they scored and on factors such as price and brand reliability.

Excellent | Very good | Good | Fair | Poor

Within types, in performance order. Gray key numbers indicate Quick Picks.

	Brand & model	Price	Overall score	Test results			Features	
	Similar models, in small type, and gas equivalent comparable to tested model.		0–100 (P F G VG E)	Drying	Capacity	Noise	Porcelain top	Drying rack
1	**GE** Profile DPSB620EC[WW] GAS: DPSB620GC[ ]	$500		Excellent	Excellent	Excellent		•
2	**Kenmore** (Sears) HE4 8586 8587[ ] GAS: 9586[ ] 9587[ ]	800		Excellent	Excellent	Excellent	•	•
3	**Maytag** Neptune MCE8000AY[W] GAS: MCG8000A[ ]	1,200		Excellent	Excellent	Very good		
4	**Kenmore** (Sears) Elite 6497[2]	580		Excellent	Excellent	Very good	•	•
5	**Kenmore** (Sears) Elite HE3 8482[1] GAS: 9482[ ]	800		Excellent	Excellent	Excellent	•	•
6	**Whirlpool** Duet GEW9250P GAS: GGW9250P	800		Excellent	Excellent	Very good	•	•
7	**Kenmore** (Sears) 6487 **CR Best Buy** 6488[ ] 6489[ ] GAS: 7487[ ] 7488[ ] 7489[ ]	470		Excellent	Excellent	Very good		•
8	**Kenmore** (Sears) Elite HE3 8483[2] GAS: 9483[ ]	900		Very good	Excellent	Excellent	•	•
9	**LG** DL-E5932[W] GAS: DL-G5932[ ]	850		Very good	Excellent	Very good	•	•
10	**Maytag** Neptune MDE9800AY[W] GAS: MDG9800A[ ]	800		Excellent	Very good	Excellent	•	•
11	**Whirlpool** LEQ8000J[Q] **CR Best Buy** GAS: LGQ8000J[ ]	400		Very good	Excellent	Very good		
12	**Kenmore** (Sears) Elite 6408[2] GAS: 7408[ ]	720		Very good	Excellent	Very good	•	•
13	**Whirlpool** Duet GEW9200L[W] GAS: GGW9200L[ ]	800		Very good	Excellent	Excellent	•	•
14	**Whirlpool** Gold GEW9868K[Q] GAS: GGW9868K[ ]	680		Very good	Excellent	Excellent	•	•
15	**Whirlpool** Gold GEW9878J[Q] GEW9878P[ ] GAS: GGW9878P[ ]	530		Excellent	Excellent	Very good		

	Brand & model	Price	Overall score	Test results			Features	
	Similar models, in small type, and gas equivalent comparable to tested model.		0 100 P F G VG E	Drying	Capacity	Noise	Porcelain top	Drying rack
16	**Bosch** Nexxt Premium WTMC6300US GAS: WTMC6500US	$800		⊖	⊖	○	•	•
17	**GE** Profile Harmony DPGT750EC[WW] GAS: DPGT750GC[ ]	1,000		⊖	⊜	⊜		•
18	**Maytag** Neptune MDE7500AY[W] GAS: MDG7500A[ ]	800		⊜	⊖	○	•	
19	**Kenmore** (Sears) Elite 6206[2] GAS: 7206[ ]	720		⊖	⊜	⊖	•	•
20	**KitchenAid** Superba Ensemble KEHS01PMT GAS: KGHS01PMT	1,100		⊖	⊜	⊜	•	
21	**Frigidaire** Gallery GLER642A[S] **CR Best Buy** GAS: GLGR642A[ ]	310		⊖	⊖	⊖		•
22	**Maytag** Atlantis MDE8400AY[W] GAS: MDG8400A[ ]	570		⊖	⊜	⊜	•	•
23	**Frigidaire** Gallery GLEQ642A[S] GAS: GLGQ642A[ ]	450		⊖	⊖	⊖		•
24	**GE** Profile DPXH46EA[WW] DSXH43EA[ ] GAS: DPXH46GA[ ] DSXH43GA[ ]	450		⊖	⊖	○		•
25	**Kenmore** (Sears) 8407[2] GAS: 9407[ ]	520		⊖	⊖	⊖		•
26	**GE** DWSR405EB[WW] GAS: DWSR405GB[ ]	370		○	⊜	⊖		•
27	**Frigidaire** Gallery GLEQ942C[S] GAS: GLGQ942C[ ]	450		⊖	⊖	⊖		•
28	**Fisher & Paykel** Smartload DEGX1 GAS: DGGX1	780		⊖	⊖	○		
29	**Maytag** Legacy Series SDE515D[W] SDE4606A[ ] GAS: SDG4606A[ ] SDG515D[ ]	400		○	⊜	⊖		•
30	**Estate** by Whirlpool TEDS840J[Q] GAS: TGDS840J[ ]	370		○	⊜	○		
31	**Hotpoint** NWSR483EB[WW] GAS: NWSR483GB[ ]	300		○	⊜	⊖		
32	**Fisher & Paykel** DE08 GAS: DG08	440		○	⊖	⊖		
33	**Roper** RES7745P GAS: RGS7746P	280		⊖	⊖	◒		
34	**Miele** Touchtronic T1303	1,250		⊜	●	⊜		
35	**Amana** NDE7800AY[W] GAS: NDG7800A[ ]	400		○	⊜	⊖		•
36	**Admiral** LNC7764A[W] GAS: LNC8764A[ ]	325		○	⊜	○		
37	**Roper** REX4634K[Q] GAS: RGX4634[ ]	200		○	⊖	○		
38	**Asko** T701	730		○	◒	⊜		

See report, page 74. Based on tests posted on ConsumerReports.org in September 2004

Guide to the Ratings

Overall score is based primarily on drying performance, capacity, and noise. Also factored in: convenience (not shown). Most were very good for convenience, though the Frigidaire (23), Ropers (33, 37), Admiral (36) and Asko (38) scored lower. **Drying** performance combines tests on various-sized loads of different fabric mixes, including cotton, permanent press, and delicates. **Capacity** is about 7.0 to 7.5 cubic feet for the largest models; all could hold our 12-pound load. **Noise** reflects judgments by panelists. **Price** is approximate retail for electric models. Under **brand & model,** bracketed letters or numbers are color codes. A **porcelain top** resists scratches, which can rust. A **drying rack** lets you dry items without tumbling.

Quick Picks

Spacious and superb at drying:

1 GE $500
4 Kenmore $580

Both are fine. The Kenmore (4) is not as quiet as the other but has rotary dials, rather than pushbuttons or touchpad controls, which may be less confusing for some.

Fine performer at a low price:

21 Frigidaire $310, CR Best Buy

Even at this price, you get ample capacity and the benefits of a moisture sensor, contributing to very good drying performance.

Modestly priced and very capable:

7 Kenmore $470, CR Best Buy
11 Whirlpool $400, CR Best Buy

For a little more money, the Kenmore (7) did a bit better with drying. It's also quieter and has a drying rack.

Expensive, but with unusual capabilities:

3 Maytag $1,200

Excellent standard dryer has drying cabinet for air-drying wet clothes and refreshing dry garments. Unit is twice as tall as a standard dryer and a few inches wider.

DVD PLAYERS

Excellent picture quality is a hallmark of virtually all DVD players. Any of the tested models would be fine for playing commercial DVD movies and audio CDs on a conventional TV. For typical use, then, you can safely buy a player by price and any special features that you want.

If you own a digital TV, you'll need to be a bit more selective. Used with a high-definition or enhanced-definition TV, the progressive-scan technology found on almost all new players (including all those in the Ratings except the Apex, 19), will yield smoother images from most DVD movies. But a few models, including the Sony (4) and Samsung (14) we tested, don't confer that image improvement. And a few, called out in the Quick Picks, also smooth the images from DVDs that originate from digital video cameras (such as those from the DVDs of recent TV programs.)

Similarly, you need to be choosy if you're an audiophile who buys music on DVD-Audio discs. These discs contain two versions of the music: a high-resolution DVD-Audio version and a Dolby Digital version of the same program. All DVD players can play the Dolby Digital version; only players that meet the DVD-Audio spec can play the high-resolution version, which provides sound that is subtly better than that of a CD.

Excellent ⊜ Very good ⊖ Good ○ Fair ◒ Poor ●

Within types, in performance order. Gray key numbers indicate Quick Picks.

Key number	Brand & model	Price	Overall score (0–100: P F G VG E)	Test results: Picture quality	Test results: Ease of use	Features: Coaxial digital-audio out	Features: Optical digital-audio out	Features: JPEG image files	Features: Video CDs	Features: WMA audio files
	PROGRESSIVE-SCAN MULTI-DISC PLAYERS									
1	**Panasonic** DVD-F86	$120		Excellent	Excellent	●		●	●	●
2	**Panasonic** DVD-F87	130		Excellent	Excellent	●		●	●	●
3	**Onkyo** DV-CP701	200		Excellent	Excellent	●	●	●	●	●
4	**Sony** DVP-NC665P	160		Excellent	Excellent	●	●		●	
	PROGRESSIVE-SCAN SINGLE-DISC PLAYERS									
5	**Panasonic** DVD-S47	100		Excellent	Excellent	●	●	●	●	●
6	**Go-Video** D2730	220		Excellent	Excellent	●	●	●	●	●
7	**Panasonic** DVD-S27	80		Excellent	Excellent	●		●	●	●
8	**Denon** DVD-910	230		Excellent	Excellent	●	●	●		●

Excellent ⊜ Very good ⊖ Good ○ Fair ◒ Poor ●

Within types, in performance order. Gray **key numbers indicate Quick Picks.**

Key number	Brand & model	Price	Overall score (0–100; P F G VG E)	Test results: Picture quality	Test results: Ease of use	Features: Coaxial digital-audio out	Features: Optical digital-audio out	Features: JPEG image files	Features: Video CDs	Features: WMA-audio files
	PROGRESSIVE-SCAN SINGLE-DISC PLAYERS *Continued*									
9	**JVC** XV-N55SL	$130		⊜	⊜	•	•	•	•	•
10	**Hitachi** DV-P745U	70		⊜	⊖	•				
11	**Sony** DVP-NS575P/B	90		⊜	⊖	•		•	•	•
12	**Aspire** Digital AD-1100	100		⊜	⊖	•	•	•		
13	**Onkyo** DV-SP301	150		⊜	⊖	•	•	•	•	•
14	**Samsung** DVD-P731M	70		⊜	⊜	•	•	•		•
15	**Toshiba** SD-3960	70		⊜	○	•		•	•	•
16	**JVC** XV-N310B	80		⊜	○	•		•	•	
17	**Samsung** P241	60		⊜	○	•		•		
18	**JVC** XV-N410B	90		⊜	○	•	•	•	•	
19	**Apex** Digital AD-1225	50		⊜	○	•	•	•	•	•

See report, page 38. *Based on tests posted on Consumer Reports.org in September 2004.*

Guide to the Ratings

Overall score is mainly based on picture quality; ease of use is also factored in. **Picture quality** indicates the sharpness and detail of video images. For progressive-scan models, the score reflects performance with both conventional TVs and HDTVs. **Ease of use** is our assessment of remote control, console front panel, setup menu, key playback functions, and features. **Price** is approximate retail. Under Features, **JPEG image files** and **video CDs** indicate ability to read digital photos and video files on CDs. **WMA-audio files** indicates ability to play music files stored on CD in this format.

Quick Picks

Best values for use with a regular TV:
Any of the single-disc players priced at $100 or less will deliver excellent picture and sound quality at a fine price, and should be first choices for typical use. Note that the Samsung P241 (17) doesn't have a true console display, so you'll need to turn on the TV and use the Samsung's onscreen menu to check the player's status while it's playing music CDs.

Best choice for use with an HD TV:
15 Toshiba, $70
17 Samsung, $60
Where almost any DVD player in the Ratings will make the most of images from a movie DVD displayed on a digital TV, these two models are unique in also producing smoother images from DVDs whose content originates from digital video cameras (such as DVDs from many recent TV programs). Although they lack a few conveniences found on some other models, they merit first consideration if you own an HD TV or ED TV and want the best possible picture from all DVDs.

Best choice if you own DVD-Audio discs:
2 Panasonic, $130
This Panasonic 5-disc carousel player is the only tested model that can make the most of both of DVD-Audio's key advantages: slightly better sound quality than CD and the parsing of sound into up to six surround channels. In addition, it also has the Dolby Digital and DTS decoders you'll need to hear those many channels should the multichannel receiver in your sound system lack the capability to decode those signals. Another plus: this player is among many tested that can read MP3 and WMA audio and JPEG image files on CDs. This Panasonic's brandmate (1) $120, offers all the same advantages except multichannel capability.

Best choice for playing digital content from a computer:
6 Go-Video, $220
This player can be networked with a home computer to play digital media files, contributing to its high price.

GRILLS, GAS

All of these grills cook at least adequately. Top scorers kick performance up a notch with more consistent temperatures across their surfaces—important when cooking lots of food at once. They're also better at grilling chicken and other delicate foods on low heat without burning them. More performance doesn't necessarily mean a higher price. While paying more buys you better grates, stainless-steel trim, and other beefier components, you'll find several moderately priced exceptions among the Ratings. More cooking space, however, typically requires more dollars.

Excellent · Very good · Good · Fair · Poor

Within types, in performance order. Gray **key numbers indicate Quick Picks.**

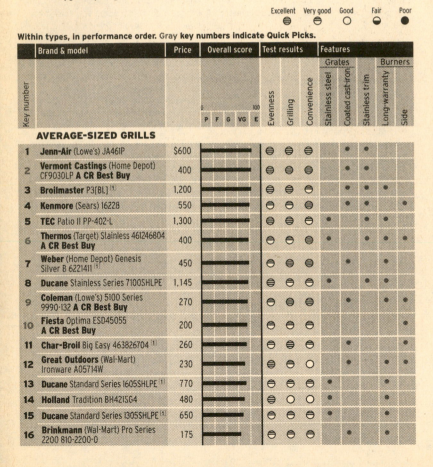

Key number	Brand & model	Price	Overall score (0–100: P F G VG E)	Test results: Evenness	Test results: Grilling	Test results: Convenience	Features: Grates: Stainless steel	Features: Grates: Coated cast-iron	Features: Stainless trim	Features: Burners: Long warranty	Features: Burners: Side
	AVERAGE-SIZED GRILLS										
1	**Jenn-Air** (Lowe's) JA461P	$600		Excellent	Excellent	Excellent		•	•		
2	**Vermont Castings** (Home Depot) CF9030LP **A CR Best Buy**	400		Excellent	Excellent	Excellent		•	•		
3	**Broilmaster** P3[BL] [1]	1,200		Excellent	Excellent	Very good		•	•	•	
4	**Kenmore** (Sears) 16228	550		Very good	Very good	Excellent		•	•		•
5	**TEC** Patio II PP-402-L	1,300		Excellent	Excellent	Very good	•		•	•	
6	**Thermos** (Target) Stainless 461246804 **A CR Best Buy**	400		Very good	Very good	Excellent	•		•	•	•
7	**Weber** (Home Depot) Genesis Silver B 6221411 [1]	450		Very good	Excellent	Excellent		•		•	
8	**Ducane** Stainless Series 7100SHLPE	1,145		Excellent	Very good	Very good	•		•	•	
9	**Coleman** (Lowe's) 5100 Series 9990-132 **A CR Best Buy**	270		Very good	Excellent	Excellent		•		•	•
10	**Fiesta** Optima ESD45055 **A CR Best Buy**	200		Very good	Very good	Very good					•
11	**Char-Broil** Big Easy 463826704 [1]	260		Very good	Excellent	Very good		•			•
12	**Great Outdoors** (Wal-Mart) Ironware A05714W	230		Excellent	Very good	Good		•		•	•
13	**Ducane** Standard Series 1605SHLPE [1]	770		Very good	Very good	Very good	•			•	
14	**Holland** Tradition BH421SG4	480		Excellent	Good	Good	•			•	
15	**Ducane** Standard Series 1305SHLPE [1]	650		Very good	Very good	Very good	•			•	
16	**Brinkmann** (Wal-Mart) Pro Series 2200 810-2200-0	175		Very good	Very good	Very good		•		•	

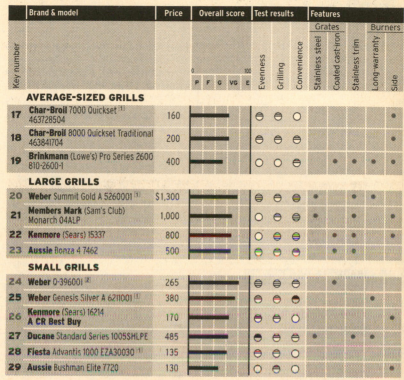

Key number	Brand & model	Price	Overall score (0–100: P F G VG E)	Test results: Evenness	Test results: Grilling	Test results: Convenience	Features: Grates – Stainless steel	Features: Grates – Coated cast-iron	Features: Stainless trim	Features: Burners – Long-warranty	Features: Burners – Side
	AVERAGE-SIZED GRILLS										
17	**Char-Broil** 7000 Quickset [1] 463728504	160		VG	VG	G					•
18	**Char-Broil** 8000 Quickset Traditional 463841704	200		VG	VG	VG					•
19	**Brinkmann** (Lowe's) Pro Series 2600 810-2600-1	400		G	G	VG		•	•	•	•
	LARGE GRILLS										
20	**Weber** Summit Gold A 5260001 [1]	$1,300		E	VG	E	•		•	•	
21	**Members Mark** (Sam's Club) Monarch 04ALP	1,000		G	VG	E	•		•		•
22	**Kenmore** (Sears) 15337	800		G	E	E		•	•		•
23	**Aussie** Bonza 4 7462	500		VG	VG	VG		•	•		
	SMALL GRILLS										
24	**Weber** Q-396001 [2]	265		E	E	VG		•			
25	**Weber** Genesis Silver A 6211001 [1]	380		VG	VG	F				•	
26	**Kenmore** (Sears) 16214 **A CR Best Buy**	170		VG	VG	G					•
27	**Ducane** Standard Series 1005SHLPE	485		F	VG	VG	•		•	•	
28	**Fiesta** Advantis 1000 EZA30030 [1]	135		VG	VG	G					
29	**Aussie** Bushman Elite 7720	130		G	VG	G					•

[1] *Price includes propane tank.* [2] *Portable model; price includes optional cart and adapter for 20-lb. fuel tank.*

See report, page 102. Based on tests published in Consumer Reports in June 2004, with updated prices and availability.

Guide to the Ratings

Under **brand & model,** brackets show a tested model's color code. **Overall score** denotes performance, features, and convenience. We tested **evenness** at high and low settings with temperature sensors, then combined scores. We verified results by searing 15 burgers on the high setting of the best and worst grills for 1½ minutes. **Grilling** is the ability to cook chicken and fish on the low setting. **Convenience** includes construction and materials, accessory burners, shelves, rack space, and ease of use. **Price** is approximate retail. **Most grills have:** A lifetime warranty for castings, 3 to 10 years for burners, and 2 to 5 years for other parts. Steel rack filled with ceramic or charcoal-like briquettes, or steel triangles or plates, to distribute heat. A painted-steel cart. Plastic handles. Natural-gas conversion kit (or similar model designed for this fuel) available. No propane tank ($25 to $30 extra). **Most average-sized grills have:** Two or three burners. **Most large grills have:** Three to six burners to cover their larger cooking areas. **Most small grills have:** One or two burners.

Quick Picks

Best for most outdoor cooks; all are CR Best Buys:

2 Vermont Castings $400
6 Thermos $400
9 Coleman $270
10 Fiesta $200

The Vermont Castings (2), sold at Home Depot, includes stainless trim and lots of shelf space. A notable value: The Thermos (6), sold at Target, delivers stainless construction at the lowest price. Also consider the Coleman (9) for its long-warranty castings and burners and the Fiesta (10) for its spacious warming rack.

If you often cook for a crowd:

20 Weber $1,300
23 Aussie $500

Both provide the even heating needed when cooking for a large group. The Weber (20) offers robust construction and plenty of features. The Aussie (23) is a fine basic choice and can function as a charcoal grill. But use a potholder; its lid handle got very hot during cooking.

For smaller groups or less patio space:

24 Weber $265
26 Kenmore $170, CR Best Buy

The high-scoring, portable Weber (24) costs $180 without a cart and 20-pound fuel-tank adapter; adding those equips it for yards and apartment terraces. The Kenmore (26) is a fine, low-priced performer. But as with the Aussie (23), you'll need a potholder to grip its handle.

Recommendations

AVERAGE-SIZED GRILLS

1 JENN-AIR JA461P **Excellent.** Lots of shelf space. Stainless-steel and aluminum lid. Stainless-steel cart, shelves, and handle. Grill base (or tray) can be removed for cleanup. Claimed output: 44,000 Btu/hr. Warranty: castings, life; burners, 5 yr.; other parts, 5 yr. Similar: Vermont Castings CF9055P

2 VERMONT CASTINGS CF9030LP **A CR Best Buy Excellent.** Lots of shelf space. Stainless-steel handle. Grill base (or tray) can be removed for cleanup. Claimed output: 36,000 Btu/hr. Warranty: castings, life; burners, 5 yr.; other parts, 5 yr.

3 BROILMASTER P3[BL] **Excellent.** Cooking grates can be adjusted to three different levels for more cooking flexibility. Stainless-steel cart and handle. Fold-down front shelf. Utensil hooks. Comes with natural-gas conversion kit. Claimed output: 40,000 Btu/hr. Warranty: castings, life; burners, 15 yr. prorated; other parts, 5 yr.

4 KENMORE 16228 **Excellent.** Stainless-steel handle. Grill base (or tray) can be removed for cleanup. Utensil hooks. Claimed output: 52,000 Btu/hr. (including side burner). Warranty: castings, 2; burners, 1 yr.; other parts, 2 yr.

5 TEC Patio II PP-402-L **Excellent.** Infrared main burners. Stainless-steel castings, lid, and handle. Grill base (or tray) can be removed for cleanup. No thermometer on lid. Claimed output: 37,000 Btu/hr. Warranty: castings, life; burners, 10 yr.; other parts, 10 yr. Similar: TEC Sterling II.

6 THERMOS Stainless 461246804 **A CR Best Buy Very good.** All stainless-steel construction. Smoker drawer for wood chips. Grill base (or tray) can be removed for cleanup. Claimed output: 50,000

Recommendations

Btu/hr. (including side burner). Warranty: castings, 99 yr.; burners, 10 yr.; other parts, 2 yr. Similar: Char-Broil Stainless Series 463244404.

7 WEBER Genesis Silver B 6221411 **Very good.** Lots of shelf space. Grill base (or tray) can be removed for cleanup. Utensil hooks. Removable thermometer on lid doubles as meat thermometer. Thermometer got hot. Claimed output: 36,000 Btu/hr. Warranty: castings, life; burners, 10 yr.; other parts, 5 yr. Similar: Silver C 6231499.

8 DUCANE Stainless Series 7100SHLPE **Very good.** All stainless-steel construction. Lots of shelf space. Folding side shelves can be removed for cleanup. Flared up more than others. No thermometer on lid. Claimed output: 28,000 Btu/hr. Warranty: castings, life; burners, life; other parts, 5 yr. Similar: Ducane Stainless Series 7100RSHLPE.*

9 COLEMAN 5100 Series 9990-132 **A CR Best Buy. Very good.** Grill base (or tray) can be removed for cleanup. Utensil hooks. No thermometer on lid. Claimed output: 52,000 Btu/hr. (including side burner). Warranty: castings, life; burners, life; other parts, 3 yr. Similar: 5110 Series 9991-132.

10 FIESTA Optima ESD45055 **A CR Best Buy. Very good.** Lots of warming-rack space. Auto electronic igniter (fires up with single knob turn). Utensil hooks. No thermometer on lid. Claimed output: 55,000 Btu/hr. (including side burner). Warranty: castings, life; burners, 5 yr.; other parts, 2 yr.

11 CHAR-BROIL Big Easy 463826704 **Very good.** Stainless-steel handle. Utensil hooks. No thermometer on lid. Claimed output: 44,000 Btu/hr. (including side burner). Warranty: castings, life; burners, 5 yr.; other parts, 1 yr. Similar: 463845804, 463845104.

12 GREAT OUTDOORS Ironware A05714W **Very good.** Cooler/sink built into side shelf. Handle got very hot. Claimed output: 40,000 Btu/hr. (including side burner). Warranty: castings, 50; burners, 10 yr. prorated; other parts, 3 yr.

13 DUCANE Standard Series 1605SHLPE **Very good.** Lots of warming-rack space. Removable side shelf doubles as cutting board. Lit-burner indicator. Flared up more than others. Handle got hot. No thermometer on lid. Claimed output: 37,000 Btu/hr. Warranty: castings, life; burners, life; other parts, 5 yr. *

14 HOLLAND Tradition BH421SG4 **Very good.** Can steam and smoke as well as grill. Smoker drawer for wood chips; smoker-drawer knob got hot. Utensil hooks. Only one temperature setting on single burner; unable to turn temperature down for keeping food warm. No sear marks when grilling. No warming rack. Claimed output: 19,500 Btu/hr. Warranty: castings, 5 yr.; burners, life; other parts, 5 yr. Discontinued, but similar Holland Heritage BH421SG5 is available.

15 DUCANE Standard Series 1305SHLPE **Very good.** Removable side shelf doubles as cutting board. Lit-burner indicator. Flared up more than others. Handle got hot. No thermometer on lid. Claimed output: 32,000 Btu/hr. Warranty: castings, life; burners, life; other parts, 5 yr. *

16 BRINKMANN Pro Series 2200 810-2200-0 **Very good.** Lots of shelf space. Stainless-steel handle. Grill base (or tray) can be removed for cleanup. Utensil hooks. Flared up more than most others when loaded with greasy foods. Claimed output: 45,000 Btu/hr. Warranty: castings, life; burners, 10 yr.; other parts, 1 yr.

17 CHAR-BROIL 7000 Quickset 463728504 **Very good.** Lots of warming-rack space. Utensil hooks. Cart judged less sturdy than most others tested. No thermometer on lid. Claimed output: 43,000 Btu/hr. (including side burner). Warranty: castings, life; burners, 1 yr.; other parts, 1 yr. Similar: 463742704, 463713304.

18 CHAR-BROIL 8000 Quickset Traditional 463841704 **Very good.** Can be used as a charcoal grill. Utensil hooks. Claimed output: 48,000 Btu/hr. (including side burner). Warranty: castings, life; burners, 3 yr.; other parts, 1 yr. Similar: 463842904, 463842704, Char-Broil 463841804.

19 BRINKMANN Pro Series 2600 810-2600-1 **Good.** Lots of shelf space. Stainless-steel handle. Grill base (or tray) can be removed for cleanup. Cooler/sink built into side shelf. Flared up more than most others when loaded with greasy foods. Claimed output: 52,000 Btu/hr. (including side burner). Warranty: castings, life; burners, 10 yr.; other parts, 2 yr.

LARGE GRILLS

20 WEBER Summit Gold A 5260001 **Very good.** Stainless-steel and aluminum lid. Stainless-steel handle. Lots of shelf space. Grill base (or tray) and side shelves can be removed for cleanup. Utensil hooks. Two side shelves with pop-up sections. Handle got hot. Claimed output: 57,600 Btu/hr. Warranty: castings, life; burners, 10 yr.; other parts, 5 yr. Similar: Summit Gold D 5290001, Summit Gold B 5270001.

21 MEMBERS MARK (SAM'S CLUB) Monarch 04ALP **Very good.** All stainless-steel construction. Lots of shelf space. Rotisserie burner, motor, and spit. Smoker drawer for wood chips. Grill base (or tray) can be removed for cleanup. Claimed output: 87,000 Btu/hr. (including side burner, rotisserie, and smoker). Warranty: castings, 1 yr.; burners, 2 yr.; other parts, 1 yr.

22 KENMORE (SEARS) 15337 **Very good.** Lots of shelf space. Stainless-steel and aluminum lid. Stainless-steel handle. Rotisserie burner included; motor and spit cost extra. Utensil hooks. Smoker drawer for wood chips. Grill base (or tray) can be removed for cleanup. Claimed output: 85,000 Btu/hr. (including side burner and rotisserie). Warranty: castings, life; burners, 1 yr.; other parts, 2 yr.

23 AUSSIE Bonza 4 7462 **Very good.** Can be used as a charcoal grill. Lots of shelf space. Grill base (or tray) can be removed for cleanup. Handle got very hot. Claimed output: 52,000 Btu/hr. Warranty: castings, 1 yr.; burners, 5 yr.; other parts, 1 yr. Similar: Deluxe 4 7462.

SMALL GRILLS

24 WEBER Q-396001 **Excellent.** Portable, single-burner model; price includes optional stand and adapter for 20-lb. propane tank. Grill base (or tray) can be removed for cleanup. Utensil hooks. No thermometer on lid or warming rack. Claimed output: 12,000 Btu/hr. Warranty: castings, 5 yr.; burners, 5 yr.; other parts, 5 yr.

25 WEBER Genesis Silver A 6211001 **Very good.** Lots of shelf space. Grill base (or tray) can be removed for cleanup. Utensil hooks. Removable thermometer

Recommendations

on lid doubles as meat thermometer. Thermometer got hot. Claimed output: 22,000 Btu/hr. Warranty: castings, life; burners, 10 yr.; other parts, 5 yr. Similar: Silver A 6218001, Silver A 6217001.

26 **KENMORE (SEARS)** 16214 **A CR Best Buy Very good.** Lots of shelf and warming-rack space. Utensil hooks. Handle got very hot. Claimed output: 43,000 Btu/hr. (including side burner). Warranty: castings, life; burners, 2 yr.; other parts, 1 yr. Similar: 16212.

27 **DUCANE** Standard Series 1005SHLPE **Very good.** Stainless-steel cart. Lit-burner indicator. Removable side shelf doubles as a cutting board. Flared up more than others. Handle got hot. No thermometer on lid. Claimed output: 25,000 Btu/hr. Warranty: castings, life; burners, life; other parts, 5 yr. Similar: 1005ASHLPE.*

28 **FIESTA** Advantis 1000 EZA30030 **Very good.** Utensil hooks. Wood handle. Cart judged less sturdy than most others tested. Flared up more than others. No thermometer on lid. Claimed output: 30,000 Btu/hr. Warranty: castings, life; burners, 3 yr.; other parts, 2 yr.

29 **AUSSIE** Bushman Elite 7720 **Good.** Handle got very hot. No thermometer on lid. Claimed output: 33,500 Btu/hr. (including side burner). Warranty: castings, 1 yr.; burners, 1 yr.; other parts, 1 yr. Similar: Bushman Deluxe 7710, Bondi II Elite 7830, Bondi II Deluxe 7820.

* Ducane is no longer in business; the company was bought by Weber. Weber has informed us that they are not obligated to honor Ducane's product guarantees, but will offer replacement parts. Call 800-446-1071 for more information.

HOME THEATER IN A BOX

Many of the systems in the Ratings—even some toward the bottom of the list—were solid performers. Models judged excellent for sound had the crispest, smoothest, fullest audio without excessive bass. Those scoring very good should suit all but the pickiest. Paying more may get you more features and inputs but won't necessarily get you better performance.

Excellent · Very good · Good · Fair · Poor

In performance order. Gray key numbers indicate Quick Picks.

Key number	Brand & model	Price	Overall score (0–100; P F G VG E)	Test results: Sound quality	Test results: Ease of use	Test results: Features	Features: DVD player: Separate	Features: DVD player: Integrated	Features: DVD player: No. of discs	VCR	6.1 surround	Front input	Onscreen display	Composite-video in/out	Component-video in/out
1	**Yamaha** YHT-450	$500		Excellent	Very good	Very good			N/A		•	•		4/1	2/0
2	**Yamaha** YHT-750	700		Excellent	Very good	Very good	•		5		•	•		4/1	2/0
3	**Kenwood** HTB-S715DV	900		Excellent	Good	Good	•		1		•	•		5/2	2/0
4	**Onkyo** HT-S777C	700		Very good	Very good	Very good	•		6		•	•		4/1	2/0
5	**Sony** DAV-FR9	800		Excellent	Good	Good		•	5		•		•	0/0	0/0
6	**Panasonic** SC-HT920	500		Excellent	Good	Good		•	5				•	0/0	0/0
7	**Sony** DAV-FR8	700		Excellent	Good	Good		•	5		•		•	0/0	0/0
8	**Sony** HT-V2000DP	400		Very good	Very good	Good		•	1	•				0/0	0/0
9	**Panasonic** SC-HT820V	400		Excellent	Good	Good		•	5	•			•	1/1	0/0
10	**Philips** MX5600D	500		Very good	Good	Good		•	5				•	0/0	0/0
11	**Cambridge Soundworks** MegaTheater 505	500		Very good	Good	Good		•	1			•	•	3/1	0/0
12	**Samsung** HT-DB390	500		Very good	Good	Good		•	1				•	2/0	0/0
13	**Pioneer** HTZ-940DV	1,200		Very good	Good	Good		•	1				•	0/0	0/0
14	**Sony** DAV-BC150	350		Excellent	Good	Fair		•	5					0/0	0/0
15	**Toshiba** SD-V55HT	300		Very good	Good	Good		•	1	•		•	•	2/1	0/0
16	**JVC** TH-M505	400		Very good	Good	Good		•	5				•	1/0	0/0
17	**JVC** TH-M303	300		Very good	Good	Good		•	5				•	1/0	0/0
18	**Samsung** HT-DS660T	600		Good	Good	Good		•	5				•	2/0	1/0

See report, page 41. Based on tests published in Consumer Reports in November 2004.

Guide to the Ratings

Overall score is based mostly on sound quality. **Sound quality** represents accuracy of the front speakers, subwoofer, center-channel speaker, and surround speakers, with tone controls adjusted for best sound. **Ease of use** reflects the design of the front panel and the remote control, legibility of controls, and ease of setup. **Features** score is based on the presence or absence of useful features. The inputs and outputs shown are on the receiver. (Does not include outputs on the DVD player, if that is separate.) **Price** is approximate retail.

Quick Picks

For the best sound and simple design:

1 Yamaha $500
2 Yamaha $700

The two Yamahas produced excellent sound and were easy to use, with lots of convenience features. Both support Dolby 6.1 and have a third rear speaker. Yamaha (1) has no DVD player and has midsized speakers; (2) has a player that's separate from the receiver and has small speakers.

For excellent sound plus sleek styling:

3 Kenwood $900
5 Sony $800
7 Sony $700

The Kenwood (3) has two slim towers, three small rear speakers, and a separate DVD player. The Sony (5) has four slim towers; (7) has two towers and two small cubes. Both have a combo receiver/DVD player. All three systems support Dolby 6.1 surround

For excellent sound at the lowest price:

9 Panasonic $400
14 Sony $350

You won't get all the bells and whistles, but you will get great performance. The Sony (14) has a receiver/DVD player. Its style is functional; speakers are small cubes. The Panasonic (9) has a sleeker design and adds a VCR to the receiver/DVD player. Its speakers are small cubes. Both lack front-panel input and volume control on the subwoofer.

If you want fewer wires:

12 Samsung $500

The Samsung has very good sound, a sleek design, and wireless rear speakers. The DVD player and receiver are combined.

For decent sound, sleek styling, low cost:

17 JVC $300

The JVC has a very slim console and tiny silver speakers. Sound was very good. The DVD player and receiver are combined.

HUMIDIFIERS

The two top-scoring tabletop units are evaporative models, which combine efficiency with good output and features. Choose a high-scoring warm-mist model, however, if you place a premium on quiet and can live with higher operating costs. All console models are evaporative. While the Lasko humidifies well, its parts may break during use. Among all types, better models have good or better humidistat and hard-water performance scores, and met or exceeded their claimed output. Lower-rated evaporative units fell short of claimed output.

The Ratings list products strictly on performance. Quick Picks considers other factors.

Excellent ⊜ | Very good ⊖ | Good ○ | Fair ◒ | Poor ●

Within types, in performance order. Gray **key numbers indicate Quick Picks.**

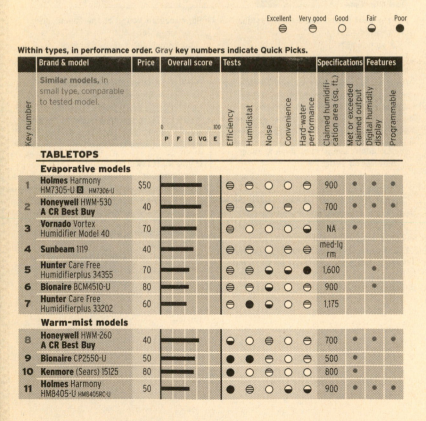

Key number	Brand & model (Similar models, in small type, comparable to tested model.)	Price	Overall score (0–100: P F G VG E)	Tests: Efficiency	Humidistat	Noise	Convenience	Hard-water performance	Specifications: Claimed humidification area (sq. ft.)	Met or exceeded claimed output	Features: Digital humidity display	Programmable
	TABLETOPS											
	Evaporative models											
1	**Holmes** Harmony HM7305-U [D] HM7306-U	$50		⊜	⊖	○	○	⊖	900	•	•	•
2	**Honeywell** HWM-530 **A CR Best Buy**	40		⊜	⊖	○	⊖	○	700	•	•	•
3	**Vornado** Vortex Humidifier Model 40	70		⊜	○	○	○	◒	NA	•		
4	**Sunbeam** 1119	40		⊜	⊖	○	⊖	⊜	med-lg rm			
5	**Hunter** Care Free Humidifierplus 34355	70		⊜	⊜	◒	◒	●	1,600		•	
6	**Bionaire** BCM4510-U	80		⊜	⊖	◒	○	⊖	900		•	
7	**Hunter** Care Free Humidifierplus 33202	60		⊖	●	◒	○	⊖	1,175			
	Warm-mist models											
8	**Honeywell** HWM-260 **A CR Best Buy**	40		◒	○	⊜	○	⊖	700	•	•	•
9	**Bionaire** CP2550-U	50		●	●	⊖	○	⊖	500	•		
10	**Kenmore** (Sears) 15125	80		●	○	⊖	○	○	800	•		
11	**Holmes** Harmony HM8405-U HM8405RC-U	50		●	⊜	○	◒	◒	900	•	•	•

Key number	Brand & model (Similar models, in small type, comparable to tested model.)	Price	Overall score (0–100: P F G VG E)	Tests: Efficiency	Tests: Humidistat	Tests: Noise	Tests: Convenience	Tests: Hard-water performance	Specifications: Claimed humidification area (sq. ft.)	Specifications: Met or exceeded claimed output	Features: Digital humidity display	Features: Programmable
	CONSOLES											
12	**Emerson** HD7005 **A CR Best Buy**	$90		⊖	○	◒	○	⊖	1,200	*		
13	**Lasko** Recirculating Humidifier 1155	110		⊖	⊖	●	◒	⊖	3,800	*	*	
14	**Kenmore** (Sears) 14411	120		⊖	⊖	◒	○	⊖	2,300		*	
15	**Bemis** BEM 821 000	100		⊖	⊖	◒	○	⊖	1,700		*	

D *Discontinued, but similar model is available. Price is for similar model.*

See report, page 105. *Based on tests published in Consumer Reports in October 2004.*

Guide to the Ratings

Efficiency is the wattage required to send a gallon of water into the air. **Humidistat** notes the presence and accuracy of this feature; models without one rated poor for this attribute. **Noise** was tested on both high and low settings with a decibel meter and by listening. **Convenience** measures how easy it is to carry, fill, and clean the unit and replace the wick, and how easy the controls are to use. **Hard-water performance** compares output and efficiency using hard water and soft water. **Claimed humidification area** is the maximum area over which humidity is kept at a target level, according to the manufacturer. **Met or exceeded claimed output** is based on our tests measuring output over two hours at the highest setting, and extrapolating the 24-hour output. **Price** is approximate retail.

Quick Picks

If quiet is paramount; a CR Best Buy:
8 Honeywell $40 (tabletop)
The Honeywell put out more moisture in our tests than claimed, is very quiet and feature-laden, and is the most efficient warm-mist model. But remember that tabletop units can humidify only one room. It costs about $60 per year to operate.

If inexpensive operation is a priority; both are CR Best Buys:
2 Honeywell $40 (tabletop)
12 Emerson $90 (console)
Both are evaporative models, so they're somewhat noisy, the Emerson (12) especially so. Both cost $19 per year to run.

If you have hard water:
1 Holmes $50 (tabletop)
8 Honeywell $40 (tabletop),
14 Kenmore $120 (console)
These models rated very good or excellent on this measure. The Holmes (1) and Kenmore (14) are somewhat noisy. The Honeywell (8) is quieter but costs more to run. The Sunbeam (4) has excellent hard water performance, but its output was much lower than claimed.

IRONS

Virtually all the tested irons were equal to the task of removing wrinkles from a range of fabrics. You don't have to spend a lot to get very good performance. Some irons selling for $20 to $30 scored better than others that sell for $60 to $100 or more. The top-scoring models were prodigious steamers, good gliders, and easy to use. All the recommended models also have auto shutoff, a safety feature that we highly recommend.

Excellent ⊜ | Very good ⊖ | Good ○ | Fair ◒ | Poor ●

Within types, in performance order. Gray key numbers indicate Quick Picks.

Key number	Brand & model Similar models, in small type, comparable to tested model.	Price	Overall score (0–100; P F G VG E)	Ironing	Steaming	Glide	Ease of use	Weight (lb.)
	CORDED IRONS							
1	**Black & Decker** Digital Advantage D2020 D2000	$50		Excellent	Excellent	Good	Very good	3½
2	**Rowenta** Perfect DX9800	140		Very good	Excellent	Excellent	Very good	3¾
3	**Hamilton Beach** Steam Excel 14770	30		Very good	Good	Excellent	Very good	2½
4	**Braun** FreeStyle Pro SI 6285	90		Excellent	Good	Very good	Very good	2¾
5	**T-Fal** Ultraglide Diffusion 1759 1769	45		Excellent	Good	Very good	Good	3
6	**Black & Decker** Steam Xpress S685 S680	30		Very good	Good	Very good	Very good	2½
7	**GE** 106671R 169153 **A CR Best Buy**	20		Very good	Good	Very good	Very good	2½
8	**Sunbeam** Simple Press 3035	25		Excellent	Good	Good	Good	3
9	**Hamilton Beach** Steam Storm Plus 14560	20		Excellent	Good	Very good	Good	2¼
10	**Sunbeam** Dura Press 4075	25		Very good	Good	Very good	Very good	2¾
11	**Proctor-Silex** Easy Press 17585 17520	25		Very good	Fair	Very good	Very good	2¼
12	**Black & Decker** Quick Press S560A	25		Very good	Good	Excellent	Good	2¼
13	**Rowenta** Powerglide 2 DM273	60		Very good	Good	Very good	Good	2¾
14	**Rowenta** Professional Luxe DM880	100		Very good	Good	Good	Good	3¾
15	**Black & Decker** Steam Advantage AS775	30		Very good	Good	Fair	Very good	2½
16	**Black & Decker** Prestige X805	40		Good	Very good	Fair	Good	3¼
17	**Black & Decker** Classic F63D	30		Very good	Fair	Poor	Fair	3¼
	CORDLESS IRONS							
18	**Maytag** MLI-7500	150		Excellent	Fair	Good	Very good	2¾
19	**Panasonic** NI-L40NS NI-L45NR	45		Excellent	Fair	Very good	Good	2½

See report, page 80. Based on tests published in Consumer Reports in September 2004.

Guide to the Ratings

Overall score is based on performance, convenience, and features. **Ironing** reflects how easily the iron removed wrinkles from silk, cotton-polyester blends, cotton, and linen, plus temperature consistency and evenness. **Steaming** indicates how much steam was produced in 10 minutes on the highest setting. **Glide** reflects how easily a hot iron moved back and forth over dry fabric, using no steam or water spray. **Ease of use** judges how easy the iron was to set, fill, and empty, and how easy it was to see water levels and markings and indicator lights. Other factors in determining convenience (not shown) were the spray pattern, leaking, how well the irons steamed at low settings, and stability when upright. **Weight** is rounded up to the next quarter-pound. **Price** is approximate retail. Scores for irons that appeared in previous Ratings may have changed due to new test procedures as well as improvements in steaming, which established a new standard for excellence.

Quick Picks

If you want excellent performance and lots of steam:

1 Black & Decker $50

With top scores for ironing and steaming, the Blacker & Decker (1) is the only tested model judged excellent overall and a fine choice for heavily wrinkled items. But note that its stainless-steel soleplate was judged only good for glide on dry fabrics. Still, if you dampen items or usé steam or spray, you'll get smooth sailing. It has a digital control for setting the temperature.

Very good choices and solid values:

3 Hamilton Beach $30
7 GE $20, CR Best Buy
8 Sunbeam $25
12 Black & Decker $25

All the models in this group were very good overall and either very good or excellent for ironing. All but the Hamilton Beach (3) have a nonstick soleplate; it has a stainless-steel soleplate, which scored excellent for glide. The GE (7) has an extra-long, 12-foot cord. At $20, it's a CR Best Buy. It is sold only at Wal-Mart.

If you want to go cordless:

10 Panasonic $45

Very good overall and excellent at ironing, the Panasonic would be fine for ironing all but the most wrinkled fabrics, which would benefit from more steam. It could also be tedious to iron large items like sheets and tablecloths, which would require frequent reheating of the iron.

LAWN MOWERS

All of these self-propelled and push mowers scored at least good overall. The best in this test cut evenly and proved easy to start, maneuver, and control. They also bagged thoroughly, courtesy of rear-mounted collection bags, which tend to fill more completely than the side-mounted bags they've displaced on most models.

High performance doesn't necessarily mean the highest price. Five of our top 10 self-propelled gasoline-powered mowers cost $500 or less, compared with $700 for the top-scoring Honda. You'll also find low-priced corded electrics, though you'll still pay a premium for cordless models without getting premium performance.

Big-name engines like those from Honda are another selling point that can boost a mower's appeal. But many models with other engines performed at least as well. What's more, the newer-design Honda engines used on many Honda and non-Honda mowers have different components than the commercial-grade engine on the Honda (7) and other pricier Honda mowers sold only at independent dealers.

The Ratings rank models by overall score. See Quick Picks for models that match the kind of mowing you do.

Excellent ⊜ Very good ⊖ Good ○ Fair ◒ Poor ●

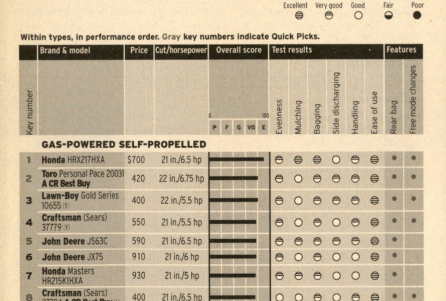

Within types, in performance order. Gray **key numbers indicate Quick Picks.**

Key number	Brand & model	Price	Cut/horsepower	Overall score (0–100; P F G VG E)	Test results: Evenness	Mulching	Bagging	Side discharging	Handling	Ease of use	Features: Rear bag	Free mode changes
	GAS-POWERED SELF-PROPELLED											
1	**Honda** HRX217HXA	$700	21 in./6.5 hp		⊖	⊜	⊜	○	⊖	⊜	•	•
2	**Toro** Personal Pace 20031 **A CR Best Buy**	420	22 in./6.75 hp		⊖	○	⊖	⊖	⊖	⊜	•	•
3	**Lawn-Boy** Gold Series 10655 [1]	400	22 in./5.5 hp		⊖	○	⊖	⊖	⊖	⊜	•	•
4	**Craftsman** (Sears) 37779 [1]	550	21 in./5.5 hp		⊖	○	⊖	○	⊖	⊜	•	•
5	**John Deere** JS63C	590	21 in./6.5 hp		⊖	⊖	⊖	⊖	⊖	⊜	•	
6	**John Deere** JX75	910	21 in./6 hp		⊖	○	⊖	○	○	⊜	•	
7	**Honda** Masters HR215K1HXA	930	21 in./5 hp		⊖	⊖	⊖	○	○	⊜	•	
8	**Craftsman** (Sears) 37784 **A CR Best Buy** [1]	400	21 in./6.5 hp		○	○	⊖	○	⊖	⊜	•	•

Key number	Brand & model	Price	Cut/horsepower	Overall score (0–100; P F G VG E)	Test results: Evenness	Mulching	Bagging	Side discharging	Handling	Ease of use	Features: Rear bag	Free mode changes
	GAS-POWERED SELF-PROPELLED											
9	**Husqvarna** 55R21HV [1]	$480	21 in./5.5 hp		○	○	⊖	○	⊖	⊖	•	•
10	**Troy-Bilt** Pro Cut 320 12A-998Q [1]	500	21 in./5.5 hp		○	⊖	⊖	⊖	⊖	⊖	•	•
11	**Toro** Personal Pace Super Recycler 20037	595	21 in./6.5 hp		⊖	⊖	⊖	⊖	○	⊖	•	
12	**Husqvarna** 5521CHV [1]	350	21 in./5.5 hp		○	⊖	○	○	⊖	○	•	•
13	**Yard-Man** 12A978Q [1]	400	21 in./5.5 hp		○	○	⊖	○	⊖	⊖	•	•
14	**Yard-Man** 12AD465E	370	21 in./6.75 hp		⊖	○	○	○	⊖	○	•	•
15	**Honda** Harmony II HRZ216TDA	530	21 in./5.5 hp		○	○	○	○	⊖	⊖	•	
16	**Troy-Bilt** TuffCut 230 12AF569Q	400	21 in./6.75 hp		○	○	○	○	⊖	⊖	•	•
17	**Ariens** LM21S (911514)	600	21 in./ 6.5 hp		○	○	⊖	⊖	○	⊖	•	•
18	**Cub Cadet** SR621 12A-977A	460	21 in./6.5 hp		⊖	⊖	⊖	⊖	◒	⊖	•	•
19	**Craftsman** (Sears) 37855 [1]	330	21 in./5.5 hp		○	⊖	○	⊖	○	○	•	•
20	**Craftsman** (Sears) 37894	280	21 in./7 hp		○	○	⊖	○	⊖	○	•	•
21	**Snapper** RP215517HC [1]	660	21 in./5.5 hp		○	○	⊖	○	⊖	○	•	
22	**Craftsman** (Sears) 37778	330	21 in./6.75 hp		○	○	◒	○	⊖	⊖	•	•
23	**Ariens** 911097 [1]	490	21 in./5.5 hp		○	◒	⊖	◒	⊖	⊖	•	•
24	**Toro** High Wheel Recycler 20016	320	22 in./6.5 hp		⊖	○	⊖	○	○	○	•	•
25	**Yard Machines** Gold 12A-288A	260	22 in./5 hp		⊖	⊖	◒	⊖	○	○		
26	**Yard-Man** DLX 12A567A	300	21 in./6.5 hp		○	○	○	○	⊖	○	•	•
27	**Honda** Harmony II HRS216K2SDA	415	21 in./5.5 hp		⊖	⊖	●	⊖	○	○		
28	**Yard-Man** 12A445E	260	21 in./6.75 hp		○	○	○	○	⊖	○	•	•
29	**Craftsman** (Sears) 37910	280	22 in./6.25 hp		○	○	◒	⊖	○	○		
30	**Yard-Man** 12A-569T	325	21 in./6 hp		⊖	○	○	○	◒	○	•	•
31	**Murray** 226111X92	215	21 in./5.5 hp		○	○	NA	○	○	○		•
32	**Murray Select** 228511X8	260	22 in./6.25 hp		○	○	○	NA	◒	○	•	•

Excellent ⊜ | Very good ⊖ | Good ○ | Fair ◒ | Poor ●

Within types, in performance order. Gray key numbers indicate Quick Picks.

Key number	Brand & model	Price	Cut/horsepower	Overall score (0–100: P F G VG E)	Test results: Evenness	Mulching	Bagging	Side discharging	Handling	Ease of use	Features: Rear bag	Free mode changes
	GAS-POWERED PUSH											
33	**Lawn-Boy** Gold Series 10654 [1]	$330	22 in./5.5 hp		Very good	Good	Very good	Good	Good	Very good	•	•
34	**Toro** 20008	350	22 in./6.5 hp		Very good	Good	Very good	Good	Good	Good	•	
35	**Yard-Man** 11A-435D **A CR Best Buy**	200	21 in./6.5 hp		Good	Good	Good	Good	Very good	Good	•	•
36	**MTD Pro** 11A588Q [1] **A CR Best Buy**	200	21 in./5.5 hp		Good	Good	Good	Good	Very good	Good	•	•
37	**Bolens** 11A-584E765	170	21 in./4.5 hp		Good	Good	Good	NA	Very good	Good	•	•
38	**Honda** Harmony II HRS216K2PDA	365	21 in./5.5 hp		Very good	Good	Poor	Excellent	Good	Very good		
39	**Bolens** 11A084E765	170	22 in./4.5 hp		Good	Good	NA	Good	Very good	Good		
40	**Craftsman** (Sears) 38746	200	22 in./4.5 hp		Good	Good	Poor	Good	Very good	Good		
41	**Craftsman** (Sears) 38855	230	21 in./6.5 hp		Good	Good	Fair	Fair	Good	Good	•	
42	**Murray Select** 204210X8	160	20 in./4.5 hp		Good	Fair	Fair	NA	Very good	Good	•	•
43	**Murray** 225112X92	155	21 in./5 hp		Good	Good	NA	Fair	Very good	Good		•
44	**Snapper** MR216517B	410	21 in./6.5 hp		Good	Good	Very good	Good	Good	Good	•	
	CORDED ELECTRIC PUSH											
45	**Bolens** 18A-V17-765	190	19 in./12 amp		Fair	Good	Fair	NA	Good	Very good	•	•
46	**Black & Decker** MM875	244	19 in./12 amp		Fair	Good	Poor	Good	Good	Very good	•	
	CORDLESS ELECTRIC PUSH											
47	**Black & Decker** CMM 1000	465	19 in./24 volt		Good	Very good	Poor	Very good	Good	Very good	•	
48	**Neuton** EM 4.1	400	14 in./24 volt		Fair	Good	Fair	Fair	Very good	Good	•	

[1] *Non-Honda mower with a Honda engine.*

See report, page 106. Based on tests published in Consumer Reports in June 2004, with updated prices and availability.

Guide to the Ratings

Overall score is based mainly on cutting performance, handling, and ease of use. **Evenness** shows average cutting performance for all available modes. **Mulching** is how evenly mulched clippings were spread over the lawn surface. **Bagging** denotes how many clippings the bag held before it filled or the chute clogged. **Side discharging** is how evenly clippings were dispersed in that mode. **Handling** includes ease of using the drive controls (for self-propelled), pushing, pulling, making U-turns, and maneuvering. **Ease of use** is ease of starting, using blade-stopping controls, changing speeds (for self-propelled), and adjusting cut height. **Price** is approximate retail and includes attachments for all applicable mowing modes.

Quick Picks

Best for most; versatile mowing:

1 Honda $700
2 Toro $420, CR Best Buy
5 Deere $590
8 Craftsman $400, CR Best Buy
20 Craftsman $280

Superb mulching and bagging with the ability to adjust both for tall or wet grass make the top-scoring Honda (1) versatile. But the high-value Toro (2) and the Deere (5) work nearly as well and distribute clippings more evenly when side-discharging. The Toro (2) has variable drive speeds that involve pushing the handlebar, which may take some getting used to. Its similar model lacks electric starting and costs $40 less. Also consider the high-value Craftsman (8) for its easy cut-height adjustment and the single-speed Craftsman (20) for its low price. Note that while Lawn-Boy has been among the more repair-prone brands in our surveys, it now shares its design with Toro. We'll see whether that affects its reliability.

For small, relatively flat properties:

35 Yard-Man $200, CR Best Buy
36 MTD Pro $200, CR Best Buy
45 Bolens $190
47 Black & Decker $465

The gas-powered Yard-Man (35) and MTD Pro (36) perform equally well, though the MTD is sold only at Sam's Club and may be harder to find. Consider the Bolens (37) if you don't side-discharge clippings and the Honda (38) if side-discharging is the mode you use most. Also consider the corded-electric Bolens (45) if entangling shrubs aren't a problem and the Black & Decker (47) if a cordless mower is worth the higher price and limited run time.

Recommendations

SELF-PROPELLED MOWERS

1 **HONDA** HRX217HXA **Excellent**. Highest scoring model. The only model with a hydrostatic transmission, which gives smooth engagement and variable speed. "Versamow System" allows partial bagging and mulching simultaneously. Has blade brake clutch. Mulching and bagging attachments included. Choke and throttle at handle bar. Similar: Honda HRX217TDA.

2 **TORO** Personal Pace 20031 **A CR Best Buy Very good.** Has Tecumseh engine with battery electric start. Mulching and bagging attachments included. "Personal Pace" variable speed system adjusts ground speed by pressure on the handlebar. Handlebar can swing up for easier bag removal and storage, but scratches the paint at the base of the handlebars. Similar: Toro Recycler 20017.

Recommendations

3 LAWN-BOY Gold Series 10655 **Very good.** Mulching and bagging attachments included. Has Honda engine. "Personal Pace" variable speed system adjusts ground speed by pressure on the handlebar. Handlebar can swing up for easier bag removal and storage, but scratches the paint at the base of the handlebars. Engine starter rope has padded, large handle. Bag has padded handle. Lawn-Boy has been among the more repair-prone brands.

4 CRAFTSMAN (Sears) 37779 **Very good.** Moderately priced. Honda engine and blade brake clutch. Throttle and choke. Options for all modes included.

5 JOHN DEERE JS63C **Very good.** Swivel wheels for easy U-turns but hard to jockey side-to-side. Has Briggs & Stratton engine. Bag hard to empty. Throttle and choke at handlebar.

6 JOHN DEERE JX75 **Very good.** Expensive. Kawasaki engine and blade-brake clutch. Easy bag handling. Drive starts abruptly. Throttle and choke. Aluminum deck.

7 HONDA Masters HR215K1HXA **Very good.** Expensive. Easy to use, with easy bag handling, though mulching requires a blade change. Blade-brake clutch. Throttle and choke. Aluminum deck.

8 CRAFTSMAN (Sears) 37784 **A CR Best Buy Very good.** Mulching and bagging attachments included. Has Honda engine. Easy deck height adjustment. Similar to Husqvarna 55R21HV.

9 HUSQVARNA 55R21HV **Very good.** Mulching and bagging attachments included. Has Honda engine. Easy deck height adjustment. Similar to Craftsman 37784.

10 TROY-BILT Pro Cut 320 12A-998Q **Very good.** An especially well-rounded choice. Honda engine. Swivel wheels for easy U-turns, though hard to adjust deck height. Single-lever deck height adjustment for rear. Hard to push and pull. Bag hard to empty. Options for all modes included.

11 TORO Personal Pace Super Recycler 20037 **Very good.** Briggs & Stratton engine. Less noisy than most. Hard to jockey side to side. Bag inconvenient to empty.

12 HUSQVARNA 5521CHV **Very good.** Mulching and bagging attachments included. Has Honda engine. Single speed. Similar to Craftsman 37855.

13 YARD-MAN 12A978Q **Very good.** Mulching and bagging attachments included. Has Honda engine. Easy deck height adjustment. Has been among the more repair-prone brands of self-propelled mowers.

14 YARD-MAN 12AD465E **Very good.** Front-drive reduces traction. Variable speed system adjusts ground speed by pressure on handle bar. Tecumseh engine. Side-to-side jockeying especially easy. Bag hard to empty. Deck height hard to adjust. Has been among the more repair-prone brands of self-propelled mowers.

15 HONDA Harmony II HRZ216TDA **Very good.** A fine, well-rounded mower. Swivel wheels for easy U-turns. Quieter than most.

16 TROY-BILT TuffCut 230 12AF5690 **Very good.** Has Briggs & Stratton engine with spring powered self starter that does not use a battery. Mulching and bagging attachments included. Variable speed system adjusts ground speed by pressure on handle bar.

Recommendations

17 ARIENS LM21S (911514) **Very good.** Briggs & Stratton engine. U-turns and jockeying side-to-side hard. Bag hard to empty.

18 CUB CADET SR621 12A-977A **Very good.** A capable though clumsy performer. Kawasaki engine. Single-lever deck height adjustment. Hard to push, pull, U-turn, and jockey from side to side. Bag difficult to empty. Options for all modes included. Similar: Cub Cadet SRE621 12AE-977C.

19 CRAFTSMAN (Sears) 37855 **Very good.** Honda engine. Mulching and bagging attachments included. Similar to Husqvarna 5521CHV.

20 CRAFTSMAN (Sears) 37894 **Very good.** Very good performance for under $300, but single speed. Has Briggs & Stratton engine with unique fuel stabilizing system. Mulching and bagging attachments included.

21 SNAPPER RP215517HC **Very good.** Honda engine. Choke and throttle at the handlebar. Snapper has been among the more repair-prone brands.

22 CRAFTSMAN (Sears) 37778 **Very good.** Tecumseh engine. Mulching and bagging attachments included. Easy deck height adjustment.

23 ARIENS 911097 **Very good.** Honda engine. Mulching and bagging attachments included. Has easy deck height adjustment. Choke and throttle at handlebar.

24 TORO High Wheel Recycler 20016 **Very good.** Has Tecumseh engine. U-turns and jockeying side to side hard.

25 YARD MACHINES Gold 12A-288A **Very good.** Briggs & Stratton engine. Hard to pull. Bag inconvenient. Handle vibrates. Has been among the more repair-prone brands of self-propelled mowers.

26 YARD-MAN DLX 12A567A **Good.** Kawasaki engine. Mulching and bagging attachments included. Available at Costco. Has been among the more repair-prone brands of self-propelled mowers.

27 HONDA Harmony II HRS216K2SDA **Good.** Drive starts abruptly. Bagging requires blade change. Throttle and choke.

28 YARD-MAN 12A445E **Good.** Tecumseh engine. Mulching and bagging attachments included. Has been among the more repair-prone brands of self-propelled mowers.

29 CRAFTSMAN (Sears) 37910 **Good.** Briggs & Stratton engine.

30 YARD-MAN 12A-569T **Good.** Briggs & Stratton engine with push-button starter. Hard to push and pull. U-turns, jockeying side-to-side, and bag emptying hard. Options for all modes included. Has been among the more repair-prone brands of self-propelled mowers.

31 MURRAY 226111X92 **Good.** Briggs & Stratton engine. Lacks bagging mode.

32 MURRAY Select 228511X8 **Good.** But there are better choices among self-propelled models. Briggs & Stratton engine. Front-drive reduces traction. Hard to push and jockey from side to side. Uncomfortable handle.

GAS-POWERED PUSH MODELS

33 LAWN-BOY Gold Series 10654 **Very good.** Expensive for a push mower. Similar deck to Lawn-Boy Series 10655 and Toro 20031. Mulching and bagging attachments included. Has Honda engine. Handlebar can swing up for easier bag removal and storage, but scratches the paint at the base of the handlebars. Engine starter rope has large, padded handle. Bag has padded handle. Has been the most repair-prone brand of push mowers.

34 TORO 20008 **Very good.** Expensive for a push mower. Similar deck to Lawn-Boy Series 10655, 10654 and Toro 20031. Has Tecumseh engine.

35 YARD-MAN 11A-435D **A CR Best Buy Very good.** A capable, well-rounded push mower. Tecumseh engine. Side-to-side jockeying, pushing, and U-turns especially easy. Bag inconvenient to empty. Cut height hard to adjust.

36 MTD PRO 11A588Q **A CR Best Buy Very good.** Has Honda engine. Mulching and bagging attachments included. Available only at Sam's Club stores.

37 BOLENS 11A-584E765 **Good.** Briggs & Stratton engine. Lacks discharge mode.

38 HONDA Harmony II HRS216K2PDA **Good.** Great for side-discharging, but pricey. Overhead-cam engine and choke. Weak in tall grass. Bagging requires blade change.

39 BOLENS 11A084E765 **Good.** Briggs & Stratton engine. Lacks bagging mode.

40 CRAFTSMAN (Sears) 38746 **Good.** Tecumseh engine. Limited bag capacity.

41 CRAFTSMAN (Sears) 38855 **Good.** Briggs & Stratton engine.

42 MURRAY Select 204210X8 **Good.** There are better choices among push models. Briggs & Stratton engine. Side-to-side jockeying, pushing, and U-turns especially easy. Bag inconvenient to empty. Cut height hard to adjust. Uncomfortable handle.

43 MURRAY 2251112X92 **Good.** Briggs & Stratton engine. Lacks bagging mode.

44 SNAPPER MR216517B **Good.** Expensive for a push mower. Briggs & Stratton engine. Throttle and choke at handlebar.

CORDED ELECTRIC PUSH MODELS

45 BOLENS 18A-V17-765 **Very good.** Lacks discharge mode. Power cord hard to keep out of the way while mowing.

46 BLACK & DECKER MM875 **Good.** Power cord hard to keep out of the way while mowing.

CORDLESS ELECTRIC PUSH MODELS

47 BLACK & DECKER CMM 1000 **Good.** Easy wheel height adjustment. Cutting power is limited.

48 NEUTON EM 4.1 **Good.** Easy wheel height adjustment. Cutting power is limited. Narrow cutting width. Battery can be replaced with a second battery (optional) for extended cutting. Has an electric powered trimmer attachment.

LAWN TRACTORS

Nearly all of these lawn tractors mow at least adequately. Top scorers combine level cutting with even clippings dispersal in the most-used side-discharge mode, along with thorough mulching and well-vacuumed results with their bagging kits. But there are subtle differences, particularly among models with higher scores.

You needn't pay a premium for that performance; nearly half of the top 10 automatic-drive models we tested cost less than $2,000. Wider decks sized 44 inches and beyond are one feature that often fetches a premium. But even here, you'll find reasonably priced exceptions.

Other attributes are important regardless of cost. A major one is stability on hills. Two models—the Bolens (19) and Toro (25)—lifted their front wheels on a moderate incline with their bags full.

The Ratings rank models by overall score. See our Quick Picks for lawn tractors with the specific strengths you need for your property.

Excellent | Very good | Good | Fair | Poor

Within types, in performance order. Gray key numbers indicate Quick Picks.

Key numbers	Brand & model	Price	Mulch/ bag kits	Cutting width/hp	Overall score (0–100; P F G VG E)	Evenness	Side	Mulch	Bag	Handling	Ease of use
	AUTOMATIC DRIVE										
1	**John Deere** L110 **A CR Best Buy**	$1,800	$285	42 in./17.5 hp		Very good	Good	Very good	Excellent	Excellent	Very good
2	**Cub Cadet** LT1018 13AL11CG	1,600	300	42 in./18.5 hp		Good	Very good	Very good	Excellent	Excellent	Very good
3	**Simplicity** Regent	2,800	135/400	44 in./16 hp		Good	Good	Very good	Excellent	Excellent	Very good
4	**White Outdoor** LT-1650	1,700	55/299	42 in./18 hp		Good	Very good	Very good	Excellent	Very good	Very good
5	**John Deere** LT160	2,600	445	42 in./16 hp		Very good	Very good	Good	Excellent	Very good	Very good
6	**Troy-Bilt** Bronco 13AJ609G **A CR Best Buy** [1]	1,350	300	42 in./18.5 hp		Good	Very good	Very good	Excellent	Very good	Very good
7	**Toro** Wheel Horse 16-38 HXL	2,150	340	38 in./16 hp		Good	Good	Excellent	Good	Excellent	Good
8	**Kubota** T1670 44"	3,400	180/891	44 in./15 hp		Good	Good	Very good	Good	Excellent	Very good
9	**Kubota** T1670 40"	3,000	180/454	40 in./15 hp		Fair	Very good	Good	Excellent	Excellent	Very good
10	**John Deere** L120	2,200	295	48 in./20 hp		Good	Good	Good	Excellent	Excellent	Very good
11	**Craftsman** (Sears) DYT 4000-27364	1,500	266	42 in./18.5		Good	Very good	Good	Good	Very good	Very good
12	**Simplicity** Regent	2,500	255	38 in./16 hp		Good	Fair	Very good	Very good	Excellent	Very good

Excellent · Very good · Good · Fair · Poor

Within types, in performance order. Gray key numbers indicate Quick Picks.

Key numbers	Brand & model	Price	Mulch/ bag kits	Cutting width/hp	Overall score (0–100; P F G VG E)	Test results: Evenness	Side	Mulch	Bag	Handling	Ease of use
	AUTOMATIC DRIVE *Continued*										
13	**Husqvarna** YTH1542XP	$2,000	270	42 in./15 hp		Very good	Very good	Good	Good	Very good	Very good
14	**Craftsman** DLT 3000-27350	2,150	266	42 in./16.5 hp		Good	Good	Good	Good	Very good	Very good
15	**Murray** Select 465600x8A	1,200	267	46 in./21 hp		Good	Good	Good	Good	Very good	Good
16	**Husqvarna** LTH1742	1,400	200	42 in./17 hp		Good	Good	Good	Good	Very good	Good
17	**Snapper** LT180H42IBV2	3,000	75/246	42 in./18 hp		Good	Good	Good	Fair	Good	Good
	MANUAL DRIVE										
18	**John Deere** L100	1,500	285	42 in./17 hp		Very good	Good	Very good	Excellent	Very good	Very good
19	**Bolens** 13AN683G [2]	1,000	30/300	42 in./17 hp		Good	Very good	Very good	Excellent	Fair	Fair
20	**Craftsman** LT1000-27275	1,000	266	42 in./18 hp		Good	Good	Good	Good	Good	Good
21	**Craftsman** DLT3000-27347	1,500	266	42 in./20 hp		Good	Good	Good	Good	Good	Very good
22	**Murray** Select 425000x8A	1,000	267	42 in./16.5 hp		Good	Good	Fair	Fair	Good	Good
	TIGHT-TURNING MODELS										
23	**John Deere** Spin-Steer SST-16	3,300	400	42 in./16 hp		Good	Excellent	Good	Very good	Excellent	Excellent
24	**Cub Cadet** Z-Force 44	3,600	349	44 in./15 hp		Good	Good	Very good	Good	Very good	Good
25	**Toro** 16-42Z Timecutter	3,100	70/400	42 in./16 hp		Good	Poor	Very good	Fair	Good	Very good
26	**Ariens** Zoom 1640-915035	3,300	49/268	40 in./16 hp		Good	Good	Poor	Fair	Good	Good

[1] *Uses a continuously variable transmission that performs like a hydrostat.*
[2] *Uses a continuously variable transmission with detents, rather than a gear drive.*

See report, page 109. Based on tests published in Consumer Reports in May 2004, with updated prices and availability.

Guide to the Ratings

Overall score denotes mowing performance, handling, and ease of use. **Evenness** is how close models came to carpetlike mowing. **Side** is how evenly clippings were dispersed from the chute. **Mulch** is how finely and evenly clippings were cut and dispersed in this mode. **Bag** denotes effective capacity when bag was full or chute was clogged. **Handling** includes drive engagement, braking, steering, turn radius, and stability. **Ease of use** is legroom, seat and steering-wheel comfort, blade and brake engagement, cut-height adjustment, bag removal, and mode changes. Scoring for ease of use has been slightly modified from previous reports. **Price** for tractor is approximate retail; prices for mulching/bagging kits are from the manufacturer.

Quick Picks

Best for most; versatile mowing at a reasonable price:

1 John Deere $1,800, CR Best Buy
6 Troy-Bilt $1,350, CR Best Buy
11 Craftsman $1,500

A notably level cut helps make the Deere (1) our top pick. The less expensive Troy-Bilt (6) gives up some evenness for better dispersal when side-discharging. Consider the Craftsman (11) if you're willing to trade some performance for an electric power takeoff and other added features. While the Cub Cadet (2) offers impressive performance and the Toro (7) superior mulching, both brands have been among the more repair-prone in our survey.

For large, wide-open spaces:

3 Simplicity $2,800
10 John Deere $2,200

Consider the 44-inch Simplicity (3) for its better mulching, the 48-inch Deere (10) for its added width and lower price. Also consider the 46-inch Murray (15) if you don't mind giving up some performance for more width at a still-lower price.

For lawns with lots of obstacles:

23 John Deere $3,300

The tight-turning Deere (23) offers agile handling using a steering wheel rather than the levers typical of this breed.

Recommendations

AUTOMATIC-DRIVE MODELS

1 **JOHN DEERE** L110 Automatic **A CR Best Buy Very good.** A top tractor at a reasonable price. Smooth drive engagement. Cruise control. Fuel level visible from seat. Kohler engine. High brake pedal awkward. Must engage override switch to cut in reverse. Must change blade to bag. Bag $285. Mulch kit included.

2 **CUB CADET** LT 1018 13AL11CG **Very good.** Very good overall, but Cub Cadet has been among the more repair-prone brands. Excellent bagging and handling. Briggs & Stratton engine. Automatic drive with foot-operated speed control. Electric blade engagement. Comfortable steering wheel. Cruise control. Won't cut in reverse. Bag $300. Mulch kit included.

3 **SIMPLICITY** Regent **Very good.** Excellent bagging and handling. Kohler engine. Hydrostatic drive with foot-operated speed control. Electric blade engagement. Deck has a fan attachment to improve grass bagging, also useful for leaf pickup. Must change blade to mulch and bag. Bag with fan assist $400. Mulch kit $135.

4 **WHITE OUTDOOR** LT1650 **Very good.** Fine overall. Precise steering and comfortable steering wheel. Cruise control. Tecumseh engine. High brake pedal awkward. Won't cut in reverse. Bag $299. Mulch kit $55. Discontinued, but similar LT1855H is available.

5 **JOHN DEERE** LT160 **Very good.** Kohler engine. High brake pedal awkward. Must change blade to mulch. Must engage override switch to cut in reverse. Bag $445. Mulch kit included.

6 **TROY-BILT** Bronco 13AJ609G **A CR Best Buy Very good.** Very good in discharge and mulching and excellent for bagging. Briggs & Stratton engine. Pedal drive (not a true hydrostatic—requires shifting from forward to reverse) with foot-operated speed control. Fuel level visible from seat. Cruise control. Won't cut in reverse. Bag $300. Mulch kit included.

Recommendations

7 TORO Wheel Horse 16-38 HXL **Very good.** A top pick for mulching, but Toro has been among the more repair-prone brands. Smooth drive engagement. Precise steering and comfortable steering wheel. Briggs & Stratton engine. High brake pedal awkward. Must engage override switch to cut in reverse. Bag $340. Mulch kit included.

8 KUBOTA T1670 44" **Very good.** Excellent handling. Kohler engine. Automatic drive with foot-operated speed control. Mower deck has a fan attachment to improve grass bagging, also useful for leaf pickup, but bagging was only Good. Must change blade to mulch and bag. Bag with fan assist $891. Mulch kit $180.

9 KUBOTA T1670 40" **Very good.** But evenness is only Fair. Excellent bagging and handling. Kohler engine. Automatic drive with foot-operated speed control. Must change blade to mulch. Bag $454. Mulch kit $180.

10 JOHN DEERE L120 Automatic **Very good.** 48-in. cutting width. Cruise control. Electric blade engagement. Comfortable seat. Briggs & Stratton engine. High brake pedal awkward. Must change blade to bag. Must engage override switch to cut in reverse. 3 blades. Bag $295. Mulch kit included.

11 CRAFTSMAN (Sears) DYT 4000 27364 **Very good.** Briggs & Stratton engine. Automatic drive with lever-operated speed control Cruise control. Electric blade engagement. Fuel level visible from seat. Comfortable steering wheel. Bag $266. Mulch kit included.

12 SIMPLICITY Regent **Very good.** But only Fair for side-discharge. Kohler engine. Automatic drive with foot-operated speed control. Electric blade engagement. Must change blade to mulch. Bag $255. Mulch kit included.

13 HUSQVARNA YTH1542XP **Very good.** Fine overall. Electric blade engagement. Kawasaki engine. Bag kit $270. Mulch kit included.

14 CRAFTSMAN (Sears) 27350 **Good.** Cruise control. Fuel level easy to read. Comfortable steering wheel. Honda engine. Bag $260. Mulch kit included.

15 MURRAY Select 465600x8A **Good.** 46-in. cutting width. Briggs & Stratton engine. Uncomfortable seat and steering wheel. 3 blades. Bag $267. Mulch kit included. Discontinued, but similar 465306x8A is available.

16 HUSQVARNA LTH1742 **Good.** Kohler engine. Bag $200. Mulch kit included.

17 SNAPPER LT180H42IBV2 **Good.** Good overall, but has shortcomings. Electric blade engagement. Briggs & Stratton engine. Mulching evenness and bag capacity among the worst. Must engage override switch to cut in reverse. Must change blade to mulch. Awkward parking brake. Bag $246. Mulch kit $75.

MANUAL-DRIVE MODELS

18 JOHN DEERE L100 **Very good.** A very good gear-drive tractor. Briggs & Stratton engine. Must change blade to bag. Must engage override switch to cut in reverse. Bag $285. Mulch kit included.

19 BOLENS 13AN683G **Good.** Gear-drive model that's only Fair in handling and ease of use. Briggs & Stratton engine. Manual drive requires setting each speed. Foot-operated brake/clutch pedal. Wide turning radius. Cut-height adjustment also engages the blades. Won't cut in reverse. Bag $300. Mulch kit $30.

Recommendations

Discontinued, but similar Troy-Bilt 13AN689G766 is available.

20 CRAFTSMAN (Sears) 27275 **Good.** Good overall, but has handling problems. Briggs & Stratton engine. Rough drive engagement. Uncomfortable steering wheel. Bag $260. Mulch kit included.

21 CRAFTSMAN (Sears) 27347 **Good.** Comfortable steering wheel. Kohler engine. Rough drive engagement. Bag $260. Mulch kit included.

22 MURRAY Select 425000x8A **Good.** Briggs & Stratton engine. Mulching evenness and dispersal, and bag capacity, among the worst. Uncomfortable seat and steering wheel. Awkward parking brake. Must change blade to mulch. Bag $267. Mulch kit included. Discontinued, but similar 425001x8A is available.

TIGHT-TURNING MODELS

23 JOHN DEERE Spin-Steer SST-16 **Very good.** A top zero-turn tractor. Steering wheel, rather than levers. Smooth drive engagement. Precise steering. Briggs & Stratton engine. Awkward cut-height adjustment. Must engage override switch to cut in reverse. Bag $400. Mulch kit included.

24 CUB CADET Z-Force 44 **Good.** A good zero-turn machine, but Cub Cadet has been among the more repair-prone brands. Electric blade engagement. Kawasaki engine. Awkward parking brake and cut-height adjustment. Bag $349. Mulch kit included.

25 TORO 16-42Z Timecutter **Good.** A tight-turning model that's Poor for side-discharge and only Fair for bagging; Toro has been among the more repair-prone brands. Briggs & Stratton engine. Automatic drive controlled by twin levers, one for each wheel. Levers do not return to the neutral position when released. Electric blade engagement. Seat lacks arm rests. Bag $400. Mulch kit $70.

26 ARIENS Zoom 1640 915035 **Good.** A good zero-turn machine, but mulching dispersal and bag capacity among the worst. Electric blade engagement. Briggs & Stratton engine. Awkward parking brake and cut-height adjustment. Control levers don't return to neutral when released. Must change blade to mulch. Bag $268. Mulch kit $49. Discontinued, but similar 915051 is available.

PDAS

The Ratings tell you which models were easiest to use, had the longest battery life, and performed best overall. The table also indicates the models' major features. But finding the best PDA for your needs also means weighing price and other considerations. Quick Picks does that for you. It highlights good values in PDAs that our experts consider full-featured or especially well designed.

Excellent · Very good · Good · Fair · Poor

Within types, in performance order. Gray **key numbers indicate Quick Picks.**

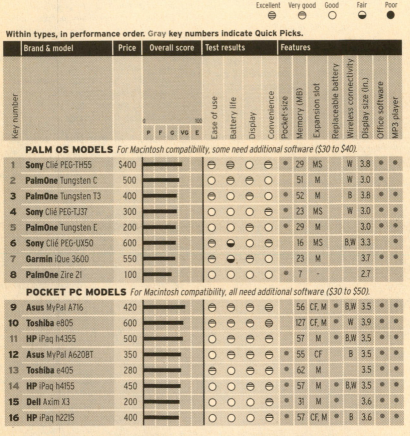

Key number	Brand & model	Price	Overall score (0–100; P F G VG E)	Ease of use	Battery life	Display	Convenience	Pocket-size	Memory (MB)	Expansion slot	Replaceable battery	Wireless connectivity	Display size (in.)	Office software	MP3 player
	PALM OS MODELS *For Macintosh compatibility, some need additional software ($30 to $40).*														
1	**Sony** Clié PEG-TH55	$400		Very good	Excellent	Good	Very good	•	29	MS		W	3.8	•	•
2	**PalmOne** Tungsten C	500		Good	Very good	Very good	Good		51	M		W	3.0	•	
3	**PalmOne** Tungsten T3	400		Very good	Good	Very good	Good	•	52	M		B	3.8	•	•
4	**Sony** Clié PEG-TJ37	300		Good	Good	Good	Very good	•	23	MS		W	3.0	•	•
5	**PalmOne** Tungsten E	200		Good	Good	Very good	Good	•	29	M			3.0	•	•
6	**Sony** Clié PEG-UX50	600		Very good	Fair	Good	Very good		16	MS		B,W	3.3		•
7	**Garmin** iQue 3600	550		Very good	Fair	Very good	Good		23	M			3.7	•	•
8	**PalmOne** Zire 21	100		Good	Good	Good	Good	•	7	-			2.7		
	POCKET PC MODELS *For Macintosh compatibility, all need additional software ($30 to $50).*														
9	**Asus** MyPal A716	420		Very good	Very good	Very good	Excellent		56	CF, M	•	B,W	3.5	•	•
10	**Toshiba** e805	600		Very good	Very good	Very good	Excellent		127	CF, M	•	W	3.9	•	•
11	**HP** iPaq h4355	500		Good	Very good	Very good	Very good		57	M	•	B,W	3.5	•	•
12	**Asus** MyPal A620BT	350		Good	Very good	Very good	Very good	•	55	CF		B	3.5	•	•
13	**Toshiba** e405	280		Very good	Good	Very good	Very good	•	62	M			3.5	•	•
14	**HP** iPaq h4155	450		Good	Good	Very good	Very good	•	57	M	•	B,W	3.5	•	•
15	**Dell** Axim X3	200		Good	Good	Good	Very good	•	31	M	•		3.6	•	•
16	**HP** iPaq h2215	400		Good	Good	Good	Very good	•	57	CF, M	•	B	3.6	•	•

See report, page 136. Based on tests published in Consumer Reports in July 2004, with updated prices and availability.

Guide to the Ratings

Overall score is based primarily on ease of use, battery life, and display. **Ease of use** considers overall design, navigation, and built-in software. **Battery life** is how long fully charged models lasted with continuous use. (For battery life and display, we scored monochrome and color models differently.) For color units: ● blob 15 hours or more; ◓ blob 8 to 15 hours, ○ blob 4 to 8 hours, ◒ blob less than 4 hours. **Display** is readability in low and normal room light and in sunlight. **Convenience** considers battery type, expansion capability, and software. **Expansion slot** indicates the type of removable media you can add: CompactFlash (CF), MultiMedia/SecureDigital Card (M), or Memory Stick (MS). **Wireless connectivity** indicates the connection type: Bluetooth (B) or Wi-Fi (W). **Price** is approximate retail.

Quick Picks

For a basic organizer at a good price:

5 PalmOne $200
13 Toshiba $280

The PalmOne (5) and the Toshiba (13) are well priced yet offer plenty. The PalmOne lets you view pictures and see daily tasks at a glance. The Toshiba has a picture viewer and a voice recorder. Another unit, the PalmOne (8), is the only monochrome unit tested. But while it's low-priced and fine for to-do lists and contacts, other monochrome units we've tested scored higher in battery life.

For a full-featured Palm OS unit:

1 Sony $400
2 PalmOne $500

The Sony (1) has a better design than most other Palm OS models, plus a large display and exceptional battery life for a color unit. For the extra cost, the PalmOne (2) has a usable keyboard and battery life eight hours longer, in tests, than that of next-ranked PalmOne (3).

For a Windows look and feel in a PDA:

11 HP $500
14 HP $450

Both are well designed and have Wi-Fi and Bluetooth capability. The HP (11) squeezes a usable keyboard and easily readable display into a slim case. The HP (14) is similar but, lacking a keyboard, costs less.

For a portable navigation system:

7 Garmin $550

The Garmin (7) is the only unit tested to include a GPS-equipped navigation system. It was easy to use, though its battery life was lacking.

Recommendations

PALM OS MODELS

1 SONY Clié PEG-TH55 **Very good.** One of the most innovative PDA designs we've seen. Overall design and user interface better than most. Fits easily in a shirt pocket. Combines camera, large display, and Wi-Fi connectivity in a small case. Has handy jog dial, LED alarm, printed manual, picture viewer, and eBook Reader. Can record voice memos. But Sony Clié organizer functions not very useful, and Sony software cannot be used with PCs running Windows 98. 6.5 oz.

2 PALMONE Tungsten C **Very good.** A good model for viewing and editing documents, accessing e-mail, and wireless Web surfing. Has one of the most readable screens we've seen, plus picture viewer, expense tracker, eBook reader, and LED and vibrating alarms. Basic organizer functions easy to use. But too bulky to fit in a shirt pocket. Doesn't include backup program. 6.3 oz.

3 PALMONE Tungsten T3 **Good.** A large display in a small size. Overall design better than most, and basic organizer functions easy to use. A good model for viewing and editing documents; display can be viewed in landscape and portrait mode. Fits easily in a shirt pocket. Has picture viewer, eBook reader, expense tracker, and LED and vibrating alarms. Can record voice memos. But battery life not as good as most. Doesn't include backup program. 5.3 oz.

4 SONY Clié PEG-TJ37 **Good.** Basic organizer functions easy to use. Fits easily in a shirt pocket. Has picture viewer, eBook reader, printed manual, and LED alarm. 5.1 oz. Similar: PEG-TJ27 lacks Wi-Fi and an MP3 player.

5 PALMONE Tungsten E **Good.** A good choice for Palm users looking to upgrade. Easily readable display. Improved datebook software lets you see daily tasks at a glance. Basic organizer functions easy to use. Has expense-tracker software, picture viewer, and eBook reader. Fits easily in a shirt pocket. But no backup program included. Battery life not as good as most. 4.6 oz.

6 SONY Clié PEG-UX50 **Good.** Multimedia-capable. Unusual design has swivel display; display is small. User interface better than most. Basic organizer functions easy to use. Has picture viewer, eBook reader, printed manual, and LED alarm. Can record voice memos. But too bulky to fit in a shirt pocket. Battery life not as good as most. 6.3 oz.

7 GARMIN iQue 3600 **Good.** A good organizer with GPS capability. Well-conceived design, with large, easily readable display. Basic organizer functions easy to use, and user interface better than most. Has handy jog dial, eBook reader, and LED and vibrating alarms. Can record voice memos. But lacks e-mail and backup software. Not much battery life for GPS functionality. Too bulky to fit in a shirt pocket. 5.8 oz.

8 PALMONE Zire 21 **Good.** Good, but there are better choices. Basic organizer functions easy to use. Fits easily in a shirt pocket. Has expense tracker and eBook reader. But doesn't include e-mail or backup programs. Disappointing battery life for a monochrome-display PDA. Display lacks backlight and is difficult to read. No external memory card. 3.9 oz.

POCKET PC MODELS

9 ASUS MyPal A716 **Very good.** A good choice if you want to add peripherals. Overall design better than most, with easily readable display. User interface better than most. Has picture viewer, eBook reader, printed manual, and LED alarm. Can record voice memos. But too bulky to fit in a shirt

Recommendations

pocket. 25 MB flash memory for storage. 7.2 oz.

10 TOSHIBA e805 **Very good.** A good organizer with laptop-like functionality, but bulky. A good choice if you want to add peripherals. Easily readable display, and user interface better than most. Has picture viewer, eBook reader, printed manual, and LED alarm. Can record voice memos. But too bulky to fit in a shirt pocket. 31 MB flash memory for storage. 7 oz. Similar: e800.

11 HEWLETT-PACKARD iPAQ h4355 **Very good.** A good organizer with laptop-like functionality and an easily readable display. Slim case design incorporates many features. User interface better than most. Has built-in keyboard, picture viewer, eBook reader, and LED alarm. Can record voice memos. But too bulky to fit in a shirt pocket. 3 MB flash memory for storage. 5.9 oz. Similar: h4350.

12 ASUS MyPal A620BT **Very good.** Easily readable display. User interface better than most. Fits easily in a shirt pocket. Has picture viewer, eBook reader, printed manual, and LED alarm. Can record voice memos. 31 MB flash memory for storage. 5.2 oz. Similar: A620 lacks Bluetooth.

13 TOSHIBA e405 **Very good.** Performance without a lot of features. Easily readable display, and user interface better than most. Fits easily in a shirt pocket. Has picture viewer and LED alarm. Can record voice memos. 31 MB flash memory for storage. 4.6 oz. Similar: e400.

14 HEWLETT-PACKARD iPAQ h4155 **Very good.** A lot of features in a small package—one of the smallest PDAs we've tested. Easily readable display, and user interface better than most. Fits easily in a shirt pocket. Has picture viewer, eBook reader, and LED alarm. Can record voice memos. 3 MB flash memory for storage. 4.7 oz. Similar: h4150.

15 DELL Axim X3 **Good.** Easier to run multiple programs than with most Pocket PCs, and user interface better than most. Fits easily in a shirt pocket. Has picture viewer, eBook reader, and printed manual. Can record voice memos. 4 MB flash memory for storage. 4.8 oz. Discontinued, but X30 is available.

16 HP iPaq h2215 **Good.** A lot of capability in a small case. A good choice if you want to add peripherals. User interface better than most. Fits easily in a shirt pocket. Has picture viewer and eBook reader. Can record voice memos. 4 MB flash memory for storage. 5.1 oz. Similar: h2210.

POWER BLOWERS

We found wide performance variations, though the best of each blower type—electric and gas handheld, backpack, and wheeled—swept and loosened debris well. But even the best tend to be better at one or the other task, and many don't vacuum, a mode you may not need.

The Ratings list products strictly on performance. Quick Picks consider specific performance strengths as well as value, which we don't score.

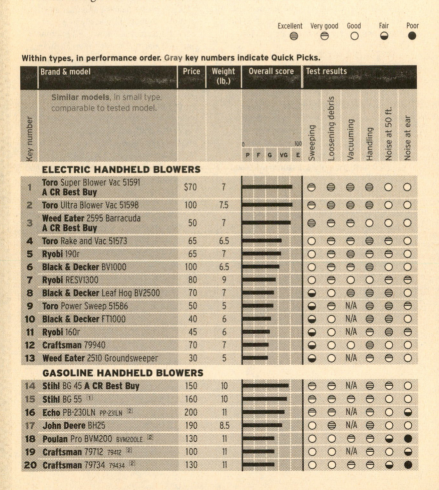

Excellent · Very good · Good · Fair · Poor

Within types, in performance order. Gray key numbers indicate Quick Picks.

Similar models, in small type, comparable to tested model.

Key number	Brand & model	Price	Weight (lb.)	Overall score (0–100; P F G VG E)	Sweeping	Loosening debris	Vacuuming	Handling	Noise at 50 ft.	Noise at ear
	ELECTRIC HANDHELD BLOWERS									
1	**Toro** Super Blower Vac 51591 **A CR Best Buy**	$70	7		Very good	Excellent	Excellent	Excellent	Good	Good
2	**Toro** Ultra Blower Vac 51598	100	7.5		Very good	Excellent	Excellent	Excellent	Good	Good
3	**Weed Eater** 2595 Barracuda **A CR Best Buy**	50	7		Excellent	Very good	Very good	Good	Good	Good
4	**Toro** Rake and Vac 51573	65	6.5		Good	Very good	Very good	Excellent	Very good	Good
5	**Ryobi** 190r	65	7		Good	Very good	Excellent	Very good	Very good	Good
6	**Black & Decker** BV1000	100	6.5		Good	Very good	Very good	Excellent	Good	Good
7	**Ryobi** RESV1300	80	9		Good	Very good	Good	Good	Very good	Very good
8	**Black & Decker** Leaf Hog BV2500	70	7		Fair	Good	Excellent	Excellent	Excellent	Good
9	**Toro** Power Sweep 51586	50	5		Fair	Very good	N/A	Excellent	Excellent	Very good
10	**Black & Decker** FT1000	40	6		Fair	Good	N/A	Excellent	Excellent	Good
11	**Ryobi** 160r	45	6		Fair	Good	N/A	Very good	Excellent	Very good
12	**Craftsman** 79940	70	7		Fair	Good	Good	Excellent	Good	Good
13	**Weed Eater** 2510 Groundsweeper	30	5		Fair	Good	N/A	Very good	Very good	Good
	GASOLINE HANDHELD BLOWERS									
14	**Stihl** BG 45 **A CR Best Buy**	150	10		Very good	Very good	N/A	Excellent	Very good	Good
15	**Stihl** BG 55 [1]	160	10		Very good	Very good	Very good	Very good	Good	Good
16	**Echo** PB-230LN PP-231LN [2]	200	11		Very good	Very good	N/A	Very good	Good	Fair
17	**John Deere** BH25	190	8.5		Good	Excellent	N/A	Excellent	Good	Good
18	**Poulan** Pro BVM200 BVM200LE [2]	130	11		Good	Good	Very good	Very good	Fair	Poor
19	**Craftsman** 79712 79412 [2]	100	11		Good	Good	N/A	Very good	Good	Fair
20	**Craftsman** 79734 79434 [2]	130	11		Good	Good	Very good	Very good	Fair	Poor

Key number	Brand & model Similar models, in small type, comparable to tested model.	Price	Weight (lb.)	Overall score 0–100 P F G VG E	Sweeping	Loosening debris	Vacuuming	Handling	Noise at 50 ft.	Noise at ear
	GASOLINE HANDHELD BLOWERS *Continued*									
21	**Echo** ES-210 ES-211 [2]	$200	9.5		○	○	◒	○	○	○
22	**Ryobi** RGBV3100	125	12.5		○	○	○	○	○	◒
23	**Husqvarna** 225B	180	12		○	◒	N/A	○	○	○
24	**Weed Eater** FL 1500 Featherlite	80	7.5		◒	○	N/A	○	⊖	○
	GASOLINE BACKPACK BLOWERS									
25	**Husqvarna** 145BT **A CR Best Buy**	350	22		⊜	⊜	N/A	⊜	○	●
26	**Makita** RBL500	400	24.5		⊜	⊖	N/A	⊜	○	●
27	**Poulan** Pro BP400	360	18.5		⊜	⊜	N/A	⊖	◒	●
28	**Stihl** BR340L	300	20.5		⊖	⊖	N/A	⊜	○	◒
29	**Echo** Pro Lite PB260L	300	16		⊖	⊖	N/A	⊜	⊖	◒
	GASOLINE WHEELED BLOWERS									
30	**Little Wonder** 9600-6HP	580	125.5		⊜	⊜	N/A	○	◒	◒
31	**Yard Machines** 652D	400	107.5		⊜	⊜	N/A	◒	◒	◒

[1] *Price includes optional bag ($35).* [2] *Similar models comply with California emissions rules and typically are sold in California only.*

See report, page 113. *Based on tests published in Consumer Reports in September 2003, with updated prices and availability.*

Guide to the Ratings

Overall score is based on sweeping and loosening performance, handling, noise, and where applicable, vacuuming. **Weight** is to the nearest tenth of a pound in blower mode. **Sweeping** is how quickly blowers moved large leaf piles. **Loosening** is how quickly models removed embedded leaf particles from the lawn. **Vacuuming** is how quickly blowers picked up leaves and how well they mulched them. **Handling** includes ease of maneuvering while blowing and ease of controls and mode changes. **Noise** includes our measurements at 50 feet and at ear level. Models rated excellent or very good at 50 feet should meet typical limits of 65 decibels (dBA). For noise **at ear,** models rated good, fair and poor emitted 86 to 99 dBA and, we think, should be used with hearing protection. **Price** is approximate retail.

Quick Picks

Best for blowing and vacuuming:

1 Toro $70
2 Toro $100
3 Weed Eater $50
15 Stihl $160

The Toro (2) is similar to the Toro (1), a CR Best Buy, but adds infinitely variable speeds and a metal fan—nice but not essential. The low-priced Weed Eater (3), a CR Best Buy, excelled at sweeping, while the Stihl (15) requires no cord.

If you need gas, but not vacuuming:

14 Stihl $150
17 John Deere $190

The Stihl (14), a CR Best Buy, is relatively quiet and the John Deere (17) light.

For large properties:

25 Husqvarna $350
29 Echo $300
30 Little Wonder $580

The Husqvarna (25), a CR Best Buy, is more powerful, the Echo (29) less noisy. Among wheeled units, better handling overall justifies paying more for the Little Wonder (30).

FEATURES THAT COUNT

Power blowers

FOR HANDHELD BLOWERS

Variable speeds. All gas-powered blowers allow maximum force for sweeping, minimum force around plants, and everything in between, courtesy of an infinitely variable throttle. Among electrics, the Toro (2) has an infinitely variable motor switch, compared with the two-speed, High and Low settings on most. The Black & Decker (10) has just one, high-speed setting.

A bottom-mounted air intake. Handheld blowers with this feature are less likely than side-intake models to pull at shirts. All the electrics we tested have it. Gas-powered models with a bottom-mounted intake include the Weed Eater (24), Poulan (18), Craftsman (19, 20), Husqvarna (23), and Weed Eater (24).

For backpack blowers

T-handle controls. Models with a T-handle let you aim the nozzle and control the throttle with one hand, rather than requiring a second hand to control the throttle. Tested backpack models without T-handle controls are the Poulan (27) and Echo (29).

FOR WHEELED BLOWERS

Adjustable air deflectors. Most wheeled blowers let you direct airflow forward or to the side. The Little Wonder (30) includes an up-and-down adjustment for added airflow control, while the Yard Machines (31) has an easy-to-use adjustment lever.

Handlebar-mounted throttle. The Little Wonder (30) has the throttle control on the handlebar, rather than the engine.

A larger fan. Bigger tends to be better. The Little Wonder (30) has a 17-inch fan, compared with a 14-inch fan for the Yard Machines (31). While both did well, the Little Wonder had slightly more air power.

POWER SANDERS

You'll find many competent sanders, especially among the versatile random-orbit and finishing types. Top performers tend to cost the most; paying more typically buys more features. Exceptions include the well-equipped Ryobi (4), a CR Best Buy. But a higher price doesn't buy less noise, particularly among the noisy belt sanders. We also found that some models that were especially good at capturing wood dust weren't the fastest at sanding. You may improve performance in both areas by attaching a wet/dry vacuum, as many allow.

Excellent ⊜ Very good ⊖ Good ○ Fair ◒ Poor ●

Within types, in performance order. Gray key numbers indicate Quick Picks.

Key number	Brand & model (Similar models, in small type, comparable to tested model.)	Price	Weight (lb.)	Overall score (0–100: P F G VG E)	Performance: Speed by type	Performance: Controls	Performance: Dust capture	Performance: Handling by type	Performance: Noise	Features: Dust bag	Features: Vac connection	Features: Easy paper change
	RANDOM-ORBIT											
1	**Craftsman** (Sears) 27957	$80	3.6		⊜	⊜	⊖	○	○	●	●	●
2	**DeWalt** DW423K	90	3.5		⊖	⊜	⊜	○	○	●	●	●
3	**Makita** BO5012K	100	3.1		⊖	⊜	⊖	⊖	○	●		●
4	**Ryobi** RS241 **A CR Best Buy**	30	3.0		⊖	○	○	⊜	○	●	●	●
5	**Porter Cable** Quicksand 333 333VS	60	3.6		○	○	○	⊖	○	●		●
6	**Craftsman** (Sears) 11623	40	2.9		○	○	◒	⊖	◒	●	●	●
	FINISHING											
7	**Makita** BO3700 (⅓-sheet)	85	3.7		○	⊖	⊜	⊜	⊖	●		●
8	**DeWalt** DW411K	55	3.0		⊖	⊜	⊖	⊖	◒	●		
9	**Porter Cable** 340K	50	2.7		⊖	⊖	⊖	⊖	◒	●		
10	**Black & Decker** FS350 (⅓-sheet)	40	2.9		⊖	⊜	NA [1]	⊜	⊖		●	
11	**Craftsman** (Sears) 11632 (⅓-sheet)	60	3.7		⊜	⊖	○	○	○	●	●	
12	**Makita** BO4552K	50	2.5		⊖	⊖	⊖	○	◒	●		
13	**Skil** 7230	20	3.0		⊖	○	NA	⊜	◒			●
14	**Craftsman** (Sears) 11627	30	2.6		⊖	○	NA	○	◒			
	DETAIL											
15	**Ryobi** CFS1500K Cat	30	1.8		○	⊖	NA	⊜	⊖			●
16	**Craftsman** (Sears) 11680 Mouse	40	1.4		○	○	NA	⊖	⊖			●

Within types, in performance order. Gray key numbers indicate Quick Picks.

Key number	Brand & model	Price	Weight (lb.)	Overall score (0–100; P F G VG E)	Performance: Speed by type	Controls	Dust capture	Handling by type	Noise	Features: Dust bag	Vac connection	Easy paper change
	Similar models, in small type, comparable to tested model.											
	BELT											
17	**Porter Cable** 352VS	$180	11.3		Excellent	Excellent	Good	Very good	Poor	•		•
18	**Makita** 9911	130	6.6		Good	Excellent	Excellent	Excellent	Fair	•		
19	**Skil** 7313	50	5.3		Good	Good	Very good	Good	Fair	•		
20	**Ryobi** BE318	50	6.8		Good	Very good	Fair	Excellent	Poor	•	•	
21	**Black & Decker** BR400	60	7.2		Good	Good	Fair	Very good	Poor	•		

[1] *NA means no collection bag.*

See report, page 115. Based on tests published in Consumer Reports in January 2004, with updated prices and availability.

Guide to the Ratings

Overall score is based on sanding speed, controls, dust capture, handling, and noise. **Speed by type** denotes the amount of hardwood and softwood removed in 5 minutes. We used coarse, 80-grit paper for belt sanders, 100-grit paper for random-orbit and finishing types, and 120-grit paper for detail sanders. Belt sanders that excelled in speed removed four times as much wood in 5 minutes as similarly rated finishing sanders. **Controls** includes handle and switch design, and other usability judgments. **Dust capture** is the percentage of sanded wood captured by the bag. **Handling by type** denotes maneuverability and freedom from vibration. We emphasized easy, one-handed operation for most sanders and two-handed use for belt sanders. **Noise** is based on tests with a sound meter. **Weight** reflects our measurement to the nearest tenth of a pound. **Price** is approximate retail.

Quick Picks

Relatively versatile and best for most:

1 Craftsman $80 (random-orbit)

4 Ryobi $30 (random-orbit), CR Best Buy

The Craftsman (1) offers fine performance, the Ryobi (4) easier handling and low price.

If getting into corners is critical:

7 Makita $85 (finishing)

8 DeWalt $55 (finishing)

11 Craftsman $60 (finishing)

Consider the Makita (7) and Craftsman (11) for larger areas, the DeWalt (8) for its fine controls.

For sanding large or uneven areas:

17 Porter Cable $180 (belt)

18 Makita $130 (belt)

19 Skil $50 (belt)

The Porter Cable (17) is best for large, horizontal surfaces, while the Makita (18) offers easier vertical sanding and better horizontal dust collection, with slightly less noise. Consider the Skil (19) if you're willing to trade some speed and a vacuum connection for a low price.

For small finishing jobs:

15 Ryobi $30 (detail)

The Ryobi (15) is less expensive and easier to handle than the Craftsman (16). But both lack a bag and a vac connection.

RANGES

Ranges prove the point that you don't have to pay a lot for high performance. As the Ratings of 30-inch-wide models show, ranges costing several hundred dollars performed on a par with models costing more than a thousand. Spending more can also buy you less convenience, especially with pro-style ranges. Several of the priciest models ranked among the smallest for oven capacity. And while nearly all ranges scored at least a good in our oven self-cleaning tests, the pro-style DCS RGSC-305 (27) and Viking VDSC305B[SS] (36) and Viking VDSC3074B (37) were only fair, despite their roughly $4,000 price tags.

Note, due to a major line change, the Kenmore models we tested for this report are no longer available and do not appear in the Ratings below.

Excellent | Very good | Good | Fair | Poor

Within types, in performance order. Gray key numbers indicate Quick Picks.

Key number	Brand & model	Price	Overall score (0–100; P F G VG E)	Test results: Cooktop High	Cooktop Low	Oven Capacity	Oven Baking	Oven Broiling	Features: Elements/Burners High	Medium	Low	Stainless available
	ELECTRIC-COIL MODELS											
1	**GE** JBP35WH[WW]	$550		Excellent	Excellent	Excellent	Good	Excellent	2		2	•
2	**Hotpoint** RB757WH[WW] **A CR Best Buy**	400		Excellent	Excellent	Very good	Very good	Good	2		2	
3	**Maytag** MER5555QA[W]	525		Very good	Excellent	Very good	Very good	Very good	2		2	
	ELECTRIC SMOOTHTOP MODELS											
4	**GE** JBP80WH[WW] **A CR Best Buy**	750		Very good	Excellent	Excellent	Very good	Very good	1	1	2	•
5	**GE** JBP82WH[WW]	850		Very good	Excellent	Excellent	Very good	Very good	1	2	1	•
6	**GE** Profile JB905TH[WW]	1,150		Very good	Excellent	Excellent	Very good	Very good	1	1	2	•
7	**Maytag** MER5775QA[W]	750		Very good	Excellent	Very good	Very good	Very good	2		2	•
8	**GE** Profile JSP46WD[WW]	1,250		Very good	Excellent	Very good	Very good	Good	1	2	1	
9	**Bosch** HES25[2]	1,500		Very good	Very good	Very good	Very good	Very good	1	1	2	•
10	**Hotpoint** RB787WH[WW]	450		Very good	Excellent	Very good	Very good	Good		2	2	
11	**GE** Profile JS968SF[SS]	1,750		Very good	Excellent	Good	Very good	Very good	1	2	1	•
12	**Whirlpool** Gold GR440LXM[P]	750		Very good	Excellent	Good	Very good	Very good	1	1	2	
13	**Jenn-Air** JES8850AA[W]	1,600		Very good	Very good	Good	Good	Good	2		2	•
14	**GE** Profile Trivection JS998SH[SS]	3,000		Excellent	Excellent	Fair	Very good	Good	1	1	2	•
15	**Whirlpool** Polara GR556LRK[P]	1,700		Very good	Excellent	Good	Good	Good	2	1	1	•
16	**Whirlpool** RF364PXM[Q]	550		Very good	Excellent	Good	Very good	Very good		2	2	

Excellent | Very good | Good | Fair | Poor

Within types, in performance order. Gray key numbers indicate Quick Picks.

Key number	Brand & model	Price	Overall score (0–100; P F G VG E)	Test results: Cooktop High	Cooktop Low	Oven Capacity	Oven Baking	Oven Broiling	Features: Elements/Burners High	Elements/Burners Medium	Elements/Burners Low	Stainless available
	GAS MODELS											
17	**GE** JGBP85WEH[WW]	$950		Very good	Excellent	Very good	Very good	Excellent	2	1	1	•
18	**Hotpoint** RGB745WEH[WW] **A CR Best Buy**	550		Very good	Excellent	Very good	Very good	Excellent	1	2	1	
19	**Magic Chef** CGR3742CD[W]	600		Good	Excellent	Very good	Excellent	Good	1	3		
20	**Maytag** Gemini MGR6772BD[W]	1,300		Very good	Very good	Excellent	Very good	Very good	1	2	1	•
21	**Whirlpool** SF367LEM[Q]	625		Good	Excellent	Very good	Very good	Very good	1	2	1	
22	**Jenn-Air** JGS8750AD[W]	1,500		Very good	Very good	Good	Very good	Excellent	1	2	1	•
23	**Amana** AGR5715QD[W]	600		Good	Excellent	Very good	Very good	Very good	1	2	1	•
24	**Maytag** MGR5875QD[W]	1,150		Very good	Very good	Very good	Very good	Very good	2	2	1	•
25	**Whirlpool** Gold GS470LEM[Q]	1,000		Good	Excellent	Very good	Good	Very good	2	1	1	
26	**GE** Profile JGB900WEF[WW]	1,000		Very good	Good	Very good	Very good	Very good	1	2	1	•
27	**DCS** RGSC-305	3,650		Very good	Excellent	Good	Very good	Good	5			•
28	**Bosch** HGS25[5]	1,750		Good	Good	Very good	Very good	Very good	2	1	1	•
29	**Viking** VGSC3064B[SS]	3,900		Very good	Fair	Fair	Very good	Excellent	4			•
30	**GE** JGBP26WEH[WW]	750		Good	Poor	Very good	Very good	Very good		4		
	DUAL-FUEL MODELS											
31	**KitchenAid** KDRP407H[SS]	3,400		Good	Very good	Good	Excellent	Excellent	4			•
32	**Jenn-Air** JDS8850AA[S]	2,150		Good	Excellent	Good	Good	Very good	1	2	1	•
33	**GE** Profile J2B915WEH[WW] **A CR Best Buy**	1,450		Very good	Very good	Very good	Very good	Very good	1	2	1	•
34	**Jenn-Air** JDS9860AA[W]	2,000		Fair	Very good	Good	Very good	Excellent		4		
35	**Dacor** ERD30S06[BK]	3,800		Good	Excellent	Good	Very good	Fair	4			•
36	**Viking** VDSC305B[SS]	3,800		Very good	Excellent	Fair	Good	Very good	4			•
37	**Viking** VDSC3074B	4,000		Very good	Excellent	Fair	Good	Very good	4			•
38	**GE** Monogram ZDP30N4D[SS]	3,050		Good	Very good	Fair	Very good	Very good	4			•
39	**Frigidaire** Gallery GLCS378D[S]	1,100		Very good	Fair	Fair	Very good	Very good	2	1	1	

See report, page 84. Based on tests published in Consumer Reports in August 2004, with updated prices and availability.

Guide to the Ratings

Overall score reflects cooktop performance, oven capacity, baking, broiling, and self-cleaning. **Cooktop high** denotes how quickly the highest-powered element heated water to a near-boil. **Cooktop low** shows how well the least-powerful element melted and held chocolate without scorching and whether the most powerful, set to low, held tomato sauce below a boil. **Oven capacity** is usable space. **Baking** shows baking evenness for cakes and cookies. **Broiling** reflects high-heat searing ability and evenness for a tray of burgers. **Elements/burners** covers the following: **High:** more than 2,000 watts for electric, 11,000 Btu/hr. for gas. **Medium:** more than 1,500 to 2,000 watts for electric, more than 6,500 to 11,000 Btu/hr. for gas. **Low:** 1,500 watts or less for electric, 6,500 Btu/hr. or less for gas. **Price** is approximate retail. In **brand & model,** brackets show color code.

Quick Picks

Best for most; lots of performance and convenience for the price:

1 GE, $550
4 GE, $750
17 GE, $950

The GE (4), a CR Best Buy, has a very useful combination of performance and oven space. The GEs (1, 17) excelled at broiling.

If you simply want the basics:

2 Hotpoint, $400
18 Hotpoint, $550

These lack high-end looks but provide very good performance. Consider the Hotpoint (2) for its fast cooktop heating and low price, and the Hotpoint (18) for its superb broiling. Both are CR Best Buys.

For high-end style and features:

32 Jenn-Air, $2,150
33 GE, $1,450

The dual-fuel Jenn-Air (32) performs well, but we don't know how reliable it will be; Jenn-Air has not been among the more reliable brands of gas or electric ranges. The GE (33), a CR Best Buy, is an affordable dual-fuel range.

Recommendations

ELECTRIC-COIL MODELS

1 **GE** JBP35WH[WW] **Very good basic range.** Similar: GE JBP48WH[ ].

2 **HOTPOINT** RB757WH[WW] **A CR Best Buy Inexpensive and very good; fairly basic.**

3 **MAYTAG** MER5555QA[W] **Very good basic model.** But Maytag has been among the more repair-prone brands of electric ranges. Door and window less hot than most during self cleaning.

ELECTRIC SMOOTHTOP MODELS

4 **GE** JBP80WH[WW] **A CR Best Buy Excellent performance at a good price.** Has warming element and dual cooktop elements. But only small elements in rear.

5 **GE** JBP82WH[WW] **Excellent performance at a good price.** Has warming element, dual cooktop elements, and bridge element.

6 **GE** Profile JB905TH[WW] **Very good overall.** Has numeric-keypad oven controls, warming element, three oven racks,

Recommendations

dual cooktop elements, and "hot" light indicator for each element. But only small elements in rear.

7 **MAYTAG** MER5775QA[W] **Very good overall, but Maytag has been among the more repair-prone brands of electric ranges.** Has dual cooktop elements and warming element. One of its two oven racks can be split. But only small elements in rear and one "hot" light for cooktop elements.

8 **GE** Profile JSP46WD[WW] **A CR Best Buy Very good.** Has numeric-keypad oven controls, dual elements, "hot" light indicator for each element, and excellent window view. Discontinued, but similar JSP47WF[ ] is available.

9 **BOSCH** HES25[2] **Very good.** Magnetic dial and touch sensitive element controls on right-hand-side of cooktop. Has meat probe for automatic shutoff. Has convection option; in our tests convection-baked cakes were better than non-convection cakes. Comes with 3 oven racks. Cooktop elements also function as warming elements. "Hot" light for each element. Has one dual cooktop element, one triple cooktop element, and warming drawer.

10 **HOTPOINT** RB787WH[WW] **Very good, basic smoothtop.**

11 **GE** Profile JS968SF[SS] **Cramped controls hamper this very good smoothtop.** Slide-in model; no side panels or backsplash. Has dual cooktop elements, warming element, bridge element, "hot" light for each element, numeric-keypad oven controls, and meat probe with automatic shutoff. Cooktop and oven controls in front, but easy to activate by mistake. Cooktop does not contain spills.

12 **WHIRLPOOL** Gold GR440LXM[P] **Very good overall.** Has warming element, dual cooktop elements, and "hot" light indicator for each element. Door and window less hot than most during self cleaning. One of its two oven racks can be split. But only small elements in rear. Similar: GR445LXM[ ].

13 **JENN-AIR** JES8850AA[W] **Very good, but has been among the more repair-prone brands of electric ranges.** Has numeric-keypad oven controls, convection option, dual elements, meat probe for automatic oven shutoff, "hot" light indicator for each element. But cooktop has no rim to contain spills.

14 **GE** Profile Trivection JS998SH[SS] **Very good.** Has microwave feature to decrease cooking time. Slide in model; no side panels or backsplash. Cooktop and oven controls in front; numeric keypad for oven temps and time. Has convection option; in tests convection-baked cakes were better than non-convection cakes. Door and window did not get as hot as others in self clean test. Comes with 3 oven racks. Has dual elements and "hot" light for each element. Cooktop does not contain spills.

15 **WHIRLPOOL** Polara GR556LRK[P] **A very good smoothtop.** Has a unique feature; a refrigeration mode that allows you to set the range to keep the food cool during the day, then cook it just before you return in the evening. Has convection option, "hot" light for each element and dual cooktop elements. Lacks storage drawer.

16 **WHIRLPOOL** RF364PXM[Q] **Very good overall.** Door and window less hot than most during self cleaning. Similar: RF364LXM[ ].

Recommendations

GAS MODELS

17 GE JGBP85WEH[WW] **Very good.** Has warming drawer.

18 HOTPOINT RGB745WEH[WW] **A CR Best Buy Very good, fairly basic range at a good price.** Has steel grates.

19 MAGIC CHEF CGR3742CD[W] **Very good, fairly basic range at a good price.**

20 MAYTAG Gemini MGR6772BD[W] **A very good model with two ovens.** Small upper oven can toast, bake, and broil. Lower oven mounted very low. Has numeric-keypad oven controls, and heavy, continuous grates. But no storage drawer, and large pot on rear burner blocked oven controls.

21 WHIRLPOOL SF367LEM[Q] **Very good overall.**

22 JENN-AIR JGS8750AD[W] **Very good.** Has numeric-keypad oven controls and continuous grates. Rangetop burners automatically reignite.

23 AMANA AGR5715QD[W] **Very good overall, but Amana has been one of the more repair-prone brands.** Door and window less hot than most during self cleaning.

24 MAYTAG MGR5875QD[W] **Very good.** Has numeric-keypad oven controls, convection option, and continuous grates. One of its three oven racks can be split. Door and window less hot than most during self-cleaning.

25 WHIRLPOOL Gold GS470LEM[Q] **Very good.** Has warming drawer and continuous grates. One of its two oven racks can be split. Similar: GS475LEM[ ].

26 GE Profile JGB900WEF[WW] **Very good overall.** Has numeric-keypad oven controls and continuous grates. Similar: JGB905WEF[ ].

27 DCS RGSC-305 **A very good pro-style range, but with only mediocre oven space.** Has convection option, heavy continuous grates, and burners that reignite if they go out. Cooktop and oven controls in front. Lacks touchpad and digital display. Only four rack positions. Large fifth burner wasn't the fastest, despite its high heat.

28 BOSCH HGS25[5] **Very good overall.** Has convection option, warming drawer, and continuous grates. Has meat probe for automatic shutoff. Comes with 3 oven racks.

29 VIKING VGSC3064B[SS] **Good and expensive stainless-steel stove.** Among the more repair-prone brands in recent years. Has convection option, continuous grates, and cooktop burners that auto reignite. But unsealed burners and window view not clear. Smallish oven and subpar simmering compromised performance.

30 GE JGBP26WEH[WW] **Good, basic model.** Door and window less hot than most during self cleaning. But unsealed burners and poor performance in cooktop low tests.

DUAL-FUEL MODELS

31 KITCHENAID KDRP407H[SS] **Very good and expensive dual-fuel stainless-steel range.** Has convection option and continuous grates. Oven dial instead of touchpad controls.

32 JENN-AIR JDS8850AA[S] **A very good dual-fuel range.** Slide-in model; no side panels or backsplash. Burners reignite if

Recommendations

they go out. Has convection option, heavy, continuous grates, meat probe with automatic oven shutoff. Door and window less hot than most during self-cleaning.

33 GE Profile J2B915WEH[WW] **A CR Best Buy Very good dual-fuel range.** Has numeric-keypad oven controls, convection option, continuous grates, warming drawer, three oven racks, and meat probe for automatic oven shutoff.

34 JENN-AIR JDS9860AA[W] **Very good.** Dual-fuel range has grill module and downdraft vent, convection option, and meat probe for auto shutoff. But fairly slow cooktop speed. Similar: JDS9860AA[P].

35 DACOR ERD30S06[BK] **Very good, dual-fuel stainless-steel model.** Has convection option, simmer plate, and continuous grates. Cooktop burners auto reignite. Baking performance very good in pure convection mode; results in regular bake mode were poor.

36 VIKING VDSC305B[SS] **Very good stainless steel dual-fuel range.** Has convection option, heavy continuous grates and burners that reignite if they go out. But has a smallish oven and unsealed burners, and is among the least effective at self-cleaning.

37 VIKING VDSC3074B **A very good dual-fuel, pro-style range.** Has convection option, heavy continuous grates and burners that reignite if they go out. Door and window less hot than most during self-cleaning. But smallish oven, and among the least effective at self-cleaning.

38 GE Monogram ZDP30N4D[SS] **Very good stainless steel dual-fuel stove.** Has convection option and continuous grates. But smallish oven, unsealed burners, and only three oven-rack positions. Discontinued, but similar ZDP30N4H[ ] is available.

39 FRIGIDAIRE Gallery GLCS378D[S] **Good overall.** Dual-fuel, slide-in model; no side panels or backsplash. Has convection option and gas burners atop glass ceramic surface. Oven controls on front panel, but are easy to activate by mistake. Has smallish oven and no rim to contain spills. Fair performance in cooktop low tests. Only four oven-rack positions.

REFRIGERATORS

Most new refrigerators will keep your milk chilled and your ice cream frozen. We'd stick with those judged very good or excellent for temperature performance, which indicates even, consistent temperatures. Lower-priced models are less likely to have spill-proof glass shelves or adjustable shelves and door bins. A malfunction can be inconvenient and costly, so be sure to check the repair history for a brand you're considering. The top-freezer models we tested are superior when it comes to price, usable space relative to external dimensions, and energy efficiency.

Excellent | Very good | Good | Fair | Poor

Within types, in performance order. Gray key numbers indicate Quick Picks.

Key number	Brand & model	Price	Overall score (0–100; P F G VG E)	Test results: Energy efficiency	Test results: Temperature performance	Test results: Noise	Test results: Ease of use	Capacity: Claimed (cu. ft.)	Capacity: Usable capacity (cu. ft.)	Features: Touchpad controls	Features: Stainless/SS-look option	Features: HxWxD (in.)
	TOP-FREEZERS											
1	**Kenmore** (Sears) 7498[2]	$820		Excellent	Excellent	Good	Very good	18.8	14.0			66 x 30 x 31
2	**Kenmore** (Sears) 7425[2]	720		Excellent	Excellent	Very good	Good	21.6	16.8			66 x 33 x 31
3	**Kenmore** (Sears) 7495[2]	670		Excellent	Very good	Good	Good	18.8	14.5			66 x 30 x 31
4	**Amana** ATB2135HR[W]	750		Excellent	Very good	Good	Good	20.7	16.9			68 x 33 x 30
5	**GE** GTS18KCM[WW]	650		Very good	Excellent	Good	Very good	17.9	14.0			67 x 30 x 31
6	**Maytag** MTF2176HR[W]	760		Very good	Very good	Fair	Very good	20.7	15.8			68 x 33 x 30
7	**Hotpoint** HTS22GBP[WW]	550		Very good	Excellent	Good	Good	21.9	16.5			68 x 33 x 32
8	**Frigidaire** Gallery GLRT186TA[W]	530		Very good	Very good	Good	Good	18.3	14.3		•	67 x 30 x 31
9	**Frigidaire** Gallery GLRT212ID[W] **A CR Best Buy**	500		Excellent	Very good	Good	Good	20.5	16.6			69 x 30 x 33
10	**GE** GTS22KCM[WW]	750		Very good	Very good	Good	Very good	21.7	16.5			68 x 33 x 32
11	**Haier** HTQ18JAB[WW]	570		Very good	Good	Fair	Good	18.2	14.3			66 x 30 x 31
12	**Hotpoint** HTS18BCP[WW]	600		Very good	Fair	Good	Fair	17.9	15.1			67 x 30 x 31

Excellent | Very good | Good | Fair | Poor

Within types, in performance order. Gray key numbers indicate Quick Picks.

Key number	Brand & model	Price	Overall score (0–100; P F G VG E)	Test results: Energy efficiency	Test results: Temperature performance	Test results: Noise	Test results: Ease of use	Capacity: Claimed (cu. ft.)	Capacity: Usable capacity (cu. ft.)	Features: Touchpad controls	Features: Stainless/SS-look option	HxWxD (in.)
BOTTOM-FREEZERS												
13	**LG** LRDC22731[WW]	$1,350		Very good	Excellent	Very good	Very good	22.4	14.7	•	•	69 x 33 x 32
14	**Samsung** RB1855S[W]	750		Good	Excellent	Good	Good	18.8	14.2	•	•	70 x 33 x 29
SIDE-BY-SIDES												
15	**GE** GSS25JFP[WW] **A CR Best Buy**	1,050		Very good	Excellent	Very good	Very good	25.0	16.9			70 x 36 x 32
16	**Kenmore** (Sears) 5538[2] **A CR Best Buy**	1,120		Good	Excellent	Very good	Very good	21.9	13.1	•		67 x 33 x 31
17	**Frigidaire** FRS26LF8C[W]	1,200		Very good	Excellent	Good	Very good	25.9	16.6			69 x 36 x 33
18	**Kenmore** (Sears) Elite 5560[2]	2,000		Very good	Very good	Very good	Very good	25.5	15.7	•		70 x 36 x 33
19	**GE** Profile PSS26NGP[WW]	1,900		Very good	Very good	Very good	Very good	25.5	16.2	•	•	70 x 36 x 33
20	**Kenmore** (Sears) 5522[2]	1,450		Good	Excellent	Very good	Very good	21.8	14.1	•		67 x 33 x 31
21	**Samsung** RS2555S[W]	1,400		Very good	Very good	Good	Very good	25.2	16.6	•	•	70 x 36 x 33
22	**Amana** ASD2624HE[W]	1,100		Very good	Very good	Good	Very good	25.6	16.1			71 x 36 x 31
23	**GE** GSL25JFP[BS]	1,150		Good	Excellent	Good	Very good	25.0	16.5		•	70 x 36 x 32
24	**Whirlpool** Gold GD5SHAXM[Q]	1,500		Very good	Very good	Good	Very good	25.5	16.7			70 x 36 x 31
25	**Hotpoint** HSS25GFP[WW]	850		Good	Very good	Very good	Good	25.0	16.7			70 x 36 x 32
26	**Frigidaire** Gallery GLRS237ZA[W]	950		Good	Good	Very good	Very good	22.6	14.6		•	70 x 33 x 33
27	**GE** GSS20IEM[WW]	975		Good	Good	Good	Very good	19.9	13.3	•		68 x 32 x 32
BUILT-IN AND CABINET-DEPTH BOTTOM-FREEZERS												
28	**Sub-Zero** 650/F	4,500		Very good	Excellent	Good	Good	20.6	15.4	•	•	84 x 37 x 26
29	**Viking** DFBB363	4,700		Very good	Excellent	Good	Very good	20.3	15		•	84 x 36 x 25

Key number	Brand & model	Price	Overall score (0–100; P F G VG E)	Test results: Energy efficiency	Test results: Temperature performance	Test results: Noise	Test results: Ease of use	Capacity: Claimed (cu. ft.)	Capacity: Usable capacity (cu. ft.)	Features: Touchpad controls	Features: Stainless/SS-look option	Features: HxWxD (in.)
BUILT-IN AND CABINET-DEPTH SIDE-BY-SIDES												
30	**Viking** DFSB423	$5,300		VG	VG	VG	VG	24.0	16.6	•	•	83 x 43 x 25
31	**Jenn-Air** JS42FWD[W]	4,650		G	E	VG	VG	26.0	14.5	•	•	84 x 42 x 27
32	**Thermador** KBUDT4270A	5,400		G	VG	VG	VG	25.2	15.9	•	•	84 x 41 x 26
33	**GE** Monogram ZISS420DR[SS]	5,700		G	VG	E	VG	26.1	14.9	•	•	85 x 43 x 26
34	**KitchenAid** KSSS42QM[W]	4,200		VG	G	E	VG	25.3	17.7	•	•	84 x 43 x 26
35	**Sub-Zero** 680	5,500		VG	VG	G	VG	23.7	16.9	•	•	84 x 43 x 26
36	**Kenmore** (Sears) Elite 4410[2]	2,000		F	VG	G	VG	20.9	12.7	•		70 x 36 x 29
37	**GE** GSC23LGQ[WW]	1,850		G	G	E	VG	22.6	13.6	•		70 x 36 x 28

See report, page 87. Based on tests published in Consumer Reports in August 2004, with updated prices and availability.

Guide to the Ratings

Overall score gives the most weight to energy efficiency and temperature performance, then to noise and convenience. **Energy efficiency** reflects consumption per the EnergyGuide (the yellow sticker) and usable volume. **Temperature performance** combines outcome of tests at different room temperatures, including high heat. We judged how closely and uniformly recommended settings matched our ideal temperatures: Most kept the main space at 37 degrees and the freezer at zero degrees with good uniformity. **Noise** is gauged with compressors running. **Ease of use** assesses features and design including layout, controls, and lighting. **Capacity** lists the manufacturer's claimed volume and our measurement of actual usable volume. **Height, width,** and **depth** (without handle) are rounded up to the nearest inch. Under **brand & model,** a bracketed letter or number is a color code. **Prices** for built-ins are for unfinished models; exterior panels cost extra. On free-standing models, a stainless-steel finish adds about $150 to $300 to the prices shown; faux-stainless metal adds about $150. Price is approximate retail; it includes the cost of an icemaker if that is not standard equipment.

Quick Picks

TOP-FREEZERS

2, 3 Kenmore (Sears), $670-$720

9 Frigidaire, $500, CR Best Buy

All three models performed well and are very energy-efficient. The 33-inch-wide Kenmore (Sears) 7425[2] (2) is quiet and has ample capacity and a water dispenser. Two 30-inch-wide models would suit smaller spaces: the Kenmore (Sears) 7495[2] (3) has a water dispenser and makes lots of ice; the Frigidaire Gallery GLRT212ID[W] (9) has the most usable space of the 30-inchers and the lowest price. It's a CR Best Buy.

BOTTOM-FREEZERS

13 LG, $1350

The 33-inch-wide LG LRDC22731[WW] (13) did well overall. It has touchpad controls. For a stainless-look metal finish, add $150. Note that we have no reliability data for this brand.

SIDE-BY-SIDES

15 GE, $1050, CR Best Buy

16 Kenmore (Sears), $1120, CR Best Buy

The 36-inch-wide GE GSS25JFP[WW] (15) and 33-inch-wide Kenmore (Sears) 5538[2] (16) scored well and are CR Best Buys. Both have a water dispenser and the Kenmore has touchpad controls.

BUILT-IN AND CABINET-DEPTH BOTTOM-FREEZERS

28 Sub-Zero, $4500

29 Viking, $4700

Both the 37-inch-wide Sub-Zero 650/F (28) and 36-inch-wide Viking DFBB363 (29) are stainless and very energy-efficient. The Sub-Zero has touchpad controls. Like all built-ins, they're tall—84 inches high—so make sure they'll fit under upper cabinets.

BUILT-IN AND CABINET-DEPTH SIDE-BY-SIDE MODELS

30 Viking, $5300

The Viking DFSB423 (30) built-in is stainless with touchpad controls.

Recommendations

TOP-FREEZERS

1 KENMORE (Sears) 7498[2] **Very good overall, with excellent energy efficiency.** Has water filter. Similar: 7499[ ].

2 KENMORE (Sears) 7425[2] **Very good overall, with excellent energy efficiency.** Has water filter and internal water dispenser. Similar: 7426[ ].

3 KENMORE (Sears) 7495[2] **Very good overall, with excellent energy efficiency.** Has water filter and internal water dispenser. Similar: 6495[ ], 7496[ ].

4 AMANA ATB2135HR[W] **Very good overall, with excellent energy efficiency.** No pull-out shelves.

5 GE GTS18KCM[WW] **Very good overall, but no pull-out shelves.** Discontinued, but similar GTS18KCP[ ] is available.

6 MAYTAG MTF2176HR[W] **Very good overall, but noisy.** Has crank-adjustable shelf.

7 HOTPOINT HTS22GBP[WW] **Very good overall and low-priced for this type of refrigerator.** No spillproof shelves, pull-out shelves, or light in freezer.

8 FRIGIDAIRE Gallery GLRT186TA[W] **Very good overall and low-priced for its type.** Discontinued, but similar GLRT185TD[ ] is available.

9 FRIGIDAIRE Gallery GLRT212ID[W] **A CR**

Recommendations

Best Buy Very good overall, with excellent energy efficiency. Low-priced for this type of refrigerator.

10 GE GTS22KCM[WW] **Very good overall.** But no pull-out shelves and manufacturer's recommended settings left fridge and freezer much too cold. Discontinued, but similar GTS22KCP[ ] is available.

11 HAIER HTQ18JAB[WW] **Good overall, but noisy.** Manufacturer's recommended settings kept both refrigerator and freezer too warm. Single control for both refrigerator and freezer. No pull-out shelves. Similar: HTQ18JAA[ ], HTQ18JABR[ ].

12 HOTPOINT HTS18BCP[WW] **Good overall.** Manufacturer's recommended setting kept freezer too warm. Single control for both refrigerator and freezer. No spillproof shelves, pull-out-shelves, or light in freezer. Similar: HTS18BBP[ ].

BOTTOM-FREEZERS

13 LG LRDC22731[WW] **Very good overall.** Bottom freezer pulls open like a drawer and tilts down for easier access. Has water filter for icemaker. Curved doors.

14 SAMSUNG RB1855S[W] **A very good, well-priced performer with dual evaporators.** Bottom freezer has a swing-open door. Exterior digital display shows internal temperature. Has door alarm and curved doors. Freezer has no light and no bins or shelves, just three pull-out drawers. No automatic icemaker available; ice-cube trays are awkward to fill. This model does not have reversible doors; it is only available with the hinge on the right. Discontinued, but similar RB1844S[ ] is available.

SIDE-BY-SIDES

15 GE GSS25JFP[WW] **A CR Best Buy A very good model** at a very good price. Has water filter.

16 KENMORE 5538[2] **A CR Best Buy Very good overall.** Produces 11 lbs. of ice per day. Has digital display and water filter. Similar: 5539[ ].

17 FRIGIDAIRE FRS26LF8C[W] **Very good overall.** Has water filter and crank-adjustable shelf. But among the more repair-prone side-by-side brands.

18 KENMORE Elite 5560[2] **Very good overall, but pricey.** Has water filter, curved front, ice bin on door, and digital control (temperature setting). Similar: 5561[ ].

19 GE Profile PSS26NGP[WW] **Very good overall.** Has water filter, curved doors, and door alarm. Similar: PSF26NGP[ ].

20 KENMORE (Sears) 5522[2] **Very good overall.** Produced 10 lbs. of ice per day. Has water filter, ice bin on door, and digital control (temperature setting). Similar: 5523[ ].

21 SAMSUNG RS2555S[W] **A very good performer with dual evaporators.** Has water filter, door alarm, and built-in deodorizers. Exterior digital display shows internal temperature. Note: This model has limited retail availability.

22 AMANA ASD2624HE[W] **Very good overall.** Has water filter.

23 GE GSL25JFP[BS] **Very good overall.** Has water filter.

24 WHIRLPOOL Gold GD5SHAXM[Q] **Very good overall.** Has water filter and beverage-chiller compartment on door. Ice bin on freezer door for easy access and removal. Discontinued, but similar GD5SHAXN[Q] is available.

25 HOTPOINT HSS25GFP[WW] **Very good**

overall and low-priced for its type. Has water filter but no spillproof or pull-out shelves.

26 FRIGIDAIRE Gallery GLRS237ZA[W] **A good performer and low-priced for its type.** Excellent at making ice—about 8.5 lb. per day. Has water filter. But among the more repair-prone side-by-side brands. Discontinued, but similar GLRS237ZD is available.

27 GE GSS20IEM[WW] **Good overall and low-priced for its type.** But meatkeeper too warm, internal temperature variations higher than most, and manufacturer's recommended setting left freezer much too cold. No spillproof shelves. Discontinued, but similar GSS20IEP[ ] is available.

BUILT-IN AND CABINET-DEPTH BOTTOM-FREEZERS

28 SUB-ZERO 650/F **Very good built-in, bottom-freezer model.** Bottom freezer pulls open like a drawer. Needs custom panels at extra cost. But Sub-Zero has been the most repair-prone brand of top- and bottom-freezer refrigerators.

29 VIKING DFBB363 **Very good model.** Bottom-freezer opens like a drawer. Needs custom panels at extra cost. Stainless option costs about $700 more. Similar: DDBB363[ ], VCBB363[ ], DTBB363.

BUILT-IN AND CABINET-DEPTH SIDE-BY-SIDES

30 VIKING DFSB423 **Very good built-in, side-by-side model.** Has door alarm. Needs custom panels at extra cost. Similar: VCSB423SS, DDSB423.

31 JENN-AIR JS42FWD[W] **Very good built-in, side-by-side model.** Has water filter, door alarm, and crank-adjustable shelf. Needs custom panels at extra cost.

32 THERMADOR KBUDT4270A **Very good built-in side-by-side model.** Has water filter, ice bin on door, and digital controls (actual temperature). No spillproof shelves. Needs custom panels at extra cost. Similar: KBUIT4250A, KBUIT4260A, KBUIT4270A, KBUDT4250A, KBUDT4260A.

33 GE Monogram ZISS420DR[SS] **Very good built-in side-by-side.** Very quiet. Has water filter, door alarm and digital controls (actual temperature).

34 KITCHENAID KSSS42QM[W] **Very good and very quiet built-in, side-by-side model.** Has water filter and door alarm. Excellent at ice-making—about 9.5 lb. per day. Ice bin on freezer door for easy access and removal. But internal temperature variations higher than most. Needs custom panels at extra cost. Similar: KSSP42QM[ ], KSSO42QM[ ], KSSC42QM[ ].

35 SUB-ZERO 680 **Very good built-in, side-by-side model.** Has water filter. No spillproof shelves. Storage compartment for meats too warm. Needs custom panels at extra cost. But Sub-Zero has been among the more repair-prone side-by-side brands. Discontinued, but similar 685F is available.

36 KENMORE (Sears) Elite 4410[2] **Good cabinet-depth side-by-side model, fair energy efficiency.** Digital controls on door (temperature setting). Has water filter and ice bin on door.

37 GE GSC23LGQ[WW] **Good cabinet-depth side-by-side model.** Has water filter. Similar: GSC23LSR[ ].

SNOW THROWERS

Our snow-thrower scores emphasize fast, effortless clearing. Most of our top performers are larger, two-stage machines, since their wider augers help them scoop more snow than single-stage models do. Convenient controls and relatively easy handling are also important. Indeed, our top performers outscored two faster, but less friendly, 30-inch models. You might also want a less noisy snow thrower. Among two-stage models, only the Husqvarna (11) was quieter than the 85 decibels or more at which we recommend ear protection. Except for the Toro (14, 15), single-stage models made less noise than two-stage models.

The Ratings rank models by overall score. See Quick Picks for high-scoring models with specific strengths and value.

Excellent ⊜ Very good ⊖ Good ○ Fair ◒ Poor ●

Within types, in performance order. Gray **key numbers indicate Quick Picks.**

Key number	Brand & model (Similar models, in small type, comparable to tested model.)	Price	Width/power	Overall score (0–100; P F G VG E)	Removal speed	Distance	Surface cleaning	Controls	Handling
	TWO-STAGE GAS								
1	**Toro** Power Max 828LXE	$1,250	28 in./8 hp		Very good	Very good	Very good	Excellent	Good
2	**Yard-Man** E5KLF **A CR Best Buy**	1,100	26 in./9.5 hp		Very good	Very good	Excellent	Excellent	Good
3	**Troy-Bilt** Storm 10030	1,300	30 in./10 hp		Excellent	Very good	Excellent	Very good	Good
4	**Craftsman** (Sears) 88790 **A CR Best Buy**	950	28 in./9 hp		Very good	Good	Excellent	Excellent	Good
5	**Frontier** ST0927 [1]	1,800	27 in./9 hp		Excellent	Very good	Good	Very good	Fair
6	**Craftsman** (Sears) 88811	1,300	30 in./11 hp		Excellent	Very good	Good	Very good	Fair
7	**Honda** HS928WAS HS928WA	2,080	28 in./9 hp		Very good	Very good	Excellent	Excellent	Poor
8	**Simplicity** 9560E	1,300	24 in./9.5 hp		Excellent	Fair	Excellent	Good	Good
9	**Yard Machines** S6FEE	700	24 in./8 hp		Very good	Very good	Excellent	Good	Fair
10	**Ariens** 8524LE [1]	1,000	24 in./8.5 hp		Good	Very good	Excellent	Very good	Fair
11	**Husqvarna** 524ST	700	24 in./5 hp		Good	Good	Very good	Good	Fair
12	**Craftsman** (Sears) 88700	600	22 in./5 hp		Fair	Good	Excellent	Fair	Good

Excellent ⊜ · Very good ⊖ · Good ○ · Fair ◒ · Poor ●

Within types, in performance order. Gray **key numbers indicate Quick Picks.**

Key number	Brand & model (Similar models, in small type, comparable to tested model.)	Price	Width/power	Overall score (0–100; P F G VG E)	Removal speed	Distance	Surface cleaning	Controls	Handling
	SINGLE-STAGE GAS								
13	**Honda** Harmony HS520AS HS520A	$750	20 in./5 hp		Good	Very good	Excellent	Good	Very good
14	**Toro** CCR 2450 GTS 38515	540	20 in./5 hp		Good	Very good	Very good	Fair	Very good
15	**Toro** Snow Commander 38602 38600	900	24 in./7 hp		Good	Good	Excellent	Fair	Very good
16	**Troy-Bilt** Squall 521	500	21 in./5 hp		Fair	Good	Good	Fair	Excellent
17	**Yard-Man** 285 S285	400	21 in./5 hp		Fair	Good	Poor	Good	Excellent
18	**Ariens** 522 522EC [1]	500	22 in./5 hp		Fair	Fair	Good	Good	Very good
19	**Yard Machines** S260	400	21 in./5 hp		Fair	Good	Poor	Fair	Excellent
20	**Craftsman** (Sears) 88140 [2]	300	21 in./4 hp		Fair	Fair	Good	Fair	Excellent
	SINGLE-STAGE ELECTRIC								
21	**Toro** 1800 Power Curve 38025	300	18 in./12 amp		Fair	Good	Excellent	Good	Excellent
22	**Toro** Electric Power Shovel 38310	100	11 in./6.6 amp		Poor	Fair	Excellent	Fair	Excellent
23	**Yard-Man** 31A-040	160	12.5 in./8.5 amp		Poor	Poor	Excellent	Fair	Excellent

[1] *3-year warranty, rather than 2-year.* [2] *1-year warranty.*

See report, page 117. Based on tests published in Consumer Reports in October 2004.

Guide to the Ratings

Overall score is based mainly on removal speed, distance, surface cleaning, controls, and handling. **Removal speed** is how quickly models could remove snow without laboring; single-stage machines were pushed as quickly as possible before the machine labored. **Distance** is how far snow was dispersed straight ahead, left, and right with the discharge chute set for maximum distance. Measured distances ranged from roughly 10 feet to more than 30 feet. **Surface cleaning** denotes how much snow the machines left on our blacktop surface after clearing with the skid shoes and/or scraper set for best clearing. The best in the test left a thin dusting; the worst left a relatively thick coating. **Controls** include ease of discharge-chute adjustment, handle height and comfort, and engine controls and speed selection. **Handling** denotes ease of pushing, pulling, and steering with the engine or motor on and off, as well as how straight machines track while clearing. **Price** is approximate retail for tested machines. Tests were performed using 2004 models. Model names reflect 2005-model name changes, and scores for handling and controls reflect 2005-model revisions, where applicable.

Quick Picks

Best for most and capable all around:

1 Toro $1,250
2 Yard-Man $1,100, CR Best Buy
4 Craftsman $950, CR Best Buy

All three offer quick cleaning, easy controls, and good handling for their size, courtesy of a trigger-release drive disengagement and a single-lever joystick for the chute. The Toro (1) offers the smoothest of these chute controls, though the Yard-Man (2) performs as well overall for less. Consider the Craftsman (4) if you're willing to trade some discharge distance for a lower price. Stronger users may also want to consider the $700 Yard Machines (9), which performs well but lacks trigger releases.

For larger driveways:

3 Troy-Bilt $1,300

A 30-inch swath helped the Troy-Bilt (3) clear faster than most. Trigger controls and a single-lever chute control add ease.

For lighter jobs:

13 Honda $750 (gas)
14 Toro $540 (gas)
21 Toro $300 (electric)

The four-stroke Honda (13) performs best and has the most accessible chute handle. The Toro (14) is the best value, though its two-stroke engine requires fuel mixing. Both are inexpensive compared with the two-stroke Toro (15), which has a wider swath but costs $900. Consider the electric Toro (21) for smaller driveways. Also consider the Toro (22) if you're simply clearing light snow from a porch or walkway.

STRING TRIMMERS

Many of these models can handle everything from trimming around fence posts to tall grass and weeds. All but five gas-powered models (noted in the Ratings) also meet the tougher emissions standards required for sale in California. Top performers add other strengths to that mix.

Noise is a major downside of most top performers. Exceptions among those that scored well include the corded-electric Ryobi (28) and the Black & Decker (29); both emitted less than the 85 dBA at which we recommend ear protection. Note that the MTD-built Ryobi models tested differ from the newly introduced Ryobi models sold at Home Depot, which are made by another company and arrived too late for inclusion.

The Ratings rank models strictly by overall performance. See our Quick Picks for tested models that deliver specific strengths and value.

Excellent ⊜ | Very good ⊖ | Good ○ | Fair ◒ | Poor ●

In performance order. Gray **key numbers indicate Quick Picks.**

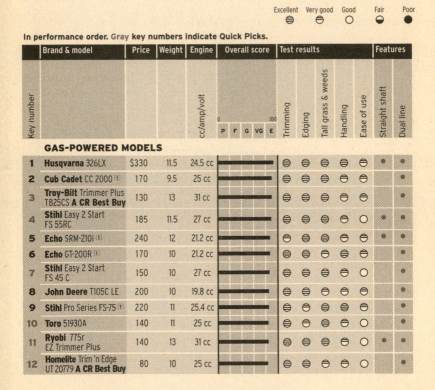

Key number	Brand & model	Price	Weight	Engine cc/amp/volt	Overall score 0–100 (P F G VG E)	Test results: Trimming	Edging	Tall grass & weeds	Handling	Ease of use	Features: Straight shaft	Dual line
	GAS-POWERED MODELS											
1	**Husqvarna** 326LX	$330	11.5	24.5 cc		⊜	⊜	⊜	⊜	⊖	•	•
2	**Cub Cadet** CC 2000 [1]	170	9.5	25 cc		⊜	⊜	⊜	⊖	⊖		•
3	**Troy-Bilt** Trimmer Plus TB25CS **A CR Best Buy**	130	13	31 cc		⊜	⊜	⊜	⊖	⊖		•
4	**Stihl** Easy 2 Start FS 55RC	185	11.5	27 cc		⊜	⊜	⊜	⊖	○	•	•
5	**Echo** SRM-210i [1]	240	12	21.2 cc		⊖	⊜	⊜	⊖	⊖	•	•
6	**Echo** GT-200R [1]	170	10	21.2 cc		⊜	⊜	⊖	⊜	⊖		•
7	**Stihl** Easy 2 Start FS 45 C	150	10	27 cc		⊜	⊜	⊜	⊖	○		•
8	**John Deere** T105C LE	200	10	19.8 cc		⊜	⊜	⊖	⊖	⊖		•
9	**Stihl** Pro Series FS-75 [1]	220	11	25.4 cc		⊜	⊖	⊜	⊜	⊖		•
10	**Toro** 51930A	140	11	25 cc		⊜	⊖	⊜	⊖	○		•
11	**Ryobi** 775r EZ Trimmer Plus	140	13	31 cc		⊜	⊜	⊜	⊖	○	•	•
12	**Homelite** Trim 'n Edge UT 20779 **A CR Best Buy**	80	10	25 cc		⊜	⊜	⊖	⊖	○		•

Key number	Brand & model	Price	Weight	Engine cc/amp/volt	Overall score (0–100; P F G VG E)	Test results: Trimming	Edging	Tall grass & weeds	Handling	Ease of use	Features: Straight shaft	Dual line
	GAS-POWERED MODELS											
13	**Husqvarna** 325CX E-tech [1]	$200	10.5	24.5 cc		E	VG	VG	E	VG		●
14	**Stihl** Easy 2 Start FS 46C	185	9	27 cc		E	VG	E	VG	VG		●
15	**Craftsman** 79612 [2]	170	16	34 cc		E	VG	VG	VG	VG	●	●
16	**Ryobi** 875r Trimmer Plus	180	13	26.2 cc		E	E	VG	VG	G	●	●
17	**Stihl** FS 110 RX	370	13.5	31.4 cc		VG	VG	E	VG	VG	●	●
18	**Craftsman** 79154	110	12	25 cc		E	E	G	VG	VG		
19	**Bolens** BL100 **A CR Best Buy**	75	10	31 cc		E	VG	VG	VG	G		●
20	**Weed Eater** Max SST MX550	100	12.5	25 cc		E	E	G	VG	G	●	●
21	**Ryobi** 700r	100	10.5	31 cc		E	VG	E	G	G		●
22	**Craftsman** 79158	140	14	32 cc		VG	VG	VG	VG	VG	●	●
23	**Troy-Bilt** Trimmer Plus TB475SS [2]	195	13.5	26.2 cc		VG	VG	VG	VG	VG	●	●
24	**Honda** HHT25SLTA [2]	310	13	25 cc		VG	VG	VG	VG	G	●	●
25	**Weed Eater** Featherlite FL20	70	9.5	20 cc		G	E	F	VG	G		
26	**Weed Eater** Featherlite Xtreme FX26	80	9.5	25 cc		G	E	F	VG	G		●
	CORDED ELECTRIC MODELS											
27	**Ryobi** 132r Trimmer Plus	75	10	5.2 A		E	VG	G	G	VG		●
28	**Ryobi** 105r	60	7.5	4.7 A		E	G	G	VG	VG		●
29	**Black & Decker** Grass Hog GH600	50	5.5	4.8 A		VG	VG	F	VG	E		
30	**Weed Eater** RTE115	35	6	4.5 A		G	VG	F	VG	VG		
31	**Toro** 51355	30	5	3.9 A		G	G	F	VG	VG		
32	**Toro** 51357	40	5.5	4 A		G	G	F	VG	VG		
33	**Weed Eater** RT112	30	5	3.7 A		G	G	F	VG	VG		
34	**Craftsman** 74524	40	5.5	4.5 A		F	G	F	VG	VG		
35	**Weed Eater** Electralite 9 EL9	20	3	2.1 A		P	F	P	G	G		
36	**Black & Decker** ST1000	25	3.5	1.8 A		P	P	P	G	G	●	

In performance order. Gray key numbers indicate Quick Picks.

Key number	Brand & model	Price	Weight	Engine cc/amp/volt	Overall score (0–100; P F G VG E)	Test results: Trimming	Edging	Tall grass & weeds	Handling	Ease of use	Features: Straight shaft	Dual line
	CORDLESS ELECTRIC MODELS											
37	**Ryobi** 155r	$100	10	15 V		◒	◒	◒	○	⊜	•	
38	**Toro** 51465	90	12	24 V		○	○	●	◒	⊜	•	
39	**Black & Decker** Grass Hog CST2000	90	9.5	12 V		◒	●	◒	○	⊜	•	

[1] Not sold in California. [2] Equipped with a relatively clean, but heavy, four-stroke engine.

See report, page 119. Based on tests published in Consumer Reports in June 2004, with updated prices and availability.

Guide to the Ratings

Overall score is based mainly on trimming near a wall, edging, cutting tall grass and weeds, handling, and ease of use. **Weight** is rounded to the nearest ½ pound and doesn't include fuel, which can add ½ pound. Engine cubic centimeters **(cc),** motor amperes **(A),** and motor electrical voltage **(V)** are from the manufacturer. **Trimming** denotes how quickly and neatly models cut grass. **Edging** is how quickly and neatly models trimmed a vertical line along a walkway. **Tall grass** denotes cutting power in tall grass and weeds. **Handling** denotes responsiveness and balance. **Ease of use** denotes ease of starting, feeding out more line, and accessing controls, along with handle comfort. **Price** is approximate retail.

Quick Picks

Best for most people:

3 Troy-Bilt $130, CR Best Buy
7 Stihl $150
10 Toro $140
12 Homelite $80, CR Best Buy
19 Bolens $75, CR Best Buy

The Troy-Bilt (3) and Stihl (7) perform nearly as well as the pro-style Husqvarna (1). The Troy-Bilt also accepts an edger blade and other tools; the Stihl (7) and Toro (10) weigh less. The lightweight Homelite (12) and Bolens (19) trade some tall-grass performance for a low price.

If longer reach matters:

4 Stihl $185
11 Ryobi $140
20 Weed Eater $100

A straight shaft allows these models to trim beneath shrubs more easily than do curved-shaft models. The Stihl (4) offers the best blend of performance and light weight. Consider the Ryobi (11) or Weed Eater (20) if you can handle the extra weight.

If handling tall grass is less critical:

28 Ryobi $60
29 Black & Decker $50

Both corded electric models are relatively quiet, lightweight performers for light-duty work. The Black & Decker (29) trades some tall-grass performance for even less weight.

TELEPHONES, CORDLESS

Phones and answerers that use analog transmission are the only ones with excellent scores in voice quality. But phones with very good voice quality should be just fine, too. As the Ratings show, multiple-handset models generally have more features.

With similar phones and phone-answerers, the performance should be like that of the tested model. Consider a similar model if you can't find a product we've tested.

The Ratings lists products strictly on performance. Quick Picks considers factors such as features and value.

Excellent, Very good, Good, Fair, Poor

Within groups, in performance order. Gray key numbers indicate Quick Picks.

Key number	Brand & model (Similar models. Many of these have similar models that differ mainly in features. They are listed with the tested model, in small type.)	Type	Price	Overall score (0–100: P F G VG E)	Test results: Voice quality	Test results: Ease of use	Test results: Talk time (hr.)	Features: Max. handsets supported (extra included)	Features: Base speakerphone and keypad	Features: Handset speakerphone	Features: Lighted keypad
	SINGLE-HANDSET PHONES										
1	**Panasonic** KX-TC1486B **A CR Best Buy**	900A	$35		Excellent	Very good	12				
2	**Uniden** EXI 5160	5.8/900A	60		Excellent	Very good	10				
3	**GE** 26938GE1 26928GE1 **A CR Best Buy**	900A	25		Excellent	Very good	11				
4	**Uniden** EXI 7246 **A CR Best Buy**	2.4/900A	30		Excellent	Very good	9				
5	**Uniden** EXI 976 **A CR Best Buy**	900A	30		Excellent	Very good	12				
6	**Bell South** MH9111SL **A CR Best Buy**	900A	30		Excellent	Very good	10				
7	**Motorola** MA350 MA300, MA351, MA352	2.4A	50		Excellent	Very good	10				
8	**Uniden** EZI 996	900A	55		Very good	Excellent	10				•
9	**GE** 27938GE6 27928GE6	2.4A	30		Excellent	Good	8				
10	**Panasonic** KX-TG2313W KX-TG2312W	2.4D	50		Very good	Very good	8			•	•
11	**Panasonic** KX-TG5050W KX-TG5055W	5.8D	90		Very good	Very good	5			•	•
12	**Bell South** GH9457BK	2.4A	30		Very good	Good	8				
13	**VTech** t2426	2.4/900A	30		Very good	Good	8				

Key number	Brand & model	Type	Price	Overall score (0–100: P F G VG E)	Test results: Voice quality	Test results: Ease of use	Test results: Talk time (hr.)	Features: Max. handsets supported (extra included)	Features: Base speakerphone and keypad	Features: Handset speakerphone	Features: Lighted keypad
	Similar models. Many of these have similar models that differ mainly in features. They are listed with the tested model, in small type.										
	MULTIPLE-HANDSET PHONES										
14	**Uniden** DXI 986-2 **A CR Best Buy**	900A	$40		⊜	⊖	12	2 (1)			
15	**Uniden** DXI 7286-2 **A CR Best Buy**	2.4/900A	50		⊜	⊖	9	2 (1)			
16	**VTech** ev 2625	2.4D	65		⊖	⊖	11	2 (1)		•	•
17	**Radio Shack** ET-3570	2.4D	60		⊖	⊖	10	4		•	•
18	**Panasonic** KX-TG2700S D	2.4D	130		⊖	⊖	7	8	•	•	•
19	**Uniden** DCT 646-2 DCT 646	2.4D	90		⊖	⊖	9	4 (1)		•	•
20	**VTech** VT20-2431 (2-line)	2.4D	160		⊖	⊖	10	8	•	•	•
21	**Bell South** GH9702BKEX	2.4D	80		○	○	6	9 (1)			
22	**Motorola** MD451 MD451sys, MD471	2.4D	60		○	⊖	6	4		•	•
23	**Southwestern Bell** GH5811 GH5812	5.8/2.4D	80		⊖	○	7	4		•	•

D *Discontinued, but similar model is available. Price is for similar model.*

Guide to the Ratings (phones chart)

Overall score mainly covers voice quality, ease of use, unobstructed range, electrical surge protection, and privacy. **Type** is as follows: 900A=900-MHz analog; 2.4A=2.4-GHz analog; 2.4D= 2.4-GHz digital spread spectrum or digital; 5.8D=5.8-GHz digital spread spectrum; some phones use two frequency bands. **Voice quality** covers listening and talking, as judged by trained panelists. **Ease of use** includes handset comfort and weight, talk time, setup and control accessibility, clarity of labels and the presence of useful features. **Talk time** is based on continuous-use tests with fully charged batteries. Features columns list features that enhance versatility. We also list the total number of handsets that multiple-handset models can support, along with the number of extra handsets supplied with the base unit. **Price** is the approximate retail. **All have:** 1-yr. warranty; flash to answer call-waiting, handset earpiece volume control, handset ringer, at least 10 memory-dial slots, last-number redial, and low-battery indicator. **Most have** caller ID and are wall-mountable.

Guide to the Ratings (answerers chart)

Overall score is the same as for phones. Here, the overall score also includes message and greeting voice quality, answerer ease of use, and recording time. **Type** is the same as for phones. **Phone tests** are the same as those conducted on phones. For **answerer, message** and **greeting voice quality** were judged by trained panelists. **Answerer ease of use** includes readability of labels, accessibility of controls, setup, ability to play new messages first and not erase unplayed ones. **Recording time** is based on tests using continuous speech. **Price** is the approximate retail. **All have:** call screening, day/time stamp, remote access, selectable number of rings, repeat, and message skip.

Within groups, in performance order. Gray key numbers indicate Quick Picks.

Key number	Brand & model (Similar models. Many of these have similar models that differ mainly in features. They are listed with the tested model, in small type.)	Type	Price	Overall score (0–100; P F G VG E)	Test results: PHONE – Voice quality	PHONE – Phone ease of use	PHONE – Talk time (hrs.)	ANSWERER – Message quality	ANSWERER – Answerer ease of use	ANSWERER – Greeting quality	ANSWERER – Recording time (min.)	Max. handsets supported (extra included)	Mailboxes
	SINGLE-HANDSET PHONES WITH ANSWERER												
24	**AT&T** 1465	2.4/ 900A	$60		⊖	⊖	8	⊖	⊜	⊖	20		1
25	**GE** 25898GE3	5.8/ 900A	70		⊜	⊖	10	○	⊖	○	15		1
26	**GE** 27998GE6	2.4A	45		⊜	⊖	11	○	⊖	◒	16		1
27	**Panasonic** KX-TG2257S **D**	2.4D	120		⊖	⊖	6	⊖	⊖	○	15		1
28	**GE** 27958GE1	2.4A	80		⊖	⊖	11	○	○	◒	16		1
29	**VTech** VT9152 **D** VT9162	900A	50		⊖	○	5	⊖	⊖	⊖	14		1
	MULTIPLE-HANDSET PHONES WITH ANSWERER												
30	**AT&T** E2600B E2555, E2525	2.4D	160		⊖	⊖	12	⊖	⊖	⊖	30	8 (1)	1
31	**VTech** i5867 i5866	5.8/ 2.4D	140		⊖	⊖	10	⊖	⊖	⊖	31	8	3
32	**AT&T** E5965C E5865, E5860	5.8/ 2.4D	180		⊖	⊖	7	⊖	⊖	⊖	30	8	1
33	**Uniden** DXAI 5188-2	5.8/ 900A	100		⊜	⊜	10	○	⊖	○	12	2 (1)	1
34	**Motorola** MD681	5.8D	150		⊖	⊖	7	⊖	○	⊖	30	6	3
35	**Panasonic** KX-TG5240M KX-TG5212M, KX-TG5210M	5.8D	150		⊖	⊖	5	⊖	⊖	○	15	4	3
36	**VTech** ip 5850	5.8/ 2.4D	125		⊖	⊖	6	⊖	⊖	⊖	20	2 (1)	3
37	**AT&T** 2256	2.4D	100		⊖	⊖	17	⊖	⊖	⊖	20	2 (1)	3
38	**Panasonic** KX-TG2770S	2.4D	150		⊖	⊖	7	⊖	⊖	○	15	8	3
39	**Uniden** TRU 8885-2 TRU 8885	5.8D	180		⊖	⊖	7	⊖	○	⊖	14	10 (1)	1
40	**Panasonic** KX-TG2344B	2.4D	100		⊖	⊖	8	⊖	⊖	○	14	2 (1)	1
41	**Uniden** DCT 6485-2 DCT 6485, DCT 648-2, DCT 648	2.4D	110		⊖	⊖	9	○	○	○	12	4 (1)	1

D *Discontinued, but similar model is available. Price is for similar model.*

See report, page 144. *Based on tests published in Consumer Reports in October 2004.*

Quick Picks

PHONES

Good choices in single-handset phones. All are CR Best Buys:

1 Panasonic $35
3 GE $25
4, 5 Uniden $30
6 Bell South $30

They offer excellent voice quality and plenty of talk time.

Good choices for a multiple-handset phone. Both are CR Best Buys:

14 Uniden $40
15 Uniden $50

Both have excellent voice quality and come with an additional handset and a charging cradle.

PHONE-ANSWERERS

A good, basic choice:

24 AT&T $60

Very good voice quality and an answerer that's very easy to use.

Good choices for a phone-answerer with multiple handsets:

30, 32 AT&T $160, $180
31 VTech $140
33 Uniden $100

AT&T (30, 32) come loaded with features and offer long recording times. The VTech (31) is less expensive but has fewer features. Those three can coexist with a wireless computer network, use rechargeable AA batteries, and can work during a power outage. The low-priced Uniden (33) combines an excellent phone with a decent answerer.

FEATURES THAT COUNT

Cordless phones

Nearly all cordless phones come with caller ID, a headset jack for hands-free use, and a base that can be wall-mounted. Other features are listed here. For features that aren't highlighted in the Ratings, we give key numbers of phones and phone-answerers that have them.

Caller ID Nearly standard these days. The display on some phones can show data on a call-waiting caller. On some VTech phones, a photo you've uploaded is displayed when that person calls.

Lighted keypad that glows or lights up when you press a key or take an incoming call makes the phone easy to use in a darkened room.

Handset-to-handset talk capability on multiple-handset phones lets you use the handsets as you would an intercom. Some models let you take handsets away from home and use them as walkie-talkies.

Speakerphones offer a hands-free way to converse or wait on hold or let others join the conversation. The speakerphone can be on the base or on the handset.

A base keypad is found on most models that have a speakerphone and makes it easy to wade through phone menus.

Wall-mountable phones include all the hardware that you need to save a bit of counter space.

Two-line capability, declining in popularity, separates business and home numbers. Found on 20, 27.

TVS, LCD

The best and highest-priced LCD TVs, all HD sets, can display a very good picture when connected to a high-quality source, such as a DVD player, satellite receiver, or digital-cable box. But the smaller a TV's screen, the less benefit you'll see from the added detail of HD unless you're close to the set. Lower-priced sets with good or fair picture quality (especially standard-definition sets) could be fine if the best image quality isn't critical—if you want to keep an eye on the news while in the kitchen, for example.

In this group, the HD sets offer the best performance and cost no more than the ED sets, so that's what we're recommending. Only one of the tested ED sets could display HD signals. If you watch a lot of DVDs, check out the DVD-playback scores, which reflect picture quality from a progressive-scan DVD player.

Scores for HD programming and DVD playback are held to a higher standard than scores for regular TV, so a very good HD picture is much better than very good picture quality with regular TV.

The Ratings list models by performance. Quick Picks highlights sets that you may want to consider based on how they scored and on factors such as price.

Excellent ⊜ Very good ⊖ Good ○ Fair ◒ Poor ●

Within types, in performance order. Gray key numbers indicate Quick Picks.

Key number	Brand & model	Price	Overall score (0–100; P F G VG E)	Screen: Shape	Screen: Size (in.)	Picture quality: HD programming	Picture quality: DVD playback	Picture quality: Regular TV via high-quality input	Picture quality: Regular TV via basic input	Sound quality	Ease of use	Rear inputs: Composite-video	Rear inputs: S-video	Rear inputs: Component-video	PC monitor option	Full warranty (mo.)
	HIGH-DEFINITION SETS															
1	**Sony** LCD Wega KDL-32XBR950	$6,000		16:9	32	⊖	⊖	⊖	○	⊜	○	2	2	2		12
2	**Sony** Wega KLV-26HG2	3,300		16:9	26	⊖	○	⊖	○	⊜	○	2	2	1		12
3	**Toshiba** 26HL84	2,500		16:9	26	○	○	⊖	◒	⊜	○	3	3	2		12
4	**Go-Video** TW1730	650		16:9	17	○	○	○	○	⊜	○	1	1	1	•	3
5	**Philips** 15PF9936/37	700		4:3	15	⊖	⊖	○	◒	⊜	◒	3	2	2	•	12
6	**Zenith** L17W36	800		16:9	17	○	○	⊖	○	⊖	○	2	1	1	•	12
7	**Philips** 17PF8946	900		16:9	17	⊖	⊖	○	◒	⊖	◒	3	2	2	•	12
8	**Zenith** L15V36	550		4:3	15	○	○	○	○	○	○	2	1	1	•	12
9	**Samsung** LT-P227W	1,800		16:9	22	◒	○	○	◒	⊜	○	1	1	2		12

Excellent / Very good / Good / Fair / Poor

Within types, in performance order. Gray key numbers indicate Quick Picks.

Key number	Brand & model	Price	Overall score (0–100; P F G VG E)	Screen: Shape	Screen: Size (in.)	Picture quality: HD programming	Picture quality: DVD playback	Picture quality: Regular TV via high-quality input	Picture quality: Regular TV via basic input	Sound quality	Ease of use	Rear inputs: Composite-video	Rear inputs: S-video	Rear inputs: Component-video	PC monitor option	Full warranty (mo.)
	HIGH-DEFINITION SETS *Continued*															
10	**LG** RU-23LZ21	$2,200		16:9	23	Fair	Good	Good	Fair	Very good	Good	2	1	1	•	12
11	**Panasonic** TC-26LX20	2,500		16:9	26	Fair	Good	Good	Fair	Excellent	Fair	1	1	2		12
12	**Polaroid** LCD-1750	800		16:9	17	Fair	Fair	Very good	Fair	Good	Good	1	1	1	•	12
13	**RCA** LCDX2620W	2,165		16:9	26	Fair	Good	Good	Fair	Excellent	Fair	1	1	1	•	12
14	**BenQ** DV-2680	2,500		16:9	26	Fair	Fair	Good	Fair	Excellent	Fair	2	2	1	•	12
15	**Gateway** GTW-L26M103	2,000		16:9	26	Poor	Fair	Fair	Fair	Excellent	Good	2	2	1	•	12
16	**V. Inc.** Vizio L6	800		4:3	20	Poor	Fair	Good	Poor	Very good	Good	1	1	1		12
17	**Westinghouse** W32701	1,700		16:9	27	Poor	Good	Fair	Fair	Excellent	Good	1	1	2	•	12
	ENHANCED-DEFINITION SETS															
18	**Panasonic** TC-20LA2	1,100		4:3	20		Good	Good	Fair	Excellent	Fair	2	2	1		12
19	**JVC** LT-17X475	1,000		16:9	17		Good	Good	Poor	Very good	Fair	1	1	1	•	12
20	**JVC** LT-23X475	1,900		16:9	23		Good	Fair	Poor	Very good	Fair	1	1	1	•	12
21	**Zenith** L20V36	850		4:3	20	Fair	Fair	Good	Good	Very good	Good	2	1	1		12
22	**Sharp** Aquos Series LC-20S2U-S	1,000		4:3	20		Fair	Fair	Fair	Excellent	Fair	2	2	1		12
23	**Sharp** Aquos Series LC-20B4U-S	1,000		4:3	20		Poor	Fair	Fair	Excellent	Good	2	1	1		12
	STANDARD-DEFINITION SET															
24	**Samsung** LT-P2035	900		4:3	20			Good	Fair	Very good	Good	1	1	1		12

See report, page 55. Based on tests published in Consumer Reports in November 2004.

Guide to the Ratings

Overall score is based primarily on picture quality; sound quality and ease of use are also figured in. **Screen shape** indicates the aspect ratio: the squarish 4:3 or wide-screen 16:9. **Screen size** is measured diagonally. Experts evaluated **picture quality** for clarity and color accuracy. **HD programming** reflects display of a 1080i signal. For ED sets, HD scores indicate how well they down-converted 1080i signals to 480p. **DVD playback** indicates how a set displayed a 480p signal, such as the output from a progressive-scan DVD player. **Regular TV** scores are for a 480i signal, such as that of a regular TV program, received via **high-quality** (S-video) and **basic** (antenna/cable) inputs. HD and DVD performance are judged by a higher standard than regular TV, so scores can't be compared. **Sound quality** is measured from the set's built-in speakers using computer-aided test equipment. **Ease of use** assesses the remote control, onscreen menus, labeling of inputs, and useful features. **Price** is approximate retail. **Full warranty** is for parts and labor except for the Go-Video (4), which has 12 months on parts and 3 months on labor. **Standard-definition models** can display only conventional TV programming. **ED models** can display 480p signals from progressive-scan DVD players or from an external digital TV tuner. Only the Zenith (21) could down-convert HD signals. **HD models** can typically display an HD picture only if connected to an external HD tuner. The Sony (1) has an integrated digital tuner. It's the only tested model with a separate control unit.

Quick Picks

If you're willing to pay a high price for the biggest screens and best performance:

1 Sony $6,000

2 Sony $3,300

Two wide-screen HD-ready models were the best of all the LCD TVs tested—and also the most expensive. The 32-inch Sony (1) and its 26-inch sibling (2) are large enough to serve as a primary TV set, and they were very good with both HD programming and regular TV via the S-video input. The Sony (1) has an integrated digital tuner (which can receive off-air HD signals via antenna) and a separate control unit; (2) is an HD-ready model. One drawback to the 26-inch Sony (2) is that it has only one component-video input. Neither set can be used as a computer monitor.

If you want the most bang for the buck in smaller HD sets:

4 Go-Video $650

5 Philips $700

6 Zenith $800

8 Zenith $550

Among 17-inch wide-screen sets, the Go-Video (4) and Zenith (6) are good TVs at modest prices. Two 15-inch 4:3 sets may suit you if low cost is a priority: the Philips (5) costs more than the Zenith (8), but had better picture quality. All four sets can be used as computer displays.

TVS, PLASMA

Most of the plasma sets we tested displayed bright, colorful images. On the better sets, picture quality was clear and crisp, especially with HD programming and with output from a progressive-scan DVD player. With regular TV programming, images weren't quite as sharp, but the picture quality was still good, and the sheer size and brightness are likely to impress you. The best ED sets did better than some HDTVs, and they cost $1,000 or so less.

Sound quality of all tested models except the ViewSonic (12) was excellent, largely because of the size and design of the front-facing speakers. The ViewSonic's sound was only fair; its speakers are on the back, facing the wall. Some models don't include speakers or tuners at the price shown; in such cases, we tested the optional speakers.

About scoring: HD programming and DVDs can look much better than regular TV programming, so we used a higher standard when judging HD and DVD content. As a result, a very good score for HD programming indicates a much better picture than a very good score for regular TV. If all content were judged on the same scale, a TV that did an outstanding job displaying regular TV programming would get an unfairly mediocre score.

The Ratings list models by performance. Quick Picks highlights models that you may want to consider based on how they scored and on factors such as price.

Excellent / Very good / Good / Fair / Poor

Within types, in performance order. Gray key numbers indicate Quick Picks.

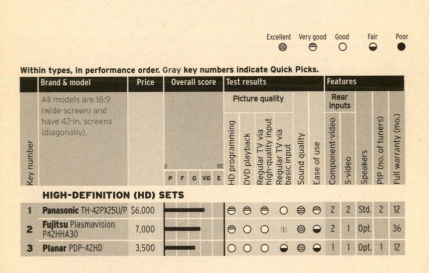

Key number	Brand & model	Price	Overall score (0–100; P F G VG E)	Test results: Picture quality: HD programming	DVD playback	Regular TV via high-quality input	Regular TV via basic input	Sound quality	Ease of use	Features: Rear inputs: Component-video	S-video	Speakers	PIP (no. of tuners)	Full warranty (mo.)
	All models are 16:9 (wide-screen) and have 42-in. screens (diagonally).													
	HIGH-DEFINITION (HD) SETS													
1	**Panasonic** TH-42PX25U/P	$6,000		Very good	Very good	Very good	Good	Excellent	Very good	2	2	Std.	2	12
2	**Fujitsu** Plasmavision P42HHA30	7,000		Very good	Good	Good	[1]	Excellent	Fair	2	1	Opt.		36
3	**Planar** PDP-42HD	3,500		Good	Good	Good	Fair	Excellent	Fair	1	1	Opt.	1	12

Key number	Brand & model	Price	Overall score	Test results: Picture quality: HD programming	DVD playback	Regular TV via high-quality input	Regular TV via basic input	Sound quality	Ease of use	Features: Rear inputs: Component-video	S-video	Speakers	PIP (no. of tuners)	Full warranty (mo.)
	All models are 16:9 (wide-screen) and have 42-in. screens (diagonally).		0–100: P F G VG E											
	ENHANCED-DEFINITION (ED) SETS													
4	**Marantz** PD4220V	4,800		⊖	⊖	○	[1]	⊜	◒	2	1	Opt.		12
5	**Fujitsu** Plasmavision P42VHA30	5,000		⊖	⊖	○	[1]	⊜	◒	2	1	Opt.		36
6	**Mitsubishi** Platinum Series PD-4225S	5,000		⊖	○	○	○	⊜	○	1	[2]	Std.	1	12
7	**Panasonic** TH-42PD25U/P	3,800		○	⊖	○	◒	⊜	⊖	2	2	Std.	2	12
8	**Philips** 42PF9936	3,200		○	⊖	○	○	⊜	◒	1	2	Std.		12
9	**Daewoo** DP-42SM	2,500		◒	○	○	[1]	⊜	◒	2	2	Opt.		12
10	**Samsung** SP-P4251	3,800		◒	○	○	○	⊜	◒	2	1	Std.	2	24
11	**Samsung** SP-P4231	3,500		◒	○	○	○	⊜	○	1	1	Std.	1	24
12	**ViewSonic** Cinema Wall VPW-425	3,000		○	○	◒	◒	◒	○	2	1	Std.	1	12

[1] *Model lacks antenna/cable input and requires external tuner to receive any channels.*
[2] *S-video connection possible only via front panel, which prohibits hiding of A/V cables.*

See report, page 55. Based on tests published in Consumer Reports in November 2004.

Guide to the Ratings

Overall score is based primarily on picture quality; sound quality and ease of use are also figured in. Expert panelists evaluated **picture quality** for clarity and color accuracy. **HD programming** reflects display of a 1080i signal. For ED sets, HD scores indicate how well they down-converted 1080i signals to 480p. **DVD playback** indicates how a set displayed a 480p signal, such as the output from a progressive-scan DVD player. **Regular TV** scores are for a 480i signal, such as that of a regular TV program, received via **high-quality** (S-video) and **basic** (antenna/cable) inputs. Scores for HD programming and DVD playback are held to a higher standard than scores for regular TV. **Sound quality** is measured from the set's speakers using computer-aided test equipment. (Std. indicates that speakers come standard with the TV; opt. indicates that they are an extra-cost option.) **Ease of use** is our assessment of the remote control, onscreen menus, labeling of inputs, and useful features. **Price** is approximate retail. **Full warranty** is for parts and labor. **HD sets** can typically display an HD picture only if connected to an external digital tuner; the Panasonic (1) has an integrated digital tuner for decoding off-air digital and digital-cable signals. **ED sets** can display 480p signals from progressive-scan DVD players or from an external digital TV tuner. The Panasonic (7) has an integrated digital tuner for off-air digital and digital cable.

Quick Picks

For a very good picture at a premium price:

1 Panasonic $6,000
4 Marantz $4,800
5 Fujitsu $5,000

The Panasonic (1), a digital-cable-ready HD model, was the best performer in this group and one of the easiest sets to use. It was also one of the most expensive. But it has a lot to offer, including higher native resolution and front speakers that come standard with the TV. Its built-in tuner can decode off-the-air signals, including HD. It can also decode some digital-cable signals without using a cable box, but it requires a CableCard (obtained through your cable operator) for premium channels and HD. You can get comparable HD and DVD picture quality at a lower price with two ED sets, the Marantz (4) and Fujitsu (5). With those sets, speakers are optional. They don't have a TV tuner; a digital-cable box or satellite receiver would supply this. Their menus and remotes weren't as user-friendly as the Panasonic's. The Fujitsu has the longest warranty.

For a decent picture at a lower price:

8 Philips $3,200

This set's picture quality is a step lower but still good. Although it's an ED set, it did a good job displaying HD when connected to an external tuner. With DVDs, the picture quality was very good. The set comes with front speakers, but its onscreen menu and remote control were fairly hard to use.

VACUUM CLEANERS

Virtually all of these vacuums cleaned bare floors quickly and neatly. Top-scoring models add impressive carpet cleaning and strong airflow through the hose for use with tools, along with extra features—something we now weigh more heavily in our scores to reflect real-world use.

More performance and convenience needn't cost more money; many $150 to $300 upright and canister vacuums offer better vacuuming and more features than pricier models. Paying less often buys less vacuuming performance and convenience, however. Nearly all of the lowest-priced models we tested were also judged poor in noise and should be used with earplugs or other hearing protection.

Prices soar when you opt for a central vacuum system. But not having to push, pull, or carry an upright or canister may be worth the roughly $500 to $1,250 you'll pay when you include the base unit, hose and tools, plus the roughly $300 to $750 you'll spend for installation if your home isn't equipped for central vacuuming. Alternatively, you could spend less by buying several conventional vacuums and storing one at each level of your home.

Legend: Excellent · Very good · Good · Fair · Poor

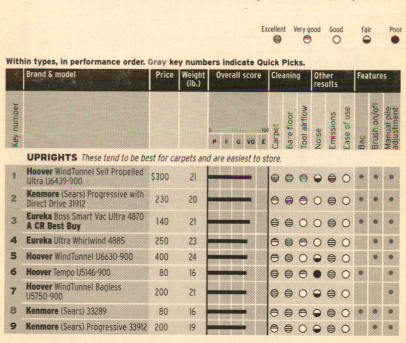

Within types, in performance order. Gray key numbers indicate Quick Picks.

Key number	Brand & model	Price	Weight (lb.)	Overall score (0–100; P F G VG E)	Cleaning: Carpet	Cleaning: Bare floor	Cleaning: Tool airflow	Other results: Noise	Other results: Emissions	Other results: Ease of use	Features: Bag	Features: Brush on/off	Features: Manual pile adjustment
	UPRIGHTS *These tend to be best for carpets and are easiest to store.*												
1	**Hoover** WindTunnel Self Propelled Ultra U6439-900	$300	21		Excellent	Excellent	Excellent	Fair	Excellent	Good	•	•	•
2	**Kenmore** (Sears) Progressive with Direct Drive 31912	230	20		Very good	Excellent	Very good	Good	Excellent	Good	•	•	•
3	**Eureka** Boss Smart Vac Ultra 4870 **A CR Best Buy**	140	21		Excellent	Excellent	Good	Good	Excellent	Good	•	•	•
4	**Eureka** Ultra Whirlwind 4885	250	23		Very good	Excellent	Very good	Good	Excellent	Good		•	•
5	**Hoover** WindTunnel U6630-900	400	24		Very good	Excellent	Good	Fair	Excellent	Good		•	•
6	**Hoover** Tempo U5146-900	80	16		Excellent	Excellent	Very good	Poor	Excellent	Good	•		•
7	**Hoover** WindTunnel Bagless U5750-900	200	21		Excellent	Excellent	Good	Fair	Excellent	Good			•
8	**Kenmore** (Sears) 33289	80	16		Very good	Excellent	Very good	Fair	Excellent	Good	•	•	•
9	**Kenmore** (Sears) Progressive 33912	200	19		Very good	Excellent	Good	Fair	Excellent	Good		•	•

Excellent (E) · Very good (VG) · Good (G) · Fair (F) · Poor (P)

Within types, in performance order. Gray key numbers indicate Quick Picks.

Key number	Brand & model	Price	Weight (lb.)	Overall score (0–100; P F G VG E)	Cleaning: Carpet	Cleaning: Bare floor	Cleaning: Tool airflow	Other results: Noise	Other results: Emissions	Other results: Ease of use	Features: Bag	Features: Brush on/off	Features: Manual pile adjustment
	UPRIGHTS *Continued*												
10	**Dyson** DC07	$400	19		G	E	VG	F	E	F		•	
11	**Kenmore** (Sears) Progressive 34612	150	18		VG	E	VG	F	VG	G	•	•	•
12	**Oreck** XL21-600 [1]	700	11		VG	E	NA	G	E	VG	•		
13	**Dirt Devil** Vision M087900	180	21		VG	VG	G	P	VG	G			•
14	**Bissell** ProLite 3560-2 [1]	200	9		VG	E	NA	F	E	G	•		
15	**Panasonic** Duel Sweep Bagless MC-V7582	180	18		VG	E	G	F	VG	G		•	
16	**Bissell** Lift-Off 3750	180	22		VG	E	G	F	G	G		•	•
17	**Dirt Devil** Jaguar M088105	70	13		VG	E	G	P	VG	G			
18	**Eureka** Whirlwind Litespeed 5843	160	19		G	VG	VG	F	E	G		•	•
19	**Electrolux** Aptitude EL5010A	350	19		G	VG	VG	F	E	G	•		•
20	**Hoover** Fold Away U5162-900	110	16		VG	VG	F	F	E	G			•
21	**Dirt Devil** Jaguar M085545	50	13		VG	E	G	P	VG	G	•		
22	**Dirt Devil** Scorpion 088100	80	13		E	E	G	P	F	G		•	
23	**Dirt Devil** Featherlite Plus 085560	60	13		VG	E	F	P	VG	G	•		
24	**Panasonic** Fold 'n Go MC-V5481	100	16		G	G	F	F	E	G		•	
25	**Westinghouse** Unplugged WST1600 [2]	295	21		F	E	P	G	E	G		•	
26	**Bosch** Turbo Jet BUH11700UC	240	20		G	E	G	F	G	F	•	•	
27	**Eureka** Whirlwind Plus 4684	150	19		G	E	G	F	E	G			•
28	**Bissell** Powerforce 3522-1	45	15		G	E	G	F	VG	G	•	•	•
29	**Kenmore** (Sears) Quick Clean Bagless 34720	90	16		F	VG	G	F	E	G			•
30	**Bissell** CleanView Power Trak 3593-1	110	17		G	E	G	F	F	F		•	•
31	**Hoover** Tempo U5154-900	90	17		VG	VG	P	P	G	G			•
32	**Bissell** CleanView Bagless 8975	75	16		G	E	G	P	P	G			•
33	**Eureka** Whirlwind Lite 4388	100	16		F	F	F	F	G	G			•
	CANISTERS												
34	**Kenmore** (Sears) 22612	230	24		VG	E	VG	F	E	VG	•	•	•
35	**Kenmore** (Sears) Whispertone 23513	230	24		VG	E	VG	F	VG	VG	•	•	•
36	**GE** (Wal-Mart) 106766	150	19		VG	E	F	G	VG	VG	•	•	

Key number	Brand & model	Price	Weight (lb.)	Overall score (0–100; P F G VG E)	Cleaning: Carpet	Cleaning: Bare floor	Cleaning: Tool airflow	Other results: Noise	Other results: Emissions	Other results: Ease of use	Features: Bag	Features: Brush on/off	Features: Manual pile adjustment
	CANISTERS *Continued*												
37	**Miele** Plus S251	$450	20		○	⊜	⊖	○	⊜	⊖	•	•	
38	**Electrolux** Oxygen EL6988A	500	21		⊖	⊜	○	◒	⊜	⊖	•	•	•
39	**Hoover** WindTunnel Plus S3639	350	22		⊖	⊜	⊖	○	⊖	○	•	•	
40	**Miele** Solaris Electro Plus S514	700	21		○	⊜	○	⊖	⊜	○	•	•	
41	**Hoover** WindTunnel Bagless S3765	500	22		⊖	⊜	○	◒	○	○		•	
42	**Sanyo** High Power SC-800P	300	22		○	⊜	⊖	◒	⊖	⊖	•	•	
43	**Fantom** Falcon FC251	190	22		⊖	⊜	●	◒	⊖	○		•	
44	**Bissell** DigiPro 6900	230	21		◒	⊜	◒	◒	⊜	⊖	•	•	•
45	**Rainbow** e-Series E-2	1,800	32		○	◒	⊖	◒	○	○		•	•
	CENTRAL VACUUM SYSTEMS												
46	**Beam** Serenity Plus 2775 with Imperial Power Team Classic 775	880	13		⊖	⊜	⊖	◒	⊖	⊜		•	
47	**Nutone** Quiet Series CV750 with CK350	910	14		○	⊜	⊖	○	⊖	⊜	•	•	•
48	**Eureka** The Boss Plus CV1801 with CV205G **A CR Best Buy**	660	14		⊖	⊜	⊖	○	⊖	⊖	•	•	
49	**MD** Silent Master S2 104SM with 424GC	1,245	16		○	⊖	○	○	⊖	⊜	•	•	•
50	**Vacuflo** 5660 with Electroglide 560	925	14		○	⊜	⊖	○	⊖	⊜		•	•
51	**AirVac** Red Series AV3500 with VM2200DS	885	14		○	⊖	⊖	○	⊖	⊜		•	•
52	**Aerus** Centralux	1,200	16		○	⊜	⊖	○	⊖	⊜		•	
53	**AirVac** BV2000KIT **A CR Best Buy**	500	12		⊖	⊜	⊖	○	⊖	⊜	•	•	
54	**Hoover** S5620 with S5682	700	12		⊖	⊖	⊖	○	⊖	⊜		•	
55	**Vacu-Maid** Silent Partner S2000 with TK-230	850	13		○	⊜	⊖	○	⊖	⊜		•	•

[1] *Comes with minicanister for cleaning with tools. Performance was fair for (14), poor for (12).* [2] *Cordless model.*

See report, page 121. Based on tests published in Consumer Reports in July 2004, with updated prices and availability.

Guide to the Ratings

Overall score mainly reflects cleaning performance, ease of use, and emissions. Under **cleaning, carpet** denotes how much embedded talc and sand the vacuum lifted from a medium-pile carpet. **Bare floor** is how well a model vacuumed sand without dispersing it. **Tool airflow** is airflow through the hose with increasing amounts of dust-simulating wood "flour"; higher-scoring models provide more airflow and maintain more of it. **Noise** denotes results using a decibel meter and, for central vacs, is noise within the room, not at the base unit. Models judged poor should be used with hearing protection. **Emissions** is the wood flour released while vacuuming and, for central vacs, is as measured within the room, not at the base unit. **Ease of use** is how easy a model is to push, pull, carry, and use beneath furniture as well as its dust capacity. **Features** note whether the model has a bag, lets you turn off the brush, and includes manual pile-height adjustment. **Weight** for uprights reflects the vacuum body; for canisters, the body, hose, and powerhead; for central vacs, the hose and powerhead. **Price** is approximate retail and, for central vacs, includes the unit and accessory kit (typically $300 to $450).

Quick Picks

UPRIGHTS AND CANISTERS

Best for most; all-around performance and value:

1 Hoover $300 (upright)
2 Kenmore $230 (upright)
3 Eureka $140 (upright), CR Best Buy
34 Kenmore $230 (canister)
35 Kenmore $230 (canister)

The Hoover (1) and Kenmore (2) are top performers in our vacuum tests. Among the upright vacuum cleaners, consider the high-value Eureka (3) if you're willing to trade some performance for a much lower price. Between the two equally priced canister vacuums, consider the Kenmore (34) if fewer dust emissions are a critical part of your shopping list.

If you accept a few compromises:

8 Kenmore $80 (upright)
36 GE $150 (canister)

Both offer lots of performance and features for the price. The Kenmore (8) was relatively noisy and somewhat hard to push. The GE (36) did a fine job overall, but early clogging in our airflow tests is likely to mean relatively frequent bag changes.

CENTRAL VACUUMS

Best for a range of home sizes:

46 Beam $880
47 Nutone $910
48 Eureka $660, CR Best Buy

All three are designed for homes roughly 6,000 square feet or more. Consider the Beam (46) for its carpet performance, the Nutone (47) for its quieter running. While the Beam (46) was noisiest in the room, it was relatively quiet at the base unit. Also consider the Eureka (48), which has fewer tool wands, but costs relatively little. Lack of a manual pile-height adjustment didn't hamper its performance.

For smaller homes:

53 AirVac $500, CR Best Buy

The AirVac (53) is a strong choice. Airvac says it can handle up to 2,400 square feet, the smallest tested. Other models are slated to handle homes roughly 6,000 square feet or more.

Recommendations

UPRIGHTS

1 **HOOVER** WindTunnel Self Propelled Ultra U6439-900 **Excelled at cleaning, but noisy.** May not fit on some stairs. Bag: $2. Similar: U6437-900, U6436-900, U6433-900.

2 **KENMORE** (Sears) Progressive with Direct Drive 31912 **Very good all around.** Bag: $4 to $5. HEPA filter: $21. Similar: 31913.

3 **EUREKA** Boss Smart Vac Ultra 4870 **A CR Best Buy. Highest performance for the dollar.** Excelled at most cleaning, but hard to pull. Bag: $2.30. HEPA filter: $20.

4 **EUREKA** Ultra Whirlwind 4885 **A very good bagless vac,** but small capacity. Note: This model has limited retail availability. HEPA filter: $20. Similar: 4880.

5 **HOOVER** WindTunnel U6630-900 **Very good, but noisy, heavy, and tippy on stairs.** HEPA filter: $20. Similar: U6660-900, U6632-900, U6617-900, U6616-900, U6607-900.

6 **HOOVER** Tempo U5146-900 **Excelled at most cleaning, but noisy.** Tippy with hose extended. Cord less convenient to wrap than others. Hose and power cord shorter than most. Had to bend to adjust rug height. Bag: $2.90. Similar: U5144-900.

7 **HOOVER** WindTunnel Bagless U5750-900 **Very good.** Bagless model with excellent performance on carpets. Less prone to tipping when hose is fully extended. Small rotating brush for stairs. HEPA filter: $30 (Replace every 3 years). Similar: U5759-900, U5758-900 U5756-900, U5752-900, U5751-900, U5722-900.

8 **KENMORE** (Sears) 33289 **A very good, inexpensive vac, but noisy.** Tippy with hose extended. Hose shorter than most. Had to bend to adjust rug height. Bag: $1.25. Similar: 33189, 33079, 33078.

9 **KENMORE** (Sears) Progressive 33912 **Very good, full-featured machine.** Bagless. Exhaust filter: $14. Chamber filter: $20. Similar: 33913.

10 **DYSON** DC07 **A very good bagless vac, but has confusing controls.** Hose longer than most. Noisy. Hard to push and pull. No headlamp. HEPA filter (washable): $17.50.

11 **KENMORE** (Sears) Progressive 34612 **Very good, with lots of features.** Bag: $3.50. Exhaust filter: $14. Similar: 34613

12 **ORECK** XL21-600 **Very good, but no overload protection.** Comes with mini-canister for cleaning with tools; we found the performance of that machine to be poor. Filter on tested models wasn't a HEPA, despite label. Bag: $3

13 **DIRT DEVIL** Vision M087900 **A very good bagless vac, but noisy.** Hose longer than most. Had to bend to adjust rug height. No upholstery tool. Filter: $25.

14 **BISSELL** ProLite 3560-2 **Very good, but noisy and awkward to carry.** Comes with minicanister for cleaning with tools; we found the performance of that machine to be fair. No overload protection. Bag: $2.

15 **PANASONIC** Dual Sweep Bagless MC-V7582 **Very good overall.** But relatively noisy. Filter: $25. Similar: MC-V7572

16 **BISSELL** Lift-Off 3750 **A good bagless vac, but noisy.** Tippy with hose extended. Comes with telescopic wand, but detaching the hose from the base is difficult. Had to bend to adjust rug height. Filter: $13

17 **DIRT DEVIL** Jaguar M088105 **A good, inexpensive bagless vac, but noisy.** Tippy

Recommendations

with hose extended. Cord shorter than most. Hose isn't attached at suction end. Note: This model has limited retail availability. Filter: $25.

18 EUREKA Whirlwind Litespeed 5843 **A good bagless vac, but noisy.** Hose longer than most. No upholstery tool. Note: This model has limited retail availability. HEPA filter: $20. Similar: 5847, 5840, 5740

19 ELECTROLUX Aptitude EL5010A **Good, but pricey and noisy.** Tippy with hose extended. Hose longer than most. Motor control has more than one speed. Had to bend to adjust rug height. No upholstery tool.

20 HOOVER Fold Away U5162-900 **Good, somewhat spartan upright.** Suction for cleaning with tools not as effective as most. Unique design enables user to fold down the handle for easier storage. But we found the handle harder to grip while vacuuming. Bagless. Primary filter: $13. Similar: U5167-900, U5163-900, U5161-900

21 DIRT DEVIL Jaguar M085545 **A good, inexpensive vac, but noisy.** Cord less convenient to wrap than others. Hose and cord shorter than most. Hose isn't attached at suction end. Note: This model has limited retail availability. Bag: $3.30.

22 DIRT DEVIL Scorpion 088100 **Good performance for the money, especially on carpet.** Relatively light: 13 lbs. But noisier, with more emissions than most. Bagless. Exhaust filter: $10. HEPA filter: $25.

23 DIRT DEVIL Featherlite Plus 085560 **Good.** No overload protection or upholstery tool. Hose and cord shorter than most. Note: This model has limited retail availability. Standard bag: $1. Microfilter bag: $3.30.

24 PANASONIC Fold 'n Go MC-V5481 **A good bagless vac, but noisy.** Tippy with hose extended. Airflow through the hose is only fair. Power cord shorter than most. No upholstery tool. Filter: $9.

25 WESTINGHOUSE Unplugged WST1600 **A good bagless vacuum, and the first upright cordless model ever.** But its performance on carpet is worse than average. Comes with two rechargeable batteries. HEPA filter: washable. Hose longer than most. Unstable on stairs. Cleaning with tools performance was poor. There are better choices. Note: This model has limited retail availability.

26 BOSCH Turbo Jet BUH11700UC **Good overall, though just so-so on emissions.** Curvy design includes front-mounted hose that we found awkward to remove. Bag: $4. Filter: $25.

27 EUREKA Whirlwind Plus 4684 **A good bagless vac, but noisy.** Tippy on stairs and with hose extended. Small capacity. Cord shorter than most. Note: This model has limited retail availability. HEPA filter: $20.

28 BISSELL Powerforce 3522-1 **Good, but noisy.** Tippy with hose extended and unstable on stairs. Hard to push. Hose and power cord shorter than most. No overload protection. Bag: $3. Filter: $3.

29 KENMORE (Sears) Quick Clean Bagless 34720 **A good bagless vac, but noisy.** Tippy on stairs and with hose extended. Hose and cord shorter than most. No upholstery tool. Tower filter: $20. Exhaust filter: $14. Similar: 34721

30 BISSELL Cleanview Power Trak 3593-1 **A good bagless vac, but noisy.** Tippy with hose extended and unstable on stairs. Hard to push. No upholstery tool. HEPA filter: $10.

31 HOOVER Tempo U5154-900 **There are**

Recommendations

better choices. Tippy with hose extended. Cord less convenient to wrap than others. Hose and cord shorter than most. Bagless. Had to bend to adjust rug height. Filter: $30. Similar: U5150-900

32 BISSELL Cleanview Bagless 8975 **There are better choices.** Upper-tank filter: $4. Premotor filter: $1.50. Postmotor filter: $3.

33 EUREKA Whirlwind Lite 4388 **There are better choices.** Bagless.

CANISTER VACUUM CLEANERS

34 KENMORE (Sears) 22612 **Very good, but noisy and heavy.** Hose longer than most. Bag: $4. HEPA filter: $21. Similar: 22613.

35 KENMORE (Sears) Whispertone 23513 **A very good canister** with better-than-average cleaning on carpet, but noisy. Hose longer than most. Wand unstable in upright position and felt heavy when using tool. Difficult to detach wand-to-wand connection. Bag: $1.25. Similar: 23512.

36 GE (Wal-Mart) 106766 **Very good, well-priced canister,** with better-than-average performance on carpet. On the downside, its suction for cleaning with tools was less effective than most. Available only at Wal-Mart. Bag: $1.97.

37 MIELE Plus S251 **Very good.** Less bulky, and heavy than most. Cord shorter than most. Bag: $2.60.

38 ELECTROLUX Oxygen EL6988A **A very good canister with better-than-average cleaning on carpet.** Hose longer than most. Cord shorter than most. Difficult to detach wand-to-wand connection and wand from hose. Similar: EL6989A.

39 HOOVER WindTunnel Plus S3639 **A very good, well-rounded vac.** Bag: $2.

40 MIELE Solaris Electro Plus S514 **Very good, and quieter than most,** but hard to push and pull. Cord and hose shorter than most. Filters and 5-bag set: $12.

41 HOOVER WindTunnel Bagless S3765 **A very good canister vac, with better cleaning than most on carpet.** But relatively noisy, and released dust when we emptied the bin. Dirt cup filter: $14.25. HEPA: $9.45. Similar: S3755.

42 SANYO High Power SC-800P **Good, but spartan for the price.** Noisy. No overload protection. Cord shorter than most. Bag: $4. Electrostatic micron filter: $9.95.

43 FANTOM Falcon FC251 **Good overall, with better-than average cleaning on carpet.** But disconnecting the power head and wiring to change tools was very difficult. Vac also was relatively noisy, and released dust when bin was emptied. HEPA filter: $30.

44 BISSELL DigiPro 6900 **There are better choices.** Noisy. Unimpressive on carpets. Hose longer than most. Cord shorter than most. Had to bend to adjust rug height. Wand unstable in upright position. Bag: $2.30.

45 RAINBOW e-series E-2 **Extremely high price not justified by performance.** Among the worst on bare floors, and relatively noisy. Unusual design utilizes water to retain dust and dirt that's been picked up; that makes the machine very heavy (32 lbs.) when filled with water. Special features include the ability to pick up wet spills (not tested), an inflator for toys and a dusting brush for plants and animals.

WASHING MACHINES

We've updated our tests to better reflect improvements in today's washers and changes in the way you use them. (See page 91 for more details.) As a result of these changes, overall scores for washing performance are lower than in the past. While excellent washing performance is harder to come by with our more demanding tests, many of the tested models did a very good job and should satisfy most users.

As the Ratings show, top-loaders priced as low as $350 got very good washing scores, as did front-loaders selling for $1,000 or more. Models differed more in energy and water efficiency, gentleness, capacity, and noise. The higher-priced models were more likely to score well on all counts.

Some of the new high-efficiency top-loaders were outstanding, but we don't yet know how reliable they'll be. There are issues besides reliability. The Maytag Neptune FAV9800A[WW] (1) set a new standard for excellent washing performance—besting even the front-loaders in the group—but it was tougher on clothes than other models. The Kenmore (Sears) Elite Calypso 2408[2] (2), which has scored among the best top-loaders since we began testing these models three years ago, tangles and wrinkles clothing. In addition, our repair data for this and the Whirlpool Calypso indicate a higher-than-average need for repairs in recent years.

Excellent | Very good | Good | Fair | Poor

Within groups, in performance order. Gray key numbers indicate Quick Picks.

	Brand & model Similar models, in small type, comparable to tested model.	Price	Overall score 0–100 (P F G VG E)	Washing Performance	Energy efficiency	Water efficiency	Capacity	Gentleness	Noise	Cycle time (min.)	Stainless-steel tub	Porcelain top/lid
	TOP-LOADERS											
1	**Maytag** Neptune TL FAV9800A[WW]	$1,300		Excellent	Very good	Excellent	Excellent	Good	Good	95	•	•
2	**Kenmore** (Sears) Elite Calypso 2206[2] 2408[ ]	900		Good	Very good	Very good	Excellent	Very good	Excellent	70	•	•
3	**Fisher & Paykel** Intuitive Eco IWL12	850		Very good	Excellent	Fair	Good	Very good	Very good	55	•	
4	**Maytag** SAV4655A[WW] **CR Best Buy**	480		Very good	Good	Very good	Very good	Very good	Good	50		
5	**GE** Profile Harmony WPGT9350C[WW]	1,000		Very good	Fair	Good	Very good	Good	Good	55	•	
6	**Fisher & Paykel** Ecosmart GWL11	600		Very good	Very good	Good	Good	Very good	Very good	50	•	
7	**Amana** NAV3330A[WW]	450		Good	Good	Very good	Very good	Very good	Fair	45		

	Brand & model	Price	Overall score	Test results						Features		
	Similar models, in small type, comparable to tested model.		0–100; P F G VG E	Washing Performance	Energy efficiency	Water efficiency	Capacity	Gentleness	Noise	Cycle time (min.)	Stainless-steel tub	Porcelain top/lid
	TOP-LOADERS *Continued*											
8	**GE** WWRE5240D[WW]	450		○	◒	○	⊜	⊜	○	50	●	
9	**Kenmore** (Sears) Elite Catalyst 2403[2] 2404[ ] 2405[ ]	750		⊜	◒	○	⊜	⊜	○	50		●
10	**Amana** NAV8800A[WW]	540		○	○	⊜	○	⊜	○	45	●	
11	**GE** WBSR3140D[WW]	350		○	○	○	⊜	⊜	◒	40		
12	**Kenmore** 1584	500		○	○	○	⊜	○	○	40		
13	**Whirlpool** LSW9700P	380		○	○	○	⊜	○	○	45		
14	**GE** WHSE5240D[WW]	450		◒	○	○	⊜	⊜	○	50		
15	**GE** WHRE5260	500		◒	⊜	◒	⊜	⊜	○	45	●	
16	**Kenmore** (Sears) Elite 2494[2] 2495[ ] 2496[ ]	580		○	◒	○	⊜	○	◒	45		●
17	**Frigidaire** FWS1339A[CN] GLWS1339C[ ]	320		◒	⊜	○	○	⊜	○	45		
18	**Admiral** LNC6760[W] LNC6762[ ]	350		⊜	◒	○	○	○	◒	50		
19	**Hotpoint** VWSR4150D[WW]	390		◒	◒	○	⊜	⊜	○	45		
20	**Kenmore** (Sears) 2462[2] 2463[ ] 2464[ ]	350		○	◒	○	○	⊜	◒	40		
21	**Maytag** Performa PAVT444A[WW] HAV4657[ ]	475		⊜	◒	○	○	○	◒	45		
22	**Estate** by Whirlpool TAWS800J[Q]	350		○	◒	○	○	⊜	◒	40		
23	**Roper** RAS8333p	290		◒	○	◒	○	⊜	○	35		
24	**Roper** RAS8244L[Q]	270		○	◒	○	○	○	◒	45		
	FRONT-LOADERS											
25	**Whirlpool** GHW9400P	1,300		⊜	⊜	⊜	⊜	⊜	⊜	65	●	●
26	**Bosch** Nexxt Premium WFMC6400UC	1,350		⊜	⊜	⊜	⊜	○	⊜	110	●	
27	**Kenmore** He4t 4598[2] 4599	1,300		⊜	⊜	⊜	⊜	⊜	⊜	70	●	●
28	**LG** WM2432HW	1,150		⊜	⊜	⊜	⊜	○	⊜	75	●	●
29	**KitchenAid** Superba KHWS01PMT	1,600		⊜	⊜	⊜	⊜	⊜	⊜	85	●	●
30	**Whirlpool** Duet GHW9100L[W]	1,000		⊜	⊜	⊜	⊜	⊜	⊜	70	●	
31	**Kenmore** (Sears) He3 4586[2]	1,100		⊜	⊜	⊜	⊜	⊜	⊜	70	●	
32	**LG** WM2032H[W]	1,030		⊜	⊜	⊜	⊜	⊜	⊜	80	●	●

Within groups, in performance order. Gray key numbers indicate Quick Picks.

	Brand & model	Price	Overall score	Test results						Features		
	Similar models, in small type, comparable to tested model.		0–100 (P F G VG E)	Washing Performance	Energy efficiency	Water efficiency	Capacity	Gentleness	Noise	Cycle time (min.)	Stainless-steel tub	Porcelain top/lid
	FRONT-LOADERS *Continued*											
33	**Whirlpool** GHW9150P	1,000		⊖	⊖	⊖	⊜	⊖	⊖	65	•	
34	**Kenmore** (Sears) 4407[2]	800		○	⊜	⊖	○	⊖	⊖	55	•	
35	**Frigidaire** FWTB830T[S]	700		○	⊜	○	○	⊖	⊖	55	•	
36	**Frigidaire** Gallery GLTR(F)1670A[S] Crown CRTR9300A[ ]	650		○	⊖	○	○	○	⊖	60	•	
37	**Miele** Touchtronic Series W1113	1,650		⊖	⊜	⊖	●	⊖	⊜	90	•	
38	**Asko** W6021	1,000		⊖	⊜	⊖	●	⊖	⊖	120	•	
39	**Maytag** Neptune MAH6500A[WW] MAH5500B[ ]	1,000		⊖	○	⊖	○	○	○	70	•	•

See report, page 90. *Based on tests posted on ConsumerReports.org in August 2004.*

Guide to the Ratings

Overall score is based mostly on performance, capacity, energy efficiency, and noise. Water efficiency and gentleness are also considered. **Washing performance** indicates how well each machine removed soil in the most-aggressive normal cycle, for both an 8-pound load and a maximum load. **Energy efficiency** is based on the energy needed to run the washer and to heat the water for a warm wash, and the amount of water extracted in the final spin (which reduces time in the dryer). **Water efficiency** reflects how much water per pound of laundry it took to do an 8-pound load and each machine's maximum load. **Capacity** measures how large a load each machine could handle effectively. Models with lower scores for **gentleness** are more likely to cause wear and tear to clothing. Panelists gauged **noise** during the fill, agitation, drain, and spin cycles. **Cycle time** is for the normal cycle, rounded to the nearest 5 minutes. **Price** is approximate retail. Under **brand & model,** bracketed letters or numbers indicate a color code.

Quick Picks

Fine performance at a modest price:

4 Maytag $480, CR Best Buy
13 Whirlpool $380

Of these two conventional top-loaders, the Maytag (4) did somewhat better in overall washing performance.

Outstanding but pricey front-loaders:

30 Whirlpool $1,000
31 Kenmore $1,100
32 LG $1,030
33 Whirlpool $1,000

Big, solid machines with top scores across the board. Note that we have no reliability data on Whirlpool or LG front-loaders.

Smaller, less expensive front-loaders:

34 Kenmore $800
35 Frigidaire $700
36 Frigidaire $650

If you wash smaller loads and would be satisfied with slightly lower scores, these can save you hundreds of dollars.

BRAND RELIABILITY

Products today are generally pretty reliable, but some brands have been more reliable than others. Every year we survey readers on repairs and on problems they encounter with household products. From their responses, we derive the percentage of a brand's products that have been repaired or had a serious problem. The graphs that follow give brand repair rates for 16 product categories. Over the 30-plus years we've surveyed brand reliability, our findings have been consistent, though they are not infallible predictors.

A brand's repair history includes data on many models, some of which may have been more or less reliable than others. And surveys of a brand's past models can't anticipate design or manufacturing changes in its new models. Still, you can improve your chances of getting a trouble-free product by getting a brand that has been reliable in the past.

Product categories include appliances such as washers and ranges, electronic products such as TV sets and computers, and lawn mowers and tractors. Note that repair histories for different products are not directly comparable.

Because the quality of technical support may be the deciding factor when you're shopping for a desktop or laptop computer, we include a recent assessment of the manufacturers' technical support as well.

QUICK GUIDE

Camcorders

Camcorders are historically one of the least-used pieces of hardware, averaging 10 to 15 hours of use a year (analog to digital), which influences the repair rate. For digital camcorders, Canon and JVC MiniDV models were more repair-prone than the others. Differences in score of less than 3 points aren't meaningful.

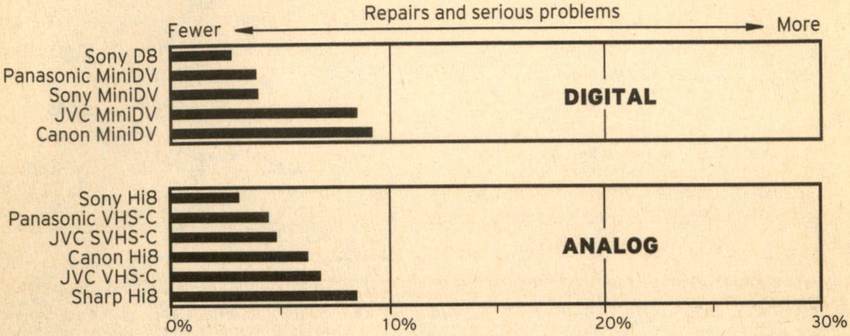

Based on nearly 32,000 reader responses to our 2003 Annual Questionnaire about camcorders bought new between 2000 and 2003. Data have been standardized to eliminate differences linked to age and use.

Cameras, digital

Repair history can be affected by the differences in models within a brand, and by design and manufacturing changes. Differences of less than 3 points aren't meaningful.

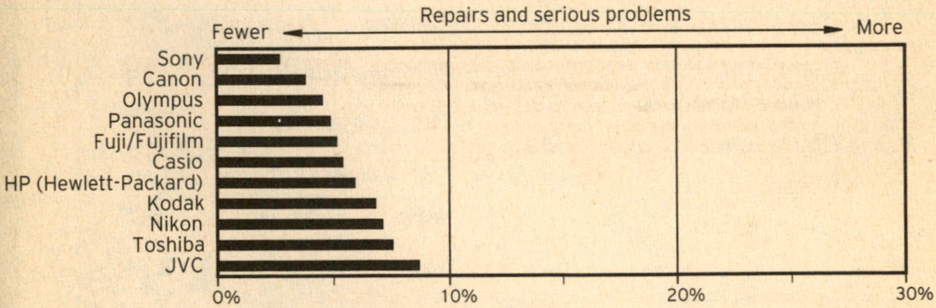

Based on more than 107,000 responses to our 2003 Annual Questionnaire about digital cameras bought new between 2000 and 2003. Data have been standardized to eliminate differences linked to age and usage.

Computers, desktop

A recent survey of more than 48,000 ConsumerReports.org subscribers found that 2 percent bought PCs that became completely inoperable in the first month; that another 6 percent had serious problems in the first month but the PCs were usable; and that over the past four years, 27 percent of PCs have needed repair. The chart shows the percent that ever had a repair to original components. Differences of 6 or more points are meaningful.

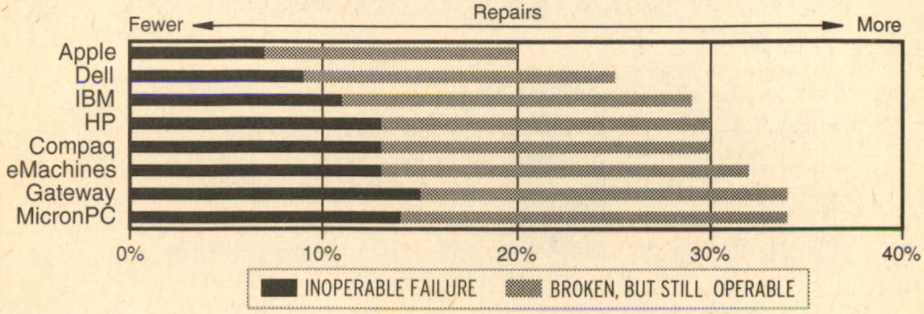

Based on computers purchased 1999-2003. Data have been standardized to eliminate differences linked to age and usage.

Computers, laptop

Over the last four years, 20 percent of laptops have needed repair. Compaq and Gateway have been among the more repair-prone brands. Differences of 3 or more points are meaningful.

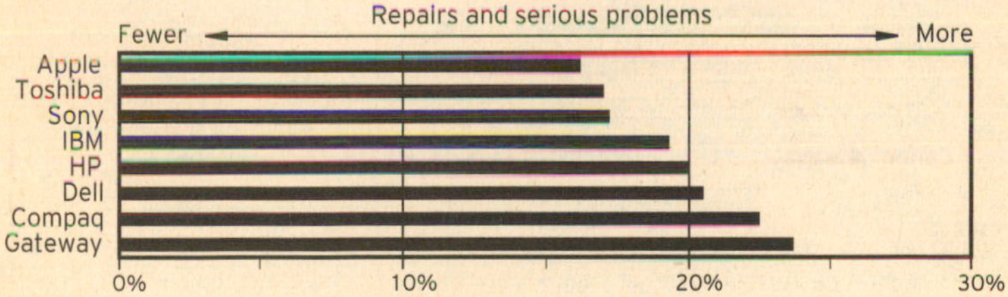

Based on responses of more than 57,000 Consumer Reports subscribers on laptops purchased between 1999 and 2003. Data have been standardized to eliminate differences linked to age and usage.

HOW THE HELP RATES

Computer tech support

Better ⊜ ⊖ ○ ◒ ● Worse

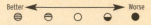

Which manufacturers did the best job of answering questions quickly and correctly.

Desktops

In order of reader score.

Manufacturer	Reader score (0–100)	Solved problem	Support staff	Waiting on phone	Web support
Apple	79	⊜	⊜	⊜	⊜
Gateway	63	○	○	⊖	○
Dell	62	⊖	○	○	○
HP	55	◒	○	○	○
Compaq	54	◒	○	○	○

Based on more than 4,900 desktop computers bought between January 1999 and January 2004.

Laptops

In order of reader score.

Manufacturer	Reader score (0–100)	Solved problem	Support staff	Waiting on phone
Apple	82	⊜	⊜	⊜
IBM	69	⊖	⊜	⊜
Gateway	64	○	⊖	○
Dell	60	⊖	○	◒
Toshiba	59	○	○	○
HP	55	◒	○	○
Sony	52	◒	○	◒
Compaq	49	●	◒	●

Based on more than 4,000 laptops bought between January 1999 and November 2003.

We conducted two surveys of subscribers to ConsumerReports.org on their most recent experiences with manufacturers' technical support. For desktop computers, the survey covered September 2002 through January 2004; for laptops, the period covered May 2002 to November 2003. The charts give the specifics. If everyone were completely satisfied, the **reader score** would be 100; 80 would mean respondents were very satisfied, on average; 60, fairly well satisfied. In the desktop survey, differences of 4 or more points are meaningful; with laptops, differences of 6 or more points are meaningful. **Solved problem** indicates how many people said the manufacturer solved their problem. **Support staff** is primarily based on how knowledgeable phone representatives seemed and whether they communicated clearly. **Waiting on phone** refers to time waiting and other phone-system problems. In the desktop survey, **Web support** indicates experiences using that type of contact to get help. We lacked sufficient data to rate laptop manufacturers on this measure. Because of differences in methodology, the charts are not directly comparable.

Dishwashers

Asko was the most repair-prone brand, followed by Bosch. Differences of less than 4 points are not meaningful. While we don't have enough data to include Fisher & Paykel in the chart, our most recent data give us concerns about this brand's reliability.

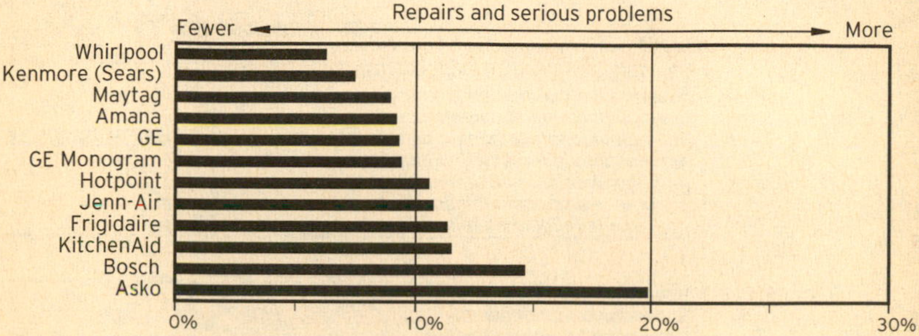

Based on nearly 104,000 responses to our 2003 Annual Questionnaire about dishwashers purchased new between 1998 and 2003. Data have been standardized to eliminate differences linked to age and usage.

Dryers

Overall, there were no meaningful differences between gas and electric dryers, and only small differences in the major brands of electric dryers. Among the six brands of gas dryers analyzed, Amana was the most repair-prone. Differences of less than 4 points are not meaningful.

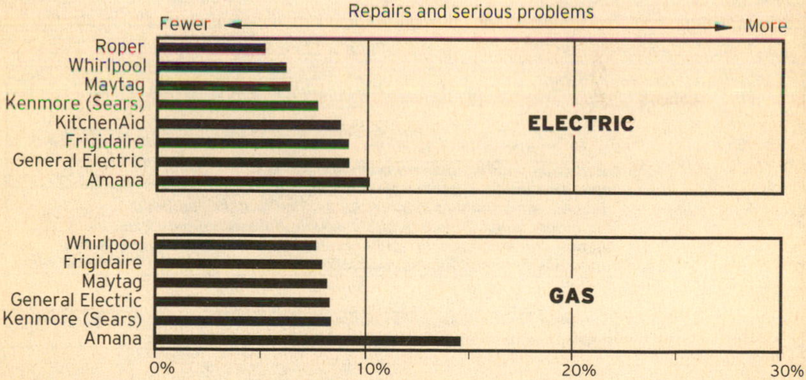

Based on more than 91,000 responses to our 2003 Annual Questionnaire about full-sized dryers bought new between 1998 and 2003. Data have been standardized to eliminate differences linked to age and usage.

Lawn mowers

Self-propelled mowers were more repair-prone than the push types. Lawn-Boy, Snapper, and Yard Machines/Yard-Man were among the more repair-prone brands for the self-propelled mowers. Lawn-Boy was the most repair-prone of the push mowers. Differences of less than 5 points are not meaningful.

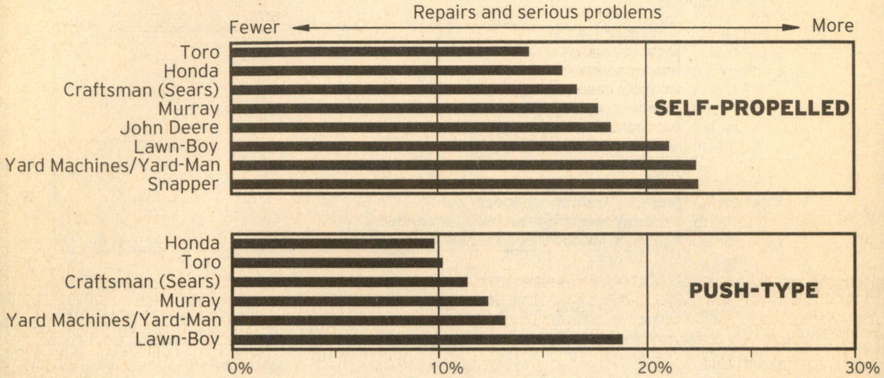

Based on 43,077 responses to our 2003 Annual Questionnaire for self-propelled and push mowers bought new between 1999 and 2003. Data have been standardized to eliminate differences linked to age and usage.

Lawn tractors and riding mowers

Lawn tractors and riding mowers are among the most repair-prone products we survey. Cub Cadet and Toro were among the more repair-prone brands for tractors. Differences of less than 6 points are not meaningful.

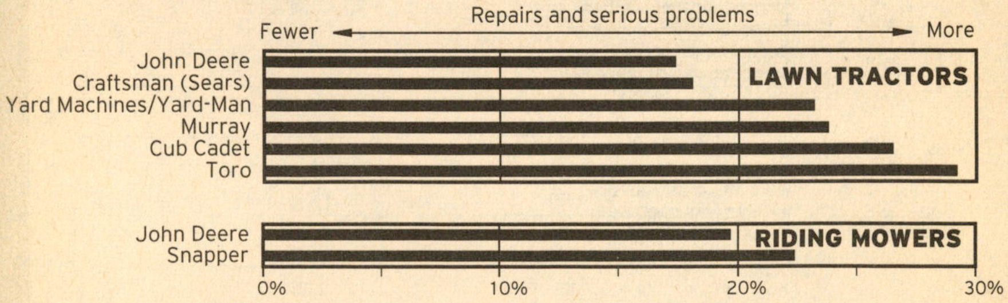

Based on 13,993 responses to our 2003 Annual Questionnaire for lawn tractors and riding mowers bought new between 1999 and 2003. Data have been standardized to eliminate differences linked to age and usage.

Microwave ovens, over-the-range models

This chart doesn't include Kenmore, KitchenAid, or Whirlpool; some OTR models were recalled in 2001, resulting in high repair rates of 35 to 48 percent for those brands. Sharp has been one of the most repair-prone brands. Differences of less than 4 points aren't meaningful.

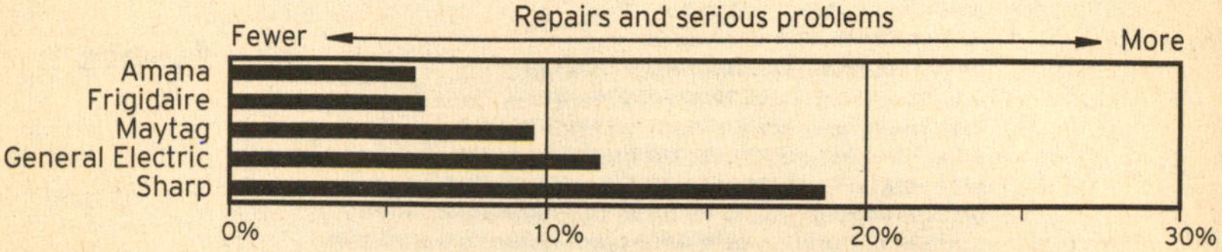

Based on 21,114 reader responses to our 2003 Annual Questionnaire about OTR ovens purchased new between 1999 and 2003. Data have been standardized to eliminate differences linked to age and usage.

Ranges

In general, electric ranges tend to hold up better than gas ranges. However, because gas and electric models were analyzed separately, the brand results cannot be compared. For electrics, the bottom five brands were more repair-prone than the top five. For gas ranges, Thermador and Amana were among the more repair-prone brands. Differences of less than 4 points are not meaningful.

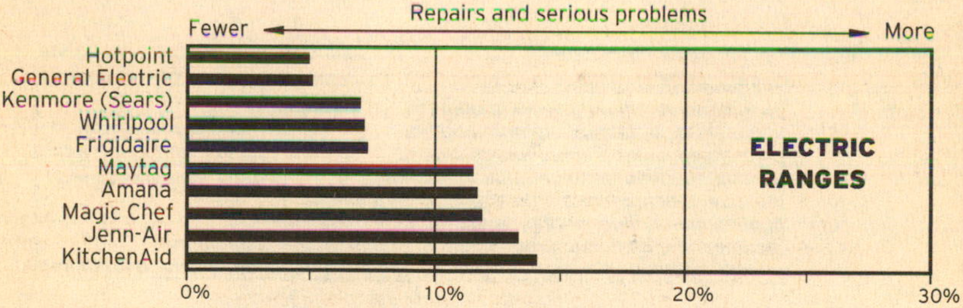

Ranges (continued)

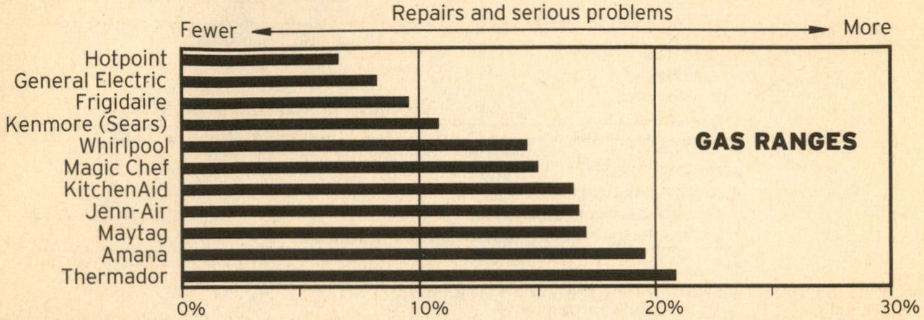

Based on almost 81,000 responses to our 2003 Annual Questionnaire for gas and electric ranges bought new between 1998 and 2003. Data have been standardized to eliminate differences linked to age.

Refrigerators

Built-in refrigerators seem to have a higher repair rate than stand-alones. And the presence of an icemaker tends to add repairs. In side-by-sides, Frigidaire and Sub-Zero were among the more repair-prone, while Maytag was the most repair-prone. Sub-Zero bottom freezers were more repair-prone than all other top- and bottom-freezer brands. Differences of less than 5 points are not meaningful.

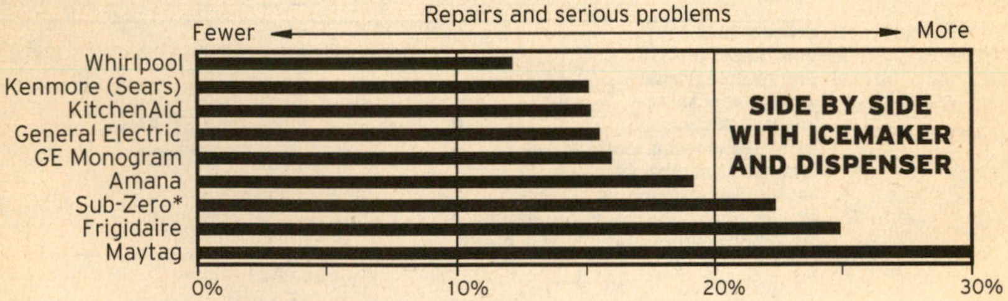

* Built-in with icemaker only

Refrigerators (continued)

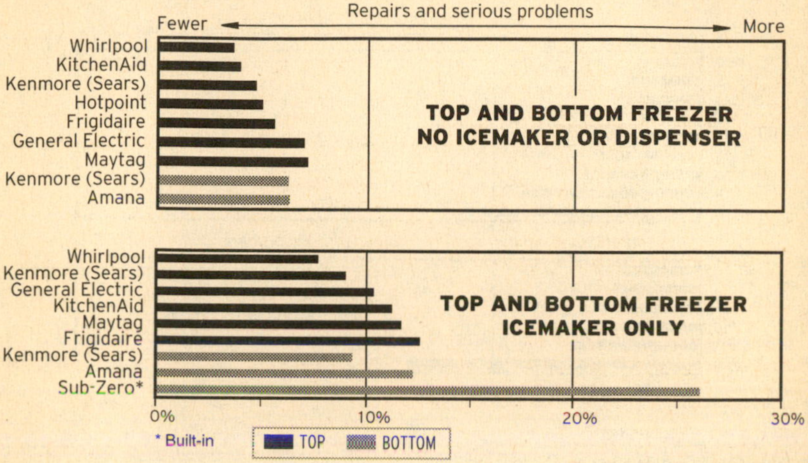

Based on almost 75,000 responses to our 2003 Annual Questionnaire about refrigerators bought new between 1999 and 2003. Data have been standardized to eliminate differences linked to age.

TVs, conventional

Of the smaller models, RCA and GE were among the more repair-prone brands. In both categories of larger models, RCA was the most repair-prone. Zenith was among the more repair-prone models of 30- and 32-inch sets. Differences of less than 3 percentage points are not meaningful.

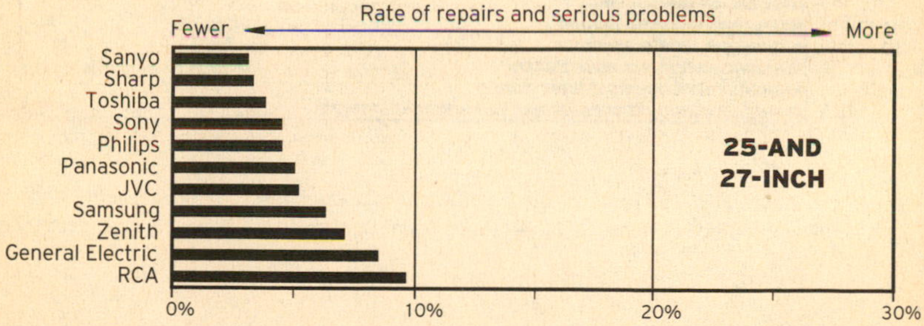

BRAND RELIABILITY

TVs, conventional (continued)

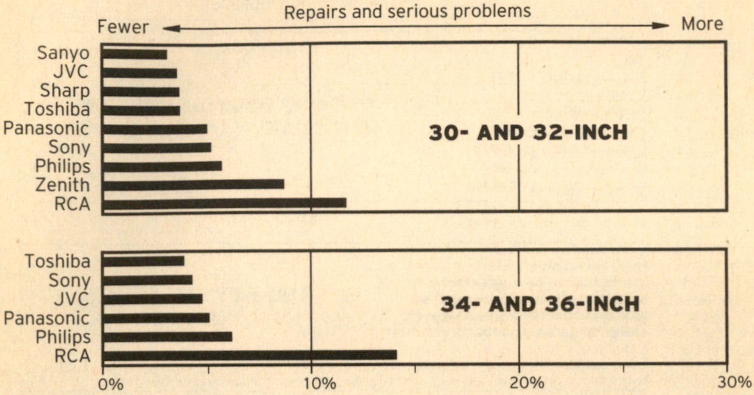

Data for 25- to 27-inch sets are based on nearly 74,000 responses to our 2003 Annual Questionnaire about sets purchased new between 1998 and 2003; data for 30- and 32-inch and 34- to 36-inch sets are based on nearly 57,000 responses. Data have been standardized to eliminate differences linked to age.

TVs, projection

HD-capable sets accounted for more than 70 percent of the sets in the sample; the rest were analog. The two types showed no difference in reliability. RCA was the most repair-prone brand. Differences of less than 4 points are not meaningful.

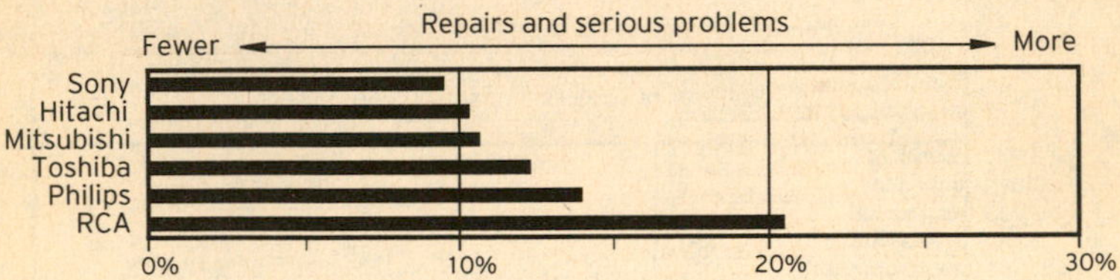

Based on more than 21,000 responses to our 2003 Annual Questionnaire for rear-projection TVs purchased new between 1998 and 2003. Data have been standardized to eliminate differences linked to age.

Vacuum cleaners

Fantom was the most repair-prone upright, while Eureka was the most repair-prone canister. Electrolux-brand vacuum cleaners are now manufactured by Eureka. Belt repairs are not included. Differences of less than 4 points are not meaningful.

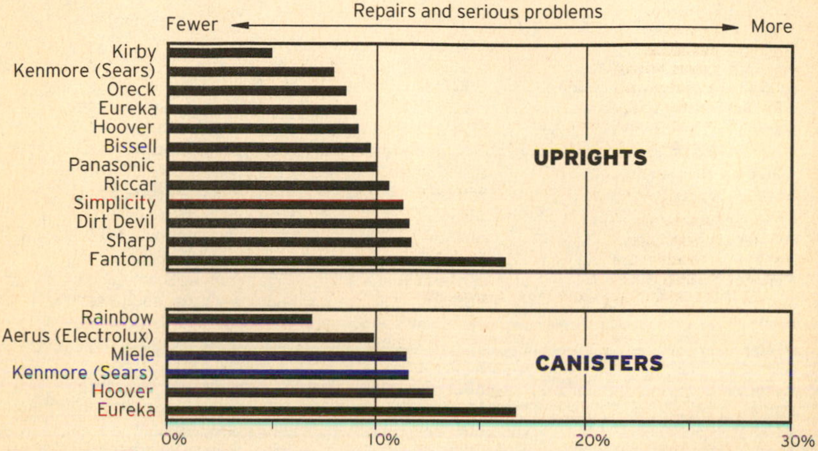

Based on more than 100,000 responses to our 2003 Annual Questionnaire about vacuum cleaners bought new between 1999 and 2003. Data have been standardized to eliminate differences linked to age and usage.

Washing machines

For top-loaders, Roper was among the more reliable brands. Front-loading Maytag washers were the most repair-prone. Differences of less than 4 points aren't meaningful.

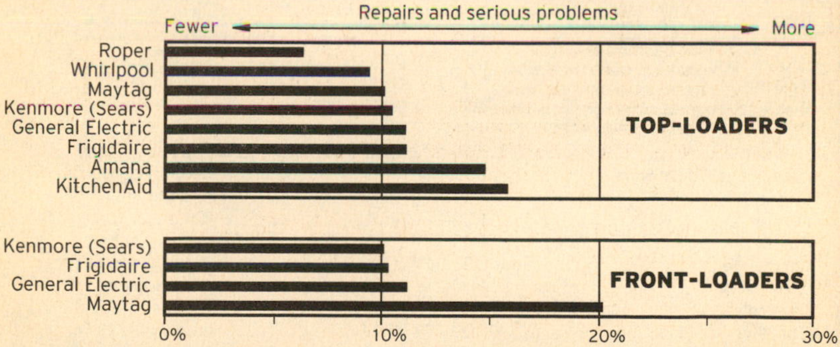

Based on more than 79,000 responses to our 2003 Annual Questionnaire about washers bought new between 1999 and 2003. Data have been standardized to eliminate differences linked to age and usage.

BRAND LOCATOR

Phone numbers and Web addresses of selected manufacturers.

A		
Acura	800 382-2238	www.acura.com
ACD Systems	866 244-2237	www.acdsystems.com
Adobe	800 833-6687	www.adobe.com
Aerus (Electrolux)	800 243-9078	www.aerusonline.com
AGFA	888 988-2432	www.agfa.com
Aiwa	800 289-2492	www.us.aiwa.com
Akai	888 697-2247	www.akaiusa.com
Amana	800 843-0304	www.amana.com
AMD	800 222-9323	www.amd.com
America Online	800 827-6364	www.aol.com
Apex	909 930-0132	www.apexdigitalinc.com
Apple	800 538-9696	www.apple.com
ArcSoft	510 440-9901	www.arcsoft.com
Ariens	800 678-5443	www.ariens.com
Asko	800 898-1879	www.askousa.com
Asus	510 739-3777	www.asus.com
AT&T	800 222-3111	www.att.com
Audi	800 367-2834	www.audiusa.com
Audiovox	800 229-1235	www.audiovox.com
B		
B&W	800 370-3740	www.bwspeakers.com
BellSouth	888 757-6500	www.bellsouth.com
BIC	888 461-4628	www.bicamerica.com
Bionaire	800 253-2764	www.bionaire.com
Bissell	800 237-7691	www.bissell.com
Black & Decker	800 544-6986	www.blackanddecker.com
BMW	800 334-4269	www.bmwusa.com
Bosch	800 944-2904	www.boschappliances.com
Bose	800 444-2673	www.bose.com
Boston Acoustics	800 246-7767	www.bostonacoustics.com
Broilmaster	800 255-0403	www.broilmaster.com
Brother	800 276-7746	www.brother.com
Buick	800 422-8425	www.buick.com
C		
Cadillac	800 333-4223	www.cadillac.com
Cambridge Soundworks	800 367-4434	www.cambridgesoundworks.com
Canon	800 652-2666	www.usa.canon.com
Carrier	800 227-7437	www.carrier.com
Casio	800 962-2746	www.casio.com
Cerwin-Vega	805 584-5300	www.cerwinvega.com
Char-Broil	800 241-7548	www.charbroil.com
Chevrolet	800 950-0540	www.chevrolet.com
Chrysler	800 422-4797	www.chrysler.com
Cingular	800 331-0500	www.cingular.com
Coleman	800 356-3612	www.coleman.com

Compaq	800 345-1518	www.compaq.com
CompuServe	800 336-6823	www.compuserve.com
Corel	800 772-6735	www.corel.com
Craftsman	Call local Sears store	www.sears.com
Creative Labs	800 998-5227	www.creative.com
CTX	877 688-3288	www.ctxintl.com
Cub Cadet	877 282-8684	www.cubcadet.com
Cuisinart	800 726-0190	www.cuisinart.com
D		
Dacor	800 793-0093	www.dacor.com
Daewoo	888 643-2396	www.daewoous.com
Dell	800 879-3355	www.dell.com
DeLonghi	800 322-3848	www.delonghiusa.com
Denon	973 396-0810	www.usa.denon.com
DeWalt	800 433-9258	www.dewalt.com
DirecTV	800 347-3288	www.directv.com
DirecWay	866 347-3292	www.direcway.com
Dirt Devil	800 321-1134	www.dirtdevil.com
Dish Network (EchoStar)	800 333-3474	www.dishnetwork.com
Disney Interactive	800 900-9234	disney.go.com/disneyinteractive
Dodge	800 423-6343	www.dodge.com
Ducane	800 382-2637	www.ducane.com
Dynamic Cooking Systems (DCS)	800 433-8466	www.dcsappliances.com
Dyson	866 693-9766	www.dyson.com
E		
EarthLink	800 327-8454	www.earthlink.net
Echo	800 673-1558	www.echo-usa.com
Electrolux	800 243-9078	www.electroluxusa.com
EMachines	877 566-3463	www.e4me.com
Emerson	800 898-9020	www.emersonradio.com
Envision	888 838-6388	www.envisionmonitor.com
Epson	800 463-7766	www.epson.com
Ericsson	800 374-2776	www.ericsson.com
Eureka	800 282-2886	www.eureka.com
F		
Fantom	800 668-9600	www.fantom.com
Fedders	217 342-3901	www.fedders.com
Fiesta	800 396-3838	www.fiestagrills.com
Fisher	818 998-7322	www.fisherav.com
Fisher & Paykel	888 936-7872	www.usa.fisherpaykel.com
Ford	800 392-3673	www.fordvehicles.com
Franklin	800 266-5626	www.franklin.com
Friedrich	800 541-6645	www.friedrich.com
Frigidaire	800 374-4432	www.frigidaire.com
Fujifilm	800 800-3854	www.fujifilm.com
Fujitsu	800 838-5487	www.fujitsupc.com
G		
Garmin	800 800-1020	www.garmin.com
Gateway	800 846-2000	www.gateway.com
GE (appliances)	800 626-2000	www.geappliances.com
GE (electronics)	800 447-1700	www.home-electronics.net
Gibson	888 203-1389	www.frigidaire.com
GMC	800 462-8782	www.gmc.com
Goldstar	800 243-0000	www.lgeus.com
Great Outdoors Grill Company	888 869-5454	www.gogrills.com
Grizzly	570 546-9663	www.grizzly.com

H		
Haier	888 764-2437	www.haieramerica.com
Hamilton Beach	800 851-8900	www.hamiltonbeach.com
Handspring	888 565-9393	web.palmone.com
Harman/Kardon	800 422-8027	www.harmankardon.com
Hewlett-Packard	800 752-0900	www.hp.com
Hitachi	800 448-2244	www.hitachi.com
Holland	800 880-9766	www.hollandgrill.com
Holmes	800 546-5637	www.holmesproducts.com
Homelite	800 242-4672	www.homelite.com
Honda (autos)	800 334-6632	www.honda.com
Honda (mowers)	800 426-7701	www.hondapowerequipment.com
Hoover	800 944-9200	www.hoover.com
Hotpoint	800 626-2000	www.hotpoint.com
Hughes	800 274-8995	www.hns-usa.com
Husqvarna	800 487-5962	www.usa.husqvarna.com
Hyundai	800 826-2277	www.hyundaiusa.com
I		
IBM	800 426-7235	www.ibm.com
Infiniti	877 647-7266	www.infiniti.com
Infinity	516 674-4463	www.infinitysystems.com
InkSaver	800 275-2410	www.inkjetsinc.com
Intel	800 628-8686	www.intel.com
Iomega	800 697-8833	www.iomega.com
Isuzu	800 726-2700	www.isuzu.com
J		
Jaguar	800 452-4827	www.jaguarusa.com
Jasc	800 622-2793	www.jasc.com
JBL	516 255-4525	www.jbl.com
Jeep	800 925-5337	www.jeep.com
Jenn-Air	800 688-1100	www.jennair.com
John Deere	800 537-8233	www.deere.com
Jonsered	877 693-7729	www.usa.jonsered.com
JVC	800 252-5722	www.jvc.com
K		
KDS	800 237-9988	www.kdsusa.com
Kenmore	Call a local Sears store	www.sears.com
Kenwood	800 536-9663	www.kenwoodusa.com
Kia	800 333-4542	www.kia.com
Kirby	800 437-7170	www.kirby.com
KitchenAid	800 422-1230	www.kitchenaid.com
KLH	818 767-2843	www.klhaudio.com
Kodak	800 235-6325	www.kodak.com
Konica	800 285-6422	www.konica.com
Kyocera	800 349-4188	americas.kyocera.com
L		
Land Rover	800 346-3493	www.landroverusa.com
Lawn-Boy	800 526-6937	www.lawnboy.com
LearningCo.com	800 395-0277	www.broderbund.com
Lexmark	800 539-6275	www.lexmark.com
Lexus	800 872-5398	www.lexus.com
LG	800 243-0000	www.lgeus.com
Lincoln	800 521-4140	www.lincoln.com
Lotus	800 465-6887	www.lotus.com
Lucent	888 458-2368	www.lucent.com

M		
Magic Chef	800 688-1120	www.maytag.com
Magnavox	800 531-0039	www.magnavox.com
Makita	800 462-5482	www.makita.com
Maxim	800 233-9054	www.esalton.com
Maytag	800 688-9900	www.maytag.com
Mazda	800 639-1000	www.mazdausa.com
McCulloch	800 521-8559	www.mccullochpower.com
Mercedes-Benz	800 367-6372	www.mbusa.com
Mercury	800 392-3673	www.mercuryvehicles.com
Micron PC	888 719-5031	www.buympc.com
Microsoft	800 426-9400	www.microsoft.com
Microsoft Network	800 373-3676	www.msn.com
Microtek	310 687-5940	www.microtekusa.com
Miele	800 289-6435	www.mieleusa.com
Milwaukee	877 279-7819	www.mil-electric-tool.com
Minolta	800 808-4888	www.minoltausa.com
Mintek	866 709-9500	www.mintekdigital.com
Mitsubishi	888 648-7820	www.mitsubishicars.com
Motorola	800 331-6456	www.motorola.com/us
MTD	800 800-7310	www.mtdproducts.com
Murray	800 224-8940	www.murray.com
N		
NEC	800 338-9549	www.necus.com
Network Associates (McAfee VirusScan)	800 338-8754	www.mcafee.com
Nextel	800 639-6111	www.nextel.com
Nikon	800 645-6687	www.nikonusa.com
Nintendo	800 255-3700	www.nintendo.com
Nissan	800 419-7520	www.nissandriven.com
Nokia	888 665-4228	www.nokiausa.com
O		
Oki	800 654-3282	www.okidata.com
Oldsmobile	800 442-6537	www.oldsmobile.com
Olympus	800 622-6372	www.olympusamerica.com
Onkyo	201 785-2600	www.onkyousa.com
Optimus	Call local RadioShack	www.radioshack.com
Oreck	800 989-3535	www.oreck.com
Oster	800 597-5978	www.oster.com
P		
PalmOne	800 881-7256	www.palmone.com
Panasonic	800 211-7262	www.panasonic.com
Pentax	800 877-0155	www.pentaxusa.com
Philips	800 531-0039	www.philipsusa.com
Pioneer	800 421-1404	www.pioneerelectronics.com
Polaroid	800 432-5355	www.polaroid.com
Polk Audio	800 377-7655	www.polkaudio.com
Pontiac	800 276-6842	www.pontiac.com
Porsche	800 767-7243	www.porsche.com
Porter-Cable	800 487-8665	www.porter-cable.com
Poulan	800 238-9333	www.poulan.com
Precor	800 477-3267	www.precor.com
Precisionaire	800 347-2220	www.precisionaire.com
Proctor-Silex	800 851-8900	www.proctorsilex.com
PSB	888 772-0000	www.psbspeakers.com

Q		
Quasar	800 211-7262	www.panasonic.com
R		
RadioShack	800 843-7422	www.radioshack.com
RCA	800 336-1900	www.rca.com
Regal	262 626-2121	www.regalware.com
Regina	228 867-8507	www.reginavac.com
Remington	616 791-7325	www.remingtonchainsaw.com
ReplayTV	866 286-3662	www.replaytv.com
Research Products	800 545-2219	www.resprod.com
Rival	800 557-4825	www.rivalproducts.com
Riverdeep	319 247-3333	www.riverdeep.net
Roper	800 447-6737	www.roperappliances.com
Rowenta	781 396-0600	www.rowentausa.com
Royal	800 321-1134	wwww.dirtdevil.com
Ryobi	800 345-8746	www.ryobi.com
S		
Saab	800 722-2872	www.saabusa.com
Sabre by John Deere	800 537-8233	www.deere.com
Salton	800 233-9054	www.esalton.com
Sampo	800 203-4429	www.sampoamericas.com
Samsung	800 726-7864	www.samsungusa.com
Sanyo	818 998-7322	www.sanyo.com
Saturn	800 522-5000	www.saturn.com
SBC Prodigy	800 776-3449	myhome.prodigy.net
Sega	800 872-7342	www.sega.com
Sharp	800 237-4277	www.sharpusa.com
Siemens	888 777-0211	www.icm.siemens.com
Sierra	425 649-9800	www.sierra.com
Simplicity (yard equipment)	262 284-8669	www.simplicitymfg.com
Simplicity (vacuum cleaners)	888 974-6759	www.simplicityvac.com
Skil	877 754 5999	www.skiltools.com
Snapper	800 762-7737	www.snapper.com
Solo	800 765-6462	www.solousa.com
Sony	800 222-7669	www.sony.com
Southwestern Bell	800 366-0937	www.sbc.com
Sprint PCS	888 253-1315	www.sprintpcs.com
Stanley	800 788-7766	www.stanleylawnmowers.com
Stihl	800 467-8445	www.stihlusa.com
Subaru	800 782-2783	www.subaru.com
Sub-Zero	800 222-7820	www.subzero.com
Sunbeam	800 458-8407	www.sunbeam.com
Suzuki	877 697-8985	www.suzukiauto.com
Symantec (Norton Antivirus)	800 441-7234	www.symantec.com
T		
Tappan	800 537-5530	www.frigidaire.com
TEC	800 331-0097	www.tecgasgrills.com
Technics	800 211-7262	www.panasonic.com
Thermador	800 735-4328	www.thermador.com
TiVo	877 289-8486	www.tivo.com
T-Mobile	800 866-2453	www.t-mobile.com
Toastmaster	800 947-3744	www.toastmaster.com
Toro	800 348-2424	www.toro.com
Toshiba	800 631-3811	www.toshiba.com
Toyota	800 468-6968	www.toyota.com

Tripp Lite .... 773 869-1234 .... www.tripplite.com
Trion .... 800 338-7466 .... www.trioninc.com
Troy-Bilt .... 866 840-6483 .... www.troybilt.com

U

Ulead .... 800 858-5323 .... www.ulead.com
Umax .... 214 342-9799 .... www.umax.com
Uniden .... 800 297-1023 .... www.uniden.com

V

Verizon Wireless .... 800 922-0204 .... www.verizonwireless.com
ViewSonic .... 800 688-6688 .... www.viewsonic.com
Viking .... 800 467-2643 .... www.vikingrange.com
Visioneer .... 925 251-6398 .... www.visioneer.com
Vivitar .... 805 498-7008 .... www.vivitar.com
Volkswagen .... 800 444-8987 .... www.vw.com
Volvo .... 800 458-1552 .... www.volvocars.us
VTech .... 800 624-5688 .... www.vtech.com

W

Walker .... 800 843-7422 .... www.radioshack.com
Waring .... 800 492-7464 .... www.waringproducts.com
Weber .... 800 446-1071 .... www.weber.com
Weed Eater .... 800 554-6723 .... www.weedeater.com
West Bend .... 800 367-0111 .... www.westbend.com
Whirlpool .... 800 253-1301 .... www.whirlpool.com
White Outdoor .... 800 949-4483 .... www.whiteoutdoor.com
White-Westinghouse .... 800 245-0600 .... www.frigidaire.com
WinBook .... 800 254-7806 .... www.winbook.com

X

Xerox .... 800 832-6979 .... www.xerox.com

Y

Yamaha .... 800 492-6242 .... www.yamaha.com
Yard Machines by MTD .... 800 800-7310 .... www.mtdproducts.com
Yashica .... 800 526-0266 .... www.yashica.com

Z

Zenith .... 877 993-6484 .... www.zenith.com
Zone Labs .... 415 922-0204 .... www.zonealarm.com

PRODUCT RECALLS

Products ranging from child-safety seats to chain saws are recalled when there are safety defects. Various federal agencies, such as the Consumer Product Safety Commission (CPSC), the National Highway Traffic Safety Administration (NHTSA), the U.S. Coast Guard, and the Food and Drug Administration (FDA), monitor consumer complaints and injuries and, when there's a problem, issue a recall.

But the odds of hearing about an unsafe product are slim. Manufacturers are reluctant to issue a recall in the first place because they can be costly. And getting the word out to consumers can be haphazard. If you return the warranty card that comes with a product, however, you're more likely to receive notification on a recall for it.

A selection of the most far-reaching recalls appears monthly in CONSUMER REPORTS. Below is a listing of products recalled from December 2003 through November 2004, as reported in issues of CONSUMER REPORTS. For details on these products and hundreds more, go to our Web site, *www.ConsumerReports.org*, in order to access our free, comprehensive list of product recalls.

If you wish to report an unsafe product or get recall information, call the CPSC's hotline, 800-638-2772, or visit its Web site, *www.cpsc.gov*. Recall notices about your automobile can be obtained from a new-car dealer or by calling the NHTSA hotline at 888-327-4236 or go to *www.nhtsa.dot.gov*. Questions about food and drugs are handled by the FDA's Office of Consumer Affairs, 888-463-6332 or *www.fda.gov*.

VEHICLES AND EQUIPMENT

'97-99 Acura (various models)
'01-04 Acura (various models)
'98-04 Audi (various models)
'01-04 BMW K and R Series motorcycles
'03-04 Buick Rendezvous
'01-03 Cadillac Escalade EXTs
'02-03 Cadillac
'04 Cadillac SRX
'02-04 Chevrolet Avalanches
'00-01 Chevrolet Malibu, Oldsmobile Alero, and Pontiac Grand Am
'00-04 Chevrolet Silverados
'93-99 Chrysler Corp. cars
'04 Chrysler 300M and Concorde
'04 Chrysler Pacifica
'04 Dodge Durango
'01-03 Ford Escape
'00-03 Ford Taurus
'01-03 Ford Windstar
'96-01 General Motors cars
'99-03 GMC Sierra
'97-99 Honda (various models)
'01-04 Honda (various models)
'02-03 Honda CR-V
'01-03 Hyundai (various models)
'04 Hyundai Elantra
'03-04 Jaguar with automatic transmission
'97-00 Kawasaki Prairie 300 and 400 all-terrain vehicles
'01-04 Kia Rio and Rio Cinco
'99-04 Land Rover Discovery II
'03 Mazda6
'01 Mazda Tribute
'00-03 Mercury Sable
'03-04 Mitsubishi (various models)
'02-03 Nissan Altima
'99-03 Nissan Frontier and Xterra
'02-03 Oldsmobile
'00-01 Oldsmobile Alero
'02-03 Pontiac
'00-01 Pontiac Grand Am
'04 Pontiac Grand Prix
'03-04 Porsche Cayenne

'03-04 Saab 9-3
'03-04 Saturn Ion
'02-04 Saturn Vue sport-utility vehicles
'99-04 Suzuki Grand Vitara
'01-04 Suzuki XL-7
Segway Human Transporter (HT)

CHILDREN'S PRODUCTS

Arctic Flash, Arctic Wind, and Air Elegance air-hockey tables
Baby Trend "Passport" strollers sold at Babies "R" Us stores
Backyard Products swings
Britax Marathon, Husky, Wizard, and Snug Seat Traveler Plus safety seats
Britax Super Elite child car seats
Cosco Rock 'N Roller baby stroller
Falls Creek Army Flight jackets sold at Meijer stores; unbranded fleece pantsuits with long waist drawstring with toggles and knots on jacket; Just Friends and Angel Fish girls hooded fleece jackets
Fisher-Price battery-powered scooters and minibikes
Graco Pack 'n' Play portable play yard with raised changing table
Graco SnugRide infant car seat and carrier
Graco Travel Lite portable baby swing
Inexpensive metal toy rings, necklaces and bracelets bought from gumball-style vending machines
Plan Toys solid wood drum
Trails End, Cottage Retreat, and Stages bunk beds made by Ashley Furniture Industries

ELECTRONICS

Apple iBook notebook computers
Apple PowerBook rechargeable battery
Batteries in LG cell phones sold through Verizon Wireless
Combination auto-air power adapter for Dell notebook computers
Fuji Power and A&T Fuji Power CR123A 3-volt lithium batteries
IBM G51 and G51t Touch Screen 15-inch CRT computer monitors
Kyocera batteries for Smartphone cell phone/PDA combos
Panasonic, Quasar, RCA, and JCPenney combination television sets and VCRs

HOUSEHOLD PRODUCTS

Bachtold Whipper, DR Field & Brush Mower, and B-800 weed and brush cutters
Black & Decker 18-volt cordless drill/drivers
Char-Broil gas barbecue grills
Cub Cadet Series 7000 compact tractors
Euroflex multisurface steam cleaners sold on QVC cable channel
Fedders, Maytag, and Comfort-Aire air conditioners that also supply heat
Frigidaire and Carrier through-the-wall combination air conditioner/heater
Hamilton Beach Cappuccino Plus electric espresso and cappuccino makers
Lakewood Sun-Sational Deluxe Radiant electric heaters
Lasko space heaters
Murray lawn mowers and tractors
Nesco deep fryers
"Real Essence" votive candles
Sauder TV/VCR carts
Turbo Power handheld hair dryers
Vicks Warm Mist humidifiers
Weber Summit and Vieluxe gas grills
Wagner cordless drill charger base

YARD AND GARDEN

Honda Harmony walk-behind lawn mowers
Husqvarna walk-behind lawn mowers

PERSONAL CARE PRODUCTS

Eyelash curlers sold at various drug, discount, and grocery store chains

SPORTING GOODS

DBX and Geartec bicycle helmets

8-YEAR INDEX TO CONSUMER REPORTS

This index indicates when the last full report on a given subject was published in CONSUMER REPORTS. The index goes back as far as 1997.

In text below, **bold type** indicates Ratings reports or brand-name discussions; *italic type* indicates corrections, followups, or Updates.

A

BUYING GUIDE INDEX

INDEX

Statement of Ownership, Management, and Circulation

(Required by 39 U.S.C. 3685)

1. Publication Title: Consumer Reports. 2. Publication No: 0010-7174. 3. Filing Date: September 13, 2004. 4. Issue Frequency: Monthly, except two issues in December. 5. No. of Issues Published Annually: 13. 6. Annual Subscription Price: $26.00. 7. Complete Mailing Address of Known Office of Publication: Consumers Union of United States, Inc., 101 Truman Avenue, Yonkers, New York 10703-1057. 8. Complete Mailing Address of Headquarters or General Business Office of Publisher: Consumers Union of United States, Inc., 101 Truman Avenue, Yonkers, New York 10703-1057. 9. Full Names and Complete Mailing Addresses of Publisher, Editor, and Managing Editor. Publisher: Consumers Union of United States, Inc., 101 Truman Avenue, Yonkers, New York 10703-1057. President: James A. Guest; Editor: Margot Slade; Managing Editor: Kim Kleman. 10. Owner: (If the publication is published by a nonprofit organization, its name and address must be stated.) Full Name: Consumers Union of United States, Inc., a nonprofit organization. Complete Mailing Address: 101 Truman Avenue, Yonkers, New York 10703-1057. 11. Known Bondholders, Mortgagees, and Other Security Holders Owning or Holding 1 Percent or More of Total Amount of Bonds, Mortgages, or Other Securities. If none, so state: None. 12. For Completion by Nonprofit Organizations Authorized to Mail at Special Rates: The purpose, function, and nonprofit status of this organization and the exempt status for federal income tax purposes has not changed during preceding 12 months.

15. Extent and Nature of Circulation:

	Average no. copies each issue during past 12 mo.	Actual no. copies of single issue published nearest to filing date
A. Total no. of copies (net press run)	4,433,615	4,448,025
B. Paid and/or requested circulation		
1. Paid or requested mail subscriptions (include advertisers' proof copies/exchange copies)	4,109,685	4,010,387
2. Sales through dealers, carriers, street vendors, counter sales (not mailed)	105,980	106,500
C. Total paid and/or requested circulation (sum of 15b(1) and 15b(2))	4,215,665	4,116,887
D. Free distribution by mail (samples, complimentary, and other free)	22,359	22,676
E. Free distribution outside the mail	14,540	14,399
F. Total free distribution (sum of 15d and 15e)	36,898	37,075
G. Total distribution (sum of 15c and 15f)	4,252,563	4,153,962
H. Copies not distributed	181,052	294,063
I. TOTAL (sum of 15g and 15h)	4,433,615	4,448,025
J. Percent paid and/or requested circulation	99.13%	99.11%

17. I certify that the statements made by me above are correct and complete.

Louis J. Milani, Senior Director, Business Affairs